lgbt

**encyclopedia
of**
lesbian, gay,
bisexual, and
transgender
**history
in america**

editorial board

lgbt

**encyclopedia
of**
lesbian, gay,
bisexual, and
transgender
**history
in america**

MARC STEIN
editor in chief

3

Race to Zulma
Appendix
Index

CHARLES SCRIBNER'S SONS®

THOMSON
™
GALE

New York • Detroit • San Diego • San Francisco • Cleveland • New Haven, Conn. • Waterville, Maine • London • Munich

THOMSON

™

GALE

Encyclopedia of Lesbian, Gay, Bisexual, and Transgender History in America

Marc Stein, *Editor in Chief*

© 2004 by Charles Scribner's Sons
Charles Scribner's Sons is an imprint of The Gale Group, Inc., a division of Thomson Learning, Inc.

Charles Scribner's Sons® and Thomson Learning™ are trademarks used herein under license.

For more information, contact
Charles Scribner's Sons
An imprint of The Gale Group
300 Park Avenue South
New York, NY 10010

For permission to use material from this product, submit your request via Web at http://www.gale-edit.com/permissions, or you may download our Permissions Request form and submit your request by fax or mail to:

Permissions Department
The Gale Group, Inc.
27500 Drake Rd.
Farmington Hills, MI 48331-3535

Permissions Hotline:
248-699-8006 or 800-877-4253, ext. 8006
Fax: 248-699-8074 or 800-762-4058

LIBRARY OF CONGRESS CATALOGING-IN-PUBLICATION DATA

Encyclopedia of lesbian, gay, bisexual, and transgender history in America / Marc Stein, editor in chief.
     p. cm.
Includes bibliographical references and index.
     ISBN 0-684-31261-1 (hardcover set: alk. paper) — ISBN 0-684-31262-X (v. 1) —
ISBN 0-684-31263-8 (v. 2) — ISBN 0-684-31264-6 (v. 3)
     1. Homosexuality—United States—History—Encyclopedias. 2. Gays—United States—History—Encyclopedias. 3. Bisexuals—United States—History—Encyclopedias. 4. Transsexuals—United States—History—Encyclopedias. I. Stein, Marc. II. Title.
     HQ76.3.U5E53 2003
     306.76′6′097303—dc22

This title is also available as an e-book.
ISBN 0-684-31427-4 (set)
Contact your Gale sales representative for ordering information

Printed in United States of America
10 9 8 7 6 5 4 3 2

lgbt

encyclopedia
of
lesbian, gay,
bisexual, and
transgender
history
in america

R

RACE AND RACISM

Responding to the September 11, 2001 attack on the World Trade Center and the Pentagon, the Audre Lorde Project's Center for Lesbian, Gay, Bisexual, Two Spirit, and Transgender People of Color Communities issued a statement condemning the scapegoating of people of color in the United States. The statement challenges other LGBT organizations to expand beyond strategies of single-issue politics and to take a stand on the crisis that incorporates a critique of xenophobia. This call speaks to the significance of race and racism within LGBT communities in the United States.

Definitions and History

Racism, roughly defined, is the belief that race determines human characteristics and capabilities, and that differences grounded in race translate into an inherent superiority of one race over others. Most scholars today are critical of biological conceptions of race, believing instead that race and racism are social, cultural, and historical constructions with powerful material effects. Racism in North America, rooted in histories of colonialism and slavery, takes many forms, ranging from physical violence to systemic white supremacy. Traci C. West in *Wounds of the Spirit* maintains that white supremacy is the most actively pervasive form of racism in the United States. In West's view, white supremacy has two key components: the institutionalized political, cultural, social, and economic power of white people; and the disproportionate access of white people to high status through the privileging of whiteness. In this framework, people of color are seen as less worthy and valuable than those con-

sidered white. White expectations and standards occupy a culturally dominant position and people of color are subjected to white judgments and decisions.

LGBT people of color are as subject to the effects of racism as are their non-LGBT counterparts. In fact, they have encountered both the racism of the larger society and the racism of LGBT communities. In terms of the former, LGBT people of color have experienced racialized, gendered, and sexualized colonialism, enslavement, segregation, capitalist exploitation, immigration exclusion, and citizenship restriction. In terms of the latter, community studies of LGBT life before the Stonewall Riots of 1969 have documented the history of racism in LGBT social and sexual worlds, examining racist ideologies and practices in neighborhoods, streets, parks, beaches, bars, clubs, restaurants, bedrooms, and bathhouses. When LGBT people began in the post–World War II era to challenge homophobia through homophile political organizing, they modeled their movement on race-based civil rights activism but failed to address both ongoing struggles against racism and the particular needs of LGBT people of color. After Stonewall, LGBT activists of color (including Anita Cornwell, Kyoshi Kuromiya, Audre Lorde, and Barbara Smith) increasingly criticized white supremacy in LGBT communities, but LGBT worlds continued to be marked by racism.

As Siobhan Somerville has argued, the links between homophobia and racism run deep. Somerville's *Queering the Color Line* (2000) examines scientific, literary, and popular discourse in the late nineteenth and early twentieth centuries, demonstrating that the language and con-

1

cepts of scientific racism played foundational roles in the invention of the language and concepts of scientific homophobia. The same impulses that led scientists to develop taxonomies of race led them to develop taxonomies of sexuality. Just as they used science to put forward notions of racial superiority and inferiority, they used science to put forward notions of sexual superiority and inferiority. And to the extent that their sexual science was aimed at improving "the race," their categories of homosexuality and heterosexuality were profoundly racialized.

Within the LGBT community, white supremacy often takes the forms of a lack of awareness about an effective critique of, and an appropriate accountability for, white privilege. Ignorance of systemic racialized power imbalances often translates into social and political strategies against heteronormativity and heterosexism that omit the concerns of LGBT people of color. Already dealing with denial, invisibility, and shame induced by homophobia and transphobia within communities of color, LGBT people of color must also negotiate white supremacy within LGBT communities.

African Americans

According to Cornel West, white supremacy is an ideology based primarily on the degradation and control of black bodies. Influenced by centuries of racial slavery, African American identity exists in the context of a long history of racism that continues to have social, economic, and political repercussions. Today the average income of African Americans remains at or near the bottom of the income scale. African Americans are disproportionately affected by HIV/AIDS and are overrepresented in the prison system. While the black body continues to be a highly visible site of public discourse about race, real African Americans still confront invisibility.

Barbara Smith submits that despite the development in the 1970s of a strong black LGBT movement and evidence of black LGBT influences in art and literature, African American LGBT people are still missing in historical scholarship. For example, during the 1920s, black LGBT people flourished in Harlem. Smith suggests that this time period may have reflected openness sparked by the wider society's racial prejudice or may simply have been an instance of structural accommodation in which black people were forced to live together in a community designed by geographic apartheid. Whatever the reasons, the Harlem Renaissance fostered and was fostered by LGBT writers and artists. And yet racism, homophobia, and transphobia have often rendered invisible their contributions. The same can be said for the activities of

Bayard Rustin, the adviser to Dr. Martin Luther King Jr. who served as chief organizer of the 1963 March on Washington for Jobs and Freedom. The roles of Cleo Glenn, president of the Daughters of Bilitis in the 1960s, and Ernestine Eckstein, who marched in early homophile demonstrations, are also rarely acknowledged. Nor are the challenges made to sexual racism in the late 1960s and early 1970s by Anita Cornwell (whose works were later collected in *Black Lesbian in White America*) and by LGBT delegates at the 1970 Black Panther Party's Revolutionary People's Constitutional Convention.

Influenced by activists and writers such as Audre Lorde and Barbara Smith, the 1970s witnessed important developments in African American LGBT political organizing. The Combahee River Collective authored an influential statement analyzing intersections between forms of oppression and resistance based on gender, sexuality, class, and race. The National Coalition of Black Lesbians and Gays was created. The 1979 LGBT March on Washington, the first national march for LGBT rights, and its associated National Third World Lesbian and Gay Conference were milestones in the development of black LGBT organizations.

African American, white, and other activists do work collaboratively within the mainstream LGBT community. Nevertheless, racism continues to thwart coalition building, fracturing the wider movement for sexual and gender equality. In the face of such racism, African American LGBT people are forced to live divided lives. They need to be connected to the wider LGBT community because of the importance of sexuality and gender in their lives. At the same time, they need to be connected with the wider black community because this is the foundation of their social identities, the "womb" that provides protection from the oppressive dominant culture. The African American family is an especially important shield against racism. The refuge provided by the African American family is, however, complicated by pervasive homophobia and transphobia within the black community.

Arab Americans

The Arab American Antidiscrimination Committee reported more than two hundred hate crimes in the week following the September 11 terrorist attack on the World Trade Center and the Pentagon. Since then, anti-Arab and anti-Muslim sentiments in the United States have heightened the feeling among LGBT Arab Americans that they are outsiders twice over. They share with other Arab and Muslim Americans the repercussions of increasingly severe policies and attitudes. At the same time, as members of ethnic and religious cultures that have been explicitly homophobic and transphobic, they struggle to make a space for themselves.

Anticipating racist backlash, LGBT Arab American and Muslim groups responded quickly to the September 11 attacks with public statements supporting the victims and condemning the terrorists. Ramzi Zakharia, a founding member of the Gay and Lesbian Arab Society (GLAS), witnessed both the attack and the subsequent threatening e-mails sent to his group's Web site. The gay and lesbian Muslim group Al-Fatiha ("the Opening") prepared a statement mourning the loss of life and condemning the tragedy. The group also endorsed the Queer Economic Justice Network's (QEJN) call for LGBT organizations to oppose war and denounce the racist and xenophobic attacks taking place against Arab, Muslim, South Asian, and Central Asian communities.

Organizing by LGBT Arab and Muslim people is a fairly recent phenomenon that has found its largest public forum via the Internet. Academic research and theorizing about the concerns of this population has emerged only in the last few years. Islamic religious discourse remains hostile to LGBT existence. Activists, however, are creating virtual and actual communities and are addressing political and social issues in increasingly organized ways. Working for visibility and safe space, their chief concerns are countering homophobia and transphobia in the Arab and Muslim world and challenging racism in LGBT communities. Organizations in the wider LGBT community such as QEJN, Pride at Work, Queers for Racial & Economic Justice, and Children of Lesbians and Gays Everywhere (COLAGE) expressed public support for Arab Americans and Muslims after September 11, 2001. Nevertheless, dealing with racist attitudes that long precede that day and urging the LGBT community to be mindful of its discriminatory ideas and practices are common themes in Arab and Muslim American LGBT public discourse.

The Gay and Lesbian Arabic Society and Al-Fatiha are two of the more comprehensive organizations. Established in 1988 and based in the United States, GLAS is an international networking organization for gays and lesbians of Arab descent. The society aims to promote positive images of gays and lesbians in Arab communities and to combat negative portrayals of Arabs within LGBT communities. Al-Fatiha, founded in 1998, is a member of an international network of LGBT Muslim organizations and has the unique goal of reconciling Muslim LGBT people with their religion. The organization promotes Islamic notions of peace, equality, and justice. Providing resources and a safe environment within the context of Arab and Muslim communities, GLAS and Al-Fatiha are committed to ending injustice and discrimination.

Asian Americans and Pacific Islanders

Representing the newly formed Lesbian and Gay Asian Collective at the 1979 March on Washington, Michiyo Cornell bore witness to the importance of that moment. In her address at the Washington Monument, she referenced the emerging network of support among LGBT Asian Americans in the context of racial and sexual oppression and the difficulty of maintaining unique identities given pervasive ignorance and racist resistance to differences. Cornell emphasized the concept of Asian America as a space apart where people who have been an integral part of the country for nearly two hundred years are not yet considered fully American but are simultaneously categorized as the country's "model minority" (Cornell, pp. 83–84). LGBT people in Asian America and LGBT Pacific Islanders share common problems with their non-LGBT counterparts, such as fear of deportation, economic discrimination, sexual objectification, and dependence on families and communities for support. These common problems differentiate their experiences of homophobia and transphobia from those of the white LGBT community. They have always had to consider not only their sexual and gender marginality but also the history of Asians and Pacific Islanders in the United States, the legacy of colonization, and the dynamics of emerging Third World struggles across the globe.

Asian American and Pacific Islander LGBT activists and writers speak of negotiating multiple identities and of making hard choices between conflicting sociopolitical commitments. Gil Mangaoang was one of many activists asserting Asian identities in white-dominated society in the early 1970s. While immersed in social justice work for Filipinos and exploring his Filipino American identity, Mangaoang struggled with his sexual orientation, feeling that the two parts of his life were irreconcilable. To come out in the Filipino community was, for him, to face double jeopardy. Being openly gay would undermine his legitimacy within the Filipino community and would compound racial discrimination with homophobia in his dealings with society at large. For a period Mangaoang spent some time in organizations geared toward Filipino causes and other time in white-male dominated gay rights organizations, encountering homophobia in the former and racist attitudes in the latter. Like Mangaoang, many LGBT Asian Americans and Pacific Islanders continue to experience the worlds of Asia/Pacific America and LGBT America as separate places and take care to keep the two worlds distant from one another.

Over twenty years after Cornell's speech, Asian and Pacific Islander LGBT people still struggle for cultural and political citizenship. Members of the Asian and

Pacific Islander LGBT community continue combating what Eric Estuar Reyes describes as representational hyphenization and stereotypes of the silent, hardworking, "good minority" with exotic (a)sexualities (Reyes, pp. 85–86). Activism and visibility, however, have increased over the last twenty years. Countering suspicions about their ethnic loyalties, many LGBT Asian Americans and Pacific Islanders use constructionist ideas about gender and sexuality to challenge essentialist tendencies often prevalent in ethnic-based narratives of identity. They are claiming LGBT identities as part of their ethnicity rather than as a "white disease" and are creating "no passing zones" or sites of resistance where marginality is transformed into empowerment and self-definition (Williams-León, pp. 159–160).

Social, political, and academic networks have grown since Asian American LGBT activists such as Kyoshi Kuromiya first rose to prominence in the 1960s and since LGBT Asian American and Pacific Islander organizations first formed in the 1970s. Nevertheless, the locus of cultural, social, and political power has not shifted much. Asian American and Pacific Islander communities remain marginal and disenfranchised in Eurocentric America, while LGBT people continue to confront homophobia and transphobia in Asian American and Pacific Islander communities. Within academia, for instance, Asian American studies has brought strong focus to cultural differences within Asian American communities, but often remains silent on the topic of sexual and gender diversity. Notwithstanding the growing number and range of cultural resources, many LGBT Asian Americans and Pacific Islanders still view themselves as on the margins of both LGBT America and Asian/Pacific America and feel especially invisible in the context of the broader society's heteronormative white supremacy.

Latinas and Latinos

Despite being the fastest-growing ethnic population in the United States and the country's largest ethnic minority, Latinas and Latinos continue to experience racial discrimination, economic exploitation, and political disenfranchisement. Language remains a contested marker of social legitimacy, a subject of heated debate on the value of having a homogenous versus a heterogeneous lingua franca. Spanish-speaking people present the most visible challenge to an "English-only" social environment and, despite hundreds of years of existence in the lands that now make up the United States, are still perceived as being outside the normative parameters of North American identity.

In addition to encountering the discrimination that Latinos/as face in general, LGBT people confront deeply engrained homophobia, heterosexism, and transphobia within Hispanic communities and are simultaneously marginalized by the larger, non-Hispanic LGBT population. Traditional gender roles are firmly established within Latino/a families and cultures. Women are generally expected to be submissive, virtuous, and willing to defer to men, who in turn are expected to exhibit aggression and control. By labeling themselves as lesbians, Latina women push their culture to reconsider its views on women's gender and sexuality and are therefore perceived as a threat to the established order. Homosexuality is generally not open for discussion. Male same-sex sexual relations, although not uncommon, are rarely discussed and usually occur within a prescribed dominant/submissive formula in which the aggressor is not considered gay. Men who exist outside of the masculine norm are at best suspect and at worst are subject to violence. Although LGBT visibility continues to grow within Latino/a cultures, it faces sustained resistance.

LGBT Latino/a activists and writers have been openly countering invisibility, homophobia, transphobia, and racism since the 1950s. In the homophile movement era, Tony Segura helped found the Mattachine Society of New York; Tony Reyes was involved in the creation of ONE, Inc.; a Filipina lesbian helped create the Daughters of Bilitis; and José Sarria ran for political office in San Francisco. Sylvia Rivera is credited with playing a key role at the 1969 Stonewall Riots in New York and shortly thereafter created Street Transvestite Action Revolutionaries. Jeanne Cordova edited and later published the *Lesbian Tide,* founded in 1971. Juanita Ramos spoke at the 1979 March on Washington and eight years later edited the first Latina lesbian anthology, *Compañeras: Latina Lesbians* (1987). The organization Gay and Lesbian Latinos Unidos was formed in 1981; three years later Lesbianas Unidas developed to serve the specific needs of women within the group. The first and second Lesbiana Encuentros took place in Cuernavaca, Mexico (1987), and Costa Rica (1990). In 1998 Nicole Ramirez-Murray, co-chair of the National Latino/a Lesbian and Gay Organization (LLEGO), endorsed the year 2000 Millennium March on Washington. Although the march was controversial among LGBT communities of color, Ramirez-Murray stressed its importance in light of intensifying assaults on both the LGBT and Latino/a populations.

Activism notwithstanding, Latino/a and LGBT identities do not easily mix. Jorge Sanchez, a Colombian immigrant who does gay outreach in the Mission District of San Francisco, describes the balancing act as "making a Faustian bargain." In the Mission, Latino/a LGBT people feel culturally at home but must deal with the same religious, family, and "machismo" influences typical of Latin American countries. In the mostly white Castro district next door, they find acceptance for their sexualities and genders. But there they have to cope with systemic racism, are subjected to erotic fetishism, and are also dismissed as gangsters or migrant workers. The diversity and divisions that characterize multifaceted immigrant and American-born Chicano/a, Puerto Rican, Cuban, Central American, South American, and other Latino/a communities are erased under the homogenizing, white supremacist gaze.

Despite virulent homophobia and transphobia in their ethnic communities, Latino/a LGBT people sustain deep attachments to those communities. Latino/a cultures generally expect that large, extended families will remain close-knit. Despite rejection of sexual and gender diversity by these cultures, LGBT members remain committed to family and community. This is especially true in the context of a wider LGBT culture whose rites and institutions, according to Eric-Steven Gutierrez, consider Latino/a LGBT people to be peripheral or an "acquired taste" (p. 242).

Native Americans

A landmark book in the long history of academic inquiry into Native American sexualities and genders, *Two-Spirit People: Native American Gender Identity, Sexuality, and Spirituality*, begins with a dedication to the memory of Native Americans who have died as a result of homophobia, HIV/AIDS, and racism. This book grew out of a series of precedent-setting conferences held in 1993 and 1994. The primary goal of the Wenner-Gren Conferences was to convene both Native American and non-Native scholars and activists for discussions about constructions of sexuality and gender in Native American cultures and for critical reconsideration of previous scholarly writings.

Native American peoples endure two ongoing legacies: first, the erasure and misrepresentation by dominant culture discourse, and second, the systematically enforced separation from their own cultural heritage through a variety of institutionalized practices, ranging from wholesale denigration of Native belief systems and re-education through the "boarding school system" to urban relocation by the Bureau of Indian Affairs. Native American contributors to the *Two-Spirit* volume attest to the persistent impact of racism, ignorance, homophobia, and transphobia. Pervasive cultural usurpation and desecration leave Native peoples' lives, land, and language severely endangered. Lost heritage and the power of internalized racism complicate efforts to counter the limited definitions of identity imposed by dominant culture.

In *Two-Spirit People*, the collaborators document the shift from European and Euro-American control of discourse to Native American and First Nations self-naming, critical theory, and activism. The authors recognize that discussions of Native American gender diversity and sexuality have too long been about, but not with, Native Americans. With the exception of Beatrice Medicine's now classic 1979 article "Changing Native American Sex Roles in an Urban Context," very little writing has dealt with the experiences of contemporary two-spirit people, thus perpetuating the erasure of their living culture. In consulting sessions for the book, Native American participants identified a need for thorough research into contemporary LGBT and two-spirit people and contemporary gender and sexual diversity in Native American communities. They also strongly recommended reevaluation of the commonly cited concept of *berdache* and more accurate studies of traditional roles historically categorized under that term. The etymology of *berdache* and the history of its application to Native American LGBT and two-spirit people serves as an example of the pervasive impact of white supremacy on the community. (*Berdache* was first applied to Native Americans by early French explorers, who simplistically employed an Arabic or Persian term for a boy slave.)

Native Americans self-identify in terms of Native categories instead of embracing terminologies imposed by others. The Native categories themselves are complex and contested, subject to social location, historical specificity, and individual experience. Activist organizations such as Gay American Indians, which was formed by Barbara Cameron and Randy Burns in 1975, have at the heart of their work a search for Indian pride in the face of pervasive racism; a challenge to sexism, homophobia, and transphobia within their communities; and a desire to mediate between tradition and change. This mediation involves both challenging inaccurate typologies and generating new categories to signify traditional and emerging identities.

The term two-spirit (or two-spirited), for example, was originated in 1990 at the third Native American/First Nations gay and lesbian conference. "Two-spirit" generally includes Native American LGBT people and people who identify with traditional tribal gender and sexual categories. Development of the term was a deliberate move to distance Native Americans from non-Native LGBT people. The identities of contemporary Native American two-spirit people emerge at what Sabine Lang describes as the intersection of traditional tribal gender models, (ways of life that have developed in LGBT urban subcultures) and awareness of being Native American as opposed to being white or of any other ethnic heritage.

Conclusion

LGBT communities of color are diverse, reflecting the unique characteristics of their various races, ethnicities, religions, languages, classes, sexes, genders, and sexualities, but they share the common experience of having to confront and negotiate racism. Like the wider communities of color, they are subject to oppression ranging from economic disadvantage, political disenfranchisement, and physical violence to ineffective health care, social ostracism, and cultural invisibility. Racism, including white supremacy, complicates their efforts to live as whole, multidimensional people able to celebrate their racial, ethnic, sexual, and gender identities. The effects of racism thwart LGBT people at social, economic, political, and personal levels, restricting growth and erasing their existence from public discourse.

LGBT activists, academics, and other architects of culture within communities of color have a substantial and multifaceted history of countering racism, heteronormativity, and gender oppression. From the civil rights movement to the LGBT movement, African American LGBT people have been full, if usually invisible, participants in struggles for social justice. Arab Americans are taking advantage of communication technologies to build LGBT communities. Those communities in turn are taking an active stand against war, racial discrimination, sexual intolerance, and gender prejudice. Stereotyped as the "model minority," Asian Americans continue to challenge both this categorization and the homophobia and transphobia of their various communities. Latino/a LGBT people confront their heteropatriarchal cultures and white supremacy in the mainstream LGBT community. In the process they assert their values, priorities, and visions for socioeconomic, sexual, and gender justice. Native American LGBT people draw on a legacy that includes the first North American resistance to white supremacist discourse. Their activism challenges both racist attitudes and the homophobia and transphobia imported into their cultures by those attitudes.

Present in—but marginalized by—every one of these communities, mixed race people complicate the struggle even further, suffering the effects of essentialist categories of identity as well as challenging them. LGBT people are complex and complicated. Those in communities of color continue to encounter racism. The movers and shakers among them challenge and change society on a daily basis. As church activist and health care practitioner Audrey Skeete declares, "We Ain't Gonna' Let Nobody Turn Us Around."

Bibliography

Ahbab. Site of the Gay and Lesbian Arab Society. Home page at http://www.glas.org

Al-Fatiha Foundation. Home page at http://www.al-fatiha.net.

Audre Lorde Project: Center for Lesbian, Gay, Bisexual, Two Spirit and Transgender People of Color Communities. Home page at http://www.alp.org

Beemyn, Brett, ed. *Creating a Place for Ourselves: Lesbian, Gay, and Bisexual Community Histories.* New York: Routledge, 1997.

Blackwood, Evelyn, and Saskia E. Wieringa, eds. *Female Desires: Same Sex Relations and Transgender Practices across Cultures.* New York: Columbia University Press, 1999.

Brandt, Eric, ed. *Dangerous Liaisons: Blacks, Gays, and the Struggle for Equality.* New York: New Press, 1999.

Bull, Chris. "Gay, Muslim, and Scared." *Advocate* 849 (2001): 54.

Chávez-Silverman, Susana, and Librada Hernández, eds. *Reading and Writing the Ambiente: Queer Sexualities in Latino, Latin American, and Spanish Culture.* Madison: University of Wisconsin Press, 2000.

Cohen, Cathy J.. *The Boundaries of Blackness: AIDS and the Breakdown of Black Politics.* Chicago: University of Chicago Press, 1999.

Cornell, Michiyo. "Living in Asian America: An Asian American Lesbian's Address before the Washington Monument." In *Asian American Sexualities: Dimensions of Gay and Lesbian Experience.* Edited by R. C. Leong. New York: Routledge, 1996.

Cornwell, Anita. *Black Lesbian in White America.* Talahassee, Fla.: Naiad Press, 1983.

Eng, David L., and Alice Y. Hom. *Q & A: Queer in Asian America.* Philadelphia: Temple University Press, 1998.

Engardio, Joel P. "'You Can't Be Gay—You're Latino': A Gay Latino Identity Struggles to Emerge, Somewhere between the Macho Mission and Caucasian Castro." *SF Weekly* (14 April 1999).

Greene, Beverly. *Ethnic and Cultural Diversity among Lesbians and Gay Men.* Thousand Oaks, Calif.: Sage Publications, 1997.

Greene, Beverly. "Lesbian Women of Color: Triple Jeopardy." *Journal of Lesbian Studies* 1, no. 1 (1997): 109–147.

Gutierrez, Eric-Steven. "Latino Issues: Gay and Lesbian Latinos Claiming La Raza." In *Positively Gay: New Approaches to Gay and Lesbian Life.* Edited by Betty Berzon. Berkeley, Calif.: Celestial Arts, 1992.

Jacobs, Sue-Ellen, Wesley Thomas, and Sabine Lang. *Two-Spirit People: Native American Gender Identity, Sexuality, and Spirituality.* Urbana: University of Illinois Press, 1997.

Kumashiro, Kevin K., ed. *Troubling Intersections of Race and Sexuality: Queer Students of Color and Anti-oppressive Education.* Lanham, Md.: Rowman and Littlefield Publishers, 2001.

Leong, Russell, ed. *Asian American Sexualities: Dimensions of the Gay and Lesbian Experience.* New York: Routledge, 1996.

Liu, Peter, and Connie S. Chan. "Lesbian, Gay, and Bisexual Asian Americans and Their Families." In *Lesbians and Gays in Couples and Families: A Handbook for Therapists*. Edited by Joan Laird and Robert-Jay Green. San Francisco, Calif.: Jossey-Bass Publishers, 1996.

Longres, John F., ed. *Men of Color: A Context for Service to Homosexually Active Men*. Binghamton, N.Y.: Harrington Park Press, 1996.

McKinley, Catherine E., and L. Joyce DeLaney, eds. *Afrekete: An Anthology of Black Lesbian Writing*. New York: Anchor Books, Doubleday, 1995.

Medicine, Beatrice. *Learning to Be an Anthropologist and Remaining "Native": Selected Writings*. Edited with Sue-Ellen Jacobs. Urbana: University of Illinois Press, 2001.

Murray, Stephen O., and Will Roscoe, eds. *Boy-Wives and Female Husbands: Studies of African Homosexualities*. New York: St. Martin's Press, 1998.

Murray, Stephen O., and Will Roscoe, eds. *Islamic Homosexualities: Culture, History, and Literature*. New York: New York University Press, 1997.

Nelson, Emmanuel S., ed. *Critical Essays: Gay and Lesbian Writers of Color*. New York: Haworth Press, Inc., 1993.

Ramirez-Murray, Nicole. "Millennium March: The Defense— 'A Public Statement by Nicole Ramirez-Murray, National Co-Chair, National Latino/a Lesbian and Gay Organization (LLEGO) Washington, D.C.'" *Gay Community News* 23, no. 4 (1998): 26–27.

Reyes, Eric Estuar. "Strategies for Queer Asian and Pacific Island Spaces." In *Asian American Sexualities: Dimensions of Gay and Lesbian Experience*. Edited by R. C. Leong. New York: Routledge, 1996.

Smith, Barbara. *The Truth That Never Hurts: Writings on Race, Gender, and Freedom*. New Brunswick, N.J.: Rutgers University Press, 1998.

Somerville, Siobhan B. *Queering the Color Line: Race and the Invention of Homosexuality in American Culture*. Durham, N.C.: Duke University Press, 2000.

Trikone. Site for South Asian gays and lesbians. Home page at http://trikone.org

West, Cornel. *Race Matters*. Boston: Beacon Press, 1993.

West, Traci C. *Wounds of the Spirit: Black Women, Violence, and Resistance Ethics*. New York: New York University Press, 1999.

Williams-León, Teresa. "The Convergence of Passing Zones: Multiracial Gays, Lesbians, and Bisexuals of Asian Descent." In *The Sum of Our Parts: Mixed-Heritage Asian Americans*. Edited by Teresa Williams-León and Cynthia L. Nakashima. Philadelphia: Temple University Press, 2001.

Aryana Bates

See also AFRICAN AMERICANS; ANTIDISCRIMINATION LAW AND POLICY; ANTI-SEMITISM; ARAB AMERICANS; ASIAN AMERICANS AND PACIFIC ISLANDERS; COMBAHEE RIVER COLLECTIVE; LATINAS AND LATINOS; MARCHES ON WASHINGTON; MATTACHINE SOCIETY; NATIVE AMERICANS; TOURISM; STEREOTYPES.

RADICAL FAERIES

During the 1970s, members of LGBT communities increasingly looked toward establishing or reestablishing spirituality as part of their everyday lives. This interest in faith, mysticism, and religion became a significant part of the organization and nature of LGBT social experiences in the final decades of the twentieth century. In some cases, this new emphasis on the spiritual meant the founding of LGBT groups within established Christian churches, as well as the establishment of LGBT congregations, synagogues, and organizations within other traditional faiths. However, the spirituality of individuals within LGBT communities was not limited to organized or established religion. Throughout the 1970s and 1980s, and to the present, there has been an efflorescence of spiritual thought, alternative religious practice, and personal exploration of faith among LGBT peoples. One of the most significant of these alternative spiritual movements has been the Radical Faeries, which emerged during the late 1970s.

Like many social movements, the Radical Faeries movement does not have a single point of origin and is rather a coalescence of various factions that grew out of the 1960s counterculture, the New Age movement, and spiritual groups with the lesbian and gay liberation movement of the early 1970s. Following these counterculture roots, Faeries have sought to create a nonhierarchical movement with an amorphous structure that allows a wide variety of expression, interpretation, and style. In this sense, there is no single Radical Faeries culture or identity. Generally, though, Faeries have celebrated sensuality, corporeal pleasures, and the natural body while rejecting the more commercial and highly muscular male body types that predominate so much of the gay media and bar culture. Moreover, faeries have sought to blur traditional gender roles and to revel in the effeminate and the "nelly."

The call for authentic gay self-representation led Faeries to develop anarchist, utopian, even romantic, visions of society, community, and the individual. In addition, non-Western customs, rituals, and cultural practices, particularly Native American as well as East Asian and South Asian, have been influential, and at times they have been appropriated by the Radical Faeries in their quest for spiritual experience, connection, and ecstasy.

As early as the mid-1970s, author and gay liberation veteran Arthur Evans began to hold in the Bay Area what he called "Fairy Circles" on sexuality, paganism, witchcraft, and other topics. During this same period longtime activist and Mattachine Society founder Harry Hay started to articulate a vision of gay liberation that evoked a distinctive and radical notion of gay identity utilizing the language of faeries. In 1978 Hay, along with Don Kilhefner and Mitch Walker, organized the first Radical Faeries gathering, which occurred in Arizona over Labor Day weekend in 1979. In utilizing the name Radical Faeries, the organizers were able to draw on a number of important references: the term "fairy," which historically had been used to refer to effeminate gay men; pagan fairy tales and magic; and finally the term "radical," which emphasized the activist and political aspects of the movement.

One of the central practices of Radical Faeries is their regular gatherings, which first began in 1979 and continue across North America and in Europe and Australia. These gatherings are most often held in rural settings; they are exercises in a communal approach to living. Rituals, pagan rites, dancing, singing, and storytelling are among the many activities. The key to these gatherings is the "faerie circles," which resemble, in part, earlier feminist and lesbian and gay consciousness-raising groups. These circles provide participants with an opportunity to not only experience fellowship, but also discuss difficult personal and political issues.

Another important aspect of Radical Faerie culture has been its attempt to promote the open expression of gay identity in a public space other than traditionally "safe" urban settings. Indeed, an emphasis on rural life, the outdoors, small towns, and the wilderness has always been a major element of Radical Faeries thought. This derives, in part, from the affinity and involvement many faeries have had with the environmental and green movements. In this sense, Radical Faeries are part of a longer American tradition that has, in the words of environmental historian Robert Gottlieb, sought "spiritual replenishment" in its conceptualization of and relationship with wilderness and nature.

One of the strongest links between the Radical Faeries and this more rural-oriented sense of sexual community has been the periodical *RFD*. First published in Iowa in 1974, *RFD* was, at its outset, a magazine for gays and lesbians living outside the urban enclaves of New York and San Francisco; the publication, in fact, derived its name from the post office designation "rural free delivery." Over the years *RFD* has become so closely associated with the Radical Faeries movement that it is often jokingly referred to as "Radical Faerie Digest."

In their rebellious ethos, activist spirit, and focus on wellness, healing, and comradeship, the Radical Faeries remain a critical link between sexual liberation's counter-

culture past and an alternative vision of what it means to be LGBT in the present and future.

Bibliography

Gottlieb, Robert. *Forcing the Spring: The Transformation of the American Environmental Movement.* Washington, D.C.: Island Press, 1993.

Hay, Harry. *Radically Gay: Gay Liberation in the Words of Its Founder.* Edited by Will Roscoe. Boston: Beacon Press, 1996.

Thompson, Mark, ed. *Gay Spirit: Myth and Meaning.* New York: St. Martin's Press, 1987.

Timmons, Stuart. *The Trouble with Harry Hay: Founder of the Modern Gay Movement.* Boston: Alyson, 1990.

Walker, Mitch. *Visionary Love: A Spirit Book of Gay Mythology and Trans-mutational Faerie.* Boston: Treeroots Press, 1980.

David S. Churchill

See also ANARCHISM, SOCIALISM, AND COMMUNISM; ANDROGYNY; ENVIRONMENTAL AND ECOLOGY MOVEMENTS; HAY, HARRY; NEWSPAPERS AND MAGAZINES; RADICAL SPIRITUALITY AND NEW AGE RELIGION; URBAN, SUBURBAN, AND RURAL GEOGRAPHIES; WITCHES AND WICCA.

RADICAL SPIRITUALITIES AND NEW AGE RELIGIONS

"WomanSpirit," "queer spirit," "hermaphrodeities," "radical faeries," and "ceremonial dykes" are all terms that sprang from spiritualities that have emerged since the early 1970s. They are generally seen as "New Age," in that they diverge from LGBT religious movements that remain within the fold of mainstream religions. Instead, they seek ancestry and inspiration from knowledge systems—ancient myths, magical systems, and Eastern, African, Aboriginal, and Native American theologies—that have been discredited and marginalized by mainstream religion in cahoots with colonization, imperialism, capitalism, misogyny, racism, and enforced heterosexism. They share with New Age movements a belief in the transformative power of consciousness and the cultivation of intuition and psychic powers. Although mainstream religion virtually taboos female divinity as well as overtly sexual divinities, radical LGBT spiritualities often invoke female, feminine, hermaphroditic, gender shifting, and markedly sexual divinities. They recognize and respect energetics, the idea that all beings are connected energetically and that one's personal energy, rooted inextricably in eroticism, is both a spiritual and political force. For these diverse LGBT movements, spirituality is always political and activism is inextricably psychic as well as physical.

WomanSpirit and Goddess Consciousness

Although its adherents often speak of themselves and those they address simply as "women," many of the feminist WomanSpirit movement's principal exponents are lesbian and bisexual women, including Paula Gunn Allen, Mary Daly, Alice Walker, Gloria Anzaldúa, Susan Griffin, Kay Gardner, Vicki Noble, Kay Turner, Emily Culpepper, and Audre Lorde. In WomanSpirit, ancient myths are reinterpreted from gynocentric perspectives and sovereign goddess images are put forth as contemporary guides for female being and becoming. Lesbian feminist spirituality recognizes a specifically female energy or "gynergy" as an erotic/political/transformative force enabling female bonding, resistance to patriarchy, and healing for the self, the community, and the planet. Some practice female separatism to deny energy to patriarchal structures and the men who uphold them, as well as to concentrate their energies. Lesbian feminist spirituality resists a global system of patriarchy, marked by domination and violence. It renames women (most markedly in the works of Daly) as Amazons, Crones, and Spinsters; redefines power as energetic force, not domination; and images a space-time outside of patriarchy, that one can realize or bring into manifestation through daring acts of sinning against patriarchal taboo, wild imagination, and courage. It embraces the body as a manifestation of divinity, reclaims "Cunt" as a name for the oldest goddess powers, resists racism, acknowledges the dark as holy, affirms the sacredness of nature, fights against animal torture and the devastation of the environment, and practices gynocentric meditations and rituals. Some lesbian and bisexual spiritualists ally themselves with witchcraft, usually Dianic Wiccan forms. The movement inspires festivals, poetry, music, fiction, theoretical writings, and communal living spaces.

Lesbian writer Peggy Kornegger in a 1980 article in *Sinister Wisdom* sums up its core concepts: "Women understand that changes in consciousness . . . are at the core of revolutionary change and that those deep, soul-shaking transformations are also the most profound energy sustainers. It is the spirit of hope within us that will keep us going when all else fails. To see being as indestructible energy, death as continuation not obliteration, and revolution as psychic as well as political movement is the vision of feminist spirituality."

Queer Spirit

Paula Gunn Allen draws upon Native American traditions to argue for the sacred role of LGBT people in gynocentric cultures, which, she argues, existed worldwide prior to patriarchal colonizations. Lesbian and bisexual women like Allen reclaim "dyke" and her "ceremonial"

character, while some radical gay men who are spiritual political activists (Harry Hay, Arthur Evans, John Burnside) take back the word "fairy," often spelling it "faerie," as an honorific that recalls gay men's spiritual link to nature and ancient magical traditions. Judy Grahn's *Another Mother Tongue* (1984) is one of the first of many works that rediscovers the ancient spiritual and tribal legacy of LGBT peoples, which, although forced underground, continues to make its existence felt.

In *Cassell's Encyclopedia of Queer Myth, Symbol, and Spirit* (1997), Randy Conner, David Sparks, and Mariya Sparks define "queer spirit" as "an eclectic movement based in the beliefs that the divine source embraces homoeroticism, lesbianism, bisexuality, and transgenderism and that persons enacting these behaviors or holding these identities have served in many cultures as spiritual functionaries, which include the role of ritual artist or craftsperson as well as that of (spiritual) warrior, priestess, prophet, shaman, and medicine person. Its practices include the reverence of divine beings or forces, healing, divination, and magic the creation of art, and a reconnection with nature."

Numerous practitioners of queer spirit (Anzaldúa, Will Roscoe), both indigenous to the Americas and not, point to Native Americans' various recognition and honoring of "Two-Spirit" persons (homosexual, transvestite, and/or transgender persons), who often have spiritual healing or shamanistic roles. Gay spiritual leader and writer Christian de la Huerta, in *Coming Out Spiritually* (1999), discusses a range of practices (including meditation, sexuality, bodywork, and conscious reading) to integrate spirituality into one's life. He too understands LGBT people as a people, with a history, traditions, and archetypal roles including "catalyptic transformers, outsiders, consciousness scouts, sacred clowns, keepers of beauty, caregivers, mediators, shamans, divine androgynes, and gatekeepers."

In *Hermaphrodeities: The Transgender Spirituality Workbook* (2001), Raven Kaldera recognizes being transgender as a "spiritual path" and offers a philosophical and ritual backdrop for understanding this, drawn from a consideration of a mixture of deities from around the world as well as interviews with contemporaries. Elias Farajajé-Jones, in a 2000 article aptly titled "Holy Fuck," denounces "erotophobia," consecrated in the desexed and all-male god of mainstream religions, as fundamentally linked to white and male supremacies as well as homophobia. For him, decolonizing the body/mind means finding the sacred in the sexual and vice versa; ritual body piercing and tattooing affirms his "Black queer body as a site of resistance" to colonization and the interdependence of sex and spirit.

On Exuberance

Gay biologist Bruce Bagemihl surveys the overwhelming incidence of homosexuality and gender variance in the animal world. He informs his science and enriches LGBT spirituality by drawing upon indigenous traditions that recognize sexual and gender variance in the animal realm as necessary to overall fecundity in nature. Hence, homosexuality and transgender ways, in humans, plants, and animals, can be understood as eminently natural, for these manifest the ecological order, which is based not in uniformity but in diversity, extravagance, and seemingly "wasteful" exuberance (for example, the endless variety of snowflakes, the profligacy of the seed). His view, marrying science and spirituality, reflects a core precept of the radical LGBT spiritual movements: the sexual fluidity, variance, and exuberance expressed by LGBT being and culture is neither sinful nor deviant but an expression of the sacred biodiversity that is essential to life processes.

Bibliography

Allen, Paula Gunn. *The Sacred Hoop: Recovering the Feminine in American Indian Traditions.* Boston: Beacon Press, 1986.

Anzaldua, Gloria. *Borderlands/La Frontera.* San Francisco: Spinsters/Aunt Lute Press, 1987.

Bagemihl, Bruce. *Biological Exuberance: Animal Homosexuality and Natural Diversity.* New York: St. Martin's Press, 1999.

Barzan, Robert, ed. *Sex and Spirit: Exploring Gay Men's Spirituality.* San Francisco: White Crane Press, 1995.

Conner, Randy P. *Blossom of Bone: Reclaiming the Connections between Homoeroticism and the Sacred.* San Francisco: HarperSanFrancisco, 1993.

Conner, Randy P., David Hatfield Sparks, and Mariya Sparks. *Cassell's Encyclopedia of Queer Myth, Symbol, and Spirit: Gay, Lesbian, Bisexual, and Transgender Lore.* London: Cassell, 1997.

Daly, Mary. *Gyn/Ecology: The Metaethics of Radical Feminism.* Boston: Beacon Press, 1978.

Farajajé-Jones, Elias. "Holy Fuck." In *Male Lust: Pleasure, Power, and Transformation.* Edited by Kerwin Kay, Jill Nagle, and Baruch Gould. New York: Harrington Park Press, 2000.

Grahn, Judy. *Another Mother Tongue: Gay Words, Gay Worlds.* Boston: Beacon Press, 1984.

Huerta, Christian de la. *Coming Out Spiritually: The Next Step.* New York: Jeremy P. Tarcher/Putnam, 1999.

Kaldera, Raven. *Hermaphrodeities: The Transgender Spirituality Workbook.* Philadelphia: Xlibris, 2001.

Kornegger, Peggy. "Cosmic Anarchism: Lesbians in the Sky with Diamonds." *Sinister Wisdom,* no. 12 (1980).

Jane Caputi

See also CHURCHES, TEMPLES, AND RELIGIOUS GROUPS; RADICAL FAERIES; WITCHES AND WICCA.

RADICALESBIANS

Until the spring of 1970, when Radicalesbians circulated its groundbreaking position paper, "The Woman-Identified Woman," the people most eager to link feminism and lesbianism were those who opposed the fledgling feminist movement. Antifeminist efforts to link the two initially dismayed many feminists, even those considered the movement's most militant. While it is true that radical feminists, including Shulamith Firestone, Anne Koedt, and Kate Millett, suggested that women's liberation would bring about a sexual liberation that would undermine the hegemony of heterosexuality, they did not make an explicit connection between feminism and lesbianism. One of the few who did was Florida radical feminist Judith Brown, who had the prescience to see that women involved in this new liberationist movement might discover through their movement work that they were capable of loving another woman, too. Most radical feminists, however, were more comfortable endorsing bisexuality rather than lesbianism.

But by the beginning of 1970 lesbianism was being discussed more and more within the movement, both by heterosexuals whose sexual horizons were expanding and by lesbians interested in claiming a place for themselves within feminism. Their efforts to explore the possible connections between feminism and lesbianism made many other feminists uneasy, not the least because they felt that lesbian femme/butch role-playing imitated the patterns of domination and subordination that they argued had so warped heterosexual relationships. Others, such as influential radical feminist Ti-Grace Atkinson, doubted that lesbians and feminists really had much in common because feminism was a theory whereas lesbianism was clearly a practice. In "Sisterhood is Powerful," an article in the *New York Times Magazine* (15 March 1970), feminist Susan Brownmiller cited National Organization of Women (NOW) founder Betty Friedan as arguing that lesbians constituted a "lavender menace" that could severely damage the feminist movement by associating feminism with this stigmatized sexuality. Brownmiller, countering Friedan, stated that radical lesbians were nothing more than a "lavender herring."

Rita Mae Brown and the Second Congress to Unite Women

While heterosexual feminists were debating whether lesbianism was a genuine threat to the women's movement, some lesbians in New York City began to question their second-class citizenship in both the women's movement and in the emerging, and predominantly male, gay liberation movement. One woman who proved particularly pesky to homophobic feminists was Rita Mae Brown, the editor of New York NOW's newsletter. After raising the issue within New York NOW, Brown was relieved of her duties as newsletter editor. She subsequently resigned from the chapter and became involved in the radical feminist group Redstockings, which she later claimed was no more accepting of lesbians than was NOW. After Redstockings she moved on to the Gay Liberation Front (GLF), a gay group that had formed in the aftermath of the June 1969 Stonewall Riots. Brown also gathered around her a small group of lesbians to travel with her to feminist conferences and events where they brought up the issue of lesbianism and forced heterosexual feminists to take a position on the relationship of feminism to lesbianism.

Brown was not the only lesbian trying to connect the dots between feminism and lesbianism. Martha Shelley, past president of the New York chapter of the pre-Stonewall lesbian group Daughters of Bilitis (DOB) and current GLF member, had been doing the same in speeches and articles since 1969. Both Brown and Shelley were involved in the earliest efforts to bring together for the first time lesbians from women's liberation with those from gay liberation. In early 1970 a group of New York women including Sidney Abbot, Ellen Bedoz, Suzanne Bevier, Ellen Broidy, Rita Mae Brown, Cynthia Funk, Barbara Gladstone, Michela Griffo, Lois Hart, March Hoffman, Arlene Kisner, Barbara Love, Linda Rhodes, Martha Shelley, Susan Silverwoman, and Fran Winant began meeting. They resolved to write a position paper that would spell out the significance of lesbians to women's liberation and that could be circulated to feminist groups.

Before they had even finished writing their position paper, they decided that the best place to introduce it would be at the upcoming second Congress to Unite Women, a NOW-sponsored conference that sought to bring together a variety of feminist groups. By this point New York NOW had developed something of a reputation for its skittish reaction to lesbians. Indeed, organizers of the first Congress, held in New York City in November 1969, had aroused the suspicions of lesbians when they accepted money from DOB but omitted its name from the press release detailing the groups that were participating in the event.

On 1 May 1970, approximately three hundred women attended the opening night of the second Congress to Unite Women, also held in New York City. They were sitting in the auditorium when the hall inexplicably went black. Next they heard the sound of women running and laughing, and when the auditorium lights came

back on they saw seventeen women wearing lavender t-shirts with the words "Lavender Menace" written across the front. Other demonstrators were strategically dispersed throughout the crowd. The women who were planted in the audience were supposed to join the seventeen Menaces. When they did, they were supposed to reveal that they, too, were outfitted in Lavender Menace t-shirts. However, as soon as the Menaces took the floor and announced themselves, women began coming up to the front of the hall spontaneously in support of the seventeen Menaces. For two hours the Menaces and their supporters held the floor and discussed what it was like living as a lesbian in a heterosexist culture. The final assembly adopted a set of resolutions advanced by the Lavender Menace, including the recommendation that whenever the movement or individual feminists were stigmatized that the label "lesbian" be affirmed rather than denied.

"The Woman-Identified Woman"

In contrast to the Lavender Menace action, which was both a clever and moving appeal for acceptance, the Radicalesbians' position paper, "The Woman-Identified Woman," argued for the centrality of lesbianism to women's liberation. A lesbian, they argued, is the fury of all women distilled to the breaking point. She is the real rebel, the true feminist, the woman who refuses to be psychically annihilated or warped by either individual men or the system of male dominance. Heterosexual women, by contrast, were unable to commit fully to feminism because they were too absorbed in trying to patch up and sustain relationships with the very men who were oppressing them. Their energies flowed back to men, not forward to their feminist sisters, as lesbians' energies did. As long as the movement continued to allow itself to be tripped up by the charge that it was really lesbian, the movement would be kept in line in the same way that most women were kept in line by the threat of the stigmatizing "lesbian" label.

In the months before the second Congress, lesbians had challenged the automatic privileging of heterosexuality both inside and outside the feminist movement. But what set "The Woman-Identified Woman" apart from these earlier efforts was its redefinition of lesbianism as a largely political choice rather than a sexual orientation, and one that was strikingly consonant with feminism. Lesbians set out to persuade feminists that lesbianism was not a bedroom issue and that lesbians were not male-identified "bogeywomen" intent on sexually objectifying and exploiting other women. Critical to their makeover of lesbianism was the term "woman identification." One woman recalls that they were searching for another term because they had found that in previous zap actions heterosexual feminists tended to recoil from the word "lesbian." As a result of these discussions, someone came up with the phrase, "woman-identified woman," which effectively turned the tables on heterosexual feminists opposing lesbianism on the grounds that it was male-identified. Far from being male-identified, lesbians, they argued, were less contaminated by male culture than were heterosexual feminists, whose sense of themselves was dependent on both men and male culture.

In many ways Radicalesbians broke with the thinking prevalent among a large number of nonmovement lesbians. They believed that hostility to lesbianism arose solely from sexist gender hierarchy rather than from any system of sexual hierarchy. Although they noted that sissy boys also provoke uneasiness in a sexist culture, they emphasized lesbians' connections to other women rather than their connections to gay men. Radicalesbians also broke with the idea of a lesbian minority, which was so popular with the homophile movement and gay and lesbian social organizations. In "The Woman-Identified Woman" any woman, indeed all women, could come out. In this respect, their understanding of sexuality was social-constructionist rather than essentialist. Nevertheless, lesbian feminists who further elaborated the arguments made in the "The Woman-Identified Woman" sometimes did reinforce common stereotypes about the ways in which sexuality is gendered. Women's sexuality, they contended, was nurturant, relational, and sensual whereas men's sexuality had all the subtlety of a speeding train, oriented as it was toward orgasm and reliant as it often was on aggression.

Although New York Radicalesbians dissolved sometime in the late fall of 1970, the group spurred lesbians elsewhere to organize. In Philadelphia, for example, a group of women numbering between 150 and 200 met as Radicalesbians in the early 1970s.

"The Woman-Identified Woman" was the founding document of lesbian feminism. Because of it thousands of women refused to be cowed into silence when the label "lesbian" was hurled their way. Radicalesbians helped to pioneer the idea that sexuality, like gender, was socially constructed. However, by the 1980s the Radicalesbians' effort to understand lesbianism solely through the prism of gender began to be called into question by some lesbians, most notably anthropologist Gayle Rubin, who argued against feminists' definitional fusion of sexuality and gender. Lesbians, she insisted, are oppressed both as queers and as women. Moreover, the group's politicizing of lesbianism and its effort to depict lesbianism as the only feminist sexuality have since been criticized by les-

bians eager to claim the erotic dimensions of lesbianism. While these criticisms have much merit, Radicalesbians' refashioning of lesbianism as a political choice should be seen as a brilliant pre-emptive strike that prevented feminists' continued disparagement of lesbianism.

Bibliography

Abbott, Sidney, and Barbara Love. *Sappho Was a Right-On Woman: A Liberated View of Lesbianism.* New York: Stein and Day, 1972.

Echols, Alice. *Daring to Be Bad: Radical Feminism in America, 1967–75.* Minneapolis: University of Minnesota Press, 1989.

Stein, Marc. *City of Sisterly and Brotherly Loves: Lesbian and Gay Philadelphia, 1945–1972.* Chicago: University of Chicago Press, 2000.

Alice Echols

See also ATKINSON, TI-GRACE; BROWN, RITA MAE; CORNWELL, ANITA; DAUGHTERS OF BILITIS; FURIES; GAY LIBERATION FRONT; LESBIAN FEMINISM; SHELLEY, MARTHA.

RADIO

Lewis Hill, poet and journalist, initiated a series of events that transformed the broadcasting world when he formed the Pacifica Foundation in 1946. Pacifica was the actualization of Hill's dream to redefine radio as a community tool for outreach and discussion. What began as one station soon became a powerful grassroots network of noncommercial community stations licensed in major cities across the United States. Small, yet powerful, collectives of radio professionals were developed within each broadcast community to address the concerns of those people previously unheard and underrepresented across commercial airwaves, including LGBT listeners.

Sixty years later, groups such as Outright Radio carried on Hill's ideas. Outright Radio, which is syndicated over Public Radio International, broadcasts what it calls "extraordinary stories of America's gay community" and has won the Edward R. Murrow Award and the National Federation of Community Broadcasters' Golden and Silver Reels for excellence in radio. Host David Gilmore is the voice of Outright, and he has taken Hill's vision to a new level of outreach. Another group, the National Lesbian and Gay Journalists Association (formed in 1990), has also consistently embraced fair and accurate coverage of LGBT issues. However, it was Hill's view of community radio that initially shaped public radio, and later, commercial radio.

Early Years

From its inception in 1946, Pacifica chose to air queer perspectives across its stations in Berkeley, California; Los Angeles; New York City; Houston, Texas; and Washington, D.C. Ten years later, Allen Ginsberg's reading of his controversial homoerotic poem "Howl" across the airwaves of KPFA in Berkeley, California, challenged conservative views toward sexuality. On November 24, 1958, KPFA also made history when it aired a documentary that centered on a discussion among a small group of physicians, lawyers, and criminologists along with the mother of a gay man and Harold L. Call, one of the editors at the homophile magazine *Mattachine Review*. This documentary was perhaps the first comprehensive attempt to dispel stereotypes about homosexuality on the radio airwaves. Thus, noncommercial radio was beginning to experiment with broadcasting LGBT programming across the airwaves. Although many of these efforts were short-lived, they succeeded in paving the way for LGBT programs on television and radio.

Noncommercial Radio

One of the first (and longest-running) LGBT programs in the United States was *Friends,* which began in 1960 on Georgetown University's campus station WGTB-FM. The show celebrated queer life with visits from actors and drag queens. It also embraced the words of activists such as Ginsberg and provided airtime to health experts who openly discussed sexual diseases and issues. Also debuting on WGTB was *Sophie's Parlor,* one of the nation's longest-running lesbian feminist programs. The show featured music that was produced by women for women.

In the mid-1970s, listeners protested to WGTB management when it dropped both shows from its schedule, but to no avail. To fill the void, Pacifica picked up both programs in 1976. However, despite that move, over the years queer activists have occasionally complained that Pacifica has not adequately addressed homosexual topics on its stations. In 1962 New York City Mattachine organizer Randolfe Wicker demanded equal time from the management of WBAI-FM, the Pacifica station in that city, in response to the station's one-hour broadcast of a discussion on homosexuality by a panel of psychiatrists. In response, the station aired another radio forum, but this time with Wicker and six other gay men. Subsequently, some listeners filed a complaint with the Federal Communications Commission (FCC) opposing the station's coverage of such topics. The FCC upheld Pacifica's view that such issues, if handled maturely on air, served the public interest.

Typically volunteer produced, LGBT radio programs represented the interests and efforts of a handful of collectives across the United States. Thirty analog recordings of *Homophile Half Hour* that aired in the early 1970s on KBOO-FM, a Portland, Oregon, noncommercial radio station, provide a time capsule of one of the earliest LGBT programs in the United States. The shows featured interviews with numerous activists and civic leaders. Another significant program debuted in 1971 when Pacifica's KPFK-FM in Los Angeles aired *IMRU* (I Am, Are You?), that city's (and perhaps the nation's) first weekly LGBT radio program. Another magazine program, *Gaydreams,* debuted the same year on WXPN-FM, the University of Pennsylvania's public radio station in Philadelphia. Producer Robert Drake revamped the show in the 1990s and changed its name to *Q-zine*. In 2003 it still aired on WXPN. *Gaydreams* founder John Zeh created another radio program of the same name on WAIF-FM in Cincinnati during the late 1970s. That show is now called *Alternating Currents*.

WBAI in New York City was among the first stations in the nation to air LGBT programming, yet only in 1982 did it do so on a consistent basis. Through the years, some of the earlier collectives have reorganized. Like *Outlooks* and *The Gay Show,* its predecessors on WBAI, *OutFM* has been dependent on the energy and resources of volunteers to survive as one of the oldest and longest-running queer programs in the United States.

As other queer radio shows began to surface through the 1980s, some in the conservative religious community challenged their on-air appropriateness. In one incident, the Reverend Larry Poland mistakenly tuned into the radio drama *Jerker* that aired on KPFK in 1986. The program dramatized the impact of AIDS on two gay friends. Poland complained to the FCC about what he considered controversial content, and subsequently the FCC pressured KPFK to refrain from airing such sensitive issues. At about this time, the FCC began to define decency based on local community standards (*FCC v. Pacifica Foundation,* 2 FCC Red 2698 [1987]) and soon enacted its "safe harbor" policies that were designed to protect children from undesirable broadcast content during the day and early evening (*Action for Children's Television v. FCC,* 932, F2d 1504 [1991]). Also, in 1991 Pacifica Radio successfully petitioned the federal Court of Appeals to lift the FCC's a twenty-four-hour indecency ban initiated by Jesse Helms. Indeed, the FCC's efforts to remove the "safe harbor" policies in favor of an outright ban on adult-oriented programming faced considerable public debate.

With so much happening, the landscape of queer radio in the United States was definitely shifting, as discussions of once closeted issues, concerns, and lyrics began airing across the country, even the world. In April 1988, Los Angeles radio producer Greg Gordon (and a volunteer staff) created the half-hour newsmagazine program *This Way Out*. It began with a weekly distribution to 26 public stations in the United States and Canada and fifteen years later aired on over 125 radio public and commercial stations across the world. *This Way Out* won the Outstanding Achievement Award from the Gay and Lesbian Press Association in 1988. The National Federation of Community Broadcasters awarded the producers the Silver Reel in 1991 for its news and public service commitment to diversity.

Commercial Radio

WFNX-FM in Boston made a giant leap forward for commercial radio when it debuted the three and one-half hour radio magazine show *One in Ten* in 1992. Other commercial stations attempted to air similar locally produced shows in the 1990s with only moderate success, perhaps due to the difficulty of building an audience in a competitive market. KGAY Radio Network was the first attempt to market a twenty-four-hour queer music and talk format in the United States. The network signed on the air on 28 November 1992 in Denver, Colorado. Owners Clay Henderson and Will Gunthrie made a fateful decision to broadcast over satellite radio. Initially, satellite transmission seemed easier and less expensive to the owners than purchasing a commercial radio station in a large or medium market. Up-linked to satellite dishes, KGAY's news and music was beamed across North America, Canada, and the Caribbean. KGAY claimed to be the first daily media vehicle for the gay and lesbian community in North America. Nearly one year after its inception, however, the network failed, with only a few sponsors to its credit. In retrospect, Henderson said that he should have first attempted to build a local queer audience in Denver; time zone differences across the United States, for example, made programming decisions especially difficult.

Also in the early 1990s, Chris DeChant founded *Aware Talk Radio*. Within a couple of years, DeChant began to syndicate his program from Chicago to major cities across the United States. It led in the discussion of HIV and other health issues and was mainly directed toward gay and lesbian audiences. DeChant's newsmagazine program *Life OUTside* debuted nearly ten years later, featuring news, entertainment, and discussion on social issues to an audience of 1.5 million, including listeners drawn from the Internet and seventy U.S. radio stations. The project, as promoted by DeChant, is the only nationally syndicated, commercial radio newsmagazine program with an all-queer on-air staff.

Another commercial radio venture soon began to command public attention after its debut in June 1994. Adult Contemporary WCBR-FM in Chicago became the home to *LesBiGay Radio*. Its founder, Alan Amberg, hosted America's only drive time gay radio show. The station signal tapped into North Chicago neighborhoods where many LGBT people resided. *LesBiGay Radio* went off the air in April 2001, but only after a successful stint of seven years. In the late 1990s Charles "Karel" Bouley II and Andrew Howard, an openly gay couple, made history when *Karel and Andrew Live* became the number one afternoon drive time radio show (from 4 P.M. to 7 P.M.) in Los Angeles after only several months at KFI-AM 640, Southern California's number one commercial talk station.

The tremendous social, cultural, political, and economic diversity within the queer community is echoed through the variety of radio programs available to listeners. *Amazon Country*, which airs on WXPN-FM, celebrates its thirtieth anniversary in 2004. The program features a lesbian feminist perspective in its music and its interviews with artists, authors, and leaders throughout the nation. In 2003 the United States was a leader in queer programming, with the broadcast of more than one hundred original LGBT shows on a regular basis.

Bibliography

Alwood, Edward. *Straight News: Gays, Lesbians, and the News Media.* New York: Columbia University Press, 1996.

Capsuto, Steven. *Alternate Channels: The Uncensored Story of Gay and Lesbian Images on Radio and Television.* New York: Ballantine Books, 2000.

Gross, Larry, and James D. Woods, eds. *The Columbia Reader on Lesbian and Gay Men in Media, Society, and Politics.* New York: Columbia University Press, 1999.

Hendriks, Aart, Robert Tielman, and Evert van der Veen, eds. *The Third Pink Book.* Buffalo, N.Y.: Prometheus Books, 1993.

Johnson, Phylis, Charles Hoy, and Dhyana Ziegler. "The Case of KGAY: Rise and Fall of the First Gay and Lesbian Network." *Journal of Radio Studies* 3 (1995–1996): 162–181.

Johnson, Phylis, and Michael C. Keith. *Queer Airwaves: The Story of Gay and Lesbian Broadcasting.* Armonk, N.Y.: Sharpe, 2001.

Laser, Matthew. *Pacifica Radio: The Rise of an Alternative Network.* Philadelphia: Temple University Press, 1999.

Schulman, Sarah. *My American History: Lesbian and Gay Life during the Reagan/Bush Years.* New York: Routledge, 1994.

Phylis Johnson

See also GINSBERG, ALLEN; MORGAN, ROBIN; WICKER, RANDOLFE.

RAINEY, Ma (b. 26 April 1886; d. 22 December 1939), blues singer.

One of the first professional women blues singers, Gertrude "Ma" Rainey performed and recorded a wide repertoire of blues songs rooted in southern rural folk traditions, vaudeville, and black minstrelsy. Engaging in relationships with both women and men, Rainey made no attempt to hide her bisexuality, which was well known to her audiences and colleagues. Rainey addressed her sexual desire for women in "Prove It On Me Blues" (1928), the period's most explicit blues song on lesbian sexuality. Rainey's sexually assertive stance and her pioneering role in classic blues position her as an important African American female performer.

Born Gertrude Pridgett in Columbus, Georgia, Rainey was the second of Ella and Thomas Pridgett's five children. Her first public appearance in 1900 as part of the Bunch of Blackberries revue was followed by performances in tent shows throughout the South. By 1902 Rainey added the blues to her repertoire and became one of its earliest public performers. At the age of eighteen, she married William "Pa" Rainey, a somewhat older dancer, comedian, and singer. The couple performed together in black minstrel productions; they were often presented as the "Assassinators of the Blues." However, by 1918 the marriage had dissolved; Rainey later remarried a younger man who worked outside of show business.

Throughout the 1910s, when Rainey appeared as a solo performer, she was billed as "Madame Gertrude Rainey"; by 1915 the shortened "Ma" eclipsed this billing. Rainey's nickname reflected the fact that she was older than many other performers as well as her friendly and compassionate personality. Despite the maternal attributes of her name, Rainey was also presented on stage as a highly experienced, attractive, and sexual woman.

Ma Rainey's sexualized image was not only forged through her performance of rough and raunchy blues: in her appearance, as well as in her songs, Rainey was not demure. Often described as a short dark-skinned woman with unruly hair and a mouth full of gold teeth, Rainey's appearance did not fall into the standard paramaters of what defined a sexually attractive African American woman; her audiences, however, viewed her as extremely desirable. Flaunting diaphanous gowns, tiaras, a gold necklace, and earrings, Rainey was, to black working-class audiences, the epitome of a successful, sexually alluring woman. Such an image challenged the period's definition of female beauty as passive, fragile, and white.

In 1923, already a celebrated performer in southern black minstrel shows, Rainey began her five-year recording career in Chicago with Paramount Records. During this period Rainey wrote and recorded "Prove It On Me Blues." Departing from the predominantly heterosexual discourse of the blues, the song not only celebrated same-sex erotic pleasure, but also highlighted the ability of black women to choose sexual partnership with other women. Rainey did not romanticize same-sex relationships—she acknowledged that they were still prone to heartache and despair—nor did she claim that being a lesbian was easy in a society that sought to condemn so-called "deviant" sexuality. Central to Rainey's composition was the claim that despite all suggestions to the contrary, she—an African American lesbian woman—was indeed a woman. Her admissions notwithstanding, Rainey's blues challenged society to prove its suspicions before condemning her. Her lyrics defiantly taunted the listener: even if society was able to prove her bisexuality, Rainey did not care. In her lyrics Rainey was perhaps referring to a 1925 incident when such "proof" emerged in her arrest for hosting an indecent party. Responding to a noise complaint, Chicago police found Rainey and a roomful of naked women engaged in intimate relations. Rainey spent the night in jail and was bailed out the next morning by her friend, blues singer Bessie Smith.

Rainey's official obituary included no acknowledgment of her important artistic contribution as the first important female blues singer, describing her as a housekeeper by occupation. Rainey's rightful place in musical history was later restored, and in 1994 her reputation gained further national prominence when her image appeared on a U.S. postage stamp. Rainey's significant contribution must be recognized in terms of her artistry. Maintaining her southern rural roots and incorporating lyrics about same-sex sexual desire in her blues, Rainey challenged her largely black working-class audiences to confront homophobic attitudes. Her music provided visibility and voice to early-twentieth-century African American bisexual and lesbian women.

Bibliography

Carby, Hazel. "It Just Be's Dat Way Sometime: The Sexual Politics of Women's Blues." *Radical America* 20, no. 4 (June–July 1986).

Davis, Angela. *Blues Legacies and Black Feminism: Gertrude "Ma" Rainey, Bessie Smith, and Billie Holiday.* New York: Vintage Books, 1998.

Harrison, Daphne Duval. *Black Pearls: Blues Queens of the 1920s.* New Brunswick, N.J.: Rutgers University Press, 1988.

Lieb, Sandra R. *Mother of the Blues: A Study of Ma Rainey.* Amherst: University of Massachusetts Press, 1981.

Laila S. Haidarali

See also FEMMES AND BUTCHES; HARLEM RENAISSANCE; MUSIC: POPULAR; SMITH, BESSIE.

RAMOS OTERO, Manuel (b. 20 July 1948; d. 7 October 1990), writer, theater director, scholar.

Jesús Manuel Ramos Otero was born and raised in Manatí, Puerto Rico, a small town on the northern coast of the island, known as the "Athens of Puerto Rico," where his grandparents owned a bakery. He attended the University of Puerto Rico High School in Río Piedras (1960–1965) and went on to receive a bachelor's degree in social sciences (major in sociology and minor in political sciences) in 1968, immediately migrating to New York after graduation. In interviews, Ramos Otero stated that he felt compelled to leave the island because of social intolerance of homosexuality. Ramos Otero spent most of his adult life in the United States, except for a brief period in 1977, when he returned to Puerto Rico, and in 1990, when he returned to die from AIDS-related complications.

In New York, Ramos Otero enrolled in film classes at the School of Visual Arts and at the New School for Social Research (1970–1971), and went on to study theater directing with Lee Strasberg (1971–1972). He also started a theater troupe called Taller Teatral Aspasguanza (1971) and collaborated extensively with other Puerto Rican theater artists. Ramos Otero received a master's degree in Spanish from New York University (1979) but died before completing his Ph.D. from the Graduate Center of the City University of New York (CUNY), where he had begun a dissertation entitled "Urban Life as Metaphor: Narrative Puerto Rican Fiction (1971–1991)." He also taught literature courses at CUNY. His lovers included John Anthes in the 1970s and the Puerto Rican gay painter Angel Rodríguez Díaz in the early 1980s.

Ramos Otero is known as the foremost Puerto Rican gay author and his work continues to be very influential. He formed part of a group of radical young writers including Rosario Ferré, Olga Nolla, and Víctor Fernández Fragoso, who shocked Puerto Rican society in the late 1960s and early 1970s with their feminist-inspired, racially diverse, and gay liberationist works. Ramos Otero's short story "Vida ejemplar del esclavo y el señor" (Exemplary Life of a Slave and a Master, 1974), published in *Zona de carga y descarga*, was widely banned in Puerto Rico for its open treatment of gay sadomasochism. Almost all Ramos Otero's works were in Spanish and were published in Puerto Rico, New York, or New Jersey, and to date most have not been translated.

Many of Ramos Otero's short stories have a Puerto Rican gay male protagonist and narrator, what Arnaldo Cruz-Malavé (1993) has identified as "personas" and Jossianna Arroyo (2001) as "masks" of the author. In fact, both Cruz-Malavé and Arroyo have seen the work of Ramos Otero as a response to dominant patriarchal, male-centered narratives by canonical authors such as René Marqués and Luis Rafael Sánchez. Migration and drug use are also central themes of his work. As Juan Gelpí (1993) has observed, there is an evolution in his stories from anonymous wanderings in New York City (such as in "Hollywood Memorabilia") through an integration of the New York gay scene (Christopher Street in "The Story of the Woman from the Sea"), and finally to the diasporic Puerto Rican community of the Lower East Side ("Blank Page and Staccato"), where the Chinese-Afro-Puerto Rican private detective Sam Fat meets the gay white Puerto Rican writer Manuel Ramos. Rubén Ríos-Avila (1998) has compared Ramos Otero's migratory experience to that of the Cuban exiled writer Reinaldo Arenas. Other narratives deal with Puerto Ricans in Hawaii ("Vivir del cuento") and a famous black female prostitute in Ponce ("La última plena que bailó Luberza").

Ramos Otero published three books of short stories: *Concierto de metal para un recuerdo y otras orgías de soledad* (Metal Concerto for a Memory and Other Orgies of Solitude, 1971); *El cuento de la Mujer del Mar* (The Story of the Woman of the Sea, 1979); and *Página en blanco y staccato* (Blank Page and Staccato, 1987). He also wrote one novel, *La novelabingo* (The Bingo Novel, 1976), and two books of poetry, *El libro de la muerte* (The Book of Death, 1985) and *Invitación al polvo* (Invitation to Dust, 1991). He was fond of performing his poetry with the help of costumes, lights, and props. His literary scholarship, published in the journal *Cupey*, includes articles on the openly gay Spanish poet Luis Cernuda and on contemporary Puerto Rican literature as well as a discussion with Olga Nolla and the Argentine writer Manuel Puig.

Jorge Merced and the Pregones Theater of the Bronx, New York, adapted one of Ramos Otero's short stories, "Loca la de la locura" (The Queen of Madness), into a one-man play with live musical accompaniment called *El bolero fue mi ruina* (The Bolero Was My Downfall). The story is a first-person narrative by a drag queen who is incarcerated in Puerto Rico for having assassinated her boyfriend Nene Lindo (Pretty Baby), a typical *bugarrón* or masculine-acting man who maintains sexual relations with effeminate men but never assumes a gay identity;

Merced plays both characters on stage. This play was in repertoire from 1997 to 2002 and was shown extensively across the United States, Latin America, and Europe.

Bibliography

Arroyo, Jossianna. "Exilio y tránsitos entre la Norzagaray y Christopher Street: acercamientos a una poética del deseo homosexual en Manuel Ramos Otero." *Revista Iberoamericana* 67, no. 194–195 (January–June 2001): 31–54.

Costa, Marithelma. "Manuel Ramos Otero." *Hispamérica* 20, no. 59 (August 1991): 59–67.

Cruz Malavé, Arnaldo. "Para virar al macho: la autobiografía como subversión en la cuentística de Manuel Ramos Otero." *Revista Iberoamericana* 59, no. 162–163 (January–June 1993): 239–263.

Gelpí, Juan. "Conversación con Manuel Ramos Otero (Nueva York, 3 de mayo de 1980)." *Revista de Estudios Hispánicos* (Río Piedras) 27, no. 2 (2000): 401–410.

———. *Literatura y paternalismo en Puerto Rico.* San Juan: Editorial de la Universidad de Puerto Rico, 1993.

La Fountain-Stokes, Lawrence. "Bolero, memoria y violencia." *Conjunto* 106 (May–August 1997): 68–69. Review of Pregones Theater's *The Bolero Was My Downfall.*

Ríos Avila, Rubén. "Caribbean Dislocations: Arenas and Ramos Otero in New York." In *Hispanisms and Homosexualities.* Edited by Sylvia Molloy and Robert McKee Irwin. Durham, N.C.: Duke University Press, 1998.

Lawrence M. La Fountain-Stokes

See also PUERTO RICO.

RAPE, SEXUAL ASSAULT, AND SEXUAL HARASSMENT LAW AND POLICY

At its worst, the history of LGBT dimensions of law and policy related to rape, sexual assault, and sexual harassment reveals a biased and prejudiced criminal justice system that seemingly attempts to control and shape sexual behavior to fit normative heterosexist and sexist views of gender and sexual orientation. At its best, this history reveals a very gradual shift toward increased protection from violence and discrimination against LGBT people. An examination of various laws and court rulings points to ongoing struggles to define terminology related to rape, sexual assault, and harassment and to determine whether those definitions provide adequate protection from discrimination and violence.

Rape and Sexual Assault Law

Each state legally defines rape, and rape and sexual assault laws can thus vary by state and even within a state.

Despite impressive reform efforts since the 1950s, no consensus exists on how to define rape, what terminology should be used to delineate various sexual crimes, and what are the purposes of rape laws. Lack of clarity influences the extent to which rape laws actually protect people. Historically, rape and sexual assault laws have not provided equal protection to LGBT people. Why is this? A historical review of trends in rape law points to at least three interconnected factors: the significance of racial, gender, and sexual orientation stereotypes; the regulation of sexual behavior; and the marginalized status of those who are LGBT.

Stereotypes

Rape and sexual assault laws have always been influenced by gender, race, and sexual orientation stereotypes. Take, for example, the definition written by William Blackstone, a British legal commentator, in 1769. Rape, he wrote, is the carnal knowledge of a woman forcibly and against her will. Blackstone's definition influenced rape law in the United States and is still used in some jurisdictions today. The limitations of this definition can be seen in the original purpose of the law: to protect the chastity of women and hence the property of men. Traditionally, survivors were acknowledged only when they were female and perpetrators only when they were male, and rape was defined with sole reference to penetration of the vagina. Historical records stretching back to the colonial period do contain evidence of prosecutions for forced same-sex sex, but in the vast majority of cases perpetrators were charged with other sex crimes (for example, sodomy), not with rape. Based on stereotypes of men as aggressive and women as passive, this understanding of rape failed to protect people of any sex who were raped within the context of marriage, same-sex relationships, hate crimes, courtship, and dating. Nor did it protect people who were sexually assaulted (by same-sex or cross-sex perpetrators) without vaginal penetration.

The significance of stereotypes in rape law can also be seen in the evolution of child molestation laws. From 1881 to 1946, as awareness grew about the abuse of children, many states took greater interest in legally protecting children, and, as a result, built on their existing seduction statutes (which generally criminalized vaginal intercourse between an adult male and a prepubescent girl) and sodomy laws (which generally criminalized anal and sometimes oral sex) to delineate various sex crimes committed by adult males on children. Even though nearly all of these new "immoral use," "indecent liberties," and "contributing to the delinquency of minors" laws attempted to protect both boys and girls, the laws often failed to consider the extent to which women and heterosexual men were abusers. In many contexts, gay men who had consensual adult sex were conflated with adult perpetrators who had sex with children and were regarded as "sexual perverts."

As with rape laws, statutory rape laws (dealing with rapes of minors) are passed at the state level. Once again, statutes vary by state, including the age at which consent can be legally given. Typically, the age today is sixteen, but as of 1996 eight states set the age at thirteen while another eight set the age at eighteen. Qualifications and exceptions (for example, if the older party is close in age to the younger party) also vary greatly. In the 1950s, reformers with the prestigious American Law Institute proposed setting an age of consent for males that would be higher than the age of consent for females (based on notions of adolescent development and on stereotypes of adult men preying on adolescent males). Statutory rape statutes become confusing when both parties are underage, and very little is written about what happens if both parties are of the same sex, let alone if they actually consent to the behavior.

Rape Law as Regulation of Sexual Behavior

In theory, rape laws are designed to regulate nonconsensual sexual behavior, but in practice, they have also been used to regulate nonnormative consensual sexual acts (including same-sex sex and black male/white female sex). Discourses of rape have also been used to justify the passage of other sex laws that regulate consensual sexual behavior. Over the course of the first few decades of the twentieth century, law enforcement efforts increasingly prioritized crimes committed by men against women and children; as a result, there were more arrests for rape, sex with and corruption of minors, and forcible sodomy. This may be explained partly by the growing acceptance of Freudian and other psychological theories of sexual development. With increased use of expert witness testimony in court, the psychiatric field, beginning in the 1930s, influenced the creation of sexual psychopath laws, often passed in the context of sensational media coverage of rape and sexual assault cases. Criminal sexual conduct was often explained as a product of mental disorders, with the individual too sick to be punished in prison and therefore requiring permanent or semipermanent institutional confinement. Between 1947 and 1957, more than half the states revised existing sexual laws or adopted the new sexual psychopath laws. William N. Eskridge Jr. (1999) documents the regulatory function of sexual psychopath statutes, stating that in most states homosexuals were the primary targets of these laws. He estimates that between 1946 and 1961, amid public concern about sexual psychopaths, as many as one million lesbians and gay

men received criminal punishments for engaging in consensual adult intercourse, dancing, kissing. and holding hands.

Although efforts to reform rape and related sex laws began soon after World War II, significant changes in these laws did not take place until the 1960s, 1970s, and 1980s. For instance, by the 1980s most states had repealed or stopped using the sexual psychopath laws. Beginning in the 1960s, the efforts of feminist and victim advocacy groups led to several improvements in the processing of rape crimes, including rape shield statutes, which prohibit the questioning of rape survivors about prior sexual activity while on the witness stand; name protection laws, which prohibit the publication of a rape survivor's name; police sensitivity training toward the emotional and physical trauma suffered by rape survivors; and the establishment of rape crisis centers. Although most LGBT critics of rape law reform have appreciated the efforts of feminist and other advocacy groups, they have critiqued the changes for inherent bias. For example, many police sensitivity training workshops and rape crisis centers are not prepared to deal adequately with LGBT survivors. Clearly, feminist analysis of sexual assault has expanded awareness about the underlying power and control dynamics involved in rape. However, emerging research into the prevalence of victimization and domestic violence in same-sex relationships points to the need to expand conceptions of power.

Rape Law and LGBT Marginalization

Perhaps the most illustrative example of how rape law enforces the marginalized status of LGBT people is the lack of protection for people raped within the context of same-sex relationships and other people raped by same-sex perpetrators. Research into same-sex domestic violence has had to contend with the prominent gendered stereotype in which only heterosexual women are abused and only men are abusers. However, initial research into the extent of same-sex partner abuse shows that violence is indeed a serious problem, probably occurring at the same rate as in cross-sex relationships.

The gender bias in conceptions of rape is said to affect several aspects of processing sexual assault claims. Krisana Hodges (1999–2000) reports that the exclusion of gay and lesbian relationships in state domestic violence laws takes place in three ways: by limiting protection to married or formerly married couples; by using ambiguous language that enables prosecutors and judges to vary how laws are applied; and by explicitly excluding gay and lesbian relationships from the statutes. The latter currently occurs in nine states. Many states have domestic violence statutes protecting "partners," "unmarried couples," "household members," and the like. But the interpretation of such language has been left up to judges and prosecutors. Only a few states have clarified that in domestic violence situations same-sex couples deserve the protection of the courts. The 1997 Kentucky case of *Ireland v. Davis* illustrates this point. John Ireland and Blake Davis had lived together as lovers. Ireland claimed that Davis had abused him. A domestic violence order was filed, which Ireland later claimed Davis violated. After an arrest warrant was issued, a district court judge set aside the warrant on the grounds that since both Davis and Ireland were men, the court lacked jurisdiction. However, the Kentucky Court of Appeals held that same-sex couples qualify as "unmarried couples" under the state's domestic violence statute. Few state courts have followed suit, and without such explicit protection, same-sex couples do not know if legal protection will be granted should they decide to seek help.

Not only do LGBT people face the ambiguity of legal language when seeking protection, but the likelihood is that an LGBT defendant or survivor will be up against the potential influence of bias and fear in the courtroom. A study by Drury Sherrod and Peter M. Nardi (1998) suggests that jury reactions to lesbian and gay men may indeed be influenced by homophobia. Lesbian and gay victims of rape are often blamed in the courtroom for attacks against them and experience indifference from prosecutors, judges, and juries. Because of a perceived lack of compliance with stereotypical gender roles, transgender people are frequent targets of physical and sexual abuse, and they also experience bias in legal proceedings. Take the experience of Teena Brandon, a biological female who cross-dressed and lived much of her life as a man. She reported that two men raped her on Christmas Day in 1993. The local sheriff warned her that if she reported the rape, they would silence her. Brandon ignored the warning and went to the police. Brandon was murdered on New Year's Eve. Her family later filed a lawsuit against local law enforcement officials, claiming that they did not take her report seriously, in part because she was a cross-dresser, and that they could have prevented her murder.

With the well-documented mistreatment of LGBT people by the police and courts, and without the reassurance of adequate legal protection, scholars such as Michael Scarce (1997) and Claire Renzetti (1992) ask whether LGBT people should use the legal system to resolve the problems of same-sex rape and same-sex domestic violence. Before the 2003 *Lawrence v. Texas* ruling that overturned the state's sodomy law, in the thirteen states in which sodomy was criminalized, males had the

added fear that if they reported rape, not only would they not be believed, but they also could be charged with consensual homosexual sex. Thus, as various scholars note, there is a need for broader conceptualizations of the power dynamics in relationships contributing to rape and domestic violence. Conceptions of power need to address more than just sex and gender; they need to consider race and ethnicity, sexual orientation, class and economic status, physical strength, mental and physical ability, and religion.

Sexual Harassment Law

As of 2003, there were no laws explicitly protecting LGBT people from workplace sexual harassment and discrimination; nor were there laws explicitly protecting people from same-sex sexual harassment. A review of cases reveals a very gradual shift over time toward increased protection. However, court systems of all levels still inconsistently resolve these cases. Inconsistency may stem from a variety of ongoing unresolved issues, namely, how to define "sex" (particularly "sex" in Title VII of the Civil Rights Act of 1964), what specifically constitutes sexual harassment, and to what extent gender stereotypes related to sexual orientation are relevant. The courts have been criticized for reproducing normative sexist and heterosexist values and for playing a role in perpetuating the workplace violence experienced by LGBT people.

Historical Overview

Sexual harassment was barely recognized in the courts prior to the passage of the Civil Rights Act of 1964; often it was dismissed as a harmless product of personal urges, an acceptable form of masculine bantering, or a symptom of relationship problems between a man and a woman. Title VII of the Civil Rights Act of 1964, as originally conceived, made it illegal for employers to discriminate in hiring, firing, or compensating, or in the terms, conditions, and privileges of employment based on race, color, sex, religion, or national origin. Congress left "sex" undefined, leaving the courts free to interpret the term in a variety of ways. According to Alba Conte (1998), sexual harassment was not recognized as a form of sex discrimination under Title VII until the 1970s. In *Williams v. Sabe* (1976), the courts ruled that a woman who had refused the sexual advances of her male supervisor, who in turn reprimanded her and gave her unfavorable reviews, had an actionable sex discrimination claim under Title VII.

Sexual harassment cases initially were based on two concepts of sexual harassment. "Quid pro quo" arguments were used for situations in which compliance with sexual advances was a term of employment. The other main argument concentrated on "hostile environment." Both arguments focused on male harassment of females. Without explicit protection from same-sex sexual harassment and from sexual orientation harassment, there have been several efforts to use existing legislation strategically.

Recent Cases

According to Jo Bennett (1996), same-sex sexual harassment makes up 9 percent of workplace sexual harassment claims. One of the first cases to be tried and found applicable under Title VII was *Wright v. Methodist Youth Services* (1981). In this case, Donald Wright filed charges with the Equal Employment Opportunity Commission (EEOC), alleging that his supervisor, Dale Hillerman, made sexual advances toward him. Wright claimed that he turned down the advances and had been fired as a result. In addition to alleging a violation of Title VII, Wright claimed that his termination violated 42 U.S. Code sections 1983 and 1985, which prohibit unconstitutional discrimination under state law and provide remedies for governmental violation of constitutional rights. Prior to this case, there had been no precedent for making a Title VII claim in a same-sex employment situation.

Whether the alleged conduct is based on gender or sexual orientation is an important legal distinction. In *Ecklund v. Fuisz Technology, Ltd* (1995), a female coworker made sexual comments and jokes to the female plaintiff. The plaintiff alleged that the coworker also stroked her hair and body, hugged and forcibly kissed her at a company event, and partially undressed in front of her. After receiving no help from her company's human resources department, the plaintiff resigned. The court determined that the identity of the harasser in a Title VII suit is not relevant and thus the harassment was recognizable, in this case as hostile environment sexual harassment. Title VII, however, limits liability in discrimination to employers, and since the coworker was not the employer, she was not liable for damages.

Despite these cases, court responses to same-sex sexual harassment continue to vary greatly. In *Goluszek v. Smith* (1988), a claim of same-sex sexual harassment under Title VII was denied. Male coworkers harassed the male plaintiff for not having a wife or girlfriend (there is no reference to his sexual orientation). In addition to explicit comments about sex, they showed him pictures of nude women, accused him of being gay or bisexual, poked him in the buttocks with a stick, and repeatedly tried to knock him off his ladder. Goluszek was then fired for lateness and unexcused absences. The judge in the case stated that Goluszek was unable to show that he worked in an environment that treated males as inferior.

For the judge, the discrimination prohibited in Title VII is related to a power imbalance that results in discrimination against a vulnerable group. She accepted that the plaintiff may have been harassed because he was male. However, since all the figures in this case were male, the judge concluded that the harassment was not the kind that created an anti-male environment. Her anti-male requirement set the precedent that in order for a gay man to claim sexual harassment he must first demonstrate an anti-male environment. Although the *Goluszek* ruling has influenced many subsequent courts to decide similarly—that same-sex sexual harassment is outside the coverage of Title VII—the judge's reasoning has been criticized. Francis Achampong (1999) points out that an imbalance of power is not a prerequisite of sexual harassment. As Alba Conte (1998) writes, the conduct considered in this case perpetuates stereotypes, drains productivity, and interferes with professional relationships.

Many courts struggle with the question of whether an employee was harassed because of sexual orientation or because of sex. Some courts have rejected sexual orientation (and same-sex sexual harassment) arguments altogether, while other courts have avoided the issue of sexual orientation by framing the issue as one related to gender. Jo Bennett (1996) makes a persuasive case for the illegality of gender stereotyping under Title VII. She argues that in *Dillon v. Frank* (1992) Dillon was indeed harassed because of his sexual orientation. Yet that harassment did violate Title VII since Dillon was treated differently because of his sex, even though someone of the same sex inflicted the harassment.

Only a few courts have decided that harassment based on the sexual orientation, perceived or not, of an employee constitutes sex discrimination. In the case of *Oncale v. Sundown Offshore Services, Inc.* (1998), the plaintiff claimed both quid pro quo and hostile environment sexual harassment by coworkers and his supervisor, who thought he was gay. The harassment involved threats of rape, restraining him, placing a penis on his neck, and pushing a bar of soap into his anus. The district court relied on *Garcia v. Elf Atochem North America* (1994), which argued that a male has no cause of action under Title VII for harassment by male colleagues. The *Oncale* case made it to the U.S. Supreme Court, which ruled unanimously that Title VII protects employees from same-sex sexual harassment. However, the Supreme Court, trying to avoid making Title VII a "general civility code," also established formal rules requiring the plaintiff to prove that the alleged conduct was not merely offensive but constituted discrimination because of sex. This decision, according to B. J. Chisholm (2001), has potential applications for claims brought by employees for harassment based on their perceived sexual orientation. Employers have used the *Oncale* decision to dismiss claims, especially when the employee is gay or perceived to be gay. The Supreme Court made it the plaintiff's burden to prove that discrimination is sex-based; the Court never reached a conclusion, according to some, that the harassment was based upon sexual orientation.

Chisolm, along with other scholars, is concerned with the motivation for harassment. Gays and lesbians are often targeted because they fail to conform to social gender and sexual norms based on their perceived biological sex and genitalia. The failure of courts to examine the sex- and gender-based nature of sexual orientation harassment leaves them basing their decisions on presumed norms of masculinity, femininity, and heterosexuality. Oncale was singled out for harassment not because of his sex, but because of his gender—for being the kind of man his colleagues disapproved of.

Recommendations

Proposals for the revision of policy and law have been developed by a variety of scholars, researchers, activists, reformers, and legislators. Common suggestions include the development of more comprehensive definitions (for instance, of sex, gender, and sexuality), more explicit prohibitions on sexual harassment and sexual orientation harassment, and passage of employment nondiscrimination laws to protect LGBT people.

Bibliography

Achampong, Francis. *Workplace Sexual Harassment Law; Principles, Landmark Developments, and Framework for Effective Risk Management.* Westport, Conn.: Quorum Books, 1999.

Bennett, Jo. "Same-Sex Sexual Harassment." *Law and Sexuality; A Review of Lesbian, Gay, Bisexual, and Transgender Legal Issues* 6 (1996): 1–29.

Berrill, Kevin. "Anti-Gay Violence: Causes, Consequences, and Responses." In *Bias Crime: American Law Enforcement and Legal Responses.* Chicago: University of Illinois at Chicago, 1993.

Chisholm, B. J. "The (Back)door of *Oncale v. Sundowner Offshore Services, Inc.*: 'Outing' Heterosexuality as a Gender-Based Stereotype." *Law and Sexuality: A Review of Lesbian, Gay, Bisexual, and Transgender Legal Issues* 10 (2001): 239–276.

Conte, Alba. *Sexual Orientation and Legal Rights.* Vol. 1. New York: Wiley, 1998.

Eskridge, William N., Jr. *Gaylaw: Challenging the Apartheid of the Closet.* Cambridge, Mass.: Harvard University Press, 1999.

Eskridge, William N., Jr., and Nan D. Hunter. *Sexuality, Gender, and the Law.* New York: Foundation Press, 1997.

Hodges, Krisana M. "Trouble in Paradise: Barriers to Addressing Domestic Violence in Lesbian Relationships." *Law and Sexuality: A Review of Lesbian, Gay, Bisexual, and Transgender Legal Issues* 9 (1999–2000): 311–331.

Island, D., and P. Letellier. *Men Who Beat the Men Who Love Them: Battered Gay Men and Domestic Violence.* New York: Haworth Press, 1991.

Kranz, Rachel, and Tim Cusick. *Gay Rights.* New York: Facts on File, 2000.

Kuehl, Sheila James. "Seeing Is Believing: Research on Women's Sexual Orientation and Public Policy." *Journal of Social Issues* 56, no. 2 (2000): 351–359.

Leonard, Arthur S. "Same-Sex Harassment and the Male Employee." In *Sexuality and the Law: An Encyclopedia of Major Legal Cases.* Edited by John W. Johnson. New York: Garland, 1993.

Renzetti, Claire M. *Violent Betrayal: Partner Abuse in Lesbian Relationships.* Newbury Park, Calif.: Sage, 1992.

Scarce, Michael. *Male on Male Rape: The Hidden Toll of Stigma and Shame.* New York: Insight Books, 1997.

Sherrod, Drury, and Peter M. Nardi. "Homophobia in the Courtroom: An Assessment of Biases against Gay Men and Lesbians in a Multiethnic Sample of Potential Jurors." In *Stigma and Sexual Orientation; Understanding Prejudice against Lesbians, Gay Men, and Bisexuals.* Thousand Oaks, Calif.: Sage, 1998.

West, Carolyn. "Lesbian Intimate Partner Violence: Prevalence and Dynamics." *Journal of Lesbian Studies* 6, no. 1 (2002): 121–127.

Kathryn A. Lyndes

See also DISCRIMINATION; EMPLOYMENT LAW AND POLICY; FEDERAL LAW AND POLICY; HATE CRIMES LAW AND POLICY; POLICE AND POLICING.

RAUSCHENBERG, Robert
(b. 22 October 1925), artist.

Among the most influential American artists of the twentieth century, Rauschenberg personifies the complicated relationship between art and sexual identity during this period. A native of rural Texas, Rauschenberg began formal studies in art after his naval service in World War II. In 1950 he married and in 1951, fathered a son while exhibiting with the Abstract Expressionists. Shortly thereafter, however, Rauschenberg joined a new avant-garde contingent centered around the composer John Cage and his lover, the choreographer Merce Cunningham. In contrast to the Abstract Expressionists' heteronormative social mores and artistic emphasis on intuitive emotional expression, Cage's circle was less masculine and more intellectual. Rauschenberg fell in love with two of the

Robert Rauschenberg. The American artist, some of whose works are seen as having coded allusions to his sexual identity, sits by one of his paintings. [Bettmann/corbis]

other young men in Cage's group in succession: Cy Twombly and Jasper Johns.

The role of sexual identity in Rauschenberg's art is intensely controversial. Although he acknowledges his homosexuality more openly than does Twombly or Johns, all three artists resist analyses of their lives or work that emphasize sexual identity. Such secretiveness contrasts with artists like Andy Warhol and David Hockney, who came of age in the 1960s. Despite Rauschenberg's resistance, however, recent scholarship suggests that homosexuality—and homophobia—played a crucial role in the development of his art.

Rauschenberg's art began to challenge the expressive premises of Abstract Expressionism during his relationship with Twombly. He gained notoriety for a 1953 series of all-white paintings, about which the artist Allan Kaprow recalled, "In the context of Abstract Expressionist noise and gesture, they suddenly brought one face to face with a numbing, devastating silence" (Katz, p. 195). Even more confrontational was Rauschenberg's 1953 *Erased de Kooning*, which is exactly what the title describes: a marred sheet of paper from which he had erased a drawing by the Abstract Expressionist painter Willem de Kooning. Jonathan Katz analyzes the silence of these works in relation to the secrecy required of homosexuals in this era, arguing that Rauschenberg's homosexuality made him painfully aware of the art world's restrictions on self-expression and prompted him to read Abstract

Expressionist brush strokes as mere symbols, rather than real traces, of emotion. Quoting Rauschenberg's statement, "'words like "tortured," "struggle" and "pain" . . . I could never see these qualities in paint,'" Katz concludes, "Rauschenberg could never see those qualities in paint precisely because they stood out in such high relief in his life, in comparison with which paint was revealed as just, well, paint" (Katz, p. 195).

Around 1953 Rauschenberg's art shifted from a blank refusal of self-expression to overwhelming the viewer with quotations from divergent visual languages. The following seven years, when Rauschenberg and Johns were a couple, were crucial to their careers, a time of enormous inventiveness when both artists defined the terms of their life-long artistic preoccupations as they led the American avant-garde away from Abstract Expressionism and toward Pop Art. During this period, Rauschenberg became famous for what he called "Combines": collages of text, abstract marks, photographs, and stuck-on objects. Some of the Combines' elements—photographs of Judy Garland, for instance—can be read as references to gay identity, although such implications were noted only by hostile critics at the time. The persistence of this stigma has prompted Rauschenberg and his art-world allies to dismiss even the most compelling arguments for the relevance of sexual identity to his famous works. His 1955 *Bed*, for example, long exhibited at the Museum of Modern Art as a monument of American modernism, derives its impact from a juxtaposition of spattered paint and scrawled pencil marks on an actual quilt and pillow. The collision between the gestural signifiers of Abstract Expressionist machismo and the feminine associations of textiles in a setting associated with sexuality is hard to separate from contests over gender roles and sexual secrets in the art world of the 1950s.

Following the disintegration of his relationship with Johns in 1961, even coded allusions to gay culture disappeared from Rauschenberg's art as he moved toward collaborative and mechanical methods of image production that resist biographical interpretations. Through the 1960s, and occasionally thereafter, Rauschenberg collaborated in performance and dance and more recently worked with artists internationally to promote cultural interchange and human rights. Most critics, however, see his earliest work as his best. Arthur Danto's review of a 1997 retrospective mourned the loss of "human investitures" in Rauschenberg's later art, attributing it to the end of his intense involvement with Cage, Cunningham, Johns, and Twombly (*The Nation*, p. 36). If so, both the influential innovations and the later dryness of Rauschenberg's art reflect his negotiation of sexual identity.

Bibliography

Danto, Arthur. "Robert Rauschenberg." *The Nation* 17 (November 1997).

Hopps, Walter, and Susan Davidson. *Robert Rauschenberg: A Retrospective.* New York: Guggenheim Museum Publications, 1997.

Katz, Jonathan. "The Art of Code: Jasper Johns and Robert Rauschenberg." In *Significant Others: Creativity and Intimate Partnership.* Edited by Whitney Chadwick and Isabelle de Courtivon. London: Thames and Hudson, 1993.

——. "Passive Resistance: On the Success of Queer Artists in Cold War American Art." *Image* (Winter 1996): 119–142.

Silver, Kenneth E. "Modes of Disclosure: The Construction of Gay Identity and the Rise of Pop Art." In *Hand-Painted Pop.* Edited by Russell Ferguson. Los Angeles: Museum of Contemporary Art, 1992.

Christopher Reed

See also ART HISTORY; CAGE, JOHN; CUNNINGHAM, MERCE; JOHNS, JASPER; VISUAL ART.

RECHY, John (b. 1934), novelist, journalist, teacher.

Around the turn of the twenty-first century, novelist John Rechy's forty-year writing career finally began to receive serious critical and institutional attention. In 1997 Rechy was awarded two lifetime achievement awards, one from PEN/USA-West, the other the William Whitehead Award from Triangle Publishing. In 2000 the publishing arm of the Annenberg Communication Center published a retrospective, multimedia CD-ROM project entitled *Mysteries and Desire: Searching the Worlds of John Rechy,* while in December 2002 Alyson Books was preparing to publish the initial volume of Carlos Casillo's *Outlaw: John Rechy,* the first serious attempt to chronicle Rechy's life in biographical form. During this same time period Rechy published his twelfth novel, *The Coming of the Night* (1999), and continued to participate actively in the world of public intellectual and cultural exchange, both as a journalist and as a teacher of writing.

Rechy's life as a writer and legendary cultural figure began with the 1963 publication of his first novel, *City of Night,* which was a bona fide bestseller and for that reason broke new ground. The success of his first novel put him in the company of prominent gay writers like Gore Vidal, James Baldwin, and William Burroughs who had already enjoyed popular and critical success with gay-themed work. *City of Night* combined intense beat lyricism in its prose style with brutal documentary realism in the choice of subject matter. Rechy's exploration of the netherworld of gay male hustling, by turns politically, poetically, and even philosophically charged, was unprecedented for its time, and continued to provide Rechy with a wealth of material to mine. He returned to the same or similar subject matter in such works as *Numbers* (1967), *The Sexual Outlaw* (1977), *Rushes* (1979), and *The Coming of the Night* (1999).

Born of Mexican parents in 1934 in El Paso, Texas, Rechy was less forthcoming in his early writing about his Mexican American identity than about being gay. However, any close reading of his early, loosely autobiographical fiction makes it clear that Rechy never denied his Tex/Mex roots. Most of Rechy's early protagonists share their author's cultural background, and he makes much of his characters' dark physical features and the exploitative fetishization of those features by non-Latino johns. A more subtle cultural politics always accompanied and informed the more spectacular and attention-grabbing sexual politics in Rechy's work. While Rechy's place in the canon of important U.S. gay writers is unquestionably secure, one cannot say the same about his position among the ranks of Chicano writers. But if Rechy's early work completed a picture only alluded to by writers such as Vidal and Burroughs, it also contributed to the literary advances of writers of Mexican descent such as José Antonio Villarreal, whose 1959 novel *Pocho,* and Arturo Islas, whose 1983 novel *The Rain God,* both trace the lives of young Chicano protagonists across simultaneously sexual, cultural, and political fields of experience.

In later work Rechy explored in greater detail experiences that fall outside the exclusive purview of the world of gay male sex; these titles include *Marilyn's Daughter* (1988), *The Miraculous Day of Amalia Gómez* (1991), and *Our Lady of Babylon* (1996), all of which cover from various angles the related but distinct terrain of female experience, as well as cultural constructions of femininity. These latter titles offer a rich context for the "male" work for which Rechy is better known, and each in its own way calls significant attention to other topics of central concern to their author: *Marilyn's Daughter* analyzes cinema's influence on the popular imagination; *Amalia Gómez* elaborates on Chicano life; and *Our Lady* fuses his views of sex, gender, and transgression into one coherent historical mythology.

Although Rechy is primarily noted as one of the most important gay novelists in the United States, he has during the course of his long career managed always to defy, and to transgress, the conventions of literary and cultural practice. In doing so, he has challenged audiences, critics, and scholars to consider his literary work within the context of a more complex and iconoclastic personal life, which for him has been chiefly an alternative form of public performance. For these reasons, that life may best be summarized in multimedia forms such as the Annenberg 2000 CD-ROM project or http://www. JohnRechy.com, one of the many Web sites devoted to Rechy's life and work. As the year 2003 marks the fortieth anniversary of Rechy's first appearance on the cultural scene in the United States, it also marks a significant and still evolving period in U.S. gay culture, one that predates Stonewall, and that will survive thanks in large part to its having been recorded so memorably by writers such as Rechy.

Bibliography

Canning, Richard. *Gay Fiction Speaks: Conversations with Gay Novelists*. New York: Columbia University Press, 2000. Contains a chapter on Rechy.

Casillo, Charles. *Outlaw: The Lives and Careers of John Rechy*. New York: Alyson, 2002.

                                                    Ricardo L. Ortíz

See also PULP FICTION: GAY.

RELIGION. see CHURCHES, TEMPLES, AND RELIGIOUS GROUPS. SEE ALSO INDIVIDUAL RELIGIONS.

REPUBLICAN PARTY

Since the pre-Stonewall era, LGBT activists have often found themselves on the defensive, responding to policy agendas that have been established by others. Conflicts over LGBT rights have been informed by the considerable efforts of Christian conservative organizers to disparage, discredit, and prevent all assimilation and liberation efforts. Over time, the Republican Party has had to negotiate its relationship to the Christian evangelical movement, while reassessing its interaction with the LGBT movements. Lesbians and gays achieved visibility within the Democratic and Republican Parties during the 1990s. But the differences between the Democrats and Republicans on issues of sexual orientation have been the source of significant conflict since the early 1980s, especially since Christian evangelicals began to infuse local, state, and national Republican Party politics by the end of that decade.

The 1980 Elections

A Gallup poll predicted that the 1980 presidential election between Ronald Reagan and the incumbent Jimmy Carter would be close, but Reagan won handily and with considerable help from the New Right and Christian Right. The political landscape was fundamentally altered with Republican victories in the White House and U.S. Senate, where Republican challenges had defeated nine incumbent Democrats, thus giving the Republican Party control of the Senate for the first time in nearly thirty years. In addition, Republicans enjoyed gains in the U.S. House of Representatives.

Understandably, the Christian Right was emboldened by the Republican Party's electoral success in the 1980 elections and sought credit for electing Reagan and defeating Democratic members of Congress. Jerry Falwell, the head of the recently created Moral Majority, was particularly vocal in celebrating the crucial role played by Christian evangelicals, citing their national voter turnout campaigns and impressive grassroots organizing abilities. The mobilizing accomplishments of Richard Viguerie, Paul Weyrich (of the Free Congress Foundation), Terry Dolan (of the National Conservative Political Action Committee), Phyllis Schlafly (of the Eagle Forum), and Howard Phillips (of the Conservative Caucus) inspired the modern conservative movement to support organizations that were dedicated to promoting traditional family, antiabortion, antifeminist, and evangelical Christian views.

How did the Christian Right contribute to the dominance of social conservatism that has characterized the Republican Party since 1980? First, it registered hundreds of thousands of new voters who could generally be counted on to support its pro-family views. Second, it successfully infiltrated the Republican Party by recruiting new people at the grassroots level to participate in party politics. Third, the Christian Right helped to reshape the political and cultural agenda by taking abortion, school prayer, and pro-family issues and placing them on the public and congressional agendas. All these developments had consequences for the LGBT movements as Ronald Reagan assumed the presidency in January 1981.

The Reagan White House

What did these political developments mean for the LGBT movements? The reality is that there was little to celebrate. Despite Reagan's previously announced public opposition to the 1978 California Briggs initiative, which would have prevented lesbians and gays from teaching in California's public schools, he had appealed to the most conservative elements of the Republican Party in his quest for the presidency. As a result, his presidency had to cater to their various demands, which meant pursuing a conservative social agenda, one that celebrated the traditional family and school prayer, while also opposing anyone who did not share his view of morality. Fundamentalist Christians continued their vigorous organizing efforts at the local, state, and national levels in an effort to capitalize on their postelection momentum and take full advantage of the Reagan honeymoon period. It was against this backdrop that Senator Roger Jepsen (R-Iowa) introduced the 1981 Family Law (Protection of Spouses and Children) Act, which would prevent lesbians and gays from receiving welfare, veteran's, or Social Security benefits. To no one's surprise, Reagan publicly endorsed Jepsen's legislation. In addition, he pleased his Christian Right supporters when he appointed Gary Bauer, a close associate of James Dobson, who was president of Focus on the Family, to the position of domestic policy advisor.

The early 1980s also ushered in the era of Acquired Immune Deficiency Syndrome (AIDS), a disease that soon grew into an epidemic as more and more gay men became infected with HIV, the virus that can eventually lead to AIDS. The outbreak of AIDS enabled Christian Right activists such as Falwell to craft new fundraising strategies that targeted homosexuality with particular vitriol, despite the fact that many people with AIDS are not gay, the vast majority of gay men would never contract HIV, and lesbians were at low risk for contracting the disease. Falwell and his Christian evangelical supporters had found what they considered to be just punishment for homosexual behavior; lesbians and gays could not argue that engaging in same-sex practices was without negative consequences. Indeed, to Falwell and his friends, AIDS

was "divine retribution for sodomy" (Bull and Gallagher, pp. 25–26).

Falwell was only one of many Republican Party conservative activists who shared this perspective and whose voices were given increased power and legitimacy during the Reagan presidency. For example, Representative William Dannemeyer (R-California) informed a Presidential Commission on AIDS hearing in March 1988 that homosexuals were receiving God's punishment in the form of AIDS. Paul Cameron, director of the Institute for the Scientific Investigation of Sexuality (ISIS) in Lincoln, Nebraska, had been conducting antigay research for a number of years. As the AIDS epidemic intensified, Cameron's work received greater publicity, especially when it was revealed that several of his studies attempted to "demonstrate that gay men brought AIDS on themselves and the rest of the world" (Bull and Gallagher, p. 26). At the national policymaking level, Senator Jesse Helms (R-North Carolina) introduced the Helms Amendment, which would eliminate federal funding for any educational material that "promotes or encourages homosexuality," and which passed both houses of Congress. From 1987 on Helms continued in his efforts to include his amendment in every major appropriations bill. With these amendments, Helms and his conservative and often Republican supporters in Congress, notably former California Representatives Dannemeyer and Robert Dornan, helped limit federal funding for safe-sex education, targeting lesbians and gays at a time when such education was desperately needed.

In the midst of this hostile environment, the lesbian and gay movements and their supporters fought a variety of legislative battles in the 1980s across all levels of government, many of which related to the various crises surrounding AIDS, including funding, antidiscrimination laws, and education. For example, California's state legislature passed an employment antidiscrimination act, but it was soon vetoed by then Republican Governor George Deukmejian in February 1984. At the national level, James Miller, Reagan's budget director, informed a Senate panel in 1986 that the care of, and funding for, people with AIDS were the responsibilities of state and local governments. This position was surely in keeping with Reagan's determination to cut back on the federal government's intervention in matters of social policy, but it reminded lesbian and gay activists and their supporters that Reagan and his allies had little interest in addressing AIDS in a serious way, especially since state and local governments were suffering fiscal crises of their own in a time of scarce resources. In response to the inability of national policymakers to address discrimination and prejudice, however, some states passed laws that prevented HIV/AIDS discrimination. But Reagan and his close political advisers also successfully prevented his surgeon general, C. Everett Koop, from discussing AIDS publicly until Reagan's second term.

This larger conservative climate enabled the Reagan administration's continued indifference toward AIDS. The administration undercut federal efforts to confront AIDS in a meaningful way by refusing to spend the money Congress had allocated for AIDS research. In the critical years of 1984 and 1985, according to his White House physician, Reagan thought of AIDS as though "it was measles and it would go away" (Cannon, p. 814). Reagan's biographer Lou Cannon claims that the president's response to AIDS was "halting and ineffective" (Cannon, p. 814). It took Rock Hudson's death from AIDS in 1985 to prompt Reagan to change his personal views, although members of his administration were still openly hostile to more aggressive government funding of research and public education. Six years after the onset of the epidemic, Reagan finally mentioned the word "AIDS" publicly at the Third International AIDS Conference held in Washington, D.C. His only proposal at the time, however, was widespread routine testing.

Reagan did appoint the Presidential Commission on the Human Immunodeficiency Virus Epidemic in the summer of 1987; it was later renamed the Watkins Commission, after its chair. The commission numbered few scientists who had participated in AIDS research and few physicians who had actually treated people with AIDS. In addition, the commission included outspoken opponents of AIDS education. The Watkins Commission's final report did recommend a more sustained federal commitment to addressing AIDS, but this recommendation was largely ignored by the Reagan and Bush administrations.

In the face of such inaction by the Reagan presidency and many Republicans in Congress, the lesbian and gay communities were forced to confront AIDS on their own, often through direct action. AIDS prevention campaigns were created, service groups were established to care for those infected with the disease, and political organizations, such as the AIDS Coalition to Unleash Power (ACT UP) and the AIDS Action Council, were formed to represent those who otherwise had little clout in the mainstream policy process.

The Bush Presidency

By the end of Reagan's two terms in office, the LGBT movements had largely turned to the Democratic Party as the party most likely to respond to their concerns. This strategic approach was reinforced when Senator Orrin G.

Hatch (R-Utah) announced at a 1987 Republican Party fundraiser that the Democrats were "the party of homosexuals" (Raben, p. 237). The differences between the two parties widened once President George H. W. Bush took office in January 1989. He identified ACT UP protests as examples of "an excess of free speech." In addition, he informed reporters that his administration would "be very sensitive to the question of babies suffering from AIDS, innocent people that are hurt by the disease." In doing so, he reinforced the widespread belief among many conservatives that gay men and IV drug users deserved AIDS due to their irresponsible personal behavior. His administration continued Reagan's policy of fiscal austerity with respect to AIDS funding at the national level and embraced the notion of mandatory testing to prevent the spread of AIDS. It was not until March 30, 1990, almost nine years after AIDS was first identified and over a year into his presidency, that Bush gave his first AIDS speech, one in which he asked the country to end discrimination against those infected with HIV.

There were, however, some modest legislative gains for the LGBT movements during the Bush presidency. Bush signed the Hate Crimes Statistics Act, sponsored by Senator Paul Simon (D-Illinois), in April 1990. The act requires the attorney general to collect statistics on hate crimes that are committed against individuals on the basis of race, religion, ethnicity, or sexual orientation. Also in 1990, Bush signed into law the Americans with Disabilities Act, which provided protection for people with HIV/AIDS from discrimination, and the Ryan White Comprehensive AIDS Resources Emergency (CARE) Act, which funded medical care for America's most severely hit inner cities.

The Clinton Years

The 1992 Republican Convention in Houston was notable for its celebration of "family values" and open hostility toward LGBT people. Unlike the 1988 Republican party platform, the 1992 platform specifically denounced lesbian and gay rights: "We oppose efforts by the Democratic Party to include sexual preference as a protected minority receiving preferential status under civil rights statutes at the federal, state and local level." In addition, the platform denounced adoption and foster care by lesbians and gays, and same-sex marriage, while renewing support for the already existing military ban. The public face of the convention was one that was openly hostile to LGBT rights. In a fiery convention speech, Pat Buchanan warned a national audience, that if elected, Bill Clinton would impose a radical gay rights agenda on the United States.

This was the backdrop against which President-elect Clinton announced in November 1992 that one of his first goals as president would be to overturn the ban on lesbians and gays in the military. Clinton's decision produced a firestorm of opposition from the military, conservative Democrats, and the Christian Right, all of whom worked to prevent Clinton's promise from reaching fruition. Clinton was stunned by the vehemence of the oppositions, and the lesbian and gay movements lacked the necessary resources or organizing capacity at the grassroots level to provide the newly elected president with the political support that he needed. As a result, in a major victory for conservatives and the Republican Party, Clinton's promise evolved into the compromise "don't ask, don't tell" policy that still persists as of 2003.

Looking for a wedge issue in the 1996 presidential election between Bob Dole and Bill Clinton, the Republican-controlled Congress introduced and quickly passed the Defense of Marriage Act, which was signed into law by Clinton in 1996. The law has two goals: "1) prevent states from being forced by the Full Faith and Credit Clause to recognize same-sex marriages validly celebrated in other states, and 2) define marriages for federal purposes as the union of one man and one woman" (Strasser, p. 127). Given its history of organizing against LGBT rights over time, it is no surprise that the Christian Right organized in opposition to same-sex marriage. For example, three days before the 1996 presidential caucuses in Iowa, a coalition of eight conservative religious groups publicly celebrated a Marriage Protection Resolution. All Republican presidential candidates that primary year signed the resolution, and three even addressed a rally sponsored by the conservative groups who had sponsored the resolution.

Although Clinton secured reelection with relative ease, he antagonized the lesbian and gay movements with his decision to sign the Defense of Marriage Act, even though he had never before promised to support same-sex marriage. In this way, same-sex marriage worked as a wedge issue just as members of the Republican Party had intended. Clinton's decision to sign a mean-spirited act into law antagonized and deeply disappointed some of his strongest supporters, who never forgave him. Some of these former Clinton supporters either stayed home or voted Republican in the 1996 elections.

Nevertheless, the Dole campaign also found itself embroiled in controversy on lesbian and gay politics during the 1996 campaign. In August 1995 Dole returned a $1,000 financial contribution from the Log Cabin Republicans, a national group representing lesbian and gay Republicans, because he did not want to be associated

Steve May. The conservative Mormon, U.S. Army Reserve officer (who survived a "don't ask, don't tell" attempt to discharge him), and board member of the Log Cabin Republicans became the first openly gay Republican state legislator in the country in 1998, when he was elected to the Arizona House of Representatives; after two terms, he lost the 2002 primary by just fifty-eight votes—a defeat attributed not to GOP homophobia but to redistricting, overconfidence, and other factors. [AP/Wide World Photos]

with this organization or what he perceived to be their policy agenda. The Dole incident produced considerable turmoil within the organization, especially since the Log Cabin Republicans ultimately decided to endorse his presidential candidacy. Founded in 1993 and based in Washington, D.C., the Log Cabin Republicans boast more than fifty chapters located throughout the United States, some of them formed well before the national organization was created. In response to the hostility displayed toward lesbians and gays at the 1992 Republican Convention, the organization's founders (including its first executive directors, Rich Tafel and Kevin Ivers) believed that a national organization was needed to counteract the notion that the Republican Party and lesbian and gay rights are inimical. But as Dole found out during the 1996 campaign, due to the growing acceptance of lesbians and gays in a variety of realms, Republican Party candidates must now devote serious attention to their political and policy relationships with the LGBT movements.

The Second Bush White House

Presidential candidate George W. Bush learned the lesson of how important these relationships are during the 2000 presidential election. Bush was understandably challenged by gay Republicans after he stated on NBC's *Meet the Press* that he would not likely meet with the Log Cabin Republicans if elected president. After he was assured of his party's nomination, Bush did meet with representatives of the organization, but they were people that he and his staff personally approved. Exit polls conducted by the Voter News Service on the day of the 2000 elections indicated that 4 percent of all voters identified themselves as gay, and that Democrat Al Gore received 70 percent of the gay vote, Bush 25 percent, and Ralph Nader (the Green Party candidate) 4 percent. Bush's 25 percent figure represented a slight improvement over Republican presidential candidate Bob Dole's showing in 1996 and a considerable increase over his father's in 1992. Given the closeness of the election, lesbian and gay Republicans claimed that Bush's ability to win the support of a quarter of lesbian and gay voters in such a close election provided the margin for his victory. Bush's response to the Log Cabin controversy proved to be an omen for the shape of things to come.

Since assuming office, Bush has done little to support lesbian and gay concerns, indicating his own personal hostility toward the LGBT by appointing former Senator John Ashcroft (R-Missouri) as attorney general, the top law enforcement officer in the United States. As a member of the U.S. Senate, Ashcroft consistently voted in support of the Christian Right's positions when lesbian and gay issues came up for consideration. And even before taking office, Bush indicated that he would eliminate the White House liaison to lesbians and gays, a position created by Clinton. Lesbian and gay activists have consistently criticized Bush for the following: his failure to fund HIV/AIDS-related programs adequately, his failure to support the Employment Non-Discrimination Act (ENDA), his opposition to a sexual-orientation provision in Texas hate crime laws when he served as governor of that state, his opposition to lesbian and gay adoptions, his unwavering support for a continuation of the current "don't ask, don't tell" policy in the military, and his vow to fight gay marriage after the 2003 *Lawrence v. Texas* decision.

However, as Bush mounts his 2004 reelection campaign, he will be forced to defend his record on issues of interest to the larger lesbian and gay movements. As he does so, he will undoubtedly attempt to balance his socially conservative policy leanings with the reality that with or without the Republican Party's support, LGBT people are slowly but surely integrating into mainstream institutions at all levels of society.

Bibliography

Andriote, John-Manuel. *Victory Deferred: How AIDS Changed Gay Life in America.* Chicago: University of Chicago Press, 1999.

Bull, Chris, and John Gallagher. *Perfect Enemies: The Religious Right, the Gay Movement, and the Politics of the 1990s.* New York: Crown, 1996.

Cannon, Lou. *President Reagan: The Role of a Lifetime.* New York: Simon & Schuster, 1991.

Herman, Didi. *The Antigay Agenda: Orthodox Vision and the Christian Right.* Chicago: University of Chicago Press, 1997.

———. "The Gay Agenda Is the Devil's Agenda: The Christian Right's Vision and the Role of the State." In *The Politics of Gay Rights.* Edited by Craig A. Rimmerman, Kenneth D. Wald, and Clyde Wilcox. Chicago: University of Chicago Press, 2000.

Raben, Robert. "Politics." In *St. James Press Gay and Lesbian Almanac.* Edited by Neil Schlager. Detroit, Mich.: St. James Press, 1998.

Rayside, David. *On the Fringe: Gays and Lesbians in Politics.* Ithaca, N.Y.: Cornell University Press, 1998.

Rimmerman, Craig A. *From Identity to Politics: The Lesbian and Gay Movements in the United States.* Philadelphia: Temple University Press, 2002.

Rimmerman, Craig A., ed. *Gay Rights, Military Wrongs: Political Perspectives on Lesbians and Gays in the Military.* New York: Garland Press, 1996.

Rollins, Joe. "Beating around Bush: Gay Rights and America's 41st President." In *Creating Change: Sexuality, Public Policy, and Civil Rights.* Edited by John D'Emilio, William B. Turner, and Urvashi Vaid. New York: St. Martin's Press, 2000.

Strasser, Mark. *Legally Wed: Same-Sex Marriage and the Constitution.* Ithaca, N.Y.: Cornell University Press, 1997.

Thompson, Mark, ed. *Long Road to Freedom: The Advocate History of the Gay and Lesbian Movement.* New York: St. Martin's Press, 1994.

Vaid, Urvashi. *Virtual Equality: The Mainstreaming of Gay and Lesbian Liberation.* New York: Anchor Books, 1995.

Craig A. Rimmerman

See also ANTI-DISCRIMINATION LAW AND POLICY; DEMOCRATIC PARTY; ELECTORAL POLITICS; FEDERAL LAW AND POLICY; HEALTH AND HEALTH CARE LAW AND POLICY; LEGG, DORR; MILITARY LAW AND POLICY; NEW RIGHT.

RESORTS

People who can afford—financially, emotionally, and psychologically—to vacation are, generally speaking, in search of one thing: a diversion from the scenes and rhythms of their everyday lives. People vacation to escape, to be free of their jobs, families, responsibilities, schedules, children, surroundings, and climates. Some specifically desire time off from partners or spouses. Vacationers also seek to experience what they cannot or will not at home. For some this takes the form of cultural and historic enrichment, viewing works of art or visiting ancient ruins. Others set their sights on recreational ventures, from modest to extreme, such as scuba diving or bungy jumping. Warm coastal destinations and quiet resort spas appeal to those seeking rest and relaxation, the clichéd "R. and R." Leisure and cultural studies have also coined the phrase "sex tourist" for those who travel overseas or simply across town to buy the services of prostitutes of the same or opposite sex.

LGBT resorts satisfy many and in some cases all of the above modes of escape. The three that have been around the longest and are the most popular on the East Coast are, from north to south, Provincetown, Massachusetts; Cherry Grove on Fire Island, New York; and Key West, Florida. All three are Dionysian, "anything goes" beach resorts with loose physical and cultural connections to the mainland, in effect "land's end" termini, communities stemming from art colonies, and towns built on historically significant and outlandish backgrounds. These resorts market themselves as having outlandish histories that relate to their current outlandish status, since they all had marginalized or unusual inhabitants or visitors in their pasts, including pirates, smugglers, pilgrims, and artists. They are all, as well, communities that once were based on seafaring economies but now survive on tourism and consumption. More specifically, they base their service industries on LGBT consumption and expenditure of space and capital as well as on the institutions and aspects of LGBT culture that vacationers seek to experience. The LGBT resorts on the East Coast that have been the next most frequently visited by gays and lesbians are South Beach, Florida; Rehoboth Beach, Delaware; and Atlantic City, New Jersey.

Provincetown

Provincetown, Massachusetts, a gay resort perched sixty miles out in the Atlantic Ocean on the tip of Cape Cod, satisfies most vacationing needs. People go to Provincetown to escape their everyday lives, visit the landing place of the *Mayflower* Pilgrims, experience the town's artistic and Portuguese cultures, and take in the sun, sand, and surf. Tourists also go to Provincetown to do what they cannot do in their own hometowns, whether that means simply holding a lover's hand in public or having anonymous sex in the sand dunes.

Also known as Land's End or Ptown, Provincetown houses just over three thousand year-round residents but over twenty thousand seasonal visitors. Ptown began as a remote refuge for Native Americans, explorers, pirates, and smugglers. Its stable residential history began, however, in the early 1800s when Yankee men and women set up salt works and whaling industries. A critical mass of Portuguese immigrants joined them in the late 1800s, and countless artists and writers converged on Land's End beginning in 1899 with the opening of the Cape Cod School of Art. From the mid-1910s onward, when World War I prevented travel to European enclaves, gender and sex dissidents, known at the time as "maiden ladies" and "confirmed bachelors," made Provincetown their seasonal home. From these migration patterns, a loosely configured community of artists and bohemians, the most famous being the Provincetown Players, took shape. The navy stationed battleships in Provincetown harbor during both World War I and World War II; hundreds of sailors cruised the streets of Provincetown during these eras.

Relationships within and between Provincetown's native and visiting populations strengthened during the interwar years as Portuguese townsfolk welcomed gay men and lesbians into their homes as boarders, into their shops and restaurants as customers, into their communities as neighbors, and into their families as kin. As in other gay enclaves, World War II and the immediate postwar period were pivotal years for Provincetown and its future as a gay resort. During this time, gay men and lesbians institutionalized their presence by setting up a queer infrastructure and daily routine based on gay- and lesbian-owned or patronized nightclubs, restaurants, and boarding homes.

The postwar period also ushered in the first waves of homophobic backlash against emerging queer tourist communities. In the 1950s and 1960s some local officials, residents, and clergy sought to rid Provincetown of its most flamboyant guests and entertainers by putting forth a series of by-laws that banned "female impersonators so-called" and other gender deviant behaviors from all licensed liquor establishments. They also called on "all decent people" in the town of Provincetown to cease accommodating queers in their homes and shops. They succeeded in shutting down the Weathering Heights Club, a nightclub featuring female impressionists that was run by an outsider, or nonnative. But when native-owned clubs were targeted, townsfolk lobbied against the twelve by-laws, known as the "ten commandments," and pleaded with their neighbors for the sake of the economy and their livelihoods to cease what they now considered arbitrary harassment. Those against the "ten commandments" succeeded, as one might tell from the subsequent state of gay affairs in Ptown, but this state, this paradise, this Queersville, U.S.A., as one tourist put it, did not come about easily.

During the second half of the twentieth century, the number of LGBT residents, tourists, business owners, and local officials increased. Gay women in particular mounted a strategic and largely successful plan during the 1980s to fashion Provincetown into one of the only resorts that actively welcomed lesbians as well as gay men. Women's Week, the Women Innkeepers of Provincetown, the Women-owned Business Guide brochure, and the lesbian section of Herring Cove Beach all promote a lesbian-friendly presence in Ptown. Today the gay and lesbian business association, established in 1978 as the Provincetown Business Guild, markets Provincetown internationally as a premier gay and lesbian resort area, gay and lesbian elected officials keep institutional homophobia in check, and gay and lesbian tourists and residents claim no small amount of ownership over Land's End. Provincetown has been gentrified as have many other gay enclaves, the result being dramatically unequal distributions of affordable housing, financial resources, and racial demographics. Still, Provincetown appeals to and satisfies the desires of thousands of LGBT vacationers every year.

Cherry Grove

Like Provincetown, Cherry Grove on Fire Island was once home to transient bands of smugglers, pirates, and explorers. Although it cannot claim national historic significance in the same way Provincetown can, it has had an equally tempting reputation as an "anything goes" beach resort with minimal connections to the mainland and maximum connections to the arts. The first LGBT vacationers to visit Fire Island, a barrier island off the southern slope of Long Island, New York, set up camp in the 1920s and 1930s. It was a time when, for various reasons, including the havoc wreaked by the hurricane of 1938, few were interested in Cherry Grove. As Esther Newton explains in her groundbreaking book, *Cherry Grove, Fire Island: A History of America's First Gay Town* (1993), LGBT people took advantage of this disinterest and built their summer capital on Fire Island. The network of friends, lovers, and associates who first made Cherry Grove their temporary home affiliated themselves with the New York City theater scene rather than with Provincetown's cast of visual artists, playwrights, and Greenwich Village bohemians.

The early LGBT Grovers were white, wealthy men and women whose urban capital bought them space and tolerance on Fire Island. Financial, racial, and class negotiations began with the gay "country clubbers," as Newton notes, many of whom led double lives as gay at Cherry Grove and closeted (if not married) back in New York City. Cherry Grove residents welcomed these clubbers and their financial investments, especially during and immediately following the Great Depression.

From the end of World War II to the 1960s, the tide turned when LGBT Grovers became more fully integrated into Cherry Grove as homeowners rather than renters and as community activists, fund-raisers, and semi-permanent citizens rather than seasonal or weekend visitors. Whereas early Grovers enjoyed what Fire Island offered regarding nature and tolerance, post–World War II LGBT Grovers valued excess and ecstasy in spaces with LGBT majorities. Cherry Grove's lack of traditional heterosexual institutions, such as schools, police forces, and churches, enabled gay men and lesbians to transgress typical gender and sexual mores more freely than they otherwise could have, all the while assuming strong political and social leadership positions. Straight Grovers and mainlanders eventually staged an antigay backlash during the postwar era, but as in the case of Provincetown, the profit motive, the capitalist service economy, democratic legal protections, and the lack of unity among locals meant LGBT Grovers would remain and continue to grow in numbers and influence on Fire Island.

Cherry Grove changed in a number of ways during the second half of the twentieth century. The long-standing elite or privileged groups of early Grove artists and theater folks witnessed the emergence of younger white men of various ethnicities who had money to spend, good looks to sport, and an inclination toward multiple sexual interludes. Working-class lesbians with femme/ butch sensibilities moved in alongside but not in community with Cherry Grove's older "gay ladies." And, finally, gay business owners with resources and clubs in New York City moved in to turn Cherry Grove from an isolated enclave into the internationally famous LGBT resort mecca that it had become by the early 2000s.

Key West

Of the three most popular LGBT resorts on the East Coast, Key West may be the best known. All varieties of tourists, from straight-acting to the flamboyantly queer, have sought out paradise in Jimmy Buffet's "margaritaville," also known by some, according to Leila Rupp, as "the rock." The southernmost U.S. gay resort (and southernmost Florida key that markets the southernmost hotel, barber, restaurant, and so on), Key West has had a compelling and colorful history. During the colonial era, Native Americans, Spanish settlers, smugglers, and pirates sought respite on this tropical anomaly. From the 1830s into the twentieth century, Spaniards, American Southerners, New Englanders, Cuban cigarmakers, English Bahamians, Jewish merchants, African Americans, and navy seamen coalesced and lent Key West a decidedly eclectic and cosmopolitan reputation. Before the overseas railroad reached Key West in 1912, thereby linking it to the mainland and tourism, cigar-making and fishing sustained this small town of just under thirty thousand inhabitants (peaking to eighty thousand in season). In the early twenty-first century, corporate chains as well as smaller, gay-owned businesses including hotels, bars, and restaurants cater to thousands of patrons each year.

Key West's artistic history and presence, which included extended stays by Ernest Hemingway (whose house is one of the main tourist attractions) and Tennessee Williams, helped set the tone for tolerance in the name of creativity. Its artistic clout, reputation for the outlandish, and populations of Cubans, bohemians, and hippies provided the foundation for Key West's development during the 1970s into a gay resort. Like Provincetown and Cherry Grove, Key West has had its share of historic and recent homophobic and gender harassment. It has also gone through its own rendition of gentrification and native displacement. The unemployment rate in Key West is relatively low; that is the good news. The bad news is that housing prices have skyrocketed and a lack of affordable housing prevents many individuals and families from remaining or becoming townsfolk. Key West also shares at its heart, again as do Cherry Grove and Ptown, a brilliant, vibrant, and talented community of drag performers. As Rupp notes, the history of places like Key West and its drag culture are integral parts of American history because the connections, however tenuous, that they maintain between themselves and the larger population speak volumes about American expectations, desires, and leisure experiences.

Other Locales

The eastern seaboard is sporadically dotted with other LGBT beach resorts. The ones that have been frequented and come to mind most often are, from south to north, South Beach, Florida; Rehoboth Beach, Delaware; and Atlantic City, New Jersey.

South Beach. From about 1990 onward, South Beach, across the bay from downtown Miami, has offered endless parades of fashion models and "south beach boys"—men sporting V-shaped torsos and the accoutrements of the late-twentieth-century cult of masculinity. Decades earlier, from the 1920s to the 1930s, South Beach was known as a harmless yet risqué tropical paradise serving mostly white, middle-class vacationers. Its popularity, however, waned during the 1940s and 1950s into the 1960s, with some referring explicitly to the earlier South Beach as "paradise lost" when working-class retirees and Cuban refugees moved in. In the 1970s artists and service-industry entrepreneurs, similar to those who took advantage of Cherry Grove, Key West, and Provincetown, hatched a plan for a "new" South Beach (SoBe) that would link it with the New York City arts scene. It was not long before SoBe became an artists' haven, then a trendy art deco destination, and finally, a popular gay enclave. During the 1980s the sunshine, inexpensive housing, and relaxed lifestyle attracted artists, entrepreneurs, tourists, and a fair number of gay men who had contracted HIV and were in search of more accommodating climates. Like Provincetown, SoBe at the beginning of the twenty-first century faces critical community issues as it becomes gentrified with souvenir shops displacing laundromats and expensive houses and condominiums replacing smaller bungalows and apartments.

Rehoboth Beach. Due north on Route I-95, past, not surprisingly, all other beach resorts and coastal towns in the conservative, old plantation South (except Fort Lauderdale, which is forming legible queer resort communities and spaces), gay men and lesbians can seek refuge in Rehoboth Beach, Delaware. In the early 1920s, Rehoboth Beach attracted a number of celebrities, such as Tallulah Bankhead and Lilly Holman, many of whom vacationed at the Dupont estate of Louisa Carpenter. As was the case in Provincetown, however, a highly visible gay community did not develop until the post–World War II period, when gay men and lesbians came out en masse. Gay men and lesbians from Baltimore, Philadelphia, and Washington, D.C., escaped to Rehoboth Beach on weekends, gathering for house parties and beach soirees in front of the old Carpenter estate at the southernmost end of Rehoboth. A few unrelated venues were reportedly gay-friendly at the time, including the Dinner Bell Inn and, in the 1960s, a boardwalk bar called the Pink Pony, which reputedly welcomed gay men at happy hour.

Some things needed to change, however, before Rehoboth vacationers enjoyed a gay entertainment ritual like that in Provincetown, perhaps the most important one being the liquor laws that prevented vacationers from carrying open containers. The 1970s ushered in a more distinct bar scene, the development of which focused on one or two bars and nightclubs. Later, with a string of social gathering places in town to boost community and collectiveness, gay men and lesbians decided that trekking down to Carpenter Beach would no longer do. Instead, they began moving their beach parties to the south end of the Rehoboth Boardwalk, an area later dubbed Poodle Beach. Hundreds of gay men and a fair number of lesbians gather there for special holiday parties, including the annual Labor Day Drag Volleyball Tournament. Lesbians in Rehoboth, however, have staked out exclusive beach space at Cape Henlopen State Park Beach. In other words, like their counterparts in Ptown, Rehoboth lesbians created a "girls beach," as it is called, which attracts hundreds of lesbian women each summer, with holiday weekends bringing in inordinate numbers.

Since the early 1980s Rehoboth Beach has witnessed a gentrification similar to Provincetown and Key West. Gay men and lesbians now flock there to vacation, buy second homes, or retire. Along with bars and beach spaces, Rehoboth offers any number of gay-owned or operated restaurants, shops, and accommodations. CAMP Rehoboth, a local service organization, offers a community center in downtown Rehoboth. There one can learn about the town's many special events such as April Women's Weekend, fund-raisers, and the like.

Atlantic City. Poised at the northern end of a thin barrier island sixty miles southeast of Philadelphia, Atlantic City was host to a LGBT resort culture during the decade of the 1970s. As Bryant Simon has noted, gay Atlantic City took root as a result of postwar "opportunistic reconfiguration," an urban phenomenon whereby white middle- and upper-class residents and tourists depart, leaving a void filled by people of color, working-class people, and gay men and lesbians in search of anonymity.

Atlantic City hosted a number of LGBT sites prior to World War II. Around 1925 Louisa Mack opened the gay-friendly Entertainers Club, and drag shows, known as pansy acts, took place in the 1930s at the Pansy Club and Cotton Club. Although the mayor banned these performances in 1933, the Cotton Club and Entertainers Club became key institutions for semi-public gay life before the war. From 1942 to 1945 city officials turned Atlantic City over to the navy, possibly with much the same effect as that in Provincetown: large concentrations of servicemen attracted similarly large and enthusiastic civilians in search of same-sex sexual interludes.

A number of guest houses and distinct cruising zones made for a loosely knit gay culture prior to WWII. Yet as in Ptown and Cherry Grove, the postwar era ushered in a witch-hunt in Atlantic City as local officials and the state's Division of Alcoholic Beverages shut down a number of clubs and banned female impersonators. The year 1967 was a turning point for Atlantic City, however,

when a gay bar won a court case against the Division, thus paving the way for numerous bars and restaurants that catered to gay men and lesbians. By 1969 Atlantic City, dubbed the "queen of resorts," boasted eight gay-friendly clubs and a number of gay-friendly hotels, shops, and restaurants all situated on or near South New York Avenue. A gay routine similar to Provincetown's took root in the 1970s, with gay people congregating at the beach before moving on to the various entertainment sites along New York Avenue.

Two significant demographic shifts influenced Atlantic City's LGBT community. The first was the "white flight" out of Atlantic City leading up to the 1960s—white disinvestment and desegregation resulted in a mostly black and Puerto Rican ghettoized community. This was when white gay men and lesbians commenced the "opportunistic reconfiguration," when they filled the void left by those disillusioned with the "world's playground." The second demographic turn and "opportunistic reconfiguration" took place in 1976, when a majority of New Jersey voters approved casino businesses in Atlantic City. It was only a matter of time before the small, entrepreneurial gay-friendly hotels, bars, and restaurants fell swiftly to the competition of casino conglomerates. It is likely that a different kind of LGBT clientele has subsequently patronized Atlantic City, but the sense of an LGBT beach resort community has certainly been lost.

This in no way exhausts the many LGBT resorts in the United States; rather, it speaks to those with at least partially known histories. Historians have yet to fully research a number of other intriguing LGBT resorts, including Ogunquit, Maine; Saugatuck, Michigan; and Palm Springs, California. Also remaining to be more fully studied are international gay resorts such as Sitges, Spain, and Mykonos, Greece.

Bibliography

Forrest, David W. "South Beach: 'Paradise' and Reality." *Gay and Lesbian Review Worldwide* 9, no. 3 (May–June 2002): 24–26.

Krahulik, Karen C. "Cape Queer: The Politics of Sex, Class, and Race in Provincetown Massachusetts, 1859–1999." Ph.D. dissertation, New York University, 2000.

Newton, Esther. *Cherry Grove, Fire Island: Sixty Years in America's First Gay and Lesbian Town.* Boston: Beacon Press, 1993.

Patron, Eugene J., and David W. Forrest. "SoBe: The Making of a Gay Community." *Gay and Lesbian Review Worldwide* 7, no. 2 (Spring 2000): 28–29.

Philipp, Steven F. "Gay and Lesbian Tourists at a Southern USA Beach Event." *Journal of Homosexuality* 37, no. 3 (1999): 69–86.

Rupp, Leila J., and Verta Taylor. *Drag Queens at the 801 Cabaret.* Chicago: University of Chicago Press, 2003.

Simon, Bryant. "New York Avenue: The Life and Death of Gay Spaces in Atlantic City, New Jersey, 1920–1990." *Journal of Urban History* 28 (2002): 300–327.

Karen Christel Krahulik

See also BOSTON; BUSINESSES; DEMUTH, CHARLES; FLORIDA; NEW YORK CITY; TOURISM.

RESTAURANTS. see BARS, CLUBS, AND RESTAURANTS.

REYES, Rodrigo (b. 24 September 1945; d. 19 January 1992), cultural activist, journalist, writer.

Rodrigo Reyes was born in Weslaco, near McAllen, Texas, to a Mexican family of migrant farmworkers. He attended Ohio State University in the late 1960s, where he majored in education and Spanish. Two years after first visiting San Francisco, Reyes moved to the city permanently in 1971 where he lived until his death. The strong manifestations of racism that he and his family had experienced as farmworkers would later fuel his creative and political trajectory as a gay Chicano organizer in San Francisco.

Nurtured in 1960s and 1970s countercultural, nationalist, and gay liberation movements, Reyes reported extensively on the Chicano movement in the 1970s through Berkeley's Pacifica radio station, KPFA. Slowly meeting other Chicanos and LGBT community organizers in his travels, he began to consider more carefully what it meant to be both gay and Chicano. In 1975, in response to regional interest in San José and San Francisco to form a LGBT Latino organization, Reyes cofounded the Gay Latino Alliance (GALA). With Manuel Hernández Valadéz, Jesús Barragán, Diane Felix, and other key organizers, Reyes put LGBT Latinos on the regional and national map, forming one of the first organizations of its kind in the country. GALA soon became a critical political and social vehicle for addressing racism in the gay movement and homophobia in the Latino community. Reyes and GALA were instrumental in facilitating many of the discussions that ensued between LGBT people and Latinos in San Francisco in the context of gentrification. Less successful in addressing sexism within the organization, GALA had a leadership that was predominantly male, a problem Reyes would consider in his work on AIDS in the 1980s.

GALA's successful run for nearly eight years relied on its successful social gatherings, events that raised funds for community-based projects in San Francisco's Mission District and its Latino community. GALA was also a key participant in the 1979 Third World Conference during the March on Washington. Reyes was central in these efforts, especially in writing about the LGBT Latino and LGBT Latin American movements of the period for regional and national audiences. In 1981 his article "Latino Gays: Coming Out and Coming Home" appeared in the national Latino *Nuestro* magazine (April) and in the Bay Area's LGBT periodical *Coming Up!* (December). As one of the first articles to reach a national Latino audience on LGBT issues, "Latino Gays" sparked great attention. Featuring a two-page photograph of GALA members marching in San Francisco's Gay Freedom Day, Reyes's article documented the important solidarity between LGBT organizations and the United Farm Workers (UFW) and other groups opposing U.S. intervention in Central America.

Reyes was also successful as an actor, writer, and producer, eventually founding his own production company, Yerba Buena Productions. With it he staged in 1983 the first play about gay Chicanos, *Reunion,* written by gay Filipino playwright Edgar Poma. He was part of the active Chicano and Latino theater movement of the late 1970s and early 1980s. With fellow gay Chicano artist Juan Pablo Gutiérrez and gay Chicano author Francisco X. Alarcón, Reyes published the first gay Chicano poetry anthology, *Ya Vas Carnal* (1985). Reyes served briefly as executive director of the Mission Cultural Center and as president of the Mission Neighborhood Centers. He was also a member of the Community Advisory Board of the University of California–San Francisco AIDS Health Project.

In 1987 Reyes once again was the key organizer for a new community project, a grassroots reaction to the growing AIDS epidemic in San Francisco. Given the general homophobia of Latino health agencies and the racism of mainstream, white AIDS institutions, CURAS (Comunidad Unida en Respuesta al AIDS/SIDA), or Community United in Response to AIDS/SIDA, was an explicitly LGBT Latino response to the epidemic. Coordinating the first meeting for the project at the gay Latino bar La India Bonita, Reyes envisioned CURAS as a community-based effort to educate the public about the disease and prevent further infections. The new gay health agency was also intended to be inclusive of the Mission's Latina transgender community. In time, CURAS, like GALA, fell prey to unresolved conflicts between Latinas and Latinos. CURAS's collapse in 1991 came at the same time that Reyes was losing his own battle against AIDS. Concerned with his community's welfare and history to the end, Reyes willed a great portion of his personal belongings to his friend and gay Chicano archivist Luis Alberto de la Garza C. In conjunction with other community efforts to preserve LGBT Latino historical archives, Reyes's personal archives have become part of the Ethnic Studies Library collection at the University of California, Berkeley.

Bibliography

Aguirre, Valentin. "Rodrigo Reyes: A Legend in His Time." *San Francisco Sentinel* 20, no. 4 (23 January 1992): 16.

Moraga, Cherríe. "Tribute." In *The Last Generation*. Boston: South End Press, 1993.

Roque Ramírez, Horacio N. "'That's My Place': Negotiating Racial, Sexual, and Gender Politics in San Francisco's Gay Latino Alliance (GALA), 1975–1983." *Journal of the History of Sexuality* 12, no. 2 (2003).

Horacio N. Roque Ramírez

See also LATINA AND LATINO LGBTQ ORGANIZATIONS AND PERIODICALS; LATINAS AND LATINOS; LITERATURE; THEATER AND PERFORMANCE.

RICH, Adrienne (b. 16 May 1929), writer.

Adrienne Cecile Rich was born in Baltimore, Maryland, into the intellectual family of Arnold Rich, a medical pathologist at Johns Hopkins University, and Helen Jones, a musician who had studied to be a concert pianist. She was home-schooled until the fourth grade, and taught to write formal poetry at a very young age by her father. Rich's superb education, through an A.B. at Radcliffe College (cum laude, 1951), groomed her as an intellectual poet. Although it took her years to claim feminism and lesbianism as poetic topics, she provided the most powerful lesbian-feminist literary voice of the 1970s. Along with her poetry, Rich consistently wrote essays, most chronicling the life and work of a political poet. Taken together her poems and essays provide a record of one of the most exciting and intelligent artists of her era.

Rich began her public career as a writer with her first book of poetry, *A Change of World,* which won the Yale Younger Poets Award in l951. W. H. Auden's condescending introduction to that volume described the poems as formally secure and emotionally modest, poetic values in the 1940s and 1950s. In the 1950s she married the Harvard economist Alfred Conrad and had three sons. The pressure of raising three children in a traditional marriage changed her poetic ideals, which she recounts in the essay "When We Dead Awaken" (1971). The poem that displays this new poetic voice and style—a looser poetic form and a more personal tone—is "Snapshots of a Daughter-in-Law" (1958–1960).

In the 1960s and 1970s, Rich, along with many of her generation, became politically active in causes such as the antiwar movement, civil rights, and feminism. Her poetry began to embrace a political, especially feminist, vision. Along with identifying as a feminist, she came out as a lesbian. She separated from her husband in 1970. He committed suicide later that year. In 1976, Rich became involved with the writer Michelle Cliff; they have lived together since then and currently reside in Santa Cruz, California.

Because her new poetry defied prevailing critical opinion, some felt betrayed by Rich's turn, while others, especially women, were inspired by her use and analysis of the political power of poetic language. Rich became an icon of lesbian-feminism. *The Dream of a Common Language,* perhaps her finest book of poetry and certainly her most optimistic, was written in this period (1978). The centerpiece of this book is a sequence of lesbian poems, "Twenty-One Love Poems," in which Rich combines lesbian love and feminist politics and which includes her only erotic lesbian poem, "THE FLOATING POEM, UNNUMBERED."

Among the ideas she fostered at this time, one in particular proved highly controversial as well as influential: the concept of the lesbian continuum. In her collection of essays from the 1970s, *On Lies, Secrets, and Silence* (1979) and in her most scholarly essay, "Compulsory Heterosexuality and Lesbian Existence" (*Signs,* Summer 1980), Rich espoused the idea of lesbianism in all women, a primary energy or attention between and among women which may be found in nonsexual as well as sexual relationships. By broadening the definition of lesbian, Rich encountered criticism from those who accused her of ahistoricism, essentialism, and failure to acknowledge sexuality as a central aspect of lesbianism.

As with other feminists of the 1970s and 1980s, Rich was moved to rethink her idea of lesbian-feminism by women of color such as Audre Lorde and Michelle Cliff. She also began to explore her own roots as the daughter of a Jewish father, especially in the sequence of poems "Sources" (1983). In her collection of essays *Blood, Bread, and Poetry* (1986), Rich expanded her definition of oppression to include a "simultaneity of oppressions" (p. xii) rather than considering all women part of a single category. Since that time her social critiques have depended on a Marxist-feminist reading of capitalism inspired in part by the writings of Raya Dunayevskaya (*Arts of the Possible* [2001]).

Rich still writes about lesbian issues, but not with the same single-mindedness she did in the 1970s. In her 1993 book of essays *What Is Found There,* Rich features a number of lesbian poets, such as Irena Klepfisz and Minnie Bruce Pratt, and praises them for their abilities to use poetic language to explore social and political issues. With her commitment to political and poetic revolutions, Rich continues to provide a powerful analysis of poetic language as a means to reimagine society. In this capacity, Rich has become a prophet in the tradition of poets who claim human freedom as their goal.

Bibliography

Cooper, Jane Roberta, ed. *Reading Adrienne Rich: Reviews and Re-Visions, 1951–1981.* Ann Arbor: University of Michigan Press, 1984.

Gelpi, Barbara Charlesworth, and Albert Gelpi, eds. *Adrienne Rich's Poetry and Prose: Poems, Prose, Reviews, and Criticism.* New York: Norton, 1993.

Keyes, Claire. *The Aesthetics of Power: The Poetry of Adrienne Rich.* Athens: University of Georgia Press, 1986.

Rich, Adrienne. *The Dream of a Common Language: Poems 1974–1977.* New York: Norton, 1978.

———. *On Lies, Secrets, and Silence: Selected Prose, 1966–1978.* New York: Norton, 1979.

———. "Compulsory Heterosexuality and Lesbian Existence." *Signs* 5 (1980): 631–660.

Women's Studies 27, no. 4 (1998). An issue devoted to Adrienne Rich.

Marilyn R. Farwell

See also AUDEN, W.H.; LITERATURE; LORDE, AUDRE.

RICHARDS, Renée (b. 19 August 1934)
athlete, activist.

In 1976, Renée Richards, a postoperative male-to-female transsexual, first garnered media attention when she decided to compete in the women's division of professional tennis and legally challenged the United States Tennis Association's (USTA) policy requiring that female competitors undergo chromosomal analysis to determine their "true" sex. The New York Supreme Court's ruling on her case in 1977 established legal precedent by declaring that Richards was legally female regardless of her XY chromosomal configuration.

Richards was born Richard Raskind, son of David Raskind, M.D., and Sadie Muriel Bishop, M.D. Richards devoted a great deal of his childhood to tennis, winning his first championship at age ten at Sunrise Tennis Club in New York. After graduation from Horace Mann High School in New York City in 1951, Richards became a third-generation Yale man, where he played intercollegiate tennis. He attended medical school in Rochester,

New York, and interned at New York City's Lenox Hill Hospital. After completing his residency at Manhattan Eye and Ear Hospital, Richards enlisted in the Navy, captained the Navy tennis team, and became the All-Navy champion. Shortly before his discharge, Richards began hormone treatments under the supervision of Dr. Harry Benjamin. Six months later, Benjamin stopped Richards' hormone regimen, apparently because he was concerned about Richards' medical career and his history of dating women. Other transsexual gatekeepers, such as Christian Hamburger and John Money, also refused Richards' requests for hormones and sex reassignment. In response, Richards, then 35 years old, tried to live as a heterosexual man—he had breast reduction surgery, married, and fathered one child.

In 1975, after years of failing to gain a transsexual diagnosis from the medical establishment, Richards finally underwent sex reassignment surgery in Queens, New York, under the supervision Dr. Roberto Granto. At the time, she was 41 years old and an accomplished tennis player who, the previous year, had been ranked third in the east and thirteenth nationally in the men's thirty-five and older division. Two years after her surgery, Richards again played in a number of high profile women's tennis tournaments. In response to Richards' request to play in the women's division of the U.S. Open, the USTA established a policy that required all female players to pass a chromosomal analysis like the one established in 1968 by the International Olympic Committee. Alleging that she was being discriminated against on the basis of her sex, Richards filed for a preliminary injunction based on New York law. On August 10, 1977, the New York State Court of Appeals ruled in Richards' favor, stating that the USTA's policy was unfair, discriminatory, and violated New York's human rights law. It was determined that given Richards' conditions, chromosomes were not a sufficient determination of sex, and, based on the testimony of medical experts, Richards was declared legally female. However, despite the ruling, Richards won only one singles title in the five years that she played women's tennis. After retiring as a competitive player, she joined Martina Navratilova's coaching staff and helped her prepare for her 1982 Wimbledon championship.

By the time Richards published *Second Serve: The Renée Richards Story* in 1983, she was as well-recognized as famous transsexuals such as Christine Jorgenson and Jan Morris and women's sports activists like Billie Jean King. A made-for-television movie based on her autobiography aired in 1986, featuring Vanessa Redgrave as Richards. Richards, who now avoids the spotlight, gave an invited speech during Navratilova's induction into the

Renée Richards. After winning a landmark court case, the former male tennis star makes her debut as a women's tennis professional at the U.S. Open in New York on 1 September 1977 (but loses here to Virginia Wade, 6–1, 6–4. [AP Photo/Dave Pickoff]

International Tennis Hall of Fame in June 2000. That same year, *Sports Illustrated* identified Richards as a player and coach who "helped to usher in the power game and the unapologetic musculature prevalent in women's sports today." As of 2003, Richards was a practicing ophthalmologist on Park Avenue in New York. She serves on the editorial board of the *Journal of Pediatric Ophthalmology and Strabismus*.

Bibliography

Richards v. USTA., 400 N.Y.S. 2nd 267 (1977).

Richards, Renée and Ames, John. *Second Serve: The Renee Richards' Story*. New York: Stein and Day, 1983.

Wertheim, L. J. "Where Are They Now? Renée Richards." *Sports Illustrated* (July 31, 2000): 103.

Cheryl Cole

See also ICONS; SPORTS, TRANSSEXUALS, TRANSVESTITES, TRANSGENDER PEOPLE, AND CROSS DRESSERS.

RIGGS, Marlon (b. 3 February 1957; d. 5 April 1994), film and video artist, writer, activist.

Marlon Riggs, Emmy Award–winning director and outspoken critic of censorship, was a leading American documentary filmmaker as well as a central figure in the black LBGT community. Born in Fort Worth, Texas, Riggs went on to graduate magna cum laude from Harvard College in 1978. He then moved to California to attend the University of California at Berkeley, where he received a master's degree in journalism in 1981. He was a professor at Berkeley's school of journalism from 1987 until his death.

Riggs had unprecedented success from almost the beginning of his career. His 1987 film, *Ethnic Notions*, which examined more than 150 years of the racial stereotyping of black Americans, won him a national Emmy Award. The following year he testified before a committee of the U.S. Senate in support of the creation of the Independent Television Service (ITVS). Riggs will perhaps be best remembered, however, for his film *Tongues Untied* (1989), a highly subjective examination of black gay subjectivity in which Riggs himself appears. The work was roundly applauded by audiences and critics alike. Indeed, it won the award for best documentary film at the prestigious Berlin Film Festival. It also placed Riggs at the center of a national controversy.

Broadcast by PBS on its series POV, *Tongues Untied* attracted the attention of a large segment of the American public, including activists on the Christian right. A copy of the film was sent to U.S. Senator Jesse Helms, a conservative from North Carolina, who suggested not only that the work was pornographic but also that, because Riggs had received $5000 from a regional regranting program of the National Endowment for the Arts (NEA) and POV itself received monies from the National Endowment as well as the Corporation for Public Broadcasting, there was ample evidence of indecency within the NEA and on PBS. Right-wing political commentator and presidential candidate Patrick Buchanan used a twenty-second, heavily edited clip from the film as part of his 1992 campaign. Riggs responded to all this with an opinion piece in the *New York Times* entitled "Meet the New Willie Horton," thus comparing himself to the black male criminal whose case had been used successfully in 1988 by presidential candidate George H. W. Bush in his run against Massachusetts governor Michael Dukakis.

Riggs continued to be undeterred, however. In 1990 he released the two short films, *Anthem* and *Affirmations*. In 1991 he completed a highly successful examination of the history of black Americans on television, *Color Adjustment*. For that work, which looked at more than forty years of television history, Riggs won the George Foster Peabody Award, the Erik Barnouw Award from the Organization of American Historians, and a second Emmy. He followed this with his 1992 piece *Non, Je ne Regrette Rien* (No Regrets). All this was celebrated by the California College of Arts and Crafts when they bestowed an honorary doctorate upon Riggs in 1993.

During this entire period Riggs was fighting not only to produce his work and to have his voice heard but also literally to save his life. Diagnosed with HIV disease long before he was well established, Riggs produced the bulk of his work while his health steadily declined. His final work, *Black Is . . . Black Ain't*, is an incredibly moving testament to his courage and tenacity. Perhaps his most personal and reflective piece, *Black Is . . . Black Ain't* asks the deceptively simple question, "What is this 'black' in black American identity?" Interviewing a host of scholars, activists, and his own family members, Riggs finally comes to settle on the notion of black American identity as a type of gumbo, the southern stew that will never taste right if any one of its ingredients is forgotten. One of the things that Riggs refuses to forget in this film is the pressing reality of AIDS in the black and gay communities and within his own life. In the film he appears often in his hospital bed as he undergoes treatment for kidney failure. Even in this state, however, Riggs is clearly in charge, giving directions to his associates and speaking directly into the camera about both the film and his illness. Riggs was not able, however, to see this final work completed. He died in April 1994 in San Francisco. *Black Is . . . Black Ain't*, which is now a classic American documentary, was finished by his coproducer, Nicole Atkinson, and codirector, Christian Badgeley.

Bibliography

Harper, Philip Brian. "Marlon Riggs: The Subjective Position of Documentary Video." *Art Journal* 54, no. 4 (Winter 1995).

Mercer, Kobena. "Dark and Lovely Too: Black Gay Men in Independent Film." In *Queer Looks: Perspectives on Lesbian and Gay Film and Video.* Edited by Martha Gerver et al. New York: Routledge, 1993.

Robert Reid-Pharr

See also FILM AND VIDEO.

RIGHTS OF ASSOCIATION AND ASSEMBLY

The rights of free association and assembly have been a double-edged sword in LGBT legal struggles. On the one hand, the recognition of such rights can prevent the government from prohibiting the association of LGBT people with one another. On the other hand, such rights can also protect the association of persons whose goal is to discriminate against LGBT people.

In either context, the rights of association and assembly are grounded in the U.S. Constitution. The First Amendment contains an explicit prohibition on government laws that would abridge "the right of the people peaceably to assemble." The First Amendment does not contain an explicit guarantee of "association," but the courts have generally interpreted the First Amendment's prohibition of laws "abridging the freedom of speech" as encompassing a prohibition of laws abridging the freedom of association for expressive (speechlike) purposes. Additionally, the courts have at times recognized a right of "intimate association," derived from the post–Civil War Fourteenth Amendment's clause mandating "due process of law." This right is more generally described as a "right to privacy" or a "right to bodily autonomy," denoting the focus on individual rights, rather than group rights, that permeates U.S. law.

To the extent that all of the above rights assert the First Amendment or Fourteenth Amendment to the U.S. Constitution, they apply only against the government or government actors. In other words, a private entity's actions cannot generally establish a denial of a person's constitutional rights of association, assembly, or other expressive speech. Instead, if a private entity is the actor, there may be remedies permitted under specific state or local laws, including state constitutions. For the most part, however, freedom of association and assembly are litigated and theorized as rights under the U.S. Constitution.

Freedom of assembly, however, has generally not been a specifically litigated doctrine in LGBT struggles. For the most part, LGBT public gatherings are constitutionally permitted, although the government may impose time, place, and manner restrictions and may require a permit process. Even when there are arguments regarding the government's infringement of the rights of freedom of assembly, these are most often conceptualized in court as limitations on freedom of speech or expression.

Whatever the outcome of particular cases or the peculiar developments of legal doctrine, the rights of freedom of association and assembly have been important inspirations to LGBT struggles for equality. The earliest known homosexual organization in the United States, the Society for Human Rights, chartered by the state of Illinois in 1924, was an expressive association that should have been protected under the First Amendment. Instead, the leaders were arrested for disorderly conduct based upon their membership in the organization.

Earliest Cases

The earliest cases in which LGBT persons implicitly asserted rights of freedom of association and assembly do not contain constitutional claims, but instead focused on the application of regulations that prohibited liquor licenses from being held by establishments that were "injurious to public morals." Perhaps one of the first judicial LGBT legal victories was the 1951 pronouncement by the California Supreme Court in *Stoumen v. Reilly* that "homosexuals" were "human beings" and their mere patronage of the Black Cat bar in San Francisco was not proof of the establishment's immorality.

The litigation surrounding police raids on the Humoresque Coffee Shop in Philadelphia, which was reputed to be a gathering place of "homosexuals and narcotic addicts," was less successful. After a raid in which police officers reportedly observed profanity and noted that the "hi-fi was blasting at a very high pitch," they arrested the owner, Mr. Haifetz, and thirty-two patrons for breach of the peace. Subsequently, Haifetz brought a civil rights action in federal court against the police department, arguing that the repeated raids and arrests violated numerous constitutional rights, including the First Amendment right to assembly. In *Haifetz v. Rizzo* (1959) the federal court rejected these claims, discrediting the testimony of the owner and patrons.

Impact of the Civil Rights Era and Student Activism

In the civil rights era, freedom of association was an important argument to protect new advocacy organizations. In 1958 the U.S. Supreme Court in *NAACP v.*

Alabama ex rel Paterson first explicitly recognized freedom of association as a constitutional doctrine in a case involving the state of Alabama's attempt to force the National Association for the Advancement of Colored People (NAACP) to produce its membership lists, and the Court thereafter applied the doctrine of freedom of association in other cases involving the NAACP. Gay and lesbian organizations were able to use similar arguments as they sought various forms of official recognition and protection. In the case of *In re Application of Thom* (1973), the litigation necessary to incorporate Lambda Legal Defense and Education Fund, New York's highest court reversed a lower court's finding that an organization to advance the interests of homosexuals was not being established for a "charitable or benevolent purpose" pursuant to the controlling statute. Important to the arguments was the organization's claim of First Amendment rights of freedom of association. In *Adolph Coors Co. v. Wallace* (1983), a court would uphold the right of a gay organization to keep its membership list confidential in litigation against the private company.

Student activism also accounted for many of the freedom of association cases affecting LGBT people. The First Amendment was used quite successfully by gay and lesbian student groups at public universities. The groups relied on the U.S. Supreme Court case *Healy v. James* (1972) that recognized the freedom of association rights of a campus chapter of Students for a Democratic Society. For example, in *Gay Students Organization of University of New Hampshire v. Bonner* (1974), the Court declared unconstitutional a university prohibition of all on-campus social activities by a gay student organization, prompted by the governor's objection to a gay dance. The Court rejected the university's argument that social activities such as dances were not covered by the First Amendment, noting that the reason for the university's prohibition was based on disapproval of the group's message about the existence of homosexuals and toleration of homosexuality. The *Bonner* court found that the student organization's mission of organization, education, and advocacy placed the students' activities at the very core of the freedom of association doctrine as it was being developed by the U.S. Supreme Court.

Using the First Amendment's protection of freedom of association as well as freedom of expression, LGBT students also successfully litigated to have their student groups recognized by universities. Students at Virginia Commonwealth University were victorious in *Gay Alliance of Students (GAS) v. Matthews* (1976), as were students from the University of Missouri in *Gay Lib v. University of Missouri* (1977). Yet both of these cases involved lengthy and costly litigation, including appeals, with the universities arguing that First Amendment freedoms were not pertinent when the exercise of such freedoms could lead to violations of the criminal laws, specifically those prohibiting sodomy.

Claiming Freedom of Intimate Association

Freedom of intimate association has historically been a less successful argument for LGBT groups and individuals. Until the landmark decision of the U.S. Supreme Court in *Lawrence v. Texas* in 2003, the courts had failed to recognize that such a right might prevail—or perhaps even exist—in the context of criminal prohibitions of sodomy or same-sex relations. One of the first cases decided by the U.S. Supreme Court to recognize a privacy right, *Griswold v. Connecticut* (1965)—dealing with the use of contraception by a married couple—mentioned the right of intimate association. Subsequent cases, however, have largely considered sexual activity under the due process clauses of the Constitution. Thus, in *Bowers v. Hardwick* (1986) the Court rejected any arguments that the Georgia statute that criminalized sodomy should be measured under First Amendment rights of intimate association. The Court distinguished a case that declared unconstitutional a statute that had criminalized the possession of obscene materials in one's home, because although obscenity is a matter for the First Amendment, sodomy is not.

Similarly, courts have rejected intimate association arguments when they have been used to challenge laws or policies that prohibit same-sex marriage; the rare cases that have held opposite-sex marriage prohibitions invalid have relied upon equality arguments. Likewise, in *Shahar v. Bowers* (1997), the courts rejected a freedom of intimate association argument made by Robin Shahar, challenging her dismissal from her position as an attorney with the Georgia Attorney General's Office when her superiors learned that she was participating in a lesbian marriage ceremony.

However, with the court's overruling of *Bowers* in the *Lawrence* case in 2003, the court declared that criminal laws against privately consensual gay and lesbian sexual acts did violate the due process clause. Although not decided on the basis of intimate association, this due process privacy ruling encompasses the idea of intimate association and provides protection for it. Further litigation will seek to expand this right.

Freedom of Association versus LGBT Rights

Since the 1970s, many states and localities have increasingly begun to prohibit discrimination against LGBT persons, but these laws have sometimes run afoul of the First Amendment's protection of freedom of association or expressive association. Thus, when faced with state or local laws that prohibit discrimination on the basis of sexual orientation, some groups have argued that their First Amendment rights would be violated should they be forced to comply with such antidiscrimination laws.

For example, in many cities in the United States the annual St. Patrick's Day celebration includes a festive parade celebrating Irish heritage. In several cities, controversies have erupted between the organizers of the parades and members of local LGBT Irish American communities who wish to march in the parade. In Boston in the 1990s, when organizers again refused to allow the LGBT contingent, the group brought suit in state court, relying upon constitutional provisions as well as Massachusetts's recently passed law prohibiting discrimination on the basis of sexual orientation in several situations, including public accommodations. The case reached the Massachusetts Supreme Court, which ruled that the parade constituted a place of "public accommodation," occurring as it did on city streets, and that the parade organizers violated the state law prohibiting sexual orientation discrimination. The U.S. Supreme Court accepted review and in its unanimous opinion written by Justice David Souter reversed the Massachusetts Supreme Court on the basis of the First Amendment. In *Hurley v. Irish-American Gay, Lesbian, and Bisexual Group of Boston* (1995), the Court does not explicitly confront the freedom of association doctrine. *Hurley* takes pains to distinguish this case from a previous one that had held that the Jaycees' freedom of association was not infringed when the state declared that the organization must comply with the state's antidiscrimination laws and admit women into its membership.

Yet in *Dale v. Boy Scouts of America* (2000), the Court explicitly held that the Boy Scouts had a First Amendment right of expressive association, which would be violated if the Boy Scout organization was forced to include gay men as members in order to comply with the state of New Jersey's antidiscrimination statute. In so ruling, a majority of the Court found that the Boy Scouts was an expressive association and that part of its expressive activity included disapproval of homosexuality. Although there was some factual controversy regarding whether a stance on sexuality was actually part of the Boy Scout's policy, the Court decided that an association's statements about its expressive intent must be given deference, that all members of an association need not agree, and that an association need not associate for the "purpose" of a certain expression. The Court held that weighed against the state's interest in nondiscrimination against sexual minorities, the Boy Scouts' freedom of expressive association should prevail. Thus, in this case freedom of association was used to undermine a claim of equality made by an LGBT person.

In *Dale* a majority of the Court theorized the First Amendment's freedom of association as a bulwark to protect minority views. The rhetoric of the Court's opinion posits discrimination against LGBT persons as an unpopular position requiring the safeguard of the Constitution. Given such a perspective, *Dale* is consistent with earlier cases that sought to protect organizations such as the NAACP during the 1950s. *Dale* would also be consistent with the efforts of LGBT organizations to be recognized under corporate laws and by universities, and even with arguments that LGBT persons should be permitted to assemble in private establishments such as bars and coffeehouses without governmental harassment or arrests. There remain, however, bitter disputes about the use of the First Amendment's guarantee of freedom of association and expression to insulate parties who wish to discriminate against LGBT persons.

Bibliography

Carpenter, Dale. "Expressive Association and Anti-Discrimination Law After Dale: A Tripartite Approach." *Minnesota Law Review* 85 (2001): 1515.

Eskridge, William N., Jr. *Gaylaw: Challenging the Apartheid of the Closet.* Cambridge, Mass: Harvard University Press, 1999.

Haifetz v. Rizzo, 178 F. Supp. 828 (E.D. Pa. 1959) (The Humoresque Coffee Shop).

Leonard, Arthur S. *Sexuality and the Law: An Encyclopedia of Major Legal Cases.* New York: Garland, 1993.

Mazzone, Jason. "Freedom's Associations." *Washington Law Review* 77 (2002): 639.

Murdoch, Joyce, and Price, Deb. *Courting Justice: Gay Men and Lesbians v. The Supreme Court.* New York: Basic Books, 2001.

Robson, Ruthann. *Sappho Goes to Law School: Fragments in Lesbian Legal Theory.* New York: Columbia University Press, 1998.

Ruthann Robson

See also BARS, CLUBS, AND RESTAURANTS; CRIME AND CRIMINALIZATION; DISCRIMINATION; FEDERAL LAW AND POLICY; LAMBDA LEGAL DEFENSE; LIQUOR CONTROL LAW AND POLICY; POLICING AND POLICE; PRIVACY AND PRIVACY RIGHTS; SOCIETY FOR HUMAN RIGHTS; SOCIETY FOR INDIVIDUAL RIGHTS.

RITTS, Herb (b. 13 August 1952; d. 26 December 2002), photographer, videographer.

Born to Herb and Shirley Ritts in Los Angeles, California, Ritts grew up in southern California, where his father owned a furniture company. Photographing family occasions became an interest of his during childhood. He attended Bard College, where he studied economics and art history; returning home after graduation, he began work as a sales representative in his father's business. Ritts soon thereafter revealed his homosexuality to his parents, who remained supportive of their son. Ritts's sexual orientation is central to appreciating his art. The raw, but gentle sensuality of his photos and the distinctive machismo and fragility of his male models became an enduring characteristic of Ritts's work both as a photographer and a videographer.

Adult education night classes in photography further improved Ritts's artistic skills, and by the early 1970s he found work taking pictures of friends in the arts, particularly aspiring actor Richard Gere. Ritts's highly sensual 1978 photograph of a sweaty Gere in a dirty T-shirt and jeans taking a break from repairing a flat tire attracted significant attention. Within a year, Gere was a major film star, and Ritts, continuing to hone his skills, found employment in fashion photography, mostly for Italian magazines. The images he created had a strong narrative thrust and carefully designed period settings, and this led Ritts to establish a relationship with the film industry. When he visited the set of the remake of *The Champ* in 1979, he persuaded stars Jon Voight and Ricky Schroeder to pose for him, and one of his shots appeared in *Newsweek*'s "Newsmakers" section soon after.

If Robert Mapplethorpe, the groundbreaking, often controversial photographer of highly sensual, homoerotic images, established a new frontier in contemporary photography, Ritts provided a more mainstream aesthetic in which to explore both male and female sexuality in high-concept, erotic photography. For a fashion shoot on blue jeans, Ritts rented a ramshackle garage and posed his athletic male models as 1950s auto mechanics. The photos, particularly one entitled "Fred with Tires" (1984), create images of a rough and virile sexuality set against the backdrop of an evocative environment. In Ritts's photos the muscular male models often appear to be glistening, smoothly textured classical statues enlivened by a potent sexuality, although in his more erotic work, the photographer's gaze is that of a dispassionate observer.

By the early 1980s, Ritts was one of the world's most sought-after fashion photographers; he worked for many celebrated designers, including Donna Karan, Calvin Klein, Gianni Versace, and Giorgio Armani. He pho-

Herb Ritts. The noted fashion and celebrity photographer, whose works are often very sensual, stands between two of his prints at an exhibition. [Bembaron Jeremy/corbis Sygma]

tographed numerous spreads in leading magazines such as *Vogue, Vanity Fair, Harper's Bazaar, GQ, Interview Magazine,* and *Rolling Stone,* among many others. In 1980, his photos of Richard Gere on the set of *American Gigolo* were used for that film's publicity.

Ritts photographed celebrities of every kind, mythologizing his subjects while simultaneously revealing them in new and often surprisingly unguarded ways. Screen legend Elizabeth Taylor revealed her shaved head and the scar from brain surgery to Ritts, and he captured paralyzed actor Christopher Reeve in stark profile breathing through a respirator. In a sexier vein, Ritts photographed five completely nude supermodels, including Cindy Crawford, Christy Turlington, and Naomi Campbell, huddled together, and in one of his most controversial images, he captured a scantily clad Crawford provocatively straddling a barber chair to shave singer k. d. lang, dressed in male drag, for a cover of *Vanity Fair.* He photographed countless movie stars (Jack Nicholson, Glenn

Close, Michelle Pfeiffer, and Brad Pitt), pop music icons (Mick Jagger and Dizzy Gillespie), sports heroes (Dennis Rodman, Jackie Joyner-Kersee, and Michael Jordan), public figures (George Wallace, Nelson Mandela, Ronald Reagan, and Kofi Annan), and contemporary artists of every variety (John Huston, Merce Cunningham, and Keith Haring).

By the mid-1990s, Ritts was widely recognized as an artist. Major exhibitions of his photographs were held in New York (1988), Boston (1996), and Paris (2000). Ritts branched out to direct music videos in the 1990s; Ritts-directed videos featuring Janet Jackson and Chris Isaak both received MTV Best Video Awards. Ritts also directed critically acclaimed music videos for Madonna, *NSYNC, Jennifer Lopez, and Britney Spears.

Although a deeply private person, Ritts publicly revealed his homosexuality on a 1993 NBC news program. He also became involved in raising funds for the American Foundation for AIDS Research (AMFAR), donating the royalties from his 1991 photographic collection *Duo,* a study of a gay couple—one of whom was Mr. Universe—to AMFAR.

Following a short January 1993 visit to East Africa, Ritts returned there to travel extensively the following summer. His photographs from this trip were published in a 1994 book, *Africa,* which featured photos of animals, the African landscape, and the Massai people. The choice of subject might have seemed uncharacteristic for a celebrity photographer, but the collection was nonetheless well received.

Diagnosed HIV-positive several years earlier, Ritts died on 26 December 2002 at the UCLA Medical Center, following the completion of a difficult desert shoot. Ritts's death inspired controversy when his obituaries, released by his longtime partner Erik Hyman, indicated that he had died of complications from pneumonia. The opinion pages of newspapers and magazines nationwide were soon filled with comments condemning the use of "Reagan-era euphemisms" to obscure Ritts's AIDS-related death at the height of the pandemic. Despite such controversy, Ritts's final photographs appeared for months after his death, and his work continues to gain appreciation.

James Fisher

See also FASHION, STYLE, AND CLOTHING; VISUAL ART.

RIVERA, Sylvia (b. 2 July 1951; d. 19 February 2002), activist.

Sylvia (formerly Ray) Rivera achieved legendary status in the LGBT community as one of the street queens who fought in the riot at the Stonewall Inn that helped launch the modern gay and transgender liberation movements.

Rivera, of Puerto Rican and Venezuelan descent, had it rough from the start. She was born feet-first in the back of a taxicab outside Lincoln Hospital in the Bronx, New York. When Rivera was three, her twenty-two-year-old single mother attempted to take both their lives with a concoction of rat poison and milk, but succeeded only in killing herself. Rivera, always effeminate, was raised by a grandmother who beat and abused her, and she suffered constant bullying and harassment at school. Consequently, she ran away at age ten to make a life for herself on the streets, working as a child prostitute on 42nd Street near Times Square. Rivera became a drug addict in the process, and endured repeated arrests and rapes. Fortunately, Marsha P. ("Pay It No Mind") Johnson, an older transgender sex worker, befriended Rivera and

schooled her in the survival strategies of the urban street queen subculture. Johnson remained involved in Rivera's life for several years and shared with her an activist zeal bred by the hardships they both had suffered.

On 27 June 1969, seventeen-year-old Rivera was dancing to the jukebox in the Stonewall Inn, a gay bar on Christopher Street in Greenwich Village, when the lights brightened and the police marched in. The patrons were surprised by the raid, even though raids on gay bars were relatively frequent occurrences at that time, because the usual bribe to the police department had been paid earlier that week. When Rivera and the others were taken outside to waiting police wagons, the assembled crowd began throwing pennies, nickels, and dimes at the cops. Bottles soon followed—Rivera is sometimes credited with throwing the first—and the police retreated back inside the Stonewall to call for help. Three days of street fighting between gays and the police followed, and the militant phase of the gay liberation movement was off and running.

Neither the Gay Liberation Front nor the Gay Activists Alliance had much understanding of, nor sympathy for, transgender issues. Consequently, in 1970, after nearly a year's frustration with the movement they helped launch, Rivera and Johnson founded the Street Transvestite Action Revolutionaries (STAR), to help young street queens make a better life for themselves. They eventually were able to rent a building on East Second Street and establish STAR House, a loosely knit collective crash pad that provided food and shelter and a support network to street queens in need.

STAR was committed to multi-issue political activism and revolutionary politics, drawing connections between homophobia, sexism, race, class, poverty, and police violence in the analyses of its members. Rivera was also briefly involved with the Young Lords, a revolutionary Puerto Rican youth group, and met with Huey Newton of the Black Panther Party at the 1970 Revolutionary People's Constitutional Convention in Philadelphia. She always considered the liberation of street queens to be part of a broader radical struggle for social justice.

Rivera was deeply alienated from the gay movement in 1973, when lesbian feminists who considered drag to be disrespectful of women threatened to boycott the fourth annual march and rally commemorating the Stonewall riots if Rivera was allowed to speak. The gay men organizing the event agreed, believing that this decision showed solidarity with their feminist sisters. Rivera tried to storm the stage to speak but was physically prevented from doing so.

Rivera thereafter retreated from active involvement in gay politics for many years. She and her partner Frank lived for nearly twenty years in Tarrytown, New York, where Rivera found work as a food services manager with the Marriott Corporation. She struggled with addiction throughout this period, however, and eventually wound up homeless, alone, and destitute on the piers of New York City's West Village.

By 1997 Rivera had turned her life around once again. She found a new home in Transie House, a Brooklyn commune embodying the former ideals of STAR, and found herself lionized by a new generation of transgender activists who considered her a foremother of their movement. She found a new love, Julia Rivera-Murray, another transgender woman. Reinvigorated, Rivera threw herself into a fresh round of political activism.

After a long fight with liver cancer at the end of a harsh but fiercely proud life, Rivera died among friends in New York on 19 February 2002.

Bibliography

Bronski, Michael. "No Longer on the Back of a Bumper." *Z.* Online archives, http://zena.secureform.com/znet/zmag/zmag.cfm

Duberman, Martin. *Stonewall.* New York: Plume, 1994.

Feinberg, Leslie. "Leslie Feinberg Interviews Sylvia Rivera." *Worker's World* (2 July 1998).

Isay, David. "Sylvia Rivera." *New York Times Magazine* (27 June 1999).

Susan Stryker

See also DRAG QUEENS AND KINGS; POOR PEOPLE'S MOVEMENTS; PUERTO RICO; STONEWALL RIOTS; TRANSGENDER ORGANIZATIONS AND PERIODICALS; TRANSSEXUALS, TRANSVESTITES, TRANSGENDER PEOPLE, AND CROSS-DRESSERS.

ROBBINS, Jerome (b. 11 October 1918; d. 29 July 1998), dancer, choreographer, director.

Born Jerome Rabinowitz in New York City to Russian-Jewish immigrants who had fled the pogroms, Robbins was still small when his family moved to Weehawken, New Jersey, where his father opened a delicatessen and later became a corset manufacturer. Robbins and his only sibling, older sister Sonia, studied music and dance at the Gluck Sandor studios. He attended New York University for a single year, then began intensive study in ballet and modern dance.

He joined the American Ballet Theater in 1940 and debuted as a soloist in *Petrouchka* in 1942. On 18 April 1944, Robbins premiered his breakthrough choreographic success, the character ballet *Fancy Free,* set to a commissioned score by Leonard Bernstein. The patriotic work featured three sailors on a day of shore leave in New York City who pursue two women in a high-spirited format of comic vignettes and challenge dances. An immediate success, the work was expanded into the hit Broadway musical *On the Town,* which opened 28 December 1944.

Robbins's choreographic style combined popular social dance movements with classical ballet to underscore the dramatic impulse of dance for its characters. From then on, he maintained fertile and highly successful parallel careers as a director and choreographer of ballets and Broadway musicals.

Robbins's exceptional Broadway work encompassed several of the most important musicals of the twentieth century. He staged inventive dances for *Billion Dollar Baby* (1945), *High Button Shoes* (1947), *Look, Ma, I'm Dancin'* (1948), *Call Me Madam* (1950), and *The King and I* (1951), among others, then moved to directing and choreographing musicals on a level of unprecedented stagecraft and narrative flow. His productions of *Peter Pan* (1954), *Bells Are Ringing* (1956), *West Side Story* (1957), *Gypsy* (1959), and *Fiddler on the Roof* (1964) achieved an extravagant integration of dance, music, and character development.

West Side Story, written with gay and bisexual collaborators Bernstein (composer), Stephen Sondheim (lyricist), and Arthur Laurents (librettist), retold the tragedy of Romeo and Juliet as an encounter between rival New York City street gangs. Its jazz-inflected yet operatic score and balletic dance sequences described an ineffable angst among feuding Italian and Puerto Rican teenagers. *Fiddler on the Roof,* inspired by Sholom Aleichem stories, explored Jewish cultural heritage through the story of Tevye, a poor Russian dairyman, and his attempts to preserve tradition among his family of five daughters. Robbins revisited his Broadway successes with the staging of *Jerome Robbins' Broadway* (1989), a retrospective of his greatest dance numbers.

Robbins's choreographic success in ballet included works that mingled social dance styles with classical form, as in *Interplay* (1945), and extended theatrical possibilities of the idiom, as in the unexpected vocalized scream of the ballerina in *Facsimile* (1946), a work about a love triangle between two men and a woman. In 1948, Robbins joined the newly created New York City Ballet at George Balanchine's invitation and attracted critical acclaim dancing the title character in Balanchine's *Prodigal Son.* In the next decade he created a series of important ballets that explored gesture, character, and repressed desire framed in a patent theatricality, including *Age of Anxiety* (1950), based on a W. H. Auden poem with music by Bernstein; *The Cage* (1951), about a tribe of man-eating female insects; *Moves* (1955), an abstract group work without music; *Afternoon of a Faun* (1953), an oblique erotic encounter by dancers in a rehearsal studio; and *The Concert* (1956), a campy spoof of a classical music concert.

In 1958, Robbins formed a short-lived pick-up company, Ballets: USA, for which he created several works, including *New York Export: Opus Jazz* (1958) and *Events* (1961). He returned to the New York City Ballet, where he remained until 1990, when he gave his official farewell at the Festival of Jerome Robbins's Ballets. Among his more than fifty ballets for that company are many significant offerings, including *Dances at a Gathering* (1969), *The Goldberg Variations* (1971), *Watermill* (1972), *Dybbuk Variations* (1974), and *Glass Pieces* (1983).

Firmly closeted and deeply ambivalent about his sexuality, Robbins had brief affairs with many men and women, including the actor Montgomery Clift, the dancer Buzz Miller, the dancer Christine Conrad, the filmmaker Warren Sonbert, and the artist Jesse Gerstein. A self-proclaimed perfectionist, he earned the enmity of nearly all of his collaborators for his virulent emotional manipulations in the rehearsal hall.

In 1953, Robbins testified before the House Un-American Activities Committee, naming names of various Communist Party members, apparently in order to avoid public disclosure of his homosexuality. In general, his work tended to treat sexual identity as a catalyst for violence, as in *The Cage* and *Events* (the latter depicting the rape of a man), although *Watermill* (1972) offered, to some audiences, a visual meditation on a solo male dancer's physical beauty. Robbins died after a stroke in July 1998.

Bibliography

Conrad, Christine. *Jerome Robbins: That Broadway Man, That Ballet Man.* London: Booth-Clibborn Editions, 2000.

Kisselgoff, Anna. "Jerome Robbins, Seventy-nine, Is Dead; Giant of Ballet and Broadway." *New York Times* (30 July 1998): A1.

Lawrence, Greg. *Dance with Demons: The Life of Jerome Robbins.* New York: G. P. Putnam's Sons, 2001.

Thomas F. DeFrantz

See also DANCE.

RODWELL, Craig (b. 31 October 1940; d. 18 June 1993), gay activist, bookstore owner, movement organizer.

Craig Rodwell was central to the militant homophile initiative that took place in the 1960s on the East Coast. Following the Stonewall Riots in 1969, he played a pivotal role in transforming the drive for civil rights and social assimilation into a multifaceted movement for sexual and sex role liberation.

Born in Chicago, Rodwell was sent to a Christian Science boarding school for boys after his parents divorced. Private sexual experimentation in same-sex intimacy was common at his school, and Rodwell soon discovered that it came naturally to him. When caught having sex with another boy, he did not apologize.

As a teenager, having returned to public high school in Chicago, Rodwell sought homosexual intimacy via the cruising and sex scenes that flourished in public places in that city. An episode at seventeen led to his first grating experiences with police officers, court officials, and psychiatrists. After he seduced a dishwasher twice his age, the two were apprehended by police officers who assumed that the older man had initiated the sex act.

His newfound interest in liberal politics inspired Rodwell to take a political stand about homosexuality. After learning he was too young to join Chicago's Mattachine Society, he stuffed local mailboxes with a self-composed flyer urging, "Homosexuals Unite: Tear Off Your Masks."

In 1958, upon turning eighteen and deciding to attend ballet school, Rodwell moved to Boston and then Manhattan. In New York, he blustered around town with other gay young men who styled themselves as street queens. Adults at the Mattachine Society of New York (MSNY) allowed him to do office and newsletter work until he became old enough to join the organization at twenty-one.

On 19 September 1964 Rodwell participated in the picket line that Randy Wicker and his Homosexual League organized at the Whitehall Induction Center to protest discrimination against homosexuals in the military. At the beginning of 1965 he contributed to the takeover of MSNY by militants. On 18 April 1965 he and others from MSNY joined Wicker and his league in a demonstration at the United Nations held to protest the Castro government's internment of Cuban homosexuals in labor camps. Thereafter, these New Yorkers traveled to Washington, D.C., for the historic picket lines of the homophile movement that Frank Kameny and other East Coast leaders staged at prominent federal buildings.

When these demonstrations came to an end, Rodwell suggested that the follow-up be an Annual July 4th Reminder in the form of picketing at Independence Hall in Philadelphia. From the start, however, he objected to Kameny's insistence on structure and respectability. Kameny required all picketers to wear business attire and to march in single-file ovals carrying signs printed by the organizers. Rodwell wanted participants to dress and behave as naturally as possible and to raise issues that moved them personally.

A year later, as vice-president of MSNY, Rodwell joined Dick Leitsch, its new president, in conducting a "sip-in" that established the legality of gay bars in New York City. His own communitarian preferences led him to advocate that the Mattachine become more accessible to young people. When Rodwell's proposal to establish an MSNY storefront office in Greenwich Village met with opposition, he struck out on his own.

On Thanksgiving Day in 1967, in a small space at 291 Mercer Street in Greenwich Village, Rodwell opened the Oscar Wilde Memorial Bookshop. Its shelves bore three copies apiece of the twenty-five most positive books about homosexual behavior he could find. A countertop display case offered gay political buttons for sale. A sign in the window identified the location as "A Bookstore of the Homophile Movement." It is often regarded as the very first bookstore in the world devoted to serious materials dealing with homosexuality.

In February 1968 Rodwell started a bookshop-based group called Homophile Youth Movement in Neighborhoods (HYMN). An editorial in the first issue of its newsletter, *The New York HYMNAL,* explained that the publication "will have a 'religious' fervor and crusading spirit in its treatment of the homosexual way of life and the homophile movement. We will make no pretense of speaking to the heterosexual in trying to persuade him to 'accept' homosexuals. *HYMNAL* is solely concerned with what the gay person thinks of himself. The community has the economic, political, and social potential to shape its own future. This potential only needs to be encouraged and channeled. In a sense, *HYMNAL* is bringing Gay Power to New York" (Rodwell, p. 2).

Under the headline "Mafia on the Spot," this inaugural issue of the *HYMNAL* also expanded on a recent *New York Times* article confirming what "has been common knowledge among New York's homosexual community for many years, the Mafia (or 'The Syndicate') control of New York City's gay bars. . . ." The particular bar singled out was "The Stonewall on Christopher Street . . . one of the larger and more financially lucrative of the Mafia's gay bars in Manhattan" (Rodwell, p. 1).

A year and a half later, on his way past Christopher Street after a Friday night of cards, Rodwell encountered a crowd objecting to an ongoing police raid of the Stonewall Inn. In an effort to politicize this resistance, he began chanting, "gay power, gay power." When no one joined in, after watching the crowd for a while, he went to a nearby pay phone and alerted the mainstream press to what was happening.

That Saturday night Rodwell was back at the Stonewall Inn for a more politicized protest. On Sunday, he produced and circulated a leaflet with the headline, "Get the Mafia and the Cops out of Gay Bars." Its text began by predicting that "the nights of Friday, June 27, 1969 and Saturday, June 28, 1969 will go down in history as the first time that thousands of Homosexual men and women went out into the streets to protest the intolerable situation."

The fifth Annual Reminder at Independence Hall took place as scheduled on the following weekend. Frank Kameny remained true to form by preventing the members of an openly affectionate lesbian couple from holding hands as they circled. Rodwell was so offended that he rebelled. First he organized all protesters in the New York delegation to walk hand in hand. Then he violated Kameny's rules about carefully orchestrated press dealings by telling reporters that the Stonewall Riots had transformed their drive for civil rights into a quest for "gay liberation."

Back in New York, Rodwell concluded that a very different kind of Annual Reminder was needed to sustain the impassioned community action necessary to produce gay liberation. In November 1969, at a meeting of the Eastern Regional Conference of Homophile Organizations (ERCHO), he engineered passage of a resolution that replaced the July 4th Annual Reminder with an annual Christopher Street Liberation Day in New York City's Greenwich Village.

During the next several months Rodwell used his bookshop and his apartment as a base for organizing the first set of "Gay Pride" and "Freedom Day" events. Gay organizations of every community-based kind were invited to attend. Gay people were encouraged to dress as they normally would, openly express affection, and advocate as they chose at these events. Groups in other cities were urged to hold similar observances.

On 28 June 1970 there was a march up Sixth Avenue to Central Park followed by a gay-in at its Sheep Meadow. There was also a march of comparable size in West Hollywood, a much smaller procession in Chicago, and spontaneous walks and celebrations in Boston, Provincetown, New Haven, and San Francisco. Ever since, the Stonewall Riots have been commemorated with yearly June parades and festivals in cities throughout the world.

The genius of the post-Stonewall liberation movement, which Rodwell did so much to shape, was that it encouraged loving individuals to contribute as they could and would. The resulting feelings of empowerment caused a geometrically expanding number of people to become involved in matters affecting their sexuality. This dynamic of exponential growth continues.

In 1973 Rodwell moved his Oscar Wilde Memorial Bookshop to 15 Christopher Street. Symbolically enough, this new location was just down the block from the abandoned Stonewall Inn, at the intersection of Christopher and a tiny elbow of a way named Gay Street. From here, until his death from stomach cancer, Rodwell carefully cultivated the liberation movement to which he had devoted his life.

Bibliography

Clendinen, Dudley, and Adam Nagourney. *Out for Good: The Struggle to Build a Gay Rights Movement in America.* New York: Simon and Schuster, 1999.

Duberman, Martin. *Stonewall.* New York: Dutton, 1993.

Marotta, Toby. *The Politics of Homosexuality: How Lesbians and Gay Men Have Made Themselves a Political and Social Force in Modern America.* Boston: Houghton Mifflin, 1981.

Marotta, Toby. LGBTQ Archive. Available from www.Toby Marotta.com.

Rodwell, Craig. Papers, 1940–1993. International Gay Information Center (IGIC) Archives, Manuscripts and Archives Division, The New York Public Library.

Rodwell, Craig, editor-in-chief and publisher. "HYMNAL Makes Bow" and "Mafia on the Spot." *The New York Hymnal* I, no. 1 (February 1968): 1-2.

Teal, Donn. *The Gay Militants: How Gay Liberation Began in America, 1969–1971.* New York: St. Martin's Press, 1995.

Tobin, Kay, and Randy Wicker. *The Gay Crusaders.* New York: Paperback Library, 1972.

Toby Marotta

See also BOOKSTORES; BUSINESSES; GAY LIBERATION; HOMOPHILE MOVEMENT; MARCHES ON WASHINGTON.

ROMANTIC FRIENDSHIP AND BOSTON MARRIAGE

The concept of same-sex romantic friendship belongs to eras that were largely sex-segregated, sentimental, and less willing to contemplate sexual meanings in behavior than Americans have been for most of the last century. Romantic friendship was ostensibly a universally honored institution for both men and women. Numerous traces of it are to be found in ancient literature, including the Old Testament. In Ruth 1:15–16, for example, Ruth implores Naomi in words that heterosexuals later took as part of their marriage vows, "Whither though goest, I will go; and whither thou stayest, I will stay. Your people will be my people and your God my God." David's powerful declaration to Jonathan in 2 Sam. 1.26—"Your love was wonderful to me, passing the love of women"—became part of the language of romantic friendship for both males and females in early modern Europe and was imported onto American soil with little change.

Romantic Friendship Between Women: The European Heritage

In speaking of their own romantic friendships, women sometimes reversed David's terms, as does a female character in William Hayley's *The Young Widow* (1789), who declares to another woman, "I assure you, with a love 'passing the Love of Men,' that I am yours." Obviously, we cannot be certain of the extent to which such declarations were sexual, but evidence from personal journals as well as literature shows that romantic friendships were clearly love relationships and that often they were patently sensual. Romantic friends pledged to be eternally devoted to one another. They claimed to wish to be together always, to care for one another above anything or anyone. They slept together and held each other in long embraces.

Perhaps female romantic friendship was a socially accepted institution in Europe for many centuries because it was perceived to provide necessary functions such as an innocuous release for homosocially segregated girls and unhappily married women. Though, as Faderman and Donoghue have shown, these relationships were occasionally suspected of being sexual, for the most part such possibilities seem not to have been entertained by those outside the relationships. In any case, they were generally not considered threatening to the fabric of society at a time when few jobs were open to women of the middle and upper classes and most women would have to marry, for economic reasons if no other. Perhaps, too, in a phallocentric society men had difficulty taking the notion of female same-sex sexuality seriously.

The wealth of European literature about female romantic friendship, by both male and female writers, includes Thomas Lodge's sixteenth-century play, *Rosalynde*, the seventeenth century poetry of Katherine Philips, a spate of eighteenth-century novels, including Jean-Jacques Rousseau's *La nouvelle Héloïse* (1761); Sarah

Scott's *A Description of Millenium Hall* (1762); Helen Maria Williams's *Anecdotes of a Convent* (1771); *Danebury: or, The Power of Friendship* (1771) "by a Young Lady"; Harriet Lee's *The Error of Innocence* (1786); Mary Wollstonecraft's *Mary: A Fiction* (1788); and Charlotte Lennox's *Euphemia* (1790). All of these works concern middle- and upper-class women. There is little information extant on romantic friendships between European women of the lower classes since they were seldom the focus of novels, and in a society where only the well-off read, they were seldom literate and did not record their own stories.

Romantic Friendship Between Women in America

The first published literary evidence of female romantic friendship in America is Charles Brockden Brown's 1798 novel, *Ormond: or The Secret Witness*, in which the relationship between his two heroines is described as "a master passion." Constantia exclaims, "To look and to talk to each other afforded enchanting occupation for every moment. I would not part from her side, but ate and slept … with her breath fanning my cheek…. O precious inebriation of the heart! O pre-eminent love!" (p. 207). In his 1849 novel, *Kavanagh*, Henry Wadsworth Longfellow gives some insight into why romantic friendships such as that between his heroines Cecilia and Alice were viewed as nonthreatening to the social fabric: They are "a rehearsal in girlhood of the great drama of woman's life" (p. 41), that is, the inevitable heterosexual marriage. In William Alger's 1868 historical survey, *The Friendships of Women*, the author finds yet another reason for social approval of female romantic friendships in the high number of male fatalities during the Civil War, which left many superfluous women doomed to lifelong loneliness if they had no dear woman friend.

Women's letters and journals of the period indicate that these male authors were reflecting a common phenomenon. Carroll Smith-Rosenberg's valuable pioneering archival work on nineteenth-century romantic friendships, "The Female World of Love and Ritual: Relations Between Women in Nineteenth Century America," shows the great extent to which middle- and upper-class women saw each other as kindred spirits who inhabited a world of interests and sensibilities alien to men. The material quoted by Smith-Rosenberg demonstrates that these women expressed their passion to one another without the inhibition that came to characterize discussion of same-sex love in later times.

A rare historical find, reported in Karen V. Hansen's "'No kisses is like youres': An Erotic Friendship Between Two African-American Women During the Mid-

Nineteenth Century," which presents the letters of two black women, Addie Brown and Rebecca Primus, demonstrates much the same language that is found in the correspondence of their white counterparts: for example, "I am near the[e], breathing the same air with your arm gently drawn around me, my head reclining on your noble breast in confidence and love" (p. 184). Addie, who worked as a cook in a boarding school and slept in a bed with a white girl, assured her beloved Rebecca, "my night dress was butten up so she could not get to my bosom" (pp. 185–186), suggesting perhaps that when Addie and Rebecca slept together, her nightdress was not "butten up" and leaving open to question the extent to which romantic friendships did indeed have physical expression.

Glimpses of the romantic friendships of lower-class women are also rare (for reasons mentioned above), but an interesting exception is Sarah Orne Jewett's "Martha's Lady," a short story that depicts the passionate friendship Martha, a servant, feels for an upper-class woman, which adds fortunate moral and emotional dimensions to Martha's life.

Boston Marriage, Yesterday and Today

Feminist agitation in the second half of the nineteenth century led to huge social gains for women, including the opening of higher education and professions. Women now had the capability of supporting themselves. Those "rehearsals in girlhood," as Longfellow characterized earlier romantic friendships, could now become "the great drama." That is, two women could establish a long-term domestic relationship, which would have been all but impossible for most women in earlier times. The term "Boston marriage" may have been coined by Mark DeWolfe Howe, editor of the *Atlantic Monthly*, about his good friends Annie Fields and Sarah Orne Jewett, who lived together in a committed relationship until Jewett's death in 1909. "Boston marriage" came to signify a long-term, monogamous, domestic relationship between two otherwise unmarried women. By the late nineteenth century such relationships were not uncommon among graduates of women's colleges, which were primarily in the northeastern United States: many of these women did not go home again after graduation but rather settled in cities such as Boston and became career women.

In 1993, Esther Rothblum and Kathleen Brehony reintroduced the term "Boston marriage" to describe relationships between contemporary lesbian couples that are romantic but asexual. Rothblum and Brehony suggest that in our day some women see Boston marriage as a feminist alternative to traditional heterosexual marriage.

Their work challenges the notion that sex is the sine qua non in the definition of a lesbian relationship.

Romantic Friendship Between Men: The European Heritage

In Montaigne's sixteenth-century essay, "On Friendship," he uses his romantic friendship with Estienne de La Boétie as an example of an ideal love relationship. Montaigne writes that two men could love so deeply that they "mix and blend in each other with so complete a mixing that they efface and never again find the seam that joined them" (p. 139). He speaks of falling in love with Estienne at first sight and declares, "Nothing from then on was so near to either of us as was the other." He distinguishes his love for Estienne from male same-sex love as practiced by the Greeks by pointing out that between Greek lovers there was generally a great disparity in age and vocation and that the relationship was founded on the physical beauty of the youth alone; thus true friendship was not possible. He maintains that for the same reason, relations between men and women are generally inferior to those possible between two mature men. Montaigne never deals more specifically with the sexual implications of the Greek relationships other than to say that they were based on the youth's attractiveness, and in no way does he allude to the sexual possibilities of his friendship with Estienne.

European Renaissance literature often depicted two men in passionate friendships such as what Montaigne described in his essay. Devoted males are seen "sharing one bed, one house, one table, and one purse" (Painter), or being "neither separated at bourde nor severed at bed" (Lodge, p. 18). Male romantic friends in these works generally marry women before the denouement, but their passionate friendships continue unchanged. In *The Palace of Pleasure*, for instance, after one of the men marries, Painter emphasizes that his same-sex relationship is unaltered: "Their goodes were common betweene them, and the marriage did yield no cause to hinder their assured amities." It is not clear what happened after the marriage (or before, for that matter) in the "one bed" Painter has his two romantic friends sharing.

Romantic Friendship Between Men in America

Colonial law often mandated public execution or castration for men caught in flagrante delicto with other men, and though sodomy laws became less draconian in post-colonial times, statutes prohibiting sexual acts between men were universal. Strong expressions of male romantic friendship, however, were not uncommon. Even during the most homophobic times, scholars looking back on male romantic friendships of the past preferred to see them as they were undoubtedly seen from the outside in earlier eras, as largely sentimental or rhetorical. Alexander Hamilton's 1959 biographer, John Miller, for example, discussing Hamilton's passionate "Damon and Pythias" friendship with John Laurens, observes that expressions of love such as Hamilton and Laurens, both military men, used with one another would "provoke a riot in even the best-regulated present-day barracks"; but he insists that their ostensible passion can be understood as merely a manifestation of "the high-flown literary language of [Hamilton's] day" (p. 122).

Regardless of the real nature of the connection between men like Hamilton and Laurens, "romantic friendship" was long a useful, untroubling concept by which to explain passionate male–male relationships, as was Walt Whitman's phrase, "manly love of comrades." Most of Whitman's reading public was credulous of the wildly heterosexual myths he propounded about himself, despite his "Calamus" poems (1860) in which Whitman's manly "friend" and "lover" are conflated: for example, "… [W]hen I thought how my dear friend my lover was on his way coming, O then I was happy" ("When I Heard at the Close of Day").

The general public's disinterest in presuming sexual behavior when ostensible evidence could be explained away as "romantic friendship" explains a remarkable lack of self-consciousness in other eras about overt expression of same-sex love. There is extant, for example, a wealth of photographs of nineteenth- and early-twentieth-century male couples posing before the camera in all manner of affectionate stances—hugging, intertwining bodies, holding hands—that, in later eras, would have "provoked a riot," as Miller phrased it in 1959.

When It Changed and Why

The dissemination of the work of the late-nineteenth-century sexologists, who included "sexual inversion" as a major category in their lists of sexual pathology, was a significant influence in changing the way both male and female romantic friendships were perceived. It was no longer possible for society to see them as innocuous once the sexologists insisted that same-sex passion (whether or not it had genital manifestations) was sick. For example, a Dr. G. Alder Blumer, whose 1882 article, "A Case of Perverted Sexual Instinct," may have been the first in America to question the notion of "pure" romantic friendship, writes of a Mr. X, a twenty-seven-year-old patient who told the doctor of his "ideal friend" for whom he had "a vague, platonic, transcendental longing." Mr. X's language was no different from that used by romantic friends for centuries, but Blumer, following the work of

European sexologists such as Richard von Krafft-Ebing and Havelock Ellis, classified Mr. X's yearnings as "a congenital perversion of the sexual instinct."

The work of the sexologists tolled a death knell for romantic friendships. Their theories about the pathology of same-sex love were widely accepted for several reasons. They came at a time when feminist successes brought women unprecedented opportunities and freedoms, which might have been construed to mean that if women's natural affection for one another were socially encouraged, heterosexual marriage would no longer be an inevitable path for many. Furthermore, as Christina Simmons and Jonathan Ned Katz have observed, the early twentieth century ushered in a metamorphosis in the concept of marriage. The heterosexual couple changed from being primarily a productive unit to one in which material goods and pleasures would be consumed mutually, and a man and woman would be "companions" and "kindred spirits." Same-sex romantic friendships were thus discredited in favor of heterosexual companionate marriage.

Bibliography

Blumer, G. Alder. "A Case of Perverted Sexual Instinct." *American Journal of Insanity* 39 (July 1882): 22–35.

Brown, Charles Brockden. *Ormond.* 1799. Reprint, New York: American Book Company, 1937.

Bush, Russell. *Affectionate Men: A Photographic History of a Century of Male Couples (1850's to 1950's).* New York: St. Martin's Press, 1998.

Deitcher, David. *Dear Friends: American Photographs of Men Together: 1840–1918.* New York: Abrams, 2001.

Donoghue, Emma. *Passions Between Women: British Lesbian Culture, 1668–1801.* New York: Perennial, 1996.

Faderman, Lillian. *Surpassing the Love of Men: Romantic Friendship and Love Between Women from the Renaissance to the Present.* New York: Morrow, 1981.

———. *To Believe in Women: What Lesbians Have Done for America—A History.* Boston: Houghton Mifflin, 1999.

Hansen, Karen V. "No kisses is like youres: An Erotic Friendship Between Two African-American Women During the Mid-Nineteenth Century." In *Lesbian Subjects: A Feminist Studies Reader.* Edited by Martha Vicinus. Bloomington: Indiana University Press, 1996.

Katz, Jonathan Ned. *Gay/Lesbian Almanac.* New York: Harper, 1983.

———. *Gay American History: Lesbians and Gay Men in the U.S.A.* New York: Crowell, 1976.

Lodge, Thomas. "Euphues Shadow," 1592. Reprint, in *The Complete Works of Thomas Lodge,* Vol. II. New York: Russell and Russell, 1963.

Longfellow, Henry Wadsworth. *Kavanagh: A Romance.* 1849. Reprint, Philadelphia: Henry Altemus Company, n.d.

Miller, John Chester. *Alexander Hamilton: Portrait in Paradox.* New York: Harper, 1959.

Montaigne, Michel de. "On Friendship." In *The Complete Works of Montaigne.* Translated by Donald Frame. Stanford, Calif.: Stanford University Press, 1957.

Painter, William. *The Palace of Pleasure.* Reprint, London: 1890, Vol. II.

Rothblum, Esther D., and Kathleen A. Brehony. *Boston Marriages: Romantic but Asexual Relationships among Contemporary Lesbians.* Amherst, Mass: University of Massachusetts Press, 1993.

Rupp, Leila. *A Desired Past: A Short History of Same-Sex Love in America.* Chicago: University of Chicago Press, 1999.

Simmons, Christina. "Companionate Marriage and the Lesbian Threat." *Frontiers: A Journal of Women's Studies* 4, no. 3 (Fall 1979): 54–59.

Smith-Rosenberg, Carroll. "The Female World of Love and Ritual: Relations Between Women in Nineteenth Century America." *Signs: Journal of Women in Culture and Society* 1, no. 1 (Autumn 1975): 1–29.

Lillian Faderman

See also ADDAMS, JANE; BATES, KATHERINE LEE; CUSHMAN, CHARLOTTE; FRIENDSHIP; GILMAN, CHARLOTTE PERKINS; HOMOEROTICISM AND HOMOSOCIALITY; MARRIAGE CEREMONIES AND WEDDINGS; PRIMUS, REBECCA, AND ADDIE BROWN; SAME-SEX INSTITUTIONS; SMASHES AND CHUMMING; VAN WATERS, MIRIAM.

ROOSEVELT, Eleanor

(b. 11 October 1884; d. 7 November 1962) and Lorena HICKOK, (b. 7 March 1893; d. 1 May 1968).

The triumphs of the LGBT movement have given us new dimensions for history and biography. No longer are same-sex loves obscured by deceit and denial—the perspective of the fortress, the camouflage of the closet. In the course of presenting the truths about Eleanor Roosevelt's heart, the arc of her romantic loves, a dramatic change occurred. In 1992, when volume 1 of *Eleanor Roosevelt* appeared, talk show discussions were filled with hate, horror, and vengeance. The very idea that Roosevelt was not a lonely, depressed, ordinarily neglected wife; that she actually struggled to live a full life and succeeded; that she was a desired and desiring woman, the most powerful woman in U.S. history, was unacceptable to countless people. In 1999, when volume 2 appeared, the very same talk shows with presumably much the same audiences now responded with enthusiasm or more casual interest. LGBT scholars' long effort to present complexity concerning sexuality and desire had achieved new levels of acceptance. Eleanor Roosevelt and Lorena Hickok benefited history by preserving the documents of their passionate, turbulent, ever-changing, always respectful, often stormy thirty-year friendship in long (often twelve to fifteen pages) and detailed letters. They met in 1932 during the presidential campaign of Franklin Delano Roosevelt, Eleanor's husband, when Lorena Hickok ("Hick") was a celebrated, award-winning political journalist and the highest paid woman reporter for the Associated Press. She was confident, brilliant, and determined. And she was, initially, very annoyed to be asked to cover the First Lady of New York State, since FDR, as governor, was usually her primary assignment. When the two women met, they were both at the top of their careers, surrounded by friends and allies.

After 1920, Eleanor Roosevelt became active in the League of Women Voters and lived in part in a lesbian world. Her closest friends were former suffragists and Democratic Party loyalists Nancy Cook and Marion Dickerman, the couple with whom she shared her home at Val-Kill in New York State. With them, she also bought the prestigious Todhunter School in New York City and several other enterprises. Also, she relied on Esther Lape and Elizabeth Read, two learned women and coordinators for the League of Women Voters who owned her Greenwich Village hideaway home at 20 East 11th Street, to which she retreated during most of the White House years. Lape and Read were the couple Roosevelt consulted for all her most significant political work, from the World Court to affordable housing to national health care. Read, an international lawyer, was also Roosevelt's tax accountant and financial consultant. Although her world was secure, Roosevelt at forty-eight was discontented and restless when she first met Hick. Above all, she dreaded the presidency, which FDR won in 1932, worried that her own needs would be discounted, her work devalued.

Sensitive and ardent, Hick sensed Roosevelt's emotional longing and troublous reality. As they spent more and more time together, they told each other their stories: their alcoholic fathers and abused mothers, and their past lives, loves, lingering hurts. Hick was fun to be with. Smart and generous, she drank and smoked, she told a good story, and was a generous listener. Widely perceived as "one of the boys," she was passionate about politics, sports, and music. Roosevelt was impressed by Hick's manner; she felt fortified by her pungent wit and direct, blunt style.

Although Eleanor's marriage to FDR was always more than a business partnership, she had not felt first in his life since 1918, when she discovered his affair with Lucy Mercer, which was followed by his arrangement with Missy LeHand, his live-in junior "wife," whom Eleanor always treated with respect and warmth. Actually, until Hick, there was an empty place at her heart's core.

For a time, Hick filled that place. For many years, Eleanor was first in Hick's life, and she was focused on their relationship. Eleanor was often preoccupied, busy with other people and public issues, but she loved and trusted Hick, with a renewed sense of romance. There are few ambiguities about the nature of their relationship. A letter once defined as "particularly susceptible to misinterpretation" reads: "I wish I could lie down beside you tonight & take you in my arms."

Eleanor and Hick were not involved in a schoolgirl "crush." They did not meet in a nineteenth-century Victorian storybook. They were two adult women, in the prime of their lives, committed to working out a relationship under very difficult circumstances. They appreciated the risks and dangers. They never thought it would be easy or smooth. They gave each other pleasure and comfort and traveled widely. They touched each other deeply, loved profoundly, and moved on. They sought to avoid gossip and mostly succeeded. They wrote to each other exactly what they meant to write. Sigmund Freud notwithstanding, a cigar may not always be a cigar, but "the northeast corner of your mouth against my lips" is always the northeast corner.

Roosevelt learned a great deal from Hick. At her suggestion, the First Lady held press conferences for women journalists only, and with Hick's editorial help, Roosevelt's columns and articles were professional and rousing. Indeed, Hick inspired "My Day," which became one of the most popular nationally syndicated columns from 1936 until Eleanor's death. Hick wrote: "You send all these details to me, all America would like to know about how you spend your day." When Hick was forced to quit her work as the AP's top political journalist, because she had gotten too close to her news source—and too protective of the first family—Eleanor found her other jobs, at which she performed brilliantly. From 1934 to 1938, she was the New Deal's most significant reporter on the impact the administration's changes had on the lives of people throughout the United States, from the mountains of the Northwest, through the heartland to the delta. But she had lost her newspaper byline and her sense of self. She became dependent and needy. The robust, self-starting, dedicated journalist Eleanor Roosevelt so admired was gone. By 1939, Roosevelt acknowledged that she could not fulfill Hick's needs; and she was easily bored. Ultimately, they both sought alternative enthusiasms and traveling companions. They remained close confidantes, and their friendship endured to the end of Eleanor's life. In 1954 they coauthored *Ladies of Courage*.

After Eleanor's death in 1962, Hick spent a weekend at Esther Lape's place in Connecticut, tossing countless letters into the great stone fireplace. Later, Hick explained to Roosevelt's daughter Anna that her mother was not always "discreet." Still, more than 3,500 letters survived. They represent a great gift to our ongoing study of the arc of love.

Bibliography

Cook, Blanche Wiesen. *Eleanor Roosevelt.* 2 vols. New York: Viking, 1992, 1999.

Coss, Clare. *The Arc of Love: An Anthology of Lesbian Love Poems.* New York: Scribner, 1996.

Faber, Doris. *The Life of Lorena Hickok: E.R.'s Friend.* New York: William Morrow, 1980.

Hickok, Lorena. *Eleanor Roosevelt: Reluctant First Lady.* New York: Dodd, Mead, 1962.

Lowitt, Richard, and Maurine Beasley, eds. *One Third of a Nation: Lorena Hickok's Reports on the Great Depression.* Urbana: University of Illinois Press, 1981.

Streitmatter, Rodger. *Empty Without You: The Intimate Letters of Eleanor Roosevelt and Lorena Hickok.* New York: Free Press, 1998.

Blanche Wiesen Cook

ROREM, Ned (b. 23 October 1923), composer, writer.

An American composer in the French-influenced tradition of Virgil Thomson, Aaron Copland, Paul Bowles, and others, and an illustrious diarist and essayist, Ned Rorem has attained a position unusual in both American music and literary circles during the last half of the twentieth century.

Born in Richmond, Indiana, and raised by Quaker parents in Chicago, Rorem, an atheist, studied at the Curtis Institute, the Juilliard School of Music, and elsewhere with Thomson, Copland, Rosario Scalero, Leo Sowerby, Bernard Wagenaar, and Arthur Honegger. Crucial to his development were years spent abroad, especially in Paris, where he enjoyed the patronage of the Viscountess Marie-Laure de Noailles in the 1950s. Back in America, Rorem went on to teach at the University of Buffalo, the University of Utah, and the Curtis Institute.

In a musical age of unprecedented complexity and abstraction, Rorem—as did few other renowned composers of his generation—composed in an unabashedly traditionalist style indifferent to the shifting musical trends set by avant-garde composers, whether by John Cage's aleatoric pursuits, by Pierre Boulez's and Milton Babbitt's respective brands of multiple serialism, or by the hyperintellectualism and severity of such composers as Elliott Carter. At the close of the twentieth century,

Rorem's consistency, longevity, and continuing productivity won him new audiences at the same time that other conservative approaches again came to dominate the concert scene of new music.

Despite its own complexity, the directness and unpretentious style of Rorem's music and its readiness to communicate have at times seemed almost neo-Romantic by comparison with other contemporary composers of his stature. The understatement of sentiment typical of Rorem, however, is traceable to a neoclassical French influence obtained in the first half of the twentieth century. At the turn of the twenty-first century, Rorem's reputation has excelled in concert and recital halls, where the predominant styles have partially reverted to characteristics long associated with Rorem's music, that is, to writing perceptibly tonal in nature and marked by traditional melodic gestures and rhythms, without pretense of ultracerebral design.

Though Rorem has composed choral scores, chamber works, operas, and symphonic music, even winning the Pulitzer Prize in 1976 for his orchestral suite titled *Air Music* (1974), his prolific attention to art song has distinguished his output above all else. During a century when to many art song seemed a sentimental relic from a distant past, few composers of his caliber contributed so significantly to the genre. Even fewer composers undertook setting to music such an extraordinary range of poets, numbering in the hundreds. Sensitivity and expert text setting best characterize his songs, which in these terms rival those of any living American composer, despite Rorem's relative lack of innovation in terms of actual musical procedure.

As for originality, the case for Rorem is easier to make as writer than as composer. He has published a large literary catalog comprising diaries and other autobiographical pieces, plus several volumes of belles lettres. By far, his diaries have attracted the most attention. They stand out for Rorem's uninhibited and ruthlessly honest way of beautifully recounting his queer life. The publication of his Paris diary in 1966 and his New York diary in 1967 proved quite shocking in the late 1960s. Both caused sensations. Never before had an American composer been so unashamed and explicit in outing himself and implicating so many others in print. Immediately better known than his musical works, Rorem's diaries have stayed in wide circulation.

As a group, his diaries have also been acknowledged as bearing the most sustained, intimate witness of a gay composer's life, chronicling every aspect into old age. By measures, the diaries have become ever more literary, if little by little less glamorous or exhibitionistic, and more morbid. He leaves hardly any type of thought or action unrecorded, whether pertaining to the promiscuity of his youth; to viewing friends, lovers, and strangers alike in the most unflattering light; to overcoming alcoholism; to prolonged periods of celibacy and loss of his cover boy good looks; to daily thoughts of suicide; to the death of his longtime companion James Holmes from AIDS and cancer; to lifelong sexual fantasies. If in music he has been a model of independence, in his writings he has literally set the tone like no other musical gay writer before him.

Given the openness and frankness of his diaries, Rorem was naturally an object of attention when, especially in the last decade of the last century, musicologists began to explore sexuality as a topic, that is, to the ways in which music might suggest, reflect, or affect the understanding of sexuality. Many, however, were disappointed to realize that for all Rorem's allusions to homosexuality and unusual candor, he remained quite old-fashioned on the issue of gay sensibility. In interviews and writings, he flatly refused to accept that music and musical content or style may have any real connection to homosexuality. His position that sexuality and music were necessarily unconnected appeared too curt a dismissal from one so active in developing a gay cultural presence and from one whose very life itself offers a paragon of gay integrity and accomplishment.

In addition to writing diaries and a memoir of his early years, Rorem has authored books of essays on musical topics, on works and composers, and on famous writers and other luminaries he has known. While knowledgeable and well-written, his essays unfortunately devote too little attention to his own music, which in general has also received scant critical attention from scholars in terms of techniques and influences. The relation of Rorem's musical and personal, albeit literary, identities thus awaits scrutiny.

Bibliography

Mass, Lawrence D. "A Conversation with Ned Rorem." In *Queering the Pitch: The New Gay and Lesbian Musicology.* Edited by Philip Brett, Elizabeth Wood, and Gary C. Thomas. New York and London: Routledge, 1994.

Rorem, Ned. *Knowing When to Stop: A Memoir.* New York: Simon and Schuster, 1994.

———. *The Later Diaries of Ned Rorem, 1961–1972.* San Francisco: North Point Press, 1983.

———. *Lies: A Diary, 1986–1999.* Washington, D.C.: Counterpoint, 2000.

———. *The Nantucket Diary of Ned Rorem, 1973–1985.* San Francisco: North Point Press, 1987.

———. *The Paris and New York Diaries of Ned Rorem, 1951–1961.* San Francisco: North Point Press, 1983.

Daniel E. Mathers

See also LITERATURE; MUSIC: CLASSICAL.

RULE, Jane (b. 28 March 1931), writer and activist.

Born in Plainfield, New Jersey, Jane Rule moved frequently throughout the United States while growing up, eventually settling in the San Francisco Bay Area. After receiving her B.A. from Mills College (1948–1952), she studied for a year in London before teaching briefly at the Concord Academy in Massachusetts. Disturbed by the effects of McCarthyism, she relocated to Vancouver, British Columbia, in 1956; Helen Sonthoff, with whom she had taught in Massachusetts, soon joined her there. The two obtained Canadian citizenship and lived together (first in Vancouver and then on Galiano Island) until Sonthoff's death in January 2000.

Rule started writing before 1970s lesbian feminism created visible social and political communities in which to imagine positive lesbian identities. For many readers, Rule's work provided the first opportunity to imagine alternatives to the misogynist, antisexual norms of post–World War II America. Twenty-two publishers rejected her first novel, *Desert of the Heart* (1964), because of their uneasiness with a story in which lesbian desire is not pathologized or punished, and whose protagonists do not "recuperate" by eventually embracing heterosexuality. The novel's chapters alternate between the two main characters, suggesting that the couple they ultimately form incorporates rather than erases the differences between them.

Though cognizant of the stakes communities have in individual identities and behaviors, Rule is wary of all prescriptive norms, whether they come from the mainstream or from LGBT and feminist groups. In a column for *The Body Politic* (later reprinted in *Outlander* as "Reflections") she wrote: "I do understand the appetite in the gay community for art which can celebrate, but too often that desire gets translated into a need for a narrowly correct propaganda for one lifestyle or another. Any writer who tries to please such an audience is doomed to failure, because within the gay community there are not only different but morally and politically conflicting tastes" (p. 203).

Best known for *Desert of the Heart,* which later served as the basis for Donna Deitch's 1985 film *Desert Hearts,* Rule has produced a varied body of work, including seven novels, numerous short stories, and essays for periodicals ranging from mainstream women's magazines such as *Redbook* to the lesbian periodical the *Ladder* (published from 1956 to 1972) and the Toronto gay liberationist monthly *The Body Politic* (published from 1971 to 1987). Her *Lesbian Images* (1975) was the first book-length study of lesbian writers.

Rule's second novel, *This Is Not for You* (1970), is told exclusively from the suffocating first-person point of view of Kate, a closeted lesbian who has internalized the shame that normative heterosexuality imposes on lesbian desire. Kate fails, however, to control the meanings of her own story even as she fails to control the fate of the woman who loves her. Rule exposes the corrosive effects of internalized oppression and, through the central character, links ethnic and class bias to sexual intolerance.

In the novel *Against the Season* (1971) many narrative points of view play off each other as Rule examines the intersection of public and private histories in a small Pacific Coast town. *The Young in One Another's Arms* (1977) and *Contract with the World*, both set in Vancouver, are novels that explore the often vexed interactions between individuals and communities—including unforgiving oppression by the state when it is threatened by dissent, whether political, sexual, or artistic. Although always aware of the brutal nature of power, Rule imagines possibilities for resistance and survival. In *Memory Board* (1987), Rule returns to the dual narrative form of her first novel, alternating between elderly fraternal twins (a widowed man and a lesbian in a long-term relationship with a woman who has lost her short-term memory). Her last novel, *After the Fire* (1989), told from multiple points of view, depicts both crises and ordinariness in an island community.

Rule's short stories and essays, some of which have been collected in *Theme for Diverse Instruments* (1975), *Outlander* (1981), *A Hot-Eyed Moderate* (1985), and *Inland Passage* (1985), often examine the permeability of public and private spaces. Written primarily for an LGBT or feminist readership, her essays, such as her *Body Politic* column "So's Your Grandmother," challenge the reader to contemplate difficult issues, including censorship and the sexuality of children. Rule's later essays challenge the assimilationist tendencies of contemporary activism—for example, the push for legal recognition of same-sex unions. Her lifelong resistance to convention (LGBT as well as mainstream), her insistence that the most desirable communities are heterogeneous, and her imaginative use of familiar literary forms are the core strengths of her writing—though these very same characteristics have also often created a problematic relationship with some of her readers.

Bibliography

Fiction and Other Truths: A Film about Jane Rule. Directed by Lynne Fernie and Aerlyn Weissman. Produced by Rina Fraticalli. Montreal: Great Jane Productions, 1995.

Rule, Jane. *Outlander*. Tallahassee, Fla.: Naiad, 1981.

Schuster, Marilyn R. *Passionate Communities: Reading Lesbian Resistance in Jane Rule's Fiction*. New York: New York University Press, 1999.

Zimmerman, Bonnie. *The Safe Sea of Women: Lesbian Fiction, 1969–1989*. Boston: Beacon, 1990.

Marilyn R. Schuster

See also LITERATURE; PULP FICTION: LESBIAN.

RUNNING EAGLE. see PI'TAMAKAN.

RUSSO, Vito (b. 11 July 1946; d. 7 November 1990), film critic, writer, activist.

Born in New York, Russo received his bachelor's degree at Fairleigh Dickinson University (1968) and his master of arts degree in film at New York University (1974). He worked in the film department at the Museum of Modern Art in New York City, and was an active member of the Gay Activists Alliance (GAA). In the early 1970s, at the GAA Firehouse, he programmed all-night film screenings, setting the stage for later LGBT film festivals. Today, his name is inseparable from any discussion of queer representation in Hollywood because of his groundbreaking 1981 study *The Celluloid Closet: Homosexuality in the Movies*.

The Celluloid Closet is a reflection of gay activism following the Stonewall Riots. It examines Hollywood's representations of LGBT people, and argues that if LGBT people are ever to achieve equality, these images would have to change, since they legitimize discrimination. With chapters on "sissies," LGBT villains, and self-hating homosexuals, Russo examines the Motion Picture Production Code, also known as the Hays Code, responsible for prohibiting "any inference to sexual perversion" from the 1930s to the 1960s. The censorship imposed by the code led to insidious depictions of LGBT people. A frightening appendix, "Necrology," which lists over thirty films, mostly from the 1960s and 1970s, provides the manner of the queer character's death, usually by murder or suicide.

This approach has led critics to challenge some of Russo's premises and conclusions. In his "Necrology" for instance, there is no differentiation between mainstream and LGBT-authored texts. His work has also been criticized for its simplistic distinction between positive and negative portrayals, leading to questions about who gets to make such judgments and how responses may vary across audiences and contexts. Is there consensus about accurate or realistic representation? Does queer culture lose its critical edge by choosing safe representations of LGBT people, ones that appear more normal? Other critics have remarked on the lack of attention to identification, desire, camp, and gay fandom, though he is remembered for his humorous lectures on and love of Judy Garland. Nevertheless, many are quick to acknowledge Russo's important contribution to queer scholarship, and the way this early work helped to politicize audiences and filmmakers who came to demand and produce the kinds of images seen today.

Russo also wrote on LGBT representation in film for *New York Magazine*, *Esquire*, *Newsday*, *Rolling Stone*, *Village Voice*, and the *Advocate*. In 1983, he wrote, produced, and cohosted the gay and lesbian show *Our Time* on the cable station WNYC-TV. Russo was asked to speak at numerous film festivals and the American and Swedish film institutes. He also taught and lectured at Harvard, Yale, Princeton, and Columbia universities, and the University of California at Santa Cruz, though he remained an independent scholar. In 1985, he helped create the Gay and Lesbian Alliance Against Defamation (GLAAD) in response to the *New York Post*'s coverage of the AIDS crisis.

Russo appeared in a number of documentaries about AIDS and AIDS activism, such as Stuart Marshall's *Over Our Dead Bodies* (1991); *Voices from the Front* (1991) by Robyn Hutt, Sandra Elgear, and David Meieran; and most notably Robert Epstein and Jeffrey Friedman's *Common Threads: Stories from the Quilt* (1989), which won an Academy Award for best documentary. In *Common Threads,* Russo talks about losing his lover, Jeffrey Sevcik, for whom Russo quit his job and moved to San Francisco following Sevcik's AIDS diagnosis. Epstein and Friedman went on to make a film version of *The Celluloid Closet* (1995), narrated by Russo's friend, Lily Tomlin.

Before his death in 1990 (often erroneously cited as 1991), Russo was a founding member of the AIDS Coalition to Unleash Power (ACT UP). In a speech entitled "Why We Fight," delivered at a demonstration on 9 May 1988 in Albany, New York, and later at the Department of Health and Human Services in Washington, D.C., on 10 October 1988, Russo stated: "I'm here to speak out today as a PWA [person with AIDS] who is not dying *from*—but for the last three years quite successfully living *with*— AIDS. If I'm dying from anything it's homophobia. . . . If I'm dying from anything it's indifference and red tape."

At his memorial service Larry Kramer accused closeted people in Hollywood, all gays and lesbians, and every person in the room of killing Vito Russo. Russo's panel on the AIDS Quilt reads "You left us with a broken heart" and is accompanied by an image of one. In 1991, the Pat Parker/Vito Russo Center Library was established at the Lesbian and Gay Community Services Center in New York, a research collection for those studying queer literature and film.

Bibliography

Epstein, Robert, and Jeffrey Friedman, directors. *The Celluloid Closet.* Tristar/Columbia, 1995.

Kantrowitz, Arnie. "Milestones: Vito Russo." *Outweek* 73 (21 November 1990): 37.

Kramer, Larry. "Who Killed Vito Russo?" *Outweek* 86 (20 February 1991): 26.

Russo, Vito. *The Celluloid Closet: Homosexuality in the Movies.* New York: Harper and Row, 1981.

Scott Rayter

See also AIDS AND PEOPLE WITH AIDS; AIDS COALITION TO UNLEASH POWER (ACT UP); FILM AND VIDEO; FILM AND VIDEO STUDIES; GAY ACTIVISTS ALLIANCE; GAY AND LESBIAN ALLIANCE AGAINST DEFAMATION (GLAAD); MAUPIN, ARMISTEAD.

RUSTIN, Bayard (b. 17 March 1912; d. 24 August 1987), pacifist, civil rights leader.

Raised by his grandparents in West Chester, Pennsylvania, Bayard Rustin attended a racially segregated elementary school and an integrated high school, where he excelled as a student and athlete. Moving to New York City in 1937, he encountered the left-wing politics of Depression-era New York. Rustin became a member of the Young Communist League, but broke ties with the Communist Party in 1941.

Rustin joined the staff of the Fellowship of Reconciliation (FOR), a Christian pacifist organization in 1941; he worked there until 1953, when he moved to the War Resisters League. One of only a few African Americans who were prominent in the U.S. peace movement, Rustin traveled throughout the United States many times over, preaching a message of nonviolence. As a result of his activities as a war resister, he spent twenty-seven months in federal prison during World War II. During the Cold War, Rustin opposed a peacetime draft. In the 1950s he organized demonstrations against civilian defense drills and aboveground nuclear testing and planned militant pacifist actions in the Nevada desert, the South Pacific, and the Sahara.

Rustin left his mark on history primarily through his adaptation of direct nonviolent action to the black struggle for freedom within the United States. An enthusiast of

Bayard Rustin. He played a crucial role in the civil rights movement, especially in influencing Martin Luther King Jr. and organizing the 1963 March on Washington, but his Communist Party past and his homosexuality kept him largely out of the public eye.

Mahatma Gandhi, he studied the renowned pacifist's use of nonviolence in India and devoted himself to propagating a similar message among African Americans. In the 1940s he worked closely with A. Philip Randolph, a black socialist labor leader, insinuating nonviolence into Randolph's effort to desegregate the military. A founder of the Congress of Racial Equality (CORE) in 1942, Rustin used nonviolence to desegregate restaurants, barbershops, and other facilities in the North. In 1947 he led an interracial "Journey of Reconciliation" into the South against segregated buses, and he was subsequently arrested and imprisoned for his efforts in this regard.

In February 1956, Rustin traveled to Alabama to offer his assistance to organizers of a citywide boycott of Montgomery's buses. Bonding with Martin Luther King Jr., the young leader of the effort, he tutored King in Gandhian nonviolence and convinced him of the need to create a regional organization committed to nonviolent resistance. Rustin drew up the plans for the Southern Christian Leadership Conference (SCLC) and, for the duration of the 1950s, he worked closely with King.

Early in 1963, Randolph, with Rustin's support, issued a call for a national march on Washington, D.C., and Rustin was put in charge of organizing the event. On 28 August a crowd estimated at 250,000 assembled for a rally at the Lincoln Memorial in support of federal civil rights legislation. It was the largest protest demonstration Washington had ever seen and became the prototype for many later marches. The event's success gave Rustin a high national profile.

In February 1965, Rustin published the article "From Protest to Politics" in *Commentary* magazine. He urged the civil rights movement to plunge directly into party politics. He called for a coalition with labor, white religious activists, and liberals within the Democratic Party, believing it possible for a progressive majority to shape the party's direction. However, as segments of the civil rights movement shifted toward "black power" and as President Lyndon Johnson plunged the nation more deeply into war in Vietnam, most radicals repudiated Rustin's willingness to work within the Democratic Party. In 1965, Rustin left the War Resisters League to become director of the newly created A. Philip Randolph Institute, an organization devoted to building links between civil rights groups and organized labor. He remained there until his death in 1987.

Throughout his career, Rustin was plagued by the homophobia that existed everywhere in U.S. society. His homosexuality was controversial in both the peace and civil rights movements. Police harassment of gays was commonplace during these decades, and homosexual behavior and solicitation was a crime in every state. Arrested a number of times, Rustin was convicted of public lewdness in Pasadena, California, in 1953. The incident became a scandal in religious peace circles and forced his departure from the FOR. Rustin's sexuality kept him in the background when working with King; in 1960, to avoid possible scandal, King accepted Rustin's resignation as his assistant. Concerns among civil rights leaders about the scandal almost prevented Rustin from being named organizer of the March on Washington. Two weeks before the march, U.S. Senator Strom Thurmond, a South Carolina segregationist, labeled Rustin a sex pervert and put information about the Pasadena incident into the *Congressional Record.* Civil rights forces rallied behind Rustin, but discomfort with his sexuality never fully faded and it always remained a constraint on his public role.

John D'Emilio

See also ANTIWAR, PACIFIST, AND PEACE MOVEMENTS; POOR PEOPLE'S MOVEMENTS.

S

SADOMASOCHISM, SADISTS, AND MASOCHISTS

Sadomasochism (or S/M) is an umbrella term for an assortment of sexual practices, relationship configurations, and lifestyles. Generally, it refers to sexual interest in physical restraint, dominant-submissive role-playing, wearing garments made of fetishized substances such as leather or latex, erotic play with sexually charged objects like boots or corsets, or arousal engendered by the infliction or receipt of intense physical sensations. In order to be considered sadomasochism rather than violence, these activities must be consensual. Many of those who engage in them feel that S/M is a pejorative term and prefer other terminology like leather sex, power exchange, BDSM (bondage and discipline, sadism and masochism) or D/S (dominant/submissive). There are also those who say that sadomasochistic techniques do not produce sexual excitement for them, but are used instead for spiritual purposes, to produce transcendental or altered states of consciousness.

The partner in charge of producing an S/M fantasy scenario may be referred to as a sadist, dominant or dominatrix, master or mistress, or top, while the partner who temporarily cedes power may be referred to as a masochist, submissive, slave, or bottom. This fantasy may be drawn from the imagination of the top, bottom, or both. The terms "sadist" and "masochist" are associated specifically with erotic play that involves intense sensation. A sadomasochistic encounter is referred to as a scene or session, and the bottom is normally given a code word (called a "safe word") to use to halt the action. A scene

might include activities such as bondage, use of costume and verbal fantasy, spanking or slapping, flagellation, the use of clips or clamps on sensitive parts of the body, enemas, spattering with hot wax, abrasion, piercing, catheterization, use of gags, watersports (erotic play with urine), sensory deprivation, fisting or handballing (inserting the entire hand into the rectum or vagina), humiliation, or scat (erotic play with excrement). Non-S/M or "vanilla" sex may or may not be made part of a scene. The majority of S/M play is at the light end of the spectrum, with partners engaging in role-playing, dress up, and physical restraint with little or no experimentation with painful stimulation.

S/M As an Aspect of Human Sexuality

The association of sexual excitement with bondage, discomfort or pain, and role-playing with power is an integral part of human sexuality. In *The Prehistory of Sex* (1996), archaeologist Timothy Taylor describes a prehistoric figurine of a woman with bound hands and interprets it as possible evidence of sexual bondage. In an often-cited cross-cultural survey, *Patterns of Sexual Behavior* (1951), anthropologist Clellan S. Ford and psychologist Frank A. Beach discuss several societies in which painful stimulation was considered to be a normal and mutual part of heterosexual intercourse. They also describe these societies as ones in which children and adolescents were allowed a great deal of sexual freedom and where women were seen as active and vigorous participants in all things sexual. This leads them to conclude that any man or woman is capable of positive erotic responses to mild degrees of pain. In their 1979 book *The*

The First "Sadist." The behavior found a permanent name in the wake of the life and writings of the Marquis de Sade in France during the late 1700s and early 1800s. [Corbis Corporation (New York)]

Kinsey Data, Paul H. Gebhard and Alan B. Johnson report several dimensions of the sadomasochistic experience as assessed by Alfred C. Kinsey and his colleagues. The Kinsey researchers found that 8.2 percent of white males often engaged in biting during sexual activity. For white women, the figures were 8.7 percent for those with a college education and 10.4 percent for those without. Of college-educated black men, 4.5 percent often engaged in biting during sexual activity, compared with 11.0 percent of similarly educated black women. Of the white men who were often bitten during sexual activity, 58.8 percent of those with a college education and 64.2 percent of those without were aroused by it. Among white women, 68.5 percent of those with a college education and 69.6 percent of those without were aroused by biting. The corresponding figures for college-educated black men and women were 35 percent and 55.5 percent, respectively. Among white males, 19.3 percent with a college education and 12.1 percent without experienced some degree of arousal by sadomasochistic literature. Among white females, 12.6 percent of those with a college education and 8.5 percent without had the same experience. For both black males and black females with a college education, the figure was 3.2 percent.

The majority of S/M practitioners are heterosexual. It is not known what percentage of LGBT and intersexed people engage in BDSM. However, S/M is associated much more strongly with same-sex sexuality in popular culture and especially in right-wing efforts to discredit campaigns for equal civil rights for LGBT people.

Pathologization of S/M

In the larger society, sadomasochism is stigmatized as a mental disorder. (Fetishism, sexual sadism, and sexual masochism appear as diagnoses in the American Psychiatric Association's [APA] *Diagnostic and Statistical Manual of Mental Disorders: DSM-IV-TR,* 2000.) Little distinction is made in popular culture between violent crimes like rape and consensual S/M. Even sophisticated sex researchers such as William H. Masters, Virginia E. Johnson, and Robert C. Kolodny—who estimate in *Masters and Johnson on Sex and Human Loving* (1986) that from 5 percent to 10 percent of men and women enjoy sadomasochism on an occasional basis—discuss consensual power-exchange sex as lying at one end of a dangerous continuum, with extreme acts such as torture, rape, and lust-murder at the other end.

In addition to these negative stereotypes, S/M generally meets with disapproval within the lesbian community due to a strain of feminist thought that sees this sexual style as an aspect of the male oppression of women. The existence of lesbian S/M is dismissed with the explanation that such women have been conditioned or corrupted by a society that objectifies women and normalizes sexual violence. Antipornography cultural feminists and some lesbian separatists have also identified sadomasochism with racism and fascism. During the 1980s these controversies were especially fierce, and have been termed the feminist (or the lesbian) sex wars. Spokeswomen for the antipornography movement such as Andrea Dworkin and Catharine A. MacKinnon have been vocal exponents of this viewpoint, which is ably represented in the collection *Against Sadomasochism* (1982). The opposing branch of feminism has been called anticensorship, pro-pleasure, or sex-positive feminism.

Within the gay male community, sadomasochism is often perceived as a morally neutral preference that some men have and others do not. The 1972 publication of Larry Townsend's *The Leatherman's Handbook* did not set off anything like the lesbian sex wars. However, some gay men who identify as feminists, such as Arthur Evans and John Stoltenberg, object vehemently to S/M, perceiving it as an artifact of capitalist oppression, patriarchal misogyny, a harmful cult of brutal masculinity, and gay self-hatred.

Community Structure

In every major city in the United States, there is a pansexual (open to all genders and sexual orientations), gateway organization that provides newcomers to the S/M scene with education about negotiating a scene, consent, safe technique, prevention of sexually transmitted diseases, and community norms for play and relationships. The oldest such organization is the The Eulenspiegel Society (TES) in New York City, founded by Pat Bond and others in the winter of 1971. TES has its parallel on the West Coast in San Francisco's Society of Janus, founded by Cynthia Slater and Larry Olsen in August 1974. Motorcycle clubs and other organizations serving the gay male leather community have been in existence since the late 1950s, and among the oldest extant today are Chicago's Hellfire Club (founded in August 1971) and New York City's Gay Male S/M Activists, which had its first public meeting in January 1981. Avatar was founded in Los Angeles in 1983. Other gay male leather organizations from this generation are Sigma in Washington, D.C., Dreizehn in Boston, and The Fifteen Association of San Francisco.

Although the lesbian S/M community is smaller, it is an active one. The first known American lesbian S/M support group was the short-lived Samois, which was founded in June 1978. Samois was responsible for the first collection of writings on this topic, *Coming to Power* (1981). The Lesbian Sex Mafia in New York City, founded in 1981, continues to meet as of 2003. Some members of the transgender community have also made a place for themselves in various parts of the S/M community. Female-to-male transsexuals have been especially visible in the gay men's circuit of contests for leather titles.

Found in leather communities in major cities are retail outlets that offer S/M paraphernalia and fetishwear, leather bars and bathhouses that cater to gay men, dungeon clubs open to the public, and support groups for leatherdykes. There is a large, international BDSM community that offers its members a wide range of social, educational, and sexual opportunities, including workshops, publications (there are at least two publishers who specialize in BDSM books, Daedalus Publishing and Greenery Press), contests for various leather titles such as International Mr. Leather (IML), street fairs, play parties during which S/M activity takes place in establishments furnished with specialized bondage equipment, and political advocacy work. This sexual minority has taken a leadership role in educating its members about HIV and safer sex practices, and traditionally is a strong fundraiser for a wide range of charities such as AIDS service organizations, antiviolence agencies, gay charities, and causes important to lesbians such as breast cancer.

Pat Califia. The S/M and transgender activist and author of books on "radical sex" practices what he preaches: Califia, who began taking testosterone in 1998, describes himself these days as "a sadistic but forgiving fag who also likes to have sex with girls of all genders." [Patrick Califia]

Activism within the BDSM community includes work to preserve the community's history (which culminated in the 1991 establishment of the Leather Archives and Museum in Chicago by Chuck Renslow, owner of the IML title), lobbying for the removal of sadomasochistic practices from the APA's *Diagnostic and Statistical Manual IV-TR*, confronting right-wing Christians who disrupt leather events, legal defense, antidefamation work that addresses negative images of S/M in the mass media, and efforts to halt the censorship of educational S/M material and erotica. The National Coalition for Sexual Freedom, founded in 1997 under the auspices of Susan Wright, is a public advocacy group that addresses many of these issues.

Bibliography

American Psychiatric Association. *Diagnostic and Statistical Manual of Mental Disorders: DSM-IV-TR.* 4th ed. Washington, D.C.: American Psychiatric Association, 2000.

Baldwin, Guy, and Joseph W. Bean. *SlaveCraft, Roadmaps for Erotic Servitude: Principles, Skills, and Tools.* Los Angeles: Daedalus, 2002.

Califia, Pat. *Public Sex: The Culture of Radical Sex.* 2d ed. San Francisco: Cleis Press, 2000.

———. *Sensuous Magic: A Guide to S/M for Adventurous Couples.* 2d ed. San Francisco: Cleis Press, 2001.

Dworkin, Andrea. *Woman Hating.* New York: Dutton, 1974.

Evans, Arthur. *Witchcraft and the Gay Counterculture: A Radical View of Western Civilization and Some of the People It Has Tried to Destroy.* Boston: Fag Rag Books, 1978.

Ford, Clellan S., and Frank A. Beach. *Patterns of Sexual Behavior.* New York: Harper, 1951.

Gebhard, Paul H., and Alan B. Johnson. *The Kinsey Data: Marginal Tabulations of the 1938–1963 Interviews Conducted by the Institute for Sex Research.* Philadelphia: Saunders, 1979.

Lederer, Laura, ed. *Take Back the Night: Women on Pornography.* New York: Morrow, 1980.

Linden, Robin Ruth et al. *Against Sadomasochism: A Radical Feminist Analysis.* East Palo Alto, Calif.: Frog in the Well, 1982.

MacKinnon, Catharine A. *Feminism Unmodified: Discourses on Life and Law.* Cambridge, Mass.: Harvard University Press, 1987.

Masters, William H., Virginia E. Johnson, and Robert C. Kolodny. *Masters and Johnson on Sex and Human Loving.* Boston: Little, Brown, 1986.

Samois. *Coming to Power: Writings and Graphics on Lesbian S/M.* 2d ed. Boston: Alyson, 1981.

Stoltenberg, John. *Refusing to Be a Man: Essays on Sex and Justice.* New York: Penguin, 1990.

Taylor, Timothy. *The Prehistory of Sex: Four Million Years of Human Sexual Culture.* New York: Bantam Books, 1996.

Thompson, Mark, ed. *Leatherfolk: Radical Sex, People, Politics, and Practice.* 2d ed. Los Angeles: Alyson, 2001.

Townsend, Larry. *The Leatherman's Handbook.* New York: Other Traveller, 1972.

Vance, Carole, ed. *Pleasure and Danger: Exploring Female Sexuality.* Boston: Routledge and Paul, 1984.

Patrick Califia

See also KINSEY, ALFRED C.; LEATHER SEX AND SEXUALITY; MAPPLETHORPE, ROBERT; PRESTON, JOHN; RAMOS OTERO, MANUEL; SAMOIS; SEX CLUBS; SEX TOYS; SEX WARS.

SAFER SEX

Safer sex emerged in the early 1980s as urban LGBT communities faced the devastating impact of acquired immune deficiency syndrome (AIDS). LGBT people sought information about the relationship between sexual practices and the spread of disease and developed strategies for reducing risk of HIV infection. In the face of homophobic responses to AIDS that equated all queer sexuality with death, "safe sex" (as it was initially called, until the widespread adoption of the term "safer," reflecting the emergence of risk reduction models) represented a community-based politics of survival.

Education, Behavior, Change, and Survival

In the context of fear, backlash, and scientific uncertainty in the early 1980s, community activists developed strategies to enable gay men to prevent transmission of the as-yet unidentified infectious agent. Initial safer-sex education in the LGBT media emphasized the information necessary to avoid infection. In order to make such information effective, community educators identified the importance of behavioral change and the need to challenge homophobic treatments of gay male sexuality. Educators (often working through the newly formed AIDS service organizations) began to develop workshops to eroticize safer-sex practices, especially condom use, to preserve sexual pleasure and develop the efficacy of desire to motivate behavioral change. Prevention activists also developed "safe-sex kits" including condoms and educational materials that could be distributed at bars, bathhouses, and other sexual venues.

Although these programs drew on the latest professional research, they eschewed the clinical language of researchers and used sexual vernaculars in order to be as accessible and relevant as possible. Perhaps the most influential of the early models was Richard Berkowitz and Michael Callen's *How to Have Sex in an Epidemic* (1983). This pamphlet emphasized responsibility and advocated low-risk sexual activities as an individual strategy of self-protection and a collective imperative for community survival. This "menu"-based approach, used by many safer-sex programs in the 1980s, offered information about a wide range of practices in order to illustrate how sexual responsibility, rather than abstinence, could combat the spread of sexually transmitted disease.

Safer-sex programs sought to communicate the risks of what was called, in clinical terms, the "exchange of bodily fluids" while preserving eroticism and fun. Their first goal was to encourage and promote sexual behaviors that posed no risk of HIV transmission, such as mutual masturbation. Their second objective was the promotion of barrier methods for behaviors that might involve exposure of mucous membranes or cuts to semen or blood. Massive campaigns to promote condom use (as well as latex gloves and dental dams) sought to change behavioral norms, often via workshops and instructional materials that modeled strategies for talking to partners about use of barrier methods. Workshops (such as the "Hot, Horny, and Healthy" model created in New York City), play parties, and safer-sex pornography represented powerful tools for reshaping the sexual imaginary and turning the condom into a turn-on.

Lesbian Risk

While safer-sex programs for gay men challenged homophobic responses to gay male sexuality, lesbians struggled against invisibility in the public health response to HIV/AIDS. Although public health officials characterized lesbians as a very low-risk group, lesbians questioned the reliability of such assertions. How, for example, might women evaluate the risk of cunnilingus, when little was known about concentrations of HIV in vaginal fluids? Even as AIDS activists organized to demand epidemiological analysis of lesbian risk, anecdotal accounts circulated in lesbians communities of HIV-positive lesbians whose only exposure was through their female partners. Drawing on prior experience in the feminist health movement, lesbian safer-sex activists, such as the New York ACT UP Women's Caucus, developed a menu-based approach for lesbian sexual behaviors, describing a wide range of specific sexual activities. Such programs advocated the use of barrier methods for women, including gloves, finger cots, and dental dams-plastic wrap. Women who identified as S/M (sadomasochistic) dykes were especially active in the movement to develop lesbian safer-sex programs, drawing on strategies for negotiating safety and consent to promote the normative, consensual use of latex barriers.

Lesbian safer sex remained more controversial and less widely adopted than safer-sex models for gay men. Fundamental questions persisted about the degree of risk and the necessity of behavioral change. Although such programs raised awareness about the need for lesbian education on sexually transmitted disease, some lesbians challenged their fundamental premises, arguing that such efforts represented an attempt to control women's sexuality. Technological problems exacerbated such debates, as many women complained that thickness and unavailability made dental dams a poor solution. The AIDS epidemic also provoked discussion about injection drug use in lesbian communities and lesbians who had sexual contact with men, illustrating the complex issues surrounding the relationship between identity and behavior that continue to challenge safer-sex programs. The more transient and informal nature of lesbian institutions meant that only a few programs such as the Gay Men's Health Crisis Lesbian AIDS Project provided ongoing programming for lesbians.

Clubs, Condoms, and Controversy

A 1987 study of seroconversion rates in San Francisco revealed a dramatic decline in rates of HIV infection to under 2 percent, widely seen as evidence of the efficacy of safer-sex programs in dispersing information and increasing condom use. Despite these successes, safer sex provoked a number of controversies. Spaces of sexual expression, particularly bathhouses, raised some of the most heated debate about behavioral change when public health officials in San Francisco and New York closed bathhouses in 1984 and 1985. In the mass media, these commercial spaces provided an effective symbol to link gay male sexuality, danger, and disease. Closure revealed divisions within the LGBT community. While some argued that AIDS demanded an enforced end to the kind of sex enabled by such establishments—a position widely publicized by gay journalist Randy Shilts in his influential book *And the Band Played On* (1987)—others argued that such spaces played an important role in community building and represented an effective site for the distribution of prevention materials. Advocates of this latter position were not uncritical of commercial bathhouses and called for a number of changes including condom availability, visibly posted education materials, and changes to design and layout to encourage safer sex.

Condoms also provoked controversy. Although their importance for anal sex was widely accepted, simmering debate about HIV and oral sex highlighted international differences in safer-sex approaches. In the 1980s, Canadian and British AIDS organizations described oral sex without a condom as a relatively low-risk activity, while U.S. organizations advised against such practices, given the lack of definitive scientific data. Condoms were also a source of controversy in debates about safer-sex pornography, where there was not a clear consensus on what counted as safer sex. While some activists were satisfied with the presence of a visible condom during sex, others called for the inclusion of scenes showing performers donning condoms.

The efficacy of community-based prevention strategies, which often employed explicit sexual vernaculars, provoked conservative political resistance. In 1987, U.S. Senator Jesse Helms learned that the explicit Gay Men's Health Crisis "Safe Sex Comix" had been partly funded with federal dollars. Congress swiftly passed the Helms amendment, which prohibited federal funding for any AIDS education project that might "encourage or promote homosexual sexual activity." Although the courts overturned the Helms amendment in 1992, it had a chilling effect on the availability of funding for LGBT-positive safer-sex and prevention programs.

Challenges to Safer Sex

Safer-sex programs faced important challenges in the 1990s. The release of protease inhibitors in the mid-1990s provided the first effective treatments for HIV infection, and although AIDS educators argued that the high cost, severe side effects, and danger of resistance required a continuation of prevention efforts, the representation of AIDS as a chronic rather than fatal condition changed the context of such efforts. Simultaneously, new studies reported rising rates of HIV infection, especially among young gay men and men of color. Heated community debates about barebacking (anal sex without condoms) revealed a new eroticization of unsafe sex.

Space re-emerged as the subject of political debate in the 1990s. As sexually explicit businesses, some specifically devoted to safer sex, began to reappear on the urban landscape, Mayor Rudolph Giuliani kicked off a campaign to "clear up" New York City. Sex clubs and gay bars faced increased policing and arbitrary closure, policies justified in part by HIV prevention. Activism on public sex challenged the information-oriented strategies of public health agencies and increasingly bureaucratized AIDS service organizations and resituated safer sex within a politics of queer liberation by focusing on sexual practice, rather than identity. Controversies about the use of the virtual space of the Internet to solicit risky sexual behavior underscored the role of public space in articulating sexual norms.

A 2000 Centers for Disease Control and Prevention study on rising rates of HIV transmission among gay men of color, who exceeded the numbers of white gay men with AIDS for the first time, underlined the limitations of identity-based HIV prevention. The historical segregation of American cities, racism in gay communities, and culturally specific forms of sexual identities limited the relevance and utility of information directed at gay men to the diverse population of men who had sex with men (many of whom do not identify as gay). The disproportionate impact of HIV on gay men of color and women of color suggest that safer-sex programs must address sexuality in more complex ways and address more effectively the intersection of sexuality, race, gender, and class.

Bibliography

ACT UP New York Women and AIDS Book Group. *Women, AIDS, and Activism.* Boston: South End Press, 1990.

Callen, Michael and Richard Berkowitz. *How to Have Sex in an Epidemic: One Approach.* New York: News from the Front, 1983.

Dangerous Bedfellows, ed. *Policing Public Sex: Queer Politics and the Future of AIDS Activism.* Boston: South End Press, 1996.

Hollibaugh, Amber L. *My Dangerous Desires: A Queer Girl Dreaming Her Way Home.* Durham, N.C.: Duke University Press, 2000.

King, Edward. *Safety in Numbers: Safer Sex and Gay Men.* New York: Cassell, 1993.

Odets, Walt. *In the Shadow of the Epidemic: Being HIV-Negative in the Age of AIDS.* Durham, N.C.: Duke University Press, 1995.

Patton, Cindy. *Fatal Advice: How Safe-Sex Education Went Wrong.* Durham, N.C.: Duke University Press, 1996.

Shilts, Randy. *And the Band Played On: Politics, People and the AIDS Epidemic.* New York: St. Martin's Press, 1987.

Turner, Dwayne. *Risky Sex: Gay Men and HIV Prevention.* New York: Columbia University Press, 1997.

Meredith Raimondo

See also AIDS AND PEOPLE WITH AIDS; AIDS COALITION TO UNLEASH POWER (ACT UP); AIDS SERVICE ORGANIZATIONS; HEALTH; HEALTHCARE, AND HEALTH CLINICS; SEX EDUCATION; SEXUALLY TRANSMITTED DISEASES.

SAGARIN, EDWARD. see CORY, DONALD WEBSTER.

SAHAYKWISA. see MASAHAI AMATKWISAI.

SALSA SOUL SISTERS. see AFRICAN AMERICAN LGBTQ ORGANIZATIONS AND PERIODICALS.

SAME-SEX INSTITUTIONS

Same-sex sexual interactions and relationships have flourished in a wide variety of same-sex institutions throughout the history of the United States. In some cases individuals sought out such institutions, on a temporary or permanent basis, because of their same-sex desires. In other cases, single-sex environments fostered engagement in same-sex sexual activities and the formation of love relationships. Across schools, colleges, mining camps, Chinese bachelor societies, brothels, boardinghouses, settlement houses, the Young Men's and Young Women's Christian Associations (YMCA and YWCA), military institutions, and religious orders, same-sex institutions have touched the lives of women and men from all classes and all racial and ethnic groups.

Schools and Colleges

Sex-segregated schools and colleges have long fostered intimate relationships among students. Boys' schools are notorious for the sexual abuse of younger and weaker boys, sometimes as a form of hazing, but they also have nurtured loving and sexual relationships among students, not all of whom identified then or later as gay. Girls' schools and women's colleges into the twentieth century were the scenes of openly acknowledged "smashes" in which one girl courted another with poetry, gifts, and devotion until she was won over. Thus, at boarding school fourteen-year-old Sarah Butler Wister adorned the portrait of sixteen-year-old Jeannie Field Musgrove with flowers. Taking on a male nom de plume, Sarah wrote of her love and devotion to Jeannie. Like many such relationships, theirs lasted throughout their lives and marriages. Jeannie addressed Sarah as "my dearest, dearest lover" and sent "a thousand kisses" (Smith-Rosenberg, p. 5). In the 1850s two Georgia women, Alice Baldy and Josie Varner, met in college and formed a loving attachment. More than ten years after their meeting, Baldy wrote to Varner that she would never have a more devoted lover and that "if you only touch me, or speak to me there is not a nerve or fibre in my body that does not respond with a thrill of delight" (Knowlton, p. 48).

Such school or college relationships between women might, like Sarah and Jeannie's, continue alongside heterosexual ones, or they might—particularly as opportunities for women's economic independence increased—become the major relationships in a woman's life. Wellesley College became known as a haven for female couples. M. Carey Thomas, president of Bryn Mawr College from 1894 to 1922, formed what she called a marriage with her childhood friend Mamie Gwinn when they were both students in Switzerland. Thomas never married, and her relationship with Gwinn only ended after she had also taken up with another woman, Mary Garrett, who fully returned Thomas's love and passion.

Women's schools and colleges fostered the formation of intense and loving ties, and such relationships fit with the notion that women were emotional, spiritual, and so fundamentally different from men that they would naturally be drawn to one another. But that does not mean, especially with increasing public recognition of women's sexuality, that such loves never aroused suspicion that sexual activity was involved. By the 1920s, as a novel about Vassar College put it, "Intimacy between two girls was watched with keen distrustful eyes" (Faderman, p. 35). African American poet Angelina Weld Grimké, who expressed her love for her school friend Mamie Burrill, veiled her same-sex desires in her published poetry. Jeannette Marks, a Mount Holyoke College professor who herself lived in an intimate relationship with college president Mary Woolley, denounced intense college friendships between women as abnormal and insisted that only heterosexual marriage could be complete. Yet women's colleges, like other single-sex institutions, remained populated by coupled women.

Romantic friendships begun in school often lasted a lifetime for women, whereas men who became beloved friends in school were expected to part ways when they

married. Albert Dodd and Anthony Halsey met in college in the 1830s, and Albert wrote of his joy at sharing a pillow with his adored Anthony and of how sweet it was to hold him and kiss him. Daniel Webster and James Hervey Bingham met at Dartmouth College and then went on to study law, teach school, and serve as law clerks together. Webster described Bingham as "the only friend of my heart" and announced that his friend's little bed would be just wide enough to share (Rotundo, p. 3). But despite the similarity of such friendships to those that flourished between women classmates, the middle-class male professional and business worlds called for a competitive spirit among men that made such youthful devotion difficult. Being a man meant marrying and moving beyond the childish romance and affection of school ties, although friendship remained important. Furthermore, physical affection between men began to arouse suspicion by the end of the nineteenth century, especially with the rise of male same-sex sexual subcultures in urban areas. Nevertheless, there were men who never married and maintained their male friendships. Evan Stephens, director of the famous Mormon Tabernacle Choir from 1890 to 1916, lived with a series of what a Mormon publication called, with no disapproval, his "dear boy chums" (Quinn, p. 237). Most of them married but kept a close friendship with Stephens. The director, who was fifty-seven when the last of his companions, eighteen-year-old Tom S. Thomas Jr., came to live with him, left his position to move to the East Village when Thomas entered medical school in New York City.

Attachments among school or college friends, based in part on the conviction that only same-sex friends could truly understand one another, involved kissing, hugging, caressing, and bed sharing. That such relationships did not generally carry connotations of deviant sexuality until the turn of the nineteenth century does not mean, however, that sexual activity never took place. It was simply that the loves of the middle- and upper-class young women and men who attended boarding schools and colleges seemed to most observers to have nothing to do with sex.

The mid-nineteenth-century letters of African American domestic servant Addie Brown to her beloved Rebecca Primus make clear that physical intimacy could be a part of boarding school life. Brown worked at a girls' school in Hartford, Connecticut, and wrote to Primus, a schoolteacher working in the South, about the students' friendliness toward her and their desire to sleep with her. Brown forthrightly promised Rebecca that she would keep her breasts safely buttoned up in her night dress, suggesting at the very least that these romantic friends, as well as the schoolgirls with whom Addie worked, engaged in the caressing of breasts. In the 1820s white southerner Thomas Jefferson Withers wrote to James H. Hammond to ask whether he still slept in his shirttail and had "the extravagant delight of poking and punching a writhing Bedfellow with your long fleshen pole—the exquisite touches of which I have often had the honor of feeling" (Duberman, p. 155). Whether this represented teasing or sexual play in the tradition of boys' schools, the exchange suggests that sexual contact may have been part of school relationships, whatever commentators assumed.

Mining Camps, Chinese Bachelor Societies, and Brothels

Brown's experiences suggest that same-sex sexuality within single-sex institutions was by no means a phenomenon confined to the middle and upper classes, where romantic friendships flourished. Nor were same-sex interactions unique to urban areas. The unbalanced ratio of women to men on the western frontier of white settlement in the nineteenth century created a variety of single-sex institutions where same-sex relationships flourished. Mining camps were both heavily male and unrelentingly masculine. At all-male dances, miners paired off, one sometimes taking on the role of a woman. Across the border in British Columbia, one gold miner killed himself after the death of his partner, leaving a note that he could not go on living without him. Likewise, the Chinese bachelor society, a response to the very small numbers of Chinese women allowed to enter the United States, may have fostered sexual relationships among men. Given that, in San Francisco, women made up barely 10 percent of the Chinese population in 1920, large numbers of men in Chinatown lived in single-sex bunkhouses and opium dens. Commentators at the time focused on illicit heterosexual relationships (with Chinese prostitutes, concubines, or fallen white women), but same-sex relationships likely flourished in that world as well. Labor contractors provided male prostitutes for Chinese, Japanese, and Filipino workers in Pacific Coast cannery plants in the 1920s and 1930s, confirming the existence of same-sex sexuality in these male workplaces.

Prostitution also, somewhat ironically, created a single-sex institution of sorts in the form of the brothel. Although men were integral to the business of prostitution, women in brothels sometimes formed intense attachments and engaged in sexual acts with each other, and not just for paying customers. Calamity Jane, in the Comstock lode in Nevada, was, according to local lore, ejected from a brothel for corrupting the inmates. In the same area, a flirtatious gentleman turned out to be a

woman. Jeanne Bonnet, in San Francisco in the 1870s, dressed as a man and visited local brothels as a customer, in the process working to win women away from their pimps. She was killed by an angry man in the act of undressing to get in bed with her lover, Blanche Buneau. If a cross-dressing woman talking prostitutes into leaving their brothels was a rare phenomenon, same-sex relationships in the world of prostitution were not. In the working-class lesbian bars of the 1950s, prostitutes and lesbians, with some women fitting in both categories, shared space and faced the same dangers from male violence and police repression.

Boardinghouses, Settlement Houses, and the YMCA-YWCA

In growing urban areas of the East and Midwest, young working-class women and men encountered different kinds of same-sex institutions. Boardinghouses for those who had moved to the city, settlement houses (largely single-sex for the middle- and upper-class residents), and, most famously, the YMCA and YWCA, all fostered, in different ways, the formation of same-sex relationships.

"Women adrift"—young working-class women who moved away from their family homes to take up jobs in the cities—moved in a heterosocial world, but they frequently paired up with another woman to share a room in a boardinghouse. Sometimes such arrangements were simply a temporary expedient for women who earned very little, but sometimes women formed long-term friendships and partnerships with their roommates. One working woman explained, "We like each other … and we get along very well" (Meyerowitz, p. 95). Cora Anderson, a Native American student nurse, formed a partnership with another nursing student by passing as a man and living with her partner as husband and wife. Young urban working women, both African American and white, also sometimes lived at girls' clubs or other institutions set up and supervised by middle-class women. But young women often chafed at the restrictions they encountered from the middle-class women in charge, particularly rules designed to enforce sexual respectability. For that reason, in 1892 a group of working women founded the Jane Society, named after the settlement worker Jane Addams. It was a cooperative living arrangement with no external supervision and no rules of conduct.

Settlement houses served a mixed-gender clientele, but the majority of the residents were women, many of them living in coupled relationships. Here middle- and upper-class women, many of whom had attended women's colleges, found a way to live in a community of women and to pursue a calling. Ironically, these mostly single women tended to guide their poor and working-class neighbors into heterosexual marriage and family life. Within settlements and other institutions designed to serve and uplift disadvantaged women, class and generational conflicts between older middle- and upper-class women—both white and African American—and younger working-class women broke out over the issues of sexuality and appropriate leisure activities. Styles of dancing, appropriate behavior with men, and closing hours for residences all sparked intense disputes.

Both the YMCA and YWCA represented responses to the fear of immorality in boardinghouses—as well as taverns, dance halls, and other sites of commercial entertainment—in the burgeoning working-class neighborhoods of cities across the United States. As immigrants and rural migrants swelled the urban population, the reformers who brought the Y concept from England hoped to provide wholesome living and healthy activity to save young men and women from moral decline. Originally a primarily religious organization, the Y became a very different kind of institution as a result of the move toward provision of leisure-time activities, the acquisition of buildings, and the need to hire full-time staff to manage the institution.

Although the YWCA and YMCA had similar missions, it was the YMCA that gained a reputation for facilitating same-sex sexual contacts. When the U.S. Navy launched an investigation of deviant sexual activities in Newport, Rhode Island, in 1919, it was the local YMCA that was featured as the center of a gang of "fairies" who sought out sex with other men. Seven years earlier, and all the way across the country, an even bigger scandal broke out at the Portland, Oregon, YMCA, when police raided the local Y and eventually indicted over fifty men for indecent conduct. Unlike the sailors who hung out at the Newport Y, the men arrested in Portland came mostly from the respectable middle class.

Beginning as an organization that celebrated male friendship and bonding, the YMCA in the late nineteenth century introduced a physical education and sex education program that paradoxically both called attention to the potential dangers of men's relationships at the same time that it created the very institutions—the gymnasium and dormitory—that facilitated men's sexual encounters. As any kind of intimacy and emotional connection between men became suspect, and as the traditional bachelor leadership of the YMCA began to be eased out in favor of married men, the Y became exactly the kind of cruising ground that its new leadership feared. Yet YMCAs remained major cruising sites for men interested in sex with other men up to the 1970s, when the organization cracked down on such encounters and worked hard to enforce a heterosexual family-values agenda.

It is especially intriguing when the largely (although not entirely) class-separated worlds of romantic friendship and same-sex sexual interaction overlapped. In the case of the Newport YMCA, that happened when the navy charged two middle-class men, a clergyman and a YMCA worker, with engaging in sex acts with their charges. The defense claimed that what seemed to the navy to be deviance was simply "Christian brotherhood." That the two men visited sailors in the hospital, lent them money, showed affection and concern, and opened their homes and beds to them seemed to the prosecution a sign of effeminate behavior and inappropriate interest, while to the defense these were normal expressions of concern by helping professionals.

Prisons and Reformatories

An even more direct connection between working-class and middle-class same-sex institutions emerges in the life story of Miriam Van Waters, the superintendent of the Massachusetts Reformatory for Women from 1932 to 1957. Van Waters formed a deeply romantic relationship with her benefactor Geraldine Thompson, herself a married woman. The two met in the 1920s, when the concept of homosexuality was no mystery, and Van Waters, no stranger to psychology, had read the work of the sexologists. Yet they struggled to define their relationship, concealed it in certain situations, and although Van Waters expressed doubt about her own sexuality, she differentiated herself from the lesbians she encountered among the prison's inmates. It is this connection between her own relationship and those of women in prison that is so intriguing. When she came under attack in the 1940s for, among other things, condoning homosexual behavior among her charges, she systematically burned her correspondence with Thompson.

Van Waters was a liberal prison reformer, and she and her staff rejected the labeling of women in the reformatory as lesbians, even when they were discovered in bed together. Criminologists at the time assumed that African American women in prison were sexual aggressors, but Van Waters resisted this notion, too. She distinguished between "true" homosexuals and women who entered into sexual relationships in prison out of boredom. The former, she believed, could be cured, and the creation of "situational" lesbians could be avoided by providing appropriate activities and facilitating healthy female bonding.

There is no comparable story about men in prison, where same-sex sexuality was noted and punished much earlier. Older and younger male prisoners sometimes entered into relationships in which they shared possessions and a bed, but as of 2003, discourse focuses on the prevalence of rape or coercive relationships, in both cases an assertion of power rather than an expression of desire. The likelihood of rape in male prisons is in some ways presented as an added deterrent to criminal activity. In contrast, women's sexual relationships in prisons and reformatories continue to be viewed as either consensual "making do" in the absence of men or part of the formation of substitute families. Even the criminologists who began in the 1930s to denounce cross-racial relationships in women's prisons and to target African American women as masculine aggressors portrayed these relationships as romances in which black inmates courted willing white ones. One white woman at the New York City House of Detention smuggled a love letter to her black female husband, promising her "Sugar dady" that "'if I could sleep with you for one little night, I would show you how much I hon[es]tly and truly I love you,'" according to Estelle Freedman in her 1996 essay "The Prison Lesbian." The markedly different nature of female and male prison relationships served as one basis for the satirical claim in a humorous feminist tract that men and women belong to different species.

The Military

If the prison system seems at times to condone at least male same-sex sexuality, the same cannot be said of another authoritarian institution, the military. Nevertheless, close bonding and sexual relationships between men have been part of armies and navies throughout history, from ancient Greece through the eighteenth-century British navy to the twenty-first century. Walt Whitman, when he worked as a nurse in Civil War military hospitals, formed deep and romantic attachments to the men he tended, and he reported that the soldiers returned his affection. That sailors engaged in same-sex sexual activity on board ship is clear from the record of floggings for such misconduct.

The issue of homosexuality first troubled military officials on a national scale during World War II, when screening attempted to keep out men and women perceived as homosexual. At the same time, the sex-segregated nature of military life facilitated such contacts. Pre-induction psychological testing of men included for the first time frank questions about sexual conduct and desires, and these had the potential to raise consciousness about same-sex feelings or experiences. With no such screening in place for women until late in the war, les-

bians flocked to the military. And as the need for male and female bodies increased, the authorities looked the other way.

But despite finding a place in the military, LGBT people had to be careful. Homosexuality was cause for imprisonment, although psychiatrists persuaded the brass during the war to institute instead a system of dishonorable discharges. Only criminal offenders guilty of same-sex rape or sex with a minor would be subject to imprisonment. Others, judged "true" homosexuals who engaged in consensual sex, would be discharged, while "normal" young men who had same-sex sex because they were drunk or curious would be "rehabilitated" and kept in the service. After the war, the purge of LGBT people spread from the military to the civilian sector of government in the atmosphere of McCarthyism. The "don't ask, don't tell" policy of the late twentieth century represented a new twist on the old conviction that same-sex desires and relationships represented a danger to esprit de corps and discipline.

Conclusion

The public scandal in the first years of the twenty-first century about the sexual abuse of boys by priests in the Catholic Church reveals, among many other things, the attraction of single-sex institutions for people with same-sex desires. Single-sex religious institutions have long fostered intimate relationships, whether sexual or not. Lesbian ex-nuns have told of their loves for a "particular friend," despite the church's admonitions against such friendships. Priests and ex-priests have written of their struggles with their same-sex desires. As in the case of prisons, what is striking are the different patterns that emerge in the contemporary stories of religious men and women, women tending to form relationships with one another, and men more frequently engaging in coercive sex acts with boys in subordinate positions.

Single-sex institutions, then, have throughout U.S. history created environments that facilitated a range of same-sex interactions, from rape to mutual love and companionship. In some cases, individuals with same-sex desires sought out institutions in which they might form intimate same-sex relationships, and it made a difference whether or not those institutions condoned or forbade such bonds. In other cases, people found themselves in a single-sex world and, for whatever reason, turned to others whom they might not have chosen otherwise for sex or partnership. As the variety of interactions described here makes clear, there are not simple conclusions to be drawn about sex and love in same-sex institutions in general, either now or in the past.

Bibliography

Bérubé, Allan. *Coming out under Fire: The History of Gay Men and Women in World War II.* New York: Free Press, 1990.

Curb, Rosemary, and Nancy Manahan. *Lesbian Nuns: Breaking Silence.* Tallahassee, Fla.: Naiad Press, 1985.

Duberman, Martin Bauml, Martha Vicinus, and George Chauncey Jr., eds. *Hidden From History: Reclaiming the Gay and Lesbian Past.* New York: New American Library, 1989.

Faderman, Lillian. *Odd Girls and Twilight Lovers: A History of Lesbian Life in Twentieth-Century America.* New York: Columbia University Press, 1991.

Freedman, Estelle B. *Maternal Justice: Miriam Van Waters and the Female Reform Tradition.* Chicago: University of Chicago Press, 1996.

———. "The Prison Lesbian: Race, Class, and the Construction of the Aggressive Female Homosexual, 1915–1965." *Feminist Studies* 22 (1996): 397–423.

Gustav-Wrathall, John Donald. *Take the Young Stranger by the Hand: Same-Sex Relations and the YMCA.* Chicago: University of Chicago Press, 1998.

Hansen, Karen V. "'No Kisses Is Like Youres': An Erotic Friendship between Two African-American Women during the Mid-Nineteenth Century." *Gender and History* 7 (1995): 153–182.

Horowitz, Helen Lefkowitz. *The Power and Passion of M. Carey Thomas.* New York: Knopf, 1994.

Knowlton, Elizabeth W. "'Only a Woman Like Yourself'— Rebecca Alice Baldy, Dutiful Daughter, Stalwart Sister, and Lesbian Lover of Nineteenth-Century Georgia." In *Carryin' on in the Lesbian and Gay South.* Edited by John Howard. New York: New York University Press, 1997.

Meyerowitz, Joanne J. *Women Adrift: Independent Wage Earners in Chicago, 1880–1930.* Chicago: University of Chicago Press, 1988.

Mjagkij, Nina, and Margaret Spratt, eds. *Men and Women Adrift: The YMCA and the YWCA in the City.* New York: New York University Press, 1997.

Quinn, D. Michael. *Same-Sex Dynamics among Nineteenth-Century Americans: A Mormon Example.* Urbana: University of Illinois Press, 1996.

Rotundo, E. Anthony. "Romantic Friendship: Male Intimacy and Middle-Class Youth in the Northern United States, 1800–1900." *Journal of Social History* 23 (1989): 1–25.

Shah, Nayan. *Contagious Divides: Epidemics and Race in San Francisco's Chinatown.* Berkeley: University of California Press, 2001.

Smith-Rosenberg, Carroll. "The Female World of Love and Ritual: Relations between Women in Nineteenth-Century America." *Signs: Journal of Women in Culture and Society* 1 (1975): 1–29.

Leila J. Rupp

See also BATHHOUSES; BONNET, JEANNE; BOY SCOUTS AND GIRL SCOUTS; CATHOLICS AND CATHOLICISM; COLLEGES AND UNIVERSITIES; GOVERNMENT AND MILITARY WITCHHUNTS; GRIMKÉ, ANGELINA WELD; HAMMOND, JAMES HENRY; INTERGENERATIONAL SEX AND RELATIONSHIPS; MILITARY; PRIMUS, REBECCA, AND ADDIE BROWN; PRISONS, JAILS, AND REFORMATORIES: MEN'S; PRISONS, JAILS, AND REFORMATORIES: WOMEN'S; ROMANTIC FRIENDSHIP AND BOSTON MARRIAGE; SITUATIONAL HOMOSEXUALITY; SMASHES AND CHUMMING; THOMAS, M. CAREY; VAN WATERS, MIRIAM; WHITMAN, WALT; WIGGLESWORTH, MICHAEL; WOOLLEY, MARY, AND JEANETTE MARKS.

SAMOIS

Founded in San Francisco in June 1978 and disbanded in May 1983, Samois was the first known public organization devoted to lesbian sadomasochism (S/M) and was a key player in the early phases of the feminist sex wars. Samois grew out of the confluence of the feminist, gay and lesbian, sexual freedom, and S/M movements of the 1970s. "Samois" is a place-name taken from the famous S/M novel *Story of O* (1965), in which it is the location of the home of the sole female dominant and a site for S/M activities conducted entirely among women. Like other early S/M organizations, such as the Eulenspiegel Society (New York City, 1971) and the Janus Society (San Francisco, 1974), Samois chose an obscure name intended to evade unwanted attention yet provide legible signals to the knowledgeable.

Emergence of Lesbian S/M Groups

Samois and other early lesbian S/M groups attempted to create social worlds where kinky lesbians could find friends and partners and to carve out protected space in otherwise increasingly antagonistic lesbian communities. Prior to the formation of Samois, lesbians who practiced S/M apparently did so primarily in small, private networks or isolated couples, or else socialized along the borders of the more institutionally established S/M populations of heterosexuals and gay men. Public discussion of lesbian S/M expanded in the mid-1970s as S/M women became more visible in their communities and more vocal in the lesbian, feminist, and gay press. This amplified visibility of S/M among gay women in turn sparked a barrage of condemnation asserting fundamental incompatibilities between lesbian feminism and S/M. The escalating hostility toward S/M provided additional motivation for S/M lesbians to mobilize in self-defense.

Ironically, several acrimonious battles over the relationship of S/M and feminism enhanced the process of nascent community formation. Extensive coverage of these debates in the feminist and lesbian press telegraphed the presence of activist S/M women in several cities, including Philadelphia, Boston, Iowa City, and Los

Angeles. As they made contact, these women formed larger networks and began to assemble organizational resources. Nationally, networking among S/M women intensified from about 1975. By 1978 a critical mass was reached in the San Francisco Bay Area that resulted in the formation of Samois. Controversy over Samois further raised the public profile of lesbian S/M and propelled the formation of groups in other cities. LSM was founded in New York City in 1981, quickly followed by Leather and Lace in Los Angeles and Urania in Boston. While LSM is the only survivor of that first wave of lesbian S/M groups, large and diversified lesbian S/M communities have since become well established in many of the major urban centers.

Defending S/M

Samois articulated a bold defense of S/M as a legitimate eroticism, even among feminists. The Samois statement of purpose proclaimed:

> We believe that S/M must be consensual, mutual, and safe. S/M can exist as part of a healthy and positive lifestyle....We believe that sadomasochists are an oppressed sexual minority. Our struggle deserves the recognition and support of other sexual minorities and oppressed groups. We believe that S/M can and should be consistent with the principles of feminism. As feminists, we oppose all forms of social hierarchy based on gender. As radical perverts, we oppose all social hierarchies based on sexual preference. (Samois, 1979, p. 2)

Samois never claimed that S/M was particularly feminist, only that there was no inherent contradiction or intrinsic conflict between feminist politics and S/M practice. Moreover, while addressing the prevailing feminist discourse on sexuality, Samois did not frame its critique in purely feminist terms. It was instead groping toward a proto-queer politics that contained a broader and more inclusive sense of sexual oppression based on specifically sexual inequalities.

Samois projected these ideas through bold public events and original publications. In addition to informational presentations at local women's bookstores and lesbian bars, Samois produced the first Women's Leather Dance (1981), the first Ms. Leather Contest (1981), and the first Lesbian Pride Leather Dance (1982). In 1978 Samois printed the first women's "Hankie Code," adapted from the gay male hankie codes then in widespread circulation. Samois published the booklet *What Color is Your Handkerchief* in 1979 and the landmark anthology *Coming to Power* in 1981.

Many feminist and lesbian newspapers published excoriating reviews of these two Samois publications,

refused to print supportive commentary, and rejected paid advertisements, while some feminist bookstores simply banned them outright. Despite the vociferous censure, the books were wildly popular and sold out quickly. *What Color is Your Handkerchief* went into five printings and *Coming to Power* three editions. The publications, as well as the prominence and passion of the arguments they provoked, all helped consolidate the emerging lesbian S/M community. In addition, the books marked San Francisco as a known location for lesbian perverts, making the city a magnet for migration in much the way steamy pulp novels drew lesbians to Greenwich Village in the 1950s and 1960s.

Feminist Sex Wars

Samois's greatest notoriety came from its role in the feminist sex wars, the first skirmishes of which took place in the San Francisco Bay Area between Samois and Women against Violence in Pornography and Media (WAVPM). Founded in 1976, WAVPM was the first group dedicated to opposing pornography on feminist grounds. However, much of what WAVPM actually found objectionable in pornography was S/M content, and its attacks on pornography invariably included denunciations of S/M imagery and practice. For example, WAVPM demanded the "end to all portrayals of women being bound, raped, tortured, mutilated, abused, or degraded in any way for sexual or erotic stimulation" (September 1977, p. 3). WAVPM repeatedly condemned any visual representation, pornographic or not, in which any women were shown "bound, gagged, beaten, whipped, and chained" (November 1977, p. 1). The organization conducted street protests against S/M images and picketed theaters showing the film version of *Story of O*. Since WAVPM was treating all visual portrayals of S/M as violent and calling for their elimination, Samois and WAVPM were on a collision course.

While WAVPM denied having a position on S/M, members of Samois quickly perceived that WAVPM's program was as much anti-S/M as antipornography and that its critique of pornography entailed a series of negative presumptions about S/M. In the course of confronting such implicit suppositions, Samois challenged the fundamental credibility of both the logical structure and empirical claims of WAVPM's case against pornography. Samois and WAVPM thus engaged in a series of disputes over both pornography and S/M that prefigured a decade of subsequent struggle in feminism over sexual practice and sexual representation.

WAVPM rebuffed several attempts by Samois to engage in principled dialogue and debate. The accelerating tensions between the groups peaked in 1980 when

WAVPM held a public forum to castigate S/M and especially to vilify S/M in the lesbian community. Samois leafleted the event, protesting that

> WAVPM, without taking an "official" position on S/M has nonetheless promoted a false image of S/M sexuality and helped to create a climate that is oppressive and dangerous to S/M-identified people.... We demand that WAVPM cease equating consensual S/M with rape, murder, and violence; cease to single out S/M erotica for picketing; and either admit to having a position on S/M (which may then be discussed) or take a position supporting S/M between consenting adults. (Samois, 1980)

Although WAVPM steadfastly declined to adopt any official position on S/M, several of its fervently anti-S/M members went on to produce the anthology *Against Sadomasochism* (1982). S/M continued to be a potent flashpoint throughout the feminist sex wars, in part because the plausibility of the antipornography argument was so dependent on its indictment of S/M. Despite the fact that WAVPM had no explicit stance, the organization pioneered a characteristic fusion of anti-S/M and anti-pornography propositions that shaped virtually all subsequent feminist antipornography ideology and activity. S/M has always served as a major subtext to the feminist antipornography movement, being indispensable to its analytic coherence, the source of its most rhetorically persuasive examples, and a primary target of its prescriptions for social change. Samois was present to resolutely bear witness and dissent when this program was still embryonic in its stages.

As a result of its early resistance to the antipornography movement and its anti-S/M implications, Samois helped shatter the hegemony of antipornography positions and opened up possibilities for broader discussions of sexuality within feminism. In its brief five-year history, Samois facilitated the establishment of social worlds for lesbian sadomasochists; helped inaugurate the feminist sex wars; developed innovative critiques of sexual oppression; and fundamentally changed the lesbian community, the feminist movement, and the politics of sexuality. It was one of the most influential lesbian organizations of its era.

Bibliography

Linden, Robin Ruth et al., eds. *Against Sadomasochism: A Radical Feminist Analysis.* East Palo Alto, Calif.: Frog in the Well Press, 1982.

Samois. *What Color is Your Handkerchief: A Lesbian S/M Sexuality Reader.* Berkeley, Calif.: Samois, 1979.

Samois. "This Forum is a Lie about S/M." 1980. A leaflet. Collection of Gayle Rubin.

Samois. *Coming To Power: Writings and Graphics on Lesbian S/M.* Berkeley, Calif.: Samois, 1981.

Women against Violence in Pornography and Media. *Newspage* 1, no. 4 (September 1977).

———. *Newspage* 1, no. 6 (November 1977).

———. "A Forum on S&M in the Women's Community." 1980. A leaflet. Collection of Gayle Rubin.

Gayle Rubin

See also LESBIAN FEMINISM; PORNOGRAPHY; SADOMASOCHISM, SADISTS, AND MASOCHISTS; SEX WARS.

SAMSON, Deborah (b. 1759; d. 29 April 1827)

On 23 May 1983 Governor Michael Dukakis signed a proclamation declaring Deborah Samson the "Official Heroine of the Commonwealth of Massachusetts." Two news services stated that this was the first time in the history of the United States that any state had proclaimed anyone as the official state hero or heroine.

Deborah Samson was a descendant of Mayflower colonists William Bradford and Miles Standish. When she was not quite six, her father vanished, and her mother was forced to relinquish control of her seven children, including Samson. After living for a while with an elderly spinster and then with an ailing widow, Samson was taken to the daughterless Middleborough home of Deacon Jeremiah Thomas and his wife, who had ten sons.

Samson spent ten years with the Thomas family, growing to be about 5 feet, 8 inches tall, almost a foot higher than the average woman of her day and taller than most men. Hard work broadened her shoulders and hardened her muscles. Farm girls of that era received no formal schooling, and Samson was no exception. However, she obtained an education by studying with the Thomas boys each evening after all chores were done.

When she turned eighteen, she secured a job as a schoolteacher and supplemented her income by spinning and weaving. An excellent whittler, Samson carved many household utensils that she sold to customers at Sproat's Tavern, where she could listen to patrons talking of other places and doings, particulary about the Revolutionary War.

Samson knew she was far stronger than most men and that she was an excellent shot and could handle horses and repair tools. She was certain she would make a better than average soldier. Patriotism and a thirst for adventure finally got the best of the tall schoolmarm. There is inconclusive evidence that she disguised herself

as a man—"Timothy Thayer" of Carver (a nearby town)—and signed Muster Master Israel Wood's sheets, but changed her mind overnight and did not report to enlist the following day. Regardless, on 20 May 1782, in Bellingham, Massachusetts, Deborah Samson enlisted as Robert Shurtliff.

Although the last major battle of the Revolution had been fought the previous October at Yorktown, Virginia, a guerilla war was still being fought in some areas by determined Tories loyal to the British Crown. "Shurtliff" was paid sixty pounds bounty money, and with forty-nine other recruits marched from Worcester to West Point, New York, where they were issued uniforms and equipment. Samson's bold and legible signature still exists in Massachusetts records.

Robert Shurtliff became known for his valor and endurance, and although various biographers provide details about the wounds Shurtliff suffered, Samson in later life stated that the only injury she suffered in her seventeen months in the army was a dislocated limb.

Somehow it was discovered that Robert Shurtliff was a woman, and on 23 October 1783, she received an honorable discharge. Samson returned to her mother in Plympton, Massachusetts, but Mrs. Samson argued with her about enlisting until finally Samson donned male clothing and walked nearly twenty miles to the home of her aunt, Alice Winters, in Stoughton, Massachusetts. Aunt Alice greeted her by calling her "Ephraim," mistaking Samson for an older brother.

Samson worked on the Winters farm until she met Benjamin Gannett, who lived on a nearby farm in adjacent Sharon, Massachusetts. They were married on 7 April 1785. The Gannetts lived in a tiny three-room hovel opposite the corner of what would later be East and Billings Streets in Sharon. They had three children and in spite of their poverty also adopted an orphan.

The famous nightrider Paul Revere became aware of Samson's financial difficulties. He obtained for Samson a pension of thirty-four pounds with interest for her services in the army.

In 1797, Herman Mann wrote a biography of Samson titled *The Female Review, Or Memoirs of An American Lady.* Mann commissioned Joseph Stone of Framingham to paint a portrait of Samson for the frontispiece of the book. The portrait is in the John Brown Museum in Providence, Rhode Island.

In 1802 Samson was again desperate for funds, and used the publicity generated by Mann's book to become one of the first American professional lecturers. She was billed in posters as "The American Heroine" and "Equipt in complete uniform will go through the manual exerci[s]es." The tour took her to cities in Massachusetts, Rhode Island, and New York.

Decades of research by the late Professor Emil F. Guba, author of the only factual book on Samson as of the early 2000s, *Deborah Samson, Alias Robert Shurtliff, Revolutionary War Soldier;* Charles H. Bricknell, Plympton historian; and Patrick Leonard have found no indication that Samson was lesbian or bisexual in a sexual sense or that she cross-dressed for any other than practical purposes.

In 1813, Samson's son, Earl, married and built a beautiful mansion at 300 East Street in Sharon. There she lived until her death from a stomach ailment. She was buried in nearby Rock Ridge Cemetery in Massachusetts. Her gravestone is located a short distance from the hill on which her grandson, George Washington Gay, erected a monument for Samson and the Sharon Civil War soldiers many years later. A bas-relief of Samson is on the monument, faithfully reflecting the Stone portrait of 1787.

Bibliography

Guba, Emil F. *Deborah Samson, Alias Robert Shurtliff, Revolutionary War Soldier.* Plymouth, Mass.: Jones River Press, 1994.

Leonard, Patrick J. "Deborah Samson: Official Heroine of the State of Massachusetts," Canton Massachusetts Historical Society. Available from http://www.canton.org/samson/. Also printed in *Minerva Quarterly Report on Women in the Military* 6, no. 3 (fall 1988).

Mann, Herman. *The Female Review. Life of Deborah Sampson the Female Soldier in the War of the Revolution.* Introduction and Notes by John Adams Vinton. Boston: J.K. Wiggin & Wm. Parsons Lunt, 1866.

"Personality." *Military History Magazine* (April 2001): 16.

Thornton, Patrick J. *Famous Women of the American Revolution.* New York: Power Kids Press, 2003

Wilson, Barbara A. "Woman Soldiers in the American Revolutionary War." Available from http://userpages.aug.com/captbarb/femvets.html

Patrick J. Leonard

See also MILITARY; TRANSSEXUALS, TRANSVESTITES, TRANSGENDER PEOPLE AND CROSS-DRESSERS; WAR.

SAN FRANCISCO

By any standard, San Francisco stands out as an uncommonly queer place. The city's Castro District functions as an almost entirely queer neighborhood, openly gay and lesbian candidates dot the political landscape, municipal law protects LGBT civil rights, and the city hosts a slate of queer cultural events, including one of the largest LGBT pride parades in the world. As a result, San Francisco has become a destination for LGBT migrants and tourists. What accounts for this phenomenon? Why is San Francisco such a gay town? Historically, many factors have contributed to San Francisco's reputation as a haven for lesbian, gay, bisexual, and transgender populations.

Early Developments

The lawlessness of San Francisco's early colonial history set the foundation for San Francisco's LGBT history. San Francisco was founded in 1776 as a Spanish colonial outpost when settlers constructed a mission and presidio near the territories of the Coast Miwoks, Wintuns, Yokuts, and Costanoans. Originally called Yerba Buena, San Francisco sat at the northern edge of the Spanish Empire, and when Mexico won its independence from Spain in 1821, the town was barely governable. In 1848, when the United States acquired California through the Treaty of Guadalupe Hidalgo and gold was discovered near the Sacramento River, San Francisco was a rough-and-tumble frontier town with a mixed-race population of just over eight hundred people. The Gold Rush turned San Francisco into a boom town, and migrants from Chile, Peru, Mexico, China, and the eastern United States flocked there in search of wealth. As documented by historian Susan Lee Johnson, some of these gold seekers were same-sex couples, men who did not identify as gay or homosexual—these are twentieth-century terms of self-identification—but who lived their lives together in the pattern of traditionally married couples. One such couple was Jason Chamberlain and John Chafee, who lived together in the Central Valley for fifty years. During this period there were also a number of "passing women" or female-to-male transgender individuals who made San Francisco their home. Babe Bean, or Jack Garland, was one such person. Born in 1869 as Elvira Virginia Mugarietta, in the 1890s Mugarietta was known as Babe Bean. Bean wore men's clothes and lived for a time in Stockton, California, working as a journalist. In 1898 he enlisted in the army (as a man) and served in the Spanish-American War. After the war he settled in San Francisco and worked as a male nurse and freelance social worker under the name Jack Bee Garland. When Garland died in 1936, he was discovered to have a woman's body, surprising longtime friends who had known him for years as a man.

San Francisco's mix of people, particularly its large Catholic and immigrant populations, contributed to a wide-open quality of life that was distinct from that of other large U.S. cities. The Gold Rush and subsequent migrations brought an abundance of single men to California, and San Francisco's vice and entertainment district, the Barbary Coast, became famous for its gaming and prostitution. The Barbary Coast is especially important to San Francisco's queer history because it encouraged the development of gender-transgressive and queer entertainments. The Barbary Coast emerged along Pacific Street, or Terrific Street as it was called in the 1890s, and it hosted a battery of cheap amusements—grogeries, wine and beer dens, gambling halls, and concert saloons. Prostitution was an important aspect of Barbary Coast amusements, and alongside female prostitutes, male prostitutes plied their trade. In 1908, for instance, a place called the Dash opened, featuring female impersonators who entertained customers and sold sex in booths for a dollar. Female impersonators were also common on the burlesque and vaudeville stage, and in San Francisco female impersonator shows were popular through the early 1900s. San Francisco's most famous female impersonator, Bothwell Browne, ran a dance studio by day and staged elaborate impersonations at night. In 1904, at the Central Theater on Market Street, Browne staged a performance called "Around the World in Eighty Days" and in 1905, at the Chutes Theater, his troupe, the Gaiety Girls, performed "Mikado, on the Half Shell." The theatrical world of female impersonation overlapped with a network of drag queens, fairies, and homosexuals in the city's urban center, but in the 1910s and 1920s, morality and public decency crusades transformed the city's prostitution and entertainment districts. The criminalization of prostitution in the 1910s shifted prostitution zones away from centrally located brothels to the streets and small taverns near the Tenderloin. Morality concerns also curtailed the stage presence of female impersonators, who provided public access to a nascent queer culture. Because female impersonation was often linked to sexual immorality and prostitution, anti-prostitution crusades also worked to shift queer public space away from large costume balls and big-house theater to smaller venues like bars, taverns, and nightclubs.

The impact of Prohibition was different in San Francisco than it was in East Coast cities like New York because in San Francisco, city officials openly defied the state and federal laws that enforced the ban on alcohol. During Prohibition, drag shows continued to exist in speakeasies like Finocchio's, and when the laws were repealed in 1933, California voters did not prioritize vice control as they legalized the liquor industry. In fact, California granted complete control of liquor sales and distribution to the State Board of Equalization, the state's tax agency, so while the financial aspects of the liquor industry were regulated, the control of bars and taverns was minimal. As a result, the 1930s saw the mushrooming of small venues that hosted a variety of licentious entertainments. Nightclubs were not only less expensive to open than larger venues, but they circumvented a post-Prohibition liquor regulation that limited the sale of hard liquor within hotels, clubs, and restaurants. The intimate nature of nightclubs also made the surveillance of activities inside the bar difficult, and female impersonators were often sought out to draw a specialized clientele into the bar. In San Francisco the circumstances of Prohibition and Repeal resulted in the consolidation of vice and the transformation of a nascent queer culture into an overt and quasi-legitimate form of urban entertainment.

At the same time that Prohibition and Repeal changed the form and function of policing in San Francisco, a tourist industry began to take shape. In the 1930s both the San Francisco Golden Gate Bridge and the San Francisco–Oakland Bay Bridge were completed, and to celebrate the city hosted the 1939 World's Fair. Billed as the Golden Gate International Exposition, San Francisco's World's Fair brought an unprecedented number of tourists to the West Coast. With an increase in tourist trade, tourist entertainments took root in San Francisco, and in the tradition of the Barbary Coast, sexualized entertainments became a tourist favorite. As part of this phenomenon, through the late 1930s and 1940s, nightclubs that featured female and male impersonators became a standard on Broadway, San Francisco's tourist strip. In fact, two of San Francisco's most popular nightclubs, Finocchio's and Mona's, were impersonator clubs. During Prohibition, Finocchio's had been a speakeasy that featured informal female impersonators, and after Repeal it moved to a larger and more centrally located venue—on Broadway—and expanded its floor show of opulently dressed impersonators. Mona's opened just after Repeal in a basement café, but by 1939 it too had moved to a space on Broadway. Through the 1940s, Mona's maintained a steady tourist clientele, but it was also a public space for lesbians and gay men who came to watch male impersonators perform. Male impersonators at Mona's performed a typical nightclub act where they sang and danced, but they used their voice as entertainers to speak directly about lesbian and gay life in San Francisco. As sex tourism and the spectacle of gender transgression became an important part of San Francisco's tourist industry, it bolstered the emergence of publicly visible queer cultures in the North Beach District.

From World War II to 1969

As John D'Emilio and Allan Bérubé have demonstrated, World War II was a turning point in San Francisco's lesbian and gay history. With much of the war effort focused on the Pacific theater, San Francisco became both a port of embarkation and a strategic stronghold during the war. Over a million servicemen and women traveled through San Francisco on their way to and from war, and because San Francisco was crucial to national security, the city functioned as an extended military base. Demographic shifts forced the city to adopt new social practices during wartime, and these practices influenced the growth and development of the city's gay and lesbian communities.

Among Friends. Individuals, couples, and families fill the streets for the annual Gay Pride Parade in the world-renowned LGBT haven of San Francisco. **[AP/Wide World Photos]**

The heightened military presence returned San Francisco to the unbalanced sex ratio of its mining camp years, and with thousands of furloughed sailors and soldiers traversing the city, entertaining the troops became an important focus of San Francisco's underworld entertainments. To accommodate both the vast influx of military personnel and the quick pace of shore leave, gay and lesbian bars clustered in areas close to the center of town. Queer life, as a result, became much more accessible to both locals and military personnel looking for a good time. Gay officers and enlisted men cruised upscale hotel bars like the Oak Room at the St. Francis Hotel or the Top of the Mark at the Mark Hopkins Hotel on Union Square. But they also frequented rough bars in the Tenderloin and on the waterfront, like the Silver Rail and the Old Crow. The increased popularity of gay bars in the city center during wartime hastened the development of both a gay sensibility within the city and an urban infrastructure that supported it.

The military's presence in San Francisco also brought new modes of policing. Along with city police and state liquor control agents (who theretofore had played a minimal role in policing gay and lesbian bars), the war brought the heightened presence of military police to the city. Military police coordinated their efforts in one unit, the Armed Forces Disciplinary Control Board, and this unit controlled the leave activities of military personnel, but it also had an impact on the lives of locals in that the Board established a threatening presence inside bars and taverns. Military police communicated with San Fran-

cisco police and state liquor agents, instigating raids or other kinds of harassment that might otherwise have been avoided. During and after World War II, gay bar owners and their patrons determined new ways to manage policing. They sometimes cooperated, sometimes cajoled, and often manipulated policing agencies. As these strategies increasingly failed during the postwar years, bar owners began to fight police harassment through the courts. For instance, in 1942 several gay bars were targeted by military police and state liquor authorities and citations were issued to Finocchio's, the Black Cat, and the Top of the Mark. While each of these bars survived its investigation, the proprietor of the Black Cat, a bohemian bar in San Francisco's North Beach District, later fought charges against the bar in court, and the resulting California Supreme Court decision disrupted the ability of federal, state, and local police to control gay and lesbian bars.

The Black Cat case, *Stoumen v. Reilly* (1951), began in 1949 when the Board of Equalization suspended the bar's liquor license on the grounds that it was "a hangout for persons of homosexual tendencies" (*Stoumen v. Reilly* 234 P. 2d 969 [Calif. 1951]). Using unique sources of evidence, including the recently published Kinsey Report, attorney Morris Lowenthal argued that homosexuals had the right to assemble in bars and restaurants. After numerous appeals, in 1951 the California Supreme Court agreed with Lowenthal, overruling the Board of Equalization's decision and ordering the Black Cat's liquor license restored. In the period following *Stoumen v. Reilly,* liquor control agents stopped trying to revoke the liquor licenses of gay bars, local police stopped raiding gay bars, and the Armed Forces Disciplinary Control Board was unable to do much more than set certain bars and taverns off-limits to military personnel. It was during this period, from 1951 to 1955, that San Francisco's gay and lesbian bar culture began to grow, and gay and lesbian bars were increasingly gay owned and operated. This was also the period when the Beat Generation began to take up residence in the city, bringing a whole new level of publicity to San Francisco's queer communities.

D'Emilio and literary critic Catherine Stimpson have noted the homoerotics of Beat culture and the contributions that the Beat movement made to the consolidation of San Francisco's queer cultures and communities. Most Beat poets were not native to San Francisco, however, and brought a combination of influences (including Buddhism, pacifism, and anarchism) to San Francisco by way of Boston, Denver, and New York City. Beat culture combined the elements of confessional poetry, mind-expanding drugs, and sexual liberation, and Beat poetry, particularly the writings of Allen Ginsberg and Jack Kerouac, embraced the power of men together. But it was the publication of Allen Ginsberg's sexually explicit poem *Howl* and the subsequent censorship trial surrounding its publication that put San Francisco's homosexuality and Beat poetry on the map. *Howl* celebrates male homosexuality as painfully joyous, remembering those "who let themselves be fucked in the ass by saintly motorcyclists, and screamed with joy" and those "who copulated ecstatic and insatiate with a bottle of beer a sweetheart a package of cigarettes a candle and fell off the bed" (Ginsberg, in Charters, p. 64). The censorship case began on 21 May 1957, when an officer from San Francisco's Juvenile Bureau arrested Lawrence Ferlinghetti for publishing the poem. City Lights Bookstore manager Shigeyoshi Murao was arrested for selling *Howl* to undercover agents. The American Civil Liberties Union threw its weight behind the case, and when the verdict came back in favor of Ferlinghetti and Murao, it was a victory for free speech. Because the trial generated a tremendous amount of publicity, it fixed in the minds of many the association between San Francisco, the Beat movement, and homosexuality.

At the same time that lesbian and gay bars became an important aspect of San Francisco's queer public culture and Beat poets plied their trade in San Francisco's North Beach District, two important gay and lesbian civil rights organizations made their home in San Francisco. In 1951 the Mattachine Society was founded in Los Angeles, but it moved its national headquarters to San Francisco in 1955. In 1955 eight lesbians, among them Del Martin and Phyllis Lyon, formed the Daughters of Bilitis in San Francisco, which was the nation's first known lesbian civil rights organization. Both the Mattachine Society and the Daughters of Bilitis were small groups in that membership rosters remained relatively short and attendance at monthly meetings rarely surpassed twenty. But as Martin Meeker suggests, these organizations touched many more people through their social service activities. Both the Mattachine Society and the Daughters of Bilitis provided lay counseling, employment and housing referrals, and referrals to sympathetic lawyers and psychologists. Also, they both produced monthly publications, the *Mattachine Review* and the *Ladder,* respectively. Through these publications, the Mattachine Society and the Daughters of Bilitis reached significant numbers of readers, particularly since the publications were often passed from friend to friend. Homophile organizations thus had an immense impact on San Francisco's reputation as a gay-friendly town simply by the fact of their existence. The readers of the *Mattachine Review* and the *Ladder* got to know San Francisco as the home of the nation's foremost gay and lesbian emancipation organizations.

Through the 1960s a queer public culture took shape in the city as gay and lesbian bar owners and patrons negotiated better relationships with the police and new and more militant homophile organizations took shape. Three such organizations were the League for Civil Education, the Society for Individual Rights, and the Council on Religion and the Homosexual. The League for Civil Education initially focused on police harassment and entrapment, but it also supported the first openly gay candidate for public office. In 1961 José Sarria ran for a seat on the city's Board of Supervisors. Sarria was well-known in San Francisco for his campy drag shows at the Black Cat bar, but he was also the secretary of the League for Civil Education and aware of the need for San Francisco's gay community to express a political voice. He did not win election to the board, but with about six thousand votes, he demonstrated the possibility of an influential gay vote in municipal elections. After Sarria's candidacy, the League for Civil Education fell into disarray and was succeeded by the Society for Individual Rights, an umbrella organization that offered social, cultural, and political activities. With over three hundred members, the Society for Individual Rights was the city's largest homophile organization through the 1960s, and in April 1966 it opened the city's first gay community center on Sixth Street near Market Street.

In 1964 San Francisco's Council on Religion and the Homosexual was formed to address the relationship

Gay Pride Parade. Exuberant participants in the annual San Francisco event pass crowds of spectators on 24 June 2001. [AP Photo/Peter Lennihan]

between homosexuals and the church. To raise money for the organization, other homophile groups planned a costume ball to be held on New Year's Day in 1965. The costume ball became what many historians consider an important turning point in San Francisco's queer history. When ticket holders arrived for the event, many of them dressed in drag, they were greeted by scores of uniformed and undercover police who took their photographs and harassed them on their way into the ball. The next day the ministers attached to the Council on Religion and the Homosexual staged a press conference that blasted the San Francisco Police Department. The mayor and a city judge took the side of the Council, and the police were humbled into an apology. This event is thought by some to be the equivalent of New York City's Stonewall Riots in that it brought San Francisco's LGBT communities together and inaugurated a new phase of gay organizing. Membership rosters at the Society for Individual Rights rose to over a thousand in the wake of the event, an organization called Citizen's Alert was formed to track police abuse in the city, and the chief of police found it necessary to appoint a liaison to the city's gay and lesbian communities.

The first liaison to San Francisco's gay and lesbian communities was Elliot Blackstone, a police lieutenant who had long advocated the establishment of a police community relations unit. After his appointment in 1965,

Blackstone worked to improve the credibility of the police in neighborhoods with a proliferation of gay bars. In 1966 he also began to work with the Central City Anti-Poverty Program to improve the city's Tenderloin District. Through the 1960s, because of police crackdowns and urban renewal, a concentration of gay, transgender, and female impersonator bars opened in the Tenderloin. Because this district had also long been a prostitution zone and a place where heterogeneous transgender populations congregated, by the mid-1960s the Tenderloin had become the locus of an emergent transgender movement. In July 1966 a Tenderloin youth organization sponsored by San Francisco's Glide Memorial Methodist Church began to picket Compton's, an all-night cafeteria located at the intersection of Turk and Taylor, because it imposed a twenty-five cent surcharge on its customers. Tenderloin activists claimed that this surcharge was discriminatory and designed to drive away Compton's late-night clientele of gay hustlers, drag queens, and transgender youth. Blackstone attempted to mediate the conflict but was unable to do so, and in August an altercation occurred between drag queens, hair fairies, hustlers, and the police that marks the beginning of transgender activism in San Francisco. After the event, a number of organizations sprung up in San Francisco to help transgender and transsexual individuals negotiate contentious relationships with the police and doctors who often sought to control and limit transsexual lives.

Official Support. Mayor Willie Brown (center, with his left arm holding a line) helps to hang the rainbow flag, symbolizing gay pride, from San Francisco's City Hall on 21 June 1999—an act believed to be unprecedented for a major U.S. city. [AP Photo/Ben Margot]

Two such organizations were COG, Conversion Our Goal, and CATS, the California Association of Transsexuals.

From 1969

The transgender movement that took off in the late 1960s can be seen as part of a culture of resistance that dovetailed with the antiwar and third world liberation movements that characterized those years. Similarly, the gay liberation movement in San Francisco was as much a product of student and antiwar activism as it was a manifestation of the homophile movements that preceded it. Historian Justin Suran argues that early gay liberation activism in San Francisco stemmed from University of California at Berkeley's student movements against the war. In 1969 the Bay Area's first gay liberation group, the Committee for Homosexual Freedom, picketed the company that fired U.C. Berkeley student Gale Whitington after he came out of the closet in a student newspaper. Coming out of the closet was an important aspect of San Francisco's gay liberation movement, as were pickets, publishing, and public demonstrations. In fact, gay liber-

ation activists played a visible role in the 1969 San Francisco protest observing the national Vietnam Day Moratorium. In 1970 gay liberationists picketed and disrupted the San Francisco meetings of the American Psychiatric Association, angry that psychiatrists perpetuated the notion of homosexuality as a mental disorder requiring psychiatric intervention. Through the 1970s other gay liberation groups, including chapters of the Gay Liberation Front and the Gay Activists Alliance, sprung up in San Francisco and played an active role in defining a more militant and publicly visible LGBT community.

During this period, gay men and lesbians did not always see eye to eye, and lesbian feminist organizations began to separate from gay liberation groups. Some lesbian activists, under the influence of the women's movement, argued that lesbians faced different oppressions than did gay men, and others began to argue that gender oppression was at the root of both gay and women's oppressions. Some lesbians continued to engage directly in gay activist groups. For instance, lesbians and gay men worked together in California to defeat the 1978 Briggs Initiative, which would have banned gays and lesbians from teaching in public schools. But many others left gay activist groups to become involved in lesbian separatist institutions. Olivia Records in Oakland was one of the first record companies to produce what was called womyn's music, and it provided a space for lesbian culture to grow. Lesbian feminist collectives and communal houses also began to cluster in San Francisco's Mission District along Valencia Street, where small craft shops, cafés, and women's bookstores opened through the 1970s and 1980s. Old Wives' Tales, a women's bookstore, opened in 1976 on Valencia Street; the Artemis Café, a women's coffee house, ran from 1977 to the late 1980s, also on Valencia; and lesbian feminists were integral to the founding in 1979 of the Women's Building, a Valencia Street space that became the home to a cross-section of lesbian and feminist organizations.

Perhaps the person most emblematic of the politicization of the gay liberation movement in San Francisco was Harvey Milk, whose political career fueled the development of San Francisco's Castro District. In the early 1970s Castro Street was not known as a gay neighborhood, but by 1977, when Milk was elected to the San Francisco Board of Supervisors, the district had become a gay enclave. Milk first ran for office (unsuccessfully) in 1973 out of his camera store on Castro Street, and on his inauguration day in early 1978, he led a procession of supporters from Castro Street to City Hall, demonstrating the movement of gay issues from the margins to the center of local government. The assassination of Milk and

Mayor George Moscone on 27 November 1978 cut short Milk's promising career but enlivened and consolidated a political movement that demanded justice and civil rights for San Francisco's LGBT communities. Dan White, a disgruntled city supervisor, was responsible for the double murder, and when he was convicted of manslaughter rather than murder, the city exploded in protest. On 21 May 1979 over five thousand protestors stormed City Hall, smashing windows and setting police cars on fire.

Through the 1970s, tens of thousands of gay men and lesbians migrated to San Francisco, and many of them took up residence in the Castro District. Gay culture was at a high point despite frequent gay bashings and periodic bar raids. Gay discos, baths, bookstores, and theaters created an environment where gay men could meet, socialize, and have sexual encounters. Because of the high numbers of gay men in San Francisco and the culture of sexual freedom that had developed there, in the early 1980s it was one of the first cities to notice the mysterious disease initially called GRID, or Gay-Related Immune Deficiency, but which was soon renamed Acquired Immune Deficiency Syndrome (AIDS). AIDS divided San Francisco's gay community into advocates of sexual abstinence (and the closure of gay bathhouses) and those that argued for research funds for AIDS and support and services for people with AIDS. Among the latter were organizations like the San Francisco AIDS Foundation and the Shanti Project. As elected officials ignored the growing epidemic, informational and activist organizations formed, including Cleve Jones's Names Project, which was founded in 1986 in the Castro District, and the AIDS Action Coalition, which was founded in 1987 and spun off to become ACT UP/SF in 1988.

In the 1990s San Francisco remained one of the U.S. urban centers hardest hit by the AIDS epidemic, but the city increasingly became known for its queer cultural expression and as a center of LGBT political clout. Since Harvey Milk's election, San Francisco has been at the forefront of LGBT civil rights legislation. While in office, Milk helped pass a gay rights ordinance to protect gay and lesbian residents from discrimination in housing and employment, and in 1995 San Francisco became one of the first cities in the United States to protect transgender individuals from the same discriminations. In November 1994 city voters passed an ordinance providing domestic partner benefits to city residents, and in June 1997 the San Francisco Board of Supervisors passed a controversial bill requiring companies doing business with San Francisco, including the airlines that fly in and out of San Francisco's International Airport, to provide domestic partner benefits for its employees. In doing so, San Francisco has led the way in stimulating corporate domestic partner benefits. In May 2001 San Francisco's Board of Supervisors voted 9 to 2 to provide medical coverage to city employees seeking sex-reassignment surgeries, becoming the first governmental body in the United States to support the health care needs of transsexuals. Meanwhile, San Francisco has become a tourist destination for LGBT tourists, and gay tourism brings up to $100 million to the city each year. San Francisco has indeed been a uniquely queer town, where a history of lawlessness and sex tourism contributed to the construction of a culture where LGBT residents are taken seriously as an important social and political constituency.

Bibliography

Bérubé, Allan. *Coming Out under Fire: The History of Gay Men and Women in World War Two.* New York: Plume, 1990.

Boyd, Nan Alamilla. "Bodies in Motion: Lesbian and Transsexual Histories." In *A Queer World: The Center for Lesbian and Gay Studies Reader.* Edited by Martin Duberman. New York: New York University Press, 1997.

———. *Wide-Open Town: A History of Queer San Francisco to 1965.* Berkeley: University of California Press, 2003.

D'Emilio, John. *Sexual Politics, Sexual Communities: The Making of a Homosexual Minority in the United States, 1940–1970.* Chicago: University of Chicago Press, 1983.

———. "Gay Politics and Community in San Francisco since World War II." In *Hidden from History: Reclaiming the Gay and Lesbian Past.* Edited by Martin Bauml Duberman, Martha Vicinus, and George Chauncey Jr. New York: New American Library, 1989.

Ginsberg, Allen. *Howl.* In *The Portable Beat Reader.* Edited by Ann Charters. New York: Viking, 1992.

Johnson, Susan Lee. *Roaring Camp: The Social World of the California Gold Rush.* New York: Norton, 2000.

Meeker, Martin. "Behind the Mask of Respectability: Reconsidering the Mattachine Society and Male Homophile Practice, 1950s and 1960s." *Journal of the History of Sexuality* 10, no. 1 (January 2001): 78–116.

Members of the Gay and Lesbian Historical Society of Northern California. "MTF Transgender Activism in the Tenderloin and Beyond, 1966–1975: Commentary and Interview with Elliot Blackstone." *GLQ: A Journal of Gay and Lesbian Studies* 4 (1998): 349–372.

Shilts, Randy. *The Mayor of Castro Street: The Life and Times of Harvey Milk.* New York: St. Martin's Press, 1982.

Stein, Arlene. *Sex and Sensibility: Stories of a Lesbian Generation.* Berkeley: University of California Press, 1997.

Stimpson, Catherine. "The Beat Generation and the Trials of Homosexual Liberation." *Salmagundi* 58–59 (1982–1983): 373–392.

Stryker, Susan, and Jim Van Buskirk. *Gay by the Bay: A History of Queer Culture in the San Francisco Bay Area.* San Francisco: Chronicle Books, 1996.

Suran, Justin David. "Coming Out against the War: Antimilitarism and the Politicization of Homosexuality in the Era of Vietnam." *American Quarterly* 53 (2001): 452–488.

Nan Alamilla Boyd

See also AIDS COALITION TO UNLEASH POWER (ACT UP); AIDS MEMORIAL QUILT—NAMES PROJECT; AIDS SERVICE ORGANIZATIONS; BEAN, BABE; BEATS; BLACK AND WHITE MEN TOGETHER (BWMT); BONNET, JEANNE; BUDDHISTS AND BUDDHISM; BURNS, RANDY; CALL, HAL; CAMERON, BARBARA; CHRYSTOS; CHUNG, MARGARET; COMEDY AND HUMOR; DAUGHTERS OF BILITIS; DRAG QUEENS AND KINGS; GIDLOW, ELSA; GINSBERG, ALLEN; GRAHN, JUDY; HAY, HARRY; JEWS AND JUDAISM; KEPNER, JAMES; KLUMPKE, ANNA; *LADDER*; LAWRENCE, LOUISE; LIQUOR CONTROL LAW AND POLICY; LYON, PHYLLIS, AND DEL MARTIN; MATTACHINE REVIEW; MATTACHINE SOCIETY; MAUPIN, ARMISTEAD; MILK, HARVEY; OLIVEROS, PAULINE; OLIVIA RECORDS; POMA, EDGAR; PRESTON, JOHN; PRINCE, VIRGINIA; QUEER NATION; RIGGS, MARLON; RIGHTS OF ASSOCIATION AND ASSEMBLY; SAMOIS; SARRIA, JOSÉ; SEX CLUBS; SOCIETY FOR INDIVIDUAL RIGHTS; STEIN, GERTRUDE, AND ALICE B. TOKLAS; SULLIVAN, LOU; TRANS ORGANIZATIONS AND PERIODICALS; WITTMAN, CARL; WOO, MERLE.

SÁNCHEZ, Luis Rafael (b. 17 November 1936), writer.

Luis Rafael Sánchez Ortiz was born into a family of humble means in the eastern coastal town of Humacao in Puerto Rico. In the late 1940s, his family moved to the capital city of San Juan as part of the great social shifts generated by the state-sponsored industrialization process that transformed the Caribbean island. Sánchez went to live with relatives in the old quarter and studied within the newly reformed public education system. He graduated from high school in 1956 and started his college education at the Río Piedras campus of the University of Puerto Rico, majoring in drama.

His college years, as well as his intense encounter with the modern dynamics of San Juan, were crucial to Sánchez's early formation as a writer. He became part of the university's theater companies, participating in stage productions as well as acting. Acting was indeed Sánchez's first vocation. During his high school years, he had worked as a soap opera actor for several radio stations, where he became familiar with the development of dramatic plots and characters and sensitive to the use and modulations of the voice.

However, with the arrival of television in Puerto Rico in 1954, Sánchez soon found his acting career blocked because television producers deemed that the physical appearance of the young, handsome mulatto actor did not meet the standards of white beauty. Cut off from this valuable source of livelihood, Sánchez found an alternative venue for his artistic passion in the university's troupes, encouraged by one of the pioneers of modern Puerto Rican theater, director Victoria Espinosa.

Under the guidance of an eminent professor, Robert Lewis, he also studied and benefited from the theoretical innovations of playwrights Luigi Pirandello and Bertolt Brecht. Sanchez's first plays date from this period: *La espera* (The Waiting, 1958), an attempt to engage surrealism and the fantastic, modeled on the works of Federico García Lorca; *Cuento de cucarachita viuda* (Story of a Widowed Little Cockroach, 1959), a children's play based on a well-known Hispanic folktale; and *La farsa del amor compradito* (Farce of a Little Love for Sale, 1960), an experimental diversion in which he creolized the characters of the commedia dell'arte and sharply juxtaposed farce and drama.

In 1959, while still a student, Sánchez received a summer grant to study creative writing at Columbia University. This was his first encounter with the modern metropolis and the beginning of an unending love affair with New York City. He returned in 1962 to obtain an M.A. from New York University. During this time, he attended playwriting workshops at the Actor's Studio, established an important friendship with James Baldwin, and witnessed the emergence of the U.S. civil rights movement. He has continued to travel regularly to New York City, serving as distinguished visiting professor at the City University of New York.

For Sánchez, the 1960s marked his consecration as one of the most important writers in Puerto Rico. In 1962, he premiered, under the title *Sol 13, Interior* (13 Sun Street), two short plays devoted to the representation of marginalized characters in the slums of Old San Juan: *Los ángeles se han fatigado* (The Angels Are Exhausted), a two-act monologue of a mad prostitute; and *La hiel nuestra de cada día* (Our Daily Bitterness), a one-act play staging the desolate relationship of an older couple who have been led toward death and madness by the trials of poverty.

Unlike his earlier works, Sánchez embraced a poetically realist aesthetic in these plays and made the pitfalls of Puerto Rican colonial modernization the explicit subject of his theatrical meditations. These works achieved remarkable critical success and were quickly followed by two other highly acclaimed pieces: *O casi el alma* (A Miracle for Maggie), a metaphysical drama staged in 1964, and the most celebrated of all, *La pasión según Antígona Pérez* (The Passion According to Antigone Pérez, 1968), a rewriting of Sophocles's *Antigone* featuring a Latin American revolutionary besieged by a military dictator. As if overwhelmed by and wary of his own success, Sánchez did not stage or publish another play for more than fifteen years—with the exception of *Parábola del andarín* (Parable of the Wanderer, 1979)—until the premiere of his internationally renowned *Quíntuples* (Quintuplets) in 1984. This highly experimental piece features one of the few openly lesbian characters in Latin American drama.

Sánchez's literary reputation was further cemented by the publication in 1966 of his pioneering collection of short stories, *En cuerpo de camisa* (Shirtless), which included the first empathetic representation of a male homosexual character in Puerto Rican literature (in the story "¡Jum!"). The collection's highly poetic and theatrical stories address questions of urban marginality and disenfranchisement, and signal what is the most salient characteristic of Sánchez's mature prose: the aestheticization of orality through the intense elaboration of Puerto Rican popular Spanish as the privileged raw material for his writing. Not designed to be read in silence, these stories demand to be recited aloud to the cadences of bodily movement. The prose is pure musicality, infused with Caribbean rhythms, and it anticipates the forms of textuality that later led Sánchez to achieve resounding international recognition with the publication of his two novels: *La guaracha del Macho Camacho* (Macho Camacho's Beat) in 1976 and *La importancia de llamarse Daniel Santos* (The Importance of Being Daniel Santos) in 1988.

Sánchez is also an essayist, and at the center of his reflections are the questions of Puerto Rican cultural identity and the island's political future. Some of his essays have been collected in the volumes *La guagua aérea* (The Flying Bus, 1994) and *No llores por nosotros, Puerto Rico* (Don't Cry for Us, Puerto Rico, 1997). In 1969 he became professor of literature at the University of Puerto Rico. He received his Ph.D. from the Universidad Complutense de Madrid, Spain, in 1976, and has been awarded numerous prestigious fellowships and awards, including the Guggenheim.

Bibliography

Díaz-Quiñones, Arcadio. "Introducción." In Luis Rafael Sánchez, *La guaracha del Macho Camacho*. Madrid, Spain: Cátedra, 1977: 11–73.

Hernández Vargas, Nélida, and Daisy Caraballo Abreu, eds. *Luis Rafael Sánchez: Crítica y bibliografía*. Río Piedras, Puerto Rico: Editorial de la Universidad de Puerto Rico, 1985.

Lugo-Ortiz, Agnes. "Community at its Limits: Silence, Orality, Law, and the Homosexual Body in Luis Rafael Sánchez's '¡Jum!'" In *¿Entiendes? Queer Readings, Hispanic Writings*. Edited by Emily Bergmann and Paul Julian Smith. Durham, N.C.: Duke University Press, 1995: 115–136.

Sánchez, Luis Rafael. *La guagua aérea*. Río Piedras, Puerto Rico: Editorial Cultural, 1994.

———. *No llores por nosotros, Puerto Rico*. Hanover, N.H.: Ediciones del Norte, 1997.

Agnes Lugo-Ortiz

See also PUERTO RICO.

SARRIA, José (b. 12 December 1923), activist and performer.

A pioneering LGBT social activist and the founder of the Royal Court System (RCS), recently renamed the International Court System (ICS), José Sarria is also known as "Her Royal Majesty, Empress José the First" and the "Widow Norton."

Born to Latino parents, Maria Dolores and Julio Sarria, José Sarria was raised in San Francisco. He joined the army in 1942, was trained as a cook at Fort Ord, and spent two years in Berlin at the end of World War II as a personal attaché to a colonel. He was discharged in 1947 but stayed in the reserves until his mid-thirties.

After leaving the army, Sarria returned to San Francisco and shortly thereafter became employed at the Black Cat Cafe first as a cocktail waiter, then as a social hostess, and eventually as a female impersonator (and bar icon) doing parodies of operas. While not a gay bar in a contemporary sense, the Black Cat was widely known as a bohemian hangout where people with different sexual sensibilities were accepted and often admired. Sarria very much considered the Black Cat a place where he could be himself and had an agreement with the owner that he would perform only there (exceptions were made for charitable events). He worked there from 1947 until the bar lost its liquor license and closed in 1964.

Rejecting what he saw as the secretive focus of the Mattachine Society—many of its members remained closeted and used fictitious names—Sarria and his friends created the League for Civil Education in 1960. This was a grassroots civil rights group that set out to educate both LGBT and non-LGBT people about police raids and to provide emergency funds to those being discriminated against. As a founding member of this group, and in response to continued efforts to revoke the Black Cat's liquor license and to the harassment of other LGBT-owned businesses, Sarria became the first openly gay candidate for elected office in the United States. In 1961 he ran for a seat on the San Francisco Board of Supervisors.

José Sarria. The self-proclaimed "Empress José the First" (and the "Widow Norton"), he ran in 1961 (unsuccessfully) as the first openly gay candidate for elected office in the United States, and four years later he founded the Royal Court System (now the International Court System). [**Rick Gerharter Photography**]

Sarria lost the election and it would not be until 1977 that an openly gay individual (Harvey Milk) would finally win a seat on the board.

In 1963 the League for Civil Education split over internal conflicts and Sarria helped found a new group called the Society for Individual Rights (SIR). Monies for the SIR were largely raised from staging drag shows, such as the "Celebritycapades," with these funds often being used to help people with legal problems. Both the educational and the charitable foci of these groups became important aspects of the RCS, founded by Sarria just a few years later.

In 1964 the Tavern Guild, an association of LGBT bars, at its annual Beaux Arts Ball held every Halloween conferred upon Sarria the honorary title of "Queen of the Ball." Apparently the title was not regal enough for him—after all, being a queen in this context was somewhat common—so he declared himself "Empress José the First." This would become the RCS's first official position. To support further his status of empress, and reflecting

the importance of camp in the RCS/ICS, Sarria added the subtitle of the "Widow Norton." Joshua Norton lived in San Francisco during the Gold Rush. Once a prominent merchant in the community, he had fallen on economic hard times and began referring to himself as "Joshua Norton the First, Emperor of North America and Protector of Mexico." Whereas many cities would have ignored his proclamation, the media and the leaders and citizens of San Francisco found him quite amusing and literally treated him like royalty, providing him with free meals wherever he went and a yearly clothing stipend from the city. Emperor Norton died around the turn of the twentieth century and was buried in Woodlawn Cemetery. Sarria, the loving Widow Norton, holds an annual memorial service for his departed "husband" every year. Beginning in the early 1980s, the annual service became a more somber event and also started to be a memorial for all those lost to AIDS in the court community.

The Royal Court System was officially founded in 1965 and represents one of the oldest LGBTQ groups in the world still in existence. Today ICS is made up of sixty-five local chapters called courts (57) and baronies (8). Positions in these local chapters and throughout the court system are designated by campy titles such as empress, emperor, princess, prince, duchess, and duke. Titleholders are expected to dress their gendered parts replete with typically regal attire and appropriate accouterments (e.g., tiaras, scepters, gowns, tuxedos).

With a few notable exceptions, most female titles are held by gay drag queens while male titles are held by both gay men and lesbian women. Those holding the female titles, especially that of empress, often are the most powerful and are promoted as the leaders of the given court. While lesbian women have traditionally participated in the court in much smaller numbers than gay men, many gay court members have died from AIDS over the past fifteen years, and lesbians today seem to be taking on a more prominent role in some of the courts.

Consistent with its beginnings, each court serves as a charitable organization for those in need in the community (both LGBT and straight). Today, many of the monies raised go toward various organizations associated with AIDS. Drag shows are the primary place where money is collected (often a single dollar at a time given to the performers while on stage). The ICS raises millions of dollars each year and is one of the most successful charities, either LGBT or non-LGBT, in many communities.

In spite of the frequent rejection of drag queens by more conservative members of various gay and lesbian communities, the ICS has served as a vitally important lifeline to many LGBT people in cities throughout North America and now Great Britain.

Bibliography

Gorman, Michael R. *The Empress is a Man: Stories from the Life of José Sarria.* New York: Harrington Park Press, 1998.

International Court System. http://impcourt.org

Rosenberg, Robert, John Scagliotti, and Greta Schiller. *Before Stonewall.* New York: First Run Features, 1984.

Steven P. Schacht

See also COMEDY AND HUMOR; DRAG QUEENS AND KINGS; HOMOPHILE MOVEMENT; ELECTORAL POLITICS; THEATER AND PERFORMANCE; TRANSSEXUALS, TRANSVESTITES, TRANSGENDER PEOPLE, AND CROSS-DRESSERS.

SARTON, May (b. 3 May 1912; d. 16 July 1995), writer.

Eleanore Marie Sarton (anglicized, May Sarton) was born in Wondelgem, Belgium. An only child, she moved to England in 1914 and then to the United States in 1916 with her parents, George Alfred Leon and Eleanor Mabel Sarton. The migration of the Sarton family to England and the United States corresponded with the outbreak of World War I and was an effort to escape the German invasion of Belgium. In the United States, George Sarton, a science historian, became an instructor at Harvard University. Soon thereafter, in Boston, Massachusetts, at the age of ten, May Sarton became a naturalized U.S. citizen.

From her mother, Sarton developed a love for life, art, and creativity. In 1929, she joined Eva Le Gallienne's Civic Repertory Theatre in New York. When this group dissolved in 1933, Sarton began the Associated Actors Theatre, which was her venue for creative expression through the early 1930s. During these acting and theater years, *Poetry* magazine accepted four of Sarton's poems for publication. By the late 1930s, Sarton was crossing over artistic disciplines, for the rest of her life committing herself to creative expression through many genres of writing: poetry, fiction, nonfiction, letters, and screenplays. Sarton's first volume of poetry, *Encounter in April*, was published in 1937 and marked the beginning of a lifelong dedication to prolific authorship. At her death in 1995, Sarton had authored fifteen books of poetry, fourteen novels, one drama, several screenplay adaptations, ten journals, two children's books, a "selected" multigenre anthology, and one collection of essays on writing.

Critical responses to Sarton's writing have been guarded at best from genre scholars, but praising and celebratory from feminist scholars. In particular, her novel *Mrs. Stevens Hears the Mermaids Singing* (1965) resulted in a cult following that identified with her feminist and lesbian themes. In this semi-autobiographical novel, Sarton displays two feminist situations in particular: a woman situated as literary subject and a central "coming out" theme. As this book earned an enthusiastic and popular following of readers, genre critics irresponsibly claimed it to be a sign of her mediocrity.

Early in her career, few critics defended Sarton's poetic craft. However, as early as 1939, Basil de Selincourt, a literary critic for the London *Observer*, wrote against the tide, acknowledging that "intense experience . . . underlies and unifies [her poems and] has engendered an uncompromising determination to forge and refine the tool for its expression, a tool which is . . . deep-searching to the point of ruthlessness, and very delicate." Finally, in 1976, the renowned poetry critic Marjorie Perloff put May Sarton on the map in a review essay "Tradition and the Individual Talent" for the *Southern Humanities Review*. Despite Perloff's mention of Sarton's penchant for "turn[ing] personal suffering into hollow rhetoric," she touts Sarton's authentic contribution to women's writing, politics, and cultures: "these lines [of poetry] could well serve as epigraph for a contemporary Feminist manifesto. Here, as in her strange novel *Mrs. Stevens Hears the Mermaids Singing*, Sarton was, in a sense, ahead of her time."

In 1969, Sarton penned a groundbreaking work in the genre of women's life writing in *Plant Dreaming Deep*. In this memoir, Sarton writes about her years of self-discovery spurred by the solitude that followed buying a home in Nelson, New Hampshire. In exquisite prose, Sarton captures the details of a woman's chosen life of solitude, using the theme of home as a metaphor for a life of meditation, attention, dailiness and reflection. She begins with soul-searching questions: "if 'home' can be found anywhere, how is one to look for it, where is one to find it?" Through these inquiries, explicated through a chronicling of ordinary encounters with neighbors, the subtle and dramatic shifts in seasons, the delight and disappointment of writing and gardening in Nelson, Sarton comes to conclude, "we have to make myths out of our lives; it is the only way to live them without despair."

Since the "self-study" of *Plant Dreaming Deep*, Sarton has been considered a pioneer of women's life writing in her journals. Even in her revision of *Plant Dreaming Deep, Journal of a Solitude* (1973), Sarton maintains focus on an inward journey that contemplates women, creativity, imposed exile, and suffering. Her late-in-life journals, *At Seventy* (1984), and *Encore: A Journal of the Eightieth Year* (1993), and poetry, *Coming into Eighty* (1994), demonstrate, arguably, a surprising and authentic contemplation of aging as an arrival into a wholeness of the self and an affecting domestication of spirituality.

Bibiography

Bloom, Harold. *Women Memoirists*, vol. 2. Philadelphia: Chelsea House, 1998.

Blouin, Lenora. "'The Stern Growth of a Lyric Poet': May Sarton, Writing Poetry/Writing about Poetry and Major Critical Responses to Sarton's Poetry—A Bibliographic Survey." *Bulletin of Bibliography* 57, no. 4 (2000): 191–206.

Eder, Doris. "Woman Writer: May Sarton's *Mrs. Stevens Hears the Mermaids Singing.*" *International Journal of Women's Studies* 1 (1978): 150–158.

Fulk, Mark. *Understanding May Sarton.* Columbia: University of South Carolina Press, 2001.

Gussow, Mel. "An Obituary." *The New York Times*, 18 July 1995, B12.

Heilbrun, Carolyn G. "Introduction." In *Mrs. Stevens Hears the Mermaids Singing.* New York: Norton, 1965.

Mannocchi, Phyllis F. "May Sarton." *NWSA Journal* 7, no. 1 (1995): 131–137.

Perloff, Marjorie. "Tradition and the Individual Talent." *Southern Humanities Review* 10 (1976): 269–276.

Shelley, Dolores. "A Conversation with May Sarton." *Women & Literature* 7, no. 2 (1979): 33–41.

Swartzlander, Susan, and Marilyn Mumford. *The Great Sanity: Critical Essays on May Sarton.* Ann Arbor: University of Michigan Press, 1995.

Taylor, Henry. "Home to a Place Beyond Exile: The Collected Poems of May Sarton." *The Hollins Critic* 11, no. 3 (1974): 1–16.

MaryJo Mahoney

SEATTLE

Seattle, which by the year 2000 had become a metropolitan area with 2.5 million residents, was founded in the winter of 1851–1852. By 1900 it was a major West Coast port and the staging ground for the Alaska and Yukon gold fields. At this time, large numbers of loggers, prospectors, sailors, and fishermen from various racial and ethnic communities regularly passed through the city's Skid Road lodging district. They supported a thriving male sex trade that, in the 1910s, drew the attention of authorities concerned about the large number of local youths who participated in it. In these years middle-class gay men also made Seattle their home; several were arrested in connection with a scandal that enveloped

Portland, Oregon. Little is known of Seattle's pre-1930s lesbian history, but in the early 1890s Alice B. Toklas and her family resided there and Toklas attended local schools, including the University of Washington. The transgendered Harry Allen Livingston also lived in Seattle in the early 1900s (see sidebar).

Pioneer Square, wedged between Skid Road and the business district, emerged as Seattle's first gay space. By the mid-1960s, nearly 90 percent of the city's gay bars were located there. The Casino, which opened in 1934, was among the earliest. Military installations and the shipbuilding and aircraft industries transformed Seattle during World War II as they attracted thousands to the city. The Olympic Hotel's Marine Room became a place to pick up officers; enlisted men were available throughout the city, but the South End Steam Baths became a favored cruising ground. After the war, gay bars such as the Captain's Room and the elegant Mocambo lounge opened. Lesbian refuges included the Grand Union and the Madison. By 1955 the 318 Tavern was sponsoring a

harry allen livingston (born nell pickerell), 1882–1922

Born in Indiana, Pickerell worked on the family farm as a girl, plowing and doing other general tasks. By 1895 she had moved with her parents to Seattle, where she married while in her teens. Pickerell soon had a son and found herself a single mother. To support herself and her child, Pickerell cropped short her hair, donned male clothing, and took the name Harry Allen Livingston. As a man, Livingston worked as a farm laborer, a logger, a longshoreman, a bartender, a truck driver, and a cowboy in various parts of the Pacific Northwest. Some accounts claim, as did one from 1912, that Livingston had "an almost insane mania for making love to girls, when dressed in men's clothing" (Lola G. Baldwin Papers). Reportedly, several young women who had fallen in love with Livingston committed suicide when learning that their paramour had the body of a female. As a man, Livingston was arrested several times in Seattle, Spokane, and Portland. Mostly these were for petty crimes, but in Portland in 1912 she was arrested on suspicion of white slavery: Livingston had recently brought a known sex worker, Isabelle Maxwell, to Oregon from Washington State. By the time of his death in Seattle in 1922, Livingston was well-known throughout the Pacific Northwest, so well that the *Seattle Post-Intelligencer* (28 December 1922) ran a several-paragraph obituary that recounted the highlights of his life.

lesbian softball team. Gays, lesbians, and straights mixed at the Garden of Allah. Touted as one of the first gay-owned bars in the nation, its main staple was female impersonation. It operated from 1946 until 1956, when interest waned and McCarthy-era pressures increased.

Political Activism

Although the Mattachine Society encouraged organizing in the Seattle area as early as 1959, sustained political activism began in January 1967, just months after local police had declared that Seattle homosexuals were "out of hand." In January, gay merchants formed the Dorian Society. The Dorians fought the payoff system in which local authorities demanded bribes from gay bars to prevent their being raided by the police. The Dorians also hosted the Second Western Regional Homophile Organization Conference in December 1967, and in the summer of 1969 opened the Dorian House, a professionally staffed counseling center for homosexuals and transgender people. The Dorians also convened drag balls that grew into the Imperial Court in 1971. *The Dorian Columns* newsletter announced in September 1969 that Seattle was the only city in the country where federal funds supported transsexual operations. One of the Dorians' most daring accomplishments was the featuring of member Peter Wichern on the cover of the November 1967 issue of *Seattle* magazine.

Post-Stonewall activism included Seattle's first Gay Day, on 10 May 1970, which coincided with the formation of a local Gay Liberation Front. That same year the University of Washington's Gay Students Alliance formed. In early 1971 the Lesbian Resource Center opened. More than thirty years later, it was still operating and was the oldest such service in the United States. Also in 1971 the Dorian Society transformed into the Seattle Gay Alliance and unveiled the city's first Gay Community Center, which opened on 15 September in Pioneer Square. Stonewall, a residential treatment center for those suffering from addictions, operated between 1971 and 1976. It also began the Whitman Center, a halfway house for gay parolees. In 1972 the Gay Mother's Legal and Research Fund was founded. The *Gay Community News* appeared in 1974, became the *Seattle Gay News* in 1976, and was still publishing at the century's turn. Seattle's first gay march occurred in 1974 and three years later the mayor officially declared the last week of June as Gay Pride Week. In 1975 a new Dorian Group incorporated and became Washington's largest gay civil rights and public education organization. The Seattle Men's Chorus began in 1979. The Metropolitan Community Church held its first service in Seattle on 21 May 1972. Nine years

Seattle. Dykes on Bikes lead the thirteenth annual Gay Pride Parade—part of the officially recognized yearly Gay Pride Week—in the city's Capitol Hill district, on 30 June 1996. [AP Photo/Elaine Thompson]

later the lesbian and gay Tikvah Chadashah Jewish congregation was founded.

Troubles and Triumphs

An increase in police harassment in the early 1970s is attributable to backlash against open gay activism in Seattle but also to urban renewal plans to transform Pioneer Square into a tourist area. Gays fled to Capitol Hill, a business and residential district near downtown that had recently declined because of the routing of the I-5 Freeway. Three decades later, gay organizations and businesses flourish there. Large numbers of lesbians historically concentrated in the University neighborhood, where several of their associations emerged in the Stonewall era.

AIDS hit Seattle hard. Its first reported case was diagnosed in 1982. By late 1995 some 3,400 Washingtonians had died. In response, the Gay Men's Health Crisis in 1983 created the "buddy network," which grew into the Chicken Soup Brigade. The Northwest AIDS Foundation began in 1984. Other organizations and institutions involved in the AIDS struggle included People of Color

seattle's gay rights meet conservatism

As has been the case for sexual minorities in other American cities and states, since the late 1970s those living in Seattle and Washington State have seen their positions jeopardized by conservative efforts to repeal local and state protective ordinances and statutes and to replace them with antigay laws. The first such conservative move against Seattle's gays and lesbians came in the 1970s as part of the national reaction that Anita Bryant launched in Dade County, Florida. In this period other local jurisdictions (including Dade County; St. Paul, Minnesota; Eugene, Oregon; and Wichita, Kansas) saw the repeal of recently passed local ordinances protecting sexual minorities. In 1978 two Seattle police officers formed Save Our Moral Ethics (SOME) and filed a petition, soon known as Initiative 13, to repeal the 1973 employment and 1975 fair housing ordinances. During the campaign, SOME received funds from Bryant's Protect America's Children organization. In response, lesbians and gays organized various groups, including Citizens to Retain Fair Employment, the Seattle Committee Against Thirteen (SCAT), and Women Against Thirteen (WAT). They also formed alliances across the city and eventually received support from various local officials, mainstream churches, the National Organization of Women, the League of Women Voters, and the Young Women's Christian Association. After a rancorous several months, in November 1978 Seattle residents went to the polls and voted down Proposition 13 by 63 to 37 percent. Practically speaking, this was a major victory for gays and lesbians at the local level and affirmed Seattle's progressive spirit. But it was also significant at the national level for giving hope to sexual minorities elsewhere.

In the early 1990s, gays and lesbians in Seattle and across the state of Washington went on the offensive in forming Hands Off Washington (HOW) to counter the growing strength of conservative groups, particularly the Oregon Citizens' Alliance, that began proposing antigay laws across the Pacific Northwest. HOW's strength came from its broad appeal to diverse groups, reaching out to minorities of all types and making sure to include men and women as well as rural and urban people. In 1994 and 1995 these organizing efforts prevented four antigay initiatives from even making it onto statewide ballots. Feeling confident, in 1997 HOW introduced its own initiative, designed to protect sexual minorities in employment across Washington. Although the initiative made it onto the ballot, Washingtonians turned it down by a vote of 60 to 40 percent. In Kings County, where Seattle is located, voters also rejected the proposal by a very narrow margin, with 49.7 percent voting yes and 50.3 percent voting no.

Against AIDS Network and ACT UP. The Bailey-Boushay House, a thirty-five-bed nursing center and hospice, opened in 1992.

Ironically, despite police harassment in the early 1970s, Seattle emerged as one of the most progressive cities on gay rights. In September 1973 it became the first major American municipality to prohibit discrimination against gays in all public and private employment. Two years later, the city protected sexual minorities in its Fair Housing Code. In 1984 Seattle adopted an ordinance making physical assault and verbal harassment of lesbians and gays a criminal offense. A year later the mayor appointed the Lesbian/Gay Task Force. It achieved full commission status in 1989. In March 1990 Seattle became the largest American municipality to provide same-sex domestic partner benefits for city employees. The next year Sherry Harris was elected Seattle's first African American lesbian council member. So strong have Seattle and Washington State's commitment to progressivism been on gay issues (see sidebar) that both the city and the state have on several occasions between the 1970s and 1990s rejected anti-gay ballot measures.

Bibliography

Atkins, Gary L. *Gay Seattle: Stories of Exile and Belonging.* Seattle: University of Washington Press, 2003.

Boag, Peter. *Same-Sex Affairs: Constructing and Controlling Homosexuality in the Pacific Northwest.* Berkeley: University of California Press, 2003.

Jeske, Timothy David. "Collective Action and the AIDS Epidemic: Seattle's Gay and Lesbian Community." Ph.D. dissertation, University of Washington, 1993.

Lola G. Baldwin Papers, Portland Police Department's Women's Auxiliary Reports, June 9, 1912. Portland Police Museum, Portland, Oregon.

Marcus, Eric. *Making History: The Struggle for Gay and Lesbian Equal Rights, 1945–1990.* New York: HarperCollins, 1992.

Martinac, Paula. *The Queerest Places: A National Guide to Gay and Lesbian Historic Sites.* New York: Holt, 1997.

Mesec, Rose. "A Gender and Space Analysis of Seattle's Lesbian and Gay Communities." Master's thesis, University of Washington, 1992.

Paulson, Don, with Roger Simpson. *An Evening at the Garden of Allah: A Gay Cabaret in Seattle.* New York: Columbia University Press, 1996.

Peter Boag

See also CAGE, JOHN; KOPAY, DAVID; STEIN, GERTRUDE, AND ALICE B. TOKLAS.

SENSION, Nicholas (b. circa 1622?; d. 1689), colonist.

Nicholas Sension arrived in Windsor, Connecticut, around 1640 and married in 1645. He became a prominent and prosperous member of his community. Sension's marriage produced no children, which was unusual in colonial New England. His life appears to have been otherwise unexceptional save in one regard: in 1677 he appeared before the General Court of Connecticut, charged with sodomy. It became clear during the course of his trial that Sension had been making sexual overtures toward men in and around Windsor since the 1640s. The unusually detailed transcripts that survive from Sension's trial are revealing in several respects, not least the relative impunity with which he pursued local men for many years. Sension's sexual interest in men was apparently well known, and he had a reputation for being sexually aggressive that made at least some of his neighbors nervous. Town elders investigated his behavior and reprimanded him informally on two occasions; each of these investigations was prompted by complaints from the relatives of young men propositioned by Sension. Yet no formal action was taken against him until 1677.

Although there were those in and around Windsor who had long condemned Sension's advances toward local men, the town as a whole seems to have been remarkably tolerant of his behavior. Sension's popularity among his neighbors doubtless worked in his favor. The depositions against Sension express no hostility toward the accused save in regard to his sexual behavior. His status as one of the town's wealthiest householders would also have shielded him to some degree. Reluctance to disrupt community life by taking formal action against an established citizen and employer may well have counterbalanced disapproval of Sension's sexual proclivities. In general, New England communities preferred to handle problematic behavior through informal channels, turning to the often intractable legal system only as a last resort. Addressing a situation such as this in a manner that did not necessitate going to court would also have appealed to those who disapproved of Sension's behavior but did not want him to hang.

In addition there may have been townsfolk who did not recognize or label Sension's behavior as specifically sodomitical. Most of the men whom he approached were much younger than he; some were his own servants. Sexual aggression by a householder toward a male or female servant could be understood in terms of a master asserting his prerogative over a subordinate rather than as a distinct sexual issue. Given that Sension's advances often occurred in the context of a recognized hierarchical relationship, some observers may have reacted to his behavior as an abuse of his authority rather than separating the sexual offense from its relational context. Indeed the second local investigation of Sension's behavior focused on whether Nathaniel Pond, a servant repeatedly propositioned by Sension, had been mistreated and therefore deserved compensation.

That Sension was able to pursue his interest in men for several decades and not be prosecuted until 1677 suggests that seventeenth-century New Englanders were a good deal more pragmatic in their responses to illicit behavior than official doctrine would lead one to expect. Ministers condemned sodomy as an "unnatural" and "defiling" sin that should be punished severely. Yet ordinary colonists were in general much more concerned about the mundane interests of their communities than with moral absolutes. The community's change of heart toward Sension in the late 1670s seems to have originated with the death of Pond. Much of Sension's sexual interest had until then been focused on this young man, but in 1675 Pond was killed in an Indian war, after which Sension's advances toward other men became more frequent. The disruption and discomfort caused by these advances evidently outweighed Sension's worth as a citizen, providing his enemies with ammunition that secured the support, however reluctant, of previously loyal neighbors.

The testimony presented at Sension's trial suggests that the ways in which some colonists interpreted sexual impulses and behavior also departed from official doctrine. Ministers taught that all sinful thoughts and deeds, sexual and nonsexual, were caused by the innate corruption of fallen humanity; everyone inherited that corruption and so had the potential to commit any sin. Modern notions of sexuality and sexual orientation had no place in their ideological framework. Yet witnesses against Sension clearly recognized in him a persistent and specific attraction toward members of the same sex. Sension himself characterized his advances toward men as a distinct realm of activity: he apparently referred to such overtures as his "trade," meaning a calling or way of life, albeit an unwelcome one that he prayed God to release him from. This is not to argue that Sension or his neighbors identified in his behavior a distinct sexual orientation, but they did clearly recognize a consistent impulse that transcended specific acts. Empirical observation would seem to have been a more powerful an influence than official ideology in shaping local responses to Sension's behavior.

New England courts defined sex specifically as an act of intercourse and could convict in sexual cases only if there was clear proof that copulation had taken place; neither intention nor an unsuccessful attempt would suffice. Sodomy was a capital offense and so either confession or at least two independent witnesses were required for a conviction. Fortunately for Sension, only one witness claimed to have seen him actually penetrate another man; Sension himself denied having sodomized anyone. Therefore he could be found guilty only of attempted sodomy. Sension was whipped, shamed in public (he was made to stand under the gallows with a rope around his neck), and disenfranchised. His entire estate was placed in bond for his good behavior.

Bibliography

Godbeer, Richard. *Sexual Revolution in Early America.* Baltimore: Johns Hopkins University Press, 2002.

Katz, Jonathan Ned. *Gay/Lesbian Almanac: A New Documentary.* New York: Harper and Row, 1983.

Richard Godbeer

SEX ACTS

Although same-sex sexual activity is well-documented cross-culturally and throughout human history, wherever these sexual practices are stigmatized, details about the frequency of particular acts or the meanings assigned to them by participants is difficult to obtain. In early American history, information about same-sex sexual acts must be gleaned primarily from legal records. Vague language such as "sodomy" or "the infamous crime against nature" prevails. And the reliance on legal documents skews the sexual record toward individuals engaged in illegal activities such as same-sex prostitution or nonconsensual sex. Prior to the establishment of sexology, information about same-sex sexual acts also appeared in psychiatric case studies that provided in-depth information about a particular individual, but could not be generalized. The popularity of one sex act versus another can vary a great deal in different cultures, or during different historical periods. For instance, one response to the AIDS pandemic has been a waning in the popularity of anal sex among gay men, while a stated preference for oral sex has increased.

Kinsey Shocks America

In 1948 Alfred C. Kinsey and his associates published *Sexual Behavior in the Human Male,* a study of about 5,300 American men which revealed that 37 percent of the sample had had at least one homosexual experience leading to orgasm between the beginning of adolescence

and old age. Among unmarried men up to age thirty-five, that figure reached almost exactly 50 percent. Nearly 10 percent of married men between the ages of sixteen to twenty-five had had homosexual experiences leading to orgasm. Approximately 10 percent of all males were more or less exclusively homosexual, 4 percent being so throughout their lives.

In 1953 the companion volume, *Sexual Behavior in the Human Female,* provided equally controversial information regarding lesbianism. By age thirty, 25 percent of all females interviewed had recognized some form of erotic response to other females. By age forty, 19 percent had made specifically sexual contact with another female. Overt lesbian contact to the point of orgasm among women was 13 percent. Kinsey found that only one-half to one-third as many women were homosexual as men. From 2 to 6 percent of unmarried women, less than 1 percent of married women, and from 1 to 6 percent of previously married (divorced or widowed) women between the ages of twenty and thirty-five were exclusively homosexual.

The Kinsey reports came under attack by conservatives who were appalled by what they perceived as their advocacy of sexual immorality. The researchers themselves were also accused of engaging in deviant sexual conduct. More measured critiques have been made by sexologists who point out that Kinsey did not use probability samples, which means his respondents are not representative of the general population. These sex researchers also object to interview techniques which varied from one respondent to another.

While the Kinsey data on incidence of homosexual activity leading to orgasm are exhaustive, there is much less information in both volumes about how these orgasms were produced. Among homosexual men who had been stimulated anally (through penetration of the anus with fingers, sex toys, or the penis), these researchers found only a few who were particularly aroused, and only an occasional individual who was brought to orgasm, by such techniques. About 30 percent of the male population who had been brought to climax at least once by another male had had some type of oral relation. Kinsey found that such experimentation was much more common for men during adolescence.

The Kinsey team reported that homosexual contacts were highly effective in bringing the female to orgasm. It was also noted that 71 percent of women with any homosexual contact had restricted that activity to one or two partners. Only 51 percent of homosexual males surveyed had done so. Among women with more extensive homosexual experience, the Kinsey team found that kissing and manual stimulation of the breast and genitalia were well-nigh universal (95 to 98 percent); that deep kissing (77 percent), oral stimulation of the breast (85 percent), and oral stimulation of the genitalia (78 percent) were experienced by the great majority; and that a narrower majority (56 percent) of the sample had experienced pleasurable genital appositions—that is, tribadism, or rubbing the genitals against the partner's hips, thighs, or buttocks. Use of an object for vaginal penetration was rare. The report notes that many women, even those with long and exclusively homosexual histories, had not gone beyond kissing another woman on the lips and generalized body contact.

The Successors of Kinsey

Definitive sex research on the queer community is hampered by the seminal unanswered question: what constitutes a representative sample of LGBT and intersex people? In 1978 there appeared Alan P. Bell and Martin S. Weinberg's *Homosexualities: A Study of Diversity among Men and Women,* an official publication of the Institute for Sex Research founded by Kinsey. Their sample consisted of 575 white homosexual men, 111 black homosexual men, 229 white homosexual females, and 64 black homosexual females, drawn at random from a much larger pool of potential respondents.

Bell and Weinberg found that almost half of white homosexual males (WHMs) had sex on an average of at least two times a week, while two-thirds of black homosexual males (BHMs) had sex on average at least two times a week. The most common frequency for white homosexual females (WHFs) was one time a week, while black homosexual females (BHFs) most frequently averaged a sexual encounter two times a week or more. (The researchers attribute this difference to the younger age of their sample of black homosexual females.) The majority of men had gone cruising specifically for sex at least a few times per month during the previous year, mostly in bars, in baths, or on the street. Men looked for sexual partners much less often at private parties or in parks, beaches, public restrooms, and movie theaters. Less than 20% of women had gone out looking specifically for sex in the past year, and when they did, it was mostly at bars and private parties.

One-half of WHMs and one-third of BHMs said they had at least five hundred sex partners during the course of their homosexual careers, while one-third of WHMs and one-fourth of BHMs reported from 100 to 500 partners in their lifetime. Most WHMs and one-third of BHMs said that more than half of the men they had had sex with were people they had sex with only once.

More than one-fourth of male respondents had more than 50 partners in the previous year. One-fourth had from 20 to 50, one-fifth had fewer than 6. Most female respondents had less than 10 female sex partners during their adult lives, and most were monogamous or nearly so during the previous year.

Bell and Weinberg's male homosexual respondents were asked about seven different homosexual sexual techniques: orgasm achieved by rubbing one's body against the partner's body; masturbating the partner; being masturbated by him; giving fellatio (oral stimulation of the genitals); receiving fellatio; performing anal intercourse; and being anally penetrated. In decreasing order, the WHMs had performed the following acts: giving fellatio; receiving fellatio; being masturbated; manually stimulating a partner; performing anal intercourse; receiving anal penetration; and body rubbing. BHMs were somewhat less likely to have performed fellatio, and were more likely than whites to list performing anal intercourse as their most frequent activity. The largest number of WHMs said they liked receiving oral sex and performing anal intercourse the best. Almost half of BHMs said performing anal intercourse was their favorite sex act, while one-fifth preferred receiving fellatio.

Female homosexual respondents were asked about five different homosexual sexual techniques: orgasm achieved by rubbing one's body against the partner's body; masturbating the partner; being masturbated by her; performing cunnilingus (oral stimulation of the genitals); and receiving cunnilingus. No questions were asked about penetration. The female respondents were most likely to have used manual techniques. Whites were less likely to have performed cunnilingus or received it. Among blacks, this order was reversed. Both groups were least likely to have reached orgasm with body rubbing. Forty percent of WHFs and almost half of BHFs had given or received manual stimulation once a week or more. One-fourth of WHFs and nearly half of BHFs had used oral techniques. Significantly more black women had received cunnilingus once a week or more. One-fifth of WHFs and two-fifths of BHFs had reached orgasm at least weekly with body rubbing. The most preferred sexual technique was oral sex. For whites, the next favorite technique was being given manual stimulation, while black homosexual females next preferred body rubbing.

Same-sex sexual behavior has been paradoxically portrayed in clinical literature and popular culture as both inherently dissatisfying and so ecstatic as to be addicting. Few scientific attempts have been made to compare the incidence of sexual satisfaction or sexual problems among heterosexual versus homosexual, bisexual, transgender, or intersex people. Bell and Weinberg did find that a majority of WHMs and significantly fewer BHMs reported ever experiencing trouble getting or maintaining an erection or coming too fast. Not quite half of both races of homosexual males reported experiencing difficulty achieving orgasm. However, only 5 to 10 percent said these difficulties were much of a problem. Lesbians in this study tended to have experienced fewer sexual difficulties than the gay men.

Later books such as Felice Newman's *The Whole Lesbian Sex Book: A Passionate Guide for All of Us* (1999) and Daniel Wolfe's *Men Like Us: The GMHC Complete Guide to Gay Men's Sexual, Physical, and Emotional Well-Being* (2000) include information about a wide range of practices. In addition to anal sex, cunnilingus, and fellatio, these include, but are not limited to, fisting (insertion of the entire hand into the rectum or vagina), frottage (body-to-body contact during which the penis may be compressed between the partner's thighs but is not inserted into an orifice), manual stimulation of the partner's body (sometimes termed "mutual masturbation"), rimming (oral stimulation of the anus), tribadism (body-to-body contact between female partners), the use of sex toys for external or internal stimulation, and vaginal penetration. Some LGBT people also have more specialized sexual interests that include the use of fetish objects, sadomasochism, or watersports (erotic play with urine).

The Invisible Bisexuals

The emergence of a bisexual community with a strong sense of a unique identity is a relatively recent phenomenon in the United States, dating back to the late 1970s. Kinsey recognized the existence of a continuum of sexual orientation and devised a seven-point scale in which 0 was exclusively heterosexual, 3 was equally heterosexual and homosexual, and 6 was exclusively homosexual. But many sex researchers continue to divide their samples into homosexuals and heterosexuals only. Bell and Weinberg asked their respondents to rate themselves on the Kinsey scale for both their sexual behavior and their sexual feelings. While only a small minority of male respondents gave themselves ratings the researchers considered bisexual (4, 3, or 2), 14 percent of WHMs and 22 percent of BHMs had experienced coitus with a woman in the past year. Six percent of WHMs and 8 percent of BHMs believed they were at least as heterosexual as homosexual in their sexual feelings. Eight percent of WHFs and 17 percent of BHFs rated themselves as being at least as heterosexual as homosexual in their sexual behavior, but relatively small percentages of female respondents had experienced coitus with a man in the previous year. One-fourth of women of each race gave

themselves a score of four or less for their sexual feelings regarding women versus men. Three-fourths of WHFs considered themselves more homosexual in their behavior than in their feelings, while two-thirds of BHFs thought they were more homosexual in their feelings than in their behavior. Nevertheless, all respondents' results were interpreted as data about the homosexual experience alone, and no data were gathered about opposite-sex practices.

Transgender and Intersex Sexuality

Scant data exist on the sexual practices of transgender people. The term "transgender" potentially includes cross-dressers, pre-operative transsexuals, post-operative transsexuals, masculine women, effeminate men, intersex people, as well as other groups of people with non-normative gender expression or identity. An earlier notion that transsexuals avoided sexual activity prior to surgical modification of their genitals and after such surgery took up lives as "normal" (that is, heterosexual) men and women has been replaced by a more complex picture of people who make use of creative and playful strategies to enjoy sexual pleasure and intimate relationships regardless of what level of medical intervention they have received.

While a complete understanding of any form of sexuality must include information about that behavior's significance to the participants, this aspect of sexuality becomes especially important with people whose bodies may not match their gender identity. For example, a pre-operative transsexual woman may not wish her partner to have any contact with her genitals or may find such contact permissible if she is viewed as and described as possessing a clitoris rather than a penis. A female-to-male transsexual who identifies as a gay man may or may not permit vaginal penetration with his partner's penis, but if he did, would consider such an act to be gay sex rather than heterosexual intercourse. Post-operative transsexuals and their partners must take into account the degree to which their altered genitals possess sensation or sexual functioning.

Special problems in determining sexual orientation or engaging in pleasure-seeking behavior exist for many intersex people. If one's body contains a mixture of male and female characteristics, the ability or even the desire to identify definitively as either male or female may not exist. Notions of sexual orientation at the turn of the twenty-first century are still founded on the paradigm of binary gender. So pervasive is this paradigm that most intersex newborns are assigned a sex by medical personnel. Surgical alteration of the infant's genitals is common, even though this mutilation will very likely interfere with the intersex individual's ability to function sexually as an adult.

It is not known what percentage of transgender or intersex people identify as LGB people, only that some do. Gender specialists once refused to assist an LGB person in receiving gender reassignment. As homophobia and biphobia among doctors, psychiatrists, and therapists decreases, the number of transgender and intersex people who openly identify as LGB has increased. Acceptance of transgender or intersex women or men by the LGB community would facilitate even greater participation.

Sexual Choices and Values

Post-AIDS research on sexual behavior in the queer community focuses on so-called risk factors, or behavior that might expose the individual to sexually transmitted diseases. While the need for public health education is critical, this trend bolsters an already-endemic Western notion of sex-as-disease. Of all of the motives that shape sexual behavior, preserving or endangering one's health probably lags behind the more visceral concern of obtaining immediate physical pleasure and intimacy. A more holistic picture of queer sexual desire and fulfillment still needs to be created.

Several factors are known to affect the sexual behavior of LGBT individuals and members of associated sexual minorities. Some of these factors are spiritual, political, or ethical beliefs about the relative value of particular forms of sexual expression; knowledge gleaned about sexual possibilities from pornography, sex education literature, or mass media; previous experience with partners; anecdotal information about the sexual practices of peers; desire for the approval of one's peers or fear of censure; the range of practices permitted by the environment in which the sex takes place; a partner's desires; acts that can be exchanged for money; the individual's ability or inability to perform certain acts; the desire to conceive or avoid pregnancy; the identification of particular acts with male-masculine or female-feminine roles; the content of the individual's sexual fantasies; and, of course, the individual's personal preferences.

In June of 2003, the U.S. Supreme Court struck down the state of Texas's sodomy law. *Lawrence v. Texas* would on its face seem to render all state sodomy laws unconstitutional. The legalization of same-sex activity will have a positive effect not only on the sexual behavior of lesbians, gay men, bisexual people, and transgendered people, but on campaigns to win their civil rights as well, since sodomy laws were often used to justify homophobia and discrimination.

Bibliography

Bell, Alan P., and Martin S. Weinberg. *Homosexualities: A Study of Diversity among Men and Women.* New York: Simon and Schuster, 1978.

Kinsey, Alfred C. et al. *Sexual Behavior in the Human Female.* Philadelphia: Saunders, 1953.

Kinsey, Alfred C., Wardell B. Pomeroy, and Clyde E. Martin. *Sexual Behavior in the Human Male.* Philadelphia: Saunders, 1948.

Newman, Felice. *The Whole Lesbian Sex Book: A Passionate Guide for All of Us.* San Francisco: Cleis, 1999.

Wolfe, Daniel. *Men Like Us: The GMHC Complete Guide to Gay Men's Sexual, Physical, and Emotional Well-Being.* New York: Ballantine, 2000.

Patrick Califia

See also KINSEY, ALFRED C.; PROSTITUTION, HUSTLING, AND SEX WORK; PROSTITUTION, HUSTLING, AND SEX WORK LAW AND POLICY; PUBLIC SEX; SADOMASOCHISM, SADISTS, AND MASOCHISTS; SAFER SEX; SEX TOYS; SODOMY, BUGGERY, CRIMES AGAINST NATURE, DISORDERLY CONDUCT, AND LEWD AND LASCIVIOUS LAW AND POLICY.

SEX CLUBS

The term "sex club" sometimes denotes all commercially run spaces in which patrons may have sex with one another on the premises. More commonly, it refers to a subset of such businesses, those without the amenities of a bathhouse. (However, not every place that identifies itself as a bathhouse actually has a sauna or swimming pool on the premises.) Any group of individuals who meet informally, perhaps at one another's homes, for mutual erotic pleasure, can also be called a sex club.

Sex clubs are usually found in poor neighborhoods, red-light districts, LGBT enclaves, or industrial zones. An entrance fee is collected at the door. Patrons may be able to rent lockers or cubicles. Some cities require the removal of doors from all rooms within the club. The club may have accessories such as mattresses, cells, slings, bondage furniture, or glory holes (walls with holes in them, to facilitate anonymous oral sex). Lights are generally kept low and there is often continual music. The club may have rules about attire or the type of sexual activity allowed there. Condoms are frequently made available.

Twentieth-Century Public Sex

In the beginning of the twentieth century, a movement to promote hygiene among the poor resulted in the establishment of public bathing facilities in major U.S. cities. Gay men were quick to capitalize on these spaces, although baths were initially used only as a meeting place; sex itself usually occurred in a nearby hotel. As their popularity among the working class faded, most bathhouses closed. But some adapted to serve a more specialized population—gay men, who turned them into sexual playgrounds.

By World War I these havens of queer sensuality were well-known in urban gay subcultures throughout the United States. Historian Jonathan Katz documents the use of Turkish baths, as far back as 1914, by gay men to meet and have sex with each other in New York City, Boston, Philadelphia, and Chicago. The Mount Morris Baths in Harlem was established in 1927. "We knew that Harlem was the only place there was any freedom," Philip Johnson, a gay man who patronized the Mount Morris Baths during the 1940s, was later quoted in Charles Kaiser's *Gay New York*. In the 1930s gay San Franciscans frequented Jack's Turkish Baths and the Third Street Baths.

In the 1950s, in New York City, the Everard (also known as the Everhard) Baths was popular. There were additional gay bathhouses on West 58th Street near Columbus Circle and the Penn Post Baths across the street from Pennsylvania Station. In the 1960s a large billboard for the Rich Street Baths advertised man-to-man passion in full color at the intersection of Market and Castro Streets in San Francisco.

By the 1970s gay sex clubs (including bathhouses) in U.S. cities had proliferated in number to several hundred. Two of the most notorious were the Anvil in the meatpacking district of New York City's West Village and its even more hardcore neighbor, The Mineshaft, which was patronized primarily by leathermen.

Some LGBT critics felt that the hedonism enjoyed in sex clubs diverted gay men from political activism. They often saw the sex clubs as a form of capitalist cooptation that turned queer pleasure into a commodity. In the 1980s when AIDS, a fatal, sexually transmitted disease immune to antibiotics, emerged, these negative voices took preeminence.

Moral Panic

Sex clubs are vulnerable to closure by agencies that regulate the sale of alcohol, zoning boards, building inspectors, and the police. Crackdowns usually coincide with an election year, when candidates attempt to win votes by appealing to conservative values, or media exposés. Large-scale cleanups of sex clubs, street prostitution, and public sex in noncommercial locations coincided with the openings of the New York City World's Fairs in 1939 and 1964.

The first AIDS fatalities occurred in the early 1980s. Promiscuity was widely perceived to be the cause of this epidemic. Although some sex clubs began distributing condoms, posting safe-sex guidelines, or holding safe-sex events such as parties where only masturbation was permitted, many owners resisted. Prominent gay leaders who demanded that the baths be closed included activist Michael Callen and journalist Randy Shilts. The San Francisco Department of Public Health padlocked that city's bathhouses and other sex clubs on 9 April 1984. The following year, New York City began closing down sex clubs, including The Mineshaft and Plato's Retreat. Similar battles pitting activists and local governments, against gay men wishing to maintain the right of sexual freedom took place nationwide.

A Cautious Renaissance

The loss of commercial venues did not, however, put an end to anonymous public sex. Cruising in parks and other public locations may well have increased as a result. Because these activities placed participants at a higher risk of being gay-bashed or arrested, and condoms are not readily available in many such places, some gay men also began to host sex parties that emphasized low-risk erotic acts in their own homes.

By the end of the 1980s commercial sex clubs had begun to make a comeback. These new businesses were not as lavish as the bathhouses, and they camouflaged their presence. Agencies that focused their efforts on public health education to prevent the spread of HIV and AIDS pointed out that it was easier to perform this work in centralized locations such as sex clubs. Organizations like San Francisco's Coalition for Healthy Sex, which lobbies for social policy that will keep sex clubs in business as long as they promote safer sex practices, have sometimes been successful in obtaining a modicum of official tolerance, but the existence of sex clubs remains controversial and marginal.

Ira Tattelman's research indicates that in 1982 there were at least 160 gay baths in major cities throughout the United States. In 1994 *Steam* magazine identified sixty-one bathhouses and seventy-five sex clubs as sexual venues for gay men. The 2003 database of the Damron Company, which publishes a popular gay travel guide for men, lists about a hundred men's sex clubs, including baths.

Sex Clubs in Other Communities

Other sexual and gender minorities have adapted the sex club, a gay male sexual institution. This is especially true of the heterosexual "swinging" community. In 1978 the New York City-based Continental Baths, where entertainer Bette Midler had made her earlier singing debut, became Larry Levensen's sex club for heterosexual and bisexual men and women, Plato's Retreat. In San Francisco in the late 1970s, a gay men's fisting club, The Catacombs, was rented out for women-only S/M parties. Its successor, the Shotwell House, also was available for the same purpose. As of 2003 San Francisco's gay male 14th Street Space hosts a regular pansexual BDSM play party. The Mineshaft in New York City was occasionally opened for mixed and women-only events in the year before it closed. Heterosexual sadomasochistic/leather/fetish clubs such as the Hellfire Club and Paddles in New York City have hosted women-only parties for LBT women. A controversy currently rages about whether female-to-male transsexuals will be allowed to participate in gay men-only BDSM events like the Chicago Hellfire Club's annual Inferno party.

Since they are excluded from monogamous heterosexual courtship rituals, and since the penalties for being labeled as sexually different can be draconian, gay men and other sexual minorities have had to devise alternative social forms that would allow them to evade social control, connect with one another in a place where sexual contact was facilitated, and preserve their anonymity. The sex club is an institution that represents both social progress, in that they are safer than outdoor cruising, and repression, in that they are less luxurious and more difficult for the police, scandal-minded journalists, and potential patrons to locate.

Bibliography

Bérubé, Allan. *Coming Out under Fire: The History of Gay Men and Women in World War Two.* New York: Free Press, 1990.

Bayer, Ronald. "AIDS and the Bathhouse Controversy." In *Major Problems in the History of American Sexuality: Documents and Essays.* Edited by Kathy Lee Peiss. New York: D C Heath and Co., 2001.

Califia, Pat. "1985." In *Long Road to Freedom: The Advocate History of the Gay and Lesbian Movement.* Edited by Mark Thompson. New York: St. Martin's Press, 1994.

Kaiser, Charles. *The Gay Metropolis 1940–1996.* Boston: Houghton Mifflin, 1997.

Shernoff, Michael. "Middle-Aged, Queer, and HIV Positive." In *Male Lust: Pleasure, Power, and Transformation.* Edited by Kerwin Kay, Jill Nagle, and Baruch Gould. New York: Harrington Park Press, 2000.

Stryker, Susan, and Jim Van Buskirk. *Gay by the Bay: A History of Queer Cultures in the San Francisco Bay Area.* San Francisco: Chronicle Books, 1996.

Tattelman, Ira. "The Meaning at the Wall: Tracing the Gay Bathhouse." In *Queers in Space: Communities, Public Places, Sites of Resistance.* Edited by Gordon Brent Ingram, Anne-Marie Bouthillette, and Yolanda Retter. Seattle: Bay Press, 1997.

Patrick Califia

See also BARS, CLUBS, AND RESTAURANTS; BATHHOUSES; CRUISING; LEATHER SEX AND SEXUALITY; MONOGAMY AND NON-MONOGAMY; PUBLIC SEX; RIGHTS OF ASSOCIATION AND ASSEMBLY.

SEX EDUCATION

Although most parents approve of sex and sexuality education for their children, consideration of LGBT issues often receives less support than other topics. In fact, most school districts do not cover sexual orientation or gender identity in their curricula, except in geographic areas where LGBT people are included in civil-rights protections. Furthermore, textbooks and other educational materials rarely depict LGBT people in realistic, accurate, or positive ways. Even those that attempt to treat LGBT issues in a neutral fashion often render LGBT people as inferior and less significant. Given the lack of widespread access to accurate and age-appropriate information in the schools, most youth turn to peers, books, and the media.

Attempts to promote sex education in schools began in the late nineteenth century. The "social hygiene" programs that developed in the early twentieth century focused primarily on the control of syphilis and gonorrhea. Since then, social and educational reformers have repeatedly attempted to expand the content of such programs. However, medical perspectives that stress disease and pregnancy prevention still dominate most sex education curricula. Focused on preparing young people for heterosexual marriage and parenting, most programs attempt to socialize youth into gender-specific heterosexual roles by idealizing the heterosexual nuclear family and portraying males and females in stereotypical terms. Furthermore, due in part to government pressures, most emphasize sexual abstinence before marriage. Such approaches provide few opportunities for youth to explore their sexual desires and identities and rarely include positive appraisals of homosexuality, bisexuality, or transgenderism. They also fail to expose LGBT youth to the knowledge and attitudes that might decrease the extent of the discrimination they experience or protect them from sexual exploitation or sexually transmitted disease. They also fail to educate straight youth about LGBT issues.

Availability of Information

Until the 1990s, parents were hard-pressed to find positive depictions of LGBT families in children's books. Lesléa Newman's 1989 book, *Heather Has Two Mommies,* was one of the first children's books to depict a child with lesbian mothers. After being rejected by over fifty publishers, she and a friend finally raised enough money to publish the book themselves. The book was intended to help children with lesbian mothers feel good about themselves and their families, a goal shared by many sexuality educators. A year later, Sasha Alyson, founder and editor of Alyson Wonderland (a line of books for children with lesbian and gay parents), bought the rights to *Heather Has Two Mommies* and also published Michael Willhoite's *Daddy's Roommate,* a similar story about a child with a gay father. A variety of other titles followed. In 2001, Suzanna Danuta Walters argued in *All the Rage: The Story of Gay Visibility in America* that gay and lesbian people were visible everywhere. That may have been true for movies, television sitcoms, and children's books; however, it was clearly not the case in schools.

In *Teaching Sex* (2000), Jeffrey Moran documented that family life education materials published as early as 1968 encouraged tolerance of homosexuality even while some LGBT rights groups feared that sex education could be used to reinforce homophobia. After the Stonewall Riots in 1969 and the American Psychiatric Association's removal of homosexuality from its list of mental disorders in 1973, LGBT rights advocates worked more actively to prevent sex education from promoting anti-LGBT prejudice and discrimination.

HIV prevention programs developed independently of other approaches to sex education as a direct response to the AIDS crises. Due in part to the efforts of Surgeon General C. Everett Koop, most school districts required HIV education by the mid-1990s. Most curricula focused on the prevention of transmission of HIV through behavior change, but some shared content with other approaches to sex education. Although the AIDS crisis made it possible for the media to be more open about same-sex sexual behavior, conservative opponents of sex education increased efforts to prevent positive discussion of homosexuality in the classroom. As a result, discussion of LGBT sexuality in HIV prevention programs in schools remains extremely circumscribed.

Significant Controversies

Inclusion of material about LGBT people in school curricula has sparked controversy. A notable case was the defeat of the New York City public schools' *Children of the Rainbow* curriculum. Designed to teach respect for all kinds of families, this 443-page bibliography originally included three paragraphs that mentioned books like *Heather Has Two Mommies* and *Daddy's Roommate.* School system Chancellor Joseph Fernandez faced con-

siderable opposition to his support for the inclusion of such material in the elementary school curriculum. After the Chancellor's dismissal in 1993, due in part to his position on this issue, the curriculum was revised and any mention of LGBT families was removed.

A few years later, a film released by Women's Educational Media, *It's Elementary: Talking About Gay Issues in School* (1996), caused another uproar. Oscar-winning documentary-filmmaker Debra Chasnoff made the film in response to the name-calling and anti-LGBT violence common in schools. The film was intended to show educators how to teach respect for people who are not heterosexual. Claiming that it advocated rather than educated, groups such as the American Family Association, Focus on the Family, the Family Research Council, and Concerned Women for America financed a campaign to dissuade schools from using the film. In a September 1997 editorial, the *New York Post* claimed that the film represented a campaign to corrupt children's morals by brainwashing them into accepting homosexuality.

Government Intervention in School-Based Programs

In 2001, the Alan Guttmacher Institute (AGI) showed that nearly 80 percent of teachers believe that sexuality education should include discussion of sexual orientation, but only 50 percent included such content. Whether issues related to LGBT people were discussed in a positive or negative fashion cannot be determined from AGI's data. However, additional research indicates that while half of students discuss homosexuality in the classroom, these issues are handled negatively in many cases.

AGI also reported that between 1988 and 1999 the percentage of public school teachers in grades seven to twelve who teach abstinence as the only way to prevent pregnancy rose from one in fifty to one in four. This shift in the curriculum was the result of government funding for abstinence-until-marriage programs. Such funding began with the passage of the Adolescent Family Life Act (AFLA) in 1981. AFLA was designed to prevent teen pregnancy by promoting abstinence and self-discipline. Although its original restrictions were modified somewhat after a lengthy court battle, AFLA received $19 million in federal funding in fiscal year 2000.

Abstinence-only sexuality education programs received further support in 1996 when the U.S. Congress allocated money to states to promote abstinence. According to the statute (Section 510, Title V of the Social Security Act, Public Law 104–193), to qualify for funding schools must teach, among other things, that "sexual activity outside of marriage is likely to have harmful psychological and physical effects." This approach ignores the needs of people who do not identify as heterosexual given that they cannot legally marry. It also ignores research findings demonstrating that abstinence-only programs are ineffective.

At the state level, legislatures have attempted to control students' access to information about homosexuality by prohibiting or restricting school-sponsored clubs (in order to suppress gay-straight student alliances), by limiting sex education to discussions of monogamous heterosexual marriage, and by supporting outright bans on discussions of homosexuality in the classroom. In 1996, teachers in Charlotte, North Carolina, received a list of words they were forbidden to use in the classroom. These included "bisexual," "gay," "homosexual," "lesbian," "transsexual," and "transvestite." As late as 2000, talking about contraception in the classroom, let alone LGBT sex, could lead to loss of jobs or funding.

Comprehensive Sexuality Education

Advocates of comprehensive sexuality education tend to support acceptance of sexual diversity. For example, since its founding in 1964, the Sexuality Information and Education Council of the United States (SIECUS) has advocated comprehensive sexuality education that includes age-appropriate information about sexual orientation.

At the federal level, SIECUS and other advocates have supported the Family Life Education Act (FLEA). If enacted, this legislation would provide funds to support comprehensive sexuality education that would likely include accurate information about sexual orientation. The bill (H.R. 3469) was introduced for the first time in December 2001. However, most school curricula remain devoid of content specific to the lives of LGBT youth.

Potential Harbingers

Some state legislatures have prohibited anti-gay harassment, discrimination, and violence in schools. Massachusetts became the first state to support fully its gay and lesbian students when Governor William Weld signed into law the Gay and Lesbian Student Rights Law on 10 December 1993. The law prohibits discrimination on the basis of sexual orientation; guarantees students redress when they suffer antigay harassment, violence, or unfair treatment at school; and encourages schools to develop programs that will promote understanding of gay and lesbian students' rights.

In June 2001, U.S. Surgeon General David Satcher released *The Surgeon General's Call to Action to Promote*

Sexual Health and Responsible Sexual Behavior. In addition to encouraging respect for a diversity of sexual values, supporting open discussion about sexuality, and recognizing what science shows to be effective, this was the first federal report in many years to support proactive programs and advocacy for LGBT youth in schools. In contrast to federal policy, it encourages abstinence until people are involved in committed, enduring, and mutually monogamous relationships.

Similarly, in February 2002, the National Education Association's board of directors adopted a plan that encourages schools to develop factual, age-appropriate, nonjudgmental materials for classroom discussions on homosexuality.

These events have developed in an era when the vast majority of students regularly hear anti-LGBT comments from their peers and teachers, and few sexuality education programs allow discussion of homosexuality and transgenderism. Perhaps these incidents of LGBT support foreshadow curricular and policy changes that will provide students access to age-appropriate, scientifically accurate information about LGBT people and will support the health and well-being of all students.

Bibliography

Dailard, Cynthia. "Sex Education: Politicians, Parents, Teachers, and Teens." *The Guttmacher Report on Public Policy* 4, no. 1 (February 2001). Available from http://www.agi-usa.org

Irvine, Janice M. *Talk about Sex: The Battles over Sex Education in the United States.* Berkeley: University of California Press, 2002.

Moran, Jeffrey P. *Teaching Sex: The Shaping of Adolescence in the Twentieth Century.* Cambridge, Mass.: Harvard University Press, 2000.

Rienzo, Barbara A. "The Politics of School-Based Programs Which Address Sexual Orientation." *Journal of School Health* 66, no. 1 (1996): 33–40.

Sears, James T. "The Impact of Culture and Ideology on the Construction of Gender and Sexual Identities: Developing a Critically Based Sexuality Curriculum." In *Sexuality and the Curriculum: The Politics and Practices of Sexuality Education.* Edited by James T. Sears. New York: Teachers College Press, 1992.

Stevenson, Michael R., and Jeanine C. Cogan, eds. *Everyday Activism: A Handbook for Lesbian, Gay, and Bisexual People and their Allies.* New York: Routledge, 2003.

Michael R. Stevenson

See also EDUCATION; EDUCATION LAW AND POLICY; GAY, LESBIAN, AND STRAIGHT EDUCATION NETWORK (GLSEN); SAFER SEX; SEXUALLY TRANSMITTED DISEASES.

SEX PANICS

Sex panics, or widespread hysteria over perceived cultural, social, and political threats posed by allegedly deviant or dissenting populations, have punctuated U.S. history with regularity. Many of these panics have been marked by fear of sexual excess or sexual difference, as during the Salem witch trials in seventeenth century Massachusetts. During the twentieth century, as sexuality emerged as a more distinct arena of life relatively separable from marriage, family, and reproduction, some moral panics began to take shape specifically as sex panics—and some of these focused on the threat posed by LGBT and queer populations or on sexual and gender practices perceived as characteristic of such populations.

Institutions of government—law and legislatures, the military and the courts, the police and prisons—have been prime sites for sex panics since the early twentieth century. An especially well-documented sex panic seized the U.S. Navy in Newport, Rhode Island, during 1919–1921. The panic began when then Assistant Secretary of the Navy Franklin D. Roosevelt asked Attorney General A. Mitchell Palmer to initiate a Justice Department investigation of Newport's Naval Training Station and the Young Men's Christian Association (YMCA). The request was motivated by complaints of "moral vice" including drug use, prostitution, financial corruption, and sexual immorality. When Palmer, occupied with his anticommunist investigations and prosecutions, refused the request, Roosevelt ordered a secret undercover investigation. The lead investigators, Dr. Erastus M. Hudson and Ervin Arnold, distributed instructions including, "Men attached to and serving on this staff, must keep their eyes wide open, observing everything and ears open for all conversation and make himself free as he pumps these men for information, making him believe that he is what is termed in the Navy as 'boy humper,' making dates with them and so forth. Be careful not to arouse suspicion." Evidence was to be gathered concerning "cocksuckers and rectum receivers and ring leaders of this gang, arranging from time to time meetings whereas to catch them in the act" (Brenkert, pp. 13–15).

During April and May of 1919, the Foster Court of Inquiry held hearings and made recommendations, including prohibiting unmarried enlisted men from renting rooms at the YMCA. Several men accused of homosexual activities by the vice investigators were prosecuted in military or civil courts and received court-martials, prison sentences, or dishonorable discharges. YMCA regular Albert Veihi, for instance, was found guilty of three counts of sodomy and one of oral coition and was sentenced to twenty years in prison.

But the Navy's investigation faltered when Navy chaplain Samuel Neal Kent, head of the sailors' welfare organization, was invited for a drink by investigator Charles Zipf, who wrote in his report that "Kent threw his arms around me, and kissed me about the face. Repeatedly he tried to put his tongue in my mouth. His hand strayed and he felt of my penis. . . . Kent made me promise not to say anything to the gang down at the YMCA." Kent was tried on charges of homosexual activity twice, but he countercharged the Navy with using immoral methods and he was ultimately acquitted. Objections to the Navy's methods spread, and the investigators then found themselves under investigation. The Dunn Board of Inquiry convened in Newport in January 1920 to respond to a letter of complaint to the President of the United States by the Newport Minister's Union. The exposure of the undercover sting's methods later led to some dropped charges and reduced sentences for the men who were entrapped—Albert Veihi's twenty-year sentence, for example, was reduced to seven years, and later to five years. The military ultimately managed to protect its own personnel, however, while many of those harassed or persecuted by the Navy's vice investigators suffered lasting harm and humiliation.

Sex panics focused on the sexual identities or behaviors of LGBT military personnel continued throughout the twentieth century, escalating periodically during "purges" in which allegedly homosexual servicemen and women were investigated, court-martialed, and discharged according to military policy following World War II. Postwar purges of alleged "sexual perverts" also extended well beyond the military. Beginning in 1950 when a State Department official testified in Congress that several dozen employees had been fired because of homosexual activities, charges that sexual "deviates" had infiltrated the government proliferated. In June 1950 the U. S. Senate authorized an investigation into the employment of "moral perverts" in government, and by December the resulting report argued, "These perverts will frequently attempt to entice normal individuals to engage in perverted practices. . . . One homosexual can pollute a government office." Homosexuals were alleged to be especially vulnerable to blackmail and recruitment by foreign spies.

The results of the postwar sex panics were deep and lasting—an executive order barred homosexuals from all federal jobs, the Federal Bureau of Investigation initiated a system of surveillance to keep lesbians and gay men out of government, and the armed forces stepped up its antigay purges. Local police forces were encouraged to harass gay and lesbian bars and gathering spots, and mass arrests were a periodic reality for many urban homosexuals. In Boise, Idaho, in 1955, a fifteen-month investigation of the city's gay men followed the arrest of three men on charges of sexual activity with teenagers. The town hired an outside investigator and the police called in fourteen hundred residents for interrogation. Over 150 newspaper stories appeared in the local press, generating substantial coverage in neighboring states as well. Convictions and long prison sentences followed.

Twentieth-century sex panics often fed off and reproduced assumptions about the dangerous, predatory nature of gay male sexuality particularly. In Boise, the *Idaho Daily Statesman* referred to a "sex ring" of older men who seduced and preyed on young boys. This unsubstantiated charge intersected with widely publicized psychiatric portraits of gay men as supposed child molesters, portraits that helped feed the frenzy that lent support to the passage of the so-called "sexual psychopath laws" from the 1930s through the 1950s. Such assumptions about gay male dangerousness persisted long after they were challenged by the homophile movement and gay liberation forces from the 1950s on. In 1977, passage of a gay rights ordinance banning discrimination against gays in Dade County, Florida, led the entertainer Anita Bryant to organize a repeal campaign based in large part on fear of homosexual child molestation. Bryant's organization, Save Our Children, Inc., focused on child safety and warned that "They can only recruit children, and this is what they want to do." Supported by the Catholic Church, conservative rabbis, and local daily newspapers, the Bryant campaign won a resounding and influential victory, repeated in subsequent similar campaigns in other states.

During the 1980s, as LGBT resistance to persecution and discrimination grew, another sex panic threatened to undercut the substantial gains of political organization and cultural visibility. A new infectious disease affecting many gay men in U.S. cities, Acquired Immune Deficiency Syndrome (AIDS), incited widespread fear. Spread through the exchange of bodily fluids, especially during some sexual practices, the virus that was found to cause AIDS was sometimes represented as some form of social, biological, or religious avenger, punishing gay men for their unnatural as well as immoral promiscuity. The cover of Jerry Falwell's *Moral Majority Report* pictured a white family wearing masks under the headline, "Homosexual Diseases Threaten American Families." Some New Right groups and politicians called for quarantine, raising the specter of concentration camps for gay men, while others argued to restore draconian sodomy statutes and penalties. Magazines ran stories with titles like "The Gay

Plague." In many cities, bathhouses catering to gay men were closed rather than used for HIV prevention education. This sex panic atmosphere generated massive and sustained organized responses from LGBT organizations, writers, health care professionals, and activists, however. By the end of the 1980s, AIDS still threatened the health of millions, but the hysterical focus on the dangers of the "gay male lifestyle" and the spread of draconian legal and informal antigay discrimination ebbed as the worldwide threat of the disease to many populations and new public health initiatives and drug treatments led to a more expanded and diffuse set of battles for funding, prevention, treatment, humane care, and self-representation of people with AIDS and HIV infection.

As the antigay hysteria surrounding AIDS subsided in the late 1980s, another sex panic crescendoed. Attacks on public funding for "homoerotic" art fed attempts to destroy the National Endowment for the Arts, as well as to outlaw or discredit the work of many LGBT artists and performers. One of the most highly visible efforts in this long span of attacks and publicity was directed against the work of Robert Mapplethorpe, and began when the Corcoran Gallery of Art canceled a retrospective of the photographer's work in June 1989. In October of that year, a letter printed and distributed by the Christian Coalition and signed by Reverend Pat Robertson declared,

Dear _____,

The enclosed red envelope contains graphic descriptions of homosexual erotic photographs that were funded by your tax dollars. I'd never send you the photos, but I did want you to know about the vile contents of your tax funded material. You'll be as outraged as I am when you open the envelope.

The red envelope contained a list of descriptions of Mapplethorpe photographs, not all of them accurate, headlined, "Tax-Payer Funded. Photographs Too Vulgar to Print." Such sex panic–generating tactics marked the long political effort to defund and stigmatize LGBT and queer erotic art, writing, and performance as "indecent." This effort garnered much success, as arts funding was both restricted and cut, and institutions and artists were routinely attacked and sometimes prosecuted. But these "arts wars" attacks also generated substantial creative as well as political opposition, and sometimes paradoxically helped to publicize precisely those images and words most vilified.

The attack on public institutions for promoting homosexuality and sexual perversion was not confined to the arts. Educational institutions became prime targets as well. During 1997, a women's studies conference at the State University of New York (SUNY) at New Paltz titled "Revolting Behavior: The Challenges of Women's Sexual Freedom" became the focus of sensational publicity nationwide when conservative Republican SUNY trustee Candace de Russy and conservative pundit Roger Kimball complained in the local and national press about the lesbian content at the conference, especially the lesbian sadomasochism and safer-sex workshops. As Kimball lamented in an essay in *The Wall Street Journal* entitled "A Syllabus for Sickos": "'Revolting Behavior' was in fact a celebration of perversity and sexual libertinage." Such attacks were supported by politicians and groups eager to slash funding and restrict curricula and programming for public higher education in the state of New York . This sex panic succeeded in alarming university officials and bringing scrutiny and surveillance to women's studies programs in particular. But defenses of academic freedom, women's studies, lesbian visibility, and higher education's critical mission limited the scope of the damage, and galvanized support for public education as well.

Sex panics during the past century have consistently had this kind of paradoxical impact. On the one hand, they have resulted not only in the persecution and harassment of individuals, organizations, and institutions, but they have also left layers of repressive sex laws and reinforced anti-LGBT prejudice. On the other hand, they have generated opposition as well, publicized alternative sexual and gender possibilities as they are denounced, and motivated the organization of LGBT populations.

Bibliography

Bérubé, Allan. "The History of Gay Bathhouses." In *Policing Public Sex: Queer Politics and the Future of AIDS Activism.* Edited by Dangerous Bedfellows et al. Boston: South End Press, 1996.

Brenkert, Benjamin. "The Newport Sex Scandal, 1919–21." *The Gay and Lesbian Review* 10, no. 2 (March–April 2003): 13–15.

D'Emilio, John, and Estelle B. Freedman. *Intimate Matters: A History of Sexuality in America.* New York: Harper & Row, 1988.

Freedman, Estelle. "'Uncontrolled Desires': The Response to the Sexual Psychopath, 1920–1960." In *Passion and Power: Sexuality in History.* Edited by Kathy Peiss and Christina Simmons. Philadelphia: Temple University Press, 1989.

Gerasi, John. *The Boys of Boise: Furor, Vice and Folly in an American City.* New York: Macmillan, 1966.

Katz, Jonathan Ned. *Gay American History: Lesbians and Gay Men in U.S.A.: A Documentary.* New York: Crowell, 1976.

Meyer, Richard. *Outlaw Representation: Censorship and Homosexuality in Twentieth-Century American Art.* New York: Oxford University Press, 2002.

Murphy, Lawrence R. *Perverts By Official Order: The Campaign Against Homosexuals by the United States Navy.* New York: Haworth Press, 1988.

Rubin, Gayle. "Thinking Sex." In *Pleasure and Danger: Exploring Female Sexuality.* Edited by Carol S. Vance. Boston: Routledge & K. Paul, 1984.

Lisa Duggan

See also GOVERNMENT AND MILITARY WITCHHUNTS; POLICING AND POLICE; POLITICAL SCANDALS; SEXUAL PSYCHOPATH LAW AND POLICY.

SEX TOURISM. see TOURISM.

SEX TOYS

Sex toys—objects specifically designed for erotic stimulation—may well be as old as human technology. (Fetish objects that might, to a nonparaphiliac, seem entirely innocuous; specialized sadomasochism [S/M] gear; and ordinary objects put to erotic uses are not included in this definition of "sex toy.") Model phalluses, the oldest surviving sex toys, have been found at archaeological sites from China to Cairo, and there is ample literary evidence as to what use such objects were put by the women and men of Egypt, Greece, and Rome. One must be careful, however, about interpreting all such artifacts with a prurient eye. The *herms*—phallic good-luck charms—that decorated Greek thresholds, for instance, were clearly devices intended to ward off the evil eye, while bakers' ovens in Pompeii sported erections as an exercise in sympathetic magic intended to get the bread to rise.

Nonetheless, the dildo has a long and proud history. Even that giant in the history of sex, the Marquis de Sade, while in prison, had his long-suffering wife Renée-Pélagie provide him with *prestiges*—writing cases and other oblong objects made to his very exacting specifications—and, when these were denied him by his jailers, fashioned his own from candle wax.

Before the Twentieth Century

The history of the modern sex toy as an object of consumption, provocation, and legislation begins with the medical profession's concern for women's bodies. Rachel Maines, in her *Technology of Orgasm,* details the two-thousand-year history of "hysteria," a vague complaint first described by Hippocrates. Symptoms of hysteria could range from excessive appetite or loss of appetite to fainting, emotional excitement, and behavior that annoyed one's husband or family. Its cause, however, was known quite definitely: the wandering of the uterus in the body, brought about by a lack of the sexual release thought to be derived solely from penetrative heterosexual intercourse. Needless to say, women who rejected heterosexual norms or who experienced same-sex desires often found themselves diagnosed with hysteria.

The treatment for hysteria, according to physicians from Galen to Avicenna, was marriage and vigorous lovemaking—or, if these measures failed, or if the woman's condition was unalterably single—use of a dildo or a doctor's massage of the woman's genitalia until a "hysterical paroxysm" (that is, an orgasm) was produced. By these means, female needs for sexual satisfaction were transformed into a disease requiring allopathic treatment. This transformation placed women, and by extension their desires, in the position of the patient—an object to be acted upon by the (inevitably male) doctor-savant. (Such treatments were most likely also performed by midwives, but since midwifery was an oral, not written, tradition, this is difficult to document.)

Performing such cures for hysteria proved morally difficult, as well as fatiguing, for the emerging professional caste of physicians. This problem was solved by the invention of devices such as the "hydriatic massage" in which the hysterical paroxysms were induced by a jet of water, available at fashionable American spas as early as the 1760s, and the *trémoussior*, an early wind-up vibrator, invented in France in 1734 and available to American colonists as early as the 1750s. Such "therapies" allowed the doctor to remove himself from the object under "scientific" scrutiny and treatment, the female body, though they also led to frequent complaints that women were taking matters into their own hands, going to "take the waters" without first seeking a medical opinion.

Though Charles Goodyear's vulcanization process, patented in 1844, allowed for the mass manufacture of cheap rubber dildos to more efficiently produce hysterical paroxysms, the great breakthrough in industrial orgasm technology came in 1869 with the introduction of a device ominously named the "Manipulator." Invented by an American physician named George Taylor, the Manipulator was a steam-powered vibrator consisting of a flat table on which the patient lay with her pelvis positioned over a vibrating ball connected by a drive train to a steam engine. An electromechanical vibrator appeared in 1883, but it was not until the introduction of a battery-powered version in 1899 that relief from hysteria became truly convenient. No longer did this relief depend on heavy, unwieldy, clunky contraptions, only practical for institutions and spas; now it could be obtained from devices readily available to anyone with a room of his or her own.

Interestingly, because of their "therapeutic" use, the Comstock Act of 1873, which made the distribution of "obscenity" illegal, was never applied to the sale and production of vibrators. Thus, they were openly advertised in women's magazines and even sold through the Sears and Roebuck catalogue. It was not until the 1920s and 1930s, when early pornographic movies made apparent to the men of America for what purpose their sisters, wives, sweethearts, and daughters were using these vibrators, that such devices disappeared from the public eye.

Sexual Revolutions

Much to the disappointment of orthodox Freudians—who, following another ancient myth, fervently argued that the "mature" female orgasm is centered in the vagina—sexologist Alfred Kinsey, in his *Sexual Behavior in the Human Female* (1953), reported that 88 percent of women masturbated by stroking their labia minora and clitoris. About 20 percent had used "vaginal insertions" in conjunction with other masturbation techniques, but "the insertions that are made are usually confined to the introitus or intended to stimulate the anterior wall of the vagina at the base of the clitoris" (p. 581). Furthermore, "Douches, streams of running water, vibrators, urethral insertions, enemas, other anal insertions, and still other methods were occasionally employed, but none of them in any appreciable number of cases" (p. 163).

Kinsey also noted that "Many males, basing their concepts on their understanding of coitus and upon their conceit as to the importance of the male genitalia in coitus, imagine that all female masturbation must involve an insertion of fingers or of some other object into the depths of the vagina," but this hardly reflected the actual practices of "homosexual females," who "have a better than average understanding of female genital anatomy" (pp. 162, 581). (Interestingly, however, Kinsey found that 18 percent of childhood sex play was by vaginal penetration among lesbian-identified interviewees, as opposed to 3 percent of heterosexual women.)

The information on the comparative rarity of autoerotic insertions in the *Female* report matched what Kinsey had found five years earlier in *Sexual Behavior in the Human Male:* "Urethral insertions and other masochistic techniques, and anal stimulation and anal insertions occur only very occasionally. Sometimes devices which simulate the female genitalia may be used for masturbation, but they are rarely employed" (p. 510).

Of course, Kinsey was writing at a time when sex in America had not yet been transformed by market forces. Sex toys became an increasingly profitable industry during the early years of the post–World War II sexual revo-

a bestiary of sex toys

In our modern society of commodified eros, a wide variety of sex toys have become available to the consumer market. These include, but are not limited to:

- Beads, balls, and other small insertable objects: These take a great variety of forms, with their most common attribute being a round shape (so as not to abrade delicate tissues) and string to facilitate removal. Two of the most common forms are ben-wa balls, two balls joined by a string and designed to be held in the vagina, and anal beads, a string of beads intended to be inserted into the anus.

- Butt plugs: Similar to a dildo but designed with a distinctive flared shape specifically for anal use. Butt plugs are usually flared at the base to facilitate removal and prohibit them from entering too far into the body.

- Cock rings: A ring or collar, constructed of metal, leather, rubber, or other material, designed to be worn around the base of the penis so as to restrict the draining of blood from the erectile tissue, thus producing (at least in theory) longer-lasting, firmer erections. Health experts point out that cock rings should be used with caution, as a poor-fitting one, or one that is left on for too long, can damage vascular tissue.

- Dildos: Simply put, a dildo is an artificial phallus. Dildos come in a great variety of shapes, sizes, ethnic variants, colors, and materials, and can be vibrating or nonvibrating. They can be made to resemble an organic penis or constructed in a completely abstract and fanciful manner. Some are wearable ("strap-ons"), some are "soft packs" made for male impersonators, some are double-ended for simultaneous use by two partners, some have prongs or extensions designed to stimulate a female user's anus and/or clitoris simultaneously with vaginal penetration, and some are even S-shaped for prostate or G-spot stimulation.

- Mannequins and dolls: Essentially, a mannequin or doll is an attempt to create a surrogate partner.

Products range from campy inflatable dolls (available as men, women, and sheep) to Abyss Creations' individually customized silicone "Real Doll," which comes in male, female, and male-to-female ("she-male") transsexual forms and sells for several thousand dollars each. The idea of an artificial surrogate partner taken to its logical end would be an android such as those depicted in the movies *Westworld, Blade Runner,* and *Cherry 2000,* as well as Dr. Frank N. Furter's "creation" from the *Rocky Horror Picture Show.*

- Prosthetic orifices: The obverse of a dildo, sex toys designed to be penetrated by the user have a somewhat smaller market. They range from comparatively crude facsimiles to the state-of-the-art Fleshlight, which comes with oral, anal, or vaginal attachments.

- Penis pumps: Originally designed as a cure for impotence, manually or mechanically operated vacuum pumps are today often marketed as penis-enlarging devices. Pumps are often used in conjunction with a cock ring to maintain the artificial erection; however, bruising is a distinct possibility.

- Vibrators: A vibrator is any device designed to stimulate the user by means of vibration. Some are marketed specifically as sex toys, while others bear the time-honored euphemism of "personal massagers." Waterproof vibrators are also manufactured, as are wearable versions and models shaped like butterflies, flowers, and dolphins.

Not included in this list are ordinary objects put to sexual uses. Medical journals document the insertion, and subsequent emergency-room removal, of such objects as plastic spatulas, Coke bottles, jeweler's saws, teacups, and a plastic waste trap from the U-bend of a sink. Items that serve a function not dissimilar to that of sex toys include chemical sexual enhancers such as amyl nitrate ("poppers"), Viagra, or Spanish fly; foodstuffs such as fruits and vegetables and liver, as erotically described by writers such as Audre Lorde and Philip Roth; lubricants, condoms, and other such "ordinary" accessories; and the specialized accoutrements of BDSM and leather subcultures.

lution, and, with increased social tolerance for pornography and other once-taboo subjects, began to be sold openly in the sex shops of major cities. These stores were often located in or near LGBT neighborhoods such as Greenwich Village in New York City and the Castro in San Francisco and sold their goods to both straight and LGBT customers. Despite the fact that, in order to circumvent possible prosecution, they were still ostensibly manufactured as "marital aids" for heterosexual couples, there is evidence that sex toys achieved market penetration within the LGBT community as well. With a history of being more creative, playful, inventive, and adventurous about sex, LGBT people have probably been more willing to experiment and use sex toys than straight people. In fact, some sex toys, such as dildos ostensibly based on the genitalia of male porn stars such as Jeff Stryker, were specifically designed to appeal to queer customers. At least among certain crowds, owning sex toys became a sign that one had become freed from unhip hang-ups about sex; for instance, in her book *Liberating Masturbation* (1974), New York–based bisexual writer, artist, and educator Betty Dodson stressed masturbation and orgasm as important components of overall emotional health, and recommended the use of vibrators as express tickets to orgasm.

One notable sex toy entrepreneur was Ted Marche, a Venice, California, ventriloquist who had honed his woodworking skills carving his own dummies. Marche started out in the sex-toy business by making wooden "prosthetic phalluses" for the Gem medical supplies company in 1966, but soon branched out on his own, involving his wife and son in making and selling dildos through ads in pulp magazines and novelty-store distributors. Using new plastic-molding techniques, Marche Manufacturing was able to manufacture a wide variety of lifelike phalluses (both vibrating and nonvibrating), vaginas, and other novelties, until, by its tenth year of operation, the company was selling nearly five million units a year. Unfortunately, the Marche rubber dildos were stiffened by wires, one of which ripped a male customer's colon and resulted in a jury awarding $14 million in damages to the victim. Marche was forced to sell his company in 1976 to porn baron and sex-shop entrepreneur Reuben Sturman, owner of the Doc Johnson line of sex toys, and returned to the ventriloquism circuit.

Critiques of the Sex Toy

The earliest known legislation against sex toys in the United States was an 1879 Massachusetts law prohibiting the sale of "an instrument or other article intended to be used for self-abuse." However, most statutes criminalizing such objects were not introduced until the New Right began its reaction against the sexual revolution in the late 1960s. South Dakota introduced a statute against "equipment, machines, or materials" that appealed to "the prurient" in 1968 (it was overturned in 1990). This was followed by laws passed in 1969 by Kansas (overturned in 1990); in 1975 by Georgia; in 1977 by Texas and Nebraska; in 1981 by Colorado (overturned in 1985); in 1983 by Indiana and Mississippi; in 1985 by Louisiana (overturned in 2000); and in 1998 by Alabama.

The wording of most such legislation followed Texas's lead in defining sex toys as devices "designed or marketed as useful primarily for the stimulation of the human genitals," though Nebraska's 1977 law specified only articles or devices "having the appearance of either male or female genitals." The Louisiana statute overturned as "arbitrary and capricious" in the 2000 case *State v. Brennan* combined the two definitions to prohibit the sale of "an artificial penis or artificial vagina, which is designed or marketed as useful primarily for the stimulation of human genital organs." Whether such laws, which Maines refers to as "judicial novelties" in a 2001 affidavit concerning the Alabama statute, will be upheld in the post–*Lawrence v. Texas* judicial climate, and whether enforcement of such laws is even possible in an age when one can buy a butt plug anonymously through the Internet, remains to be seen.

Some of the most strenuous opposition to sex toys—dildos in particular—has come from lesbian feminists. While "girl-girl" porn produced for straight men, and straight men's popular conception of lesbian sex, often includes a dildo—perhaps a relic of the outdated notion that phallic penetration is necessary for female sexual pleasure—many lesbians have railed against the use of such objects. The question, simply put, is why, in woman-to-woman sex, is an artificial penis necessary?

As was the case with feminist anti-bondage and sadomasochism arguments, the anti-dildo position took on political overtones: the dildo was seen by some lesbian feminists, such as the publishers of the newspaper *off our backs,* as symbolic of "phallic imperialism," rubber embodiments of an unjust social order that subjugates women. These objections were countered by pro-sex feminists, such as the publishers of the magazine *On Our Backs,* who argued, essentially, that no one has the right to dictate someone else's sexual expression, that pleasure is its own justification, and that women in particular have much to gain from exploring new realms of sexual pleasure. These arguments continue today, as both sides have proven utterly unable to compel each other to use sex toys or to remove them from the other side's bedrooms.

The Sex Toy in Postgay and Queer Contexts

To a large extent, the pro-sex/anti-sex argument has been obviated by the generation of entrepreneurs, authors, and activists that emerged in the 1990s. Educators such as Tristan Taormino have emphasized the use of sex toys in blurring the lines between straight and gay, and between "normal" sex acts and "deviant" ones. For instance, the popular *Bend Over Boyfriend* series of porn films, in which women use strap-ons to anally penetrate their ostensibly straight male partners (a sex act christened "pegging" by gay advice guru Dan Savage) has forced viewers to question whether sexual identity is predicated on the role one plays, the acts one performs, or the apparent sex or gender of one's object of desire. In a similar vein, drag kings' use of dildos in "packing"—stuffing one's trousers to appear to have a penis—for purposes of male impersonation has helped subvert the entire idea of masculinity. The use of dildos by female-to-male transsexuals who want to experience what it is like to be a penetrator—and to fulfill their partners' willingness to be penetratees—has also posed a significant challenge to the feminist critique of sex toys.

In a more mainstream sense, vibrators, dildos, and other sex toys have come to be seen as essential accessories for the sophisticated urban professional woman, be she straight or queer. Stores such as San Francisco's Good Vibrations, billed as a "clean, well-lit place to buy a butt plug," and New York City's Toys in Babeland are a far cry from Sturman's sleazy sex emporiums. They are friendly, woman-staffed spaces that, while directed toward a primarily female clientele, will sell to anyone with a credit card, regardless of sexual preference. One of the most popular models of vibrator, the Hitachi Magic Wand, is sold partially on the strength of the Hitachi brand, while another best-selling model features the likeness of the popular Japanese cartoon character Hello Kitty. In this respect, sex toys have come full circle, from a treatment considered necessary for female health, but only when sanctioned from above by medical authority, to a consumer item purporting to sell self-administered, battery-powered empowerment.

Bibliography

Allyn, David. *Make Love, Not War.* New York: Little, Brown, 2000.

Heidendry, John. *What Wild Ecstasy.* New York: Simon and Schuster, 1997.

Kinsey, Alfred C. *Sexual Behavior in the Human Female.* Philadelphia: Saunders, 1953.

Kinsey, Alfred C., Wardell Baxter Pomeroy, and Clyde E. Martin. *Sexual Behavior in the Human Male.* Philadelphia: Saunders, 1948.

Maines, Rachel. *The Technology of Orgasm.* Baltimore: Johns Hopkins University Press, 1999.

———. "Affidavit of April 30, 2001." Available from http://www.libidomag.com/nakedbrunch/maines.html.

Mondschein, Ken. *A History of Single Life.* Los Angeles: Feral House, forthcoming.

Taylor, Emma, and Sharkey, Lorelei. *The Big Bang: Nerve's Guide to the New Sexual Universe.* New York: Plume Books, 2003.

Ken Mondschein

See also FETISHES; LEATHERSEX AND SEXUALITY; SADOMASOCHISM, SADISTS, AND MASOCHISTS; SEX ACTS.

SEX WARS

During the 1980s, a series of debates among feminists in the United States over issues of sexual politics, sexual representation, and sexual practice became known as the "sex wars." Such debates about sexuality were not new, but had split feminists along various lines since the nineteenth century. In 1873, the feminist free-love advocate Victoria Woodhull argued, "I will love whom I may; I will love for as long or as short a period as I can; I will change this love when the conditions indicate that it ought to be changed; and neither you nor any law you can make shall deter me," while in 1891, the temperance-movement leader and women's suffrage advocate Frances Willard asked, "Are our girls to be as free to please themselves by indulging in the loveless gratification of every instinct . . . and passion as our boys?" At the turn of the century, the antilynching activist Ida B. Wells criticized the rationale that supposedly "justified" lynching—that brutal black men raped pure white women—and was attacked by Willard, during the latter's late-nineteenth-century lecture tours in the American South. Willard defended the rationale because it was offered by "the best white people." In 1971, the Women's National Abortion Conference adopted demands for repeal of all anti-abortion laws, an end to sterilization abuse, and no restrictions on contraceptives, but split over a demand for "freedom of sexual expression," which was voted down and generated a walkout. The issues and ideas that generated such divergences of opinion shifted over the twentieth century and shaped the bitter conflicts of the sex wars years.

The Early 1970s

During the 1970s, issues of sexuality became central to second-wave feminism in the United States. Sexual freedom (including the freedom to be lesbian, as well as to have heterosexual sex with or without reproductive consequences), sexual violence, sexual representation (in all media), and sexual practice all generated new ideas, organizations, institutions, publications, and controversies. During the early 1970s, lesbians began to leave many women's groups to organize separately, and Betty Dodson published her widely popular pamphlet *Liberating Masturbation* (1974). During the same period, feminists offered a wide range of criticisms of the sexualized portrayal of women on television, in advertising, in films, and in print. Antirape and antibattering organizations

On the Battlefield. Verbal combatants in the "sex wars" wage a campaign in New York against pornography. [corbis]

began to create hotlines and shelters as early as 1971, and radical feminists offered analyses of sexual, as well as gender, dynamics underlying these forms of violence against women.

Many of these positions were criticized for their race and class biases by black feminists and other women of color, who offered analyses of the interconnection of sex, gender, race, class, and issues of violence and representation, as, for example, in the Combahee River Collective's 1977 "A Black Feminist Statement" and in the 1983 anthology *This Bridge Called My Back: Writings by Radical Women of Color,* edited by Cherríe Moraga and Gloria Anzaldúa. Black feminists were especially pointed in their criticisms of radical feminist analyses of the history of rape, such as Susan Brownmiller's 1975 book *Against Our Will: Men, Women, and Rape,* that tended to focus solely on the victimization of women by men while ignoring the role of racial antagonisms, especially the history of lynching and its specious justification as retaliation for rape.

Organizations Founded to Combat Violence against Women

The sex wars took off in the late 1970s and early 1980s, as issues of sexuality and violence began to converge in feminist campaigns against pornography, prostitution, and sadomasochism (S/M). In 1976, Women Against Violence Against Women (WAVAW) was formed in Los Angeles, and it generated wide publicity with the defacement of a billboard advertising an album by the rock band the

Rolling Stones, which WAVAW believed glorified sexualized violence against women. Women Against Violence in Pornography and the Media (WAVPM) formed in San Francisco in the same year and sponsored a 1978 conference called "Feminist Perspectives on Pornography," which generated a march by 7,000 women demanding an end to pornography. In 1979, Women Against Pornography (WAP) formed in New York City, where it showed versions of the slide shows developed by WAVAW and WAVPM and led tours of Times Square, pointing out the sites of pornography and prostitution. In addition to such activism, antipornography and antiprostitution feminists published a long list of books and articles that supplied the political and intellectual foundations for the movement. These writers, including Kathleen Barry, Andrea Dworkin, and Catharine A. MacKinnon, argued that gendered sexual norms often defined male domination of women as pleasure and as sex and that women's bodies were commodified and used in a range of related, exploitative sexual representations and practices.

Criticism of antipornography and antiprostitution feminism appeared at each stage of the development of this movement's ideas and institutions. The San Francisco lesbian S/M group Samois provided the earliest public forum for such criticism in 1979, at the Old Wives Tales bookstore. Articles and books by Ellen Willis, Deirdre English, and Pat Califia, as well as collections of essays by sex workers and sex-radical activists, challenged the conflation of sexuality and violence, the erasure of distinctions between representation and action, and the abandonment of demands for sexual freedom by antipornography feminists.

The most visible and significant clash of the antipornography feminists and their critics occurred in 1982 at the annual Barnard College conference "The Scholar and the Feminist," which focused on women and sexuality. Conference organizers, led by Carole S. Vance, defined the issues as pleasure versus danger, a framing they hoped would allow for a continuing conversation about the range of conflicts over sexual politics. But the conference became the scene of protests and controversy, as WAP members distributed leaflets criticizing the conference and its participants, and the Barnard College administration confiscated the conference program as suspected pornography. Vance's edited 1984 anthology *Pleasure and Danger: Exploring Female Sexuality* includes papers from the conference, as well as an account of the controversy and its extended aftermath.

Debates Move into the Mainstream

These debates within feminist circles moved dramatically into the wider society when Dworkin and MacKinnon developed a model antipornography ordinance and helped introduce it as proposed legislation in Minneapolis, Minnesota, in 1984, where it was passed but was vetoed by the mayor. Dworkin and MacKinnon argued that their model ordinance was a civil rights law and not censorship. Another version of this antipornography ordinance was then introduced and passed in Indianapolis, Indiana, where it was supported not only by feminists and their allies but also by the local chapter of the Moral Majority, the right-wing Eagle Forum member and City Council representative Beulah Coughenour, and the Republican Party. These events generated a new level of feminist opposition, as the Feminist Anti-Censorship Taskforce (FACT) formed in New York City and in Madison, Wisconsin, in 1984, for the purpose of challenging the ordinance in legislatures and in court. Versions of the ordinance were subsequently introduced in city councils and defeated by just one vote in both Los Angeles and Suffolk County, New York, in 1984 and 1985. A referendum in Cambridge, Massachusetts, was also soundly defeated in 1985. FACT groups formed in each city where an antipornography ordinance was proposed. In 1985, the U.S. Court of Appeals for the Seventh Circuit struck down the Indianapolis ordinance as unconstitutional, and the Supreme Court affirmed this decision. Also in 1985, U.S. Attorney General Edwin Meese appointed a commission "to address the serious national problem of pornography." Feminist antipornography advocates participated in the Meese Commission hearings and were represented in a final report issued in 1986.

The final report condemned "violent" pornography, a category that appeared to include both sadomasochism and representations of rape, but the commissioners were divided on whether to condemn all explicit depictions of sex outside marriage.

The mainstream debates over pornography subsumed the feminist conversation and ignored the wider range of issues generating conflict during the feminist sex wars, including the legal status of prostitution, the meanings attached to sadomasochism, and role-playing in sexual relationships. Overall, the sex wars issues dramatically affected lesbians active in feminist politics, and lesbian activists were divided along with other feminists. The discussion of S/M, for instance, focused on lesbian S/M organizations and practices, and the debates over role-playing centered on "butch" and "femme" roles among lesbians. Many lesbians actively led and participated in antipornography campaigns and produced related analyses on other issues. Other lesbians opposed antipornography feminism, and during the mid-1980s, some began publishing sexually explicit magazines, including *Bad Attitude* (Boston) and *On Our Backs* (San Francisco).

The sex wars debates primarily involved the activism and writing of white women active within American feminism. Black, Latina, Native American, and Asian feminists, allied as women of color, continued the conversation about race, gender, class, and sexual politics launched by the Combahee River Statement and *This Bridge Called My Back,* producing activism and writing that paralleled the sex wars issues, but dissented from their racially and geographically parochial framing. Lesbians and bisexual women of color, notably Audre Lorde, Cherríe Moraga, and Cheryl Clarke, contributed substantially to this conversation.

The sex wars tapered off during the late 1980s, as other issues of sexual politics rose to prominence, including controversies over AIDS and HIV prevention and treatment, and over public funding for sexually explicit art. But the issues and ideas at stake during these 1980s debates remained both central and vexed within feminist, LGBT, and queer politics in the early twenty-first century.

Bibliography

Barry, Kathleen. *Female Sexual Slavery.* New York: New York University Press, 1984.

Dodson, Betty. *Liberating Masturbation: A Meditation on Self Love.* New York: privately printed, 1974.

Duggan, Lisa, and Nan D. Hunter. *Sex Wars: Sexual Dissent and Political Culture.* New York: Routledge, 1995.

Dworkin, Andrea. *Pornography and Civil Rights: A New Day for Women's Equality.* Minneapolis: Organizing Against Pornography, 1988.

Feminist Anti-Censorship Taskforce et al., eds. *Caught Looking: Feminism, Pornography, and Censorship.* New York: Caught Looking, 1986.

Lederer, Laura, ed. *Take Back the Night: Women on Pornography.* New York: William Morrow, 1980.

Moraga, Cherríe, and Gloria Anzaldúa, eds. *This Bridge Called My Back: Writings by Radical Women of Color.* New York: Kitchen Table Press, 1983.

Vance, Carole S., ed. *Pleasure and Danger: Exploring Female Sexuality.* New York: Routledge, 1984.

Lisa Duggan

See also CENSORSHIP, OBSCENITY, AND PORNOGRAPHY LAW AND POLICY; FEMINISM; INTERGENERATIONAL SEX AND RELATIONSHIPS; LESBIAN FEMINISM; PORNOGRAPHY; SADOMASOCHISM, SADISTS, AND MASOCHISTS; SAMOIS.

SEXISM AND MISOGYNY. see FEMINISM; LESBIAN FEMINISM.

SEXOLOGY. see PSYCHOLOGY, PSYCHIATRY, PSYCHOANALYSIS, AND SEXOLOGY.

SEXUAL ASSAULT. see RAPE, SEXUAL ASSAULT, AND SEXUAL HARRASMENT LAW AND POLICY.

SEXUAL ORIENTATION AND PREFERENCE

The twentieth-century terms "sexual orientation" and "sexual preference" are sometimes used as synonyms for "sexual identity," a concept that is based on the gender of an individual and his or her sexual object choice—which might be homosexual (either lesbian or gay), heterosexual, or bisexual. At other times, these two terms are invested with contrasting meanings, with "sexual orientation" indicating a relatively fixed, biologically based condition, and "sexual preference" referring to a more flexible, mutable, environmentally shaped choice.

Sexology

The contemporary meanings of these terms underscore a distinction that appeared in most nineteenth-century sexology texts focused on "deviant" sexualities—the distinction between congenital conditions and acquired behaviors (later transformed into sexual "orientation" and "preference," respectively). Most nineteenth-century sexologists argued that sexual desire and behavior are biologically based and largely inherited. Richard von Krafft-Ebing and a wide circle of other European physicians catalogued sexualities they deemed abnormal and

the result either of incomplete evolutionary development (of an entire race or class considered "lower" on the scale of civilization) or of an arrested, neuropathic, or degenerate individual biological constitution. Krafft-Ebing also suggested, especially in the later editions of his major work, *Psychopathia Sexualis*, that sexual inversion (or same-gender sexual object choice) might sometimes be considered a benign anomaly of nature rather than a pathology when found in the "higher" type of civilized European. Other sexologists, before and after Krafft-Ebing, represented sexual inversion more consistently as either a benign or a noble condition. Karl Ulrichs, Magnus Hirschfeld, Edward Carpenter, John Addington Symonds, and Havelock Ellis all stressed the importance of social tolerance for sexually inverted individuals, sometimes referred to as "intermediate types" or members of a "third sex" who lived with an unalterable biological condition.

Yet all the nineteenth- and early-twentieth-century sexologists who focused their studies on congenital sexual variation, whether considered pathological, or inherited, or not, also proposed a kind of residual category for learned, mutable, relatively voluntary sexual deviance—acquired conditions that might be absorbed from the environment, either through a kind of social contagion or as an individual habit or vice; acquired sexual interest in members of the same gender might be picked up in single-sex boarding schools, in the military, or in prison, for example. The sexologists considered such acquired inversion a moral issue, entirely separable from their attitude toward the congenital condition. Though many were ambivalent about the moral evaluation of congenital sexual deviance from established sexual conventions and were also condescending toward the sexual behaviors of those considered "lower" in the evolutionary hierarchy, most excoriated acquired sexual deviations as immoral.

The distinction between congenital conditions and acquired behaviors was effectively erased within the psychoanalytic tradition established by Sigmund Freud. Though Freud considered the sexual libidos of individuals to be based in biological drives, he treated the polymorphous potential of those drives as malleable, shaped by cultural and historical forces into "civilized" social sexual conventions. In the United States in the twentieth century, the psychoanalytic profession generally treated homosexuality as a pathological acquired state, and many analysts attempted to convert homosexual patients to heterosexual behavior. But Freud himself did not consider homosexuality to be a pathology. And from the 1970s on, increasing numbers of psychoanalytic writers and practitioners moved away from treating sexual difference as deviance and began to accept a broad range of human sexual variation as healthy.

Biology

Outside of psychoanalysis and many religious traditions, which have viewed sexual behavior as an individual moral choice, homosexuality was widely regarded as biologically based throughout the twentieth century. Within psychiatry, psychology, sociology, history, literature, and the arts, and in popular and high culture, conceptions of sexual identity as fixed versus evaluations of sexual behavior as learned or chosen were combined in contradictory, unarticulated groupings of attitudes and beliefs. But most research into what began to be called sexual orientation, from the mid-twentieth century and thereafter focused squarely on finding the location for sexuality in the bodies of individuals. These studies have included research into the neuroanatomy, endocrinology, or genetic determination of sexuality, investigations of the inheritance of sexual orientation, and speculations about the historical, biological evolution of human sexual behavior.

Research into the hormones, genes, and brain regions that underlie human sexuality, particularly the determination of homosexuality versus heterosexuality, has continued throughout the twentieth century, generating scientific and political debate. Periodically, new versions of the argument that homosexuality is a congenital biological condition have appeared. Such arguments have been forwarded both to isolate, attack, and "treat" homosexuals considered pathological or abnormal and to defend homosexuality as a normal variation of human behavior. During the 1990s, the explicitly homophile work of Simon LeVay and Dean Hamer received especially wide attention and publicity. LeVay and his associates claimed that they had located the brain regions and mechanisms that control sexual desire and behavior; they argued that particular structures in the brains of homosexual men are more similar to the same structures in the brains of women than they are to those in heterosexual men. LeVay presented his research as grounded in evolutionary biology as well as genetics and endocrinology. Hamer and his colleagues announced that they had found the "genes" for homosexuality through a study of a group of gay men and their relatives. This research resonated with studies of identical versus fraternal twins undertaken by Richard Pillard and Michael Bailey and others, who argued that identical twins are more likely to share sexual orientations. In addition to these experimental scientific investigations of individual bodies, evolutionary or sociobiological studies have claimed a specific role for homosexual individuals in the reproduction of the species. Edward O. Wilson, for instance, argued that homosexuals assist their kinship networks, increasing reproductive success and genetic survival. Versions of Wilson's argument have been repeated often, in a wide range of popular and scientific contexts.

Social Sciences and Humanities

These studies received critical attention in the scientific world, where none have been accepted as definitive. They have also appeared with a parallel stream of social science studies undertaken throughout the twentieth century—including large comparative surveys as well as more focused ethnographic descriptions, both sociological and anthropological. Such studies, most notably Alfred Kinsey's controversial studies of male and female sexual behavior published and debated during the 1940s and 1950s, have been more concerned with reporting sexual variation than with explaining it and have generally left the question of whether sexuality is congenital or acquired, biological or environmentally determined, aside as relatively irrelevant. So while the biological research has generally focused on sexual orientation as a condition located within the body, the sociological and ethnographic studies have generally examined sexual preference as a question of sexual behavior within a social context. But these two streams of research have not necessarily been at odds, since the sexual surveys do not contest the assertion of a biological basis for sexuality, but rather tend to ignore that issue.

Another body of research and writing, appearing in the United States from the mid-1970s, has contested the view that human sexuality is primarily a biological or evolutionary phenomenon. These studies, influenced by Marxism, gay liberation, feminism, and poststructuralism, have argued that sexuality is a historical construction, shaped by culture and inflected with politics. Social construction theory of the 1970s and 1980s, located primarily within history, sociology, and anthropology, was expanded, elaborated, and complicated by poststructuralist treatises influenced by the work of Michel Foucault and located primarily within the literary humanities and in media and performance studies during the 1980s and 1990s. This work displaces the question of whether LGBT and queer people have fixed sexual orientations or learned and variable sexual preferences with the question, "'Why do we care?" At the turn of the twenty-first century, the language of sexual orientation appears primarily within the biological sciences and in the law and legal studies. The term itself often carries the assumption of sexuality as biologically fixed, but not always. In some texts, sexual orientation is simply meant as descriptive and not explanatory and may appear along with sexual preference as its synonym. Sexual preference alone appears primarily in psychology and sociology and occasionally in anthopology, where it serves as a descriptive term that generally leaves aside the question of the "cause" of sexual behavior. In history, the literary humanities, media and performance studies, and activist politics, "sexual identity" appears more often, referring to a culturally shaped social phenomenon located in specific historical contexts, and not individual bodies.

Eve Kosofsky Sedgwick, literary critic and proponent of queer theory and politics, noted in 1990 that "minoritizing" views of homosexuality as a fixed condition among a minority population and "universalizing" notions of sexuality as polymorphously variable across time and space have persisted side by side since the nineteenth century. These competing notions echo the contrast in meanings between fixed sexual "orientation" and flexible sexual "preference." And, Sedgwick argues, both conceptions have been available for both homophobic and homophile uses. Minoritizing views have supported forced experimental treatment and institutionalization of homosexuals, as well as provided the ground for defenses of lesbian and gay sexual orientation as immutable and requiring acceptance and respect. Universalizing arguments have both generated hostile moralizing and conversion efforts and inspired utopian visions of enriching sexual variety. The point, Sedgwick indicates, is not to choose one of these conceptions, but to historicize them and then to deploy them to promote and expand the possible meanings of sexual equality, justice, and freedom.

Bibliography

Abelove, Henry. "Freud, Male Homosexuality, and the Americans." In *The Lesbian and Gay Studies Reader*. Edited by Henry Abelove, Michele Aina Barale, and David Halperin. New York: Routledge, 1993. Reprint, Cambridge, Massachusetts: MIT Press, 1996.

DeCecco, John P., and David Allen Parker, eds. *Sex, Cells, and Same-Sex Desire: The Biology of Sexual Preference*. Binghamton, N.Y.: Harrington Park, 1995.

Fausto-Sterling, Anne. *Sexing the Body: Gender Politics and the Construction of Sexuality*. New York: Basic Books, 2000.

Foucault, Michel. *The History of Sexuality, Vol. 1: An Introduction*. Translated by Robert Hurley. New York: Pantheon, 1978.

Hamer, Dean, and Peter Copeland. *The Science of Desire: The Search for the Gay Gene and the Biology of Behavior*. New York: Simon and Schuster, 1994.

———. *Living with Our Genes: Why They Matter More Than You Think*. New York: Doubleday, 1998.

Kinsey, Alfred C., et al. *Sexual Behavior in the Human Female*. Philadelphia: Saunders, 1953.

Kinsey, Alfred C., Wardell B. Pomeroy; and Clyde E. Martin. *Sexual Behavior in the Human Male*. Philadelphia: Saunders, 1948.

Krafft-Ebing, Richard von. *Psychopathia Sexualis with Especial Reference to Contrary Sexual Instinct*. Translated from the 12th and final ed. by Brian King. Burbank, Calif.: Bloat, 1999.

LeVay, Simon. *The Sexual Brain*. Cambridge, Mass.: MIT Press, 1993. Reprint, New York: Basic Books, 2000.

———. *Queer Science: The Use and Abuse of Research into Homosexuality*. Cambridge, Mass.: MIT Press, 1996.

Puterbaugh, Geoff, ed. *Twins and Homosexuality: A Casebook*. New York: Garland, 1990.

Rosario, Vernon, ed. *Science and Homosexualities*. New York: Routledge, 1997.

Sedgwick, Eve Kosofsky. *Epistemology of the Closet*. Berkeley: University of California Press, 1990.

Stein, Edward. *Uncovering Desire: The Science, Theory, and Ethics of Sexual Orientation*. New York: Oxford University Press, 1999.

Stein, Edward, ed. *Forms of Desire: Sexual Orientation and the Social Constructionist Controversy*. New York: Garland, 1990.

Terry, Jennifer. *An American Obsession: Science, Medicine, and Homosexuality in Modern Society*. Chicago: University of Chicago Press, 1999.

Lisa Duggan

See also HOMOSEXUALITY AND HETEROSEXUALITY; BISEXUALITY, BISEXUALS, AND BISEXUAL MOVEMENTS; HOMOEROTICISM AND HOMOSOCIALITY; PSYCHOLOGY, PSYCHIATRY, PSYCHOANALYSIS, AND SEXOLOGY; SITUATIONAL HOMOSEXUALITY; SEX ACTS.

SEXUAL PSYCHOPATH LAW AND POLICY

From 1935 to 1965, thirty-five states enacted sexual psychopath statutes. Although the wording and parameters of the statutes varied from state to state, each was based on the belief that certain sex offenders lacked the ability to control their perverted sexual impulses, thus constituting a danger to public safety, and that theirs was a treatable medical condition. With only a few exceptions, sexual psychopath laws allowed for the involuntary and indefinite civil (as opposed to criminal) commitment of those who met the established criteria. Typically, those charged with any number of illegal sex acts, from rape and sodomy to child molestation and lewdness, could be recommended for assessment under this new legislation. However, some states did not require that a person be found guilty of a crime, or even for a crime to have been committed. Those merely deemed likely to offend could be committed to a mental institution for an indefinite length of time. Although many sexual psychopath laws were passed in response to a perceived rise in sexual assaults against children and minors, adult homosexual men engaging in consensual sex with other adult males or male adolescents made up a significant proportion of those who were subjected to incarceration and treatment under these statutes.

The Origins of Sexual Psychopath Laws

Sexual psychopath laws were a novel experiment in American criminal law, but the notion that criminal behavior was a treatable medical problem was not entirely new. After the end of the Civil War, Progressive Era reformers searched for innovative solutions to the social, economic and moral problems plaguing modern urban society. The rise of the mass media heightened public awareness of crime and social disorder, and social scientific studies of criminal populations revealed high rates of recidivism among the "dangerous" classes, reaffirming the belief that prison alone has neither a reformative nor a deterrent effect. At the same time, forensic psychiatrists proposed alternative models for understanding criminal behavior. Specifically, they argued that some offenders were unable to control their impulses, and that their problem was a health, not a criminal, matter.

Psychopathic offenders were not viewed as insane, but neither were they considered normal. Instead, they were thought to lack the self-control that enabled most people to live within the bounds of acceptable society. In the 1910s and 1920s, the diagnosis of psychopathy was most likely to be used against unemployed men and "hypersexual" women. Since they were determined to be ill and in need of treatment, psychopathic criminals could be committed to mental institutions or special wards of prisons for an indefinite period of time. Indefinite sentences were justified as a humane alternative to traditional incarceration since it was intended to facilitate medical treatment, but it often amounted to extended terms of imprisonment.

Sexual psychopath laws were the first to fully integrate psychiatric treatment with formal criminal statutes on a widespread basis. In 1935, Michigan passed the first such law, establishing a procedure that enabled the courts to refer those convicted of "indecent crimes" to a state hospital if certain criteria were met. Although revised shortly thereafter, initially the law was wide-ranging and applied in cases involving everything from sodomy and gross indecency to "indecent language in the presence or hearing of any woman or child," "any disorderly conduct involving sex," and "any other crime or offense of like

nature." One had only to "appear to be psychopathic, or a sex degenerate, or a sex pervert, with tendencies." The revised statute was more limited in scope, but this early example provides a revealing glimpse of exactly who were targeted by these laws. Later in the 1930s, Illinois, California, and Minnesota passed sexual psychopath laws. After World War II, a majority of states followed suit.

Unlike traditional prison sentences but like earlier psychopath laws, sexual psychopath statutes allowed courts to commit those who fit the designated criteria for an indeterminate length of time, not to be released until they were determined to be either "cured" or assessed as no longer a danger to society. As a result of these laws, many people were incarcerated for much greater periods of time than they would have been under traditional sentencing practices. Moreover, not all states were ready to abandon punishment altogether. Some required sexual psychopaths to serve a prison sentence for the original crime after release from treatment.

The Sex Crime Panic Gains Momentum

Historians point to several important factors to explain the popularity of sexual psychopath laws. Changing sexual norms and practices during the first sexual revolution in the 1920s, the decline of female purity as an ideology that regulated male sexuality, and the subsequent disruptions to traditional family and gender arrangements caused by the Great Depression led to growing concern about male masculinity in the 1930s. Once objects of ridicule and pity, unemployed hoboes and tramps roaming city streets and riding the rails in search of work and food and the dandies and pansies who had been a part of the nighttime urban spectacle increasingly became objects of fear. Male sex "perverts," especially effeminate homosexuals and aggressive sex offenders (both homosexual and heterosexual), helped define the boundaries around normative masculinity and male sexuality in a period of change.

These shifts were aided by the pre–World War II political maneuverings of J. Edgar Hoover, director of the Federal Bureau of Investigation. His 1937 call for a "war on sex crime" was instrumental in turning public attention toward "stranger danger." Over the next few years, the number of media reports on sex crimes rose substantially, and with these came the first wave of sexual psychopath laws. The panic subsided as Americans became increasingly concerned with World War II, but Hoover renewed his call for a war on sex crime as soon as the dust over Europe and Asia settled. While the war effectively ended the economic depression, a sharp rise in marriage and birth rates in the years immediately following the allied victory created favorable conditions for a second panic about sex "perverts." Young parents anxious to raise their children according to the most modern, scientific methods proved to be responsive to both medical ideas about sexual normality and deviancy and legislative campaigns aimed at curbing sexual assaults against children. Indeed, extensive crime coverage of assaults against children played on parental fears. The introduction of sexual psychopath statutes was typically preceded by a widely reported murder, disappearance, or attack against a child.

Parents had good reason to push for new measures. Prosecuting cases of heterosexual or homosexual assault against children was next to impossible since the testimony of a child alone was rarely enough for a conviction. Moreover, even in instances where a guilty verdict was rendered, sentences were often negligible. The shame attached to sexual assault as well as the court's failure to serve as a venue for justice deterred the majority of parents from laying formal charges against their children's assailants. Given these conditions, it is little wonder that parents of the baby boom generation were happy to support a law that required no trial to have a suspected pedophile put away. Openly supporting laws that appeared to take the matter seriously was in part an organized effort by parents, whose goal was to force authorities to improve the way sexual assault against children was handled. That these measures were perceived to be a compassionate and humanitarian response to a mental health problem helped widen support among liberal-minded citizens, while at the same time garnering support among more conservative Americans who favored longer sentences. Finally, the peculiar Cold War convergence of communism and homosexuality as perceived threats to the American way of life served to further entrench the vilification of sexual psychopaths. The cultural climate was such that nonconformists of almost every type were suspect, but male homosexuals were perceived to be the enemy within, not only because they shirked heterosexual responsibilities, but because, according to medical, legal, and police authorities, they constantly recruited young boys into their fraternity. This was a claim that neatly echoed fears of communist conversion and subversion and rendered homosexuality a threat to both sexual stability and national security. Consequently, even consensual forms of sexual "perversion" were cast as dangerous, and the prosecution of nonviolent sex offenders under sexual psychopath laws was supported by politicians and the public.

The Impact of Sexual Psychopath Laws

Although coined by psychiatrists themselves, "sexual psychopathy" was never a formal medical diagnosis and was used so broadly that it had little value as a medical term. In fact, by midcentury psychopathy was widely regarded as a "waste basket category" into which all manner of unusual or nonconforming behavior was tossed. Many psychiatrists and other medical experts were highly ambivalent about sexual psychopath statutes. In 1950, criminologist Edwin Sutherland and sociologist Paul Tappan advised against the adoption and implementation of sexual psychopath statutes. Legal expert Morris Ploscowe followed suit in 1951, and two years later psychiatrist Karl Bowman expressed grave concern about using sexual psychopath laws to incarcerate sex offenders for long periods of time; he instead called for more research and an expansion of hospital care services.

Studies have consistently shown that violent offenders and child molesters were less likely than other groups to be targeted by sexual psychopath laws. Despite the fact that public support for the treatment approach to sex crimes focused on violent sexual assaults against children, men who engaged in consensual homosexual sex and those merely found in "known homosexual haunts" were among the most likely groups to be targeted by law enforcement officials. This was partly due to policing practices. Media reports invariably directed the public's gaze onto local police forces. Anxious to appear to be doing something, they frequently responded by undertaking mass arrests in places known to have gay clientele. They also conducted sweeps of parks, beaches, and other places frequented by men seeking homosexual sexual contact after dark. For example, in 1952, Dr. E. Kelleher, the director of the Chicago Psychiatric Institute, complained that the police, acting under pressure from the media and "various public organizations," conducted a campaign to clean up North Clark Street. The campaign seemed to consist of raiding gay clubs and making mass arrests. On one particular night, forty-two suspected homosexuals were brought to his institute, overloading the staff with "patients" for whom they had neither interest nor resources. In Sioux City, Iowa, police referred to this practice as "fruit picking." Mass arrests such as these were remarkably common in the 1950s and early 1960s and have been documented elsewhere, including California, Philadelphia, and Florida.

Sexual psychopath laws tended to be used most often in districts that had a facility dedicated to the treatment of those subjected to the law. Facilities ranged from freestanding clinics to beds in a state mental institution to a wing of a prison. The type and quality of treatment were equally uneven: Those who fell under the purview of these statutes could be subjected to psychotherapy, behavior modification, psychotropic drugs, estrogen, aversive conditioning techniques, or electroshock therapy. Much to the dismay of treatment "experts," many homosexuals proved highly resistant to change and insisted on their right to be different. Frustrated with patients who refused to admit to their problem, doctors turned to increasingly coercive means to effect reformation. In most cases, however, inadequate staffing and a lack of facilities meant that treatment amounted to little more than an intake consultation with a social worker, psychologist, or psychiatrist.

Ironically, the implementation of sexual psychopath statutes led to a debate over whether or not sex between men should be a criminal offense at all. For example, in a 1949 article published in *Psychosexual Development in Health and Disease,* Alfred Kinsey and his research associates at the Kinsey Institute in Bloomington, Indiana, argued that the notion of a sexual norm was scientifically sophistic. Norms, they argued, are an expression of religious and moral values and do not come within the domain of science. Legitimate researchers and practitioners can lay no claim to authority over such definitions, they insisted. Nor should the law be regulating morals. Instead, it should limit itself to crimes causing harm.

Overall, psychiatrists tended to come to the agreement that homosexuals were overrepresented among those institutionalized under sexual psychopath laws. In New Jersey, which first passed a sexual psychopath law in 1949, almost half of the first one hundred people judged to be sexual psychopaths were convicted of homosexual lewdness, sodomy, or fellatio. In 1957, psychiatrist Bernard C. Glueck Jr. argued that sexual psychopathy was frequently equated with male homosexuality and that the male homosexual "tends to bear the brunt of prosecution under these laws." By the end of 1961 in Pennsylvania, half of that state's ninety-four sexual psychopath cases that resulted in institutionalization in state correctional facilities or mental hospitals were sodomy related, and only 15 percent of these involved the use of force. By the 1960s, many "experts" rallied behind the harm model of sexual danger, but definitions of harm proved to be highly elastic and mutable, especially at a time when Freudian and other behavioral models of sexual development were at their peak in popularity. For instance, it was entirely common to argue that gay men caused harm to themselves by indulging in perverted sexual behavior. But even more compelling was the argument that most gay men recruited adolescent males into their secret society, thus making them both predators and pedophiles. Persistently linked with pedophiles, men who did not appear to conform to the married, heterosexual ideal appeared suspect and dangerous. Furthermore, they continued to face civil or criminal commitment under sexual psychopath laws.

From Psychopath to Predator

In the late 1960s, a series of exposés on the inhumane use of medical treatments in prison helped facilitate a shift in public opinion away from an optimistic faith in science as a means to solve social problems. Even more effective in shifting public opinion were media accounts of violent sexual crimes committed by men who were released from sexual psychopath treatment programs. Despite more than twenty years of "treatment," sexual psychopath laws were clearly not working. Psychiatrists themselves had long been ambivalent about treatment for sex offenders, and by the early 1970s most had abandoned the field, leaving the area open for other experts. In 1977 a report of the Group for the Advancement of Psychiatry denounced sexual psychopath laws as a social experiment that had failed and called for their immediate repeal. By that time, LGBT activists had already successfully campaigned for the removal of homosexuality as a disorder in the American Psychiatric Association's *Diagnostic and Statistical Manual.* A small number of states repealed their laws against sodomy shortly thereafter, thereby automatically excluding adult male consensual sex from sexual psychopath statutes in those states.

Beginning in the 1960s, a series of Supreme Court decisions introduced restrictions on the use of sexual psychopath statutes, and a number of states either repealed or simply stopped using them. Others began the process of replacing them with new "sexual predator" laws that emphasized community protection over treatment for offenders, a process that continued well into the 1990s. Like sexual psychopath laws, these new laws single out sex offenders as more dangerous than other offenders and permit the use of indeterminate sentencing. The new generation of laws also focuses more squarely on the original target of sexual psychopath laws: violent sexual offenders, especially those whose victims are children. "Predator laws," however, represent a departure from sexual psychopath laws insofar as they reflect popular disenchantment with treatment and an increasingly punitive attitude toward sex offenders. Thus, indeterminate sentencing, which had been legally and politically palatable because it permitted "compassionate treatment," is now used to keep sex offenders locked up indefinitely, a practice that would not likely have passed the initial round of judicial challenges to sexual psychopath laws. Although treatment programs for sexual disorders (as defined by the medical community) continue to operate in state hospitals and private clinics, contemporary law focuses on community protection from violent predators rather than offender rehabilitation.

Sexual psychopath laws were a North American phenomenon: Canada and the United States were the only two countries to enact them. However, the medicalization of sexual "perversion" and the legitimization of medical science in the field of human sexuality were global developments of significant importance in the twentieth century.

Bibliography

Bayer, Ronald. *Homosexuality and American Psychiatry: The Politics of Diagnosis*. New York: Basic Books, 1981.

Chauncey, George, Jr., "The Postwar Sex Crime Panic" In *True Stories form the American Past*. Edited by William Graebner. New York: McGraw-Hill, 1993.

Cole, Simon A. "From the Sexual Psychopath Statute to 'Megan's Law': Psychiatric Knowledge in the Diagnosis, Treatment, and Adjudication of Sex Criminals in New Jersey, 1949-1999." *Journal of the History of Medicine* 55 (July 2000): 292–314.

D'Emilio, John. "The Homosexual Menace: The Politics of Sexuality in Cold War America." In *Passion and Power: Sexuality in History*. Edited by Kathy Peiss and Christina Simmons. Philadelphia: Temple University Press, 1989.

Eskridge, William N., Jr. *Gaylaw: Challenging the Apartheid of the Closet*. Cambridge, Mass.: Harvard University Press, 1999.

Fejes, Fred. "Murder, Perversion, and Moral Panic: The 1954 Media Campaign against Miami's Homosexuals and the Discourse of Civic Betterment." *Journal of the History of Sexuality* 9, no. 3 (July 2000): 305–347.

Freedman, Estelle. "'Uncontrolled Desires': The Response to the Sexual Psychopath, 1920–1960." In *Passion and Power: Sexuality in History*. Edited by Kathy Peiss and Christina Simmons. Philadelphia: Temple University Press, 1989.

Glueck, Bernard C., Jr. "An Evaluation of the Homosexual Offender." *Minnesota Law Review* 41, no. 2 (1957): 187–210.

Group for the Advancement of Psychiatry. *Psychiatry and Sex Psychopath Legislation, Vol. 9: The 30s to the 80s*. New York: Group for the Advancement of Psychiatry, 1977.

Horwitz, Andrew. "Sexual Psychopath Legislation: Is There Anywhere to Go But Backwards?" *University of Pittsburgh Law Review* 57: 35–78.

Jenkins, Philip. *Moral Panic: Changing Concepts of the Child Molester in Modern America*. New Haven, Conn.: Yale University Press, 1998.

Kinsey, Alfred, et al. "Concepts of Normality and Abnormality in Sexual Behavior." In *Psychosexual Development in Health and Disease*. New York: Grune and Stratton, 1949.

Robertson, Stephen. "Separating the Men from the Boys: Masculinity, Psychosexual Development, and Sex Crime in the United States, 1930s–1960s." *Journal of the History of Medicine and Allied Sciences* 56, no. 1. (January 2001): 3–35.

Sutherland, Edwin H. "The Diffusion of Sex Psychopath Laws." *American Journal of Sociology* 56 (1950): 142–148.

Terry, Jennifer. *An American Obsession: Science, Medicine, and Homosexuality in Modern Society*. Chicago: University of Chicago Press, 1999.

Elise Chenier

See also CRIME AND CRIMINALIZATION; DISCRIMINATION; FEDERAL LAW AND POLICY; HEALTH AND HEALTH CARE LAW AND POLICY; MEDICINE, MEDICALIZATION, AND THE MEDICAL MODEL; PSYCHOLOGY, PSYCHIATRY, PSYCHOANALYSIS, AND SEXOLOGY; POLICE AND POLICING.

SEXUAL REVOLUTIONS

In January 1964 *Time* magazine announced the arrival of the "second sexual revolution," signaled, in the magazine's view, by an increase in sexually explicit culture—what it called "Spectator Sex." Over the next few years, articles about the sexual revolution also appeared in *America* (March 6, 1965), a magazine published by the Jesuit order, and *Ebony* (August 1966), a mass-market magazine with a predominately African American readership.

Time's report on the sexual revolution was in some ways an impressively learned essay on the history of sexuality, a field not then acknowledged by many historians. What is equally interesting is that *Time* authoritatively identified the sexual revolution of the sixties as the second sexual revolution, the first having taken place in the years following World War I. But in differentiating between a first and second sexual revolution and making the essay an example of comparative historical analysis, the magazine also suggested that there are systematic social factors that may underlie shifting sexual attitudes and behavior. The *Time* piece never mentioned homosexuality, raising questions about just how revolutionary the sexual revolution was, but later that year *Life* (June 1964), owned by the same publisher, ran an article on "Homosexuality in America" that suggested that it continued to be depressing to be homosexual in the United States.

Despite the scholarly aspects of *Time's* essay, "sexual revolution" has only recently entered the historian's discourse as a legitimate topic of research and as an analytic framework for examining changes in sexuality. Yet to take the term seriously as a historical phenomenon—or as a series of historical events—requires an examination of underlying assumptions. The very notion of sexual revolution—defined by significant changes in sexual behavior, attitudes, and mores—is implicitly an exercise in periodization. Such periodization requires definitions of measurements, causal effects, and theoretical frameworks within which to assess changes.

For the most part, American historians have continued to explore the periodization that *Time* magazine proposed in its 1964 essay. There is some presumption that the twentieth century experienced two sexual revolutions—one in the years during and after World War I and the second in the 1960s and 1970s. What is not clear, however, is whether or not periods before the twentieth century experienced comparable shifts in sexual attitudes and conduct. Fluctuations in the regulation of sexual activity have taken place in many historical periods and cultures. One of the earliest histories of sexuality in Europe and North America, Rattray Taylor's *Sex in History,* is based on a generalization of that model—"the history of civilization is the history of a long warfare between the dangerous and powerful forces of the id, and the various systems of taboos and inhibitions . . . erected to control them" (Taylor, p. 13). Such a generalization, however, is too sweeping to be useful.

Recently, Richard Godbeer has suggested that a sexual revolution took place in several seventeenth- and eighteenth-century colonial American communities. He describes a "fundamental shift in sexual culture during the eighteenth century away from an ethos rooted in organic conceptions of society and toward a more individualistic marketplace of sexual desire and fulfillment," ultimately producing a more permissive sexual climate and reduced parental control (Godbeer, pp. 10, 237–38). The result was "a steady rise in premarital pregnancy," which rose from a mere 2 percent of the women married in the 1670s to 19 percent during the 1690s. By the revolutionary era, the proportion of pregnant brides was between 30 and 40 percent (p. 228). Godbeer found this shift from a communal to individualistic morality taking place across the three different North American colonial regions that he examines—New England, Virginia and the Carolinas, and Philadelphia. But despite the shift in the moral authority that regulated sexual life in the colonies and the fact that the ratio of men to women in certain colonies was very high, same-sex relations were never openly tolerated, even if they were not always vigorously persecuted.

"Sexual revolution" was first conceptualized by Wilhelm Reich, one of Freud's most brilliant protégés. Reich argued that human suffering could not be alleviated solely by individual therapy, but required social action—in fact, that sexual reforms were impossible without radical political action. Conversely, he also stressed that political revolution, including socialist revolution, was doomed to failure unless it was accompanied by the abolition of sexual repression. In *The Sexual Revolution* (1932), Reich analyzed the failure of the Russian Revolution—which had originally included many progressive sexual reforms such as easy access to birth control, eliminating the laws against homosexuality, sex education, and women's rights—and the rise of sexual conservatism in the Soviet Union. Reich also applied his analysis to fascism. In *The Mass Psychology of Fascism* (1933), which was written against the backdrop of Hitler's rise to power, Reich argued that fascism relied on the unsatisfied orgastic longing of the masses.

The term "revolution" often implies something that occurs rapidly and dramatically, but sexual revolution as it emerged in the twentieth century is based on a different model of historical change. The time frame of sexual revolution in this sense is much longer—the "longue durée." It resembles the time frame of "the industrial revolution"—the transition from an agricultural society to one built on new technologies and industrial production. It was an immense and contradictory process, often not very obvious, stretching out over the life span of several generations. Sexual revolution radically alters the sex/gender system, as anthropologist Gayle Rubin (in the essay "Traffic in Women") has called the cultural code that translates biological capacities into the cultural and social patterns that constitute our lives as gendered and sexual human beings. Sexual revolution in this sense includes intentional political action and fundamental sexual reforms of the sort that Reich proposes and the structural changes produced by large-scale social forces.

The first sexual revolution of the twentieth century—if indeed it was a legitimate example of large-scale structural change in sexual behaviors and attitudes—emerged from the political and cultural dislocations of World War I and the longer-term social transformations accompanying urbanization, immigration, and industrialization. The emergence of the flapper and the New Woman signaled a challenge to the sexual double standard and led to a greater emotional expressiveness and sexual vulnerability in the male gender role. But there is no unequivocal evidence of significant changes in sexual behavior. Daniel Scott Smith in his interesting examination of rates of premarital coitus (as measured by premarital pregnancies among white women) found no sudden increase in the early twentieth century—only a slow and steady rise in the number of such pregnancies. He also found that dramatic increases in premarital pregnancies occurred only after 1960.

To some degree, an increasingly liberal view of homosexuality began to emerge in the 1920s, but the period also displayed a growing public expression of homophobia. George Chauncey and Kevin Mumford both have found flourishing new sexual subcultures among gay men and in the black/white sex districts in major cities like New York and Chicago between 1900 and the late 1920s. For a short time, these subcultures also attracted sexual tourism from bohemians and upper-class dilettantes, but in the 1930s homosexuals and other sexual minorities were stigmatized and repressed. Judith Schwarz's work on the Heterodoxy Club in Greenwich Village similarly documents the emergence of lesbian subcultures in the early twentieth century but also the rise of antilesbian hostility and fear in the 1920s. Meanwhile, Christina Simmons has argued that the modernizing discourse of companionate marriage, which became popular in the 1920s, contained significant antilesbian elements.

The sexual revolution that followed World War II undoubtedly produced the most dramatic shifts in sexual conduct and mores to take place in the last century. These significant transformations resulted from the cumulative effects of an enormous number of more modest changes, including the invention of the birth control pill, large-scale entry of married women into the labor force, decline of the family wage, increased divorce rates, and the emergence of a new consumerism. While the early stages of this sexual revolution were initially signaled by shifts in public sexual discourses and struggles over freedom of sexual speech, the sexual revolution of the 1960s and 1970s was driven by a series of social and cultural movements: first, the explosion of youth culture (and student movements), which reinforced the thirst of young men and women for sexual experience before marriage; second, the emergence of feminism and the women's movement at the end of the sixties; and third, the gay liberation movement's dramatic Stonewall rebellion in 1969. Each of these developments spurred new forms of nonreproductive sexual relations.

Some feminists believe that the sexual revolution, from the perspective of women, was a failure, simply encouraging the objectification and exploitation of women. But as Barbara Ehrenreich, Elizabeth Hess, and Gloria Jacobs have demonstrated, women achieved gains in sexual freedom and in the balance of power in relationships. It was a genuine revolution in sexual attitudes and behavior—the double standard was effectively challenged, new sexual knowledge about female sexuality was developed and widely disseminated, and women achieved new kinds of sexual relationships and identities.

The gay liberation movement (as it was initially called) that followed on the heels of the women's movement sought to achieve a combination of things: sexual liberation, civil rights, alternative social activities, and the empowerment of lesbians and gay men through consciousness-raising groups. After Stonewall and into the mid-1970s, the gay and lesbian movement was organized primarily around the political act of "coming out," of making full public disclosure of one's homosexuality. The emphasis on coming out and on the building of communal institutions became the basis of creating a new "gay identity." No previous generation of lesbians and gay men had created a political movement organized around "being homosexual."

The sexual revolution of the 1960s and 1970s was not only a revolution in sexual behavior per se but also a cultural revolution that was intertwined with many other significant social changes. Women's sexuality was redefined, and new stress was laid on clitoral orgasm and female sexual satisfaction. A culture of sexual experimentation (swinging, sadomasochist clubs, singles bars) emerged that contributed to the development of new sexual norms. The women's movement, the counterculture, new sexual lifestyles, lesbian and gay liberation, a greater acceptance of pleasure, and all kinds of improvements in the quality of life overlap with the sexual revolution. The sexual revolution of post–World War II America has changed sexual and gender roles permanently.

Sexual revolutions emerge from permutations of sexual desires, sexual activities, and gender roles, setting in motion what Jonathan Dollimore has called the "perverse dynamic" (similarly, Michel Foucault spoke of the "perverse implantation"). Freud argued that perverse sexual desires (i.e., all nonreproductive forms of sexual behavior, including kissing or oral sex) were incompatible with a stable social order; instead, they must be transformed, through repression and sublimation, into forms of energy more compatible with "civilized society." Freud believed that sublimated sexuality put extraordinarily large amounts of energy at the disposal of social activities. In *Eros and Civilization* (1955), Herbert Marcuse sought to develop the emancipatory potential of Freud's theories. He argued for the possibility of "nonrepressive sublimation," which would allow for new forms of work based on nonalienated labor as well as the creation of new kinds of libidinal communities. Marcuse identified the homosexual as the radical standard bearer of sex for the sake of pleasure, a form of radical hedonism that repudiates those forms of repressive sexuality organized around genital heterosexuality and sex exclusively for biological reproduction. However, by the mid-1960s, Marcuse was increasingly concerned that advanced industrial society had made sexual liberation impossible—not through intensified repression, but by harnessing "de-sublimated" energies through increased productivity and mass consumption. Instead, the de-sublimated sexuality released by the sexual revolution was channeled into commercialized forms of advertising and entertainment and institutionalized forms of aggression, and it was isolated from broader forms of erotic life.

Both Freud and Marcuse assumed that society governed perverse sexual energies primarily through repression and sublimation. However, Foucault argued that the proliferation of discourses on sex have played a major role in the development of sexualities. In the *History of Sexuality: An Introduction,* Foucault showed that late-eighteenth-century and nineteenth-century discourses (such as medical and psychiatric discourse) promoted certain types of sexual persons: the masturbating child, the hysterical woman, the Malthusian couple (who practiced birth control), and the homosexual. Through the construction of discourses about these "identities," society is able to govern what would otherwise be an uncontrolled underground sexuality. Thus, in Foucault's theory, sexual revolution and its discourses of sexual liberation paradoxically both emancipates those who are stigmatized for their sexuality, and facilitates the governing of the newly emancipated identities.

In time, the sexual revolution provoked a profound and powerful counter-revolution—the religious fundamentalist right and the New Right—that continues to wage a battle against the forces and over the issues (homosexuality, abortion, sex education, and non-marital sexuality) that originally ignited the revolution. Many of the social changes and the conflicts (such as the sex wars and the culture wars) engendered by the sexual revolution continue on into the present and are still working themselves out.

Bibliography

Allyn, David. *Make Love, Not War: The Sexual Revolution, An Unfettered History.* Boston: Little Brown and Company, 2000.

Bailey, Beth. *Sex in the Heartland.* Cambridge, Mass.: Harvard University Press, 1999.

Chauncey, George. *Gay New York: Gender, Urban Culture, and the Making of the Gay Male World, 1890–1940.* New York: Basic Books, 1994.

D'Emilio, John, and Estelle Freedman. *Intimate Matters: A History of Sexuality in America.* New York: Harper & Row, 1988.

Dollimore, Jonathan. *Sexual Dissidence: Augustine to Wilde, Freud to Foucault.* Oxford: Clarendon Press; New York: Oxford University Press, 1991.

Echols, Alice. *Daring to Be Bad: Radical Feminism in America, 1967–1975.* Minneapolis: University of Minnesota, 1989.

Ehrenreich, Barbara, Elizabeth Hess, and Gloria Jacobs. *Re-Making Love: The Feminization of Sex.* Garden City: Anchor Press/Doubleday, 1986.

Escoffier, Jeffrey. *American Homo: Community and Perversity.* Berkeley: University of California Press, 1998.

Foucault, Michel. *The History of Sexuality: An Introduction.* New York: Pantheon, 1978.

Freud, Sigmund. *Civilization and Its Discontents.* The Standard Edition, translated by James Strachey. New York: W. W. Norton, 1961.

Godbeer, Richard. *Sexual Revolution in Early America.* Baltimore: The Johns Hopkins University Press, 2002.

Heidenery, John. *What Wild Ecstasy: The Rise and Fall of the Sexual Revolution.* New York: Simon & Schuster, 1997.

Marcuse, Herbert. *Eros and Civilization: A Philosophical Inquiry into Freud.* Boston: Beacon Press, 1955.

———. *One-Dimensional Man: Studies in the Ideology of Advanced Industrial Society.* Boston: Beacon Press, 1964.

Mumford. Kevin J. *Interzones: Black/White Sex Districts in Chicago and New York in the Early Twentieth-Century.* New York: Columbia University Press, 1997.

Reich, Wilhelm. *The Sexual Revolution: Toward a Self-Governing Character Structure.* Translated by Theodore P. Wolfe. New York: Farrar, Straus, and Giroux, 1969, 1974.

———. *The Mass Psychology of Fascism.* Translated by Vincent R. Carfagno. New York: Farrar, Straus & Giroux, 1970.

Robinson, Paul A. *The Freudian Left: Wilhelm Reich, Geza Roheim, Herbert Marcuse.* New York: Harper & Row, 1969.

Rubin, Gayle. "The Traffic in Women: Notes on the Political Economy of Sex." In *Toward an Anthropology of Women.* Edited by Rayna R. Reiter. New York: Monthly Review Press, 1975.

Smith, Daniel Scott. "The Dating of the American Sexual Revolution: Evidence and Interpretation." In *The American Family in Social-Historical Perspective* 2d ed. Edited by Michael Gordon. New York: St. Martin's Press, 1978.

Taylor, G. Rattray. *Sex in History: The Story of Society's Changing Attitudes to Sex throughout the Ages.* New York: Harper & Row, 1973.

White, Kevin. *The First Sexual Revolution: The Emergence of Male Heterosexuality in Modern America.* New York University Press, 1993.

———. *Sexual Liberation or Sexual License? The American Revolt against Victorianism.* Chicago: Ivan R. Dee, 2000.

Jeffrey Escoffier

See also COLONIAL AMERICA; GAY LIBERATION; FEMINISM; STONEWALL RIOTS.

SEXUALLY TRANSMITTED DISEASES

Sexually transmitted diseases (STDs), like the flu, seem to have been endemic to humankind. And, like the flu, they are constantly changing and adjusting to new treatments, drugs, and living conditions. At the beginning of the twenty-first century, STDs remain among the most common infectious disorders in the world, affecting men and women of all backgrounds and economic levels. While it is important to emphasize that STDs are spread by particular sexual acts and not by contact with particular social groups, statistical data reveal that gay men suffer disproportionately from many STDs, while lesbians (unless they are members of other risk groups) are less affected by many of them. This is in part because of anatomical and physiological differences in prevalent forms of sexual intimacy and also because of greater gay male promiscuity.

Abstinence—no sex at all—is the best preventive for any STD, but safer sex practices can considerably reduce the risk of STD transmission. In particular, condoms (designed originally for purposes of contraception), when used along with specific types of gels and foams, are very effective for preventing many STDs. Prior to the 1980s, condoms were rarely used by gay males, but the danger posed by acquired immunodeficiency syndrome (AIDS) encouraged their use among those who engaged in same-sex sexual activities. Special models have appeared that claim to be superior for anal (as distinct from vaginal) penetration, and the fear of disease has even inspired the use of the sheath for oral-genital contact. Female condoms and dental dams are used by some lesbians. Individuals at high risk of STDs include those who are under age thirty, those who are single, those who are sexually active with multiple partners, and those who engage in unsafe sex practices. While researchers do not always agree about how to categorize the level of risk associated with particular sexual activities, most agree that unsafe sexual practices include activities that bruise or tear internal tissues of the vagina, anus, throat, or mouth; anal, oral, or vaginal intercourse without a condom or dental dam; wet or open kissing; and masturbation on broken skin or sores. Safer sexual practices include masturbating (but not on broken skin or sores), massaging, watching, hugging, holding hands, dry kissing, and intercourse with a condom or dental dam.

Pre-AIDS History

Little research has been conducted on the history of pre-AIDS STDs in LGBT communities. Most general histories of STDs pay scant attention to LGBT people, and most LGBT historians have paid little attention to STDs before AIDS. There are, however, glimpses of pre-AIDS STDs in historical scholarship focusing on other subjects. Research on late nineteenth-century and early twentieth-century sexology reveals that many scientific experts in effect regarded homosexuality and transgenderism themselves as STDs—contagious diseases that could be transmitted sexually. Jennifer Terry's work indicates that some medical authorities of this period expressed concern that many male and female homosexuals had STDs and were responsible for spreading them. Terry's work also shows that police often forced gay men arrested in gay bar raids to undergo what were labeled VD inspections.

Some scientific studies of homosexuality in the 1930s drew subjects from STD clinics and then represented LGBT people (and in particular male prostitutes) as posing STD risks to the larger society. In the mid-twentieth century, the psychiatrist Edmund Bergler accused LGBT people of masochistically craving STDs to punish themselves. In short, there is a long history of blaming LGBT people for STDs and using the fear of STDs to mobilize anti-LGBT attitudes and actions.

Other scholars examined the heterosexism of many twentieth-century pre-AIDS anti-STD campaigns, which generally expressed concern only about cross-sex transmission. Heterosexist campaigns, however, could have unintended consequences. The sex educator Robert Eberwein showed that some commentators expressed concern that the heterosexual focus of anti-STD campaigns, which might discourage cross-sex sex, could lead to increases in homosexuality. The social historian George Chauncey's work on early twentieth-century New York suggests that some gay men were able to convince straight men to have sex with them by using the anti-STD campaign's focus on cross-sex dangers to suggest that sex with men was safer than sex with women.

Little is known about pre-Stonewall (pre-1969) homophile activism related to STDs, but evidence indicates that local homophile groups helped individuals with STD questions and needs. Marc Stein's work reveals that homophile activists in Philadelphia in the 1960s warned LGBT people to be suspicious about police involvement in STD contact tracing, advising education, treatment, and checkups by trustworthy physicians for those who were promiscuous. The historian Martin Duberman notes that in the late 1960s, the national gay and lesbian newsmagazine the *Advocate* published work on the question of whether, given fears of police involvement, LGBT people should cooperate with public health authorities on matters concerning STDs. In this atmosphere of justifiable suspicion and distrust, LGBT activists developed their own initiatives, oftentimes encountering resistance in LGBT communities. According to the *Advocate,* the Committee to Eradicate Syphilis established a clinic in heavily gay West Hollywood in 1967. In the early 1970s, LGBT-oriented health centers and clinics

113

(including the Howard Brown Health Center in Chicago and the Fenway Community Health Center in Boston) were founded to provide STD treatment and services to LGBT people. Also in this period, LGBT-oriented STD projects like the Gay Men's V.D. Clinic in Washington, D.C., and the Los Angeles Venereal Disease Control Project were established, and the Los Angeles Gay Community Services Center (later the Los Angeles Gay and Lesbian Center) published what it claimed was the country's first pamphlet dealing with gay STD issues. In 1974, *San Francisco Chronicle* reporter Randy Shilts warned *Advocate* readers that syphilis and gonorrhea were pandemic in the LGBT community, noted that LGBT STD workers blamed the high rates on the failings of the public health establishment, and made recommendations about STD prevention and treatment for LGBT people. Some scholars argue that LGBT community initiatives related to STDs in the 1970s laid the groundwork for responses to AIDS in the 1980s. Yet the history of pre-AIDS STDs in LGBT communities continues to receive little scholarly attention.

Hepatitis, Syphilis, and Gonorrhea

Gay men have been particularly prone not only to AIDS but also to infectious hepatitis (hepatitis A), a disease of the liver that is commonly acquired through the practice of rimming (oral-anal contact). Until the introduction of a vaccine in 1980, the rate of hepatitis in gay males was ten times the U.S. average. Hepatitis B, or serum hepatitis, may be transmitted by sexual intercourse, sharing needles used for injecting drugs, or ingestion of contaminated food. Although a vaccine is available, gamma globulin given within seven days after blood exposure or fourteen days after sexual contact will also prevent the disease. Other forms of hepatitis are not classified as STDs.

Prior to the appearance of AIDS, which was first reported in the United States in 1981, syphilis was the most feared STD. Although there are scholarly debates about the original source of syphilis, it became endemic early in the sixteenth century, when it was carried by sailors, soldiers, travelers, and explorers throughout the world. Syphilis is caused by the spirochete *Treponema pallidum* and starts out as a fairly mild disease. A hard, nonpainful ulcer called a chancre appears, usually on the genitalia, but heals within four to six weeks. The second stage of the disease, which begins several weeks later, is marked by a rash, which in most cases can most easily be seen on the hands and feet. Again, this phase is not particularly uncomfortable, although like the first stage it is highly infectious. The disease then recedes into a latent and noninfectious phase, but in a significant percentage

of cases (about 30%) *T. pallidum* begins to invade the tissues of the central nervous system (including the brain), the heart, and the bones, and can appear in any organ system. In the process, syphilis can imitate almost any disease, and later complications include insanity, blindness, deafness, heart disease, ulcerous tumors, seizures, coma, and ultimately death.

Syphilis was incurable until the development of Salvarsan by Paul Ehrlich and Sahachiro Hata in 1910. The treatment was so laborious and debilitating—Salvarsan contained arsenic and, given in improper doses, could cause deafness, blindness, or the destruction of living tissues at the injection site—that there was concern about which would kill the patient first, the disease or the cure. Treatment of the disease was complicated in the United States by the fact that open discussion of STDs in public forums was more or less forbidden, except among medical professionals. The cure came with the development of penicillin in the 1940s, and the results seemed miraculous, with syphilis almost disappearing. Unfortunately, strains resistant to some antibiotics developed, and syphilis has periodically reappeared in almost epidemic form. To keep up with the disease, the Centers for Disease Control (CDC) regularly issues guidelines for antibiotic therapy and recommended drugs. The reporting of syphilis (which is compulsory) is closely tracked, because it is regarded as a monitor for the rates of increase or decrease in the incidence of other STDs.

During much of the 1990s, there was a steady decline in the incidence of syphilis in the United States, but the number of cases began to rise rapidly in 2001, most noticeably among men having sex with other men. The cause of the increase is unclear, but since it is calculated that syphilis infection increases the risk for transmitting or acquiring HIV infections by two to five times, the CDC and other public health officials came to believe that many in the gay community were not taking the precautions they had been earlier.

Gonorrhea, which as late as the nineteenth century was thought to be another type of the same disease as syphilis, is often asymptomatic in women but can eventually spread into the internal pelvic organs, causing pelvic inflammatory disease. In males, it causes an acute, purulent, anterior urethritis, with extremely painful urination. Gonorrhea is caused by *Neisseria gonorrhoeae*, a bacterium that can grow and multiply easily in mucous membranes of the body. The effects of gonorrhea were very noticeable in World War I, when large numbers of American soldiers were unable to fight for the week or so during which the symptoms of the disease were at their most painful. This led the U.S. military to adopt prophylactic measures during World War II, including the mass issuance of condoms. Gonorrhea is now successfully treated with antibiotics, particularly doxycycline.

Other Common STDs

Worldwide, AIDS, syphilis, and gonorrhea are three of the six most common STDs, according to standard statistics collected in most countries. The other three are chancroid, lymphogranuloma venereum (LGV), and granuloma inguinale. Chancroid, which is caused by the bacterium *Hemophilus ducreyi,* produces a soft, destructive ulcer and painful sores in the groin area that begin to appear three to seven days after infection and that can grow, rupture through the skin, and form abscesses called buboes. If untreated, the disease can destroy male genitalia. It can be treated with antibiotics, but some buboes may require piercing with a needle. Some women do not develop sores but experience other symptoms including vaginal discharge and rectal bleeding. The disease is relatively uncommon in the United States.

LGV is a chronic, progressively destructive, and usually curable infection of the lymphatic system caused by a particular strain of *Chlamydia trachomatis,* the bacteria that causes chlamydia. Symptoms appear from three days to three weeks after contact, and like syphilis, the disease has three phases. In the first phase, there is a transient, primary genital lesion, which is more likely to be detected in men; in the second, lymphadenitis (swelling of the lymph nodes) with bubo (soft sore) formation; and in the third phase, lymphodema (chronic swelling) of the genitalia and rectum. LGV can be treated with antibiotics. Granuloma inguinal, or granuloma venereum, also known as donovanosis, is a chronic infection of the genitals caused by the bacterium *Calymmatobacterium granulomatis,* which contaminates food and water. It is only mildly contagious and needs repeated sexual exposure to thrive. Rare in the United States, the disease can only be cured by long-term antibiotic therapy.

In addition to these STDs, there are others, sometimes called the "new generation" of STDs, for which no reliable worldwide statistics exist. The most common of all STDs may be chlamydia, which is caused by the bacterium *Chlamydia trachomatis.* It only became classified as an STD in the 1970s. The disease is often asymptomatic, more so in women than men. In men, it is often marked by a scanty white or clear discharge, burning or itching, and frequent and painful urination. In women, it is marked by vaginal itching or burning, dull pelvic pain, vaginal discharge, and irregular bleeding. Untreated in women, chlamydia, like gonorrhea, can cause sterility. One form of chlamydia, chlamydia trachomatis, can

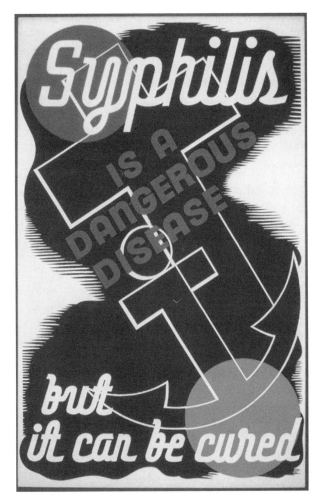

Public Health. The message of this advertisement reads: "Syphilis is a dangerous disease but it can be cured"—which is not necessarily the case with a host of other sexually transmitted diseases, some of them increasingly resistant to available treatments. [Library of Congress]

cause blindness if untreated. Treatment for chlamydia involves antibiotics of the tetracycline group. Penicillin is no longer used to treat chlamydia because many strains of the bacterium have become resistant to the drug.

Genital herpes, or herpes simplex virus (HSV), is a treatable, but not curable, infectious viral disease characterized by recurrent episodes of acute, painful, red-based blisters or open sores, particularly on females. Infected men, if they have symptoms, can develop blisters as well but often have only mild urinary complaints. The intensity of the attacks varies in the same individual over time. HSV can be treated with the antiviral drug acyclovir.

Genital or venereal warts have a long and ancient history. They are raised, rough, cauliflowerlike growths on the vulva, penis, perianal area, or vaginal or rectal walls, and are caused by the human papilloma virus, a number of varieties of which infect different areas of the body. Lesions appear six to eight weeks after exposure in moist area of the genitalia or anus in 60–70% of individuals who had contacts with an infected person or persons. Once established, they tend to grow in clusters. There is no remedy or cure except for surgical or chemical removal. The warts often reappear, but most are more of a nuisance than harmful.

There are a number of other STDs, some of which seem to infect females more than males, or vice versa. Molloscum contagiosum is a highly contagious viral skin infection, similar in some ways to venereal warts. It can be transmitted through sexual contact, and when it is, the lesions, which are small, discrete, waxy-pink, dome-shaped growths with depressed centers, usually appear on the genitalia. On most patients, they disappear, but not on immune-suppressed patients such as those with AIDS. If the lesions do not disappear, they may have to be cut away. The disease can be treated with retinoids such as retin A.

Infection with cytomegalovirus (CMV), a member of the herpes virus group, only became noticeable in the United States in the 1980s. Close and sometimes repeated contact is necessary for infection. The virus can cause hepatitis, mononucleosis, pneumonia, retinitis (infection in the eyes), and Guillain-Barré ascending paralysis. It can be devastating to people whose immune systems are compromised, as in those who have AIDS, and it is related to Kaposi's sarcoma in gay men. There is, as yet, no cure.

Trichomoniasis is a genito-urinary tract infection caused by the parasitic protozoan *Trichomonas vaginalis* and affects both men and women. In women, it is marked by a vaginal discharge that is thin, frothy, greenish gray or yellow, and may be accompanied by vulvar irritation and itching, painful urination, and painful coitus. Men are commonly asymptomatic (as are large numbers of women), but if there are symptoms, they include urethral discharge and mild urethral irritation that may result in painful intercourse. Treatment is by the antibiotic metronidazole.

Gardnerella, a commonly acquired bacterial infection, previously called hemophilus vaginalis, is marked by a unique vaginal discharge that is thick, frothy, and yellow green, with a fishy odor. Like trichomoniasis, it is probably transmitted by sexual contact and is treated with metronidazole.

Candidiasis is a common vaginal yeast infection transmitted sexually (including female-to-female contact), although it can also occur without sexual contact.

The fungus is a normal inhabitant of the vagina, mouth, and digestive tract of most adult women. If the pH in these areas is altered, however, the fungus will grow, and in immune-compromised males, it may spread to the esophagus. In women, candidiasis is marked by a discharge that looks like cottage cheese, irritation of the inner thighs, and intense itching in the vulvovaginal area. Most men are asymptomatic, but in those who are not, there is an inflammation or rash of the external genitalia. Uncircumcised men may harbor *Candida* under the foreskin. There are a number of treatments, including topical antifungal agents such as nystatin, clotrimazole, and ketoconazole.

Pubic lice and scabies move from person to person through sexual or other intimate contact or through contact with an affected person's underwear or bedding. Scabies can be cured by topical applications of permethrin, crotamiton, and lindane, and over-the-counter remedies are available for lice.

Giardasis, an intestinal illness caused by the protozoan *Giardia lamblia,* and amebiasis, an intestinal illness caused by the microscopic parasite *Entamoeba histolytica,* are due to rectal-oral sexual activity and can be treated with metronidazole. Bacteria of the genus *Campylobacter* are a major cause of what is sometimes called the "gay bowel syndrome" of diarrhea and dysentery, although the disease can also be transmitted to women. It can be cured with antibiotics.

The dangers posed to LGBT communities by STDs are manageable if precautions are taken. These entail knowing the sexual and STD history of partners; using prophylactic barriers; and washing with soap and water those body areas that have contacted genitals, feces, urine, or saliva. Regular self-inspections of the body, noting, among other things, bumps that get bigger or painful areas, are also important. If one is sexually active with a number of different partners, a cautionary step would be to visit an STD clinic regularly, or at least once a year. Although preventing an STD is far better than curing one, each person has to decide which precautions to take.

Bibliography

Bell, Alan P., and Martin S. Weinberg. *Homosexualities.* New York: Simon and Schuster, 1978.

Bergler, Edmund. *Homosexuality: Disease or Way of Life?* New York: Hill and Wang, 1956.

Centers for Disease Control. National Center for HIV, STD, and TB Prevention, Division of Sexually Transmitted Diseases. "Sexually Transmitted Diseases Treatment Guidelines." Updated 10 May 2002. Available from http://www.cdc.gov/std/treatment/default.htm

Chauncey, George. *Gay New York: Gender, Urban Culture, and the Making of the Gay Male World, 1890–1940.* New York: Basic, 1994.

Clinical Evidence Concise: The International Source of the Best Available Evidence for Effective Health Care. Kingsport, N.Y.: BMJ Publishing Group, 2002.

Eberwein, Robert. *Sex Ed: Film, Video, and the Framework of Desire.* New Brunswick, N.J.: Rutgers University Press, 1999.

Holmes, King K., et al., eds. *Sexually Transmitted Diseases.* New York: McGraw-Hill, 1999.

Ostrow, David G., Tony A. Sandholzer, and Yehudi M. Felman, eds. *Sexually Transmitted Diseases in Homosexual Men: Diagnosis, Treatment, and Research.* New York: Plenum, 1983.

Stein, Marc. *City of Sisterly and Brotherly Loves: Lesbian and Gay Philadelphia, 1945–1972.* Chicago: University of Chicago Press, 2000.

Terry, Jennifer. *An American Obsession: Science, Medicine, and Homosexuality in Modern Society.* Chicago: University of Chicago Press, 1999.

Thompson, Mark, ed. *Long Road to Freedom: The Advocate History of the Gay and Lesbian Movement.* New York: St. Martin's Press, 1994.

Vern Bullough

See also AIDS AND PEOPLE WITH AIDS; HEALTH AND HEALTH CARE LAW AND POLICY; HEALTH, HEALTH CARE, AND HEALTH CLINICS; SAFER SEX; SEX EDUCATION.

SHAW, Anna Howard (b. 14 February 1847; d. 2 July 1919), minister, physician, orator, suffrage leader.

Anna Howard Shaw, born in Newcastle-on-Tyne in the United Kingdom, immigrated to the United States in 1851 with her family and, after a few years in Massachusetts, homesteaded with the family in rural Michigan. Shaw attended Albion College and then graduated in 1878 from the Theological Seminary at Boston University. After serving for seven years as a pastor on Cape Cod, where she struggled with the church over ordination, Shaw returned to Boston University for a medical degree, which she received in 1885. In spite of this training, Shaw devoted the rest of her life to the cause of women's rights, especially suffrage. She was the greatest orator of the woman's suffrage movement and the longest-serving president of the National American Woman Suffrage Association (NAWSA), holding that post from 1904 to 1915. During World War I, Shaw was chair of the Women's Committee of the Council of National Defense. She was also a self-supporting, woman-identified woman who fought for a variety of women's issues. Her life partner was Lucy Anthony, with whom she lived from 1890 until her death.

According to her autobiography, Shaw was always drawn to nontraditional gender roles and activities. She was a tomboy, preferring construction tools, outdoor work, and what was men's work at the time. On two occasions early in her life, Shaw was forced to fulfill the traditional male role for her family. When all of the older men were absent from the farm for months, twelve-year-old Shaw assumed such responsibilities as planting, harvesting, and digging a well. Later her father and brothers all enlisted to fight in the Civil War and Anna, through school teaching, struggled to keep the rest of the family fed and the taxes paid.

At the age of twenty-three, Shaw found herself called to preach and began the journey that took her to Albion, Boston University, and eventually the women's rights movement. As a pioneering woman professional in the ministry and medical fields, Shaw made several concessions to fashion in order to mollify her critics. For example, she let her hair, which she had worn short since college, grow out. She also cultivated an appropriately womanly appearance and presence. Once committed to the suffrage cause and women's rights, Shaw earned her living as a speaker. With Anthony functioning as her private secretary and manager, Shaw traveled, most often alone, throughout the United States. Dependent upon her own earnings, she could only accept the presidency of the NAWSA after Susan B. Anthony worked with M. Carey Thomas, the president of Bryn Mawr College, and her partner, heiress Mary Garrett, to raise an endowment that would pay Shaw a salary. Thomas became a close friend and adviser for the rest of Shaw's life.

Feminist historians and theorists have long debated the social roles and identities of women such as Anna Howard Shaw. Though Shaw lived in what has been called "the golden age of spinsters," her life illustrates the complexity of systems of oppression and privilege that women such as Shaw faced in the nineteenth-century United States. As a white woman, she used the educational opportunities open to her to achieve, however tenuous, a middle-class status. But it was essential that she cloak all of her pioneering and nontraditional views and activities in a robe of respectability that often included a religious aspect. For example, early on Shaw stated that she would not include a vow "to obey" when she performed marriages, but not for reasons related to women's equality. Shaw argued instead that a woman's true obedience should only be to God. Not only was her effectiveness as a national and international woman leader built

Anna Howard Shaw. Shown here (in front seat) with younger colleagues, she spent most of her life as a champion of women's rights and was president of the National American Woman Suffrage Association for an unequaled eleven years. [Hulton-Deutsch Collection/corbis]

on such an image, but so was her ability to continue earning a livelihood that allowed her to support herself, her partner, and several of her nieces, and to contribute to the support of her parents. While this public image included a presumed asexuality, Shaw's private life revolved around women. From her earliest and longest relationships with childhood friends through her first great love, Persis Addy, and her life companion, Lucy Anthony (who was a niece of Susan B. Anthony), Shaw's most intimate and passionate relationships were with women.

While Shaw's life challenged the gender roles of her era, she had to craft a public persona that won her acceptance and admiration. For her generation, the broaching of public gender roles and of formal barriers to economic independence was risky enough. Though sexologists were developing their ideas concerning women's sexuality during this time, there is no research suggesting that Shaw claimed or acknowledged a sexual identity. From the sources available to us, it appears that Shaw never attempted to conceal her marital status or her living arrangement, but also left little evidence of any discussion of women's sexual choices. However, because many of the letters between Shaw and Lucy Anthony were destroyed, we may never have a complete picture of this woman pioneer.

Bibliography

Flexner, Eleanor. *A Century of Struggle: The Woman's Rights Movement in the United States.* Cambridge, Mass: Belknap Press of Harvard University, 1959.

Graham, Sarah Hunter. *Woman Suffrage and the New Democracy.* New Haven: Yale University Press, 1996.

Shaw, Anna Howard. *Anna Howard Shaw: Story of a Pioneer.* Cleveland, Ohio: Pilgrim Press, 1994. Originally published in 1915.

Trisha Franzen

See also ANTHONY, SUSAN B.; FEMINISM; THOMAS, M. CAREY.

SHAWN, Ted (b. 21 October 1891; d. 9 January 1972), dancer and choreographer.

In 1933 Ted Shawn founded the first all-male dance company in the United States, Ted Shawn and his Men Dancers. He began dancing in 1911 as a way to regain his strength after a serious bout of diphtheria. In 1914 he married Ruth St. Denis, one of the pioneers of modern dance. They toured and taught together, opening Denishawn schools throughout the country. After their separation (they never divorced) in 1931—caused, at least in part, by both of them falling in love with the same man—Shawn focused his attentions on promoting dance for men. Two years later, his company, named Ted Shawn and His Men Dancers, gave its first performance. Between 1933 and 1940, the company gave more than 1,250 performances in over 750 cities. Many dance writers argue that Shawn opened the door for men in modern dance in the United States.

The main goal of Shawn's company was to raise the status of male dancers in the United States and to eliminate the kind of opposition that had greeted his own decision to dance in the 1910s. Shawn hoped to overturn the prejudice against men's dancing by promoting a virile form of dance that would be seen as suitable for U.S. men. In his many essays, Shawn blamed the widespread presumption of effeminacy in dance on two things: first, a lack of recognition of the importance of dance and art in U.S. culture, and second, a failure to choreograph specifically for the "natural" qualities of the male body. In other cultures, Shawn claims in his book, *The American Ballet* (1926), dance was an important, and therefore male, activity in which women simply clapped accompaniment or sang along. He hoped to establish male dominance in modern Western dance and while he did not explicitly acknowledge the consequences of this for women dancers, he made it clear that their proper role was a lesser one.

Shawn's was a perfectly binary view of gender that matched the prevailing attitudes of his time. He strongly believed in natural, fundamental differences between male and female movement. He thought that choreographing for these sex differences would make the manliness of male dancers obvious to the U.S. public and thus make dance easier for men to watch and do. But even Shawn knew that it was not enough simply to define an acceptable range of movements for male dancing; without shifting the context of those moving bodies they could still be pegged as effeminate. Therefore, an important part of Shawn's project was to see dance move from the proscenium to the gymnasium. To speed along the transition, Shawn's company included experienced athletes who were trained by him to dance. He performed and taught regularly in physical education faculties. He choreographed works that were based on sports. He costumed his dancers in athletic attire. In *The American Ballet*, Shawn wrote that he wanted to see dance regain the position it had held in ancient Greece as the "most perfect athletic accomplishment" (p. 97).

Shawn's virile choreography provided a protective closet for himself and for the other homosexual men in the company. But it would be a mistake to see his emphasis on manliness as a contradiction of his own homo-

erotic desires. Shawn's personal identity and his work were both strongly influenced by the writings of Walt Whitman, Havelock Ellis (the English sexologist and author of *Dance of Life,* 1923), and Edward Carpenter (the English socialist, writer, and homosexual reformer). A meeting with Ellis and then one with Carpenter in 1924 had reassured Shawn about his own homosexual feelings. Homosexuality and effeminacy were not necessarily synonymous, as popular stereotypes suggested. Shawn's homosexuality, therefore, was not at odds with the type of virile masculinity he wanted to project in his dancing.

Shawn's preferred notions of homosexuality were based on a romanticized Greek ideal. Love between men was love in its highest form, while the male body epitomized physical beauty. But while Shawn's work celebrated the beauty and, especially, the strength of male bodies, his choreography presented those bodies as chaste, as dance historian Susan Foster has noted. His dancers, for instance, never touched unless all members of the group came together to make a design or tableau. Pairs of dancers never assisted each other, never took each other's weight; the spaces between the dancers remained consistently broad. Despite the overt asexuality of the work, its valorization of masculinity and its reverence for the male body generated an audience of homosexual men—helped, no doubt, by the fact that Shawn's dancers rarely performed fully clothed.

Shawn disbanded the company in 1940 when many of his dancers took up military service. But his sense of his own success at changing the face of male dancing in the United States is evident in a letter he wrote to *Dance Magazine* in July 1966. He took pride in the fact that the new generation of modern dancers was "almost male dominated," referring to Alvin Ailey, Merce Cunningham, and Glen Tetley, among others (p. 16).

Ted Shawn died in Orlando, Florida, in 1972. Jacob's Pillow, the Lee, Massachusetts, farm that was home to his company, continues today as the inspiration for the Jacob's Pillow Dance Festival in Becket, Massachusetts.

Bibliography

Desmond, Jane C., ed. *Dancing Desires: Choreographing Sexualities On and Off the Stage.* Madison: University of Wisconsin, 2001.

Shawn, Ted. *The American Ballet.* New York: Holt, 1926.

———. "Open Letter." *Dance Magazine* 40 (July 1966): 16.

———. *Dance We Must.* New York: Haskell House, 1974.

Walter, Terry. *Ted Shawn, Father of American Dance: A Biography.* New York: Dial, 1976.

Mary Louise Adams

See also AILEY, ALVIN; CUNNINGHAM, MERCE; DANCE; PERFORMANCE, THEATER, AND DANCE STUDIES.

SHELLEY, Martha (b. 27 December 1943), activist, writer.

Martha Shelley (née Altman) grew up in a Jewish family in Brooklyn, New York. She worked as a Barnard College secretary and as a social worker at the Harlem Welfare Center during her young adulthood. According to Dudley and Nagourney, Altman "determined that she was a lesbian after making love with a married woman she met at a judo class, as the woman's husband slept in the next room" (p. 42).

In November 1967, Altman joined the Daughters of Bilitis (DOB), a homophile movement organization for women, simultaneously adopting a new surname in honor of her favorite poet, Percy Bysshe Shelley. In rapid succession, she became treasurer and later president of DOB's New York chapter, not because of her hard work and articulate manner, but because "nobody else wanted the office[s]" (Marcus, p. 177).

In late 1968, Shelley joined the Student Homophile League (SHL), which had chapters at several East Coast colleges. She and activist Rita Mae Brown were the women most notably associated with SHL, but its male leaders' unwillingness to comprehend lesbian oppression caused Shelley to move on quickly.

Shelley's most important contribution to DOB and a revitalized LGBT movement lay in her powerful articles in *The Ladder* from as early as 1968 until at least 1970. John D'Emilio writes that she "drew analogies between the condition of gay women and men and other oppressed minorities, and she continually urged a more forthright, less apologetic posture" (*Sexual Politics, Sexual Communities*, p. 210). In the spring of 1969, however, Shelley left her organizational post as a new wind (its tone more militant and less apologetic than that of the homophile movement before it) blew into gay politics, culminating in New York City's Stonewall Riots. (While walking with Brown near the Stonewall Inn on the first night of the riots, Shelley perceived it as just another gay men's bar riot, and both hastily departed.) After Stonewall, Shelley cofounded (helped organize) the Gay Liberation Front (GLF), a group that expressed her style of realpolitik. In contrast with Gay Activists Alliance, which focused solely on gay issues (primarily civil rights–oriented), GLF concerned itself with "radical" politics and liberation (sexual and otherwise). Unfortunately, GLF's efforts on behalf of other groups were not similarly reciprocated, and the group's anarchic nature led to the splintering that divided and ultimately dissolved GLF.

In GLF, created just weeks after Stonewall, Shelley discovered that despite its "lack of structure and promises of equality for all, [it was] a place where [she] could have influence. Here, assertiveness and loudness counted more than size." Around that time, she also "felt overwhelmed by anger. When anyone disagreed with her, she would yell louder and louder" (*Out for Good*, pp. 41–42). GLF firmly rejected what it perceived as the timid, assimilationist strategies of the homophile organizations and declared war against straight society.

Beginning in October 1969, GLF New York published *Come Out!*, a newsletter that included some of Shelley's most militant and radical musings. Shelley "wrote for it, typeset it, helped with the paste-up, and sold it on street corners" (correspondence with the author). She described it to Rodger Streitmatter as "that marvelous moment at the very beginning of a new adventure when everything—absolutely everything—seems possible. Every topic was on the table" (*Unspeakable*, p. 118). Shelley participated in many GLF demonstrations and spoke at several events during the year following the Stonewall Riots.

As Shelley told Eric Marcus, GLF "got involved in these endless theoretical debates about what we should do and what our relationship was to other organizations. I think we just talked ourselves to death" (*Making History*, p. 185). After GLF split ideologically over giving money to the Black Panthers in December 1969, many GLF members formed the more pragmatic Gay Activists Alliance (GAA). Reluctant to join the new group and despairing about the old, Shelley "dropped out" (in that generation's lingo) almost as suddenly as she had joined. While Shelley "never split with GLF," she also "wasn't terribly interested in what [GAA was] doing" (interview with the author). Instead, Shelley produced a lesbian radio program on WBAI for the next two years.

Around May 1970, Shelley briefly explored lesbian feminism in Radicalesbians as "one of [its] poets and theorists," but it disintegrated by 1971, in part because "we couldn't do anything except by consensus, so that one person could (and did) stop the entire group from embarking on any action." Shelley believes that one of her major movement contributions was "creating and promoting a theoretical framework that fused anarcho-communist, feminist, and gay politics" (correspondence with the author).

Shelley resurfaced briefly in the mid-1970s as one of four women driving Oakland, California's Women's Press

Collective (WPC), but it folded in the early 1980s. Meanwhile, WPC published Shelley's first book of poetry, *Crossing the DMZ*, and in 1982 Shelley released another poetry book, *Lovers and Mothers*. Shelley also wrote *Haggadah,* a radical feminist seder prayer published in 1997, and has been working on a trilogy of biblical-historical novels.

Although hardly typical of any historical era, Shelley exemplified the brashness and brilliance of that decade spanning the mid-1960s to the mid-1970s, when rhetoric outshone and outshouted the status quo. Though Shelley's active participation in the LGBT movement was brief, her importance during a pivotal period of American LGBT history should not be discounted.

Bibliography

Brownmiller, Susan. *In Our Time: Memoir of a Revolution.* New York: Dial, 1999.

Clendinen, Dudley, and Adam Nagourney. *Out for Good: The Struggle to Build a Gay Rights Movement in America.* New York: Simon & Schuster, 1999.

D'Emilio, John. *Sexual Politics, Sexual Communities: The Making of a Homosexual Minority in the United States, 1940–1970.* University of Chicago Press, 1983.

D'Emilio, John, and Estelle Freedman. *Intimate Matters: A History of Sexuality in America.* New York: Harper & Row, 1988.

Hogan, Steve, and Lee Hudson. *Completely Queer: The Gay and Lesbian Encyclopedia.* New York: Henry Holt, 1998.

Marcus, Eric. *Making History: The Struggle for Gay and Lesbian Equal Rights, 1945–1990: an Oral History.* New York: HarperCollins, 1992.

Shelley, Martha. Correspondence with Paul D. Cain, 27 May 2003.

Shelley, Martha. Interview with Paul D. Cain, 17 June 2003.

Streitmatter, Rodger. *Unspeakable: The Rise of the Gay and Lesbian Press in America.* Boston: Faber and Faber, 1995.

Teal, Donn. *The Gay Militants.* New York: St. Martin's Press, 1971.

Paul D. Cain

See also ANARCHISM, SOCIALISM, AND COMMUNISM; BISEXUALITY, BISEXUALS, AND BISEXUAL MOVEMENTS; BROWN, RITA MAE; DAUGHTERS OF BILITIS; *LADDER*; LESBIAN FEMINISM; GAY LIBERATION FRONT; RADICALESBIANS.

SHOCKLEY, Ann Allen (b. 21 June 1927), writer.

The author of the first American novel to address an interracial lesbian relationship, Ann Allen Shockley disputes the notion that writers who deal with same-sex sexual themes must necessarily also have personal experience in same-sex sexual relationships.

A notably prolific writer and honored librarian, Shockley began life in Louisville, Kentucky. After attending local schools, she majored in history at Fisk University in Nashville, Tennessee. Her 1948 graduation was followed by marriage to teacher William Shockley in Maryland in 1949. The couple produced two children, a son and a daughter, before divorcing.

Already a published author of short stories and a contributor to many African American newspapers, Shockley returned to school and received an M.S. in Library Science from Case Western Reserve University in Cleveland, Ohio, in 1959. Her career as an academic librarian and archivist took her to the University of Maryland, Eastern Shore Branch (1960–1969) and then back to Fisk.

Shockley continued to write through these years, winning the National Short Story Award in 1961 from the American Association of University Women, but she focused her professional energies on her library career. Many of her publications cover the field of black librarianship, and it is for these contributions that she initially acquired renown. Shockley's *Afro-American Women Writers, 1746–1933* (1988) is the most acclaimed of her bibliographic writings.

In the early 1960s, Shockley decided to write about lesbianism in an attempt to create understanding and compassion for people who were out of the mainstream. *Loving Her* (1974), Shockley's first major work of fiction and the only one still in print, explores racism in LGBT communities and homophobia in black communities.

Set in the 1960s, the story in *Loving Her* involves a black musician and mother who leaves her abusive, alcoholic husband for a rich white female writer. Renay, the main character, is nearly beaten to death and loses her child when her ex-husband discovers that she is romantically involved with a lesbian. Following a bout of soulsearching, Renay accepts her homosexuality and is in the arms of her white woman lover at the end of the book.

A notorious 1975 review of *Loving Her* in a prominent African American journal, *Black World,* delivered a serious blow to Shockley's writing career. The male reviewer categorized the subject matter as "bullshit" that should not be encouraged. The attack from within the black community retarded the growth of public and professional regard for her fiction. Shockley responded some years later by charging that insecure African American males and the women who humored them would forever cause the marginalization of writers who took a positive approach to black lesbianism. *Loving Her* has since acquired a second life as a popular text in college and university classes.

A pessimist by nature, Shockley fully expected to remain a minor literary figure. Her reclusive behavior has contributed to this low profile. She has shunned television and radio appearances as well as public readings, while refusing to provide more than the briefest biographical information. Her sexual orientation is unknown, and only her prominence in library science publicized her race.

This anonymity is a deliberate attempt by the author to avoid being placed in a box. Stating that she has never written heterosexual or homosexual fiction, Shockley believes that her sexual orientation and race are irrelevant to discussions of her work. She argues that it is limiting to categorize every African American woman who tackles the topic of lesbianism as a lesbian because a writer should be able to choose any point of view.

Shockley's best-known works have the same point of view, that of a black lesbian dealing with racism and sexism, but she has also focused on the refusal of black communities to accept gay men. *The Black and White of It* (1980) collects ten previously published short stories about lesbians that were written as far back as the early 1960s. *Say Jesus and Come to Me* (1982) is Shockley's second novel. It uses the romance between two prominent black women, a singer and a minister, to explore the homophobia of African American churches and the reluctance of African American women to join the women's movement. The short story "Soon There Will Be None" (1994) addresses the stigma surrounding black men with AIDS. While her works of fiction have broken new ground thematically, they have been faulted for a stilted style and poor character development.

The vast majority of African American literature ignores same-sex romantic relationships. Shockley began writing about lesbian themes to fill this void. By recently shifting to the topic of gay black men, she has continued her efforts to end the silence surrounding homosexuality in the African American world.

Bibliography

Bogus, Sdiane Adams. "Theme and Portraiture in the Fiction of Ann Allen Shockley." Ph.D. Diss., Miami University, 1988.

Dandridge, Rita B. *Ann Allen Shockley: An Annotated Primary and Secondary Bibliography.* New York: Greenwood Press, 1987.

Josey, E. J., and Ann Allen Shockley, eds. *Handbook of Black Librarianship.* Littleton, Colo.: Libraries Unlimited, 1977.

Caryn E. Neumann

See also LITERATURE.

SHURTLIFF, ROBERT. see SAMSON, DEBORAH.

SITTING IN THE WATER GRIZZLY. see QÁNQON-KÁMEK-KLAÚLA.

SITUATIONAL HOMOSEXUALITY

Situational homosexuality, sometimes called transient homosexuality or circumstantial homosexuality, refers to widespread same-sex sexual behavior in institutions where no partners of the other sex are available. Whether the term is valid or not has become a matter of some debate. Jonathan Katz, for example, argues that all homosexuality is situational, influenced and given meaning and character by its location in time and space. The term itself was invented in the middle of the twentieth century, when the boundary between homosexuality and heterosexuality was held to be hard and fast. Regina Kunzel describes the use of the term as a rhetorical maneuver by social scientists to contain the disruptive meanings of same-sex sexual acts apparently unlinked to, and therefore unsettling to, sexual identity.

The behavior implied by the term is most noted and studied in jails, prisons, and reformatories, where the inmates are there involuntarily. But it has also been described as existing in monasteries, nunneries, ships that spend long periods of time at sea, the military, sex-segregated schools, isolated all-male mining and lumber camps, and similar places and institutions where participation in such activities is more freely chosen.

The term has also been applied to same-sex sexual relations that are tolerated, if not encouraged, during late adolescence and early adulthood, in many areas of the world and many historical periods where the sexes are so strictly segregated that little contact between them is possible until marriage. The assumption behind such toleration is often that individuals who engaged in such behavior will revert to heterosexuality when their situation changes. This may be true at least in part, although it is also clear that a significant number of those who engage in situational homosexuality may continue to prefer their own sex even after other options become available. It is also true that many people, perhaps even the majority, who spend significant time in sex-segregated institutions never voluntarily engage in homosexual acts no matter how long or how intense their deprivation from heterosexual contacts.

Estimates of male prisoners who take part willingly or often unwillingly in same-sex sexual relations while serving in U. S. prisons range from 15 to 86 percent, with most experts putting the figures at the higher end. This is despite the fact that prison policy usually has been to separate the more obvious homosexuals from other prisoners, with a "daddy tank" for the more masculine lesbians and a "queens tank" for the more effeminate men.

In female prisons, it has been claimed that the majority of women engage in same-sex sexual relations but with much less coercion, and much more affection is displayed by women than men. For a time in the 1950s and 1960s female homosexuality behind bars was widely hinted at and even featured in pulp fiction, while the topic of male homosexuality was ignored. Scores of semi-pornographic novels depicted innocent young women being exploited by both brutish guards and butch lesbian prisoners. Interestingly, current research has tended to demonstrate that butch lesbians were more likely to be victims of prison violence and least likely to commit violent acts. The criminologist Karlene Faith concludes that most lesbian relations in prisons involve mutual, non-coercive intimacy.

The so-called sea shanty songs, which go back to the nineteenth century and perhaps earlier in both the United States and England, reflect a casual acceptance of sex among sailors, although while in port the heterosexual activities are emphasized. In the period between 1806 and 1816, the first decade of the Napoleonic wars, 28.6 percent of all executions in the British Navy were for buggery. Winston Churchill is said to have remarked that the three traditions of the British Navy were "rum, sodomy, and the lash." Sailor slang characterized the passive homosexual partner on ships as "sea pussy," a legitimate substitute for females while on board ship. Herman Melville in his novel *White Jacket* (1850) has a character declare that "sailors as a class, entertain most liberal notions concerning morality . . . or rather, they take their own views of such matters."

What seems clear in any discussion of situational homosexuality is that no matter how it is defined there are many issues involved. Some of it, especially among adolescents, develops out of homosociality during this stage of life, and is usually replaced by heterosexuality at a later phase. But it is also clear that situational homosexuality emphasizes the bisexual element that exists in so many of us, and many people wanting intimacy, friendship, or some form of sexual release engage in situational same-sex sexual relationships as an alternative to heterosexuality. At the very least, the use of such a term implies that sexual identity does not necessarily have the hard and fast boundaries that current society may have tried to erect between heterosexuality and homosexuality.

Bibliography

Bullough, Vern L., and Bonnie Bullough. "Homosexuality in Nineteenth Century English Public Schools." *International Review of Modern Sociology* 9 (1979): 251–76.

Deming, Barbara. *Prisons That Could Not Hold*. San Francisco: Spinsters Ink, 1985.

Gilbert, Arthur N. "Buggery and the British Navy, 1700–1861." *Journal of Social History* 10 (1977): 72–98.

Katz, Jonathan. *Gay American History: Lesbians and Gay Men in the U.S.A.: A Documentary Anthology*. New York: Crowell, 1976.

Kunzel, Regina G. "Situating Sex: Prison Sexual Culture in the Mid-Twentieth-Century United States." *GLQ* 8 (2002): 253–270.

Propper, Alice M. *Prison Homosexuality: Myth and Reality*. Lexington, Mass.: Lexington Books, 1981.

Vern L. Bullough

See also MILITARY; PRISONS, JAILS, AND REFORMATORIES: MEN'S; PRISONS, JAILS, AND REFORMATORIES: WOMEN'S; SAME-SEX INSTITUTIONS.

SLAVERY AND EMANCIPATION

The history of large-scale slavery in the United States dates to the early seventeenth century, when the first European colonists purchased or abducted Africans, transported them to American soil, and forced them to work on Southern agricultural plantations. The dominant white culture justified these actions by claiming moral and intellectual superiority over black people. By characterizing blacks as savage, animalistic, and hypersexualized, white Americans sought to differentiate themselves from the enslaved population. Slavery thus functioned as a mechanism of social control that was explicitly calibrated through an ironic altruism: whites legitimized the practice of slavery by depicting it as their moral obligation to protect American culture from the supposedly inherent depravity of blacks and to protect black people from themselves. To support this point of view, advocates of slavery subjugated black men and women through an intricate combination of racial and sexual ideologies.

Popular stereotypes, for example, characterized black men as sexual predators who threatened the purity of white women. Black women, by comparison, were perceived as sexually licentious, always available for (and desirous of) sexual relations. As a consequence of these characterizations, white culture rationalized both extreme physical violence toward black men and the extreme sexual abuse of black women. On the one hand, slavery was seen as a means of protecting the sanctity of white womanhood from the threat of an allegedly rampant black male sexuality, and black men suspected of violating this interracial boundary faced the likelihood of severe whipping and the possibility of lynching. At the same time, the slave system legitimized the exploitation of black female slaves for the sexual gratification of white slave owners and overseers. Although black women often resisted these advances, white men faced no reprisals for their actions. Under the law, slaves could not be raped since they were defined solely as property.

Slavery's historical union of racial and sexual subjugation, however, does not fit easily within an overview of LGBT history for at least two significant reasons. First, slavery predates modern-day understandings (and definitions) of homosexual identity. While some scholarship suggests that African slaves may have brought same-sex sexual traditions with them to the United States, "homosexuality," as a term, did not emerge until the late nineteenth century, after slavery had been abolished. It may be historically inaccurate, therefore, to speak of homosexual identity within slavery, since this nomenclature may misrepresent the nature of same-sex eroticism in the antebellum era. Second, history does not provide very much direct evidence of homosexual activity within slavery. Unlike the slave and mixed-race children that were born of black/black and black/white heterosexual unions, there exists no comparable physical "proof" of homosexual relations between slaves or between slaves and their masters.

The figure of the mulatto, for example, calls attention to the sexual availability of black women within slavery through its literal embodiment of race-mixing. Because the light-skinned slave is the result of heterosexual union (and because the likelihood that female slave owners would seduce male slaves is low, given antebellum mores), the mulatto represents a white, male sexual aggression that is explicitly heterosexually oriented. Nineteenth-century literature thus often refers to mulatto women as "tragic" figures, since their light skin embodies the threat of sexual subservience that their (female) ancestors also faced. The light-skinned male slave, by contrast, faces no comparable threat; antebellum ideologies (and the lack of bodily "evidence") do not take into account the possibility of homosexual assault. Nevertheless, one might reasonably presume that proof of interracial sexual relations points also to the likelihood of same-sex unions, even if contemporary definitions of homosexuality do not translate easily into this earlier historical period. In this regard, literature produced during the antebellum era—especially narratives written by former slaves—may offer one way to identify traces of same-sex eroticism within slavery. Such references are rare and

usually very oblique, but they are suggestive of a nonheterocentric view of the sexual dynamics between masters and slaves.

The narrative of the ex-slave Harriet A. Jacobs, for instance, provides a telling, although very brief, glimpse of the possibility of such relations. In *Incidents in the Life of a Slave Girl* (1861), Jacobs recounts her experiences within bondage, as well as those of her fellow slaves. She mentions the particular cruelties confronted by her friend Luke, a neighboring slave who was chained to the bedside of his master and forced to submit to "the strangest freaks of despotism." "Some of these freaks," Jacobs tells us, "were of a nature too filthy to be repeated" (p. 192). One might plausibly wonder whether these "freaks" allude to a form of homosexual aggression against Luke, especially since scholarship on sexual racism suggests the existence of a homoerotic gaze in which white men focus on black men's bodies (and in which white women focus on black women's bodies). While the incident Jacobs describes carries heavily homoerotic overtones, she does not elaborate further on this scene.

Jacobs's reticence in detailing Luke's predicament is notable in a text that explicitly describes the sexual subjugation female slaves faced at the hands of their masters. Ironically, then, her prim refusal to offer further information on Luke's situation may provide a clue to the dynamics of same-sex eroticism within slavery. Yet because sex between men did not hold the same meaning in the antebellum United States as it does in contemporary culture, the possibility of Luke's sexual subservience ultimately seems to say less about sexuality per se than it does about the power hierarchies between masters and slaves. Luke's case thus points to the possibility of homosexual abuse under slavery, but it also demonstrates the difficulty in locating such incidents with any degree of historical certainty.

Sexual Ideologies Following Emancipation

The freedom from slavery granted by the Emancipation Proclamation (1863) appeared to signal a new era in the history of race relations in the United States, as did the subsequent passage of the Thirteenth, Fourteenth, and Fifteenth Amendments to the Constitution (which abolished slavery, conferred citizenship on ex-slaves, and guaranteed black men the right to vote). The black population's newfound civil liberties were significantly compromised, however, by the dominant culture's ongoing efforts to prevent social equality between the races. Just as pro-slavery advocates had merged racial and sexual ideologies to subjugate black people under slavery, so were similar techniques used to protect white supremacy after the slave system had been dismantled.

The stereotypes ascribed to black men and women in the antebellum era, for example, were revived with great fervor in the years following the Civil War. Popular assumptions that black women were naturally licentious served as justification for rape and other forms of extreme sexual abuse—both by Southern whites furious over the outcome of the war, and by Northern white soldiers acting on their own racist beliefs. Black men also faced serious social repercussions as a result of the sexual stereotypes promulgated under slavery. By claiming, once again, that black men's animalistic sexuality threatened the sanctity of white womanhood, whites rationalized lynching as a necessary form of social control. Through such acts, white culture attempted to keep intact the racial boundaries (and social inequalities) that were now challenged in the postbellum United States.

Efforts to maintain black subjugation were not confined solely to acts of physical violence, however. Scientific methodologies such as comparative anatomy and anthropometry also legitimized racial disenfranchisement by claiming that visible differences between people (such as skin color and body size) provided indisputable evidence of blacks' "natural" inferiority to whites. A complex intersection of scientific and social propaganda thus validated racial inequality in postbellum America—a condition that was ultimately institutionalized in the 1896 U.S. Supreme Court decision of *Plessy v. Ferguson*, which legalized segregation in the United States.

Concurrent with scientific attempts to categorize bodies racially were scientific efforts to identify (and thereby control) homosexual persons. Cultural perceptions of sexuality began to shift in the late nineteenth century, and same-sex desire came to be understood as a distinct category of sexual identity. In an effort to describe this new understanding, the emergent field of sexology began to define archetypes for homo- and heterosexuality. Significantly, sexologists such as Havelock Ellis and Richard von Krafft-Ebing often turned to the methodologies of comparative anatomy to explain their theories. The cultural ideologies that endorsed studies of racial difference (and which sanctioned their racist conclusions) proved useful in developing a scientific language for sexual "inversion." In this way, as literary critic Siobhan Somerville has demonstrated, quasi-scientific studies of race were deeply intertwined with late-nineteenth-century definitions of homosexual identity.

The association between racial and sexual identities was not always used to detrimental ends, however. One of the earliest supporters of homosexual rights, Edward Stevenson, invoked the figure of the mulatto to illustrate how the natural existence of "mixed races" found its corollary in "mixed sexes" (since homosexuality was thought to represent a new species of "intersexed" people). Against those views that privileged purity over fusion, Stevenson argued that intersexed and mulatto bodies were regular, biological occurrences and should be acknowledged as such. His arguments thus attempted to overturn attitudes that pathologized racial and sexual difference by utilizing the same cultural and scientific evidence to alternative ends.

Such ideological reversals are not as contradictory as they might first appear. Because racial and sexual identities are subject to fluctuations in cultural definitions, they are also subject to fluctuations in cultural understandings. It would be a mistake, however, to assume that such fluidity ultimately renders categories of difference unimportant or irrelevant. As the complicated history of race and sexuality demonstrates, what often matters most in culture is not how minority groups are defined—but how they are understood (and treated) by others.

Bibliography

Blassingame, John W. *The Slave Community: Plantation Life in the Antebellum South.* New York: Oxford University Press, 1972.

D'Emilio, John, and Estelle B. Freedman. *Intimate Matters: A History of Sexuality in America.* Chicago: University of Chicago Press, 1997.

Fout, John C., and Maura Shaw Tantillo, eds. *American Sexual Politics: Sex, Gender, and Race since the Civil War.* Chicago: University of Chicago Press, 1993.

Gutman, Herbert G. *The Black Family in Slavery and Freedom, 1750–1925.* New York: Pantheon, 1976.

Jacobs, Harriet A. *Incidents in the Life of a Slave Girl, Written by Herself* (1861). Edited by L. Maria Child. Introduction by Jean Fagan Yellin. Cambridge, Mass.: Harvard University Press, 1987.

Somerville, Siobhan B. *Queering the Color Line: Race and the Invention of Homosexuality in American Culture.* Durham, N.C.: Duke University Press, 2000.

Van Leer, David. "Reading Slavery: The Anxiety of Ethnicity in Douglass's *Narrative.*" *Frederick Douglass: New Literary and Historical Essays.* Eric J. Sundquist, ed. Cambridge, U.K.: Cambridge University Press, 1990.

Wiegman, Robyn. *American Anatomies: Theorizing Race and Gender.* Durham, N.C.: Duke University Press, 1995.

Williamson, Joel. *The Crucible of Race: Black-White Relations in the American South since Emancipation.* New York: Oxford University Press, 1984.

Michael Borgstrom

See also THOMPSON, FRANCES.

SMASHES AND CHUMMING

Nineteenth-century American culture and social practice appear to have recognized, even accommodated, various forms of intense same-sex attachment that would later become stigmatized as deviant. "Smashes" and "chumming" were popular terms for particular types of passionate friendship between individuals of the same sex.

"Smashes" referred to the romantic friendships young women developed in the all-female schools of the mid- and late nineteenth century. As an 1873 article in the *Yale Courant* put it: "When a Vassar girl takes a shine to another, . . . enters upon a regular course of bouquet sendings, interspersed with tinted notes, mysterious packages of 'Ridley's Mixed Candies,' locks of hair perhaps, and many other tender tokens, until at last the object of her attentions is captured, the two become inseparable, and the aggressor is considered by her circle of acquaintances as—*smashed*" (Sahli, p. 21). It is impossible to know how often "smashing" involved explicit sexual contact, but surviving diaries and letters detail the intense homoeroticism of the bond, which encompassed hugging, caressing, sleeping together, and kissing.

"Chumming" as a term for romantic friendships derived from the common nineteenth-century use of the word "chum" to designate a close companion and tended to be associated with intimate relationships between males. Sometimes chumming referred simply to boyhood crushes, the counterparts of girlhood smashes. Often, though, "chumming" described the sexually charged intimacy that arose between adult men thrown together by circumstance in the close quarters of the sailing ship or military encampment. Civil War diaries and reminiscences, for example, speak of the ardent devotion and loving personal arrangements that developed between foxhole "chums" or prisoners of war. Male "chumming" became a common motif of nineteenth-century American literature, where it often served to frame the contact between men of different cultural backgrounds. Variants appear throughout James Fenimore Cooper's Leatherstocking Tales (1823–1841) and Herman Melville's seafaring novels (culminating in the relationship of Ishmael and Queequeg in *Moby-Dick,* 1851). In Charles Warren Stoddard's 1873 fictionalized reminiscence, *South-Sea Idyls,* a chapter titled "Chumming with a Savage" describes the narrator's sojourn with a beautiful native young man (of "sleek figure, supple and graceful in repose") for whom he experiences a compelling, although unnamed and unrealized, sexual desire.

As a practice of the school years, "smashes" and "chumming" were generally short-lived, but ardent same-sex attachments could survive for years. Reformers Susan

B. Anthony, M. Carey Thomas, and Jane Addams all entered primary, long-term, relationships with other women. Author Sarah Orne Jewett lived with her partner Annie Adams Cushing for over thirty years. Men, too, engaged in romantic friendships, characterized by poet Walt Whitman as "the manly love of comrades" in the "Calamus" poems of *Leaves of Grass.* Expressions of this "manly love" ranged from bunking together to fairly explicit erotic teasing to constant social companionship. Among the famous men involved in intense male friendships were Abraham Lincoln, Daniel Webster, and Ralph Waldo Emerson. Most fully studied among educated, white men and women in mid-nineteenth-century America, these practices have also been documented between African American women and (as "particular friendships") among female garment workers in the early twentieth century.

Many historians identify "smashes" and "chumming" with a bygone era of sexual innocence, a time when the belief that males and females were fundamentally different in temperament and social roles and had far more in common with members of their own sex than with members of the other sex, permitted same-sex bonds to thrive without exciting social disapproval, or even much notice. Various nineteenth-century utopian movements—perhaps most notably Transcendentalism—celebrated the purity of passionate but nonsexual affection between friends of the same sex.

And yet there are indications that "smashes," "chumming," and other types of intense same-sex relationships occupied an ambiguous cultural space even in the mid-nineteenth century. Both "smashing" and "chumming" were practices of situations clearly marked as atypical and temporary. "Smashing" was a phenomenon of the all-female boarding school and of the period before marriage. In its literary version, "chumming" was distinctly racially marked and transpired well outside of dominant white culture. In a letter to Emerson, Whitman suggested that even the more amorously moderate "manly love"—although in his view virtually ubiquitous—had assumed a somewhat clandestine character by the early 1850s: "As to manly friendship, everywhere observed in The States, there is not the first breath of it to be observed in print."

The Decline of Smashing and Chumming

By the end of the nineteenth century, tolerance of passionate same-sex attachments was clearly on the wane, as the women's suffrage movement, emancipation, immigration, and the economic dislocations of industrial capitalism fostered new anxieties about "normal" sex roles. Educators warned that "smashes" distracted students from their studies. Some doctors cautioned that too much education would lead to reproductive collapse among women, a contention that reflected anxieties over the decline in the birth rate of native-born white women and mounting evidence that college-educated women tended to marry later than non-college-educated women, or not to marry at all. Other observers worried that American masculinity had grown palsied in the face of the assertiveness of the "New Woman." Practitioners of the new medical specialization known as "sexology" identified the source of this social turmoil in a condition they labeled sexual "inversion." Amounting to inappropriate gender presentation, sexual inversion was assumed to drive the formation of passionate same-sex attachments. Male inverts, described as small of body and overly delicate in their sensibilities, sought to enact an essentially passive, feminine social role. Portrayed as large, muscular women who smoked, drank, and cursed, female inverts were presumed to crave same-sex intimacy as a milieu in which to perform an aggressive and unsuitable masculinity.

Theories of inversion paved the way for a discourse of homosexuality and heterosexuality that regarded passionate same-sex attraction as abnormal. In his influential *Psychopathia Sexualis* (1886), the German psychiatrist Richard von Krafft-Ebing reduced sexual identity to three categories based on object choice: homosexuality (an unnatural erotic desire for the same sex), heterosexuality (a natural erotic desire for the opposite sex), and "psychosexual hermaphrodism" (an unnatural desire for both sexes). This paradigm defined "smashes" and "chumming" and most other Victorian same-sex attachments as sexually deviant, since all involved a same-sex partner. By the 1920s such theories had absorbed and been absorbed into a popularized version of Freudianism that emphasized object choice (male or female) as the heart of presumed healthy sexual development. While close same-sex attachments among children aroused little concern, at puberty boys and girls were expected to make a transition from same-sex to cross-sex attraction. Thus, by the early twentieth century, practices like "smashes" and "chumming" had become, at best, evidence of incomplete sexual development—at worst, proof of socially dangerous perversion.

Bibliography

Chauncey, George, Jr. "From Sexual Inversion to Homosexuality: Medicine and the Changing Conceptualization of Female Deviance." *Salmagundi* 58/59 (fall 1982/winter 1983): 114–146.

Cook, Blanche Wiesen. "Female Support Networks and Political Activism; Lillian Wald, Crystal Eastman, Emma Goldman." *Chrysalis* 3 (1977): 43–61.

Duggan, Lisa. *Sapphic Slashers: Sex, Violence, and American Modernity.* Durham, N.C.: Duke University Press, 2000.

Hansen, Karen V. "No Kisses Is Like Youres: An Erotic Friendship between Two African-American Women during the Mid-Nineteenth Century." *Gender and History* 7 (August 1995): 53–182.

Katz, Jonathan. "The Invention of Homosexuality." *Socialist Review* 20 (January–March 1990): 6–20, 28–30.

Rotundo, E. Anthony. *American Manhood: Transformations in Masculinity from the Revolution to the Modern Era.* New York: Basic Books, 1993.

Sahli, Nancy. "Smashing: Women's Relationships before the Fall." *Chrysalis* 8 (summer 1974): 17–27.

Smith-Rosenberg, Carroll. "The Female World of Love and Ritual: Relations between Women in Nineteenth-Century America." *Signs: A Journal of Women in Culture and Society* 1 (autumn 1975): 1–25.

Jeanne Boydston

See also ADDAMS, JANE; ANTHONY, SUSAN B.; COLLEGES AND UNIVERSITIES; JEWETT, SARAH ORNE; ROMANTIC FRIENDSHIP AND BOSTON MARRIAGE; SAME-SEX INSTITUTIONS; STODDARD, CHARLES WARREN; THOMAS, M. CAREY.

SMITH, Barbara (b. 16 November 1946), writer, activist, scholar.

Writing on and organizing around issues of liberation for blacks, women, lesbians, and gay men, Barbara Smith is at the forefront of contemporary movements in connecting various forms of discrimination and liberation struggles. She demonstrates the importance of the intersections of race, gender, sexual orientation, and class in LGBT history.

Smith's training for a life of scholarship-activism began in the racially segregated community of Cleveland, Ohio. Following the death of her mother, her aunt, who was instrumental in inspiring Smith's early love of literature, raised Barbara and her twin sister, Beverly. As a teen, Smith found her perspectives on racism and social justice influenced by the Congress of Racial Equality (CORE), a nonviolent, direct action-based organization that challenged racism through sit-ins, jail-ins, and freedom rides to desegregate public facilities. Smith participated in the Cleveland chapter's efforts to desegregate the area's schools and provide accessible education for all.

In 1965 Smith began undergraduate studies at Mount Holyoke College, pursuing an interdisciplinary major in English and sociology. In the introduction to her collection of essays *The Truth That Never Hurts*, Smith discusses the racism and sexism that she encountered from professors as she attempted to emulate the writing life of James Baldwin. In college Smith continued her activism in the civil rights and anti–Vietnam War movements. During this period Smith began to feel some of the tensions around her identity as black and female as she attempted to bridge her civil rights and antiwar activism. In particular, after attending the 1969 mass antiwar demonstration in Washington, D.C., Smith contemplated ending her activism rather than endure demands that she choose race or gender as her primary allegiance.

This dilemma of conflicting allegiances followed Smith to graduate school at the University of Pittsburgh. However, with the rise of the women's movement, Smith found her perspectives on identity and social justice further altered. During the late 1960s and early 1970s she was "haunted by the question of [her] sexuality." She recalls, "I wondered if I were really to commit myself to writing, what in the world would I write about, since there was this central fact of my existence that I was not able to reveal. Coming out in the mid-1970s was a crucial factor in finding my voice" (*Truth*, p. xiv).

Smith did, in fact, make this commitment to writing, but she also fully devoted herself to defining a black feminist theory that recognized simultaneously her lesbian, black, female, and working-class identities. Smith's central contribution to LGBT history is her unique ability to bridge socially constructed identities, as well as identifying writing and theory as critical to activism. In 1974 Smith, her sister, Beverly, and Demita Frazier formed the Combahee River Collective, a black-socialist-lesbian-feminist group. They co-wrote *A Black Feminist Statement*, which cogently outlined the history of black women's resistance to gender oppression in the black community and their stance against class-based oppression, an antiracist position, as well as a challenge to homophobia in black communities.

Also evolving from Smith's work with the Combahee River Collective was the Kitchen Table Women of Color Press, founded in 1980. Smith and black lesbian-feminist-poet Audre Lorde founded the press to establish an autonomous publishing outlet for women of color (*Truth*, p. xv). Kitchen Table published several works pivotal to the women's movement, black feminism, and lesbian feminism. Smith's role with the press ended in 1995.

Smith's challenge to the erasure of the black LGBT experience is evident throughout her writings, particularly in her literary criticism and social theory. Her work has appeared in *The Black Scholar*, *Gay Community News*, *The New York Times Book Review*, *The Village Voice*, *Ms.*, *The Guardian*, and *The Nation*. Smith's activism and scholarship are widely recognized. Her current work

includes constructing a thematic history of African American lesbian and gay experience as it has shaped, and been shaped by, America.

Smith continues to bring an incisive analytical mind and black lesbian feminist presence to contemporary radical organizing across communities. In 1998 Smith spoke at the Black Radical Congress, a coalition of feminist, nationalist, socialist, lesbian/gay, and youth organizations mobilizing for continued black struggle and liberation. Significantly, this was the first time Smith, as an out black lesbian, was invited to speak alongside her sixties black liberation contemporaries. Smith consistently questions how we, as a society, can come to collective solutions to our ills if we continue to parse identities and attempt to rank oppressions. Through this questioning she challenges the invisibility imposed by discrimination.

Bibliography

Anzaldúa, Gloria, and Cherríe Moraga, eds. *This Bridge Called My Back: Writings by Radical Women of Color*. New York: Kitchen Table Women of Color Press, 1984.

Bell-Scott, Patricia. "Barbara Smith: A Home Girl with a Mission." In *Still Lifting, Still Climbing: African American Women's Contemporary Activism*. Edited by Kimberly Springer. New York: New York University Press, 1999.

Bulkin, Elly, Minnie Bruce Pratt, and Barbara Smith. *Yours in Struggle: Three Feminist Perspectives on Anti-Semitism and Racism*. Ithaca, N.Y.: Firebrand Books, 1988.

Hull, Gloria T., Patricia Bell-Scott, and Barbara Smith. *But Some of Us Are Brave: Black Women's Studies*. Westbury, N.Y.: The Feminist Press, 1986.

Mankiller, Wilma, Gwendolyn Mink, Marysa Navarro, Barbara Smith, and Gloria Steinem. *The Reader's Companion to U.S. Women's History*. Boston: Houghton Mifflin, 1998.

Smith, Barbara. *Home Girls: A Black Feminist Anthology*. New York: Kitchen Table Women of Color Press, 1983. [2nd ed., New Brunswick, N.J.: Rutgers University Press, 2000.]

———. *The Truth That Never Hurts: Writings on Race, Gender, and Freedom*. New Brunswick, N.J.: Rutgers University Press, 1998.

Kimberly Springer

See also COMBAHEE RIVER COLLECTIVE; LITERATURE; PUBLISHERS.

SMITH, Bessie (b. 15 April 1894?; d. 26 September 1937), singer.

Bessie Smith was an African American singer renowned for her earthy voice, her tough manner, and her heavy drinking. Twice married, Smith engaged in affairs with both women and men and made little effort to hide her bisexuality. Rising to stardom in the 1920s, Smith was instrumental in shaping the sexualized "classic blues"— an African American music form that explored sexuality in humorous, poignant, and often explicit ways. Smith's toughness and her status as a blues singer created the necessary space to explore her sexual attraction to both women and men without condemnation.

One of seven children, Smith was born into an impoverished family in Chattanooga, Tennessee. By the time she was nine years old, both of her parents were deceased. With her brother Andrew accompanying her on guitar, Smith took to the Chattanooga streets where she sang for nickels and dimes. In 1912, Smith auditioned for the Moses Stokes Show and won the role of dancer and comedian; shortly thereafter, she was singing the blues with the traveling show. During these early years, Smith traveled and performed in tent shows in the South, which provided the largest audiences for black performers. It was also during this time that Smith met the blues singer Gertrude "Ma" Rainey, and their friendship endured throughout their careers. Both women were bisexual, but there is no conclusive evidence that an affair occurred between them.

Between 1912 and 1921, Smith toured with various troupes and amassed great popularity among rural southerners. During this period, Smith's first individual show performance was at 81 Theatre in Atlanta and the singer included male impersonation in her repertoire. In 1920, Smith met and married her first husband, Earl Love, who died one year later. By 1923, when her first record "Downhearted Blues" appeared under the Columbia label, Smith was already a successful blues singer. The song sold a record-breaking 780,000 copies, signaling the beginning of a prosperous recording career. By 1924, Bessie Smith, "Empress of the Blues," was the highest-paid black female performer in America.

Smith did not rely solely on lyrics to produce an image of the sexualized powerful black woman. As a performer, she had license to be excessive in her manner of dress, and her costumes included ermine minks, ostrich feathers, and outrageous headdresses. Competing with this image of great success was her troubled personal life: Smith's heavy drinking and fierce temper worsened as she ascended to star status, and her 1923 marriage to Jack Gee was an explosive union. A cheating husband exacerbated bouts of jealousy, and Smith, a six-foot, two-hundred-pound woman, was always quick to brawl.

Indulging in extramarital affairs with both women and men, Smith was often fearful of Jack Gee's detection and the violence that would ensue. No document reveals Smith's first liaison with a woman, but evidence confirms a romance with a young chorus girl, Lillian Smith, between December 1926 and February 1927. Bessie and Lillian shared the same bedroom, and after some inhibitions, Lillian grew as bold as Bessie and welcomed her lover's public displays of affection. Always afraid that Gee's impromptu visits would reveal the affair, Lillian left the troupe in February 1927. Soon after Lillian's departure, Gee discovered Smith in bed with another chorus girl, Marie. By all accounts, this was his first exposure to his wife's bisexuality. The couple reconciled, but there was no happy ending. After years of violent confrontations, jealous shout-downs, and continual infidelities, the couple parted in April 1929.

Following the stock market crash in October of that year, the classic blues, already in decline, was no longer in vogue. Although the heyday of Smith's recording career was over, between 1929 and 1933 she still found performance venues, often in the South. In 1933 Smith recorded her final records under the Okeh label—including "Down in the Dumps," recognized by many as her swan song. Smith's extensive recorded blues offer the best biographical statement on her life. While most of the classic blues situated heterosexual love at its center, many of Smith's songs heralded black women's ability to choose and to control their sexuality. Often cited as an empowered statement of sexual maturity, Smith's "Young Woman Blues" (1926) asserted that black women should not conform to society's pressure to marry, but should freely explore their sexual desires. Smith's legacy highlights the power held by black female blues singers in the 1920s and testifies to the early attempt to create a discourse on sexual expressiveness unrestrained by heterosexual marriage. Smith died in a car accident on 26 September 1937. She was forty-two.

Bibliography

Albertson, Chris. *Bessie.* New York: Stein and Day, 1972.

Carby, Hazel. "It Just Be's Dat Way Sometime: The Sexual Politics of Women's Blues." *Radical America* 20, no. 4 (June–July 1986): 9–24.

Davis, Angela. *Blues Legacies and Black Feminism: Gertrude "Ma" Rainey, Bessie Smith, and Billie Holiday.* New York: Pantheon, 1998.

Harrison, Daphne Duval. *Black Pearls: Blues Queens of the 1920s.* New Brunswick, N.J.: Rutgers University Press, 1988.

Laila S. Haidarali

See also FEMMES AND BUTCHES; MUSIC: POPULAR; RAINEY, MA.

SMITH, Lillian (b. 12 December 1897; d. 28 September 1966), writer.

The seventh of ten children, Lillian Eugenia Smith was born into an affluent family in Jasper, Florida, where she lived until her high school graduation in 1915. Her parents, Calvin Warren Smith and Annie Simpson Smith, gave her a strict Calvinist upbringing, emphasizing God's love and shame about the naked body. Smith also learned that white superiority and separation of blacks and whites was a natural extension of God's will in an era when segregation was entrenched in southern law and custom.

When World War I decimated her father's export lumber business, the Smiths moved its permanent residence to its summer home in Clayton, Georgia, in the foothills of the Blue Ridge Mountains. There the family established a summer camp for girls called Laurel Falls. From 1915 to 1916 Smith attended Piedmont College in nearby Demorest, Georgia, then began study of the piano at Peabody Conservatory in Baltimore in 1917. She worked as a teacher and principal in a small school in Tiger, Georgia, in 1918, and returned to the Peabody Conservatory in 1919 to continue her studies in piano until 1922. Deciding that her talents as a pianist were too creative for formal concerts, she accepted a position as head of the music department at the Virginia School in Huchow, Chekiang Province, China. Her experiences with the segregation of westerners and Chinese raised her consciousness about the injustices of racial segregation in the United States.

Smith reluctantly returned to Georgia in 1925 to direct Laurel Falls when both of her parents became too ill to oversee the camp's day-to-day operations. Determined to change the emphasis of camp activities from competitive sports to creative activities such as painting, sculpture, and dance, she fired most of the camp staff and oversaw construction projects that improved the camp's aesthetics. In the summer of 1928 she purchased Laurel Falls from her parents.

After her father's death in 1930, Smith became her mother's caretaker, nursing her for three years after a 1935 heart attack; Smith's mother died in 1938. Smith continued to run Laurel Falls in the summers while spending winters in Macon, Georgia, with her companion, math teacher and Laurel Falls counselor Paula Snelling, who encouraged Smith's efforts to write about her personal experiences. From 1930 to 1935 Smith wrote two novels, one of which was rejected by publishers because of its references to lesbian relationships between American missionaries and Chinese students, and three novellas. None of these works were published, but they helped Smith develop as an autobiographical writer. Only the novella, "Julia," survived a 1955 fire at Smith's Clayton house.

In 1936, Smith and Snelling founded the quarterly literary magazine *Pseudopodia*, which became the *North Georgia Review* in 1937 and *South Today* in 1942. Smith, Snelling, and other contributors wrote book reviews and feature articles that often discussed race relations in the South. Viewing America's entry into World War II as an opportunity to highlight the hypocrisy of promoting democracy abroad while denying it to African Americans at home, Smith publicly called for an end to segregation in the spring 1942 issue of *South Today*. She also criticized establishment-oriented liberals for their reticence in speaking out against segregation, focusing on the debilitating effects of segregation on blacks and whites. The publication of her novel *Strange Fruit* in 1944 demonstrated Smith's views that all southerners, white and black, were psychologically damaged by white supremacy. Set in a small town in south Georgia, *Strange Fruit* uses the town's violent reaction to a sexual affair between a white man and a black woman as an indictment of the social structure in the South.

Smith paid the price for challenging conventional beliefs about race. In 1949, the controversy surrounding her autobiographical *Killers of the Dream*, which clarified her views of segregation and white southerners' psychosexual maladjustments, contributed to the closing of Laurel Falls. She continued publishing novels such as *One Hour* (1959), a personal response to McCarthyism and the mob mentality of the 1950s, and nonfiction works such as *The Journey* (1953) and *Now is the Time* (1955); however, she believed many northern magazine editors and book publishers found her too controversial to publish because she violated acceptable gender roles as an outspoken female writer.

From 1950 to her death in 1966, Smith won numerous honorary degrees and literary awards including the Southern Authors' Award (1950), the Georgia Writers' Association Award (1955), and the Charles S. Johnson Award from Fisk University (1966). In the early 1960s she raised money for the Congress of Racial Equality (CORE) and the Student Non-Violent Coordinating Committee (SNCC) because of her admiration for their emphasis on mass nonviolent civil rights demonstrations. However, before her death in 1966 she denounced both groups for what she perceived as their abandonment of nonviolent principles and advocating African American nationalism. She died at her home in Clayton after a thirteen-year battle with cancer.

While few of her papers survived the 1955 fire, bits of her correspondence may be found in the following collections: nine letters between Smith and Martin Luther King Jr. at the University of Georgia Library in Athens, Georgia; correspondence in the Glenn W. Rainey Papers, Special Collections Department of the Woodruff Library of Emory University; correspondence in Congress of Racial Equality records at the State History Society of Wisconsin; correspondence in the Theodore Dreiser papers, Special Collections, Van Pelt Library, University of Pennsylvania; and author file papers of New York drama and motion agent Annie Laurie Williams, Columbia University's Rare Book and Manuscript Library.

Bibliography

Blackwell, Louise, and Frances Clay. *Lillian Smith*. New York: Twayne, 1971.

Gladney, Margaret Rose. "Personalizing the Political, Politicizing the Personal: Reflections on Editing the Letters of Lillian Smith." In *Carryin' On in the Lesbian and Gay South*. Edited by John Howard. New York: New York University Press, 1997.

Gladney, Rose, ed. *"How Am I to Be Heard?": Letters of Lillian Smith*. Chapel Hill: University of North Carolina Press, 1993, 1996.

Loveland, Anne C. *Lillian Smith: A Southerner Confronting the South: A Biography*. Baton Rouge: Louisiana State University Press, 1986.

Miller, Kathleen Atkinson. "Out of the Chrysalis: Lillian Smith and the Transformation of the South." Master's thesis, Emory University, 1984.

Will C. Holmes

SOCIALISM. see ANARCHISM, SOCIALISM, AND COMMUNISM.

SOCIETY FOR HUMAN RIGHTS

The Society for Human Rights in Chicago, Illinois, is the oldest documented homosexual emancipation organization in the United States. It was incorporated by the State of Illinois on 10 December 1924. The society's stated purpose was:

> To promote and to protect the interests of people who by reasons of mental and physical abnormalities are abused and hindered in the legal pursuit of happiness which is guaranteed them by the Declaration of Independence, and to combat the public prejudices against them by dissemination of facts according to modern science among intellectuals of mature age.

From 1920 to 1923, Henry Gerber, founder of the society, was stationed with the U.S. Army in Germany, where he was exposed to the thriving German homosexual emancipation movement. The name of his organization, Society for Human Rights, is a direct translation of Bund für Menschenrecht, the name of a German group organized in 1919. Gerber conceived of the society as a tool to "ameliorate the plight of homosexuals" (*ONE*, September 1962, p. 5). His plan had four components. First, the society would recruit homosexual men in Chicago to join the group. Second, it would engage in public education efforts. Lectures for homosexuals would instruct them about social perceptions of their behavior and urge them to avoid encounters with adolescents. Third, the society would publish a periodical entitled *Friendship and Freedom*. Finally, the organization would attempt to influence legislation by educating lawmakers about the latest medical and scientific research on homosexuality. The enlightened view at the time (relative to more conservative views) was that homosexuality was an illness, and thus expressions of homosexual behavior should not be criminalized.

Gerber knew he could not achieve such lofty goals on his own. He therefore recruited a board of directors for the society from among his acquaintances. Unfortunately, the only men he was able to interest in the effort were poor and illiterate. Consequently, Gerber did all the work and paid for all the expenses involved in keeping the operation afloat. The group only had approximately ten members.

The society published two editions of *Friendship and Freedom*, the name a translation of *Freundschaft und Freheit*, a German homosexual periodical. Gerber wrote all the material for the newsletter. No copies of *Friendship and Freedom* are known to exist today. The April 1925 issue of the French journal *L'Amitie* published a brief excerpt from the first issue of the publication.

Gerber wrote letters to distinguished physicians and social reformers in the United States and abroad in an attempt to win support for the society and its objectives. He was largely unsuccessful, as leaders of the medical establishment were unwilling to endanger their reputations by endorsing an organization whose members engaged in behavior classified as criminal.

The society came to an abrupt end in the summer of 1925. On Sunday, 12 July, Gerber returned home alone around 2:00 A.M. He answered a knock at the door, only to find a police detective. The detective searched the room without a warrant, confiscated materials of the society, and hauled Gerber off to jail. He was never charged with a crime. Al Meininger, the society's vice president, had informed the police where Gerber lived. Meininger had been arrested prior to Gerber in his own apartment with another man present and was charged with disorderly conduct.

Gerber endured three court appearances and paid $600 in attorneys' fees, resulting in the dismissal of his case due to the lack of a search warrant. He was fired from his job as a postal clerk in August for "conduct unbecoming a postal worker." With Gerber's savings depleted and income terminated, the Society for Human Rights ceased to exist.

A single thread connected the Society for Human Rights to the next organization that attempted to organize homosexuals, the Mattachine Society. Harry Hay founded Mattachine in 1950. Champ Simmons, whom Hay met in 1929, had previously been involved with a former member of the society. Simmons told Hay of Gerber's efforts to organize homosexuals, an idea that germinated in Hay for another two decades.

The incorporation papers, dated 10 December 1924, list the headquarters of the Society for Human Rights as 1710 North Crilly Court, a residence where Gerber rented a room. On 6 June 2001 the Chicago City Council designated 1710 North Crilly Court a Chicago landmark. A plaque commemorating the Society for Human Rights is imbedded in the sidewalk in front of the residence and was dedicated on 18 June 2002.

Bibliography

Coughenour, Jim. "The Life and Times of an Ordinary Hero." *Windy City Times* (22 June 1989).

Gerber, Henry. "The Society for Human Rights—1925." *ONE* 10, no. 9 (September 1962): 5–11.

———. "60 Years Ago—America's First Gay Rights Group." *GayLife* (6 December 1984).

Katz, Jonathan Ned. "1924–1925: The Chicago Society for Human Rights; 'To combat the public prejudices.'" In *Gay American History: Lesbians and Gay Men in the U.S.A.* Edited by Jonathan Ned Katz. New York: Crowell, 1976.

———. "1925, June 4, The Society for Human Rights, Chicago" and "1940, January 27, Henry Gerber to Manuel Boyfrank: 'Our proposed movement is of great social value.'" In *Gay/Lesbian Almanac: A New Documentary.* Edited by Jonathan Ned Katz. New York: Harper and Row, 1983.

Kepner, Jim, and Stephen O. Murray. "Henry Gerber (1895–1972): Grandfather of the American Gay Movement." In *Before Stonewall: Activists for Gay and Lesbian Rights in Historical Context.* Edited by Vern L. Bullough. New York: Harrington Park Press, 2002.

Sprague, Gregory. "Chicago Past: A Rich Gay History." *Advocate* (18 August 1983).

Timmons, Stuart. *The Trouble with Harry Hay: Founder of the Modern Gay Movement.* Boston: Alyson, 1990.

Karen C. Sendziak

See also GERBER, HENRY; HAY, HARRY; MATTACHINE SOCIETY; RIGHTS OF ASSOCIATION AND ASSEMBLY.

SOCIETY FOR INDIVIDUAL RIGHTS

In San Francisco on 26 May 1964, the board of directors of the bankrupt League for Civil Education, a bar-based gay rights organization, voted to dissolve the group and walked across the street to the home of Bill Plath to discuss the formation of a new organization. Calling itself the Society for Individual Rights, or SIR, the new organization took on many of the aims of the League for Civil Education, such as fighting police entrapment, but its structure expanded to encompass a larger group of members and a wider slate of activities. In July 1964 the Society for Individual Rights, wrote its constitution, and in September it was incorporated as a nonprofit corporation in the state of California. In January 1965, after six months of active recruitment, SIR's membership of roughly three hundred surpassed that of all other gay and lesbian organizations in San Francisco. By membership standards alone, it was charting new territory in gay and lesbian organizing.

Unique Characteristics

SIR was different from other San Francisco–based homophile organizations in that it utilized a bold language of social activism that was more aligned with civil rights organizations like the Student Non-Violent Coordinating Committee (SNCC) or the Congress of Racial Equality (CORE) than with homophile organizations like the Mattachine Society. Using the language of dignity, self-respect, and self-worth, SIR's leaders stressed the idea that social change depended on political organizing, and they urged the organization's members to defend their rights. On page one of the first issue of the group's monthly magazine, *Vector*, president Bill Beardemphl outlined the organization's agenda of political action, commitment to responsible legal counsel, cooperation with churches, and education in citizenship rights, as well as its desire "to provide our people with an honorable social fabric." The statement goes on to note the strengths and failures of other organizations, and promises that SIR would not fall into "inwardness," personality conflicts, or dictatorial control. Instead, SIR would pursue an open and democratic structure to "produce the most potent weapon possible in our fight for the elimination of sexual puritanism, social-political apathy, and personal irresponsibility. This weapon is fraternity."

Committee Structure

SIR's early leadership adopted a powerful tone, but the organization's success rested on its committee structure. The organization's constitution required that members elect a president, vice president, and board of directors, but leadership also came from elected committee chairs who worked autonomously to plan activities and organize events. In February 1965, for instance, members recognized eight committees: Political, Community Service, Membership, Publications, Religious, Legal, Social, and *Vector.* While the Community Service Committee worked to educate members about public health dangers such as venereal disease and the Membership Committee strove to expand the organization's roster, the Political Committee took on such tasks as reaching out to elected officials and encouraging gay people to vote. Later, this committee organized candidates' nights and advertised the concept of a gay voting bloc. In the late 1960s, several candidates for public office appealed to the gay community for support. In this way, SIR's Political Committee set the foundation for lesbian and gay political organizations such as San Francisco's Alice B. Toklas and Stonewall Democratic Clubs.

Legal Guidance

As the Political Committee worked to make itself known to San Francisco's City Hall, SIR's Legal Committee worked to protect its members from harassment and arrest. Legal Committee meetings were often attended by attorneys who were willing to give free legal advice, and *Vector* ran a regular column where attorneys answered legal questions. The Legal Committee also published a pocket-sized pamphlet that gave instructions on what to do in the case of arrest. The *Pocket Lawyer* insisted that when confronted by a police officer, one must not resist but instead should ask to see the officer's identification, make a note of the officer's badge number, and deny everything: "Although you must give your name and an address, DO NOT TELL ANYONE WHERE YOU WORK. The ONLY exception to this will be your bail bondsman. Answer ALL other statements or questions about you as follows: 'I DENY THAT' [or] 'MAY I CALL MY LAWYER'" (Smith). SIR lawyers reasoned that most cases would not be prosecuted unless the individual disclosed harmful information at the time of arrest.

Social Activities and a Community Center

Perhaps the most important committee that SIR developed, and the one that had the highest level of member participation, was the Social Committee. Social Committee members hit on the idea of selling tickets to private dances. Same-sex dancing was not allowed in bars in San Francisco at the time, so SIR dances often sold out. The Social Committee sold tickets to members ahead of time, so access to dances was a tremendous incentive for individuals to join the organization. In addition to dances, the Social Committee staged elaborate drag shows and popular theatrical productions such as *The Boyfriend, Little Mary Sunshine, Once Upon a Mattress,* and *A Funny Thing Happened on the Way to the Forum,* which encouraged San Francisco's transgender communities to participate more fully in SIR activities and events. These productions also planted the seeds for the emergence of gay and lesbian theater companies such as San Francisco's Theater Rhinoceros. The Social Committee also organized a slate of social activities such as bowling nights, tennis matches, hiking expeditions, a softball league, card games, discussion groups, and camping trips. Social events were planned for almost every night of the week, and team activities like the bowling league continued to draw a heavy turnout long after SIR had ceased to exist.

In May 1965 the SIR Board of Directors proposed to its membership that the organization open a community center to house all of its activities and events. They imagined that the center would serve the entire homosexual community and function as a clearinghouse for any gay and lesbian organizations. By early 1966 SIR had raised over $2,500 for its building fund, and in a March 1966 fund-raising letter to its membership, SIR's president set the opening date for 17 April 1966. Located at 83 Sixth Street, just south of Market Street, the center boasted office space, a boardroom, a library, a kitchen, and a public assembly area large enough to hold five hundred people. Publicity fliers announced that the center would be a symbol of unity, demonstrating the effective cooperation of San Francisco's LGBT communities and organizations.

One Voice

SIR functioned as an active organization for seven years, and while its list of social and political accomplishments is impressive, its most important contribution was to bring together the disparate communities that framed queer life in San Francisco. SIR leadership emphasized cooperation, and this allowed the organization to shape and articulate the concept of a shared community. In a 1966 letter to SIR members, for instance, Beardemphl stressed the need for "the community" to vote as one voice in an upcoming election. "We are in agreement. Even the Mattachine [Society] and the *Citizen's News,* who always are miles apart, agree on this. The Bars agree, the DOB [Daughters of Bilitis] agrees. Our straw poll has overwhelmingly shown that the whole gay community, when it becomes informed, agrees on these issues" (Beardemphl, 1966). Through a wide range of social and political activities and a commitment to cooperative participation, SIR was able to shape the notion of a "gay community" into an effective political tool.

Bibliography

Beardemphl, Bill. "S. I. R.'s Statement of Policy." *Vector 1* (1964): 1.

———. "Gold Sheet." José Sarria Papers. GLBT Historical Society of Northern California, c. 1966.

Boyd, Nan Alamilla. *Wide-Open Town: A History of Queer San Francisco to 1965.* Berkeley: University of California Press, 2003.

D'Emilio, John. *Sexual Politics, Sexual Communities: The Making of a Homosexual Minority in the United States, 1940–1970.* Chicago: University of Chicago Press, 1983.

Smith, Evander. "In Case of Arrest." *The S. I. R. Pocket Lawyer.* Ephemera Collection. GLBT Historical Society of Northern California.

Stryker, Susan, and Jim Van Buskirk. *Gay by the Bay: A History of Queer Culture in the San Francisco Bay Area.* San Francisco: Chronicle Books, 1996.

Nan Alamilla Boyd

See also HOMOPHILE MOVEMENT; SAN FRANCISCO.

SOCIOLOGY

Like the word "homosexuality," "sociology" is a nineteenth-century European neologism. In both instances, the new term became an organizing principle, though each also could be applied to earlier phenomena.

Early Research

The earliest American academic sociologists focused on the breakdown of the inhibiting bonds of family, religion, village, and other institutions as individuals moved out on their own and sold their labor in increasingly industrial, urban, and "modern" societies. Disinhibition of same-sex and gender-deviant desires was not discussed explicitly in their writings about moral "disorganization" in urban slums, but the breakdown of "tradition" and traditional restraints was central to the reformist discourse of American sociologists—many of whom were Protestant clergymen or sons of clergymen—in the decades around the start of the twentieth century.

Soon, however, the "social gospel" reformers lost influence to secularists seeking an objective science of society and social control. The academic program producing the most sociologists, that of the University of Chicago, specialized in "urban ecology," which mapped patterns of various phenomena—particularly "social pathologies" such as juvenile delinquency and suicide—across Chicago. Some analysis on which much later writing about LGBT communities drew, notably articles by Louis Wirth on urbanism and minority group ghettoes, were published in the department's journal, the *American Journal of Sociology.* Some urban sociology students observed local drag balls and bars frequented by "homosexuals," but these observations were not published in sociology journals, nor were they the focus of any doctoral dissertations. The Chicago School also pioneered in collecting life histories of immigrants, hoboes, juvenile delinquents, and other social "deviants." Some of these included passing mention of homosexuality and transvestism, but this information was not collected and systematically analyzed in print. Moreover, there were no M.A. or Ph.D. dissertations focusing on homosexuality during the Chicago "golden age" before World War II, although there was an M.A. thesis by Earle Bruce in 1942 and some term papers, fieldnotes, and life histories that are preserved in the Ernest Burgess Collection.

Life histories from forty male and forty female homosexuals were the basis for psychiatrist George Henry's 1935 book *Sex Variants.* Systematic documentation that homosexual behavior was not rare came from zoologist Alfred Kinsey. Having conducted sexual life history interviews with thousands of Americans and gained entrée to gay networks, Kinsey surprised many people, including more than a few who identified themselves as homosexuals, by reporting in a 1948 best-selling book that the homosexual "outlet" was far more common than almost anyone had supposed. Although Kinsey focused on behavior rather than on identity or patterns of association, demonstrating that the phenomenon of sex between males was not rare prepared the way for questioning whether it is pathological and unnatural. (The later Kinsey volume on females, published in 1953, proved even more controversial, despite the fact that it reported considerably less-frequent occurrence of female-female than of male-male sex.) Henry's and Kinsey's work had significant influence on the development of sociological approaches to LGBT issues.

Writing under the pseudonym Donald Webster Cory, Edward Sagarin relied on analogies to the "Negro" struggle for equality and drew from his own participation in American life as a homosexual in *The Homosexual in America* (1951). He argued that homosexuals were mostly like everyone else and that their problems were a result of prejudice and discrimination. Later, however, Sagarin undertook postgraduate study in sociology at New York

University and increasingly espoused a view of homosexuality as pathological. In a 1966 doctoral dissertation he took his revenge on the New York Mattachine Society (MSNY), whose members had rejected his leadership. In the dissertation and in subsequent published work, Sagarin extolled objectivity without revealing his own involvement in the homophile movement and in homosexual behavior. Although the dissertation was not published until decades later, Sagarin drew on it in work that represented "homosexuals" as a collection of psychopaths seeking to raise its status and protect its members under the guise of being a minority group.

Between Cory's book and Sagarin's dissertation, some observations of urban American male homosexuality were published in *Social Problems*, the journal of the Society for the Study of Social Problems (SSSP), an organization of politically engaged sociologists. In 1956, the second volume of the journal included a synopsis of an M.A. thesis by Maurice Leznoff on Montreal homosexual circles, coauthored by his Chicago-trained mentor, William Westley. In a 1961 issue of the journal, Albert Reiss published an analysis of complementary *queer* and *trade* roles in Nashville, Tennessee. Both of these pioneering studies combined Chicago School "look at what's out there" observation with assumptions from the functionalist paradigm, which asserts that there is a single moral community that everyone affirms, even those deviating from its standards. In Reiss's analysis, playing the stigmatized role of "the queer" reinforced the valuation of masculinity and the inferior status of the "queer." This interpretation flowed from the functionalist notion that some visible deviants from any moral norm are necessary to highlight the boundaries and superiorities of propriety.

In *Tearoom Trade* (1970), his study of males engaging in sex in a public park restroom, Laud Humphreys also found allegiance, indeed hyperconformity, which he characterized as buckling on "the breastplate of righteousness" (p. 131), to conventional attitudes and morality. He found this pattern of compensating for criminal behavior as especially typical of tearoom (restroom) denizens who were married to women. By then, British sociologist Mary McIntosh, in a classic functionalist analysis published in 1968 in *Social Problems*, had sketched the abjectifying role society had for "homosexuals."

Further Developments of the 1960s and 1970s

During the 1960s and early 1970s, sociologists—both functionalists and symbolic interactionists—observed and theorized stirrings of resistance by homosexuals and the primarily social but incipiently political associations of sex and gender "deviants." This work, along with challenges in psychology to views of homosexuals as psychopaths, relativized the notion of "deviant." In the SSSP/symbolic interactionist wing of American sociology, "labeling theory" focused on societal reaction to behaviors rather than on the intrinsic sickness or evil of those so behaving. At the Kinsey Institute, Chicago-trained sociologists John Gagnon and William Simon applied Chicago concepts such as "deviant career" and "script" to sexual conduct by lesbians as well as gay men. Their 1973 book *Sexual Conduct* contains revisions of their foundational papers of the late-1960s. Also during the mid-1960s, Peter Berger and Thomas Luckmann synthesized symbolic interactionist concepts with European sociology of knowledge approaches in *The Social Construction of Reality*.

A number of articles and books describing the lifeways and associations of American gays and lesbians and the burgeoning of lesbian and, especially, gay institutions were published by sociologists during the 1970s (see Harry and DeVall; Levine). Gay and lesbian sociologists did some of this research, but insider status was rarely explicit in publications, even by those who were "out of the closet." Silence about participation and identification with those studied somewhat lessened the stigma of studying "those kind of people," while maintaining a facade of nonparticipant objectivity at a time when anyone writing about his or her "own kind" (whatever that kind was) was suspected of "special pleading."

Nevertheless, the Sociologists' Gay (later LGBT) Caucus of the American Sociological Association (ASA) was founded in reaction to a presentation by Edward Sagarin at the ASA's 1974 meeting in Montreal. The caucus published a regular newsletter into the 1990s, prompted ASA to set up a task force on discrimination against gay/lesbian research and researchers, and proposed session organizers for annual ASA meetings, including many openly gay or lesbian sociologists.

During the late 1970s, empirical work on deassimilation and challenges to the stigmatization and abjection of "homosexuals" began to be eclipsed by a fashion of French deconstructionism, in particular by the oracular pronouncements by Michel Foucault (appearing in English in 1978) about the supposed "invention" of a new "species," "the homosexual," in the late nineteenth century. The notion that no such entity existed was consistent with the earlier views of Kinsey and Sagarin. While stimulating research by historians, Foucault's assertions did not lead to empirical sociology research, although Foucault had advocated studying social practices, and his earlier work on asylums and prisons influenced criminology and the sociology of social control.

During the 1970s, sociologists and psychologists seemed to be the primary scholars researching and writing about LGBT lifeways. During the 1980s, however, historical research (by John Boswell, John D'Emilio, Lillian Faderman, and others) became more important in setting interdisciplinary gay/lesbian research agendas than what sociologists wrote.

Some sociologists (including Barry Adam, David Greenberg, and Stephen Murray) developed typological comparative history of homosexualities, showing that there are different social organizations of homosexuality, but that only a few of the many imaginable types recur. At the most general level, there is a distinction between the organization of sexual roles in terms of status differences—of which gender (masculine dominating feminine) and age (older dominating younger) are the most prominent—and organization in which sexual roles are not based upon or set by status differences. Greenberg presents more of an unlinear evolution (age-based organization, followed by gender-based organization, followed by modern organization) than the University of Toronto–trained sociologists (Adam and Murray), who stress the simultaneous existence of different homosexualities in a society. All three apply the same typology to woman-woman sexual relations, though there is considerably less documentation for age-stratified female homosexual relations than for male ones.

Another comparativist sociologist, Frederick Whitam, approximated the much-denigrated "essentialist" view in writing about what he claimed was a universal rate of transvestitic homosexuals (1–2 percent of all postpubescent males), based on his observations in four places (all former colonies of Iberian countries with a tradition of heterogender homosexuality).

Sociology of the 1970s generally focused on "modern" lesbian and gay relations that were endogamous in gender and identity (in contrast to exogamous relations with one partner being straight-identified and gender-conventional). Just how egalitarian "modern" lesbian relations are was vociferously questioned by lesbians of color challenging white lesbian feminists and the desexualized conceptions of woman-identified woman and the lesbian continuum. It was also undercut by intensive observation of "domestic labor" and egalitarian self-representation by Christopher Carrington in *No Place Like Home* (1999) and by a resurgence in the visibility and valorization of heterogender (butch/femme) lesbian relationships.

Attention to racial/ethnic minority females who love females and minority males who have sex with males increased during the 1980s and 1990s, as did comparative attention to non-U.S. societies in the context of the globalization of homosexualities not structured by status differences. Also, research on sexual cultures in relation to HIV-transmission risks became a pressing analytic concern and fundable research topic, though this was pursued more by medical anthropologists than by medical sociologists. Some sociologists also took up "queer theory" during the latter half of the 1990s (see Seidman) without discernible influence either on American academic sociology or on romantic notions of "resistance" and "transgression" embedded in "queer theory."

New Social Movements

Identity-crafting, community-building, and political organizing are hallmarks of "new social movements" ("new" in contrast to working-class organizing). Various sociologists have conducted comparative and historical analyses of LGB organizations and their successes in challenging sodomy laws, extending antidiscrimination laws, and securing domestic partnership protections. One of the tenets of the founding (fore)fathers of sociology is that consciousness of being part of a "kind" is not an automatic result of sharing a characteristic. Class consciousness, for instance, is not automatic in working-class persons. This perspective has been applied by sociologists to LGBT contexts, so that self-identification as part of a "homosexual" or "transgender" community is understood not as an automatic product of having sex with persons of the same sex or crossing genders.

Moreover, before trying to change existing practices (such as the policing of bars) stigmatized people have to conclude that the practices are both intolerable and potentially changeable. The formation of a critical mass of persons who viewed themselves as defined to some extent by homosexual or transgender desires was the central precondition for mobilization for LGB and transgender rights. The feasibility of better treatment and less abject status was itself disproportionately facilitated by even tiny organizations making even equivocal challenges to the legitimacy of the dominant society's conceptions of sex and gender "deviants." The research of Humphreys, Adam, and others has shown that a prerequisite of any gay and/or lesbian political organizing is the existence of social space (beyond private-party networks and cruising sites) in which people can develop lesbian and gay identities. Both protecting and enlarging the range of these spaces are recurrent goals of LGBT movements.

Comparative research has shown that some repression against which to mobilize is a prerequisite to politicization. In a sense, some repression is good for organizing, though this is a good of which it is easy to get too much, making activism excessively high-risk and even lethal (as in most Arab countries). Research on LGBT movements has looked at cultural differences in opportunity for organization, not only from country to country, but from locality to locality. In places with multiple LGBT organizations, AIDS organizing has competed with gay organizing, though in places without developed gay organizations, AIDS has provided cover for some organizing of gender and sexual minorities. (On organizing dilemmas in the U.S. context, see Gamson; Adam, 1998.)

Bisexuals and the Transgendered

In addition to the research by Reiss, Humphreys, and others on heterosexually identified participants in homosexual sex, former Kinsey Institute sociologists Martin Weinberg and Colin Williams conducted extensive questionnaire research on those self-identifying as bisexual, whom they characterized as disconnecting sexual pleasure from the physical sex of sexual partners. Many bisexuals in their study described themselves in transition to or from primarily heterosexual relations, and, despite being recruited for study from San Francisco's Bisexual Center, did not think that there was a "bisexual lifestyle," although many portrayed their wider experience (compared with those whose sexual relations have been exclusively homosexual or heterosexual) as giving them superior wisdom about sex, gender, love, and the like. Weinberg and others concluded that the number of self-identifying bisexuals in the 1980s was declining, though the timing of their recruitment of subjects (1983–1985) coinciding with negative publicity about (male) bisexuals spreading HIV/AIDS to (female) partners. Questionnaire-based research has consistently shown that bisexual males are more hated than are lesbians, gay males, or bisexual females.

Paula Rust's 1999 book *Bisexuality in the United States* reviews the multidisciplinary (mostly not sociological) academic literature about bisexuality and reprints some of the most significant texts. This work suggests that while bisexuality formerly was more commonly conceptualized as "situational homosexuality," as a "stage" in "coming out" as gay or lesbian, or as a "phase" before commitment to heterosexuality, over time it has increasingly come to been seen as providing the basis for bisexual behavior, identity, and/or mobilization.

Research on female impersonators, transsexuals, and transgendered roles in the cultures of the world has been conducted primarily within the domains of psychiatry and anthropology, rather than sociology, with the exception of the feminist attack on transsexualism in Janice Raymond's *The Transsexual Empire* (1979).

Conclusion

Conceptions of the social construction of genders and sexualities have become common currency in other disciplines. Having pioneered description of the lifeways of those departing from the society's scripts for "normal" genders and sexualities and having produced important analyses of the social construction of gender and sexual realities, however, sociology has become peripheral to LGBT studies. Research on representative samples—whether the research is on sexual conduct or on reception of bits of pop culture—requires funding that has not been available in the United States since the 1970s. This has left the developing field to what relatively unfunded researchers can do by themselves (cull archives, essay bits of popular culture, and so on). Sociologists nevertheless continue to engage in research on LGBT topics and to be at the forefront of comparative studies of social movements and of societal accommodations of sex and gender variances.

Bibliography

Adam, Barry D. *The Rise of a Gay and Lesbian Movement.* Rev. ed. New York: Twayne, 1995.

——. "Anatomy of a Panic: State Voyeurism, Gender Politics, and the Cult of Americanism." In *Social Perspectives in Lesbian and Gay Studies: A Reader.* Edited by Peter Nardi and Beth Schneider. London: Routledge, 1998.

Adam, Barry D., Jan Willem Duyvendak, and André Krouwel. *The Global Emergence of Gay and Lesbian Politics: National Imprints of a Worldwide Movement.* Philadelphia: Temple University Press, 1999.

Berger, Peter L., and Thomas Luckmann. *The Social Construction of Reality.* New York: Doubleday, 1966.

Bruce, Earle W. "Comparison of Traits of the Homosexual from Tests and from Life History Materials." Unpublished M.A. thesis, University of Chicago, 1942.

Carrington, Christopher. *No Place Like Home: Relationships and Family Life among Lesbians and Gay Men.* Chicago: University of Chicago Press, 1999.

Cory, Donald Webster. *The Homosexual in America: A Subjective Approach.* New York: Greenberg, 1951.

Gagnon, John, and William Simon. *Sexual Conduct: The Social Sources of Human Sexuality.* Chicago: Aldine, 1973.

Gamson, Joshua. "Silence, Death, and the Invisible Enemy: AIDS Activism and Social Movement 'Newness.' " *Social Problems* 38 (1989): 351–367.

Greenberg, David. F. *The Construction of Homosexuality.* Chicago: University of Chicago Press, 1988.

Harry, Joseph, and William DeVall. *The Social Organization of Gay Males.* New York: Praeger, 1978.

Henry, George W. *Sex Variants: A Study of Homosexual Patterns.* New York: Hoeber, 1941.

Humphreys, Laud. *Out of the Closets: The Sociology of Homosexual Liberation.* Englewood Cliffs, N.J.: Prentice-Hall, 1972.

———. *Tearoom Trade: Impersonal Sex in Public Places.* New York: Aldine, 1975.

Johnson, David K. "The Kids of Fairytown." In *Creating a Place for Ourselves: Lesbian, Gay, and Bisexual Community Histories.* Edited by Brett Beemyn. London: Routledge, 1997.

Kinsey, Alfred, Wardell Pomeroy, and Clyde Martin. *Sexual Behavior in the Human Male.* Philadelphia: Saunders, 1948.

Kulick, Don. *Travesti: Sex, Gender, and Culture among Brazilian Transgendered Prostitutes.* Chicago: University of Chicago Press, 1998.

Laumann, Edward, et al. *The Social Organization of Sexuality.* Chicago: University of Chicago Press, 1994.

Levine, Martin P., ed. *Gay Men: The Sociology of Male Homosexuality.* New York: Harper & Row, 1979.

Leznoff, Maurice, and William A. Westley. "The Homosexual Community." *Social Problems* 3 (1956): 257–263.

McIntosh, Mary. "The Homosexual Role." *Social Problems* 16 (fall 1968): 182–192.

Murray, Stephen O. *Social Theory, Homosexual Realities.* New York: New York Academic Union, 1994.

———. *American Gay.* Chicago: University of Chicago Press, 1996.

———. *Homosexualities.* Chicago: University of Chicago Press, 2000.

Ponse, Barbara. *Identities in the Lesbian World: The Social Construction of Self.* Westport, Conn.: Greenwood, 1978.

Raymond, Janice G. *The Transsexual Empire: The Making of the She-male.* Boston: Beacon, 1979.

Reiss, Albert J. "The Social Integration of 'Queers' and 'Peers.'" *Social Problems* 9 (1961): 102–120.

Reiss, Albert J., ed. *Louis Wirth on Cities and Social Life: Selected Papers.* Chicago: University of Chicago Press, 1964.

Rust, Paula C. Rodríguez. *Bisexuality in the United States: A Social Science Reader.* New York: Columbia University Press, 1999.

Seidman, Steven, ed. *Queer Theory/Sociology.* New York: Blackwell, 1996.

Warren, Carol A. B. *Identity and Community in the Gay World.* New York: Wiley, 1974.

Weinberg, Martin S., and Colin J. Williams: *Male Homosexuals: Their Problems and Adaptations.* New York: Oxford University Press, 1974.

Weinberg, Martin S., Colin J. Williams, and Douglas J. Pryor. *Dual Attraction: Understanding Bisexuality.* New York: Oxford University Press, 1994.

Whitam, Frederick L., and Robin M. Mathy. *Male Homosexuality in Four Societies.* New York: Praeger, 1986.

Stephen O. Murray

See also ANTHROPOLOGY; CORY, DONALD WEBSTER; GENDER AND SEX; KINSEY, ALFRED C.

SODOMY, BUGGERY, CRIMES AGAINST NATURE, DISORDERLY CONDUCT, AND LEWD AND LASCIVIOUS LAW AND POLICY

Sodomy, buggery, crimes against nature, disorderly conduct, and lewd and lascivious behavior are crimes with a storied history, following a complex trajectory from the establishment of Great Britain's North American colonies to the present. With origins in the late medieval and early modern experience in England, the codes that referred to these offenses initially regulated specific sexual acts, both heterosexual and homosexual, and not the LGB identities that define expressions of homosexuality in the twenty-first century. The criminalization of lesbian and gay sexual expression thus has origins that significantly predate the labeling of persons who engage in same-sex sexual behavior as lesbian or gay.

Popular usage and legal definitions of the terms "sodomy" and "buggery," the crimes most commonly associated with LGBT people, have changed significantly over nearly four centuries in what is now the United States. Formal legal definitions of sodomy today include copulation (penetrative intercourse) involving any orifice of the human body, including the rectum or mouth, except for the vaginal opening of a woman. Sodomy has been defined as "oral or anal copulation between humans, esp. homosexuals," as well as "buggery; crime against nature; abominable and detestable crime against nature; unnatural offense; unspeakable crime" (*Black's Law Dictionary*, p. 1396).

Colonial America

In 1553, England established buggery as a capital offense; English courts subsequently interpreted buggery to include sodomy, which was defined as anal intercourse between two men or between a man and a woman, and bestiality, which was defined as intercourse between a human and a non-human animal. Britain's North American colonies applied the British law against buggery or enacted their own statutes. Plymouth, the first colony to enact its own law, made sodomy and buggery two of eight capital crimes in 1636. The New Haven Colony was unique in specifically prohibiting sex between women in its 1656 sodomy statute.

Overall, as many as nineteen people were prosecuted and five were executed for same-sex sexual acts in the colonial era. The social function of sodomy and other sex laws was to direct all sexual expression towards marriage and procreation. The law and culture did not maintain sanctioned social space for homosexual behavior, much less a same-sex sexual identity. The disciplinary regime was-by design-public and stern, and could include the death penalty. This ultimate penalty did not apply to those convicted of "sodomitical" acts not involving penetration (such as public masturbation), who were treated with more leniency. Women's same-sex sexual activity generally garnered the charge of lewd behavior rather than sodomy and was punished in a relatively lenient manner. Sara Norman of Plymouth, for example, was obliged to make a public acknowledgement of "unchaste behavior" with Mary Hammon, a far more lenient punishment than that which awaited those convicted of sodomy.

Early Republic and Nineteenth Century

Within several decades of independence from Great Britain, all of the original thirteen states and most of the new ones passed laws criminalizing sodomy, buggery, and/or crimes against nature. By 1868, thirty-two of thirty-seven states had such laws. Beginning with Pennsylvania in 1786, however, the death penalty for these crimes was eliminated (the last to repeal the death penalty were North Carolina in 1869 and South Carolina in 1873). Moreover, despite the widespread existence of such laws, enforcement was relatively limited, almost never applied to same-sex female sex, and almost always concentrated on non-consensual cross-sex, adult-child, or human-animal sex. Between 1796 and 1873, New York City courts issued only twenty-two indictments for sodomy, mostly in cases involving force or children. The country as a whole mirrored this limited enforcement-in 1880, the Census Bureau reported that only sixty-three prisoners were incarcerated in the entire country for sodomy. Of these, more than two-thirds were people of color or foreign-born, reflecting selective, racist, and nativist law enforcement practices.

Late Nineteen Century and Early Twentieth Century

As industrialization and urbanization contributed to the development of LGBT subcultures in the late nineteenth and early twentieth centuries, states across the country began revising their sodomy and other sex laws to facilitate governmental control over sexual expression. Until the 1870s, sodomy laws in the United States generally prohibited only anal sex. Pennsylvania's 1879 sodomy statute was the first to specify that women and men receiving or giving oral sex could be convicted of sodomy. Other states soon passed similar laws or created new laws

against "gross indecency," "lewd and lascivious acts," "private lewdness," or "oral copulation" to prohibit oral sex. In still other states, new judicial interpretations of existing laws had the same effect. By the 1920s, all states with large cities except for Texas had made consensual oral sex a felony.

The rapid expansion of laws governing sexual activity reflected the increasingly "reformist" orientation of various social elites concerned about vice and immorality in U.S. cities. Working through organizations such as the Society for the Prevention of Vice, the Society for the Prevention of Cruelty to Children, the Vigilance Society, and the Society for the Prevention of Crime, these elites often targeted LGBT cultural institutions. By 1890, the U.S. Census reported 224 people incarcerated for sodomy, an increase of more than 300 percent over 1880. According to statistics compiled by William Eskridge Jr., sodomy arrests in Boston, Chicago, New York City, and Philadelphia increased from 65 in the 1880s to more than 450 in the 1920s. Arrests in some cities continued to grow; in New York they rose from 230 in the 1920s to 536 in the 1950s. Consensual same-sex adult cases accounted for approximately 27 percent of reported sodomy cases between 1880 and 1925, fell to 21 percent between 1926 and 1970, and then dropped to 4 percent between 1971 and 1995.

While more and more LGBT people were arrested for sodomy through much of this period, even larger numbers were charged under new laws prohibiting disorderly conduct, cross-dressing, public indecency, lewdness, loitering, solicitation, vagrancy, and a variety of other crimes. "Disorderly conduct" arrests became a particularly convenient method used by states and cities to control "vice." In New York City, for example, disorderly conduct was outlawed in 1882 and became a focus of efforts to prosecute "degenerates"; over forty thousand men were arrested as "degenerates" under this law from 1922 to 1962. Many were arrested simply for being present in LGBT bars or other LGBT institutions or for consensual expressions of same-sex sexual interest and affection. California's vagrancy law, adopted in 1872 and amended in 1891 and 1903, was used in a similar fashion. Increased enforcement affected not only gay men, but also lesbians and transgendered women and men.

Late Twentieth Century

Beginning in the 1950s, homophile groups protested the existence and the enforcement of these various types of laws, lobbying for their repeal, launching investigations of police practices, meeting with police and political leaders, staging public demonstrations, advising people of their

Fight against Sodomy Laws. A portion of a flyer for a 1976 rally to repeal laws against sodomy—an early stage of a long legal struggle that was won in 2003 with the U.S. Supreme Court decision in *Lawrence v. Texas.*

rights, and pursuing court cases. In the 1960s, their efforts contributed to a significant curtailing of arrests in specific municipalities, and these efforts became increasingly successful in the 1970s.

All fifty states had sodomy laws until Illinois, following the recommendations contained within the American Law Institute's Model Penal Code, repealed its statute in 1961. Connecticut followed in 1969. Another legal revolution began in 1965, when the U.S. Supreme Court recognized a constitutional right to marital privacy in its birth control ruling in *Griswold* v. *Connecticut* (1965). The Court later expanded its privacy doctrine to cover individual decisions about birth control and abortion in *Eisenstadt* v. *Baird* (1972), and *Roe* v. *Wade* (1973).

The growth of the LGBT movement following the Stonewall Riots of 1969 contributed to further legal change. The Lambda Legal Defense and Education Fund and the American Civil Liberties Union Lesbian and Gay Rights Project were particularly active in challenging sodomy laws. In some states, legislatures repealed existing sodomy laws; in others court challenges declared these laws unconstitutional or non-enforceable; and in still others crimes were reduced from felonies to misdemeanors. By 1986, when the U.S. Supreme Court ruled on the constitutionality of state sodomy laws, twenty-four states and the District of Columbia still had such laws on the books. In the context of conservative backlash against

LGBT rights, however, several states (including Texas) decriminalized cross-sex sodomy only, leaving sodomy a specifically same-sex crime for the first time.

In bringing the case of *Bowers* v. *Hardwick* to the U.S. Supreme Court in 1986, legal advocates sought to expand the right to privacy to reverse Georgia's sodomy law, which barred both heterosexual and homosexual sodomy. The facts of that case reflected the discriminatory intent behind sodomy law enforcement. Police went to the home of Michael Hardwick, who had been the target of police harassment for drinking in public, with an outdated warrant. The officer found him engaged in oral sex with another man and arrested him for sodomy. In a much-criticized 5-4 vote, the Court decided that Georgia had the right to prohibit sodomy. Using an interpretation of history that suggested that early sodomy laws had targeted "homosexuals," even though that identity and word were of more recent vintage, even though such laws had not applied to oral sex until the late nineteenth century, and even though such laws had applied to cross-sex sex as well, the Court declared that it was "unwilling" to announce "a fundamental right to engage in homosexual sodomy" (*Bowers*, p. 191). A key member of the majority, Justice Lewis Powell, publicly stated after retiring from the Court that he regretted his vote. Powell was far from alone as a broad range of constitutional scholars and political activists sharply criticized *Bowers*'s reasoning and holding. *Bowers* nonetheless undermined a broad array of LGB rights efforts.

After 1986, legal activists stepped up their effort to overturn the twenty-five remaining sodomy statutes (including that of the District of Columbia). By 2003, when the next major case reached the Supreme Court, thirteen states still had laws against sodomy; four of these criminalized homosexual sodomy only. One of the remaining laws was that of Texas, whose Homosexual Conduct Law, passed in 1973, criminalized same-sex sodomy, but decriminalized both heterosexual sodomy and bestiality. In its 2003 ruling in *Lawrence* v. *Texas*, the Court decided to extend the notion of privacy that it had developed in *Griswold* and its progeny, overturn Bowers, and apply due process and equal protection concepts to protect consensual, private, same-sex sexual expression by adults.

In *Lawrence*, which involved a fact pattern remarkably similar to that of Bowers, Texas attempted to defend its sodomy law in part by resorting to the argument that the law did not discriminate against homosexuals, merely against their conduct. The 6-3 majority held that the privacy protections established in *Griswold* and its progeny did in fact extend to private same-sex sexual conduct by consenting adults. The Court carefully reviewed the history of sodomy law enforcement, finding that *Bowers* had relied on a misinterpretation of history. The Court referenced the sharp criticism from legal and historical scholars of *Bowers*'s reasoning and challenged the notion that sodomy laws were rooted deeply in western civilization by noting the fact that the European Court of Human Rights, along with other nations, have affirmed the right of adults to engage in private, consensual sexual conduct.

The *Lawrence* Court, in an apologetic note, stated that *Bowers* "was not correct when it was decided and is not correct today. It ought not to remain binding precedent." *Lawrence* eloquently and forcefully closed the centuries-long story of sodomy laws in the United States. The decision's strong language likely will render enforcement of other sex and "vice" laws, including disorderly conduct, more difficult. However, *Lawrence* explicitly refers to adult, consensual, and private conduct, leaving states and localities with the power to enforce such laws insofar as they prohibit public conduct, conduct by those defined as minors, and conduct defined as nonconsensual.

Bibliography

Apasu-Gbotsu, Yao, et al. "Survey on the Right to Privacy in the Context of Homosexual Activity." University of Miami Law Review 40, no. 521 (1986).

Black's Law Dictionary. 7th ed. St. Paul, Minn.: West Group, 1999.

Bowers v. *Hardwick*, 478 U.S. 186 (1986).

D'Emilio, John, "Capitalism and Gay Identity." In *Lesbians, Gay Men, and the Law*. Edited by William B. Rubenstein, 26-31. New York: New Press, 1993. Originally published in *Powers of Desire: The Politics of Sexuality*, Edited by Ann Snitow, Christine Stansell, and Sharon Thompson. New York: Monthly Review Press, 1983.

D'Emilio, John, and Estelle B. Freedman. *Intimate Matters: A History of Sexuality in America*. 2d ed. Chicago: University of Chicago Press, 1997.

Eisenstadt v. *Baird*, 405 U.S. 438 (1972).

Eskridge, William N., Jr. *Gaylaw: Challenging the Apartheid of the Closet*. Boston: Harvard University Press, 1999.

Eskridge, William N., Jr. "Challenging the Apartheid of the Closet: Establishing Conditions for Lesbian and Gay Intimacy, Nomos, and Citizenship, 1961-1981." Hofstra Law Review 25, no 817 (1997).

Eskridge, William N., and Nan D. Hunter. *Sexuality, Gender and the Law*. Westbury, N.Y.: Foundation Press, 1997.

Godbeer, Richard. *Sexual Revolution in Early America*. Baltimore: John Hopkins University Press, 2002.

Griswold v. *Connecticut*, 381 U.S. 479 (1965).

Homosexual Conduct Law. Texas Penal Code Annual § 21.06. St. Paul, Minn.: West 2001.

Jones v. *State*, 200 N.W.2d 587 (1972).

Katz, Jonathan Ned. *Gay/Lesbian Almanac*. New York: Harper & Row, 1983.

Katz, Jonathan Ned. *Gay American History: Lesbians and Gay Men in the U.S.A.: A Documentary History*. New York: Avon Books, 1976.

Lawrence v. *Texas*, (2003).

Locke v. *State*, 501 S.W.2d 826 (Tenn. Crim. App. 1973).

Robson, Ruthann. *Lesbian (Out)law: Survival Under the Rule of Law*. Ithaca, N.Y.: Firebrand Books, 1992.

Rubenstein, William B., ed. *Lesbians, Gay Men, and the Law*. New York:S New Press, 1993.

Thomas v. *State*, 326 So. 2d 413 (Fla. 1975).

Darren Rosenblum

See also ATLANTA; BOSTON; COLORADO; CRIME AND CRIMINALIZATION; DISCRIMINATION; FEDERAL LAW AND POLICY; POLICE AND POLICING; PRIVACY AND PRIVACY RIGHTS; PROSTITUTION, HUSTLING, AND SEX WORK LAW AND POLICY; PUBLIC SEX; PUERTO RICO; RIGHTS OF ASSOCIATION AND ASSEMBLY; SENSION, NICHOLAS; SEX ACTS.

SOLANAS, Valerie (b. 9 April 1936; d. 26 April 1988), writer.

Valerie Jean Solanas was born in Ventor, New Jersey, where she lived with her parents, Louis and Dorothy Bondo Solanas, until her sexually abusive father abandoned the family. Valerie and her mother then moved to Washington D.C., where her mother met and married Red Moran in 1949. In 1951, at age fifteen, Valerie had a child out of wedlock whom she put up for adoption. Solanas graduated from public high school in 1954. She went on to attend the University of Maryland at College Park, where she studied psychology. She supported herself by working at the Psychology Department's animal laboratory and by prostitution. In 1958 Solanas enrolled in a master's program in psychology at the University of Minnesota. She dropped out the following year, complaining that the program taught nothing that was relevant to women.

In 1966 Solanas moved to New York City's Greenwich Village, where she wrote a play, *Up Your Ass*, about a man-hating panhandler who murders her son. In 1967 Solanas contacted Andy Warhol, a famous pop artist and filmmaker, to see if he might produce her play. Warhol told journalist Gretchen Berg that the play was "so dirty" he suspected Solanas of being an undercover vice officer. Warhol subsequently lost Solanas's only copy of her play in the chaos of his studio. Solanas began calling Warhol on the telephone, doggedly insisting that he return her play to her. Warhol eventually did pay Solanas for appear-

Valerie Solanas. The author of the radically anti-male *S.C.U.M. Manifesto* is interviewed while in police custody, a few hours after shooting Pop artist Andy Warhol on 3 June 1968. [Bettmann/corbis]

ing in two films that he produced in 1967, *I, a Man* and *Bikeboy.*

Over the course of 1967, Solanas wrote what would become a landmark text of radical feminism, the *S.C.U.M. Manifesto,* with S.C.U.M. standing for the Society for Cutting Up Men. Both violent and funny, the *S.C.U.M. Manifesto* was anti-male and anti-capitalist. In it Solanas denounced men of all political stripes as self-centered, insecure, and power hungry: "No genuine social revolution can be accomplished by the male, as the male on top wants the status quo, and all the male on the bottom wants is to be the male on top. The male rebel is a farce" (p. 21). Solanas brilliantly used hyperbole and sarcasm to underscore the inapplicability of all other radical critiques for women. In 1970 an excerpt from the manifesto appeared in Robin Morgan's anthology, *Sisterhood is Powerful,* ensuring Solanas's place in the canon of U.S. feminist theory.

Early in 1967 Solanas met Maurice Girodias of Olympia Press. He agreed to publish her manifesto, which appeared in print in 1968. But the contract she had signed with Girodias troubled Solanas. Over the next few months, Solanas grew more and more worried that it gave Girodias legal control over all that she might write in the future. Seeing a plot masterminded by Warhol, Solanas believed that Warhol had used Girodias to steal her work. In the spring of 1968, Solanas plotted to kill her publisher.

On the morning of 3 June 1968, Solanas waited for Girodias at the Chelsea Hotel. When he did not return, she went to Warhol's studio. At 4:15 P.M. Solanas shot Warhol three times. Warhol was pronounced clinically dead when he arrived at Columbus-Mother Cabrini Hospital, but survived after undergoing five hours of surgery. At 8:00 P.M. Solanas turned herself in and stated that she had shot Andy Warhol because he had too much control of her life.

On 13 June 1968 Solanas appeared at the New York State Supreme Court with radical feminist lawyer Florynce Kennedy. Kennedy complained that Solanas was being improperly detained because she was a woman and that her actions were "politically, not sexually, motivated." Kennedy submitted the *S.C.U.M. Manifesto* as a legal brief to the court. The judge denied the motion. On 28 June 1968 Solanas was indicted for attempted murder but shortly thereafter was declared incompetent and was sent to Ward Island Hospital. Radical women began calling Solanas "the first political prisoner of the women's movement."

Solanas was released pending sentencing in the fall and winter of 1968–1969. She again pestered Warhol for money. Solanas tried to join October 17, a New York City radical feminist group, but abruptly denounced the organization and threatened to kill Ti-Grace Atkinson, one of her staunchest supporters and the group's founding member. On 9 June 1969 Solanas pleaded guilty to shooting Warhol and was sentenced to three years at the Women's Penitentiary at Bedford Hills, New York.

Solanas was released in September 1971. In both 1973 and 1975 Solanas was placed in psychiatric hospitals for treatment. On 26 April 1988 Solanas was found dead in a San Francisco welfare hotel room.

Bibliography

Baer, Freddie. "About Valerie Solanas." In *S.C.U.M. Manifesto.* By Valerie Solanas. San Francisco: AK Press, 1996.

Echols, Alice. *Daring to Be Bad: Radical Feminism in America, 1967–1975.* Minneapolis: University of Minnesota Press, 1989.

Solanas, Valerie. *S.C.U.M. Manifesto.* San Francisco: AK Press, 1996.

Jane Gerhard

See also ATKINSON, TI-GRACE; FEMINISM; LESBIAN FEMINISM; WARHOL, ANDY.

SONDHEIM, Stephen (b. 22 March 1930), composer and lyricist.

Born in New York City, Stephen Sondheim was the only son of the couturier Herbert Sondheim and his clothing designer wife Janet Fox ("Foxy") Sondheim. Descendants of German Jewish immigrants and among New York City's nouveaux riches after making the transition from working poor to middle class, the Sondheims occupied apartments in the San Remo on Central Park West. Stephen's early educational experiences took place at the Ethical Culture School, founded by Felix Adler, a nineteenth-century social reformer. Here, Stephen showed an early fascination for both words and music, possibly due to his continuous hearing of the show tunes played by his father at the family piano. Indeed, Stephen began piano lessons at an early age himself. When his parents split in 1940, Stephen was sent to the New York Military Academy at Cornwall on Hudson, New York, which he attended from 1940 to 1942. During this time his mother, in reaction to her husband's departure, became a suffocating presence in the young man's life. The resulting traumatic experiences led to Sondheim's guarded relationship with other women.

In 1942, Sondheim met Oscar Hammerstein II, the lyricist for composers Jerome Kern (*Show Boat,* 1927) and Richard Rodgers, who was to have a profound effect on shaping the composer-lyricist's career. Sondheim's interaction with the Hammerstein family provided an important balance to the unstable, often irrational behavior of his mother. From 1942 to 1946 Sondheim attended the George School, a coeducational college preparatory school in Bucks County, Pennsylvania. There he actively participated in several theater productions and made his first attempt at writing songs. In 1945, Sondheim collaborated with a classmate on a musical about student life at the school. The result was *By George* (1946), a two-act work, complete with dance numbers, twenty songs, and a cast of fifty. From 1946 to 1950 Sondheim attended Williams College, where he studied with Irwin Shainman and Joaquín Nin-Culmell, brother of Anaïs Nin. Here, Sondheim produced his earliest musicals, *Phinney's Rainbow* (1948) and *All That Glitters* (1949). Upon completion of his undergraduate degree, he was awarded the Hubbard Hutchinson Prize for Music, which allowed him to study privately with Milton Babbitt at Princeton University. When it became clear that Sondheim's real musical interest was in writing for the Broadway stage and not the production of "serious" orchestral literature, he and Babbitt parted ways.

After a brief career writing for television, most notably for the series *Topper,* Sondheim began his Broadway career in earnest. His initial success on the Broadway stage occurred in 1957 as lyricist for the Leonard Bernstein (composer), Arthur Laurents (playwright), and Jerome Robbins (choreographer) production of *West Side Story.* Two years after this auspicious entrance into the bright lights of Broadway, Sondheim was tapped to provide lyrics for *Gypsy,* the Jule Styne musical based on the life of Gypsy Rose Lee, starring the inimitable Ethel Merman. Sondheim's Broadway debut as a composer occurred in 1962 with his music for *A Funny Thing Happened on the Way to the Forum,* a production derived from the ancient Roman playwright Plautus and starring Zero Mostel. It was not until 1970, however, with the appearance of *Company,* that the composer came into the consciousness of the American theatergoing public. His best-loved works remain *A Little Night Music* (1973), *Sweeney Todd* (1979), *Sunday in the Park with George* (1984), and *Into the Woods* (1987).

Sondheim himself has stated that he was never at ease with being homosexual. As was the case with the English composer Benjamin Britten, this aspect of Sondheim is conveyed more confidently and pridefully in musical terms on stage rather than in private. Sondheim now writes exclusively for the theater, but giving greater importance to the character and the plot. In approaching a new work, Sondheim looks at the tools that have been set up for him—the characters, the dramatic situation, the ambience of the scene—and finds ways to convey these intersecting values musically. The characters in a Sondheim musical are often "others" in society, those who live on the fringe. The composer's significance as a dramatist-musician is founded on conflicting polarities between the art and the man—an avant-garde artist working in a populist medium, a cynical personal outlook on life that captures the passion and pain of life, and an unabashed intellectual capable of producing bawdy, low comedy. This juxtaposition finds its way into Sondheim's music, where a lighthearted accompaniment may be paired with a bloody or horrific lyric and vice versa.

Sondheim remains a cult figure for many musical theatergoers who were raised on the works of such "traditionalists" as Irving Berlin, Jerome Kern, and Richard Rodgers. Indeed, until the late 1990s Sondheim's works were somewhat neglected. Only now can we clearly see how significant his contributions to the American musical theater have been and the myriad ways in which he has transformed the genre, once thought of as completely moribund.

Bibliography

Citron, Stephen. *Sondheim and Lloyd-Webber: The New Musical.* New York: Oxford University Press, 2001.

Gordon, Joanne, ed. *Stephen Sondheim: A Casebook.* New York: Garland, 1997.

Gottfried, Martin. *Sondheim.* Rev. ed. New York: Abrams, 2000.

Horowitz, Mark Eden. *Sondheim on Music: Minor Details and Major Decisions.* Lanham, Md.: Scarecrow Press, 2003.

Martin, George Whitney. "On the Verge of Opera: Stephen Sondheim." *Opera Quarterly* 6, no. 3 (Spring 1989): 76–85.

Secrest, Meryle. *Stephen Sondheim: A Life.* New York: Knopf, 1998.

James P. Cassaro

See also BENNETT, MICHAEL; MUSIC: BROADWAY AND MUSICAL THEATER; ROBBINS, JEROME.

SPORTS

U.S. LGBT athletes today enjoy considerable support and visibility in a wide range of recreational sports leagues, and LGBT visibility on the Olympic and professional levels has increased significantly in the last three decades of the twentieth century. Still, homophobia and heterosex-

ism in U.S. sports are rooted deeply in the nation's history, posing significant problems. Except in LGBT sports leagues, the overwhelming majority of LGBT athletes continue to live closeted lives. This is true even in sports long thought to have significant numbers of LGBT participants, including men's figure skating and diving and women's golf, basketball, softball, and tennis.

LGBT athletes have faced not only the general homophobia and heterosexism pervasive in U.S. society but also problems specific to the sports world. Most sports are organized along single-sex lines, and homosocial activities in the United States have long been subject to anti-LGBT policing. Activities involving bodily display and performance also have been regarded with anti-LGBT suspicion, and athletic bodies, in particular, have been thought to elicit same-sex desire. Because athletic achievement has been linked with masculinity, female athletes have been attacked as mannish lesbians, and lesbianism in sports has been regarded as a taboo subject to be avoided at all costs, under the assumption that it would scare sponsors and fans. Meanwhile, because male athletes have been viewed as strong, aggressive, and hypermasculine and gay men have been seen as effeminate and weak, most male sports have been assumed to be gay-free. While some sports, such as figure skating, are deemed sissy sports, others, such as football, ice hockey, basketball, and baseball, are bastions of antigay machismo. Gay male athletes also fear that in sports worlds where men openly show physical affection toward one another, their actions might be misconstrued as sexual advances toward their heterosexual teammates.

Despite these obstacles, many LGBT people have been drawn to sports. Many participate for the same reasons that straight people do. In addition, LGBT people are active in sports because they provide opportunities for challenging homophobia and heterosexism. Sports cultures celebrate bodily achievement and beauty, sports experiences often include intense same-sex bonding, positive sports activities provide opportunities for recovering from anti-LGBT sports experiences, and participation in sports can create ways to affirm distinctive LGBT genders and sexualities.

Twentieth-Century Pioneers: Bill, Babe, and Tom

Before the 1970s, three U.S. LGBT athletes rose to prominence in their sports. William Tilden, considered the greatest tennis player of the first half of the twentieth century, was not openly gay, yet he did not entirely hide his homosexuality; his younger male lovers were his frequent companions on and off the tennis circuit. Tilden became an easy target for homophobes, resulting in harassment and exclusion from tournaments in the 1930s and legal troubles in later decades. The all-around sports legend Mildred ("Babe") Didrikson Zaharias remained closeted during her entire life. She excelled in many sports but was best known as a track-and-field Olympian and a champion professional golfer. Continually dogged by disparaging media depictions of her as "mannish" and a "muscle moll," she quelled some of the negative rumors by marrying the professional golfer George Zaharias in 1938. She also changed her style of dress to conform to mainstream standards of femininity. Nonetheless, she had a female lover who remained by her side until her death from cancer in 1956. Not until the late 1960s did another LGBT athlete rise to prominence. Tom Waddell, an army physician, finished sixth in the decathlon in the 1968 Mexico City Olympics.

Recreational Sports

Recreational sports leagues began to proliferate in the early 1900s. For women, large-scale participation in team sports began at women's colleges and corporate-sponsored baseball teams. By World War II, softball had become one of the country's most popular sports. In the 1940s, 1950s, and 1960s, closeted lesbians were significant participants and created a vibrant softball subculture centered on teams and the urban bars that sponsored them. These women formed close-knit communities in which lesbians could socialize.

Women's softball teams were among the first pioneers of LGBT sports leagues. In 1974, for instance, the Atlanta Lesbian Feminist Alliance (ALFA) formed an openly lesbian softball team called the Omegas. That same year in Houston, the local chapter of the National Organization for Women sponsored an all-lesbian softball team that competed in city leagues. During the summer of 1975, ALFA sponsored a softball tournament sanctioned by the Amateur Softball Association for female-led city teams. Each day as the tournament began, participants and fans joined together in singing the lesbian folk singerMeg Christian's "Ode to a Gym Teacher."

LGBT recreation leagues began to proliferate in the late 1970s in a wide range of sports, including wrestling, swimming, bowling, and rugby. Softball remains one of the most popular sports. The North American Gay Amateur Athletic Alliance, created in 1977, is made up of dozens of LBT softball leagues and associations nationwide. Its annual world softball championship draws thousands of athletes and spectators each year. The largest LGBT athletic event in the world is the Gay Games. Held every four years, the Gay Games were the brainchild of Waddell. He dreamed of having an international athletic competition that would attract athletes of all sexualities and abilities. By the time the first event was held in 1982 in San Francisco (with more than 1,300 participants), there were LGBT recreation leagues in every major city in the United States. Many of these leagues have competed in the Gay Games, which are run by the Federation of Gay Games. The Games initially were called the Gay Olympics, but in 1987 the U.S. Olympic Committee successfully sued Waddell, claming that his use of the word "Olympics" was property infringement. By 2002, when the Games were held in Sydney, Australia, the number of participating athletes had soared to more than thirteen thousand.

Professional and Olympic Sports

Near the end of the twentieth century, LGBT professional and Olympic athletes began coming out in larger numbers. What started as a trickle in the 1980s increased dramatically in the 1990s. This phenomenon coincided with higher and more positive LGBT visibility in American society in general, as celebrities, politicians, and other high-profile members of society made their sexualities and gender identities public.

Reneé Richards is the lone out transsexual athlete to have competed professionally. After she underwent a male-to-female sex-change operation in 1975, the United States Tennis Association barred her from competing in the U.S. Open. She sued, won the right to compete, and entered the tournament in 1977. In 1981, the tennis great Billie Jean King and the Czech-born player Martina Navratilova were outed as lesbians. King was outed when a former female lover filed a palimony suit against her. In the case of Navratilova, a newspaper reporter published, against her wishes, an interview in which she talked about her relationship with the novelist Rita Mae Brown. Both women lost major endorsement deals when their relationships were publicized. In 1983, the world champion bodybuilder Bob Paris came out in an interview in *Ironman* magazine. In 1988, Dave Pallone, a National League baseball umpire, was fired shortly after he told the National League president that he was gay.

Several former professional athletes, including football and baseball players, came out in the 1990s. Glenn Burke, an African American Major League Baseball player, had a short career and blamed homophobia for his downward trajectory. In 1995, he died, penniless, from AIDS. At the fourth Gay Games in New York City in 1994, the Olympics champion diver Greg Louganis, who is HIV positive, revealed that he was gay. That same year, the lesbian mountain biker Missy Giove won the world championships in her sport. She repeated the feat in 1996 and

Gay Games. Two female ice-skaters celebrate winning the gold at the Gay Games, which first took place in 1982 and had more than thirteen thousand participants twenty years later. [Darlene/Photo Graphics]

1997. Muffin Spencer-Devlin, a mainstay on the Ladies Professional Golf Association (LPGA) circuit, came out in 1996 in an interview with *Sports Illustrated*. The same year, the Mexican American figure skater and men's national champion Rudy Galindo also came out. Several other male figure skaters followed suit.

The Women's National Basketball Association (WNBA), the LPGA, and the Women's United Soccer Association (WUSA) have very visible lesbian fan bases and strong participation by closeted lesbians, but the professional leagues have been slow to acknowledge either. In the first six years of the WNBA, which was founded in 1997, New York Liberty forward Sue Wicks was the only out player, and the team's general manager, Carol Blazejowski, was the only openly lesbian official. Wicks retired in 2003, leaving a league with a massive lesbian fan base but no out lesbian players. The WNBA initially ignored its lesbian fans, even going so far as to print a list of married players for the media. Special interest features shown during games continued to portray players as straight or straight-acting, glowing about their married lives and boyfriends. By its fifth year, owing to complaints and protests by lesbian fans that attracted significant media attention, the WNBA began to conduct advertising and community promotions in the LGBT community.

Lesbian golf fans sometimes are marketing targets for the regional sponsors of local LPGA events. The most

significant example is the Kraft Nabisco Championship (formerly called the Dinah Shore Tournament) in Palm Springs, California. Overall, however, the league has been fairly silent on lesbian issues and has depicted its players as straight and married. The younger WUSA does not acknowledge its lesbian fans at all and admits that it markets primarily to traditional families of soccer moms and their daughters.

In the relatively young women's professional football leagues, there are teams that are made up almost entirely of lesbians. An example is the Chicago Force of the Independent Women's Football League, which was founded in 2002. In 2001, however, when Alissa Wykes, a player for the Philadelphia Liberty Belles, came out in an issue of *Sports Illustrated*, the league owner reprimanded her for allegedly sabotaging its marketing and sponsorship opportunities.

In the late 1990s, some corporate sponsors began to maintain their support of players who openly acknowledged their sexuality, instead of swiftly ending their contracts. Nike and Dunlop rallied behind the French tennis player Amélie Mauresmo when she came out in 1999, even as higher-ranked players, such as Martina Hingis (ironically named after Navratilova), made homophobic comments about her to the press. Spencer-Devlin also has retained her endorsement deals.

Although several additional professional male athletes have come out as gay after their careers were over and basketball player Dennis Rodman played around with public transgenderism while still competing professionally; men's football, ice hockey, and basketball continue to have no out players. Rumors about active players such as the baseball player Mike Piazza have been denied as quickly as they have circulated. Nevertheless, some professional baseball teams began to hold LGBT pride days in the late 1990s to extend their fan base and show appreciation of their LGBT fans.

College and University Sports

On the campus front, widespread homophobia in the worlds of high school, college, and university sports continued to be an insidious influence into the twenty-first century. Young LGBT athletes, coaches, and administrators risked ostracism and became the targets of verbal and physical abuse if they came out. Compared with other areas of college and university life, athletics have occupied a hinterland of closeted students and coaches. They have continued to live in a world in which many LGBT people knew and socialized with each other but chose collectively to remain closeted. In 2000, the National Collegiate Athletic Association (NCAA), prodded by the efforts of the National Center for Lesbian Rights and the Women's Sports Foundation, began tackling homophobia and anti-LGBT harassment with diversity training and other educational activities. A handful of athletes, coaches, and athletic directors came out or made no secret of their sexualities and gender identities in the next few years.

Hostility nonetheless has persisted. College and university coaches have tried to attract the best high school athletes with homophobic slander about the members and coaches of rival teams. Some coaches have had unofficial homophobic policies. Pennsylvania State University's women's basketball coach Rene Portland's "no alcohol, no drugs, no lesbians" team guidelines became public in 1991. The policy caused an uproar and resulted in sensitivity training for the entire athletic department. The school's openly lesbian softball coach, Sue Rankin, was largely responsible for the university's response and later became Penn State's coordinator of LGBT equity. The homophobia that some college and university athletes faced became so unbearable that some of them left teams after coming out (or being outed). This was the case for Dwight Slater, an African American member of Stanford University's football team, in 1998.

In contrast, the Nordic skier Ryan Quinn, who came out while he was a member of the University of Utah's championship skiing team in 2001, had a positive experience when he told his teammates and coach that he was

gay. Michael Muska, an openly gay athletic director at Oberlin College in Ohio, became a visible advocate for fighting homophobia in sports when he was inadvertently outed in the *Chronicle of Higher Education* in 1998. A few out coaches have had flourishing careers. Stanford University's women's basketball coach Tara VanDerveer is an example. Her perpetually nationally ranked team twice won the NCAA title. She also was the head coach of the gold medal–winning 1996 U.S. Olympic women's basketball team.

In 2003, a major milestone was reached when the National Gay and Lesbian Athletics Foundation held the first national conference focused on LGBT athletes at the Massachusetts Institute of Technology. More than three hundred participants attended the National Gay and Lesbian Athletics Conference, which brought together athletes, coaches, and administrators to have frank discussions about homophobia and LGBT visibility.

Bibliography

Anderson, Eric. "Openly Gay Athletes: Contesting Hegemonic Masculinity in a Homophobic Environment." *Gender and Society* 16, no. 6 (December 2002): 860–877.

Bull, Chris. "The College Sports Closet." *Advocate* (5 March 2002): 26–31.

Cahn, Susan K. *Coming on Strong: Gender and Sexuality in Twentieth-Century Women's Sport.* New York: Maxwell Macmillan International, 1994.

De St. Jorre, John. "Out in the Open." *Women's Sports and Fitness* (September-October 1999): 114–117.

DuLong, Jennifer. "Out in the Field." *Advocate* (19 February 2002): 32–35.

Galst, Liz. "The Sports Closet." *Ms.* 9, no. 2 (September–October 1998): 74–78.

Griffin, Pat. *Strong Women, Deep Closets: Lesbians and Homophobia in Sport.* Champaign, Ill.: Human Kinetics, 1998.

Jacobsen, Jennifer. "Facing Derision in a Macho Culture, Many Gay Athletes in Team Sports Hide Their Sexuality." *Chronicle of Higher Education* 49, no. 10 (1 November 2002): A36–A38.

Muska, Michael. "Reflections of a Gay Athletics Director." *Chronicle of Higher Education* 7 (13 October 2000): B10–B12.

National Center for Lesbian Rights. "Homophobia in Sports." Available from http://www.nclrights.org/projects/sports project.htm

National Gay and Lesbian Athletics Foundation. Home page at http://www.gayconference.org

Outsports. Home page at http://www.outsports.com

Plymire, Darcy C., and Pamela J. Forman. "Speaking of Cheryl Miller: Interrogating the Lesbian Taboo on a Women's Basketball Newsgroup." *National Women's Studies Association Journal* 13, no. 1 (Spring 2001): 1–21.

Sears, James T. *Rebels, Rubyfruit, and Rhinestones: Queering Space in the Stonewall South.* New Brunswick, N.J.: Rutgers University Press, 2001.

Women's Sports Foundation. "Recruiting-Women's Sports Foundation Response to Negative Recruiting/Slander Based on Sexuality: The Foundation Position." Available from http://www.womenssportsfoundation.org

Woog, Dan. *Jocks: True Stories of America's Gay Male Athletes.* Los Angeles: Alyson, 1998.

Uselton, Ruth. "It Takes a Team: Eliminating Homophobia in Sports." Available from http://www.womenssports foundation.org

Cheryl Coward

See also ATLANTA; DIDRIKSON, MILDRID ELLA; GYMS, FITNESS CLUBS, AND HEALTH CLUBS; KING, BILLIE JEAN; KOPAY, DAVID; NAVRATILOVA, MARTINA; PHYSICAL EDUCATION; RICHARDS, RENÉE; SHAWN, TED; TILDEN, WILLIAM; WADDELL, TOM; PHYSICAL EDUCATION.

STEIN, Gertrude (b. 3 February 1874; d. 27 July 1946), writer and patron of the arts, and Alice B. TOKLAS (b. 30 April 1877; d. 7 March 1967), writer and memoirist.

Gertrude Stein and Alice B. Toklas were the most famous lesbian couple of their time. Stein was born in Allegheny, Pennsylvania, the youngest of five children in a comfortably prosperous Jewish family of German background. Although both her parents died before 1891, the family's investments, skillfully managed by the eldest son, Michael, provided good incomes for the children throughout their lives.

In 1892 Stein followed her favorite brother, Leo (b. 1872), to Harvard University, where she enrolled in the Harvard Annex (later Radcliffe College). She attended courses in philosophy with George Santayana and psychology with William James, and decided to study medicine at Johns Hopkins University. She gave up medicine in her fourth year, in 1902.

Stein spent the winter of 1902–1903 in London, sharing a house with Leo. In 1903, she moved to New York, and wrote *Q.E.D.*, a short novel that describes a love triangle between three young women. The plot was modeled closely after a personal problem she had experienced during her final year at Hopkins. Its disappointing outcome may have contributed to her decision to leave medicine. *Q.E.D.* would remain "forgotten"—according to Stein—until Toklas found it some thirty years later. It was first published in a limited edition of five hundred copies, four years after Stein's death.

A Home in France

In the fall of 1903, Stein joined Leo in Paris, where he had rented a house and an adjoining studio at 27, rue de Fleurus. This became her permanent home for the following three decades. At Ambroise Vollard's gallery they bought paintings by Gauguin, Cézanne, and Renoir, establishing the beginnings of what would become one of the most distinguished private collections of twentieth-century art. Most significant, they selected Cézanne's portrait of his wife, Hortense, depicted sitting in a red armchair, holding a fan. By Stein's own account, this painting and Flaubert's *Trois Contes* provided the inspiration for *Three Lives*, which she completed in the spring of 1906. The book, her most remarkable early work, consists of three psychological portraits, two of German servants, and one of a young black woman, Melanchta Herbert.

Around the time of the Autumn Salon of 1905—where Stein and her brother bought Matisse's sensation-causing *Femme au Chapeau*—the Steins met Pablo Picasso. The exact time of their meeting is recalled somewhat differently by each of the participants, but the fact that their profound friendship would endure for forty-one years, until Stein's death, is beyond dispute. During the winter of 1905–1906, Stein sat for her famous portrait by Picasso. At the same time, Gertrude and Leo Stein also became collectors of Picasso's paintings, as did Michael Stein and his wife, Sarah. Eventually, the Steins would come to own more than one hundred works by Picasso. The Stein household at 27, rue de Fleurus, was fast becoming one of the magnets of Parisian social and intellectual life, a place where, at weekly Saturday evening salons, French artists would mingle with American expatriates and visitors from all over the world.

Meeting Alice B. Toklas

In 1906 Michael and Sarah Stein returned to San Francisco, where they met Alice Toklas. Toklas was born and raised in San Francisco and had studied music at the University of Washington in Seattle. When Toklas made a trip to Europe in 1907 she was invited to visit the Steins there, and on 8 September she was introduced to Gertrude. "She was a golden brown presence," Toklas recalled years later, "burned by the Tuscan sun and with a golden glint in her warm brown hair" (*What is Remembered*). Alice became a regular fixture at 27, rue de Fleurus, initially helping by typing Stein's work, but by the following summer they were a couple. In September 1909, Toklas moved into 27, rue de Fleurus, permanently.

Eccentric Style

Between 1906 and 1908 Stein devoted herself to the writing of *The Making of Americans*. Subtitled "Being a History of a Family's Progress," the sprawling, 925-page novel was not published until 1925. This novel served as a laboratory for Stein's later experimental style and has come to be recognized as an influential, though widely unread, work of modernism.

In 1913, a gradually developing rift between Gertrude and Leo became final with his moving out of the rue de Fleurus apartment and settling in Settignano, Italy. Stein's unwavering devotion to Toklas, whose presence was one of Leo's chief points of contention, was further confirmed by the fact that after Leo's move she never saw her brother again.

Stein's writing reached a milestone with the composition of *Tender Buttons* (1914), a more innovative work than *Three Lives*. The collection of short pieces straddles the fence between poetry and prose, presenting her Cubist style at its most whimsical. Its publication cemented her reputation as a difficult and eccentric writer, but it also furthered the esteem of her two most influential supporters, the critics Henry McBride and Carl Van Vechten.

The outbreak of World War I found Stein and Toklas in England, where they had traveled to sign a contract for a British edition of *Three Lives*. An invitation for a weekend at the country house of the philosopher Alfred North Whitehead turned into an eleven-week enforced stay, due to the war. Once back in Paris, Stein and Toklas decided to escape the wartime rigors by taking a vacation in Spain in the spring of 1915. They ended up staying a year, eventually renting a villa in Majorca. With the war situation worsening, however, and feeling somewhat isolated and helpless, they decided to return to Paris. They ordered a Ford automobile from the United States, and offered their services to the American Fund for French Wounded. Volunteer work and dealing with mechanics for the many necessary repairs on the vehicle occasioned one of Stein's most succinct formulations of her fundamentally democratic worldview: "The important thing is that you must have deep down as the deepest thing in you a sense of equality. Then anybody will do anything for you" (Toklas, *What is Remembered*).

During the 1920s Stein and Toklas's relationship was consolidated into a stable partnership, complete with bourgeois trappings. They began to spend their summers at a rented country house in Bilignin, in a mountainous region in eastern France, close to the Swiss border. Their circle of friends, which had been shaken up by the war, began to include a growing number of young American writers who saw in Stein an avatar of the avant-garde. Most significant, they formed quasi-familial bonds with

Gertrude Stein (left) and Alice B. Toklas. The renowned modernist writer and patron—and a major focal point of artistic and intellectual life in Paris in the early twentieth century—poses with her beloved partner, with whom she lived for nearly forty years. [AP/Wide World Photos]

Ernest Hemingway, then living in Paris. Sherwood Anderson and F. Scott Fitzgerald were also brought into their intimate circle of writer friends, and in the 1930s, Thornton Wilder began to visit them as well.

Celebrity at Home

The Autobiography of Alice B. Toklas, which Stein wrote in six weeks during the fall of 1932 in Bilignin, changed their fortunes. Published in 1933, the book instantly became a best seller and a Literary Guild main selection, and it was serialized in the *Atlantic Monthly.* Breaking with her Cubist language, ostensibly emulating Toklas's cadences, Stein wrote in colloquial prose the story of her life, Alice's life, and their life together. Though not explicit about their lesbianism, the book made no pretensions about their domestic arrangements and their deep affection for each other; it was the first positive depiction of a lesbian relationship in the mainstream American media.

Stein's sudden celebrity—their joint celebrity—resulted in invitations to visit the United States, and in October 1934, they arrived for a six-month cross-country lecture tour. The trip gave occasion to see many old friends and to make new acquaintances. They were invited for tea at the White House, and in Hollywood Stein had the pick of the movie stars she wished to see at dinner. *Four Saints in Three Acts,* an opera she had written in 1927 with music by Virgil Thomson—a cause célèbre on Broadway during the previous spring, partly on account of its all-black cast—was scheduled for a week-long run in Chicago. It was Stein's first opportunity to see one of her dramatic works produced on the stage.

Nazi Occupation

By the time they returned to France in May 1935, the Nazi menace was palpable in Europe, and the Spanish Civil War was around the corner. In spite of suggestions that they move back to America, they stayed on in France. They were at Bilignin on 1 September 1939, when Hitler's troops invaded Poland. Stein was working on *Paris France,* which was published in the United States in June 1940, as France was falling to the Germans. Initially, their area was in the zone left unoccupied by German troops according to the terms of France's surrender, but as Jews, and—after Pearl Harbor—enemy aliens, they were in grave danger. How they survived the war years unharmed remains somewhat of a mystery, but it is most likely that Stein's French translator, Bernard Faÿ, who was appointed director of the Bibliothèque nationale by the Nazi-approved Vichy government, was able to exert some influence for their protection. Still, when word came of their liberation by American troops in late summer 1944, it seemed nothing short of a miracle. "Gertie," as she came to be called by the soldiers, was fêted by GIs, and their house became a home-away-from-home for them, as it had been for the American doughboys during World War I. Her war memoir, *Wars I Have Seen,* was published in March 1945. It was a great commercial and critical success.

Later Years

During the fall of 1945, Stein's first symptoms of illness began to show, but they were ascribed to fatigue. She was full of plans, including more operas with Virgil Thomson, the purchase of a new car, and putting her papers, which she would leave to the Yale University library, in order. In July 1946, however, she fell seriously ill, and she was admitted to the American Hospital in Neuilly. After an operation, which confirmed the existence of inoperable cancer, she fell into a coma, and died on the afternoon of 27 July 1946. Toklas survived her by nearly twenty-one years.

In her will, Stein provided generously for Toklas, and she in turn spared no effort to get Stein's unpublished works printed. The eight volumes of *The Yale Edition of the Unpublished Writings of Gertrude Stein* (1951–1958) are as much a monument to their author as they are to Toklas's industry in bringing them to press. At the same time, encouraged by friends who had sampled her cooking, she embarked on the writing of *The Alice B. Toklas Cookbook,* a delicious mélange of recipes and memories. The book became famous for its inclusion of "haschich fudge," recommended as a dish "anyone could whip up on a rainy day."

By the time Toklas's "real" autobiography, *What Is Remembered,* saw the light of day in 1963, she was beset by arthritis, failing eyesight, and financial difficulties. She lived another four years; on 7 March 1967 she died in an apartment on the rue de la Convention, where she had been forced to move in her eighty-seventh year by a heartless landlord. Stein's similarly ruthless heirs had also stripped her of the art collection that had been left to her and that was sold for millions after her death. In *What Is Remembered,* reminiscing about her first glimpse of Stein in 1907, she summed up her life's sole concern: "It was Gertrude Stein who held my complete attention, as she did for all the many years I knew her until her death, and all these empty ones since then."

The admission did away with any mystery that might have lingered as to the nature of their relationship. Although dainty journalists have continued to describe Toklas as Stein's "secretary" or "companion"—less dainty ones do not hesitate to call her Stein's "sidekick"—their durable relationship had been an open secret at least since the publication of the *Autobiography.* Indeed, their iconic example would later inspire lesbians, as well as gay men, while Stein's literary reputation, steadily on the rise since the late 1960s, would experience a renaissance in the era of postmodernism. Even their adoption of traditional "masculine" and "feminine" gender roles, which had been subject to criticism for seemingly conforming to an outdated paradigm, has come to be recognized by recent queer theorists as the radical appropriation, indeed deliberate parody, of heterosexual privilege.

Bibliography

Mellow, James R. *Charmed Circle: Gertrude Stein and Company.* New York: Praeger, 1974.

Stein, Gertrude. *Writings, 1903–1932; Writings, 1932–1946.* New York: Library of America, 1998.

Stein, Gertrude, Alice B. Toklas, and Kay Turner, eds. *Baby Precious Always Shines: Selected Love Notes between Gertrude Stein and Alice B. Toklas.* New York: St. Martin's Press, 1999.

Stein, Gertrude, Alice B. Toklas, and Samuel M. Steward, eds. *Dear Sammy: Letters from Gertrude Stein and Alice B. Toklas.* Boston: Houghton Mifflin, 1977.

Toklas, Alice B. *The Alice B. Toklas Cookbook.* New York: Harper and Brothers, 1954

———. *Staying on Alone: Letters of Alice B. Toklas.* New York: Liveright, 1973.

———. *What is Remembered.* New York: Holt, Rinehart, and Winston, 1963.

Wilson, Robert A. *Gertrude Stein: A Bibliography.* Rockville, Md.: Quill & Brush, 1994.

Wineapple, Brenda. *Sister Brother: Gertrude and Leo Stein.* New York: Putnam's, 1996.

André Balog

See also BARNEY, NATALIE; DEMUTH, CHARLES; FORD, CHARLES HENRI; GRAHN, JUDY; HARTLEY, MARSDEN; LITERATURE; MUSIC: CLASSICAL; MUSIC: OPERA; THOMSON, VIRGIL; VAN VECHTEN, CARL.

STEREOTYPES

A stereotype is an oversimplified, preconceived, and standardized conception, opinion, attitude, judgment, or image of a person or group held in common by others. Originally referring to the process of making type from a metal mold in printing, social stereotypes can be viewed as molds of regular and consistent patterns of evaluation. There is, however, a difference between a stereotype (for example, all gay men are effeminate) and a cultural pattern (for example, drag queens have been celebrated within and outside of gay culture for many decades). In the latter example, the parodic enactment of drag is often seen for its entertainment value. In addition, drag can elicit the functional possibility of calling into question the "masculine/feminine" binary frame on which the enforcement of gender-based roles is based and maintained.

In their 1986 article "Contact Is Not Enough," Miles Hewstone and Rupert Brown isolate three fundamental facets of stereotypes: categorizing others based on easily identifiable characteristics; assuming that certain attributes apply to most or all of the people in the category, and that people in the category are different from people in other categories with respect to these attributes; and assuming that individual members of the category have the attributes associated with their groups.

Stereotypes may have originally contained some small grain of truth, but that element has since been exaggerated, distorted, or in some way taken out of context. Stereotypes, therefore, may be based on false generaliza-tions derived from very small samples or even from a unique case. Some stereotypes have no foundation in fact at all.

When stereotyping occurs, people tend to overlook all other characteristics of the group. Individuals sometimes use stereotypes to justify the subjugation of members of that group. In this sense, stereotypes conform to the literal meaning of the word "prejudice," which is a prejudgment, derived from the Latin *praejudicium.*

Common Prejudices

Today we see evidence of a number of general themes in the popular stereotypes of LGBT people. Many of these have roots stretching back hundreds of years. They include the beliefs that homosexuality, bisexuality, and transgenderism are caused by having an overbearing and domineering mother and a hostile distant father, stem from having been sexually abused as a child, are the result of having had a bad relationship with a member of the other sex, are just a stage that LGBT people are going through, are characterized by being physically repulsed by members of the other sex, are caused by not having yet met the right person of the other sex, are abnormal and unnatural, are forms of mental illness, and are a biblical sin. Other stereotype themes include the beliefs that LGBT people make more money than heterosexuals; hate heterosexuals; are sexually attractive and "come on" sexually to heterosexuals; would rather be heterosexual; attempt to "recruit" heterosexuals and children into their "deviant lifestyle"; are pedophiles; abuse children; play "husband and wife" roles in relationships; caused AIDS; are sad because there is nothing "gay" about homosexuality or bisexuality; grow old, lonely, and self-hating; are angry, aggressive, abusive, murderous, and suicidal; flaunt their sexuality; are antifamily and destroyers of the American family and culture; and make bad soldiers and disrupt military morale. Other beliefs are that if everyone were homosexual, the human species would be extinct since they cannot reproduce; that one can always spot an LGBT person; that homosexuals have "gaydar" (gay radar) to spot one another; and that all homosexuals and bisexuals are white except for those LGBT people of color who are attempting to be white or to mimic whiteness and white culture.

Stereotypes specific to gay and bisexual males include the beliefs that they desire to be women; they are excessive, effeminate, and flamboyant; they have affectations; they lisp; they are not "real men"; they like to dress in women's clothing and wear makeup; they are drag queens; they hate sports; they have a great fashion sense; they are drawn to "female" professions like hairdressing, interior decorating, and the arts; they are child care workers and elementary school teachers; they cannot form long-term relationships; they are not monogamous; they have many one-night stands; they are never sexually satisfied and are oversexed; they have outdoor sex in parks and public toilets; and they are into sexual fetishes including sadomasochism and performing sex acts with gerbils.

Specific stereotypes of lesbians include the beliefs that they are asexual virgins; have enlarged clitorises; are ugly and cannot attract men; have had bad experiences with men; want to be men; hate men; have a predatory nature and are prone to violence; form long-term monogamous relationships; love cats; are not "real women"; are masculine; have short hair and do not wear makeup; are athletic; are gym teachers and coaches; and are often in the military.

Stereotypes of transgender people include: all gay males and lesbians are transgender; all transgender people are homosexual (thereby confusing and conflating sexual identity with gender identity); all transgender people are confused and psychologically disturbed; and all transgender people are defined as "transsexual" and want to undertake sexual reassignment surgery.

From stereotypes a pair of contradictory myths have developed. One is that LGBTs are a privileged class of rich super capitalists who manipulate banking systems and control politicians and the media. The other is that they are radical communists and socialists attempting to overthrow the capitalist system and the dominant culture.

In "Psychological Heterosexism in the United States" (1995), Gregory M. Herek discusses a common stereotype of bisexual people as either fence-sitters who are in denial concerning their true homosexuality in an attempt to avoid the stigma often associated with assumptions of a gay or lesbian identity, or as in a way station or transitional process toward either exclusive homosexuality or exclusive heterosexuality. Other popular stereotypes specific to female and male bisexuals include the beliefs that they cannot make decisions about what they really want, cannot be monogamous, cheat on their partners, are sexually insatiable and will have sex with anyone at any time (will have sex with anything that moves); and infect heterosexuals with AIDS and other sexually transmitted diseases.

Internalization by LGBT People

Since LGBT people are raised in a society saturated with these stereotypes, they often are not immune to internalizing the social messages. A joke reflecting stereotypes,

which often circulates within lesbian and gay communities in the United States, exemplifies the stereotypes each group has of the other. It begins, "What do lesbians do on their second date? They rent a moving van." (This taps into the stereotype that lesbians form instant coupling relationships and implies that they are not as concerned with sex as much as their gay male counterparts and heterosexual women.) The joke continues, "What do gay men do on their second date? What second date?" (This reflects the popular opinion that gay men do not form lasting relations and are only concerned with one-time sexual encounters.)

In addition, since LGBT people are exposed to the prejudices and stereotyping of the larger society—for example, racism, sexism, classism, religious bigotry, ageism, looksism (the ranking of other individuals on their outward appearance), and ableism (prejudice toward people with physical, mental, and emotional disabilities)—they may internalize these prejudices and project them onto others different from themselves, including others within LGBT communities.

Origins of Stereotypes

Stereotypes have evolved historically (many dating back to ancient times), and they are continually reinforced through cultural discourses or ideologies that are pervasive in popular culture through the media, educational institutions, houses of worship, peer networks, families, and other social institutions. They are sometimes expressed in proverbs, social commentary, literature, jokes, epithets, pictorial depictions, and other cultural forms. Though stereotypes have persisted and have been extended throughout the ages, it is difficult, and in some cases impossible, to determine their precise genesis.

Some of the earliest disparaging references to those who engage in same-sex sexuality appear in passages in the Hebrew Bible and the Christian testaments. There they are described as being transgressors of standard expressions of gender behavior and as potential destroyers of "civilized" societies. From these and other origins, such beliefs have been extended and amplified in the United States.

Although records dating back to antiquity have documented the universal existence of homosexual acts, it was not until the nineteenth century that the scientific community, particularly the medical profession, created categories of sexual orientation, thereby leading to the "medicalization" of homosexuality and its construction as an immutable biological type. This also extended the notion of homosexual males as feminized males and homosexual females as masculinized females. Two medical theorists of this period were the American physicians James G. Kiernan and G. Frank Lydston, who posited homosexuals and bisexuals as a kind of remnant of the primitive organisms from which humans developed.

The Cold War years witnessed changing family dynamics and, particularly, increased freedom and independence of children and youth. During the same period, sex panic and increased stereotyping and assaults on homosexuals functioned to reinscribe prewar sexual and social norms, which had weakened during World War II. Changes during that war are attributed to the fact that since the nation needed skilled and unskilled laborers to replace the men who were called up to fight, there was a relaxation of gender roles during this period. Many women who did not join the military entered the paid workforce for the first time in large numbers. This gave women not only a sense of independence from men, but also greater economic security. With the victory over the Axis powers and the subsequent return of many men to civilian life, opportunities for women declined. Women were asked to relinquish their jobs to the men, and the country returned again to strictly defined gender roles. However, the seeds of change had been planted for the permanent establishment of a true sense of LGBT community.

In the overwhelming majority of cases, child abuse and molestation are committed by close family members, primarily men who identify as heterosexual. However, the cultural perception persists that it is primarily gay men—and, by association, lesbians and bisexuals—who attack young children. Some people exploit the stereotypes of gays and lesbians as child molesters. For example, former beauty queen and Florida Citrus Commission spokesperson Anita Bryant spearheaded the tactically named Save Our Children campaign, which succeeded in overturning a gay rights ordinance in Dade County, Florida, in 1977. (The ordinance was eventually reinstated in 1998.) Using similar stereotypes, California state senator John Briggs in 1978 submitted a ballot initiative that, had it not been defeated, could have banned openly gay and lesbian teachers from public schools throughout the state. The 1992 Republican Party platform openly promoted this stereotype, stating, "We oppose any legislation or law which legally recognizes same-sex marriages and allows such couples to adopt children or provide foster care" (preamble to the 1992 Republican Party platform). In fact, several states explicitly ban LGBT people from adopting children or serving as foster parents. A 1993 poll conducted by *Newsweek* magazine found that many people still believed that LGBT people must be kept away from children and youths: only 54 percent of those sur-

veyed believed that gays and lesbians should be hired as high school teachers, and just 51 percent felt that they should be hired as elementary school teachers. The survey also reaffirmed that many believed the stereotype that gays and lesbians are immoral, as just 48 percent said they should be allowed to serve as members of the clergy. In addition, responding to Vermont's civil unions for same-sex couples, sixteen New England Catholic bishops in a June 2000 statement asserted that "the Legislature of the state of Vermont . . . has attacked centuries of cultural and religious esteem for marriage between a man and a woman and has prepared the way for an attack on the well-being of society itself" ("Bishops Join Foes of Civil Unions").

Sexual stereotypes also continue. In the video *The Gay Agenda*, produced by the Springs of Life Christian Church for the purpose of overturning "gay rights" ordinances, the announcer proclaims that 17 percent of homosexual men consume human feces for erotic thrills and that 28 percent of them engage in sodomy with more than one thousand partners, thereby spreading diseases that imperil the entire society.

Although each LGBT person is unique in many ways and is multifaceted, when they are stereotyped, their sexual or gender identity becomes reducible to a single trait. While some (and in some cases many) individuals within these social groupings may exhibit one or more of these tendencies, this is certainly not the case for all LGBT people. In fact, some heterosexual people as well as some individuals who adhere to standard conceptualizations of gender expression may manifest characteristics associated with LGBT people.

Stereotypes are often self-perpetuating, for once a stereotype is in place, individuals tend to notice behaviors or traits consistent with the stereotypes and may dismiss (consciously or unconsciously) those that are inconsistent with the stereotype. In this way, stereotypes are reinforced, regardless of social realities. Stereotypes are therefore resistant to change and tend to persist. Stereotyping is common to intergroup relations and serves a number of functions for those who hold them, but they can be profoundly damaging.

Bibliography

"Bishops Join Foes of Civil Unions." 2000. Available from http://www.rutlandherald.com

Blumenfeld, Warren J., and Diane Raymond. *Looking at Gay and Lesbian Life*. Rev. ed. Boston: Beacon Press, 1993.

Chauncey, George. "The Postwar Sex Crime Panic." In *True Stories from the American Past*. Edited by William Graebner. New York: McGraw-Hill, 1993.

Freedman, Estelle. "'Uncontrolled Desires': The Response to the Sexual Psychopath, 1920–1960." In *Passion and Power: Sexuality in History.* Edited by Kathy Peiss and Christina Simmons. Philadelphia: Temple University Press, 1989.

Herek, Gregory M. "Psychological Heterosexism in the United States." In *Lesbian, Gay, and Bisexual Identities over the Lifespan: Psychological Perspectives.* Edited by Anthony R. D'Augelli and Charlotte J. Patterson. New York: Oxford University Press, 1995.

Hewstone, Miles, and Rupert Brown. "Contact Is Not Enough: An Intergroup Perspective on the 'Contact Hypothesis.' " In *Contact and Conflict in Intergroup Encounters.* Edited by Miles Hewstone and Rupert Brown. Oxford, U.K.: Blackwell, 1986.

"Prelude to the 1992 Republican Party Platform." Available from http://www.cs.cmu.edu.

Solomon, Alisa. "The Eternal Queer: In the Symbolic Landscape of Homophobia, We Are the Jews." *Village Voice,* 27 April 1993.

Turque, Bill, et al. "Gays Under Fire." *Newsweek,* 14 September 1992.

Warren J. Blumenfeld

See also DISCRIMINATION; HOMOPHOBIA AND HETEROSEXISM.

STODDARD, Charles Warren

(b. 7 August 1843; d. 23 April 1909), writer and educator.

Charles Warren Stoddard was born to middle-class parents in Rochester, New York. In 1854 Stoddard's father moved the family to San Francisco. Here Stoddard met Bret Harte, Mark Twain, and other leading literary figures. In the early 1860s Stoddard, using the name "Pip Pepperpod," published several poems, earning the title "Boy Poet of San Francisco." These poems marked the beginning of what would become an extensive oeuvre, encompassing travel writing, journalism, religious autobiography, essays, and a novel. Stoddard wrote in a genteel style that does not well suit contemporary sensibilities, and for that reason his writing has fallen out of fashion.

Stoddard led a varied life. In what was then an unusual act for a native-born American Protestant, Stoddard converted to Catholicism, a transformation he documented in *A Troubled Heart and How It Was Comforted at Last* (1885). For a short time in London during the 1870s, he was Mark Twain's secretary. Twain, playing on the gendered language of sexuality, wrote a friend that his secretary struck him as being "a nice girl" (Austin, *Genteel Pagan,* p. 20). Starting in the mid-1880s Stoddard taught at a number of universities, including Notre Dame

in South Bend, Indiana, and Catholic University, in Washington, D.C. In Washington, Stoddard befriended Henry Adams, George Cabot Lodge, and other artists and local figures, Lilinokalani, the deposed Queen of Hawaii, among them. He set up house—"the Bungalow"—and pursued relationships with various youths, including one of the great loves of his life, Kenneth O'Connor, who was fifteen when he and Stoddard met. Catholic University dismissed Stoddard in 1902, though no evidence exists that Stoddard's sexual relationships were the reason behind his dismissal. Soon thereafter, in any case, Stoddard returned to California, where for a brief period he was a familiar figure in Carmel's bohemian literary scene.

Stoddard is best known for his South Seas travel writing and his semiautobiographical novel, *For the Pleasure of His Company: An Affair of the Misty City.* These works are representative texts of nineteenth-century male homoerotic literature. They are oblique, highly stylized depictions of intense friendship. Stoddard first traveled to the Pacific in 1864, in part to recover from nervous exhaustion. Over the years he visited both Hawaii, where he lived from 1881 to 1884, and Tahiti. He wrote numerous short stories about his travels. These tales were initially collected and published in 1873 in *South Sea Idylls.* Other volumes followed, including *Hawaiian Life* and *The Island of Tranquil Delights.* Stoddard also wrote about his travels to Europe and the Middle East.

A central theme of Stoddard's South Sea writings is his relationships with native youth. His stories are filled with loving descriptions of naked and near-naked Pacific Islanders. In "Chumming with a Savage: Kana-Ana," for example, Stoddard describes his love for Kana-Ana, a Hawaiian he met in Molokai in 1869. According to Stoddard, he and Kana-Ana spent the day lying on the beach, and at night they shared a bed. "He lay close to me. His sleek figure, supple and graceful in repose, was the embodiment of free, untrammeled youth." Stoddard wrote that Kana-Ana was devoted to his "pale-faced friend." When the youth awoke, he "resumed his single garment—said garment and all others he considered superfluous after dark—and prepared for me . . . a breakfast" (*Cruising the South Seas,* p. 37). The exotic locale of Stoddard's tales afforded him greater artistic freedom; similar descriptions of naked Euro-American youths would no doubt have led moralists to condemn his work.

During his lifetime the general public viewed Stoddard's work as little more than depictions of romantic friendship—and romantic friendships between members of the same sex were a respected part of middle-class

154

culture. This is not to say that Stoddard did not have a "gay" readership. The same year he met Kana-Ana, Stoddard wrote to Walt Whitman from Honolulu. Stoddard, an ardent reader of Whitman's homoerotic verse, shared with the poet a certain passion for the "defiant lips" and "matchless physique" of the Hawaiian people. His sojourn in the South Seas had changed Stoddard profoundly. "For the first time," Stoddard confessed, "I act as my nature prompts me. . . . You will easily imagine, my dear sir, how delightful I find this life. I read your Poems with a new spirit, to understand them as few may be able to" (Austin, *Genteel Pagan*, pp. 42–43). Whitman responded to Stoddard's fan letter by sending a photograph of himself accompanied by an invitation to visit. Despite Stoddard's admiration for Whitman, the two men never met.

By the turn of the century some of Stoddard's readers had linked his writings to the emergent discourse on homosexuality, finally making visible what had been up until then the submerged and ill-defined homoerotic content of his work. In 1908, for example, Xavier Mayne, under the pseudonym Edward Irenaeus Prime-Stevenson, discussed Stoddard's *South Sea Idylls* in his privately published study, *The Intersexes: A History of Similisexualism as a Problem in Social Life*. Stoddard's stories, wrote Prime-Stevenson, were striking examples of "American Philarrhenic Literature" (Austen, *Playing the Game*, pp. 20–27).

Set in San Francisco, Stoddard's novel *For the Pleasure of His Company* was published in 1903. Stoddard had begun writing his novel in 1883, struggling thereafter to refine its narrative. William Dean Howells and Rudyard Kipling had both encouraged Stoddard to publish the work; in fact, Kipling had provided the title. In general, critics were unimpressed. Several of Stoddard's friends, who recognized themselves in the book, were less than thrilled by the way they had been characterized. *For the Pleasure of His Company* tells the story of Paul Clitheroe, a writer and actor, and his friendships with a series of young men. None of his attempts to forge a lasting, meaningful relationship with other Euro-Americans are successful. Stoddard resolves this frustrating reality by concluding his story on a note of fantasy. At the novel's end, Clitheroe escapes to the South Seas; the final scene depicts Clitheroe joining "three naked islanders" in a canoe (p. 188). In many ways, Stoddard's novel reveals an essential truth about its author. In its disjointed plot and structure, and racially inspired sexual fantasy, *For the Pleasure of His Company* unmasks Stoddard's inability to follow through on his psychological and physical desires in anything other than a fleeting, momentary way.

Bibliography

Austen, Roger. *Playing the Game: The Homosexual Novel in America*. Indianapolis, Ind.: Bobbs-Merrill, 1977.

———. *Genteel Pagan: The Double Life of Charles Warren Stoddard*. Amherst, Mass.: University of Massachusetts Press, 1991.

Gifford, James. *Dayneford's Library: American Homosexual Writing, 1900–1913*. Amherst, Mass.: University of Massachusetts Press, 1995.

Katz, Jonathan Ned. *Love Stories: Sex between Men before Homosexuality*. Chicago: University of Chicago Press, 2001.

Stoddard, Charles Warren. *Cruising the South Seas*. Reprint. San Francisco: Gay Sunshine, 1987.

———. *For the Pleasure of His Company: An Affair of the Misty City*. Reprint. San Francisco: Gay Sunshine, 1987.

Yingling, Thomas. "Review of Charles Warren Stoddard, *For the Pleasure of His Company* and *Cruising the South Seas*." *American Literary Realism* 21 (spring 1989): 91–92.

Terence Kissack

See also INTERRACIAL AND INTERETHNIC SEX AND RELATIONSHIPS; LITERATURE; ROMANTIC FRIENDSHIP AND BOSTON MARRIAGE; SMASHES AND CHUMMING; WHITMAN, WALT.

STONEWALL RIOTS

In late June 1969, a routine police raid on the Stonewall Inn, a well-known gay bar in New York City's Greenwich Village, sparked several nights of riots. "Stonewall," as these events came to be called, quickly became the rallying cry of LGBT people as they created an increasingly visible political movement and community. Widely considered to be the beginning of the modern gay rights movement, Stonewall has taken on significance as the preeminent symbol of LGBT resistance.

New York City had a lively and extensive gay scene in the late 1960s and the Stonewall Inn at 53 Christopher Street was one of the city's most popular gay bars at the time. Opened in 1966 by three owners with ties to the Mafia, the bar was operated as a private club to circumvent the need for a liquor license. The Stonewall crowd was eclectic, typically ranging in age from the late teens to the early thirties. In the mix were underage street kids, the upscale "sweater set," college students, drag queens in full female attire, "flame" queens dressed in men's clothing with makeup and coiffed hair, and a small number of hippies. Few women were in attendance, though an occasional lesbian would frequent the bar. Some patrons recall a racially mixed crowd, but others say that it was difficult to get into the Stonewall if you were black, Puerto Rican, or Chinese.

Raid on the Stonewall Inn

At around 2:00 A.M. on 28 June 1969, New York City police officers launched a raid on the Stonewall Inn as part of a crackdown on unlicensed gay bars with ties to organized crime. Arriving on the scene late Friday night (early Saturday morning), the police had a warrant to search for the illegal sale of alcohol. They anticipated no problems, since gay men rarely put up forceful resistance during bar raids. But on this night the atmosphere was tense and nerves were strained. Many gay men were distraught over Judy Garland's death—her funeral had taken place that morning—and were fed up with the harassment of gay bars in recent weeks.

As the eight officers, including two policewomen, most in plainclothes, entered the bar, white lights on the dance floor flashed, signaling the arrival of the police. The revelers stopped dancing as the music was turned off and the two hundred or so customers were ordered to line up and have their identification inspected. While the police detained drag queens (cross-dressing was still illegal), several employees, and those without proper identification, most of the patrons were quickly escorted out of the bar. As they exited, some struck poses and camped it up for a growing audience of curious onlookers.

When a police wagon pulled up on Christopher Street, the celebratory mood outside the bar grew more agitated. As the police escorted the arrested into the van, cheers turned to boos and catcalls. The growing crowd closed in on the wagon. Tension filled the air. "You could feel the electricity going through people," recalled Sylvia Rivera, a drag queen at the scene (Duberman, p. 196). From this point on accounts of what happened vary. Some credit a drag queen escaping from the police with striking the "first blow," while others say it was a butch "bull dyke" or one of the many men in the crowd. In any case, all hell broke loose. As the *Daily News* (6 July 1969) reported, "Without warning, Queen Power exploded with all the fury of a gay atomic bomb. . . . New York experienced its first homosexual riot" (p. M1).

The Initial Riot

As the cops herded people into the police wagon and patrol cars, the crowd taunted them with cries of "Pigs!" and "Police Brutality" and chanted "Gay Power" and "We Want Freedom" (McGarry and Wasserman, p. 8). Rioters began throwing pennies, beer cans, bottles, and bricks at the eight officers until the police retreated into the bar, locking the door behind them. But the throng was not to be quelled. A parking meter was uprooted and used as a battering ram to storm the door of the Stonewall until it gave way. The cops grabbed one of the protesters, pulling

him kicking and screaming into the Stonewall, and beat him up.

Outside the crowd was in a fury as it swelled to at least four hundred—by some accounts one thousand—as word spread. One rioter threw a trash can at the plywood-backed window, shattering the glass. Someone else threw lighter fluid through the window, then matches, and flames went up in the bar. But then the Tactical Patrol Force (TPF), a special riot-control squad, arrived. Decked out in helmets with visors and armed with billy clubs, tear gas, and other weapons, two dozen TPF troops, linked arm-in-arm, moved in on the furious mob. Violence erupted as the police beat up some of the rioters, but the crowd was quickly dispersed.

The siege on the bar lasted only forty-five minutes, and the entire raid and melee from start to finish lasted around two hours. The police confiscated twenty-eight cases of beer and nineteen bottles of liquor. A total of thirteen people were arrested, seven for the unlicensed sale of liquor, the others for assault, disorderly conduct, harassment, or resisting arrest. Several protesters were injured, as were a few police officers; one of the cops broke his wrist, an injury that many gays appreciated as a bit of divine justice, given the stereotype of the limp-wristed homosexual.

Rioting Continues the Following Night

News of the riot spread quickly by word of mouth and was reported the following morning in the *New York Post* as well as on local radio and television stations. Thousands of LGBT people flocked to the Village on Saturday night, filling the streets as they chanted "Gay Power!" and blocked traffic outside the reopened Stonewall Inn on Christopher Street. As police tried to disperse the mob, rioters threw bottles and bricks and lit small fires in garbage cans. Another kind of resistance was also on display as defiant gay couples openly kissed and held hands. Yet other homosexuals, particularly the older generation, were appalled by the protesters and the threat they posed to a comfortable, if not perfect, status quo.

TPF units (some accounts placed the number of police in the hundreds) arrived on the scene around 2:15 A.M. Linking arms and forming a human chain, they swept up and down Christopher Street to clear the protest. But as the TPF marched towards the crowd, groups of rioters circled around into side streets, reappearing minutes later to charge from the rear. When the police looked back, they were confronted with a dancing chorus line of drag queens kicking up their heels and chanting:

We are the Stonewall girls
We wear our hair in curls
We have no underwear
We show our pubic hairs!

(Truscott, p. 18)

Confrontations between protesters and the police continued until 4:00 A.M., marked by violence and three or four arrests.

On Sunday, longtime homosexual activists mobilized. Members of the Mattachine Society, a homophile organization that since the 1950s had worked to urge social acceptance of homosexuals, tried to calm things down and scheduled a community meeting for later in the week. Many of the group's members were incensed at the antics of the rioters. However, other activists felt differently and tried to harness the newly manifested gay power. Some Mattachine members distributed flyers condemning the State Liquor Authority and the police and calling for the ouster of the Mafia from gay bars.

Sunday night saw renewed confrontations between the police and gay protesters as the authorities swept the streets of the Village. Touring the area late that night, poet Allen Ginsberg stopped in at the Stonewall Inn, commenting afterwards that, "The guys there were so beautiful—they've lost that wounded look that fags all had 10 years ago" (Truscott, p. 18). Only scattered incidents occurred in the Village on the following rainy Monday and Tuesday nights, but on Wednesday night an estimated one thousand people returned to the streets of the Village, again tossing beer bottles and setting garbage cans on fire. The police response was violent and bloody as the TPF units swept the streets and arrested five rioters in what was the last night of the street uprising.

Aftermath of the Riots

While no more than about two thousand LGBT New Yorkers had participated in the riots, their impact would ultimately be profound, reaching far beyond Greenwich Village. Most participants could not have known or even imagined that they were part of a truly historic event. But some immediately proclaimed the significance of what variously came to be called the Christopher Street Riots, the Stonewall Riots, the Stonewall Rebellion, the Stonewall Uprising, and ultimately, simply Stonewall. The Mattachine Society's July newsletter called the riots "The Hairpin Drop Heard Around the World" and trumpeted, "The 'Christopher Street Riots' marked a first in the history of homosexuals" (McGarry and Wasserman, p. 13).

In the days and weeks that followed, a rash of meetings occurred during which the radical concepts of "gay

liberation" and "gay power" took center stage, challenging the more moderate homophile aim of seeking society's tolerance. By late July, these early discussions had led to the founding of the Gay Liberation Front (GLF), a radical organization that sought to align the struggle of lesbians and gay men with those of other oppressed groups. Within a couple of months, a GLF had been started in Berkeley, California, and within two years, dozens of gay liberation organizations were active in cities and on campuses around the country. By the mid-1970s, hundreds of gay and lesbian organizations had been established; at the end of the decade, there were thousands.

Stonewall was hailed as the birth of gay liberation and recognized as a potentially powerful catalyst for organizing lesbians and gay men. In the fall of 1969, several activists formed the Christopher Street Liberation Day Committee to plan a commemoration of the first anniversary of the Stonewall Riots and to encourage other groups around the country to do the same. On Sunday, 28 June 1970, several hundred LGBT people gathered at Washington Square in Greenwich Village and marched up Sixth Avenue to a Gay-In in Central Park. By the time they arrived at the park, the crowd had grown to thousands in what was the largest and most visible gay power demonstration to date. LGBT people in other cities commemorated the first anniversary of the Stonewall Riots simultaneously as more than a thousand marched in Los Angeles and hundreds gathered in Chicago and San Francisco.

Stonewall: Myth and Symbol

The Stonewall Riots have assumed almost mythic significance since 1969. LGBT people have variously likened Stonewall to the storming of the Bastille, the Boston Tea Party, Independence Day, and the various boycotts and sit-ins of the black civil rights movement. Enshrined as the watershed event in gay history, Stonewall has served as a rallying cry for LGBT people as they have confronted adversity and injustice. The Stonewall Riots were invoked by White Night rioters in San Francisco in 1979, by AIDS activists in the 1980s and 1990s, and by queers reacting to the brutal murder of Matthew Shepard in Wyoming in 1998. Above all, Stonewall's abiding power has come to be honored and renewed in more than one hundred lesbian and gay pride parades held every June in cities around the nation and the world.

Implicit in this very powerful symbol is the idea that Stonewall was a spontaneous event that suddenly transformed gay consciousness as well as the position of homosexuals in society. However, this reading of the riots obscures the history that came before and after. For while

Stonewall Inn. In 1999, people gathered outside the historic New York gay bar where a routine police raid on 28 June 1969 led to rioting and—at least in the myth that has arisen about the incident—to the birth of the modern gay rights movement thirty years earlier. [corbis]

Although these mostly moderate homophile organizations, notably the Mattachine Society and the Daughters of Bilitis, had emphasized the education of society and the assimilation of homosexuals, as the 1960s progressed some of their members became increasingly militant and staged public marches at the White House, Independence Hall, and the United Nations.

A number of incidents in California in the 1960s also awakened a more radical consciousness on the West Coast years before Stonewall. In 1961, in the first campaign by an openly gay man, José Sarria sought a seat on San Francisco's Board of Supervisors. On 1 January 1965, police harassment at a New Year's Eve dance, a fundraiser for San Francisco's Council on Religion and the Homosexual (a joint effort of ministers and gays), became a radicalizing incident for gay men and lesbians in the Bay Area. And in 1967 LGBT people in Los Angeles took to the streets to protest police harassment and raids at the Black Cat bar.

In the months before Stonewall, homophile activists adopted "Gay is Good" as their motto, a gay liberation–type group—the Committee for Homosexual Freedom—started in San Francisco, and gay publications featured articles heralding the "gay revolution." In many ways, then, the Stonewall Riots, while typically seen as the beginning of an era of gay liberation, can also be seen as the culmination of an historical process that had been in motion for decades.

The Sixties

In another sense, too, the Stonewall Riots did not happen in a vacuum. They were very much part of a widespread questioning of the status quo in the late 1960s. As *Newsweek* (27 October 1969) observed in its reporting of the riots, "It began on a balmy June evening with a police raid on one of Greenwich Village's homosexual bars. In summers past such an incident would have stirred little more than resigned shrugs among the Village's homophile population—but in 1969 the militant mood touches every minority" (p. 76). Indeed, the early gay liberation activists—and some of the rioters themselves—drew on the militant tactics and radical rhetoric of the New Left; the counterculture; and the black, women's, student, and antiwar movements, in which many of them had been (and continued to be) involved. Furthermore, as products of the sexual revolution that swept the country in the 1960s, they naturally extended their critique of the system to the oppression they experienced as homosexuals. For many of the early gay liberationists, Stonewall embodied the notion—and the reality—that they could fight back as gay people.

the first night of the riots may have been spontaneous, the activism it triggered did not happen in a vacuum. Contrary to the Stonewall myth, which seems to suggest that lesbian and gay communities came into existence as a result of the riots, New York City, Chicago, San Francisco, and other large U.S. cities had highly organized and extensive lesbian and gay subcultures dating back to the late nineteenth century. Early gay liberationists did not invent a community wholesale, but drew on the resources of an existing one that they, in turn, politicized on a mass scale.

The Homophile Movement

Nor did LGBT political activism begin with the Stonewall Riots. A small but courageous gay civil rights movement had been in existence for almost twenty years prior to Stonewall and had achieved some modest successes.

Commemorating Stonewall

Despite all of the ways in which the celebration of Stonewall tends to skew U.S. LGBT history, Stonewall has been an extraordinarily appealing—and useful—creation myth for LGBT people trying to define themselves as a community. The riot has become the symbol of a common shared heritage that has deep meaning for many people. Given this enduring significance, it is not surprising that the story of Stonewall has been contested over the decades. Some of the original participants, and others, still fight over who sparked the riot. And the role of drag queens, people of color, gay street kids, and butch dykes—people on the margins who fought back because they had little to lose—has frequently been downplayed and often written out of the story. Meanwhile, legions of people, far more than seems likely, claim to have been at the riots. All of this suggests the extent to which people want to own a piece of this critical event in LGBT history.

It also indicates the extent to which they want to celebrate the event. In addition to the annual pride marches every June, major celebrations of the Stonewall Riots have been mounted for significant anniversaries. A decade of gay liberation was celebrated in 1979 as more than 100,000 marched in New York City and 250,000 in San Francisco. On the occasion of the Riots' twentieth anniversary in 1989, New York City officially designated the block of Christopher Street in front of the Stonewall Inn as Stonewall Place. In 1994, Stonewall 25 and the Gay Games attracted more than one million people to New York City for an international march for lesbian and gay rights, marked by a mile-long rainbow flag. In conjunction with Stonewall 25, several museums and libraries mounted exhibitions that explored the Stonewall Riots and gay and lesbian history.

On the thirtieth anniversary of the riots in 1999, the Stonewall Inn was listed on the National Register of Historic Places, the first site in the country recognized for its association with lesbian and gay history. Presenting a bronze historical marker in Greenwich Village on the occasion, M. John Berry, an assistant secretary of the Department of the Interior, proclaimed, "Let it forever be remembered that here—on this spot—men and women stood proud, they stood fast, so that we may be who we are, we may work where we will, live where we choose and love whom our hearts desire." Only a year later, Stonewall received a greater distinction when it was designated a National Historic Landmark (only 3 percent of National Register sites are so designated) and deemed by the National Park Service "nationally significant because it is associated with events that outstandingly represent the civil rights struggle in America."

Officially honored and popularly celebrated, in the early twenty-first century Stonewall retains enormous power as a symbol of collective resistance and an inspiration for lesbians and gay men around the world.

Bibliography

Duberman, Martin. *Stonewall.* New York: Dutton, 1993.

McGarry, Molly, and Fred Wasserman. *Becoming Visible: An Illustrated History of Lesbian and Gay Life in Twentieth-Century America.* New York: Penguin Studio, 1998.

"Remembering Stonewall." Produced by David Isay. Pacifica Radio, 1989.

Smith, Howard. "Full Moon over the Stonewall." *Village Voice,* 3 July 1969, pp. 1, 25, 29.

Teal, Donn. *The Gay Militants.* New York: Stein and Day, 1971.

Truscott, Lucian IV. "Gay Power Comes to Sheridan Square." *Village Voice,* 3 July 1969, pp. 1, 18.

Fred Wasserman

See also BARS, CLUBS, AND RESTAURANTS; DRAG QUEENS AND KINGS; GAY LIBERATION; GAY LIBERATION FRONT; GINSBERG, ALLEN; HOMOPHILE MOVEMENT; LATINA AND LATINO LGBTQ ORGANIZATIONS AND PERIODICALS; MATTACHINE SOCIETY; NEW YORK CITY; PRIDE MARCHES AND PARADES; RIVERA, SYLVIA; SEXUAL REVOLUTIONS.

STRAYHORN, Billy (b. 29 November 1915; d. 31 May 1967), composer, musician.

Although he was responsible for hundreds of compositions (including the signature theme "Take the A Train") and arrangements for Duke Ellington's band from 1939 until his death in 1967, Billy Strayhorn, one of jazz's few openly gay figures, was largely unknown and uncredited outside the jazz world until a reawakening of interest in his work began in the 1990s. Some commentators have argued that his lack of fame during his lifetime stemmed from Strayhorn's choice to stay behind the scenes instead of subjecting himself to the scrutiny of a society that was not ready to accept him as a proud gay black man.

Born in Dayton, Ohio, William Thomas Strayhorn was a small, sickly baby. Strayhorn's parents were temperamental opposites. His mother, Lillian, was a soft-spoken, formal woman with some college education. James, Strayhorn's father, was a spontaneous, adventurous man who quit school to work after the eighth grade. From childhood, Billy Strayhorn was more like his mother than his father: quiet, creative, and studious, he loved to read and quickly developed an affinity for music. Unfortunately, James, frustrated by his lack of occupational success, began drinking heavily and took out his disappointments on his children. Billy, especially, became the target of his abuse. Lillian made a special effort to protect Strayhorn from his father's mistreatment, frequently sending him to his paternal grandparents' home in North Carolina. During these visits, Strayhorn acquired a love of the piano from his grandmother, who was her church's pianist. While still in grade school, Strayhorn worked hard to buy himself an upright piano and pay for his own sheet music and lessons.

By the time he graduated from high school, Strayhorn was already an accomplished classical pianist and composer; he had also established a personal style of refinement—studying French, dressing stylishly, subscribing to the *New Yorker,* speaking precisely and eloquently—that set him apart from his peers. Though Strayhorn achieved popular regional success after high school with the 1935 show *Fantastic Rhythm,* for which he wrote the book, dialogue, and music, classical music remained his primary interest. However, at the time few opportunities existed for African American concert pianists or composers. In 1936, when Strayhorn entered the Pittsburgh Musical Institute, he also began to play around the city with old high school friends. During this time Strayhorn's interest in jazz grew, thanks to the influence of his musician friends.

It is unclear whether Strayhorn had entered into any romantic or sexual relationships up to this point. Neither family nor friends recall him dating either men or women. Strayhorn did have a close, secretive relationship with an older musician with whom he collaborated, but it is not known whether this relationship went beyond friendship. There was a small gay social world in Pittsburgh at the time, but those involved do not remember Strayhorn being active in it. Nevertheless, the lyrics of some songs he wrote at the time, including the well-known "Lush Life" and "Something to Live For," express intense romantic, and perhaps homoerotic, desires.

Strayhorn spent the following years composing and arranging music and playing gigs around Pittsburgh. His professional and personal lives changed dramatically when a friend of an acquaintance introduced him to Duke Ellington in 1938. After hearing Strayhorn play and having him arrange a composition, Ellington offered Strayhorn work. From the beginning of their association, Ellington established a peculiarly familial relationship with Strayhorn that worked both to Strayhorn's advantage and disadvantage. Having no contract or even a verbal agreement, Strayhorn had a great deal of freedom but not much security. Strayhorn soon moved to New York City, where he lived with Ellington and his family.

Ellington covered all of Strayhorn's expenses and, according to Ellington's son Mercer, treated Strayhorn like a son. Though this relationship would later cause some problems for Strayhorn when he sought more control over his musical product, Strayhorn blossomed under Ellington's sponsorship.

Within a year of arriving in New York City, Strayhorn began a romantic relationship with Aaron Bridgers, a twenty-one-year-old pianist from North Carolina. Introduced by Mercer Ellington, Strayhorn and Bridgers soon became inseparable, and before long they were living together. Remarkably for the times, they were open to family and friends about their relationship. They remained together for eight years, until Bridgers left to live and work in Paris. Strayhorn had two other notable romances after Bridgers. One, with black sailor Francis Goldberg, lasted the longest but was also the most tumultuous. The other, with white graphic designer Bill Grove, was briefer but perhaps more nurturing, since Grove and Strayhorn were together the last three years of Strayhorn's life, when he struggled with, and finally succumbed to, esophageal cancer.

For the last twenty-five years of his life, Strayhorn worked constantly and successfully, both with Ellington and apart from him. One or more of his compositions or arrangements were included in almost every performance and recording of Duke Ellington's band between 1939 and 1967. Additionally, Strayhorn contributed to a variety of independent projects. Finally, despite Strayhorn's severe illness, he became involved in the civil rights movement, even attending the 1963 March on Washington for Jobs and Freedom.

Bibliography

Ellington, Edward Kennedy (Duke). *Music Is My Mistress.* Garden City, N.Y.: Doubleday, 1973.

Hajdu, David. *Lush Life: A Biography of Billy Strayhorn.* New York: Farrar, Straus, Giroux, 1996.

Leur, Walter van de. *Something to Live For: The Music of Billy Strayhorn.* New York: Oxford University Press, 2002.

Jon Panish

See also MUSIC: POPULAR.

STUDENT MOVEMENTS. see NEW LEFT AND STUDENT MOVEMENTS.

SUBURBS. see URBAN, SUBURBAN, AND RURAL GEOGRAPHIES.

SUICIDE

Deliberate self-destruction is a major public health issue for all Americans: it has been estimated that someone in the United States commits suicide once every seventeen minutes. Suicide ranks third for cause of death of Americans under the age of twenty-one, and it is the second leading cause of death for college and university students. From 1987 to 1996, more men under the age of thirty-five died of suicide than of AIDS. (Women are twice as likely as men to say that they are depressed, but men are four times more likely to commit suicide.) The World Health Organization reports that suicide is responsible for almost 2 percent of deaths worldwide in 1998, ahead of war and homicide.

According to social science scholarship, LGBT people are generally thought to have a heightened risk of experiencing clinically significant levels of depression, suicide attempts, suicide, and parasuicidal behaviors. Activities that fall into that last category include engaging in high-risk recreational activities or sports; using dangerous drugs and alcohol; avoiding the diagnosis of or medical attention for potentially fatal conditions, such as cervical or breast cancer; or refusing to take protective measures against life-threatening sexually transmitted diseases.

While some have posited a genetic connection between depression and homosexuality, the thinking among most mental health professionals is that despair, hopelessness, and self-hatred are an understandable response to living in a society where LGBT people face stigma, discrimination, and violence. Alan P. Bell and Martin S. Weinberg, in *Homosexualities: A Study of Diversity Among Men and Women* (1978), found that 36 percent of black lesbians (compared to 21 percent of white lesbians) and 32 percent of black gay men (compared to 27 percent of white gay men) in their sample had attempted suicide before age eighteen. The effects of racism on black lesbians and gay men likely play a role in these differentials. The high overall figures are largely confirmed by later research. In 1987, it was reported that three large, well-designed studies had found that gay men and lesbians attempted suicide two to seven times more often than heterosexual comparison groups. In 2000, another study of a random population sample of about four thousand men, ages seventeen to thirty-nine, found that 3.5 percent of heterosexual men had attempted suicide, compared to 20 percent of those with same-sex partners.

Queer Youth

Suicide is on the rise for young people in general. The rate of youth suicide has increased more than 200 percent since the 1950s, compared to only 17 percent in the general population.

In 1989, Paul Gibson's government-sponsored report on suicide among sexual minority youth generated some shocking and controversial statistics. Gibson pointed out that young lesbians and gay men belong to two groups at high risk of suicide, youth and homosexuals. Gibson claimed that gay youth are two to three times more likely to attempt suicide than other young people and may constitute up to 30 percent of all completed youth suicides annually. He suggested that transsexual youths are perhaps the most outcast of all young people and face a grave risk of suicidal feelings and behavior.

The government, at the time led by President George H. W. Bush, initially suppressed the Gibson report in response to pressure from right-wing groups and conservatives in Congress who opposed including information about homosexuality in sex education programs or funding research on or social services for gay teens. In a letter to Representative William Dannemeyer (R-CA), U.S. Health and Human Services Secretary Louis Sullivan wrote that the study "undermined the institution of the family" (Bull, p. 37). But Gibson's findings were leaked to the press and finally released; other studies later confirmed the findings. In 1996, researchers gathered data from organized youth groups in metropolitan lesbian/gay centers across the United States (Hershberger, Pilkington, and D'Augelli). Forty-two percent of the 194 participants had attempted suicide on at least one occasion, and sixty percent had thoughts about killing themselves at the time the survey was taken. The same survey showed that males reported more trouble with their sex lives, depression, anxiety, and AIDS. Significantly, youth who had attempted suicide were more precocious in recognizing their sexual orientation and disclosing it to others and had greater numbers of same-sex sexual experiences. They were more open about their identity but also lost more friends because of it. They also experienced a greater level of victimization and had greater psychopathology than those who had not tried to kill themselves. Additional studies in Massachusetts in 1997 and Minnesota in 1998 (Remafidi et al.) echoed the findings of the Gibson report and the Hershberger article and showed LGBT youth to be at a much higher risk of suicide than their straight counterparts.

When racism is added to the burden of sexual prejudice, the risk of suicide among youth may be enhanced. In a study of young men in gay and lesbian college organizations and gay rap groups, in which 55 percent reported thinking of suicide, racial/ethnic minorities tended to be overrepresented among the suicidal respondents (Schneider, Farberow, and Kruks). Twenty percent of the total reported suicide attempts, most often while closeted or after being rejected due to sexual orientation. In another study of 500 youth seeking services at an agency serving predominantly black and Latino lesbian and gay adolescents in New York City, 41 percent of the girls and 34 percent of the boys who had experienced violent assaults reported having attempted suicide (Hunter). Forty-one percent of the sample reported having suffered violence from families, peers, or strangers, and 46 percent of that violence was LGBT-related.

Transgendered Adults

"Transgender" is an umbrella term that includes cross-dressers, the intersexed, feminine men, masculine women, those who live in both or neither gender role, and transsexuals. Little research has been done on the mental health needs of such a diverse community. But transsexuals, specifically, are thought to be at a heightened risk of suicide at two junctures in their lives: first, if they feel that they may be unable to get the help they need to live in a gender other than the one they were assigned at birth, and second, ironically enough, after sex reassignment surgery, when the limitations of medical technology and continued stigma and discrimination place unbearable pressure upon them. While scant research has been done, most studies confirm the former, but not the latter, hypothesis.

In an early 1980s study of transgendered people seen at a gender clinic in Palo Alto, California, about 25 percent of the male-to-female and 19 percent of the female-to-males had attempted suicide prior to transition (the results of the study were discussed in an unpublished paper by Anne Lawrence). Another study by Bodlund and Kullgren reported that 12 percent of the male-to-females and 21 percent of female-to-males in one practice had attempted suicide prior to entering treatment. These attempts at self-destruction were attributed to intense frustration over gender dysphoria. None of the transpeople had attempted suicide since beginning therapy for gender issues.

The largest study of postsurgical outcomes for transsexuals who used medical technology found that, in a group of more than two thousand transsexuals who had received hormones or surgery or both, only sixteen possible suicide deaths—fourteen male-to-female (MTFs), one female-to-male (FTM), and one with gender not specified—had occurred. Five of the sixteen deaths may actually have been accidental medication or drug overdoses (Pfafflin and Junge).

Female-to-male transsexuals are assumed to be somewhat less susceptible to suicide than MTFs (this assumption may be based on negative stereotypes of transwomen), although FTMs are a comparatively under-researched population. In a 1994 study of forty-five FTMs interviewed outside of a clinical setting, 60 percent reported one or more types of severe childhood abuse. Ninety-six percent of those who reported abuse also reported childhood or adolescent fear, anxiety, or depression, compared to 33 percent of those without abuse histories. Fifty-one percent of respondents had either considered or attempted suicide (Devor).

Euthanasia and Physician-Assisted Suicide

Euthanasia (in which another person terminates a sick person's life) and physician-assisted suicide (PAS) became important issues in the early days of the AIDS pandemic, before life-prolonging combination drug therapies were developed. In 1997, Oregon passed the Death with Dignity Act and became the only state in the United States where physician-assisted suicide is legal. From 1998 to 2001, only 129 terminally ill Oregonians requested physician assistance in ending their lives. In a 1985 study of the rate of suicide in New York City among residents diagnosed with AIDS (Marzuk et al.), the relative risk of suicide in men with AIDS aged twenty to fifty-nine years was found to be more than thirty-six times that of men the same age without an AIDS diagnosis, and more than sixty-six times that of the general population. The authors concluded that AIDS represented a significant risk factor for suicide at that time.

Does a terminally ill person have the right to take his or her own life, and can a physician ethically assist such a patient in accomplishing this desire? In November of 2002, Attorney General John Ashcroft tried to use the Controlled Substances Act to nullify Oregon's Death with Dignity Act. He lost in a lower court and appealed to the Ninth Circuit. In other cases, the Supreme Court has held that it is not illegal for a state to ban physician-assisted suicide but also found that patients have a right to aggressive treatment of pain and other symptoms even if the treatment hastens death. The Court called for more discussion of the issue.

Suicide Prevention in the LGBT Communities

Gay educator and health activist Eric Rofes must be given considerable credit for drawing attention to the problem of suicide in the LGBT community. His 1983 classic, *I Thought People Like That Killed Themselves*, drew together academic research and personal accounts in a moving call to action. Throughout the United States, during the late

1970s and the 1980s, activists established LGBT health centers and crisis lines and did outreach and education to suicide prevention hotlines to sensitize them to callers who had issues with sexual orientation. The transgender community had only begun to mobilize to provide crisis intervention.

The most powerful organization of allies that the LGBT community has, Parents and Friends of Lesbians and Gays, was founded by Sarah Montgomery, whose son Charles committed suicide along with his lover. Such deaths continue to mobilize many queer people to radical action. The Trevor Helpline (1-866-4UTREVOR), a nonprofit endeavor, was created by the makers of a short film about a thirteen-year-old boy coming to terms with his sexuality, to promote tolerance for LGBT and questioning youth, and to aid in suicide prevention among that group. Founded on 11 August 1998, The Trevor Helpline is a toll-free suicide hotline for LGBT and questioning youth that is open twenty-four hours a day, seven days a week. More information on the organization can be found at www.thetrevorproject.org.

Suicide takes a tremendous toll on those around the person who commits suicide, a toll that can never be fully measured. As tolerance for LGBT people increases in the larger community, there is hope that suicide will no longer be seen as "the only way out."

Bibliography

Bodlund, O., and G. Kullgren. "Transsexualism—General Outcome and Prognostic Factors: A Five-year Follow-up Study of Nineteen Transsexuals in the Process of Changing Sex." *Archives of Sexual Behavior* 25, no. 3 (June 1996): 303–316.

Bull, Chris. "Suicidal Tendencies." *Advocate* (5 April 1994): 37.

Cochran, S. D., and V. M. Mays. "Lifetime Prevalence of Suicide Symptoms and Affective Disorders Among Men Reporting Same-Sex Sexual Partners: Results from NHANES III." *American Journal of Public Health* 90, no. 4 (2000): 573–578.

Devor, Aaron H. "Transsexualism, Dissociation, and Child Abuse: An Initial Discussion Based on Nonclinical Data." *Journal of Psychology and Human Sexuality* 6, no. 3 (1994): 49–72.

Dixen, J. M., H. Maddever, J. van Maasdam, and P. W. Edwards. "Psychosocial Characteristics of Applicants Evaluated for Surgical Gender Reassignment." *Archives of Sexual Behavior* 13 (1984): 269–276.

Friedman, Richard C., and Jennifer Downey. "Internalized Homophobia and Gender-Valued Self-Esteem in the Psychoanalysis of Gay Patients." *Psychoanalytic Review* 86, no. 3 (1999): 325–347.

Garofalo, Richard, Cameron Wolf, Lawrence S. Wissow, Elizabeth R. Woods, and Elizabeth Goodman. "Sexual Orientation and Risk of Suicide Attempts Among a Repre-

sentative Sample of Youth." *Archives of Pediatrics and Adolescent Medicine,* issue 153 (1999): 487–493.

Gibson, Paul. "Gay Male and Lesbian Youth Suicide." In *Report of the Secretary's Task Force on Youth Suicide.* Edited by M. R. Feinleib, Volume 3. U.S. Department of Health and Human Services, 1989.

Hershberger, Scott L., Neil W. Pilkington, and Anthony R. D'Augelli. "Categorization of Lesbian, Gay, and Bisexual Suicide Attempters." In *Gay and Lesbian Mental Health: A Sourcebook for Practitioners.* Edited by Christopher J. Alexander. New York: Haworth Park Press, 1996.

Hunter, Joyce. "Violence Against Lesbian and Gay Male Youths." *Journal of Interpersonal Violence* 5, no. 3: 295–300.

Lawrence, Anne. "Transsexual Surgery: Its Pros and Cons." Unpublished paper for the Institute for the Advanced Study of Human Sexuality. Available from http://jenelle rose.com/htmlpostings/transsexual_surgery_its_pros_ and_cons.htm

Marzuk, Peter M., Helen Tierney, Kenneth Tardiff, Elliot M. Gross, Edward B. Morgan, Ming-Ann Hus, and J. John Mann. "Increased Risk of Suicide in Persons with AIDS." *Journal of the American Medical Association* 259, no. 9 (1988): 1333–1337.

Massachusetts Youth Risk Behavior Survey, Massachusetts Department of Education, 1997.

Pfäfflin, Friedemann, and Astrid Junge. *Sex Reassignment, Thirty Years of International Follow-up Studies After Sex Reassignment Surgery: A Comprehensive Review, 1961– 1991.* Translated from German into American English in 1992 by Roberta B. Jacobson and Alf B. Maier. No print version available. Available from http://209.143.139.183/ ijtbooks/pfaefflin/1000.asp

Remafedi, G., S. French, M. Story, M. Resnick, and R. Blum. "The Relationship Between Suicide Risk and Sexual Orientation: Results of a Population-Based Study." *American Journal of Public Health* 88, no. 1 (1998): 57–60.

Rofes, Eric. *"I Thought People Like That Killed Themselves": Lesbians, Gay Men and Suicide.* San Francisco: Grey Fox Press, 1983.

Saunders, Judith M., and S. M. Valentine. "Suicide Risk Among Gay Men and Lesbians: A Review." *Death Studies* 4, no. 1 (1987): 1–23.

Schneider, Stephen G., Norman L. Farberow, and Gabriel N. Kruks. "Suicidal Behavior in Adolescent and Young Adult Gay Men." *Suicide and Life-Threatening Behavior* 19, no. 4 (1989): 381–394.

Solomon, Andrew. *The Noonday Demon: An Atlas of Depression.* New York: Scribner, 2001.

Xavier, Jessica. *Final Report of the Washington Transgender Needs Assessment Survey.* Administration for HIV and AIDS, Government of the District of Columbia, 2000.

Patrick Califia

See also ARENAS, REINALDO; HEALTH, HEALTH CARE, AND HEALTH CLINICS; MATTHIESSEN, F. O.; MITCHELL, ALICE;

PARENTS, FAMILIES AND FRIENDS OF LESBIANS AND
GAYS (PFLAG); TRANSSEXUALS, TRANSVESTITES,
TRANSGENDER PEOPLE, AND CROSS-DRESSERS;
VIOLENCE; YOUTH AND YOUTH GROUPS.

SULLIVAN, Harry Stack (b. 21 February 1892; d. 14 January 1949), psychiatrist, social scientist.

A third-generation Irish American, Sullivan spent his childhood on his parents' farm in Chenango County, New York. His closest childhood friend was Clarence Bellinger, who also became an esteemed psychiatrist. Sullivan's precocious academic talent was encouraged by his aunt Margaret Stack, who lived in New York City, and his school principal Herbert Butts. Sullivan attended Cornell University on scholarship funding (1909–1910), but received poor grades and was suspended in his first year. Information about the following year is scant. Sullivan sometimes described himself as suffering a breakdown, which Michael Allen attributes to emerging awareness of his homosexuality. Sullivan subsequently enrolled in the Chicago College of Medicine and Surgery where he had an undistinguished student career (1911–1915) but was ultimately awarded a medical degree (1917).

Information on the following years is questionable, as Sullivan represented himself differently on later applications and other documents. Helen Perry describes him working as a surgeon for the Illinois Steel Company (1915) and being physically disqualified from the National Guard (1916). He practiced medicine privately in Chicago (1916–1918), for the Army Medical Reserve Corps (1918), and for the Division for the Rehabilitation of Disabled Soldiers, Sailors, and Marines (1919–1920). In Washington, D.C., he was next employed at St. Elizabeth's hospital as a neuropsychiatrist (1921–1922), where he worked under William Alanson White, a psychiatrist who held social determinist theories of psychopathology.

Sullivan worked at Sheppard Pratt hospital in Towson, Maryland (1922–1930). Appointed director of clinical research (1925), he set up a six-bed ward for the rehabilitation of young male schizophrenics in 1929. Other shy, sensitive, young male assistants worked on the ward; all professional medical personnel were excluded, expressing Sullivan's theory that "like cures like." Sullivan theorized that schizophrenics had missed a crucial developmental experience of participating in an adolescent "gang," which the ward was to provide. The project's success brought Sullivan considerable fame within psychiatry. Kenneth Chatelaine's research suggests that Sullivan's ward was, in effect, a gay male subculture. Most of the patients and attendants were gay, Sullivan was known as

"Miss Sullivan" by his attendants, and other hospital staff avoided the ward for homophobic reasons. Sullivan theorized a homosexual phase associated with the adolescent gang as essential to the development of later heterosexuality. Given the conflation of male homosexuality with schizophrenia at the time, Sullivan could have found several gay men among Sheppard Pratt's working-class schizophrenic population.

Sullivan became close friends with anthropologist Edward Sapir in 1926. Through Sapir he developed a network of social scientists with interests in psychiatry, most notably political scientist Harold Laswell. In 1927 Sullivan met James ("Jimmy") Inscoe with whom he lived as kin until his death. Inscoe was fifteen when they met, and Sullivan often described Jimmy as his adopted son. Inscoe changed his name to James Inscoe Sullivan and worked as Sullivan's private secretary in the 1930s and 1940s. In 1929 Sullivan and Laswell traveled to Berlin, where they met the psychoanalyst William (Billy) Silverberg, who took over Sullivan's ward at Sheppard Pratt.

Sullivan left Sheppard Pratt in 1930 and moved with Jimmy to Manhattan where they lived until 1939. His first book manuscript, *Personal Psychopathology* (1932), was viewed as poorly written by colleagues and remained unpublished until after his death. Sullivan was frequently in debt in New York and filed for bankruptcy in 1932. Allen describes Sullivan as actively homosexual during this period. While in New York his closest friends included the psychoanalysts Erich Fromm, Karen Horney, and particularly Clara Thompson, and the author Ralph Ellison and the artist John Vassos.

Harry and Jimmy Sullivan moved to Bethesda, Maryland, in 1939. As psychiatric consultant to the Selective Service of the U.S. military (1940–1941), Sullivan contributed to its "Medical Circular no 1." that introduced community physicians to basic psychiatry, and he gave two-day seminars on psychiatric screening across the country. Neither this circular nor Sullivan's lectures described homosexuality as grounds for exclusion from the military. Under his guidance, during the war, the Washington School of Psychiatry flourished in response to the increased need for military psychiatric personnel. The school aimed to train psychiatrists along eclectic lines, rather than strict psychoanalytic ones. All Sullivan's books, except *Personal Psychopathology,* are based on transcriptions of his lectures from the last ten years of his life. After 1945 he became involved in the UNESCO Tensions Project, which examined contributions of psychiatry to world peace, through his Canadian colleague, psychiatrist G. Brock Chisholm. Sullivan died in a Paris hotel en route to a UNESCO meeting.

Bibliography

Allen, Michael S. "Sullivan's Closet: A Reappraisal of Harry Stack Sullivan's Life and His Pioneering Role in American Psychiatry." *Journal of Homosexuality,* 29, no. 1 (1995): 1–18.

Chatelaine, Kenneth L. *Harry Stack Sullivan: The Formative Years.* Washington, D.C: University Press of America, 1981.

Perry, Helen Swick. *Psychiatrist of America: The Life of Harry Stack Sullivan.* Cambridge, Mass.: Belknap Press, 1982.

Peter Hegarty

See also MILITARY; MILITARY LAW AND POLICY; PSYCHOLOGY, PSYCHIATRY, PSYCHOANALYSIS, AND SEXOLOGY; SAME-SEX INSTITUTIONS.

SULLIVAN, Lou (b. 16 June 1951; d. 2 March 1991), transsexual activist.

Lou Sullivan, a female-to-male (FTM) transsexual gay man who became a leading advocate for transgender rights, grew up in modest economic circumstances in a tightly knit Catholic family in Wauwatosa, Wisconsin, a Milwaukee suburb. He began keeping a diary (now part of the Louis G. Sullivan collection at the GLBT Historical Society, San Francisco) at age ten and continued this practice until shortly before his death. Sullivan thus produced an intimate, detailed record of a transgender life that is as historically significant as his many accomplishments as an activist.

In the unpublished diary, Sullivan described "playing boys" as a youngster and realized even then that it "meant more to [him] than it did to the other kids." By his early teens, Sullivan's writing voiced deeper questions about gender identity and expressed a fascination with male homosexuality. Attracted to drag queens, Sullivan began a long-term relationship at age seventeen with a self-described "feminine" male lover, and mutual play with gender roles characterized the relationship from the beginning. Both Sullivan and his companion embraced the gender-bending aesthetic then evident in the youth and pop music countercultures, and both participated in local gay liberation movement activities.

After graduating from high school in 1970, Sullivan worked as a secretary in the Slavic Languages Department of the University of Wisconsin-Milwaukee. In 1973 he self-identified as a female transvestite and began his activist career by publishing two articles in the *Gay People's Union [GPU] News*: "A Transvestite Answers a Feminist" and "Looking towards Transvestite Liberation," both of which remain notable for their early critique of anti-transgender ideology in the gay and feminist movement cultures. Though female and still living publicly as a cross-dressing woman, Sullivan participated regularly in the men's caucus of the GPU. He contributed articles, reviews, and editorial services to the *Gay People's Union News* through 1980. Most of his published pieces dealt with passing women, female transvestites, and other gender-variant individuals. Considered collectively, these articles can be considered an important effort to reclaim an FTM history and to foster a sense of historical memory in an emergent FTM community.

Sullivan self-identified as a female-to-male transsexual by the time he moved to San Francisco in 1975. Although still employed as a female, Sullivan spent most of his time outside of work cross-dressing and presenting himself as a gay man. Sullivan first sought sex-reassignment surgery in 1976, but was denied on the basis of his openly declared homosexual orientation. As a result of his own frustrations, Sullivan led an eventually successful campaign to remove homosexual orientation from the contraindications for sex reassignment. He pioneered methods of obtaining peer support, professional counseling, endocrinological services, and reconstructive surgery outside of the institution of the gender dysphoria clinics, and he disseminated this information at the grassroots level through his booklet *Information for the Female to Male Cross-Dresser and Transsexual* (1980), which remains an initial point of contact with the transgender community for many FTMs. Sullivan's efforts are responsible to a significant degree for the rapid growth of the FTM community during the 1980s.

Sullivan began taking testosterone in 1979, and after chest reconstruction surgery in 1980, he began living full-time as a gay man. At this time he changed his name from "Sheila" to "Lou" in honor of his favorite rock star, Lou Reed. Throughout the 1980s, Sullivan wrote about FTM issues in the gay and transgender press and became a popular public speaker on the subject in San Francisco and the surrounding area. He served as the first FTM peer counselor at the Janus Information Facility, an important transgender referral service and information clearinghouse. He took a leading role in educating the male-to-female transgender community about FTM needs and helped transform the Golden Gate Girls into the Golden Gate Girls and Guys, the first social and educational transgender organization in the Bay Area to offer support to FTMs. Sullivan was also a founding member of the San Francisco Gay and Lesbian Historical Society, whose newsletter he helped edit and publish. In 1984 he began work on a biography of Jack B. Garland, a northern California female who lived as a man for forty years in the late nineteenth and early twentieth centuries. Alyson Press published it in 1990.

In 1986 Sullivan finally underwent the genital reconstruction surgery he had long desired. That same year he founded the first FTM support group on the West Coast (later FTM International, the largest such organization in the United States) and began editing and publishing the *FTM Newsletter*. Tragically, 1986 was also the year Sullivan learned he had AIDS. He continued his many community activities until his death in San Francisco from an AIDS-related illness in 1991.

Bibliography

Califia, Pat. *Sex Changes: The Politics of Transgenderism*. San Francisco: Cleis Press, 1997.

Coleman, Eli, and Walter O. Bockting. "'Heterosexual' Prior to Sex Reassignment—'Homosexual' Afterwards: A Case Study of a Female-to-Male Transsexual." *Journal of Psychology and Human Sexuality* 1: 2 (1988): 69–82.

Stryker, Susan. "Portrait of a Transfag Drag Hag As a Young Man: The Activist Career of Louis G. Sullivan." In *Reclaiming Genders: Transsexual Grammars at the Fin de Siècle*. Edited by Kate More and Stephen Whittle. London: Cassell, 1999.

Susan Stryker

See also TRANSGENDER ORGANIZATIONS AND PERIODICALS; TRANSSEXUALS, TRANSVESTITES, TRANSGENDER PEOPLE, AND CROSS-DRESSERS.

SYMBOLS

The pink triangle, rainbow flag, lambda, labrys, red ribbon, strategically placed bandanna, and double Venus or Mars symbol all have significance to the LGBT community. While some are joyfully celebratory, others are symbols of persecution or sorrow that have been reclaimed in positive ways. For decades LGBT people have worn these symbols on their bodies, named their organizations and businesses after them, decorated their homes with them, used them on their posters, banners, and flags, and appropriated them for many other purposes.

Gay men incarcerated in the Nazi concentration camps were forced to wear the pink triangle as an identifying symbol of their "crime," just as Jews had to wear the yellow Star of David. Wearing pink, the color associated with femininity, was intended to humiliate gay men by implying that they were like women. After the liberation of the camps, when nongay Jewish and political prisoners were set free and nursed back to health, gay men wearing the pink triangle were often transferred to regular prisons to serve out their sentences.

The pink triangle is an example of a symbol, originally negative, that has been reclaimed and transformed into an image of pride. Although sometimes worn as a symbol of gay pride by both men and women, it is primarily identified with males. Lesbians in the concentration camps, much fewer in number, did not wear the pink triangle. Instead, they were made to wear the black triangle worn by incarcerated prostitutes (a fact that is less well known). The black triangle has not caught on, however, as a symbol of lesbian pride.

A symbol with more resonance for lesbians is the labrys, a goddess symbol from the Minoan period on the island of Crete. Actually, the symbol goes all the way back to the Paleolithic caves of southern Europe. The labrys is a double-sided ax that served as both a weapon and a harvesting tool. Amazons, legendary women warriors, were said to wield the labrys as a battle weapon. Demeter, a grain goddess of ancient Greece, had a scepter shaped like a labrys, which shows its association with agriculture as well.

To some, the labrys is a lesbian and feminist symbol of strength and self-sufficiency, but it can also represent nebulous sexuality. It is also the primary symbol of the Yoruban (African) deity Shango, who is male but sometimes represented in sexually ambiguous ways. He is a protector of expectant mothers, and his altars are usually populated by large-breasted female figures with the labrys as a headdress. In Afro-Caribbean religions, he is syncretized with a female saint, Santa Barbara.

Some scholars believe that the labrys comes from the butterfly, a shape it resembles, which is a symbol of transfiguration and rebirth. Mary Daly describes it as "an instrument of change, of Metamorphosis" (*Pure Lust*, p. 407). Although goddess religion is sometimes accused of gender essentialism, the labrys can have the opposite meaning: it can represent the power of gender ambiguity. Interestingly, it is the only symbol from the goddess-oriented branch of the feminist spirituality movement to have caught on with the lesbian community generally.

The planetary symbols of double Venus and Mars represent women together and men together, respectively, while the combination of Venus and Mars together mean heterosexual coupling. The astrological sign of Mercury is sometimes adopted by transgender people. In classical mythology, Mercury (Greek Hermes) is said to have fathered a child named Hermaphroditus with the love goddess Venus (Greek Aphrodite). That child possessed both male and female sexual organs, hence the term "hermaphrodite."

Another symbol rooted in the classical world is the lambda (λ). New York City's Gay Activists Alliance selected the Greek letter lambda as its emblem in the early

1970s, after the Stonewall Riots. Member Tom Doerr suggested it to signify "kinetic potential," based on its use as a symbol for energy change in physics. It also represented scales, and therefore balance, to the ancient Greeks. To the Spartans, it represented unity. Finally, in some ancient Greek graffiti the capital lambda appears with the meaning "fellate," representing the first letter of either *lambazein* or *laikazein*. The latter meaning would obviously have no particular relevance for lesbians. The Romans adopted the letter to represent "the light of knowledge shed into the darkness of ignorance," which fits the goals of LGBT activists.

One of the most visible symbols of LGBT pride is the rainbow flag, which has resonance for men and women equally. Gilbert Baker of San Francisco designed and made the first rainbow flag in 1978. Although in general it can be used to represent the diversity of the LGBT community, it originally had eight stripes with specific symbolic meanings for each color: pink (sexuality), red (life), orange (healing), yellow (sun), green (nature), blue (art), indigo (harmony), and violet (spirit). One of the colors, hot pink, was not commercially available, so eight became seven, but was further reduced to six (dropping indigo). The San Francisco Pride Parade required an even number of stripes, so that three could be draped along each side of the street on the route. Today it is recognized by the International Congress of Flag Makers, and is flown in LGBT pride marches worldwide.

One of the most poignant symbols to emerge in recent years is the red loop of ribbon representing AIDS awareness and a commitment to the fight against HIV. Created in 1991 by a group of art professionals in New York called Visual AIDS, the red ribbon helps to create greater awareness of the threat that AIDS poses to the LGBT community. The color red was chosen for its "connection to blood and the idea of passion—not only anger, but love, like a valentine," states Frank Moore of Visual AIDS.

Some lesbians, adapting the red ribbon idea to a specifically female disease, have begun to wear a pink ribbon representing breast cancer awareness. Some LGBT people have worn a rainbow-patterned ribbon in the familiar looped shape to commemorate Coming Out Day.

Another color symbol for LGBT people is simply the color lavender (or purple) itself. It is the combination of pink and blue, the traditional symbols of maleness and femaleness, and is used to indicate a deliberate blurring of gender boundaries.

Bandannas worn in the rear pockets of jeans have significance for some gay men, although they may function more as a signal than a symbol. A bandanna in the right pocket indicates the desire for the passive role in sex, while the left signifies the more active role. The same used to apply to earrings, but now that earrings have become a popular fashion statement for heterosexual men, they rarely are invested these meanings. Some gay men have a color-coded system for their bandannas to indicate more specific sexual practices and preferences, but these apply only to males. Nothing comparable exists in the lesbian community.

The symbols that have significance to the LGBT community are constantly changing. Some of the earlier ones that had significance only for gay men but were worn by lesbians as well, such as the pink triangle, seem to be gradually fading in favor of more universal symbols, such as the rainbow flag, which more fully reflects the diversity of the community.

Bibliography

Alyson Publications Staff, eds. *The Alyson Almanac: A Treasury of Information for the Gay and Lesbian Community*. Boston: Alyson, 1990.

Anderson, Steven. "The Rainbow Flag." *Gaze*, no. 191 (May 1993): 25.

Daly, Mary. *Pure Lust: Elemental Feminist Philosophy*. Boston: Beacon Press, 1984.

Goodwin, Joseph P. *More Man Than You'll Ever Be: Gay Folklore and Acculturation in Middle America*. Bloomington: Indiana University Press, 1989.

Hogan, Steve, and Lee Hudson. *Completely Queer: The Gay and Lesbian Encyclopedia*. New York: Henry Holt, 1998.

Lori Rowlett

T

TATTOOS. see PIERCING, TATTOOS, AND SCARS.

TAVERA, Hank M. (b. 19 January 1944; d. 27 February 2000), activist, cultural worker, health counselor.

Hank M. Tavera (Enrique Manuel Lugo Tavera III) was born in East Los Angeles, the son of Stella Lugo and Enrique Tavera. He was raised and educated in Catholic schools. Tavera's political and artistic roots developed in the United Farm Workers movement and the Chicano theater movement of the 1960s and 1970s. After he and his partner of twenty-three years, Kehau Wessel, moved from Los Angeles to San Francisco's Mission District in 1979, Tavera became a prominent figure in the city's Latino, LGBT, public health, and arts communities. During his twenty-one years in San Francisco, he worked on behalf of Latino and LGBT communities, people living with HIV and AIDS, LGBT Catholics, and queer cultural activists of color. Tavera was well known for over two decades as a LGBT Chicano activist and community organizer in the Bay Area and as a LGBT Chicano cultural worker and educational advocate throughout California.

In the 1970s Tavera was an actor with the theater collective El Teatro de la Esperanza in Santa Barbara. In the 1980s he became a director and active member of Teatro Gusto in San Francisco. A past board chair of TENAZ (Teatro Nacional de Aztlán, or National Theatres of Aztlán), Tavera coordinated the Eleventh International Chicano and Latino Theatre Festival in 1981 in San Francisco. He produced many shows at the Mission Cultural Center for Latino Arts (MCCLA), including the 1987 *People of Color Visual Art Exhibit.* This exhibit became the precursor to his annual creation, *Visual Arts Exhibit and Performing Arts Festival of Latino/a Gay, Lesbian, Bisexual and Transgender Artists,* in which dozens of queer Latina and Latino Bay Area and California artists participated. Tavera also directed several plays in San Francisco, including Herbert Sigüenza's *The Leash* (1981), Edgar Poma's *Reunion* (1983), and Alfonso Ramírez's *The Watermelon Factory* (1992). In 1995 he directed Joseph Castle's *The Black Cat,* the first play about San Francisco's LGBT movement pioneer, José Sarria.

A tireless organizer, Tavera combined his community-based work with his professional role as a health worker. Between 1986 and 1990 he was the Client Services Director for the San Francisco AIDS Foundation (SFAF). There he established a bilingual, multicultural, and women's services program. In the streets Tavera also organized the first rally in San Francisco in support of needle exchange programs. He was part of an underground needle exchange collective that provided clean needles to intravenous drug users in exchange for used ones, taking direct action to prevent further HIV infections. As chair of the Third World AIDS Advisory, he helped spawn black, Latino, and Asian AIDS coalitions. In 1989 he began to produce the annual National AIDS Theatre Festival, and in 1993, the Latino/a AIDS Theatre Festival.

Tavera was especially known among his neighbors in the Latino Mission District, where he made his home. Combining his health advocacy against AIDS and his artistic talents, Tavera organized in 1989 the annual "We

Will Survive!" safe sex performance show by male-to-female transgender Latina artists in the Mission's famed Sixteenth Street gay Latino strip. In this annual HIV awareness event, well-known artists like Ronnie Salazar and Adela Vázquez performed for and educated the local gay Latino community. For years Tavera worked on the front lines of the AIDS epidemic at the San Francisco City Clinic as an HIV/AIDS intervention specialist. He was also the co-founder of National LLEGÓ (Latina/o Lesbian, Gay, Bisexual and Transgender Organization) and LLEGÓ California and was a voting delegate to LIFE, California's LGBT and AIDS lobby group in Sacramento. With LIFE he led several Latino delegations to lobby legislators on HIV, health, immigration, and civil rights bills affecting the state.

As an openly gay Catholic, Tavera played a central role in Dignity San Francisco, a self-governing faith community of LGBT Catholics, their families, and friends. There he was an Eucharistic minister, and in 1992 he formed a people of color support group for the organization. Beginning in 1993 Tavera coordinated the yearly Feast of Our Lady of Guadalupe, and in 1995 he coauthored the "Multicultural Plan for Dignity/San Francisco."

For his multiple public roles Tavera received many awards and other forms of recognition. In October 1997 he was presented with the first Premio Cultura (Culture Award) from National LLEGÓ in San Juan, Puerto Rico. On 22 May 2000 San Francisco's Harvey Milk Gay, Lesbian, Bisexual, Transgender Democratic Club honored Tavera posthumously with one of its Bill Kraus Awards in recognition of his advocacy and service on behalf of people living with HIV and AIDS. Tavera passed away on 27 February 2000 in San Francisco. Kehau Wessel, his lover Vladimir Maldonado, his mother Stella, his son Mario Nicolás, his daughter Cecilia Luz, and his granddaughters Alexis and Annalise Villa survive him.

Bibliography

Huerta, Jorge A. *Chicano Drama: Performance, Society, and Myth.* Cambridge, UK: Cambridge University Press, 2000.

Horacio N. Roque Ramírez

See also LATINA AND LATINO LGBTQ ORGANIZATIONS AND PERIODICALS; SARRIA, JOSÉ; THEATER AND PERFORMANCE.

TAYLOR, Valerie (b. 7 September 1913; d. 22 October 1997), writer, activist.

Taylor identified herself in her poem "The Sweet Little Old Gray-Haired Lady in Sneakers" as "an eight-time loser." Not only was she a writer, a lesbian, a senior citizen, and a peace worker and gay activist, but she was also of Pottawatome extraction, working class, and "handicapped" by scoliosis beginning in childhood. Her poem asks, "how shall I not be a revolutionary?"

Born Velma Nacella Young in rural Illinois, Taylor had one sister, Rose Marie, and a brother born with spinal bifida who died at eight weeks. She attended land grant Blackburn College at the height of the Depression. In 1935 (or 1936), she joined the American Socialist Party with two fellow students, the labor activist Hank Mayer and his wife, Ada, who became lifelong friends. In 1939 she married William Jerry Tate. Her son Marshall was born in 1940 and the twins James and Jerry in 1942.

Supplementing her income as rural schoolteacher and office worker from the 1930s through the 1950s, Taylor sold verse under the names Nacella Young, Velma Tate, and Velma Young to magazines as varied as *American Weave*, *Canadian Poetry Magazine*, the *Franciscan Messenger*, and *Good Housekeeping* for as little as five dollars apiece. She sold confession genre stories for one hundred dollars each to magazines like *True Love* and *True Story*. In 1953, as Valerie Taylor, she sold her first novel, *Hired Girl*, a heterosexual rural romance later republished as *The Lusty Land*. The $500 she made from the sale of this book enabled her to divorce her alcoholic, abusive husband that same year and eventually move with her sons to Chicago.

Taylor achieved her initial popularity writing lesbian fiction for the voracious post–World War II publishing industry of paperback originals. Her first, *Whisper Their Love* (1957), sold two million copies for Fawcett–Gold Medal–Crest; she was paid $3,200 for domestic and foreign rights. She had seven books in print during the 1960s, with titles like *Stranger on Lesbos* (1960) and *Unlike Others* (1963). Even with the garishly illustrated covers proclaiming "unnatural love," the quality of Taylor's writing garnered loyal readers, especially since four of her early novels could be read as a series with overlapping characters. Taylor, who assumed that name in her public life in the mid-1960s, later decried the enforced publishing formulas of the day that prohibited healthy relationships or happy endings for lesbian novels.

In the 1960s, Taylor contributed poetry and reviews to the Daughters of Bilitis magazine, the *Ladder*. Dr. Jeannette Howard Foster (1895–1981), who self-published *Sex Variant Women in Literature* (1956) and contributed to the *Ladder* from 1953 until 1972, began a correspondence and friendship with Taylor through their contact with the magazine. Over the years, Taylor exchanged letters with many other writers, including Elsa

Gidlow and May Sarton, about their work and the future of lesbian literature.

In Chicago, Taylor worked from 1956 to 1961 as proofreader and copy editor for the publishing house Henry Regnery and Sons. She continued to contribute poetry to respected small journals like *Choice*. When she left Regnery and began writing for trade magazines, a closeted former coworker, from whom she obtained the plot for *Stranger on Lesbos,* invited her to meet her Mormon partner. These friends, who had met as students at the University of Chicago in the 1930s, introduced Taylor to their social circle of gay and lesbian couples, mostly from the academic community. The women in the group were white Anglo-Saxon Protestants (WASPs), with the exception of Renee Hanover, a communist and a Jew, who was accepted with reluctance only because she was the lover of a popular member. Hanover was a protégée and student of a prominent civil rights attorney, Pearl Hart.

In 1962, after returning from a year in the Canary Islands, where she had hoped to support herself by writing, Taylor was invited to lecture on lesbian literature by the Chicago chapter of the Mattachine Society. Taylor was fifty when she first met chapter cofounder Pearl Hart, who was then seventy-three. Attracted by Hart's intellect and passion for social justice, Taylor entered into what she would say was the defining relationship of her life. Taylor moved into a studio apartment less than a block from Hart's home. Hart, closeted in her professional life and with her family, shared her house with her estranged first love and her new partner—an arrangement Taylor described as "gothic."

In 1965, Hart and others created Mattachine Midwest, and Taylor was soon writing and editing the group's newsletter. Frequently called upon to be the woman's voice of the organization, Taylor was interviewed on radio in 1971 by the Pulitzer Prize winner Studs Terkel and appeared with sexologists William Masters and Virginia Johnson on Phil Donahue's nationally syndicated television talk show. With other Mattachine members, Taylor marched on picket lines for LGB rights, the post-1968 Democratic Convention Chicago Seven trial, anti–Vietnam War demonstrations, and the Kent State murders protests. She also worked with the Women's International League for Peace and Freedom.

In 1968, Taylor met Marie Kuda, who also wrote for the Mattachine Midwest newsletter. In the early 1970s, Kuda introduced Taylor and her lectures on literature to Chicago's lesbian separatist community. This became the impetus for Taylor, Kuda, and Susan Edwards, of the *Lavender Woman* newspaper collective, to found the national Lesbian Writers' Conference (LWC) in 1974,

which took place in Chicago over five years in the mid-1970s. Kuda's Womanpress published Taylor's keynote address for the 1974 LWC, *For My Granddaughters,* as well as *Two Women: The Poetry of Jeannette Foster and Valerie Taylor* (1976).

Hart died in February 1975. Hospital policy prohibited all but the family to be present during a patient's final days. Taylor prevailed upon Hart's friend Hanover to use her influence to intervene, but by the time permission was granted, Hart was in a coma. Distraught, Taylor relocated from Chicago to Margaretville, a small town in upstate New York near the farm of her friends from Blackburn, the Mayers. She supplemented her early retirement income from Social Security by continuing to freelance for trade magazines. Returning to Chicago that autumn for the LWC, she met the keynote speaker, Barbara Grier, of the nascent lesbian-feminist Naiad Press. From 1977 through 1989, Naiad published Taylor's new novels, featuring nonstereotypical women living rich lives. These included *Love Image* (1977); *Prism* (1981), which she called her geriatric novel; and *Rice and Beans* (1989), which was imbued with poverty and activism. Naiad also reprinted three of her earlier pulps under the Volute imprint. Naiad cofounder Anyda Marchant credited Taylor's name recognition and popularity with helping push the publishing house into profitability.

In late 1979, Taylor moved to Tucson, Arizona, to escape the climate and closeted mentality of Margaretville, and became the resident lesbian grandmother at the local lesbian center, Casa Nuestra. Her series of lectures on lesbian literature at Casa were recorded. She conducted poetry and journal-writing workshops at the senior center, joined the local Quaker meeting, and organized and agitated as a Gray Panther against Tucson Electric and others. In 1980, when Jeannette Foster was having difficulties in an Arkansas nursing home, Taylor organized a "Sisterhood Fund" that brought donations for Foster's care from women all around the country. Taylor also began lobbying for an "old dykes home." In 1993, after Taylor was seriously injured in a fall, the writer Lee Lynch and Taylor's literary executor, Tee A. Corinne, launched a similar fund for her; the contributions enabled her to get in-home assistance and remedy dental problems that Medicare and her slender income did not cover.

Corinne, through her connection with the Austin, Texas, publisher Banned Books, brought out Taylor's last novel, *Ripening* (1988), and an expanded edition of Foster and Taylor's poetry, *Two Women Revisited* (1991). Corinne also included shorter pieces in two anthologies she edited, *Intricate Passions* and *The Poetry of Sex.*

Many of Taylor's Tucson letters were filled with memories of Hart, and Taylor kept Hart's photograph above the bed, but in her last years Taylor wrote to a friend that she had a "*sub rosa* new lover." In the 1990s, Taylor continued to write poetry, revise her unpublished novels, and grant interviews, some of which were not printed until years after her death. In 1995, she contributed essays on the poet Denise Levertov and the author May Sarton to the reference book *Feminist Writers* (1996). On 10 October 1997, Taylor fell from her wheelchair while reaching for a book and died in hospice twelve days later. In 1992, Taylor was inducted into the Chicago Gay and Lesbian Hall of Fame by Mayor Richard M. Daley, an honor recognizing her achievements and contributions to the quality of life of the city.

Bibliography

Corinne, Tee A. *Valerie Taylor: A Resource Book.* Sunny Valley, Ore.: The Estate of Valerie Taylor, 1999.

Dobschuetz, Barbara. "Pearl Hart." In *Women Building Chicago, 1790–1990: A Biographical Dictionary.* Edited by Rima Lunin Schultz and Adele Hast. Bloomington: Indiana University Press, 2001.

Poling, John D. "Mattachine Midwest: History of a Chicago Gay Rights Organization, 1965–1986." Thesis, Illinois State University, 2002.

Terkel, Studs. "Valerie Taylor, Seventy-nine: Tucson, Arizona." In *Coming of Age: The Story of the Century by Those Who Lived It.* New York: The New Press, 1995.

"Valerie Taylor Papers." Human Sexuality Collection, Kroch Library, Cornell University, Ithaca, N.Y. Available from http://rmc.library.cornell.edu/eGuides/manuscripts/7627 .html.

Wolt, Irene. "An Interview with Valerie Taylor." *The Lesbian Review of Books* 4, no. 3 (spring 1998): 3–4.

Marie J. Kuda

See also FOSTER, JEANETTE; LADDER; LITERATURE; MATTACHINE SOCIETY; NATIVE AMERICANS; PUBLISHERS; PULP FICTION: LESBIAN.

TEAROOMS (BATHROOMS)

Tearooms have been a crucial and contested site in U.S. same-sex sexual subcultures for well over a century. Tearooms, or public washrooms, gained greater public and academic attention in 1970 with the publication of Laud Humphreys's now classic study, *Tearoom Trade: Impersonal Sex in Public Places.* While the ethics of Humphreys's methodology continue to be much debated—Humphreys tracked men to their homes using license plate numbers, and then posed as a public health surveyor to secure information about their domestic and familial situations—his findings underscored the importance of tearooms as sites for men searching for sex with other men. Perhaps most significantly, Humphreys's work, along with later sociological inquiries such as Edward Delph's *The Silent Community: Public Homosexual Encounters,* confirmed what Alfred Kinsey discovered three decades earlier: many men who frequent tearooms do not identify as homosexual or gay but lead otherwise "normal" lives, often married with children. And herein lies the functional brilliance of the multi-purpose tearoom. Outwardly conventional men seeking occasional sex with other men can avoid gay-identified social-sexual spaces, such as bars and bathhouses, while the tearoom becomes a meeting place for men of all manner of erotic persuasions.

The History of Tearooms

Historians have been slower than sociologists to turn to tearooms, but we now have a growing literature that offers important historical and material perspectives on sex in public washrooms. Beginning in the late nineteenth century, many cities, spurred on by the urban and public health reform movements, constructed elaborate systems of public washrooms. Many of these aptly named comfort stations were constructed below city streets and in subway systems, constituting a cornerstone of what was, often quite literally, a (homo)sexual underground. Writing about New York City, George Chauncey notes that gay men referred to public washrooms as tearooms; "T-room" being an early twentieth-century slang term for "toilet-room," which allowed men to communicate about the tearoom trade with others in the know (p. 197). Tearooms could also be found in other public places, such as parks, train stations, libraries, highway rest stops, and later, shopping malls. As John Howard discovered in his queer history of the South and as Jerry Lee Kramer likewise notes about the Midwest, tearooms associated with highway rest stops have proven particularly integral to same-sex sexual networks in rural regions, which may lack the more elaborately built environments and commercialized subcultures of city and town.

It did not take long for public washrooms, wherever they were located, to develop into a distinctive, often subterranean and nocturnal, world of sexual encounters between men. Historically, men have used tearooms for a variety of different reasons. For many men, especially those who lived in immigrant and working-class urban neighborhoods in the early twentieth century, tearooms provided a degree of privacy unavailable in crowded tenements and rooming houses. There were also financial considerations. Men of means might take a sexual partner to a hotel room, but for poor men, the tearoom offered one of the few free, albeit highly policed, spaces in increasingly commercialized sexual economies. This is not to say that only poor men frequented tearooms. For many men, from all classes, the allure of the toilet has been the erotic preference for what Humphreys termed "impersonal sex" and/or the thrill of sex associated with the risk of getting caught. We should be careful, however, not to overemphasize the element of anonymity. A public washroom can, through repeated use, develop a reputation as a particularly lively spot. Popular washrooms, with their high volume of sexual traffic and stall-wall graffiti, can take on an element of sociability, as the slang term "tearoom" suggests. To a man encountering tearoom activity for the first time, such a scene may signify a revelation of community, as opposed to impersonal or anonymous sex.

Given the obvious risks involved, men in the tearoom trade have employed a variety of nonverbal, visual signs to make sexual contact. Subtle and sophisticated signals, involving hands, feet, and eyes, are tearoom adaptations of the subaltern codes and cues used by men to cruise for sex in many other social/sexual spaces governed by threatening powers. This is a reminder that men interested in sex with other men have not been the only ones to discover the erotic potential of the public washroom. The police have always kept a close eye on men's washroom sex. Court records from the late nineteenth century on document the arrests and trials of men unfortunate enough to be apprehended in tearooms. The same historical documents also reveal the police methods of surveillance, from the use of entrapment by plainclothes officers to a host of spying techniques. To take but one example, police commissioners in Long Beach, California, hired special detectives in 1914 to stake out comfort stations; in the month of November alone, fifty men were arrested in Long Beach tearooms. As Sharon Ullman explains in her discussion of the Long Beach affair, periodic scandals over washroom sex served to make "sex seen," that is, they contributed to the emergence and increasing visibility of same-sex subcultures over the course of the twentieth century.

Privacy in Public

Much of the social and sexual conflict stirred up by the tearoom relates to its ambiguous location between the public and private. Sex between men in washrooms seems to serve as an implicit challenge to the private/public distinction so central to dominant sexual ideology, then and

now. Indeed, as literary and cultural critic Lee Edelman has suggested in a provocative essay on the Walter Jenkins affair (Jenkins, Lyndon Johnson's chief of staff, made front-page news in 1964 when he was arrested in a YMCA tearoom two blocks from the White House), the very architecture of the lavatory—its "spatial juxtaposition of public urinals and the relatively greater privacy of individual stalls" (p. 159)—captures its uncertain positioning between the public and the private. Within the dominant cultural order, however, there has been little uncertainty about the tearoom's status as public space, something underscored by its designation as a "public convenience." Men engaged in the tearoom trade, however, often make a conscious effort to carve out a relative degree of privacy in public, either by simply choosing the privacy of a stall or, more elaborately, by posting someone to watch for police and other patrons. Holes bored in the partitions between washroom stalls —called "glory holes"—are perhaps the clearest architectural evidence of men's determination to turn the toilet to their own sexual ends. The seemingly endless battle between those who desire to discourage sex in washrooms, often by riveting metal sheets to stall walls, and the determined efforts of men to bore holes through them, constitute the tearoom as a key site of sexual struggle, including men's everyday acts of rebellion against the arbitrary designations of private and public, proper and improper sex.

Lesbian Tearooms

It is frequently said that a lesbian equivalent of tearoom trade does not exist. Yet, we should not be so quick to dismiss the possibilities. Joan Nestle's evocative recollections of the Sea Colony, a working-class lesbian bar in New York City during the 1950s and '60s, revolved around "The Bathroom Line." "Because we were labelled deviants, our bathroom habits had to be watched," recalled Nestle. "Only one woman at a time was allowed into the toilet because we could not be trusted. Thus the toilet line was born." Just as men appropriated the tearoom for their own sexual purposes, lesbians at the Sea Colony turned the oppressive conditions of the bathroom line into an erotic act: "We joked, we cruised . . . we made special pleas to allow hot-and-heavy lovers in together. . . . Our eyes played the line, subtle touches, gentle shyness weaved under the blaring jokes, the music, the surveillance. We lived on that line; restricted and judged, we took deep breaths and played" (pp. 38–39).

Tearooms in the Early 2000s

Tearooms, of course, are not a thing of the past. Indeed, with the partial decriminalization of gay sex within the limited bounds of the private sphere in some jurisdictions, what we have witnessed is an increase in the policing of sex in so-called public places, such as parks and washrooms. Periodic arrests of celebrities, such as pop singer George Michael, caught with his pants down in a Los Angeles public washroom in 1998, are sensational reminders that the tearoom trade continues to thrive. Washroom sex, like public sex more generally, remains a sticky issue for both the police and the LGBT movement. The evolution of police technology, notably the use of video surveillance in men's washrooms, results in the continued arrest of countless men. And while a rare queer activist group, such as Sex Panic! during the late 1990s, sporadically springs up to speak in defense of the zones of public sex, many more mainstream gay activists continue to distance themselves from what they consider unrespectable and undefendable sexual behavior. This much seems certain: after well over one hundred years of the trade, the tearoom will remain for the foreseeable future a highly charged site for both sexual policing and pleasure.

Bibliography

Chauncey, George. *Gay New York: Gender, Urban Culture, and the Making of the Gay Male World, 1890–1940.* New York: Basic Books, 1994.

Delph, Edward William. *The Silent Community: Public Homosexual Encounters.* Beverly Hills, Calif: Sage, 1978.

Edelman, Lee. "Tearooms and Sympathy; or, the Epistemology of the Water-Closet." In *Homographesis: Essays in Gay Literary and Cultural Theory.* New York: Routledge, 1994.

Howard, John. *Men Like That: A Southern Queer History.* Chicago: University of Chicago Press, 1999.

Humphreys, Laud. *Tearoom Trade: Impersonal Sex in Public Places.* Chicago: Aldine, 1970.

Kramer, Jerry Lee. "Bachelor Farmers and Spinsters: Gay and Lesbian Identities and Communities in Rural North Dakota." In *Mapping Desire: Geographies of Sexualities.* Edited by David Bell and Gill Valentine. London: Routledge, 1995.

Maynard, Steven. "Through a Hole in the Lavatory Wall: Homosexual Subcultures, Police Surveillance, and the Dialectics of Discovery, Toronto, 1890–1930." *Journal of the History of Sexuality* 5 (1994): 207–242.

Nestle, Joan. *A Restricted Country.* Ithaca, N.Y.: Firebrand Books, 1987. (See "The Bathroom Line.")

Ullman, Sharon R. *Sex Seen: The Emergence of Modern Sexuality in America.* Berkeley: University of California Press, 1997.

Steven Maynard

See also CRUISING; KINSEY, ALFRED C.; PUBLIC SEX.

TELEVISION

Television was the dominant mass medium of the second half of the twentieth century, a time of tremendous change in public perceptions of sexual and gender minorities. This influential medium both reflected and shaped popular views about LGBT people. In the new millennium, it continues to hold an influential place in society, though increasingly it shares that place with such media as DVDs and the Internet. In the United States, television traditionally has reached its largest audience via the major commercial broadcast networks, which tend to underdevelop and desexualize LGBT characters. More unapologetic portrayals could be found in less heavily censored areas of television: public broadcasting, premium cable, and—to a lesser extent—basic cable. Since the 1970s, there have also been up-front channels and programming targeted specifically at sexual and gender minorities, often distributed via local community-access or leased-access cable stations and satellite.

The Major Commercial Networks

In the 1940s and 1950s, television was censored heavily in the United States. Industry and government leaders reasoned that because TV signals reached into every home, reverence and good taste were necessary. U.S. television's commercial nature compounded the need for censorship. Early sponsors often urged producers to avoid unpleasant or controversial subjects. In an era when homosexuality was considered a crime, an illness, and a sin, and when many people assumed that homosexuals were child molesters, TV was not about to deal openly with sexual and gender minorities. Transgenderism could be discussed in limited, vague ways, as a medical curiosity. Male homosexuality could only be hinted at, and lesbianism and bisexuality remained invisible on television for years.

The first ongoing "queer" depictions were in professional wrestling shows, a staple of early TV. One of the most famous television personalities was Gorgeous George, a hulking, sissified "villain" wrestler. George and his imitators made a fortune acting out gay stereotypes in the wrestling ring. In varying ways, other types of shows also marked homosexuality and gender nonconformity as a worrisome form of otherness, whose mere mention on television was somehow an act of naughtiness. What started as a cultural taboo quickly became an official act of transgression. In 1952, the major networks adopted a set of decency rules called the Television Code. Among other things, the Code prohibited depicting sex crimes and "sex abnormalities" and ruled that "illicit" sex relations could not be presented sympathetically. Despite this, shows could still play with LGBT stereotypes as long as there was no hint of actual same-sex desire.

Some male comedians got big laughs by lisping, mincing and flailing their wrists, or acting giddy and effeminate on screen. Sitcoms and dramas sporadically presented prissy male secretaries, florists, gossip columnists, and fashion photographers as objects of ridicule or scorn. Their professions marked them as different as clearly as did their speech and mannerisms. The most famous of these roles was comedian Ernie Kovacs's regular character of Percy Dovetonsils, a purse-lipped, lisping Greenwich Village poet. Lesbians were only depicted later.

Clearer references slipped through when sexual and gender minorities were in the news. Starting in 1952, after headlines announced that Danish surgeons had successfully turned American George Jorgensen into Christine Jorgensen, there were prime-time jokes about Denmark and gender-reassignment surgery. Jorgensen herself made some TV appearances in the 1950s as the first celebrity transsexual. After 1954's televised Army-McCarthy hearings discussed male homosexuality as a threat to national security, the subject of gay men migrated to talk shows, then drama scripts. TV dramas' rare gay roles were supporting characters whose gayness was conveyed in indirect ways. They had fey speech patterns and gestures, and other characters referred to them as "perfumed," "delicate," and so on. In the late fifties, sketch-comedy shows were allowed a bit more leeway in portraying both sissies and topical humor about gay men. However, even taken together, all of these types of visibility did not amount to much. For the average person watching television day to day in 1950s America, there was no affirmation or acknowledgment of sexual or gender minorities.

Only in the mid-1960s would a more sustained visibility develop. Even then, it was indirect visibility and almost exclusively portrayed gay men. Apparently, the only lesbian role in prime time in the 1960s was a psychiatric patient, a guest character on NBC's *The Eleventh Hour* in 1963.

From roughly 1963 to 1968, TV tended to refer to gay men as strange people who presumably existed somewhere off camera and whose mere mention was cause for laughter or concern. Television did not make jokes *about* homosexuality: homosexuality *was* the joke. In 1966, on *The Hollywood Palace*, Joan Rivers quipped that it was hard for women to meet a potential husband in show business, because "everybody you meet is either married (pause) or a dancer." Johnny Carson joked that in New York's tickertape parades, after the motorcade goes down Wall Street and businessmen throw memoranda out the windows, the hero reaches Greenwich Village, where the businessmen throw kisses. In a Christmas show, the

Monkees camped it up and flicked their wrists while singing "Don we now our *gay* apparel." Dramas like *Espionage* and *The Nurses* could depict homophobia, as long as the targeted guest character was a wrongly victimized straight man. In other words, gay people could be talked about or laughed at but could not appear on screen as three-dimensional people.

Even so, many viewers interpreted some prime-time characters as gay. Often, people would speculate—seriously or in jest—about characters like Miss Hathaway, the "old maid" banking assistant on *The Beverly Hillbillies*; Dr. Smith, the cowardly, campy, high-strung villain on *Lost in Space*; or Batman and Robin. Dialogue clearly marked most of these characters as straight. Only in an era of profound invisibility could they stand out as leading lights of gay visibility.

When talk shows from the 1950s to the mid-1960s discussed sexual minorities (again, usually male homosexuality), the producers invited psychiatrists, vice squad police, and criminologists to speak as the experts. Seldom were open LGBT people allowed to speak for themselves. When they were, they had to debate doctors and other authorities whom most viewers would take more seriously. The best a panelist could hope for was to appear with liberal therapists who believed that homosexuality was only a minor illness and that gay people deserved pity, not punishment.

An Era of Social Change

All that changed around 1967, amid the sudden growth of syndicated talk shows. Programs like David Susskind's and Phil Donahue's sometimes had gay men and lesbians as the sole guests. Bisexual and transgender people broke into the talk show circuit in noticeable numbers in the 1970s, but as early as 1967 Christine Jorgensen could get television bookings to promote her new autobiography. Finally, LGBT people were being listened to rather than talked about behind their backs.

For prime-time television, the breakthrough year for gay male visibility was 1967. That March, *CBS Reports* broadcast its much-hyped, long-delayed documentary, "The Homosexuals." It portrayed gay men as unhappy, lonely, sex-obsessed, and troubled. However, at least they were finally considered palatable enough to show on camera on a major network at an hour when people would be watching. That fall, ABC's police drama *NYPD* debuted with a gay-positive episode about criminals who extort money from closeted gay men. It marked the first time a TV character identified himself as "a homosexual." *NYPD* was not the only series of the 1960s or 1970s to deal with homosexuality in its pilot or first regular-production episode. *Alice, WKRP in Cincinnati,* and others did the same, presumably to make clear up front what a hip, daring, topical series it would be. Except for *NYPD,* such series almost never dealt with sexual minorities after that initial episode.

In the 1960s, the show that did the most to accustom viewers to gay references was the hit sketch-comedy series *Rowan and Martin's Laugh-in* (NBC, 1968–1973). Almost every *Laugh-in* featured gay or transsexual jokes and sissy characters (as usual, however, gay women were ignored). The premiere included allusions to an alleged gay scandal in California governor Ronald Reagan's cabinet and poked fun at the supposed homosexuality of effeminate singer Tiny Tim. "Well," said cohost Dan Rowan after Tim's performance, "it kept him out of the service." Dick Martin replied, "I bet the *Army* burned *his* draft card." Series regular Alan Sues played a string of bubbly, lovable, camp-queen characters, including swishy sportscaster Big Al and a prisoner apparently involved with his cellmate.

To capitalize on the rapid social changes of the early 1970s, TV writers sought nonthreatening ways to incorporate controversial subjects into familiar genres. "Relevance" was the industry's new buzzword. Even advertising agencies were open to controversial scripts, since many advertisers suddenly preferred reaching young, college-educated urban audiences, who were perceived as interested in the era's social-change movements. At the height of "relevance," ABC aired a landmark TV movie about a divorced gay father: 1972's *That Certain Summer,* starring Hal Holbrook and Martin Sheen. Its success in the Nielsen ratings and at the Emmy Awards proved that gay content was viable in prime time. Nonetheless, such TV movies remained rare. Instead, gay guest characters—mostly gay men—were incorporated into 1970s series through two main types of scripts: coming-out stories and stories about gay villains.

The coming-out stories preached that one cannot spot a homosexual just by looking, and that lesbian and gay people are as trustworthy as anyone else. The lesbian and gay guest characters were gender conformists: macho, athletic men who were often former pro football players, and feminine lesbians who were teachers or health-care workers. Their roles usually were a straight regular's relative or old friend. Typically, the lesbian or gay character came out just before the mid-show commercial, the straight regular reacted badly, and they reconciled before the closing credits. The lesbian or gay person was not in a relationship, nor was there any indication that he or she knew other homosexual people. A viewer knew these people were lesbian or gay because the dialogue *said* so, but it was invariably a very theoretical kind of homosexuality. Among sitcoms, Norman Lear's revolutionary, issue-oriented *All in the Family* pioneered this formula in 1971, and other sitcoms imitated it for the next decade. A variation of the coming-out script had a show's protagonist interested romantically in a guest character who turns out to be lesbian or gay. Here homosexuality was defined negatively, as the inability to love someone of the other sex rather than the ability to love someone of the same sex. Such portrayals turned up on *Medical Center, The Mary Tyler Moore Show,* and the sitcom *The Practice,* among many others. Whether an old friend or an unavailable potential lover, the lesbian or gay character never was heard from again after the one episode.

LGBT Villains

Scripts featuring lesbian and gay villains allowed more varied plots and characterizations. It was easy to spot "bad" lesbian and gay characters: unlike "good" lesbian and gay people, they had a sex drive and could be in long-term relationships. In the 1970s, lesbian characters in TV dramas were far more likely to turn up as violent criminals than in any other context. The trend toward queer villains peaked in the fall 1974 TV season, when a half-dozen nationally aired dramas portrayed sexual-minority characters. *All* were violent criminals, from a child-raping male teacher on *Marcus Welby, M.D.* to three lecherous, deadly lesbians on *Police Woman*; from a lustful male couple who worked together as hit men on *Harry O* to a murderous drag performer with multiple personality disorder on *The Streets of San Francisco.* The uniformly unsavory portrayals convinced some prominent lesbian and gay organizations to make media activism a priority.

Lesbian and gay activists had targeted entertainment shows as early as 1970, when the New York–based Gay Activists Alliance tried to open negotiations with the producers of *The Tonight Show* and *The Dick Cavett Show.* (In the latter case, they succeeded: several gay activists appeared on Cavett's show.) In 1973, NBC began using the Gay Media Task Force (GMTF) as a technical consultant on scripts that included LGBT characters and references. However, lesbian and gay groups in different parts of the country seldom talked to one another or worked together. That changed after the prime-time portrayals started to turn ugly. In late 1974, television inspired the gay liberation movement's first coordinated, national campaigns. Tactics included sit-ins, picketing, and letter-writing campaigns. Activists pressured sponsors and built alliances with such professional organizations as the American Psychiatric Association, which then contacted the networks to raise concerns.

In the mid-1970s, the New York–based National Gay Task Force and the Los Angeles–based GMTF met with high-ranking executives from all of the networks and most of the major production companies. Given recent portrayals, their argument was easy to make. Most executives were willing to concede that the depictions of LGBT people had become very lopsided. The activists handed out an eight-point platform that asked the networks to use the same guidelines for lesbian and gay characters as for other minorities. "Homosexuality isn't funny," it began. "Sometimes, of course, anything can be a source of humor. But the lives of twenty million Americans are not a joke." "If all blacks (or Jews, Irish, Chicanos, etc.) were presented as anguished, oddball or insane, blacks (etc.) would be angry," it said. "Gays are angry." By late 1975, the three major networks agreed to run all relevant scripts past GMTF for suggestions. This practice continued into the 1980s. Newt Deiter, the driving force behind GMTF, insisted that he did not want only saintly, heroic, or non-stereotyped characters. LGBT criminals were fine, he said, as long as there were LGBT cops as well. Stereotypes were fine—butch lesbians and screaming queens do exist—as long as there are also other portrayals.

The negotiations paid off. The criminal characters vanished almost completely, replaced by more sympathetic (and often more complex) roles. In the fall of 1976, numerous TV episodes featured likeable gay roles, and the sitcom *The Nancy Walker Show* had a gay male regular character. *Newsweek* and *TV Guide* called 1976 television's "Year of the Gay." The swing toward sympathetic roles continued in the late 1970s, when the newly politicized Religious Right movement mounted a well-publicized crusade against LGBT people's civil rights. Antigay organizers like Anita Bryant were making blatant statements on national TV, encouraging discrimination in employment and housing. Their campaigns turned "gay rights" into one of the top news stories of 1977 and 1978. One could hardly turn on a television or pick up a magazine or newspaper without hearing about Bryant's crusade and the LGBT-friendly backlash it was generating in some areas. For years, activists had struggled to convince the public that homosexuals were a legitimate minority that faced oppression. Bryant and California state senator John Briggs succeeded where gay organizers had failed: they convinced the media to reconceptualize homosexuality as a civil rights issue. The assassination of openly gay politician Harvey Milk in 1978 added fuel to the fire. From 1977 to 1980, lesbian and gay characters on TV were saintly, put-upon, squeaky-clean characters who were—as often as not—fighting prejudice and discrimination.

During this period, ABC's serialized sitcom *Soap* premiered. Regulars included openly gay Jodie, played by comedian Billy Crystal. He was not the first gay regular on a series, but he was the first one on a hit show. He was also in a more prominent role and with a better developed character than previous gay regulars. Although Jodie dated a professional football quarterback for a time, he spent much of the 1977–1981 series involved with women, even though the dialogue continued to mark him as "gay" and "a homosexual." Around the same time, Norman Lear coproduced two syndicated comedies with groundbreaking roles. On *Mary Hartman, Mary Hartman*, Gloria DeHaven played Annie (aka Tippytoes), television's first openly bisexual regular. Meanwhile, on Lear's *All That Glitters*, future *Dallas* star Linda Gray played TV's first transsexual regular, a fashion model. Previously, transgenderism had only turned up in a handful of prime-time scripts, usually medical dramas. *All in the Family* had a recurring role in the mid-1970s—an implicitly gay drag performer named Beverly LaSalle (played by drag headliner Lori Shannon).

In 1979 and 1980, the networks considered several series with gay protagonists, and numerous gay-focused TV movies and specials. Scripts for such shows were flying in and out of the office of GMTF. Then, suddenly, all of those projects were canceled.

The Pullback

The 1980s were a time of political and moral conservatism. Early in the decade, the networks faced two strong incentives to pull back from gay TV characters. First, Ronald Reagan and a host of conservative candidates swept the 1980 elections. In many cases, candidates backed by Religious Right groups replaced liberal politicians who had held office for more than a decade. Network executives took this to mean that risqué or controversial shows no longer reflected public tastes. Word went out in Hollywood that scripts with sexual-minority roles were unwelcome. The second incentive to avoid such characters was the growing public awareness of AIDS, especially in 1982 and 1983. Here was a terrifying, oftentimes fatal disease whose means of transmission was unknown, and that seemed primarily to affect gay and bisexual men. An absolute public terror of being around (or even hearing about) gay people set in. The networks, which had switched largely to escapist entertainment, deemed gay men too depressing and frightening to portray on television.

However, ABC and NBC had already committed to two series with gay regulars. ABC's *Dynasty*—a prime-time soap about a ruthless oil magnate—debuted in

January 1981. The magnate's son, Steven Carrington, spent much of the series romantically and sexually involved with women, though the producers insisted that he was gay, not bisexual. According to Ed DeBlasio, whose job it was to turn *Dynasty* plotlines into scripts, the producers paired Steven with women during years when AIDS received heavy news coverage and paired him with men in between. NBC's *Love, Sidney* caused Religious Right groups to threaten sponsors with boycotts long before the sitcom's fall 1981 debut. It starred Tony Randall as the first gay title character on a TV series. Groups like the National Federation for Decency had fits over the idea of a middle-aged gay hero who helps his lodger—an unwed mother—raise the bastard baby she conceived in an affair with a married man. The morality groups called off their protests once they saw that the hero was rather closeted, permanently celibate, and just as morally conservative as they. It was one of the most family-oriented series of the early 1980s. Only shortly before its 1983 cancellation did it start to deal with Sidney's sexual orientation in concrete terms.

AIDS's impact on television was multifaceted. Behind the scenes, the deaths of many creative people and executives in the industry led to greater and more open support for LGBT equality and AIDS causes among TV professionals—especially starting in the late 1980s and early 1990s. On entertainment shows, before the fall of 1985 only *St. Elsewhere* had dealt with the disease in a gay or bisexual context. In 1982 and 1983, the networks mostly shunted AIDS and gay issues into newscasts while ignoring them in prime time. In the mid-1980s, around the time of Rock Hudson's death, a number of shows dealt with gay or bisexual characters with HIV or AIDS: most notably a late 1985 episode of CBS's *Trapper John, M.D.* and a landmark NBC TV movie, *An Early Frost*. AIDS also led—directly and indirectly—to more visibility for lesbian characters. Homosexuality was still useful as evidence of how edgy a show was, but gay men were more or less off limits. That left lesbians. No longer pigeonholed as killers, corpses, and victims of discrimination, lesbians began to appear in sitcom episodes. Increasingly, LGBT negotiating groups were led by women, so the networks and producers had more of an incentive and context for lesbian inclusiveness. The first series with a lesbian regular, a full sixteen years after TV's first gay male regular, was the short-lived 1988–1989 medical drama *HeartBeat*. By the end of the decade, no network had yet presented an openly bisexual or transgender regular.

The Queer 90s and Beyond

The 1990s were a revolutionary period in the diversification and growth of mainstream TV's LGBT images. Same-sex couples were increasingly visible. The old tendency to portray LGBT people as white, gay men in their twenties to forties began to break down, with more portrayals of lesbians, people of color, teenagers, and older characters. Yet the biggest change was the sheer number of depictions. Some fifty series had regular or recurring LGBT roles during this decade, more than twice the combined total for all previous decades. *L.A. Law* introduced TV's first bisexual regular, C.J. Lamb (Amanda Donohoe), whose two-second, on-screen kiss with a female coworker made headlines. At the time, in early 1991, the networks' only other ongoing LGBT roles were Blaine and Antoine, the campy snap-diva film critics on Fox's *In Living Color*. However, things changed quickly. *Roseanne*, one of the top-rated shows of the 1990s, eventually introduced no fewer than six recurring LGB roles, including same-sex couples and an elderly lesbian. The early and mid-1990s brought an explosion of queer characters. In 1996 alone, there were ongoing portrayals on *The Crew, Cybill, E.R., Ellen* (though not yet the title role), *Fired Up, Friends, High Society, Lush Life, Mad About You, Melrose Place, NYPD Blue, Party Girl, Party of Five, Relativity, Roseanne, The Simpsons, Spin City,* and *Unhappily Ever After,* and the daytime serials *All My Children* and *The City*. Gay male roles, at least, were so mainstream that even family-oriented shows like *Touched By an Angel* and *Dr. Quinn, Medicine Woman* could air gay-positive episodes.

The late 1990s brought series television's first out-and-proud lesbian and gay leading roles. Comedian Ellen DeGeneres's *Ellen* paved the way. In 1996, two years into its run, rumors circulated that the title character, Ellen Morgan, would come out. DeGeneres's own lesbianism was something of an open secret, and neither she nor the sitcom's writers thought her character's attempts at straight romance were convincing. ABC approved the idea pending acceptable scripts. However, the network kept stalling, finally approving the script in early 1997. The hour-long, star-laden coming-out episode in April pulled impressive Nielsen ratings, after which the show returned to its usual viewership levels. The coming out of both DeGeneres and her character neither helped nor hurt the show. When *Ellen* returned in the fall, it became an unprecedented lesbian romantic comedy. By midseason, however, the bitterness of the producers' battles with ABC censors over lesbian and gay content started to seep into the scripts. By spring 1998 the ratings dropped, and ABC cancelled *Ellen*. However, the precedent had been set. Over the next three years, at least three sitcoms would debut with openly gay protagonists, among them the wildly successful *Will and Grace*.

From 1999 to 2002, established characters on several shows came out mid-series. Notable examples include

Jack on *Dawson's Creek,* Willow on *Buffy the Vampire Slayer* and Dr. Kerry Weaver on *E.R.* These last two were notable for both the prominence of the characters and the nuanced, complex development of their love lives. In the 2001–2002 season, more than a half century into the networks' handling of LGBT images, a network series finally included a prominent transgender regular: a college professor played by Helen Shaver in CBS's drama *The Education of Max Bickford.*

In the early 2000s, the rise of the reality TV genre of game shows—*Survivor, Big Brother, The Amazing Race,* and so on—allowed viewers to get to know real-life lesbians and gay men on an ongoing basis. Building on the tradition of earlier PBS and cable "reality" shows, it has become almost a cliché to include out-of-the-closet participants.

Despite the increases in visibility, commercial networks continued to desexualize and in some ways marginalize LGBT figures. An obvious example is *Will and Grace,* touted for its gay inclusiveness. In its first four years, the sitcom's straight heroine had a well-developed love life, but audiences were shielded from her gay best friend's romances. Except for such unusual series as *Ellen* and *Buffy the Vampire Slayer,* ongoing LGBT characters always bordered on celibacy or lived their love lives safely off camera.

PBS and Mainstream Cable

Since the 1960s, public television has been a prime source of unapologetic, up-front portrayals of LGBT people. More recently, cable television, with its ability to "narrowcast" to specific target audiences, has also broken considerable ground in terms of portraying homosexuality, bisexuality, and—less often—transgenderism.

PBS grew out of the earlier NET, which had aired relatively gay-positive educational programming as early as 1961. When Congress created PBS in the late 1960s, its mission was to broadcast types of programs that were not commercially feasible on the major networks. These included documentaries and cultural shows, which were meant to include voices of underserved minorities. From the 1970s to the mid-1990s, PBS was almost the only venue for unapologetic LGBT content, whether in dramas such as *The War Widow* or in politically charged documentaries such as *The Times of Harvey Milk.* Much of PBS's queer-inclusive programming was imported from Britain. Notable examples include the TV movie *The Naked Civil Servant,* and such miniseries as *The Roads to Freedom, Brideshead Revisited,* and *Portrait of a Marriage.* In addition, many PBS stations bought other inclusive productions from the United Kingdom, such as *Oranges*

Setting a Precedent. Ellen Degeneres (shown here speaking onstage about the homophobic murder of Matthew Shepard) played a character who came out in a much-publicized April 1997 episode of her sitcom, *Ellen,* which then continued for one season as the first lesbian romantic comedy series on network television. [Getty Images]

Are Not the Only Fruit. Since the 1990s, however, cable stations have been overtaking PBS in this area, by not only being inclusive of LGBT people, but also actively courting them as a market.

Pushing the envelope has long been a selling point for cable TV. Premium channels like HBO and Showtime have traded on their uncensored content for decades as a subscription incentive. One way to prove that daring was to include sexual content not seen on mainstream TV, including same-sex activity. In the 1980s, that largely meant lesbian scenes in soft-core porn targeted at straight men. In the early 1980s, however, HBO began developing a weekly, no-holds-barred sitcom based on Armistead Maupin's *Tales of the City* novels. The books' LGBT characters were to be left intact, as was the casual portrayal of drug use. However, by the time the show was ready for casting, the mood of the country had changed, and the show was scrapped. There seemed no way to set it in the present in an era of AIDS and antidrug campaigns. (PBS aired a British production of *Tales of the City* a decade later.) HBO's rival, Showtime, ran its gay-inclusive sitcom *Brothers* from 1984 to 1989. It focused on three brothers, one of whom came out in the premiere. Cable's uncensored nature cut both ways though when it came to LGBT issues. Standup comedians—notably Eddie Murphy and Sam Kinison—were able to use AIDS as an excuse to spout hate-filled screeds. In the early 2000s, Showtime and other cable stations began explicitly courting LGBT viewers through shows like *Queer as Folk*, a drama series whose characters are almost all gay men or lesbians. HBO series have been willing to sexualize both sympathetic gay roles (as in *Six Feet Under*) and unsympathetic ones (as in the prison serial *Oz*).

Since the 1990s, even some advertiser-funded basic-cable stations have provided a level of LGBT inclusiveness not seen on the mainstream networks. MTV cable made a commitment to LGB inclusiveness and to promoting acceptance of sexual diversity. LGB housemates appeared in almost every season of the "reality-based soap opera" *The Real World,* though as of the early 2000s no openly transgender housemates have appeared. MTV's low-budget late-night serial/anthology series *Undressed* has portrayed many same-sex couples of diverse backgrounds and situations. In the late 1990s, amid heavy news coverage of the antigay murder of college student Matthew Shephard, MTV began promoting tolerance of LGB people in all sorts of shows as part of that network's "Stop The Hate" campaign. In the early 2000s, a few basic-cable shows such as the FX network's police drama *The Shield* were willing to show same-sex couples being affectionate and even sexual.

Niche Marketing

The growth of cable and home video machines in the late twentieth century changed the nature of television profoundly. Shows no longer had to be multimillion-dollar productions aimed at a broad viewership.

In New York City and Miami, Florida, where cable TV was in place as early as the 1970s, there were early shows created by and for LGBT people. The video committee of the Gay Activists Alliance created several documentaries about early 1970s LGBT events in New York, including the first Gay Pride Day. In Miami, the man behind the porn magazine *Blueboy* packaged a regular gay series that he sold to pay-TV outlets under several titles. Back in New York, the late 1970s and 1980s brought such cultural cable series as *Emerald City* and *Out in the '80s.* In the late 1980s and 1990s, several companies marketed gay cable "networks," which were actually branded, prerecorded programming blocks that aired at different times and dates in different cities. They had such names as Gay Cable Network and Gay Entertainment Television.

Innovations of the 1990s included *Network Q*, a monthly gay newsmagazine distributed on VHS via subscription. Shows by and for the community also appeared on PBS stations—notably *In the Life*, which debuted in 1992. Series such as *DykeTV* were distributed primarily to small educational cable outlets.

By 2000, slick, mainstream channels started to target LGBT people as a niche market. In 2000, Showtime cable launched a massive marketing and merchandising campaign for its U.S. adaptation of the British series *Queer as Folk*. It advertised the show via LGBT periodicals, booths at Pride Day events, and giveaways at LGBT film festivals. The series is generally credited with boosting Showtime's subscription levels. Through *Queer as Folk* and other programs, Showtime has positioned itself as *the* LGBT-friendly premium station.

Bibliography

Alwood, Edward. *Straight News: Gays, Lesbians, and the News Media.* New York: Columbia University Press, 1996.

Capsuto, Steven. *Alternate Channels: The Uncensored Story of Gay and Lesbian Images in Radio and Television, 1930s to the Present.* New York: Ballantine, 2000.

Gamson, Joshua. *Freaks Talk Back: Tabloid Talk Shows and Sexual Nonconformity.* Chicago: University of Chicago Press, 1998.

Gross, Larry. *Up from Invisibility: Lesbians, Gay Men, and the Media in America.* New York: Columbia University Press, 2001.

Johnson, Phylis, and Michael C. Keith. *Queer Airwaves: The Story of Gay and Lesbian Broadcasting.* Armonk, N.Y.: M.E. Sharpe, 2001.

Montgomery, Kathryn C. *Target: Prime Time: Advocacy Groups and the Struggle over Entertainment Television.* New York and Oxford: Oxford University Press, 1989.

Ringer, Jeffrey, ed. *Queer Words, Queer Images: Communication and the Construction of Homosexuality.* New York: New York University Press, 1994.

Tropiano, Stephen. *The Prime Time Closet: A History of Gays and Lesbians on TV.* New York: Applause, 2002.

Tyler, Parker. *Screening the Sexes: Homosexuality in the Movies.* New York: Holt, Rinehart and Winston, 1972.

Walters, Suzanna Danuta. *All the Rage: The Story of Gay Visibility in America.* Chicago: University of Chicago Press, 2001.

Steven Capsuto

See also ACTORS AND ACTRESSES; AIDS AND PEOPLE WITH AIDS; ADVERTISING; CENSORSHIP, OBSCENITY, AND PORNOGRAPHY LAW AND POLICY; COMEDY AND HUMOR; GAY ACTIVISTS ALLIANCE; ICONS; JORGENSEN, CHRISTINE; NATIONAL GAY AND LESBIAN TASK FORCE (NGLTF); NEW RIGHT.

THEATER AND PERFORMANCE

As with the arts in general, the performing arts have been a haven and arena of excellence for LGBT people. The worlds of theater and performance are no exception, and any listing of LGBT people's contributions to these lively arts would be long and include some of the most well-known and respected artists in their fields, from playwrights like Tennessee Williams and Tony Kushner to actors and actresses like Eva Le Gallienne, Cherry Jones, and Nathan Lane; costume designers like Irene Sharaff and William Ivey Long; directors like George C. Wolfe and Michael Mayer; and performance artists like Holly Hughes and Kate Bornstein.

What Is LGBT Theater?

Plays with central characters that are LGBT or deal in a substantial fashion with themes or issues of same-sex sexuality or transgenderism may safely be considered LGBT plays or theater. Some argue that an author, director, or actor's LGBT aesthetic or imprint is in many works that seemingly have little to do with LGBT subject matter or themes. Any full analysis of a work is surely enriched with a consideration of the creator's sexuality and gender identity, whether or not the work is overtly LGBT.

LGBT theater can also describe a group of fairly recent theater companies and artists. Arising after the Stonewall Riots in 1969, this largely community-based theater phenomenon can be seen as an agitprop arts movement that came about in part to satisfy LGBT people hungry to see more positive representations of themselves. Denied these images on television or in film, LGBT people began their own theaters, staging plays that arguably reflected their realities more accurately as well as extending their own community through the bonding experiences that come along with the intensive task of staging plays. Companies like The Other Side of Silence and The Glines in New York City or the Theater Rhinoceros in San Francisco were established across the country. Yet as defined above, the history of LGBT theater in America begins much earlier.

Early LGBT Theater

Ceremonies involving Native American *berdache* (or two-spirit people) are arguably the starting point of LGBT theater in America. Highly regarded by their tribes, these mixed gender individuals undertook a variety of roles, including performative ones, in their communities.

LGBT characters, subjects, and themes were dealt with in European and Asian dramas long before their American counterparts. A European legacy can be traced through plays from Christopher Marlowe's *Edward II* (1594) to such works as Carle Lionel Dauriac Armory's *The Gentleman of the Chrysanthemums* (1908). Likewise, in Asia as early as 1603, characters, themes, and aesthetics that today we would consider LGBT are found in kabuki dramas.

The first plays to be performed in the United States with LGBT content or characters were European imports. While LGBT people were most certainly involved in theater from the colonial period onward at all levels, from playwrights and directors to performers and producers, only a few, like nineteenth-century actress Charlotte Cushman and possibly actor Edwin Forrest, are recognized as LGBT today. The first known U.S. play with same-sex desire at its core is *At Saint Judas's*, by Henry Blake Fuller. Published in 1896, its Chicago-born author is best-known as a novelist. *At St. Judas's*, a highly stylized play, is a closet drama in that it appears to have been written for reading rather than performance and no record of performance is known to exist. It is also a closet drama in that it concerns the intense friendship between two men. With characters known simply as the Bride Groom and the Best Man, the play is set before a wedding ceremony where the Best Man confesses his obsessive love for the Bride Groom. Fuller's stage directions, which include changes in the postures of the figures in the stained glass windows, leave the final images of his allegorical play of same-sex desire ambiguous, but one of the men dies on a sword.

Broadway

The first Broadway plays with major LGBT characters and themes appeared in the 1920s. This decade also saw the establishment of censorship laws that forbade the production of such plays on these stages. In this period the plays staged on Broadway with major LGBT themes or characters were European in origin and concerned lesbian desire. Sholom's Asch's *The God of Vengeance*, first written in Yiddish in 1907 and presented in English on Broadway in 1923, concerns a Jewish family that runs a brothel out of its basement. The sheltered daughter of this religious home becomes involved with one of the female prostitutes. While the play had been successfully produced around the world, only after being translated into English and presented on Broadway did it attract much of an outcry over its content. *The Captive*, by Edouard Bourdet, translated from the French and presented on Broadway in 1926, concerns the pull a mysterious offstage female admirer has on a young bride. At the end of the play, the bride walks out on her husband.

The U.S. playwright who can rightly be credited with putting gay male characters center stage for the first time

Tennessee Williams. The playwright, whose poetic and introspective explorations of human frailties included references to homosexuality (some less veiled than others), makes an appearance onstage. [AP/Wide World Photos]

is Mae West. Primarily remembered for her over-the-top vampy film performances, West's career began on stage, where she was enormously successful as a performer and playwright. Her 1927 play *The Drag,* written under the pseudonym Jane Mast, concerns the hidden gay life of a newlywed who hosts a drag ball. Rife with period camp dialogue, a sea of swish characters, and medical and legal ponderings on the subject of same-sex desire, the play was never formally presented on Broadway, but its New Jersey production caused a scandal and contributed to West's arrest.

The production of *The Captive* on Broadway and the imminent threat of West's *The Drag* resulted in police raids of several Broadway productions on the night of 9 February 1927. These raids led to revision of the New York State penal code. Section 1140A was amended in 1927 to prohibit the production of stage plays "depicting or dealing with the subject of sex degeneracy or sex perversion." Known as the Wales Padlock Law, under it any commercial theater presenting such work could be padlocked for a year. While enforcement of the law was threatened more than carried out in the years to come, the law remained on the books until 1967.

Broadway can be read as a cultural barometer of America's taste and attitudes. Over the years it has had a tempestuous relationship with LGBT content but has produced many works with significant LGBT characters or concerns, including Lillian Hellman's *The Children's Hour* (1934), Robert Anderson's *Tea and Sympathy*

(1953), and Frank Marcus's *The Killing of Sister George* (1965). Harvey Fierstein's *Torch Song Trilogy* (1982) stands as an important coming-out play as well as one of Broadway's longest-running plays. More recently, such dramas as David Henry Hwang's *M. Butterfly* (1988), Tony Kushner's *Angels in America* (1993), and Richard Greenburg's *Take Me Out* (2003) have added to the legacy and diversity of LGBT works that have played Broadway.

Off-Broadway, Alternative, and Community Theaters
Like Broadway, Off-Broadway is also a commercial theater form. Its somewhat more adventurous reputation and audiences make it a potentially richer ground for LGBT theater work. In fact, the birth of the idea for a separate category of Off-Broadway theaters is credited to the 1958 production of Tennessee Williams's *Suddenly Last Summer,* whose central story revolves around the grisly death of its offstage gay character at the hands of a band of boy street urchins.

Mart Crowley's *Boys in the Band* (1968) is a landmark in LGBT plays as well as Off-Broadway theater, where it ran for over one thousand performances. In the play an eclectic group of gay men gather to celebrate a birthday at which a party game of telephone turns ugly. Off-Broadway has also produced any number of LGBT plays and playwrights from Maria Irene Fornes and Terrence McNally to works like Charles Busch's *Vampire Lesbians of Sodom* (1985) and John Cameron Mitchell's *Hedwig and the Angry Inch* (1998).

Like the Off-Broadway movement, the noncommercial Off-Off Broadway movement can also be credited to a gay man. Joe Cino and his Café Cino, which opened in 1958, are viewed as the creators of Off-Off Broadway. The stage of his small New York City coffee bar nurtured early works by LGBT dramatists, including Lanford Wilson, H. M. Koutoukas, Robert Patrick, and Jeff Weiss, as well as directors like Andy Milligan.

The post-Stonewall era saw the formation of any number of LGBT theater companies across America. Mainly community theaters, these groups dedicate themselves to the production of plays with LGBT content. Developing resilience in the face of discrimination, these groups assert independence through representation. Some of the better-known companies have included San Francisco's Theater Rhinoceros, New York City's W.O.W. Café and The Other Side of Silence (TOSOS), Los Angeles's Celebration Theater, and Minneapolis's Out and About Theater Company. These theaters have nurtured many original works, such as Jane Chambers's *Last Summer at Blue Fish Cove* (1980) and Ana Maria Simo's *Bayou* (1977).

Types of LGBT Plays

Today, the most obvious type of LGBT play is the coming-out play. In it characters reveal their sexuality to someone who does not know or come to accept themselves as worthwhile individuals. This type of play is exemplified by *Torch Song Trilogy*.

The LGBT problem play is another type. The sexuality of the character or characters is the work's central conflict or problem, which must be resolved. In many such problem plays, the LGBT character is eliminated by the final curtain in any number of ways, from suicide to sickness or murder. Closely related to the LGBT problem play is the conversion play. There, the LGBT character is tempted by a heteronormative life. *Tea and Sympathy* is the classic example of a conversion play. Common plot devices in all of these types include whispering campaigns or outright accusations, as well as denials and confessions.

LGBT history plays are works in which actual events in LGBT history are enacted. While the events are historical, the dialogue is largely fictitious. Such works include Doric Wilson's *Street Theater* (1982), about the Stonewall Riots, and Martin Sherman's *Bent* (1979), about the experience of LGBT prisoners in Nazi concentration camps. Related to this is the LGBT docudrama, in which a real life event in LGBT history is enacted and most dialogue is based on original source materials. Examples include Emily Mann's *Execution of Justice* (1984), about the mur-

Out of the Mainstream. Gay performance artists the Pomo Afro Homos wear their trademark hot pink polka-dotted costumes. [Jill Posener]

der trial of Dan White, the man who killed openly gay San Francisco city supervisor Harvey Milk, and Moisés Kaufman and the Tectonic Theater Company's *The Laramie Project* (2000), which deals with the brutal murder of gay student Matthew Shepard. His story brought the issue of hate crimes to the fore and the docudrama was the second most produced play in America during the 2001–2002 season.

A category of theater works particular to LGBT theater are "cute boys in their underpants" plays. These works are characterized by the inordinate amount of time the performers are asked to appear in varying stages of undress and in sexually suggestive or explicit situations.

AIDS hit the performing arts communities particularly hard. Many plays and theater pieces deal with the epidemic as a subject. AIDS plays include William Hoffman's lyrical *As Is* (1985), the first Broadway play to deal with the disease; Larry Kramer's angry Off-Broadway *The Normal Heart* (1985); Robert Chesley's *Jerker* (1986); and Harry Kondoleon's *Zero Positive* (1988). The theatrical community also responded to AIDS by founding organizations like Broadway Cares/Equity Fights AIDS, which raises money for AIDS-related services across America.

Angels in America. A scene from Tony Kushner's critically acclaimed 1993 Broadway hit. [corbis]

LGBT Performance

Performance or performance art is distinguished from theater in that it is frequently much more intimate and boundary breaking than traditional theater. Many of the form's best-known artists are LGBT. Frequently, their work is highly autobiographical and provides direct reflection and sly relation of their experiences as an LGBTQ person. The works of solo performance artists like Holly Hughes, Tim Miller, and Kate Bornstein tell stories and spin fantasies from their authors' lives. Miller's *Naked Breath* (1994) tells intimate stories of past boyfriends. Hughes's *World without End* (1989) looks at her queer Michigan childhood. Bornstein's *Virtually Yours* (1994) turns its transgender author and performer's life into an Internet game. Performance groups expressing a range of LGBT life experiences include Pomo Afro Homos, Medusa's Revenge, the Five Lesbian Brothers, and Split Britches.

In the 1990s the work of four performance artists who had received funding from the National Endowment of the Arts became the focus of a heated national debate about the content of tax-dollar-supported art. The work of three of the performance artists, Hughes, Miller, and John Fleck, dealt directly with LGBT subject matter and was labeled offensive and inappropriate for public monies by anti-LGBT activists and politicians. The NEA Four, as they became known, brought the issues of government funding, sexuality, and censorship dramatically to the foreground.

Varieties of Performance and Beyond

Recently, some scholars and artists have argued that everything can be studied as performance. Beyond nar-

rower notions of performance or performance art lies a large swath of live art that should be adopted into the tent of LGBT theater and performance. This type of LGBT performance work includes any situation in which a performer-audience relation exists. This expansive notion includes but is not limited to such things as pride parades and nightclub, ball, or circuit party experiences. An entire and little-examined tradition of fan dancing exists in the gay male community. LGBT choirs, like the Portland Lesbian Choir or Connecticut's Gay Men's Chorus, as well as male burlesque theaters, including the Gaiety in New York City or the Nob Hill in San Francisco, where men strip for the pleasure of other men, are also part of the tradition. The umbrella also properly shelters "passing" as straight and "reading" as gay as a type of performance. Bathhouses and cruising can also be thought about in this way. Gay stand-up comics, singers, and performers who play a wide range of comedy clubs, piano bars, and cabarets across the country should be brought in as well. Activist demonstrations and tactics are clearly theatrical and more than merit inclusion.

Arising out of private performances at parties and LGBT bars, drag performance is perhaps indigenous to LGBT peoples and is a type of performance most frequently and closely associated with them. Female impersonation has found an appeal in mainstream theater from the days of vaudeville female impersonators like Julian Eltinge and Karyl Norman to more recent examples like RuPaul. Variously outlawed and policed across the country at various times, the LGBT community has always supported and championed drag performers like Jose Sarria, Ethyl Eichelberger, and Lypsinka and drag theater troupes like San Francisco's The Cockettes and New York City's Theater Couture.

As the lines of identity politics shifted in the 1990s, the notion of queer theater, as distinct from lesbian or gay theater, gained popularity. Queer theater, like queer politics, is more in your face and aggressively skewed in aesthetics or approach than LGBT theater, much in the same way that theater is distinct from performance.

Is "LGBT" Still a Useful Category?

The tradition of LGBT theater and performance traces its origins deep into the taproots of U.S. drama. LGBT peoples have historically proven some of the genre's most elite and accomplished artists.

Plays with LGBT content can still cause protests and firestorms. However, as LGBT characters become an increasingly more integrated presence on stages, a call for a special category for LGBT plays or performance seems less and less useful. This has not always been the case. Immediately after the Stonewall Riots in 1969, the idea of a category of LGBT works, whether they be in theater, literature, or visual arts, took hold. As identity politics solidified, the notion of LGBT works was empowering and established a tradition. Artists of all types, however, like playwright and Ridiculous Theatrical Company founder Charles Ludlam, resist labels. They argue that the term LGBT theater ghettoizes their work.

Any play or performance should be judged on its own merits. Consideration of themes and sexuality are frequently relevant to a full appreciation or understanding. A great play or performance, however, is a great play or performance regardless of its themes or the sexuality of its creators or performers.

Bibliography

Brecht, Stefan. *Queer Theatre*. New York: Metheun, 1986.

Clum, John M. *Acting Gay: Male Homosexuality in Modern Drama*. New York: Columbia University Press, 1992.

———. *Something for the Boys: Musical Theatre and Gay Culture*. New York: Palgrave, 2001.

Curtin, Kaier. *"We Can Always Call Them Bulgarians": The Emergence of Lesbians and Gay Men on the American Stage*. Boston: Alyson, 1987.

De Jongh, Nicholas. *Not In Front of the Audience: Homosexuality on Stage*. New York: Routledge, 1992.

Koestenbaum, Wayne. *The Queen's Throat: Opera, Homosexuality, and the Mystery of Desire*. New York: Poseidon Press, 1993.

Lucas, Ian. *Impertinent Decorum: Gay Theatrical Manoeuvres*. New York: Cassell, 1994.

Marra, Kim, and Robert A. Schanke, eds. *Passing Performances: Queer Readings of Leading Players in American Theatre History*. Ann Arbor: University of Michigan Press, 1998.

Miller, Carl. *Stages of Desire: Gay Theatre's Hidden History*. New York: Cassell, 1996.

Miller, D. A. *Place for Us: Essay on the Broadway Musical*. Cambridge, Mass.: Harvard University Press, 2000.

Román, David. *Acts of Intervention: Performance, Gay Culture, and AIDS*. Bloomington: Indiana University Press, 1998.

Schanke, Robert A., and Kim Marra, eds. *Staging Desire: Queer Readings of American Theatre History*. Ann Arbor: University of Michigan Press, 2002.

Senelick, Laurence. *The Changing Room: Sex, Drag, and Theatre*. New York: Routledge, 2000.

Shewey, Don, ed. *Out Front: Contemporary Gay and Lesbian Plays*. New York: Grove Press, 1988.

Sinfield, Alan. *Out on Stage: Lesbian and Gay Theatre in the Twentieth Century*. New Haven, Conn.: Yale University Press, 1999.

Solomon, Alisa, and Framji Minwalla, eds. *The Queerest Art: Essays on Lesbian and Gay Theatre*. New York: New York University Press, 2002.

Joe E. Jeffreys

See also ACTORS AND ACTRESSES; ALBEE, EDWARD; BENNETT, MICHAEL; BOURBON, RAY (RAE); CENSORSHIP, OBSCENITY, AND PORNOGRAPHY LAW AND POLICY; CHAMBERS, JANE; CUSHMAN, CHARLOTTE; EICHELBERGER, ETHYL; ELTINGE, JULIAN; FIERSTEIN, HARVEY; FORNES, MARIA IRENE; HANSBERRY, LORRAINE; ICONS; KRAMER, LARRY; KUSHNER, TONY; LUDLAM, CHARLES; MCNALLY, TERRENCE; MUSIC: BROADWAY AND MUSICAL THEATER; PERFORMANCE, THEATER, AND DANCE STUDIES; PIÑERO, MIGUEL; POMA, EDGAR; REYES, RODRIGO; SÁNCHEZ, LUIS RAFAEL; SARRIA, JOSÉ; TAVERA, HANK; THURMAN, WALLACE; WILLIAMS, TENNESSEE; WILSON, LANFORD.

THEATER STUDIES. see PERFORMANCE, THEATER, AND DANCE STUDIES.

THIRD WORLD GAY REVOLUTION

Third World Gay Revolution was a product of the radical movements of the late 1960s and early 1970s that sought fundamental social change. It focused on oppression based on gender, sexuality, race and ethnicity, and class and pioneered in exploring how various oppressions interlocked.

The group began as a caucus of the New York City Gay Liberation Front (GLF) in 1970. Founded in the aftermath of the June 1969 Stonewall riots, GLF believed that heterosexism should be fought not by reforming existing institutions, but through revolutionary changes in social structure and ideology. Members advocated increasing queer visibility through coming out and direct action protest, building coalitions with other leftist groups that believed socialism would lead to a more just society, and changing oppressive sexual ideas and practices. GLFs soon appeared in cities across the country. Some members, however, felt that the GLF was not doing enough to deal with multiple forms of oppression and that, in fact, it replicated some of those oppressions. They decided to deal with this problem by either forming caucuses within local chapters or establishing their own groups. Third World Gay Revolution was one of several caucuses and independent groups that were spawned by the New York City chapter in 1970. Others focused on women, youth, and transgendered people. Nonwhites created their own groups in at least two other cities with GLF chapters, Chicago and Detroit. Other queer political organizations of the period, such as the Gay Activists Alliance, had similar experiences.

Relations with the Black Panthers

Soon after Third World Gay Revolution formed, its black and Latino members engaged in several activities, such as organizing consciousness-raising groups, that increased the group's visibility. Third World Gay Revolution was probably best known for its involvement in the 1970 Revolutionary People's Constitutional Convention, which was organized by the Black Panther Party. The Black Panthers, a group founded by Huey Newton and Bobby Seale in Oakland in 1966, advocated black economic, political, and cultural self-determination through socialist revolution. Before the convention, the Panthers invited sexual and gender liberation activists to participate in an attempt to build a broad-based coalition of people who supported their agenda. Newton, in a letter originally published in the Black Panther newspaper in August 1970 and subsequently reprinted in several leftist and queer periodicals, called on revolutionaries to rethink their ideas about women and homosexuals. He saw both groups as being among the most oppressed in society and argued that they should be respected and welcomed into the liberation movement, not denigrated and cast out. He believed that the sexes were equal and that people should have the right to use their bodies as they wished. This was very different from what other Panthers had been saying about homosexuals. Eldridge Cleaver and Bobby Seale, for example, both claimed that homosexuality was a result of capitalist decadence and saw no place for it in the brave new world they were trying to create. While Newton admitted that he did not fully understand the issue, he was willing to learn more and include sexuality and gender on his agenda for revolutionary social change.

Encouraged by Newton, members of Third World Gay Revolution and other sexual and gender liberation activists became involved in a variety of convention-related activities. These and subsequent interactions with the Panthers and with other black nationalists, however, showed that while some took queer and gender activists seriously and valued their involvement, not everyone shared Newton's views regarding sexuality and gender. At events, queers and feminists sometimes encountered ridicule or hostility. This led to racial tensions between Third World Gay Revolution members, who wanted to continue supporting the Panthers and officially proclaim them as "the vanguard of the people's revolution in Amerikkka," and those sexual and gender liberationists who did not.

Blueprint for a Queer Revolution

It was within the context of these convention activities that Third World Gay Revolution formulated its best-known position statements, "3rd World Gay Revolution Platform" and "The Oppressed Shall Not Become the Oppressor." Both leaflets were reprinted in various forms in several underground periodicals and early gay liberation anthologies. Other Third World caucuses also published their ideas. "Gay Revolution and Sex Roles," co-written by Third World Gay Revolution and the GLF in Chicago, was another widely distributed tract. Together, these statements explored how various oppressions—particularly racism, sexism, and heterosexism—intersected and how they should be dealt with. Third World queers believed that a person should have the right to use their bodies for sex and/or reproduction, and to dress as they wished; that traditional gender roles oppressed both women and homosexuals; and that oppressive institutions like the nuclear family, organized religion, and capitalism should be abolished. They were also critical of revolutionaries who engaged in oppressive practices. They challenged white and male gay liberationists, as well as black nationalists, on their racism, sexism, and heterosexism. This did not prevent them, however, from borrowing ideas they thought were promising from those whose revolutionary consciousness supposedly needed work. Third World Gay Revolution's platform, for example, mirrored the Black Panther Party's Ten Point Platform and Program, which called for, among other demands, socialism as a means to achieve self-determination and control over one's communities, full employment, guaranteed income, good housing, fair trials, and an end to police brutality. The adjustments Third World Gay Revolution made to the Panthers' platform reflected its concerns about sexism and heterosexism.

Little was heard from Third World Gay Revolution or the other caucuses after they published these statements. Presumably, they did not survive the collapse of the GLF and other groups advocating radical approaches to sexual freedom in the early 1970s. They are important, however, in that they were among the first to focus on addressing the political issues of and creating communities among queer people of color. They were also among the first to explore the interlocking nature of various forms of oppression and to see consciousness raising as a key liberation strategy. Others—such as the black feminists who were part of the Combahee River Collective of the mid-1970s— would further develop these ideas.

Bibliography

Jay, Karla, and Allen Young. *Out of the Closets: Voices of Gay Liberation.* 2d ed. New York: New York University Press, 1992.

Kissack, Terence. "Freaking Fag Revolutionaries: New York's Gay Liberation Front, 1969–1971." *Radical History Review* 62 (1995): 104–134.

Lane, Alycee J. "Newton's Law." *BLK* (March 1991): 11–15.

Marota, Toby. *The Politics of Homosexuality.* Boston: Houghton Mifflin, 1981.

Teal, Donn. *The Gay Militants: How Gay Liberation Began in America, 1969–1971.* New York: St. Martin's Press, 1994.

Third World Gay Revolution (New York City). "The Oppressed Shall Not Become the Oppressor." In *We Are Everywhere: A Historical Sourcebook of Gay and Lesbian Politics.* Edited by Mark Blasius and Shane Phelan. New York: Routledge, 1997.

Third World Gay Revolution. "3rd World Gay Revolution: 16 Point Platform and Program." *Kaleidoscope* 4 (January 1971): 8.

Gregory Conerly

See also GAY LIBERATION; GAY LIBERATION FRONT.

THOMAS, M. Carey (b. 2 January 1857; d. 2 December 1935), educator, feminist.

M. Carey Thomas was born in Baltimore, Maryland, the daughter of prominent Quakers and reformers. A lively girl, Thomas was nurtured in the close-knit world of her deeply religious family. Convalescence after a life-threatening burn at age seven turned her to reading. At age fifteen she entered the Howland School, an academy for girls in Union Springs, New York. After graduation and additional preparation at home, she went to Cornell University, graduating in two years, receiving a B.A. degree in 1877.

Returning to Baltimore, Thomas entered the graduate program of Johns Hopkins University. Discouraged because women could not attend seminars, she withdrew

after a year and studied at home. In this period she formed intimate friendships with Mamie Gwinn and Mary Garrett, daughters of powerful and wealthy men. The three joined with two other friends to form the Friday Evening Club. Their discussions of music, art, poetry, and sexuality helped shape Thomas's enthusiasms for the rest of her life. In 1885 the five women created the Bryn Mawr School for Girls in Baltimore, and in 1889 four of them developed the campaign to endow the planned Johns Hopkins medical school and guarantee that it would be a graduate medical school open to women. In fact, it opened on a coeducational basis in 1892.

In 1879 Thomas traveled with Gwinn to study philology at Leipzig University in Germany, where as a woman Thomas could not receive a degree. She moved to the University of Zurich in Switzerland, where in 1882 she received her Ph.D. *summa cum laude.* In the years abroad, Thomas and Gwinn reveled in their aesthetic passions, especially in the poems of Algernon Charles Swinburne and Pre-Raphaelite paintings. At this point in their understanding of sexuality, Thomas and Gwinn had no comprehension of the new medical discussion of lesbianism, but they loved each other deeply and likened their relationship to a marriage.

Prior to their return to Baltimore, family news had informed them of the founding of Bryn Mawr College outside of Philadelphia, and Thomas began her campaign to be named president. In 1884 the trustees chose a male president and created for her the office of dean. In that position she turned the tiny college into a center of scholarship through high entrance requirements, a graduate school, and the gathering of a distinguished faculty. As professor of English, Thomas taught the required lecture course in literature and took Gwinn as her first graduate student and teaching assistant. The two lived in the Deanery, the house on campus that was Thomas's home until late in her life. In 1893, as Thomas continued her life in the Deanery with Gwinn, Thomas and Mary Garrett became passionately involved and committed to each other. Garrett, perhaps the wealthiest woman in her own name in the United States, offered the college $10,000 for each year that Thomas served as president, an offer the trustees accepted when they appointed Thomas to the position in 1895. Thomas served until her retirement in 1922.

As Thomas's commitment to Garrett deepened, Gwinn fell in love with Alfred Hodder. (The story of the Thomas-Gwinn-Hodder triangle is the springboard for Gertrude Stein's novella, *Fernhurst*, published in 1971.) Through the Oscar Wilde trial in England and the new medical literature, particularly the work of Richard von Krafft-Ebing, Thomas learned new understandings of homosexuality. Always passionate, she now came to understand herself as lesbian. She had been used to hiding her aesthetic enthusiasms from Quaker eyes. With her new sexual knowledge, she did not alter her relationships, but she did intensify her use of upper-class privilege to shield her private life from public view.

Thomas's early years as president were difficult, for she served under an all-male board that attempted to hold the college to its religious origins and opposed her desire for expansion. As Thomas became a national educational figure, she used her growing celebrity to overcome trustee conservatism. The college built one of the finest examples of collegiate gothic in the United States, sustained its intellectual quality, and added women professors to its largely male faculty. In her final years as president, Thomas supported new progressive programs, including the Summer School for Women Workers in Industry. Thomas believed in women, science, and progress; with many of her era, she joined those commitments to nativism, racism, and anti-Semitism. Within the institutions she served, she sought to limit opportunity to white Protestants of British descent. Although narrow and calculating, she could be visionary, and she spoke brilliantly about women, higher education, and creativity.

In the years following retirement, she focused on creating facilities for women to study abroad. A suffrage advocate, she headed the National College Equal Suffrage League, and in the 1920s supported an equal rights amendment to the U.S. Constitution. Honors came to her in abundance, including an honorary LL.D. from Johns Hopkins in 1922. She spoke in public for the last time at Bryn Mawr College's fiftieth anniversary commemoration in November 1935. She died in Blue Ridge Summit, Pennsylvania.

Bibliography

Finch, Edith. *Carey Thomas of Bryn Mawr*. New York: Harper and Brothers, 1947.

Horowitz, Helen Lefkowitz. *The Power and Passion of M. Carey Thomas*. New York: Knopf, 1994.

Thomas, M. Carey. *The Papers of M. Carey Thomas in the Bryn Mawr College Archives*. Edited by Lucy Fisher West. Woodbridge, Conn.: Research Publications, 1982. Microfilm.

Helen Lefkowitz Horowitz

See also COLLEGES AND UNIVERSITIES; FEMINISM; SAME-SEX INSTITUTIONS; SHAW, ANNA HOWARD; SMASHES AND CHUMMING; STEIN, GERTRUDE, AND ALICE B. TOKLAS.

THOMPSON, Frances (b. ?; d. 1 November 1867), slave and freedwoman.

As a freedwoman, Thompson negotiated the urban public space of Memphis, Tennessee, with courage and fortitude. One of five African American women to testify before a U.S. congressional committee investigating the Memphis riots that took place from 1 May to 3 May 1866, Thompson recounted her experience of sexual violence inflicted by a group of white men.

Although little is known about Thompson's life, including her place and date of birth, scholarship argues that Thompson was anatomically male. Her early life was spent in Maryland as an enslaved person. By 1866, after the Civil War and emancipation, Thompson lived in South Memphis, Tennessee, with Lucy Smith, another former enslaved woman. Both women engaged in work typically designated as African American women's labor; they laundered, sewed, and ironed to maintain themselves.

During the riots, Irish policemen and firemen, along with white laborers and small businessmen, attacked black residents of the shanty settlement near Fort Pickering, a Union military installation on the outskirts of the city. Although the rioters first focused on former black soldiers, they eventually targeted civic institutions and property in the black community where Thompson and Smith lived. The riots erupted in a city whose African American occupants were still negotiating their freedom to appear in public places. Some lower-class white men, including the policemen, resisted this new utilization of city streets and other public venues, and the violent consequences of the riots demonstrated the volatile atmosphere of one southern city in the early Reconstruction era.

On one night of the riots, seven white men stormed into Thompson and Smith's home demanding food, money, and sexual favors, and questioned the women about their relationships with African American Union soldiers. The women's connection to the soldiers, indicated by the red, white, and blue quilts they had made for them, inspired further violence by their attackers. The long history of the desexualization and hypersexualization of African American women remains central to an understanding of the riots. By raping African American women and targeting those who maintained relationships with black Union soldiers, the rioters attempted to reassert the superiority of white manhood and the debasement of black womanhood.

In her testimony before the congressional committee, Thompson recalled that, after demanding food, the men insisted on sexual appeasement. Although she resisted these requests by asserting that she and Smith were respectable, she was beaten by one rioter and raped by four. Emphasizing the dishonorable conduct of the white rioters, the committee's final report was circulated and excerpted in newspapers throughout the United States to demonstrate that the South was not prepared for self-rule and to underscore the need for radical Reconstruction politics under the leadership of the Republican Party. The women's testimony also validated the rights of black women to attest to their sexual misuse.

In 1876, ten years after giving her testimony, Thompson was arrested for cross-dressing. Sensationalized in the local press, her arrest provided conservative whites with the necessary ammunition to discredit the earlier rape testimonies. Her transgender identity was utilized to denounce both the earlier assertion of black southern womanhood as respectable and radical Republican politics. As Thompson's own statement had figured prominently in the committee report, conservative forces utilized this news to re-ascribe value to racist ideas of black women's lascivious sexuality. Thompson's transgender reality was exploited to prove that black women were truly excluded from the realm of southern womanhood, which, at its center, mandated respectability and virtue. The conservative media did not evoke the rhetoric of transgender behavior as being bizarre to discredit Thompson's testimony. Rather, the press engaged her transgender status to denounce her womanhood and declare untrue the testimony of all five women.

Thompson suffered greatly from the discovery of her biological sex. Forced into men's clothing, she spent one hundred days doing hard labor under the scrutinizing and scornful eyes of media-informed crowds. After her release from prison, Thompson was found in a cabin in North Memphis, alone and gravely ill. Community members assisted her, moving her to the city hospital, where she died with dignity. Despite Thompson's unfortunate end, her life as a woman contributed to the assertion of African American women's rights as citizens. Her testimony about the brutality experienced at the hands of five white men elucidates an important moment in the history of the American South, when black women were finally recognized as deserving the full rights of citizenship. Anatomically a man who lived as a woman, Thompson is proof that, despite the social and legal parameters that made transgender living dangerous and difficult, some courageous individuals found ways to express their innate gendered realities.

Bibliography

Hardwicke, Kevin R. "'Your Old Father Abe Lincoln Is Dead and Damned': Black Soldiers and the Memphis Race Riot of 1866." In *A Question of Manhood: A Reader in U.S. Black Men's History and Masculinity.* Vol. 2, *The Nineteenth Cen-*

tury: From Emancipation to Jim Crow. Edited by Darlene Clark Hine and Earnestine Jenkins. Bloomington: Indiana University Press, 2001.

Rosen, Hannah. "'Not That Sort of Women': Race, Gender, and Sexual Violence during the Memphis Riot of 1866." In *Sex, Love, Race: Crossing Boundaries in North American History.* Edited by Martha Hodes. New York: New York University Press, 1999.

"Testimony of Frances Thompson." In *Memphis Riots and Massacres,* 39th Cong., 1st sess., 1865–1866, H. Rept. 101, 196–197.

                                                    Laila S. Haidarali

See also SLAVERY AND EMANCIPATION; TRANSSEXUALS, TRANSVESTITES, TRANSGENDER PEOPLE, AND CROSS-DRESSERS; WAR.

THOMSON, Virgil (b. 25 November 1896; d. 30 September 1989), composer, music critic, author.

Although less recognized than colleagues like Aaron Copland, Leonard Bernstein, and Ned Rorem, Virgil Thomson may well have been the most brilliant and influential member of a remarkably brilliant and influential group of New York–based queer modernist composers. In the 1930s and 1940s this circle—which also included Marc Blitzstein, Paul Bowles, and David Diamond—largely defined the idiom heard even today as "America's sound," most famously in works like Copland's *Billy the Kid* (1938), *Rodeo* (1942), and *Appalachian Spring* (1944).

This American sound has roots in Thomson's creative epiphany of 1926. Inspired by dada and by lesbian writer Gertrude Stein's artistic method of "spontaneity," he conceived a musical language based on simplicity, tonality, and indigenous folkish tunes—by contrast to the standard modernist fare of the day, which was dissonant, complex, and difficult. Thomson's first major work in this idiom was a groundbreaking American opera, *Four Saints in Three Acts* (1928), the first of two operatic collaborations with Stein. For all the simple and vernacular elements of its textual and musical language, *Four Saints* was a decidedly avant-garde work, presenting some thirty saints—real and imaginary, in the form of sixteenth-century Spanish nuns and monks—within four acts eschewing plot, narrative, and any indicated action. Its 1934 premiere was a cause célèbre, and the opera has been an important touchstone for other American artists, including Philip Glass. But *Four Saints* never had the broad appeal of a work like *Appalachian Spring,* with its more conventional themes (as bestowed by modern dance choreographer Martha Graham) of pioneer life and work, and heterosexual love and marriage, on the American prairie.

Virgil Thomson. A 1984 photograph of the influential avant-garde composer and music critic, best known for his opera *Four Saints in Three Acts* (1928), a collaboration with Gertrude Stein.
[Richard Schulman/corbis]

Thomson grew up in Kansas City, where he played the organ at Calvary Baptist Church. After military service during World War I, he studied music at Harvard College, and then at Fontainebleau near Paris with the greatest composition teacher of the century, Nadia Boulanger. A resident of Paris for much of the 1920s and 1930s, Thomson was part of the city's thriving expatriate arts and literary scene up until the Nazi invasion in 1940. Making passage to New York, he settled into an apartment in the Chelsea Hotel (home to queer artists and bohemians including Tennessee Williams, William S. Burroughs, and Robert Mapplethorpe) and resided there until his death nearly a half-century later. Throughout most of his life Thomson enjoyed a primary relationship (1925–1986) with Maurice Grosser, a realist painter and the scenarist for *Four Saints*.

As a composer Thomson was renowned for his masterful prosody—for the naturalism and dramatic effectiveness of his musical settings of the English language. Less appreciated is the considerable extent to which this urbane "fairy" composer pioneered the music of spare and virile Americanism, that sound of prairie cowboys and western plains now ubiquitous via Copland's compositions and in radio, television, and movie soundtracks. These idioms and their associations with Americana landscapes and characters derive substantially from Thomson's musical settings in *Four Saints*, in Depression-era documentary films *The Plow that Broke the Plains* (1936) and *The River* (1937), and in his ballet *Filling Station* (1937). Still less recognized is the degree to which Thomson encoded queer meanings in his compositions, including *Four Saints* and various other works on religious themes and texts; as well as his second opera with Stein, *The Mother of Us All* (1947), treating the life and work of Susan B. Anthony and her partner in life and work Elizabeth Cady Stanton; and a final opera, *Lord Byron* (1972), written with the gay poet-playwright Jack Larson.

During his lifetime Thomson was best known for his work as a critic. His was a singular voice in musical commentary, a potent combination of Kansas City plain speech and Parisian wit and elegance. Throughout his 1940–1954 tenure as chief music critic for the *New York Herald Tribune*, Thomson's trenchant observations and lucid, cogent style helped to make him the most important music critic in America. So did his unorthodox approach, equally erudite and demotic: Thomson was as likely to review the Easter Sunday service of an electric-guitar-playing Harlem preacher as a symphony concert or Met program.

Thomson's oeuvre includes over 150 musical portraits—comparable to Stein's verbal portraits—composed from live sittings with nearly all his colleagues, friends, and lovers, as well as other subjects, from the 1920s through 1980s. The author of several books on music and composers, Thomson also published a 1966 memoir, *Virgil Thomson by Virgil Thomson*. His many honors and awards included the 1949 Pulitzer Prize in music for *Louisiana Story*, the first Pulitzer awarded to a film score, and 1983 Kennedy Center Honors for lifetime achievement in the arts.

Bibliography

Hubbs, Nadine. *Composing Oneself: Gay Modernists, American Music, and National Identity.* Berkeley: University of California Press, 2004.

Tommasini, Anthony. *Virgil Thomson: Composer on the Aisle.* New York: W. W. Norton, 1997.

Nadine Hubbs

See also MUSIC: CLASSICAL; MUSIC: OPERA; STEIN, GERTRUDE, AND ALICE B. TOKLAS.

THURMAN, Wallace (b. 16 August 1902; d. 22 December 1934), writer, editor.

Wallace Thurman was born into a middle-class African American family in 1902 in Salt Lake City, Utah. It is perhaps only fitting that this unlikely spot would spawn one of the most complex figures of the Harlem Renaissance. After attending the University of Utah for two years and then transferring to the University of Southern California for two more years without graduating, Thurman arrived in New York City in 1925 determined to make a name for himself as a writer. However, Thurman's ambivalence about his homosexuality and the often abrasive manner he adopted in an attempt to camouflage it, while frustrating his attempts to achieve literary distinction, made him one of Harlem's best-known cultural provocateurs in the 1920s. His arrest for committing an "indecent" act in a men's room soon after his arrival in New York City made his homosexuality common knowledge in the small circle of Harlem intellectuals, and he spent much of his time in New York experimenting with various literary and sexual personae in an effort to achieve the cultural authority for which he longed and that this incident had fundamentally compromised. Ironically, the role of cultural arbiter to which Thurman aspired was exemplified by the self-confidence and influence of the homosexual, but safely closeted, Howard University philosopher Alain Locke.

Despite his insecurities, the work Thurman produced over the course of his short career was impressively wide-ranging, consisting of plays, film scripts, novels, essays, and innumerable book reviews. He revealed his taste-making ambitions most notably in the two short-lived but now almost legendary journals he created and edited—*Fire!!* (1926) and *Harlem: A Forum of Negro Life* (1928). In *Fire!!*, in addition to his editorial services, Thurman contributed the short story "Cordelia the Crude," a nonjudgmental account of a teenage girl's decline into a life of prostitution. This story later became the basis for Thurman's most financially successful work, the Broadway play *Harlem* (1929), which he coauthored with the white playwright William Jourdan Rapp. It was exactly this kind of transgressive material that made Thurman one of the primary critical targets for more sexually conservative members of the Harlem elite like W. E. B. DuBois.

Thurman is best known today for his novels *The Blacker the Berry* (1929), an examination of intraracial prejudice, and *Infants of the Spring* (1932), a roman à clef and satire of the Harlem Renaissance offering thinly disguised depictions of most of the well-known members of the Harlem intelligentsia. The climax of *The Blacker the Berry*, the revelation of the dark-skinned heroine's light-skinned lover's bisexuality, provides striking evidence of Thurman's conflicted relationship to both his homosexual desires and his own physical blackness. However, Thurman's major and significantly more positive contribution to the homosexual culture of the period was and remains *Infants of the Spring*. In this novel, the character of Paul Arbian, based on Richard Bruce Nugent, the Harlem Renaissance figure who came closest to being "out" in the modern sense, places Thurman directly in the line of queer expression stemming from the self-conscious aestheticism of Oscar Wilde. In fact, it is the essential "queerness," racially and sexually, of Thurman's novels that may have led to his relative absence from early discussions of the Harlem Renaissance and to his still unstable and marginalized position in the canon of significant African American writers.

Finally, it may have been Thurman's self-consciously and, too often, self-destructively "jazz age" lifestyle, the lifestyle classically represented in *Infants of the Spring*, that contributed most decisively to his failure to produce a body of work fully reflective of the brilliance that even his detractors recognized and to his general physical exhaustion and early death from tuberculosis in the charity ward of City Hospital on December 22, 1934.

Bibliography

Blackmore, David. "Something . . . Too Preposterous and Complex to Be Recognized or Considered: Same-Sex Desire and Race in *Infants of the Spring*." *Soundings* 80.4 (1997): 519–529.

Jarraway, David R. "Tales of the City: Marginality, Community, and the Problem of (Gay) Identity in Wallace Thurman's 'Harlem' Fiction" *College English* 65, no. 1 (September 2002): 36–52.

Notten, Eleonore van. *Wallace Thurman's Harlem Renaissance.* Amsterdam/Atlanta, Ga.: Rodopi, 1994.

Terry Rowden

See also HARLEM RENAISSANCE; HUGHES, LANGSTON; LITERATURE; LOCKE, ALAIN; NUGENT, RICHARD BRUCE; THEATER AND PERFORMANCE.

TILDEN, William (b. 10 February 1893; d. 5 June 1953), tennis athlete, writer.

William "Big Bill" Tilden is the Oscar Wilde of the sports world. A notorious showman, sometime writer and actor, Tilden exuded a flamboyance unrivaled among athletes of his time. Like Wilde a half-century before, though, his public reputation and fortune were brought down in a court of law for sex crimes, and he died penniless, exiled from all but a few friends and associates.

Born into a prominent Philadelphia family, Tilden was not a promising athlete in his youth. He failed to make the tennis team his first year at the University of Pennsylvania, but the following decade, Tilden became the most dominant tennis player of his era. He also became the game's first theorist, writing the book *Match Play and the Spin of the Ball* (1925), which is still relevant to a game that has changed dramatically since Tilden's day.

Tilden won seven U.S. singles championships and three Wimbledon titles, and he led the United States to seven consecutive Davis Cup victories in the 1920s. In 1950, despite his public humiliations, he was voted, in a poll by the Associated Press, the greatest tennis player in the first half of the twentieth century.

While playing his best tennis, Tilden was also writing fiction and plays, trying to become an actor, and cultivating his celebrity. He lost much of his modest fortune trying to finance a career on the stage. In the 1930s he became a professional tennis player during the amateur era. He toured with a small group of players (including the much younger Bobby Riggs), playing exhibition tournaments for pay, which rendered him ineligible for competition on the international circuit. (Tennis did not become a professional sport—a sport for pay—officially until the late 1960s.)

Tilden's homosexuality was an open secret in the tennis community. The United States Lawn Tennis Association was concerned that public knowledge of his homosexuality would be detrimental to the game. On the professional tour, where he served as a kind of executive, he was often accompanied by his favorites, teenage boys who were somewhat promising on the tennis court. Once, when Tilden was a player and coach for the U.S. Davis Cup team, he played doubles with one of his favorites, a fifteen-year-old named Junior Coen, in a match against China—a move some regarded as rather scandalous.

Tilden's boys traveled everywhere with him. Although there was much talk, nothing serious ever came of it. However, in the mid-1940s, when Tilden was living in Los Angeles and keeping company with the likes of movie stars Charlie Chaplin and Errol Flynn, everything changed when he was arrested on Sunset Boulevard in November 1946 for "lewd behavior" with a teenager. He was convicted of "contributing to the delinquency of a minor" and served almost eight months in jail. Arrested again in 1949, this time for making a pass at a sixteen-year-old hitchhiker, he served ten more months. This conviction was his final undoing. Most of his friends abandoned Tilden, except, interestingly enough, Marion Anderson, whose teenage son Arthur was one of his students—and favorites.

Acclaimed sports journalist Frank Deford set out to write a feature on Tilden in the early 1970s for *Sports Illustrated,* but he found the man and his story so fascinating that he wrote a surprisingly sympathetic biography called *Big Bill Tilden: The Triumphs and the Tragedy* (1976). Depicting the tennis star as flamboyant and self-centered, Deford argues that most of Tilden's relationships with his favorites were that of a teacher and student, and none of the favorites claimed that Tilden ever made sexual advances.

After Tilden's first arrest, Deford sets the scene: "Nervous when first arrested, then nonchalant, Tilden grew increasingly uncooperative and even a bit cavalier with his lawyer" (p. 246). This posturing echoes Wilde's when the Marquess of Queensberry, the father of Wilde's lover Lord Alfred Douglas, accused Wilde of "posing as a somdomite [sic]." Wilde's perceived arrogance in the courtroom contributed to his spectacular downfall, as did Tilden's. As Deford tells it: "Tilden was unconcerned, and he acted as if indestructible, certain that no court would dare put the great American world champion behind bars" (p. 250). He could not have been more wrong. His Hollywood friends were of little help. Indeed, both Chaplin and Flynn had been in trouble for their involvement with teenage girls.

His 1949 jail time was Tilden's ultimate humiliation. He was barred from nearly every tennis club and professional venue in Los Angeles. On 5 June 1953, Tilden died of an aneurysm. The sixty-year-old former star was found in his modest Hollywood apartment with his bags packed, about to depart to play in the U.S. professional championships.

Bibliography

"Bill Tilden." ESPN's *Sportscentury.* 26 February 2000.

Borges, Ron. "Tilden Brought Theatrics to Tennis." Available from http://www.espn.go.com/sportscentury/features.

Deford, Frank. *Big Bill Tilden: The Triumphs and Tragedy.* New York: Simon and Schuster, 1976.

Tilden, William. *My Story: A Champion's Memoirs.* New York: Hellman, Williams, 1948.

Chris Freeman

See also SPORTS.

TIPTON, Billy (b. 29 December 1914; d. 21 January 1989), musician.

Billy Lee Tipton was born Dorothy Lucille Tipton in Oklahoma City, Oklahoma. When Dorothy's parents divorced in 1928, she and her brother went to live with an aunt in Kansas City, Missouri, where Dorothy became a proficient piano player. During the Great Depression Tipton found work as a jazz musician in Oklahoma City. Dressed as a young man, she took the name of Billy Tipton. No one in the family was happy about Dorothy's transformation into Billy, but times were tough and jobs were scarce.

Itinerant Career, Female Companions

Billy Tipton lived and worked as a jazz pianist, saxophonist, and vocalist in and around Oklahoma City until 1941. Except for a brief period (1939–1940), Tipton dressed full-time as a man in an environment where many people knew him to be female-bodied. During this time Tipton began living as husband (1934–1943) to a sturdy, nonconformist, former farm girl named Non Earl Harrell, who also knew of Tipton's femaleness. In 1941 the couple moved to Joplin, Missouri, where Tipton permanently took up full-time life as a man and began to work with the band George Mayer and His Music So Rare. In 1943 Tipton and Non Earl broke up, and Tipton formed his own band, the Billy Tipton Quartet.

Shortly thereafter, Tipton started living with his second common-law wife, a singer named June. Over the next few years (1943–1946), June and Billy moved from Joplin to Springfield, Missouri, to Corpus Christi, Texas, and back to Joplin while Tipton worked in various jazz bands. By the end of 1946 June and Billy had ended their relationship. June subsequently intimated to others that Billy was a hermaphrodite.

Tipton continued his career in Joplin for another year, during which he met and began a seven-year relationship (1946–1954) with Betty Cox, then an eighteen-year-old just off the farm. Betty and Billy lived and traveled together as husband and wife through Texas, Missouri, and the Pacific Northwest. Many years later, when confronted with the fact of Billy's female body, Betty said, "I cannot in my wildest dreams accept the fact I finally know to be true" (Middlebrook, p. 175). During his Pacific Northwest years, Tipton at first joined up again with Mayer in George Mayer and His Sophisticated Swing Trio (1949–1951), after which he formed the Billy Tipton Trio.

No sooner had Betty and Billy parted ways in 1954 than Billy began living with a Jewish call girl around his own age named Maryann Cattanach. Maryann happily traveled with the Billy Tipton Trio but did not partake of the nightlife that went with Billy's role as an entertainer. Throughout their relationship (1954–1961), Maryann always respected Tipton's fastidious need for personal privacy, and she reported that she never doubted Billy's maleness in any way.

Peak Year and Decline

The year 1956 was a banner one for Tipton as a musician. The trio backed him on two record albums, *Sweet Georgia Brown* and *Billy Tipton Plays Hi-Fi on Piano*. However, in 1958, at the age of forty-five, Tipton decided that he had had enough of the itinerant life and settled with Maryann in Spokane, Washington, where he worked part-time as a musician and full-time as a booking agent at the Dave Sobol Theatrical Agency.

It was at the jazz gigs that Billy met and courted a twenty-year-old stripper named Kitty Kelly while still living with Maryann. By 1961 Maryann had moved out and Kitty had moved in. The following year Tipton staged a wedding with Kitty before a fraudulent justice of the peace, using forged documents. During their relationship, Kitty had little interest in sex and she later reported that she, too, never had any reason to doubt Tipton's maleness. In 1963, 1965, and 1969, respectively, they adopted three sons, John Thomas, Scott Lee, and William Alan (Little Billy). The family lived together until 1980, when disagreements about disciplining the boys resulted in Billy and the boys leaving Kitty.

Arthritis had by this time ended Tipton's career as a musician. He tried taking over the booking agency but was not very good at collecting fees and rapidly slipped into debt. Tipton eked out a small living at the agency during his final years while living with his youngest son. By 1988 Tipton was nearly destitute and very ill, but he refused to seek treatment. He died in 1989 of untreated hemorrhaging ulcers with his son William by his side in his Spokane home.

A Focus of Controversy

The paramedic attending Tipton at the time of his death observed Tipton's female body and remarked on it to William's astonishment. The coroner who examined Tipton's body leaked the story to the press, and a minor media frenzy ensued. Headlines proclaimed that Tipton was "really" a woman. Tipton's story became an inspiration for newspaper and magazine articles, a play and a video, at least one all-female jazz band, academic treatises, and a full-length biography.

The story of the life of Billy Tipton became a contested arena for theories of sex, gender, and sexuality. On the one hand, many women's, feminist, and lesbian groups claimed Tipton as a woman who followed in the centuries-old tradition of females who defy gender conventions to pursue their dreams of lives otherwise closed to women. From this perspective, Tipton and the five Mrs. Tiptons might all have been thought of as lesbian women, whether they knew it or not.

By contrast, many transgender people and others expressed the opinion that Tipton was clearly a transgender person in action and deed, if not by his own proclamation. They argued that Tipton purposefully hid his femaleness in all ways possible for almost half a century, died of a treatable illness rather than allow a doctor to examine him and discover his femaleness, and requested that one of his trusted cousins have his body cremated immediately after his death (which did not happen) so that his secret could die with him. Speaking to a cousin in 1983, Billy Tipton summed it up this way: "Some people might think I'm a freak or a hermaphrodite. I'm not. I'm a normal person. This has been my choice" (Middlebrook, p. 278).

Bibliography

Cromwell, Jason. *Transmen and FTMs: Identities, Bodies, Genders, and Sexualities.* Urbana: University of Illinois, 1999.

Dekker, Rudolf, and Lotte van de Pol. *The Tradition of Female Transvestism in Early Modern Europe.* New York: St. Martin's Press, 1989.

Halberstam, Judith. "Telling Tales: Brandon Teena, Billy Tipton, and Transgender Biography." In *Passing, Identity, and Interpretation in Sexuality, Race, and Religion,* edited by María Carla Sánchez and Linda Schlossberg. New York: New York University Press, 2001.

Langton, James. "Jazz Musician Was Ladies' Man in Body and Soul." *Globe and Mail,* 25 February 1997, sec. D, p. 1.

Middlebrook, Diane Wood. *Suits Me: The Double Life of Billy Tipton.* Boston: Houghton Mifflin, 1998.

Smith, Dinita. "One False Note in a Musician's Life: Billy Tipton Is Remembered with Love, Even by Those Who Were Deceived." *New York Times,* 2 June 1998, sec. E, pp. 1, 4.

Aaron H. Devor

See also FEMMES AND BUTCHES; MARRIAGE CEREMONIES AND WEDDINGS; MUSIC: POPULAR; TRANSSEXUALS, TRANSVESTITES, TRANSGENDER PEOPLE, AND CROSS-DRESSERS.

TOKLAS, ALICE B. see STEIN, GERTRUDE, AND ALICE B. TOKLAS.

TOURISM

Three social processes have contributed to the emergence of U.S. LGBT tourism: the rapid development of a global consumer/commodity culture; sexual and LGBT liberation; and a fast-growing tourist industry. While U.S. LGBT communities are marked by significant class and economic differences, on the whole, their members make up an affluent and thus significant consumer group; their sexual orientation makes them an identifiable niche market; and many have considerable disposable income to spend on travel. While LGBT tourism has become increasingly visible since the end of World War II, it began much earlier, as Esther Newton has documented in her study of Cherry Grove, Fire Island.

LGBT tourism covers a broad range of activities, including any travel—individual or group, spontaneous or organized—motivated by or targeted to nonstraight orientations and interests. At least four LGBT travel trajectories are identifiable: tourism to LGBT-friendly cities in North America (e.g., San Francisco, Seattle, New York, Montreal, and Toronto); tourism to LGBT-friendly resorts in North America (Fire Island, Provincetown, and Key West are notable examples); tourism to popular LGBT non–North American destinations (Amsterdam, Paris, Berlin, Sydney, Tangier, and Bangkok, among many others); and travel by LGBT people to locations other than resorts and cities known to be LGBT-friendly.

As the involvement in LGBT tourism of an affluent, largely white traveling constituency has grown, so has the participation of people from less affluent and nonwhite groups. LGBT tourism now embraces diverse populations with a broad spectrum of motivations and activities. Also noteworthy is a set of variable and elusive, but nonetheless real, distinctions between the tourism of GBT men and LBT women that make any simple amalgamation of the two impossible.

Early History

LGBT tourism has a long history. Men and women of predominantly same-sex sexual orientation from repressed northern European and North American countries have long sought out more sympathetic, more relaxed, and more economically dependent communities in southern Europe (especially Italy and Greece). Rumors and informal networks signaled the value of certain destinations for travelers desiring same-sex sexual encounters. In the early twentieth century, while southern Europe remained popular, LGBT tourists also made a point of visiting the expatriate community in France surrounding Gertrude Stein and Alice B. Toklas, and later James Baldwin.

After World War II, the long and sometimes tortured residence of Paul and Jane Bowles in Tangier, Morocco, became a magnet for North American and European LGBT people seeking contact with an exotic and erotic avant-garde. The Bowleses' patronage of indigenous storytellers highlighted a complex dynamic between Western privilege and local culture in which some locals were attuned to how the homosexual desires of outsider patrons might be turned to the locals' advantage.

Meanwhile, LGBT travelers were making cities such as New York and San Francisco, and resorts such as Fire Island, Provincetown, and Key West, popular LGBT tourist destinations. By the early 1960s, gay guides published in the United States were listing hundreds of bars, restaurants, parks, and beaches in dozens of cities and towns around the world that were popular among LGBT people. By the time that Edmund White chronicled a tour across the United States in *States of Desire* (1980), a U.S. LGBT tourist culture was fully developed.

Recent Developments

The Stonewall Riots of 1969 ushered in a period when a liberatory sexual movement intersected with the marked intensification of Western consumer culture, including tourism. While mainstream glossy travel magazines such as *Condé Nast Traveler* have largely continued to ignore LGBT travel (mainstream travel images generally feature young heterosexual couples), an LGBT promotional print-and-image tourist industry has developed and flourished.

While several key North American cities, including San Francisco, New York, Montreal, Toronto, and Seattle, have acquired a special cachet, various city governments have recognized the enormous economic and cultural value of such events as LGBT pride marches. Consequently, productive liaisons between urban tourist organizations and LGBT groups are becoming the rule. In June 2003, for example, Toronto went out of its way to welcome gay and lesbian couples seeking marriage licenses and ceremonies in the wake of court rulings striking down restrictions on same-sex marriage. Torontonians officially and enthusiastically welcomed visitors from around the world, turning the city into an urban resort offering something not available in most other cities. This exceptional circumstance, however, also exposed another feature of tourism in general, namely its overwhelmingly economic motivation in the era of globalization, for the city's tourism had taken a large hit after a major public health crisis. The LGBT community, thus, was enlisted as part of a strategy to regain lost economic ground.

The travel industry's economic clout has long been a target for critique, especially as it relates to the vulnerability of economically struggling regions of the world. Tourism can distort and destroy local economies, promote environmental degradation, and encourage exploitative relationships between visitors and visited. Developing countries and regions, however, are heavily

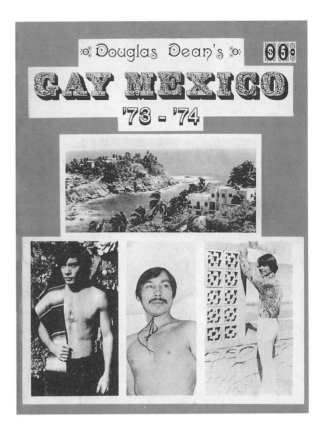

LGBT Tourism. The cover of Douglas Dean's 1973–74 guide to gay Mexico. [Barbary Coast Publications]

dependent on tourist dollars and close their doors to LGBT tourists at great cost. While there was LGBT outrage in 1998 when the Cayman Islands government denied berthing rights to the vessel *Leeward,* which was carrying more than nine hundred passengers on a chartered gay cruise, the cost to the potential host government and its tourist industry was likely not negligible. This situation highlighted disparities in economic and cultural circumstances that are paradigmatic of a larger picture.

A latter-day trend toward niche-within-niche LGBT travel marketing mirrors mainstream travel trends. In effect, much LGBT travel marketing has been a form of niche-within-niche marketing, insofar as the primary market has been middle-class, white gay men. Notwithstanding a certain degree of overlap, lesbian tourism and gay tourism have long been distinct. While gay male travel often emphasized hedonistic motivations, lesbian travel often focused on "safe" experiential spaces (though certainly erotic interests have also figured importantly for lesbians). Two early lesbian examples are Olivia, an organization that began as a music-focused business in 1973 but morphed into a cruise-and-travel company in 1990, and the Michigan Womyn's Music Festival, running since 1974. Both have been hugely successful.

Gay travel, while it has remained predominantly celebratory and hedonistic, has also hatched specialist formations, such as those catering to outdoor, adventure, and environmental activity. The history of LGBT travel confirms that, while there is an identifiable LGBT travel world for a mainstream band of that population, outside that band there are many groups whose interests may never be compatible.

Sex Tourism

In its more exclusively sexual aspects (and travel has traditionally offered sexual opportunities), LGBT tourism can be viewed less as a simple product of North American liberation and more as a venue for the problematic reproduction of white imperial/colonial practices, perpetuating the oppression of third world peoples. The economic dependency of countries such as Thailand and the Philippines makes them vulnerable to exploitation by affluent gay males as well as by straight tourists. The privileges accruing to those with disproportionate wealth, as well as the predisposition of wealthy white gay men to exoticize and eroticize tropical setting, skin color, youth, and poverty, cnable a troubling element of sexual exploitation in the global travel industry.

While there is general social outrage at the darker aspects of sexual tourism— expressed, for example, in the flurry of sociological analyses of sexual tourism that appeared in the late twentieth and early twenty-first centuries—the ethical issues are somewhat complicated. There is often a symbiotic bond between cash-strapped client economies and money coming in from sex tourists. And if the Western world has inserted the human body into the global marketplace through seductive advertising of body and clothing styles, there is often a positive response from consumers in non-Western cultures.

Despite some efforts by host governments to prosecute cases of sexual exploitation, those same governments are to one degree or another forced into silent complicity out of economic need. In Southeast Asia, in the Caribbean and Central America, and in parts of central and eastern Europe, for example, tourist dollars are an economic staple. While many travelers—LGBT as well as straight—and governments regard sexual tourism with distaste, it is by no means easy to disentangle the need to empower the host-region tourist-worker from the need to free the LGBT traveler from the risk of persecution, and both from the desire for nonexploitative travel and sex.

Conclusion

Finally, the arrival and exponential development of the World Wide Web should be noted in relation to LGBT travel. Like all advertising, the Internet is a source that both makes information accessible and invites those who access the information to pursue and consume. It has the potential to supplant rather than simply supplement print-media travel information and advertising. It can enable bookings and reservations to be made more rapidly and often more cheaply. It is hip and, supposedly, nondiscriminatory. It has also enabled virtual travel and experience, including forms that are primarily sexual. Perhaps two of the greatest challenges now facing LGBT tourism are to ensure that new opportunities for North American travelers do not represent simply movement from the gay closet into the consumer prison and that LGBT travel continues to offer rich experiential possibilities.

Bibliography

Aldrich, Robert. *The Seduction of the Mediterranean: Writing, Art, and Homosexual Fantasy.* London: Routledge, 1993.

Altman, Dennis. *Global Sex.* Chicago: University of Chicago Press, 2001.

Atkins, Gary L. *Gay Seattle: Stories of Exile and Belonging.* Seattle: University of Washington Press, 2003.

GLQ 8, no. 1 (2002). Special issue devoted to LGBT tourism.

Holland, Patrick, and Graham Huggan. *Tourists with Typewriters: Critical Reflections on Contemporary Travel Writing.* Ann Arbor: University of Michigan Press, 1998.

Kaiser, Charles. *The Gay Metropolis, 1940–1996.* Boston: Houghton Mifflin, 1997.

Littlewood, Ian. *Sultry Climates: Travel and Sex since the Grand Tour.* London: John Murray, 2001.

Newton, Esther. *Cherry Grove, Fire Island: Sixty Years in America's First Gay and Lesbian Town.* Boston: Beacon Press, 1993.

White, Edmund. *States of Desire: Travels in Gay America.* New York: E. P. Dutton, 1980.

Patrick Holland

See also BUSINESSES; CROSS-CLASS SEX AND RELATIONSHIPS; CRUISING; INTERRACIAL AND INTERETHNIC SEX AND RELATIONSHIPS; PROSTITUTION, HUSTLING, AND SEX WORK; RACE AND RACISM; RESORTS.

TRANSGENDER ORGANIZATIONS AND PERIODICALS

In the early days of transgender organizing and publishing, today's discrete categories and terms did not exist. Although the first sex-change experiments had been performed in Germany in the 1920s, the word "transsexual" was not coined until 1949, and for the first half of the twentieth century researchers concerned themselves with developing and distinguishing between categories of sexual and gender variance. In 1963, when *Female Mimics* became the first glossy magazine published about female impersonation, it included articles on related but distinct topics. The first issue included an article about the famous transsexual Christine Jorgenson, and later issues contained photo spreads on cross-dressing lesbians in Paris nightclubs.

In 1964, female-to-male (FTM) transsexual and philanthropist Reed Erickson founded the Erickson Educational Foundation (EEF) "to provide assistance and support in areas where human potential was limited by adverse physical, mental or social conditions." For twenty years, it was the main funding vehicle for "transgender" causes, and as such was a powerful hidden engine behind the explosion of medical research and social support networks and organizations.

In 1965, Virginia Prince of West Hollywood began publishing *Transvestia*. It had its roots in a mimeographed newsletter of the same name that was published sporadically since 1952. It included profiles of transvestites, photographs, readers' contributions, and makeup tips. Prince was the main spokesperson for a group that considered transvestitism to be an exclusively heterosexual phenomena and one that differed radically from both homosexual cross-dressing and transsexuality.

In San Francisco, the mid-1960s were a time of profound social change. The group Vanguard, which was sponsored by Glide Memorial Methodist Church, was a haven for gay street youth, queens, "hair fairies," and male-to-female (MTF) transsexuals. The Department of Public Health's Center for Special Problems provided health services to transsexuals. In 1967, COG (Conversion Our Goal or Change: Our Goal) became the world's first real organization of transsexuals. It was inspired by the civil rights movement, and its goals were overtly political. A splinter group, the California Advancement for Transsexuals Society (CATS) was short-lived. However, another associated organization, the National Gender-Sexual Identification Council, which was to become the National Transsexual Counseling Unit (NTCU), attracted funding from the EEF and became the first peer-run transgender social services agency in the world.

East Coast

The nascent transgender movement was stirring on the East Coast as well. In Yonkers, New York, FTM transsexual Mario Martino and his wife launched Labyrinth Foundation Counseling Service, the first group formed exclusively for the benefit of transmen. In New York City, on Halloween 1969, Lee Brewster founded QUEENS, which soon became the Queens Liberation Front. He also published the influential *Drag* magazine, which chronicled transgender struggles in a very political context. Brewster formed the Queens Liberation Front because the Mattachine Society had been reluctant to use the money he was raising for them by organizing drag balls to benefit queens rather than all gays. The Queens Liberation Front was the first transvestite organization to parade in New York City.

Also in New York City, in 1970, the teenage Puerto Rican prostitute Sylvia Rivera, together with her mentor and fellow street transvestite Marsha P. Johnson, founded Street Transvestite Action Revolutionaries (STAR). Rivera and Johnson were both veterans of the Stonewall Riots. Rivera was also involved with both the Gay Activists Alliance and the Gay Liberation Front, and STAR was formed after a sit-in at New York University by the latter. STAR opened the STAR House, which was a communal house on the Lower East Side that provided a safe shelter for young transvestites. As one of the first New York City projects to help queer street youth, STAR combined a focus on survival issues with radical political organizing. Johnson drowned in the Hudson River in 1992. Rivera continued as an activist but battled substance abuse, depression, and chronic poverty. She got "clean and sober" in the 1990s, joined the Metropolitan Community Church (MCC), and resurrected STAR as Street Transgender Action Revolutionaries. She died at age fifty of liver cancer on 19 February 2002.

In 1970, Angela Keyes Douglas founded the militant Transsexual Action Organization (TAO) in southern California. She also wrote extensively for *Moonshadow* and *Mirage*, its publications. Very much a product of its era, TAO engaged in vocal confrontation and street level protests, and at its most active boasted a thousand members in eight U.S. cities and three foreign countries.

During the mid- and later 1970s, some transsexual women who identified as lesbian or bisexual joined lesbian organizations. They were not always well received. In 1973, Beth Elliot became vice president of Daughters of Bilitis, was outed, and was forced from the organization by separatists who objected to the presence of a transsexual woman. In 1977, Sandy Stone was working as a recording engineer for Olivia Records when she was outed. Separatists threatened a boycott, and Olivia reluctantly asked Stone for her resignation.

In 1980, Joanna Clark (also known as Sister Mary Elizabeth), Jude Patton, Joy Shaffer, and others founded the ACLU Transsexual Rights Committee in southern California. The committee was active for three years, and was responsible for the establishment of separate wings for preoperative transsexuals in California state prisons.

Transgender San Francisco

In 1982 the Educational TV Channel was established in San Francisco as a social and support network mainly for male-to-female crossdressers. It has since changed its name to TransGender San Francisco, expanded its membership to include more transsexuals and female-to-male people, and become the largest transgender organization on the West Coast.

Under Construction, California's first organization dedicated solely to addressing the needs of FTMs, is also the longest running, but as a small support group meeting in the southern California home of its founder, is by no means the largest. FTM International (FTMI) holds that distinction. It was founded in San Francisco by gay FTM Lou Sullivan in 1986. It publishes the quarterly *FTMI Newsletter* and has a membership of 900 in seventeen countries. It hosted the world's first FTM Conference of the Americas, which was held in San Francisco in 1995. It also publishes the *FTM Resource Guide*.

The American Boyz (AmBoyz) is, like FTMI, an organization that aims to support people who were labeled female at birth but who feel that is not an accurate or complete description of who they are. Although FTMI is an international organization, it does not run support groups outside of San Francisco. The Maryland-based AmBoyz provides resources to regional affiliates, runs the annual True Spirit Conference, and cosponsors the Transgendered Aging Network with FORGE (For Ourselves: Reworking Gender Expression). FORGE is a national FTM organization with a Midwest focus.

The Massachusetts-based International Foundation for Gender Education (IFGE) was founded in 1987. It is an information provider and educational organization, and publishes a magazine, *Transgender Tapestry*, which covers topics ranging from medical technology and legal cases to film and book reviews. IFGE also organizes an annual conference and administers the Transgender Scholarship and Education Legacy Fund (T-SELF).

The 1990s

By the 1990s, the transgender movement was gaining speed. Where once there were just a few organizations, now many emerged. In 1990 in Atlanta, Dallas Denny launched the American Educational Gender Information Service (AEGIS), a transgender education and informa-

tion resource group. AEGIS published *Chrysalis Quarterly* from 1991 to 1998. The national grassroots civil rights group It's Time, America! (ITA) was formed during the 1994 Transgender Law Conference. ITA monitored legislation and sought to educate and influence lawmakers. In 1998, AEGIS merged with It's Time America! and became Gender Education and Advocacy (GEA). GEA has continued and expanded upon the educational mission of AEGIS and the legislative mission of ITA. It also sponsors the Remembering Our Dead project and the associated annual Day of Remembrance, which were founded by Gwen Smith to memorialize those who were killed due to antitransgender hatred or prejudice.

In 1994, Denise Anne Norris, Riki Anne Wilchins, and others founded the direct action group Transsexual Menace. Its name refers to Lesbian Menace, the 1970s grassroots lesbian activist group, and it was formed to focus attention on issues of inclusion around Stonewall 25. Its members continued to participate in direct political actions such as the vigil for Brandon Teena (the Nebraska girl murdered in 1993 and whose story was depicted in the film *Boys Don't Cry*) and the Camp Trans protest against the policy of the Michigan Women's Music Festival that excludes transsexual women. Transsexual Menace was as much a concept as an organization, and it is perhaps best known for its in-your-face dripping red logo on a signature black T-shirt. Because of its loose organization and do-it-yourself aesthetic, it continues to generate new "chapters" that have no relation to each other, much less to the original organization.

On the other end of the organizational spectrum is the Renaissance Transgender Association. It is an incorporated body that publishes the glossy monthly magazine *Transgender Community News*, runs a speakers' bureau, and sponsors regional support groups, which operate almost as franchises of the national organization.

As the 1990s progressed, so did the movement for transgender civil rights. A struggle that began on the streets moved to legislative chambers. The Washington, D.C.–based National Transgender Advocacy Coalition (NTAC) works for the civil rights for all transgender, intersexed, and gender variant people and actively opposes discriminatory acts by all means legally available. NTAC manages legal defense funds, conducts trainings, organizes lobby days, and publishes media information kits.

Although no longer a specifically transgender organization, the Gender Public Advocacy Coalition (Gender-PAC) includes significant transgender civil rights work within its scope. GenderPAC works to end discrimination and violence caused by gender stereotypes by changing public attitudes, educating elected officials and expanding legal rights. GenderPAC also organizes the national gender lobby day on Capitol Hill.

Advocacy

The Transgender Law and Policy Institute (TLPI) is another advocacy organization. The TLPI brings together advocates and legal experts to work on law and policy initiatives that advance transgender equality. TLPI tracks legal developments; writes summaries for activists, policymakers, and the media; and makes legal resources and materials available. The San Francisco–based Transgender Law Center (TLC) is a legal civil rights organization that connects transgender people to legal services in California. TLC provides direct legal services, public policy advocacy, and education.

During the 1990s the influential *Transsexual News Telegraph* was published. It was a serious magazine for transsexuals, one which featured news, history, criticism, politics, and literary and film reviews by many of the best-known transgender writers, cultural figures, and academics. In this, it reflected the tone of the times. Transgender people were increasingly out, pointedly political, and actively engaged in creating cultural niches both within and outside the gay and straight mainstreams. *Transsisters* was another publication that left a mark. This short-lived "Journal of Transsexual Feminism" was edited by Davina Anne Gabriel. The 1990s also saw an explosion of underground publishing. Magazines such as the FTM-focused *Willyboy*; *Let Them In*, published by the Lesbian Avengers in an act of solidarity with the MTF women of Camp Trans, and the Canadian *Gendertrash* coincided with the emerging genderqueer movement and its interest in interrogating and dismantling the binary gender system.

In 1998 in San Francisco, the Ella Baker Center for Civil Rights partnered with Community United Against Violence (CUAV) to create TransAction, a direct action police accountability group whose leadership is composed primarily of people of color. Recognizing that transgender people are often the targets of police abuse, TransAction exposes such abuse, and it pressures law enforcement agencies to end such systemic violence. Working from within the law enforcement system is Transgendered Officers Protect and Serve (TOPS), an organization of transgender police officers, firefighters, emergency medical personnel, and military professionals.

In 1999, San Francisco supervisor Mark Leno sponsored the San Francisco Transgender Civil Rights Imple-

mentation Task Force. The task force was charged with implementing the recommendations that the city's Human Rights Commission identified five years earlier. With supervisor Leno, it was integral in passing a historical amendment to the city health plan that removed exemptions and approved doctor-recommended treatments for transgender city employees.

San Francisco's Youth Gender Project (YGP) was formed in 1999 to provide education and resources to younger people. YGP is a peer-based, profeminist, antiracist transgender, transsexual, genderqueer, intersex, and gender-questioning (TGIQ) youth and young adult organization. Its complicated mission reflects the complex identity questions posed by young queer people at this moment in history.

Organizations for and by transgender people continue to grow and multiply. Some emerge that address the concerns of specific subgroups. While some organizations seek to gain mainstream legitimacy and access to institutional power, others adamantly reject what they see as assimilationist compromises and instead work from self-consciously and proudly marginal, militant, or single-issue positions.

Bibliography

Cartwrite, Donna. "The Resurgence of Transgender Activism: Remembering Falls City." *Against the Current* 89 (2002).

Feinberg, Leslie. *Transgender Warriors: Making History from Joan of Arc to RuPaul.* Boston: Beacon Press, 1996.

Meyerowitz, Joanne. *How Sex Changed: A History of Transsexuality in the United States.* Cambridge, Mass.: Harvard University Press, 2002.

Stryker, Susan, and Jim Van Buskirk. *Gay by the Bay: A History of Queer Culture in the San Francisco Bay Area.* San Francisco: Chronicle Books, 1996.

Jordy Jones

See also BREWSTER, LEE; ERICKSON EDUCATIONAL FOUNDATION; ERICKSON, REED; LAWRENCE, LOUISE; NEWSPAPERS AND MAGAZINES; PRINCE, VIRGINIA; RIVERA, SYLVIA; SULLIVAN, LOU.

TRANSGENDER AND GENDER IMPERSONATION LAW AND POLICY

From colonial times to the present, transgender individuals in the United States have struggled with a legal system that has sought to control the manner in which they express their sex and gender identity.

Gender Variance in Colonial America

The colonial court of Virginia grappled with sexual ambiguity and gender variance in 1629, when confronted with an apparently transgender English-born person who identified as both Thomas and Thomasine Hall. Hall varied his/her attire over time, wearing male clothing while soldiering and female clothing during years spent doing needlework and other domestic activity. After moving from England to Virginia, Hall was accused of having a sexual encounter with a plantation owner's maid. In the ensuing investigation, Hall was repeatedly examined regarding his/her gender identity and biological sex.

Initially, the plantation owner and another man, unsatisfied with Hall's explanation that s/he was both a man and a woman, physically accosted Hall and determined that s/he had a penis. Shortly thereafter, Hall was waylaid by a small band of women and men, to whom Hall explained that s/he had a piece of genital flesh about an inch long and that s/he was impotent. The colonial authorities ordered Hall to dress in women's clothing. A week later, the vigilantes again harassed Hall, asking if the protruding flesh were all s/he had. Hall answered that s/he also had a small aperture.

Ultimately, the colonial court ordered that it be made public in Hall's plantation that Hall was both a man and a woman. Rather than allowing Hall to continue alternating between male and female dress according to his/her desire, however, the court ordered Hall to wear an anomalous mixture of both, effectively ensuring that Hall would no longer pass as either male or female.

Modern Cross-Dressers and Transsexuals

More than three hundred years after the interrogation of Thomas/Thomasine Hall, American courts have continued to wrestle with defining the status of individuals whose gender expression does not conform to social norms. For more than a century, for instance, New York State had a vagrancy statute that forbid being painted, discolored, covered, concealed, or otherwise disguised in a manner calculated to prevent identification. New York had enacted the statute in response to the Anti-Rent Riots of 1845, during which Hudson Valley farmers disguised as Indian women wearing calico dresses killed law enforcement agents who were serving writs on the farmers. In 1967, in *People v. Archibald*, New York used that statute to convict Mauricio Archibald of vagrancy, although he was simply waiting for a train on a New York City subway platform while dressed in drag, which he had worn to a masquerade party earlier in the evening.

Police have attacked gender variance even in the absence of written laws. In Buffalo, New York, in the 1940s and 1950s, many women who wore traditionally male clothes were harassed by police for failure to wear at least two or three items of female clothing at all times. The police did not hesitate to arrest and beat women who violated the unwritten rule.

Similar notions of gender-appropriate dress played a part in a 1973 murder trial in Texas. Considering whether evidence of a lesbian relationship between the defendant, Maria Perez, and the deceased could be introduced into evidence, the court in *Perez v. State of Texas* allowed testimony and pictures establishing that Perez had short hair and dressed in pants at the time of the murder. Although Perez denied being a lesbian and explained that male clothing was suited to her work as a truck farmer, the court found the testimony and pictures relevant, as they supposedly suggested a lesbian relationship between the two women and therefore were somehow evidence of motive in the murder.

Statutes banning cross-dressing have at times been used to police morality. In Cincinnati, Ohio, in 1974, prosecutors charged a gay male sex worker under a local law prohibiting any person from wearing clothing not customarily worn by his or her sex, or dressing in any disguise, with the intent to commit any indecent or immoral act or to violate any state or local law. The defendant, Adams, had been wearing a blouse, brassiere, and woman's slacks, as well as a wig, earrings, and a purse, when he propositioned an undercover police officer. Although rejecting Adams's claim that his cross-dressing was protected expression under the First Amendment, the court in *City of Cincinnati v. Adams* nonetheless struck down the ordinance, finding it violated Adams's right to due process and was unconstitutionally vague.

The courts have also had mixed reactions to cross-dressing by high school students, depending on the extent of gender variance. In 1973, the Supreme Court of Idaho in *Johnson v. Joint School District No. 60*, Bringham County stuck down a local school district dress code that prohibited any clothing that might cause a disturbance and that mandated that females' dresses or skirts end no higher than two inches above the knee. Since the dress code specified a length for skirts, the school district interpreted it to mean that females could only wear skirts, not pants. Several female students, who had been sent home for wearing slacks, successfully obtained an order restraining the school from enforcing the code. On appeal, the school district unsuccessfully argued that allowing female students to wear pants might cause any of an astonishing array of dire consequences, including, among other things: harmful effects on the students' morals; the creation of unsafe conditions, safety hazards, and damage to school property; insubordination, rebelliousness, and emotional problems among the students; and increased physical contact between male and female students. Given the outlandishness of these claims and the district's inability to substantiate them, the court sided with the students and invalidated the regulation.

In contrast, the courts provided no relief to two Ohio high school students who in 1987 were physically removed from their prom by local police due to gender-variant attire: Florence Harper had worn a black tuxedo and men's shoes, while her brother Warren sported a dress, fur cape, earrings, stockings, and high-heeled shoes. In *Harper v. Edgewood Board of Education*, the siblings sued the school board, claiming an equal-protection violation, since male students were allowed to wear tuxedos and females to wear dresses. They also claimed a violation of their First Amendment right of self-expression. Rejecting both arguments, the federal district court held that the dress code did not differentiate on the basis of sex, as all students were required to dress in conformity with accepted community standards, and that the policy was based on the reasonable educational goals of teaching community values and maintaining school discipline.

Courts have at times supported cross-dressing by transsexuals, particularly as part of therapy prior to sex-reassignment surgery. In *City of Chicago v. Wilson*, from 1978, the Illinois Supreme Court struck down a local ordinance that prohibited anyone from appearing in public places in dress not belonging to his or her sex, with intent to conceal that sex. The court held that the ordinance was an unconstitutional infringement of the two defendants' liberty interest, as they were preoperative transsexuals under their doctors' care.

Title VII of the Civil Rights Act

Transgender individuals have not yet won protection from discrimination, particularly in employment. Indeed, courts have uniformly held that Title VII of the 1964 Civil Rights Act, which prohibits employment discrimination on the basis of race, color, religion, sex, and national origin, does not protect the transgendered from discrimination.

In the 1984 decision *Ulane v. Eastern Airlines*, the U.S. Court of Appeals for the Seventh Circuit rejected a sex-based Title VII discrimination claim by Karen Ulane, a highly commended airline pilot who was fired simply for transitioning from male to female. The court held that Ulane could not avail herself of the protections of Title VII, as the statute did not expressly cover transsexuals. The court reasoned that U.S. Congress, in banning discrimination on the basis of sex, meant only discrimi-

nation on the basis of one's biological sex at birth, rather than discrimination on the basis of sexual identity disorder. *Ulane* has been followed unanimously by other courts, resulting in the denial of every transsexual employment discrimination claim to date.

In an unfortunate development extending the *Ulane* reasoning beyond transsexual cases, a federal district court held in 2002 that Title VII also does not apply to employment discrimination against cross-dressers generally. In *Oiler v. Winn-Dixie Louisiana, Inc.*, the court rejected a sex-based Title VII claim by Peter Oiler, a heterosexual transvestite who was content being a biological male but enjoyed publicly dressing as a woman a few times a month. Although he never cross-dressed at work, Oiler lost his job driving trucks through rural Louisiana and Mississippi because his employer, to whom Oiler had voluntarily disclosed, was afraid of losing business if customers were to learn of the cross-dressing.

In seeking redress under Title VII, Oiler relied on *Price Waterhouse v. Hopkins*. That 1989 decision involved the defendant Ann Hopkins's claim that her bid for an accounting firm partnership was held up for a year because the existing partners in the firm thought that her behavior and clothing were insufficiently feminine. The U.S. Supreme Court held in Hopkins that such sex-role stereotyping could be evidence of sex discrimination under Title VII and remanded the case to the trial court.

In dismissing Peter Oiler's complaint and rejecting his reliance on the *Hopkins* decision, the *Oiler* court implausibly reasoned that while Hopkins may have been discriminated against for not acting womanly enough, Oiler had not been discharged for not acting sufficiently masculine, but rather for his transvestite impulses. Refusing to acknowledge the obvious point that Oiler, like Hopkins, was being punished for dressing and acting against gender stereotype, the court simply held that discrimination against transvestites was not expressly prohibited by Title VII, and therefore dismissed his claim.

Conclusion

Gender-ambiguous individuals like Thomas/Thomasine Hall in colonial Virginia have continued to fare poorly in the U.S. legal system. Sean O'Neill, for instance, was a biological female identifying as male in 1995 when he unwittingly found himself caught up in a legal nightmare in Colorado Springs, Colorado. During his late teens, he had various younger girlfriends, to whom he presented himself as male. After the girlfriends' parents suspected that he had been born female, O'Neill was charged with eleven felony counts of sexual assault, sexual assault on a child, and criminal impersonation of the opposite gender.

Prosecutors obtained a court order allowing them to drag O'Neill to a hospital emergency room, where a doctor visually inspected him to verify his biological sex. He ultimately pled guilty to one count of sexual assault. This case is extraordinary for treating O'Neill's alleged gender deception as the equivalent of rape and for the prosecutor's resort to a court-ordered visual inspection of genitalia to contest gender identity.

In all of these cases, the legal system was defining and delimiting appropriate gender expression: who is a woman, who is a man, and how should each behave and dress? Policing sex and gender boundaries is not a task at which courts and legislatures are well suited, not least because there are situations where even medicine cannot definitively resolve the ambiguity of an individual's biological sex. There are at least eight indices that might be used to determine biological sex, gender identity, or both: (1) sex chromosome constitution; (2) sex hormonal pattern; (3) gonadal sex; (4) internal sex organs other than gonads; (5) external genitalia; (6) secondary sexual characteristics, such as large breasts or facial hair; (7) the sex of rearing; and (8) the assumed or psychological sex, also called gender identity. Intersexuals, formerly known as hermaphrodites, are a ready example of medical ambiguity, as their combination of both male and female genitalia confounds many of these variables. Moreover, postoperative transsexuals demonstrate that biological traits are not necessarily fixed but can be radically altered.

Rather than balancing these complex factors, the legal system often resorts to a simple "look test," visually inspecting a person's genitalia to determine not only biological sex but gender identity. The look test was performed on Thomas/Thomasine Hall by the plantation owner and a mob of villagers in the 1600s and on Sean O'Neill by an emergency room doctor acting under a court order more than three hundred years later.

Legal sanctions against gender variance are troubling not only because biological sex is not necessarily clearly defined and unchanging, but because gender expression is ultimately no more than social performance. Looking like a "woman," for instance, often involves adopting such artifice as long hair, makeup, feminine clothing and jewelry, high-heeled shoes, and even fake breasts and padded bras. It is arguably no less artificial when a biological woman, rather than a male transvestite, uses these devices to create the illusion of "femininity." The converse is true for men or women using short hair, pants, and work boots, for instance, to project a "masculine" image. These devices are all simply props for acting out socially constructed gender roles.

If biological sex is mutable and at times indeterminate, and if gender expression is in the end merely performance, it would seem questionable to use the legal system to coerce, punish, or allow attacks on those whose gender expressions vary from those of the mainstream.

Bibliography

Butler, Judith. *Gender Trouble: Feminism and the Subversion of Identity.* New York: Routledge, 1990.

———. "Imitation and Gender Insubordination." In *Inside/Out: Lesbian Theories, Gay Theories.* Edited by Diana Fuss. New York: Routledge, 1991.

Cotton, D. Douglas. "*Ulane v. Eastern Airlines*: Title VII and Transsexualism." *Northwestern University Law Review* 80, no. 6 (1986): 1037–1065.

David, Edward S. "The Law and Transsexualism: A Faltering Response to a Conceptual Dilemma." *Connecticut Law Review* 7 (1974–1975): 288–345.

Dunlap, Mary C. "The Constitutional Rights of Sexual Minorities: A Crisis of the Male/Female Dichotomy." *Hastings Law Journal* 30, no. 4 (1979): 1131–1149.

Gould, Meredith. "Sex, Gender, and the Need for Legal Clarity: The Case for Transsexualism." *Valparaiso University Law Review* 13, no. 3 (1979): 423–450.

Green, James. "Predator?" *Bay Times* (22 February 1996): 2, 29.

Haag, Jeannine S., and Tami L. Sullinger. "Is He or Isn't She? Transsexualism: Legal Impediments to Integrating a Product of Medical Definition and Technology." *Washburn Law Journal* 21, no. 2 (1982): 342–372.

Kennedy, Elizabeth Lapovsky, and Madeline D. Davis. *Boots of Leather, Slippers of Gold: The History of a Lesbian Community.* New York: Routledge, 1993.

Minkowitz, Donna. "On Trial: Gay? Straight? Boy? Girl? Sex? Rape?" *Out Magazine* (October 1995): 99.

Newton, Esther. *Mother Camp: Female Impersonators in America.* 2d ed. Chicago: University of Chicago Press, 1979.

"Patriarchy Is Such a Drag: The Strategic Possibilities of a Postmodern Account of Gender." *Harvard Law Review* 108, no. 8 (1995): 1973–2008.

Shafiqullah, Hasan. "Shape-Shifters, Masqueraders, and Subversives: An Argument for the Liberation of Transgendered Individuals." *Hastings Women's Law Journal* 8, no. 1 (Winter 1997): 195–197.

Smith, Douglas K. "Transsexualism, Sex Reassignment Surgery and the Law." *Cornell Law Review* 56, no. 6 (1971): 963–1009.

Hasan Shafiqullah

See also ANTI-DISCRIMINATION LAW AND POLICY; BONNET, JEANNE; CRIME AND CRIMINALIZATION; DISCRIMINATION; DRAG QUEENS AND KINGS; EMPLOYMENT LAW AND POLICY; FEDERAL LAW AND POLICY; INTERSEXUALS AND INTERSEXED PEOPLE; POLICING AND POLICE; TRANSSEXUALS, TRANSVESTITES, TRANSGENDER PEOPLE, AND CROSS-DRESSERS.

TRANSSEXUALS, TRANSVESTITES, TRANSGENDER PEOPLE, AND CROSS-DRESSERS

Writing a history of transsexuals, transvestites, transgender people, and cross-dressers is immediately problematic because these words embody people, practices, and discourses that have indefinite meanings that, at different moments, contradict and also intersect with one another. From psychology and medicine, to activism, academics, and the personal, discussion focuses on both the terms that define the discipline and the people who enliven the discourse. By blending diverse points of view it becomes possible to situate the practices of gender crossings with the people who experience and perform them.

Transsexuality and European Science

As Joanne Meyerowitz points out in *How Sex Changed* (2002), transsexuality—first identified as transsexualism in 1949 by David O. Cauldwell to describe people who "sought to change their sex" (p. 5)—concerned European scientists, most notably Magnus Hirschfeld and Havelock Ellis, in the late nineteenth and early twentieth centuries. Hirschfeld, who founded the Institute of Sexual Science in Berlin, published widely on homosexuality and campaigned for homosexual rights. In *Transvestites* (1910), he distinguished what he called transvestites from what he called homosexuals. For Hirschfeld, transvestites included both those who cross-dressed and those who identified with a sex and gender that differed from their birth sex and assigned gender. Hirschfeld's transvestites included those who today would be considered transsexuals (Meyerowitz defines transsexuals as those who "hope to change the bodily characteristics of sex," p. 9). European doctors performed the first complete genital transformations, many—including those of Americans who could only receive such surgery in the United States if they suffered from disease or injury—at Hirschfeld's institute in the 1920s and early 1930s.

Changing definitions and understandings of sex and gender in the late nineteenth and early twentieth centuries contributed to more liberal approaches to sexuality. In this period, scientists began to challenge the once widely accepted notion of "opposite" sexes and separate spheres of male and female. Some, including Ellis, Hirschfeld, and Sigmund Freud, argued for the possibility of universal bisexuality, by which they meant that all human beings exhibited combined aspects of the male and the female. In the 1920s and 1930s, scientists discovered that men and women both have "male" and "female"

hormones, which supported the notion that all humans are innately bisexual. This theory reached the United States in the 1920s through medical texts and was integrated into popular sexology by the 1930s.

These innovative European concepts were primarily dependent on biological or medical definitions of sex. As Meyerowitz (2000) explains, "With hormones as the measure, sex was quantitative, literally fluid, and all humans were to greater and lesser degrees, mixtures of female and male" (p. 82). Research in social science fields such as anthropology also supported changing definitions of sex, gender, and sexuality. For example, Margaret Mead's work in the late 1920s emphasized that men and women shared masculine and feminine modes of behavior. Her work, like other work conducted in the United States, was obviously more dependent on culture than biology, but has lent potential support to the notion of sex change.

Sensationalism and Transsexuality in the United States

During this period of new research in Europe, most Americans were unaware of the possibility of sex change surgery. Historians cite isolated cases from the 1930s of Americans traveling to Europe to seek surgery, but until after World War II, what came to be defined as trans sexualism was not a widely known or understood concept in the United States. In 1949, however, American doctor David O. Cauldwell used the phrase *psychopathia transexualis* in a popular magazine article to describe the case of "Earl," who was seeking female-to-male surgery. He also distinguished transsexuals from both homosexuals and "intersexed" people (people with ambiguous genitalia). While he advocated surgery for intersexuals, for transsexuals he endorsed only psychological treatment.

In the 1930s transsexuality was popularized in the United States chiefly through personal accounts that were publicized by sensational media accounts. Magazines such as *True Confessions* and *Your Body* printed articles and letters from readers like "Miss R. R.," who confessed that she "had . . . the feeling" that "her sex was gradually changing" (Meyerowitz, 2002, p. 14). In contrast to earlier accounts of an individual's biological sex being discovered after his or her death, these stories focused on the notion that the identity of one's sex was neither obvious, nor inevitable.

Cauldwell's attention was initially brought to the subject because of these sensational accounts. For the U.S. public, transsexuality was most significantly popularized in the United States because of Christine Jorgensen's sex change operation, reported in the *New York Daily News* in

1952. In her account, Jorgensen describes a desire to be female that she had had since her youth; finally, in 1950, she traveled to Europe and sought out an endocrinologist who agreed to give her hormone treatment if she would participate in his research. Over the course of two years, she took estrogen and underwent two surgeries to transform her genitals. As is evident from the first headlines about her case, the media immediately cast Jorgensen as a personification of conventional beauty and glamour. In turn, Jorgensen's very public experiences provided a model and language for others to question the dominance of traditional medical and psychological models.

"Legitimate" Science

One of Jorgensen's doctors, Harry Benjamin, also popularized the term "transsexual" in the United States in the 1950s. He defined transsexualism as "an extreme type of transvestism, in which men wanted to be women, even anatomically" (Meyerowitz, 2002, p. 103). Benjamin challenged psychiatric models, arguing that while psychological factors contributed to the desire for sex change, psychotherapy as a treatment consistently failed and the "condition" necessitated surgery. Benjamin and others increasingly relied on the notion that one's sense of being male or female, which they referred to as psychological sex or gender identity, was immutable, while the body could be changed.

Benjamin proved to be a significant advocate and resource for those who wanted sex change surgery and was influential in a network of doctors and scientists working on transsexualism and providing sex reassignment surgery in the United States and abroad. In the late 1940s, for example, Alfred Kinsey corresponded with Benjamin, requesting his support for Val Barry, a male-to-female who sought sex change surgery; Benjamin administered hormones and tried to find Barry a surgeon in the United States. Both Benjamin and Kinsey served as points of contact for the growing transsexual population and the doctors performing sex change surgeries in the United States. They were aided by people like Louise Lawrence, a male-to-female cross-dresser who lived in San Francisco as a woman. She had a network of transvestite friends and was determined to educate the public about transvestism. She, in fact, convinced Kinsey that cross-dressing was "worthy" of scientific study (Meyerowitz, 2000, p. 75). Kinsey focused mostly on transvestites, although toward the end of his life, he began to recognize that some individuals should be allowed to have sex reassignment surgery.

Although advocates like Benjamin worked on a case-by-case basis to help those seeking surgery, most trans-

sexuals had limited funds and lacked available or willing doctors; often Benjamin had to help transsexuals travel to Europe to receive medical help. In 1964, however, with the help of the Erickson Educational Foundation (EEF), founded the same year by female-to-male transsexual Reed Erickson, Benjamin created the Harry Benjamin Foundation to fund and coordinate research on transsexualism. In 1965 Benjamin began collaboration with Dr. John Money and a committee at Johns Hopkins Hospital in Baltimore, also funded by EEF; the following year, the hospital established a Gender Identity Clinic and announced that it would perform sex-reassignment surgeries on a case-by-case basis.

Although the doctors at Johns Hopkins identified with a liberal agenda and legitimized the notion of sex change surgery, many of their practices were surprisingly conservative. For example, they often denied surgery to patients, favoring psychological "treatment" instead. The Gender Identity Clinic's work was also continually stifled by insufficient funds. By the end of the 1960s, the Johns Hopkins doctors had received hundreds of referrals for sex reassignment surgery, yet they knew they would perform few of them, not merely because of inadequate funding, but also because their focus was on research and psychological testing in order to discover the "cause" of transsexuality.

Activism and Social Networks

Nonetheless, the program at Johns Hopkins did encourage other doctors and medical centers to focus on transsexuality and the possibilities of sex reassignment surgery. At the same time, while doctors and psychologists formed professional networks, clinics, and associations on transsexuality, transsexuals developed social networks and communities. In the process, a small but organized social movement began and the first organizations for transsexuals, including Conversion Our Goal, the National Gender-Sexual Identification Council, and the Transsexual Action Organization, appeared in the late 1960s and early 1970s. Their accomplishments include increased availability of sex change surgery and increased public awareness of transsexualism. Transsexual activist groups confronted numerous challenges, much like any identity-based group. Class, race, ethnic, religious, and other differences contributed to diverse political views. Many of the early transsexual groups disbanded in the 1970s amid internal conflict and the changing political climate in the United States. However, a renewed movement flourished in the 1990s as transsexual activists joined cross-dressers, intersexed people, and others who identified as transgender to form new organizations. Some, like Transgender Nation and Transsexual Menace, are more explicitly radical than groups such as the American Educational Gender Information Service. Both types of activists work with LGB rights groups such as the National Gay and Lesbian Task Force to make certain that transsexual and transgender rights are recognized. Since the 1990s, the number of organized transsexual and transgender activist groups continued to grow, particularly via the Internet.

Border Wars

Historically, the languages and practices of transsexualism have been reliant on medical and technological intervention. However, since the late twentieth century some scholars and some transsexuals have understood the term to encompass phenomena outside of or beyond sex change surgery. Some, for example, identify as transsexual those people who longed to live as members of the other sex but were not able to obtain sex change surgery, either because they lived in the presurgery era or because of factors that limited their access to sex reassignment procedures. In addition, some people who do not wish to have sex change surgery nevertheless identify themselves as transsexual.

Engaging in intense debate, scholars and activists now distinguish between various types of gender-crossing. Judith Halberstam (1998), in her influential scholarship on female masculinity, discusses the virtual "border wars" that have taken place between lesbian butches and female-to-male (FTM) transsexuals. Using the term "gender variance" to encompass both groups, Halberstam explores the continuities and discontinuities between gender variants who retain their birth body and those who seek sex reassignment. As she states: "Some lesbians seem to see FTMs as traitors to a woman's movement who cross over and become the enemy. Some FTMs see lesbian feminism as a discourse that has demonized FTMs and their masculinity. Some butches consider FTMs to be butches who believe in anatomy, and some FTMs consider butches to be FTMs who are too afraid to make the 'transition' from female to male" (p. 144). For complex reasons, gay men generally have not been similarly steeped in debates and confrontations with male-to-female (MTF) transsexuals. MTFs have, however, experienced conflicts with female-born feminists and lesbian feminists, some of whom resist acknowledging MTFs as women (and thus restrict MTF access to women-only events such as the Michigan Womyn's Music Festival).

Another type of border war sets FTMs against MTFs. According to Meyerowitz, medical doctors in the past generally believed that MTFs greatly outnumbered FTMs, but some doctors today think that the numbers are roughly equal. Until Halberstam, Holly Devor (1997), and others drew more attention to FTMs, however, FTMs were often ignored or their experiences were conflated with those of MTFs. The politics of gender privilege may have had an impact on this phenomenon, as the desires and needs of biological men who want to change sex are often perceived as more legitimate, while FTMs are often portrayed as failed heterosexual women or even failed butch lesbians. Usually raised as males, MTFs may also be more accustomed to speaking up for themselves and claiming public space and voice than are FTMs, who are usually raised as females.

Conflict also marks relationships between transsexuals wishing to be known and visible primarily as transsexuals and those wishing to be known and visible primarily as members of their post-reassignment sexes. Many in the former group emphasize processes of sex and gender transformation, transition, and mobility, while many in the latter group affirm static sex and gender identifications. For related reasons, transsexuals who are seen to reify and authenticate categories of sex and gender have also experienced conflict with transsexuals and nontranssexuals who identify as androgynous, many of whom wish to do away with the categories of sex and gender. Another type of conflict within transsexual communities concerns class and race and their relationship to access to sex change surgery, which is very expensive. Meanwhile, while many transsexuals embrace sexual diversity, there have been conflicts between transsexuals who identify as straight and those who identify as lesbian, gay, or bisexual.

Finally, nontranssexual LGB people have engaged in border wars with transsexuals as well (beyond the wars discussed by Halberstam). Although some LGB communities and movements have embraced and included transsexuals, many have not. Some of these conflicts have concerned whether sexuality or gender should be privileged as the basis for identity and community. Some have been caused by antitranssexual beliefs, statements, and actions by LGB people and anti-LGB beliefs, statements, and actions by transsexuals. Some have been linked to conflicts about whether sex, gender, and sexuality are best conceived of within frameworks of biological essentialism or social constructionism. Perhaps the most common conflicts take place when LGB people assume that transsexuals are really people who cannot accept pretransition same-sex attraction and when transsexuals assume that LGB people are really transsexuals who lack the courage to change their sexes.

Transgender Identities

Transsexuality is clearly predicated on notions of physical or biological change. The history of the term "transgender" reveals its interconnections with the language and concept of transsexuality. The term "transgenderist" was first used in the late 1980s to describe a biological male more fully committed to living as a woman than a transvestite or cross-dresser, but not interested in changing sex biologically. The concept was also applied to biological females more fully committed to living as men. The transgenderist crossed boundaries of gender, but not sex. Many who label themselves "transgender" neither want nor desire sex reassignment surgery, but their gender-crossing actions are not limited to periodic cross-dressing. Instead, they live the majority of their lives in a gender in conflict with their biological sex, and they may identify at different times as a man, woman, neither/nor, or both/and. Many transgenderists reject the label "transsexual" because they have no intention of seeking surgery or hormonal treatment. When the concept is applied historically, women who have passed as men and men who have passed as women can be regarded as transgender.

"Transgender," however, has also acquired a second and quite different meaning, functioning as an all-encompassing term referring to the full range of gender-crossing phenomena. Ironically, this subverts the specificity originally intended by transgenderists. As used most commonly today, "transgender" is an umbrella term that describes anyone who disturbs normative gender or sex identifications or dichotomies. While an effective vehicle for building coalitions between various types of gender-crossers, this broad use of the term may simplify its important and often contested relationship to transsexuality female-to-male transsexual theorist. Henry Rubin, for example, believes that the tension between the two is the result of the transgender person's lack of definitive gender identification, while the transsexual affirms the notion of stable gender. Yet, one could counter that not everyone who identifies as transsexual seeks a finite gender identity, while not all transgenders desire a complete gender-free society.

Leslie Feinberg is one of the most influential figures who identifies as transgender. Feinberg's books, *Stone Butch Blues* (1993) and *Transgender Warriors* (1996), make clear the complexities of transgender identification. Feinberg "hirself" ("hir-" is Feinberg's constructed pronoun) epitomizes the transitivity of transgender: she/he was born biologically female, took testosterone, and underwent a double mastectomy, yet later discontinued hormone treatment and now describes hirself as a transgender lesbian.

Transvestism and Cross-Dressing

Historically, the term "transvestite" is associated with an anti-LGBT scientific taxonomy and, therefore, is rarely used in popular discourse today. Although transvestism may be used interchangeably with cross-dressing—Marjorie Garber in fact does this in her work *Vested Interests* (1992)—they are distinct terms and the histories of each sometimes bring them into opposition. Garber distinguishes between the two by what she describes as "urinary segregation." Cross-dressers who want to pass prefer to read the signs literally: "those in pants, in there; those in skirts, in here" (p. 14). However, for transvestites and transsexuals, this type of segregation connotes inflexible gender binaries. For Garber, though certainly not for all cross-dressers and transvestites, cross-dressing is implicitly temporary, an act of gender performativity, whereas transvestism is a permanent crossing. Transvestites and cross-dressers may be lesbian, gay, bisexual, or straight.

The fascination with cross-dressing, transvestism, and the related phenomenon of passing precedes the formal, scientific studies of the late nineteenth and twentieth centuries. European and American colonists were fascinated with gender ambiguity and gender-crossing, both in their own communities and in the Native American cultures that they encountered. In the eighteenth and nineteenth centuries, cross-dressing and passing provided an important means of escaping from the confines of separate spheres for women and men. This was the case especially for women, who experienced various forms of cultural, economic, legal, political, and social oppression. Many records of female cross-dressers and passing women survive, including court transcripts and newspaper accounts of those who were discovered postmortem to have been female. For women, the military proved to be an important means of escape from traditional roles. During the Civil War, for example, hundreds of soldiers were actually women who cross-dressed and passed as men. While some presume that such soldiers were moved to cross-dress by wartime patriotism or economic necessity, there were also veterans of the Civil War who were discovered at their deaths to have been women. Cross-dressing and passing women may have enjoyed the freedom they experienced as men; they may have appreciated the opportunity to perform their desired gender identity; and they may have been motivated by same-sex sexual attraction. Men also cross-dressed and passed in order to escape the confines of culturally defined masculinity and heterosexuality.

Drag Performance and Impersonation

There is also a long history of male and female impersonators on the American stage and in other aspects of entertainment and leisure culture. In the first part of the nineteenth century, male impersonators were probably more common, but toward the end of the century, female impersonation became more dominant. Both were primarily performed through burlesque or vaudeville acts, particularly as a network of railroads developed in the United States. Although many grew concerned that cross-dressing and drag shows were actually covers for homosexuality, these shows became even more popular during and after World Wars I and II. Female impersonation also increasingly appeared in American bars and nightclubs; these performers were often associated with the gay community, though not all performers identified as gay. Nevertheless, drag queen shows played an important role in the proliferation of gay public spaces. Before LGB bars could advertise publicly, for example, some announced performances by female impersonators, covertly signaling that LGB people were welcome. Esther Newton's study of female impersonators (1972) discusses the social networks they formed, in part to teach each other about stage performance and passing both on and off stage. Newton's work makes clear that male cross-dressers have a much more elaborate subculture than male impersonators.

Jennie Livingston's 1990 documentary *Paris Is Burning* is an archive that reveals the limitations of clinically defined terms such as "transvestism." Livingston's film follows several members of Harlem's drag community, most memorably as they prepare for their drag balls. Most of them are poor, homeless, and/or prostitutes, but they all belong to subsets of their larger community, like the House of Pendavis, run by "mothers" or drag queens who have matured in the extensive nonbiologically defined kinship system. Drag balls are actually an integral part of Harlem's history. The Hamilton Lodge Ball dates back to 1869, and in its early years the attendees were mostly working class. The popularity of the balls increased in the 1920s and early 1930s, but they were then forced underground because of continual harassment and raids by New York City police. Cross-dressing and transvestism are ultimately dependent on clothing choice. Some personal narratives of cross-dressing convey the sense that temporary, occasional, and periodic dressing in feminine or masculine clothes allows the narrators to achieve satisfaction. Yet for some, cross-dressing proves to be an initial step in more permanent transgenderism. Feinberg points out, for example, that because "it is our entire spirit—the essence of who we are—that doesn't conform to narrow gender stereotypes, many people who in the past have been referred to as cross-dressers, transvestites, drag queens, and drag kings today define themselves as trans*gender*" (p. xi). Her statement makes clear that, while many additional permutations exist, none of

these definitions, as categories or practices, are immutable.

Right and Wrong Bodies

In many transgender and transsexual narratives, individual subjects identify a growing sense of being in the "wrong body." In many autobiographical accounts, individuals attempt to describe the ways in which their performative gender does not align with their biological sex. In her memoir *Crossing* (1999), Deirdre McCloskey recalls trying on her mother's underwear and experiencing sexual arousal. Yet, her intense desire was to actually be a woman, not just perform a particular form of femininity. McCloskey reiterates throughout her narrative that she was a woman born with a man's body. More recently, some have raised concerns about the "wrong body" trope that has come to define discourses and ontologies of transsexuality and transgenderism. As Jay Prosser (1998) has argued, transsexuality first entered the lexicon as a medicodiscursive sign of extreme transvestism, with the body's clothing—literally the skin—seen as something that needed to be changed (p. 69). Christine Jorgensen was initially classified as a transvestite before "officially" being described as transsexual. "As a formula that continues to trope transsexuality in its medical narrative version, being trapped in the wrong body has become the crux of an authenticating transsexual 'rhetoric': language, narratives, and figures that the subject deploys to obtain access to hormones and surgery" (p. 69). Prosser's point elucidates the continued reliance on, and entrapment of, those who identify as trans to and by medical institutions and authorities that, from the beginning of its history in the United States, have had the power to authenticate and legitimate the feelings and experiences of gender variants. Autobiographical tropes as resources are infinitely important to the histories of transsexuality, transgenderism, cross-dressing, and transvestism.

The complicated and politically laden dilemmas of authority, authenticity, objectivity, subjectivity, and historiographical bias are increasingly discussed and challenged at the academic level. Who, for example, can be a "trans scholar" and who has the authority to write about transsexuality? Trans studies is both moving toward and resisting disciplinary definition. Scholars such as Jay Prosser and Jacob Hale are producing innovative and important work that makes trans more visible while they also question how the politics of visibility interpolates trans-identified people in yet another discourse.

Bibliography

Bullough, Vern L., and Bonnie Bullough. *Cross Dressing, Sex, and Gender*. Philadelphia: University of Pennsylvania Press, 1993.

Cromwell, Jason. *Transmen and FTMs: Identities, Bodies, Genders, and Sexualities.* Urbana and Chicago: University of Illinois Press, 1999.

Devor, Holly. *FTM: Female-to-Male Transsexuals in Society.* Bloomington: Indiana University Press, 1997.

Feinberg, Leslie. *Stone Butch Blues: A Novel.* Ithaca, N.Y.: Firebrand, 1993.

———. *Transgender Warriors: Making History From Joan of Arc to Rupaul.* Boston: Beacon, 1996.

Garber, Marjorie. *Vested Interests: Cross-Dressing and Cultural Anxiety.* New York: Routledge, 1992.

Halberstam, Judith. *Female Masculinity.* Durham, N.C.: Duke University Press, 1998.

McCloskey, Deirdre. *Crossing: A Memoir.* Chicago: University of Chicago Press, 1999.

Meyerowitz, Joanne. "Sex Research at the Borders of Gender: Transvestites, Transsexuals, and Alfred C. Kinsey." *GLQ* 75, no. 1 (2000): 72–90.

———. *How Sex Changed: A History of Transsexuality in the United States.* Cambridge, Mass.: Harvard University Press, 2002.

Newton, Esther. *Mother Camp: Female Impersonation in America.* Chicago: University of Chicago Press, 1972.

Prosser, Jay. *Second Skins: The Body Narratives of Transsexuality.* New York: Columbia University Press, 1998.

Kara Thompson

See also FEMMES AND BUTCHES; GENDER AND SEX; INTERSEXUALS AND INTERSEXED PEOPLE; TWO-SPIRIT FEMALES; TWO-SPIRIT MALES.

TRICKING

Tricking is a slang word used to describe a casual, quick, or short-term sexual encounter with another person. Tricking is a term commonly used by gay men, although lesbians also trick and refer to certain sexual partners as tricks. The terms "tricking" and "trick" were adopted by gay men from prostitute slang and were used originally to describe sex that involved a monetary transaction. It is difficult to determine exactly when gay men adopted the terms, but George Chauncey points out that gay men in New York City during the early twentieth century developed a language of their own to distinguish themselves from and resist dominant culture, to create solidarity, and to communicate with each other without drawing attention from straights.

Sex with a trick is generally short term, but it is not necessarily anonymous. Also, a sexual encounter that begins as a trick can sometimes lead to a longer-term relationship. Sex with a trick may involve a full range of sexual acts, but some individuals limit what types of sex-

ual acts they will do with a trick, and this limitation may be a part of how they define who is a trick and who is not.

Research on Tricking

Tricking has not received much scholarly attention, although promiscuous sex among gay men, which includes tricking, has. Scholarly attention has also focused on gay and lesbian erotica and literature, and tricking is a term and phenomenon often used in this material. These texts usually suggest that the person who is tricking knows little, if anything, about the person with whom they are tricking and that there is no, or very little, intention of having anything other than a sexual relationship. In these texts, it is unusual for a longer-term relationship to develop from a trick.

Some gay writers and commentators suggest that tricking is an institution that is particular to gay male communities. Although this can be debated, the suggestion itself speaks to the importance of tricking for many gay men. However, tricking and casual sex are also important to some lesbians.

Beginning in the 1970s, some lesbians and lesbian feminists placed increased emphasis on nontraditional sexual behaviors, including tricking, identifying these as part of a larger agenda of rejecting patriarchal institutions and conventional gender norms. Pro-sex feminists fighting for lesbian pornography and exploring lesbian sadomasochism in the 1980s and 1990s also sometimes promoted pleasure-seeking activities such as tricking.

Nevertheless, scholarly and popular writing about gay male tricking is much more common than writing about lesbian tricking. This is likely the result of gendered stereotypes about women and sex and the social restrictions placed on women's sexuality in patriarchal societies. Men, both gay and straight, have had and continue to have much more freedom to explore and enjoy their sexualities, including promiscuous sex and tricking.

Controversies about Tricking

Much of the controversy surrounding tricking and promiscuous sex concerns sexually transmitted diseases, most notably AIDS. Although not new, gay tricking and promiscuous sex entered the public spotlight during the gay liberation movement that followed the Stonewall Riots of 1969. This movement valorized sexual liberation and expression, within and outside of primary relationships. Exploring and acting on one's fantasies was encouraged, regardless of how many people this involved or whether the sex took place in the bedroom, the back room of a bar, or a public restroom.

However, not all lesbians and gay men agreed with sexual liberation. Some thought that sexual liberation made sex into the central focus of lesbian and gay identities, ignoring other, nonsexual, aspects of identity and perpetuating stereotypes about gays and lesbians. Although Larry Kramer was not the only person within lesbian and gay communities who believed this, and he did not start the debate about promiscuous sexual behavior, his 1978 novel *Faggots* galvanized the debate within gay and lesbian communities. Kramer's arguments against promiscuous sexual behavior and the damage it could cause to lesbian and gay communities surfaced again, with more legitimacy, during the AIDS crisis.

When AIDS was identified and linked to sexual behavior in the early 1980s, sexual liberation, promiscuity, and tricking were criticized more strongly, both from within queer communities and by the general public, public health officials, and the state. Although tricking did not stop after the advent of AIDS, it did take on a new, very negative connotation for many people. For these critics, tricking was no longer a way of celebrating gay identity; it could now be seen, as were all forms of promiscuous sex, as a death wish. Gay men were labeled, within and outside of queer communities, as sexual deviants and disease carriers. Many gay men responded to AIDS and the negative sexual label by shifting from sex-positive to sex-critical positions. Tricking and all other forms of promiscuous sex were discouraged, and "safe," monogamous sex was encouraged.

As more knowledge about the disease became available, however, some gay men and lesbians argued that attempts to demonize and stop promiscuous sexual behavior would be worthless and could potentially drive the behavior "underground" and thus further out of reach of sexual educators and AIDS activists. In addition, many people believed that individuals had the right to have sex any way that they wanted to, regardless of the danger of contracting AIDS. They argued that, rather than judging and policing sexual behavior, the community should be attempting to provide information about the disease and how to be as safe as possible, whether tricking or having sex in a longer-term relationship. For many gay men, tricking and promiscuous sex are viewed positively, not negatively, and nothing, including AIDS, will stop them from engaging in these activities. Latter-day controversies about barebacking (anal sex without a condom), the rerelease of 1970s and early 1980s precondom pornography, and new pornography featuring actors without condoms reflect ongoing discussions about these issues.

Tricking is also controversial for some people, regardless of sexually transmitted diseases, because it implies sex outside of a committed, monogamous relationship. Many people feel that tricking is dehumanizing and implies deception, as the literal definition of the word suggests. Some lesbians and gay men, however, continue to believe that limiting sex to the context of a committed, monogamous relationship is based on a heterosexual norm that is of questionable value for queer relationships and sexual expression.

Beyond the Controversy

Although tricking has never completely regained the positive meaning it had during the heyday of gay liberation, it is once again being viewed by many people from a somewhat more neutral stance. Tricking has been and continues to be a part of some LGBT people's sexual experiences, and, more important, many individuals are again willing to talk about tricking openly and without shame. Furthermore, technology, especially the Internet, has introduced new ways of finding tricks and has added to the casualness of tricking, since one does not even need to leave one's house to find a trick or see the person physically prior to arranging an encounter.

An example of this move toward a more sex-positive attitude among many queers, and a specific positive nod to tricking, can be found in the film *Trick*, released in 1999 by Fine Line Features. *Trick* is about two young gay men who meet in a New York City bar and spend the rest of the evening trying to find a place to have sex. The film was popular among queer audiences and even won the Audience Favorite Award at the Miami Gay and Lesbian Film Festival in the year of its release.

Bibliography

Bolton, Ralph. "Tricks, Friends, and Lovers." In *Taboo: Sex, Identity, and Erotic Subjectivity in Anthropological Fieldwork*. Edited by Don Kulick and Margaret Willson. London: Routledge, 1995.

Califia, Pat. "Unmonogamy: Loving Tricks and Tricking Lovers." In *Public Sex: The Culture of Radical Sex*. Pittsburg, Pa.: Cleis Press, 1994.

Chauncey, George. *Gay New York: Gender, Urban Culture, and the Making of the Gay Male World, 1890–1940*. New York: Basic Books, 1994.

Clum, John M. "The Time before the War: AIDS, Memory, and Desire." *American Literature* 62, no. 4 (1990): 648–667.

Colter, Ephen Glenn, and Dangerous Bedfellows (Wayne Hoffman, Eva Pendleton, Alison Redick, and David Serlin). *Policing Public Sex: Queer Politics and the Future of AIDS Activism*. Boston: South End Press, 1996.

Dawson, Jeff. *Gay and Lesbian Online: Your Indispensable Guide to Cruising the Queer Web*. 4th ed. Los Angeles and New York: Alyson, 2000.

Kramer, Larry. *Faggots*. New York: Random House, 1978.

Munson, Marcia, and Judith P. Stelboum, eds. *The Lesbian Polyamory Reader: Open Relationships, Non-Monogamy, and Causal Sex.* New York: Haworth, 1999.

Murray, Stephen O. "Self Size and Observable Sex." In *Public Sex/Gay Space.* Edited by William Leap. New York: Columbia University Press, 1999.

Sheppard, Simon. "Sex Talk: Speaking of Tricking." Available from http://www.planetout.com/pno/.

Griff M. Tester

See also CRUISING; MONOGAMY AND NONMONOGAMY, TEAROOMS (BATHROOMS).

TSANG, Daniel Chuen-Tuen
(b. 27 October 1949), activist, scholar, educator, journalist.

Daniel Chuen-Tuen Tsang was born in 1949 in Hong Kong, the youngest of three sons. His father, Kenneth, a doctor, graduated from the University of Hong Kong. His mother, Josephine, was born in the United States, graduated from the University of Washington, and moved in 1933 to Hong Kong where she worked as a librarian and later for a journalist. In Hong Kong, Tsang attended the elite Diocesan Boys School, an Anglican Anglo-Chinese school. He came to the United States to study at the University of Redlands. Upon graduating in 1971, Tsang went to the University of Michigan to pursue graduate work in political science. After completing his master's degree in political science (1973), he began his master's degree in library science, graduating in 1977.

During his time at Michigan, Tsang developed his roles in the Asian American and LGBT movements. For the next thirty years, Tsang created vehicles for networking and organization and documented and preserved the history of the Asian American and LGBT movements. Tsang was actively involved in Ann Arbor's Gay Liberation Front, the Graduate Employees Organization (GEO), and East Wing, an Asian American activist organization. Tsang's work focused on affirmative action, labor rights, and gay rights, and his writings and activism reflected a critique of restrictive stereotypes and analysis of the intersecting nature of class, race, gender, and sexuality. In 1975 Tsang was a negotiator for the GEO in what became the first strike by teachers in the history of the university. His central involvement and that of other LGBT activists led to a GEO demand that the University of Michigan include in the employee contract a sexual preference non-discrimination clause.

Tsang also mobilized his analysis through writing (publishing in *Michigan Free Press,* among other venues) to remind the late 1960s and 1970s LGBT movement of its failings. In particular, he criticized the LGBT movement for viewing Asians as foreign and only whites as gay. He directed similar critical analyses at the radical Asian American movement. In 1975, Tsang wrote "Gay Awareness," which is considered the gay Asian male manifesto. Published in *Bridge: An Asian American Perspective,* the first national Asian American magazine, Tsang's essay condemned the silence surrounding the issue of being Asian and gay, which should have been broken by a 1973 letter by Hung Nung published in *Bridge* that stated that being Asian and gay were not "mutually exclusive." After the publication of his article, Tsang began a correspondence with other Asian American lesbian and gay men, including activist Steven Lew, later the founder of Gay Asian Rap, and others who told Tsang that his writing had the effect of making it more comfortable for them to come out. Tsang's role in the LGBT and Asian American movements was not only to offer a critical voice. In 1977, Tsang began the *Midwest Gay Academic Journal* (MWGAJ) with two co-editors. By 1978, Tsang was the primary editor. In keeping with the larger goal of the MWGAJ to encourage research and writing by and about LGBT people in 1976, Tsang taught one of the earliest classes on LGBT issues at the University of Michigan, called "Politics of Gay Liberation." In 1977, he co-taught "Lesbian and Gay Experience."

Upon moving to Philadelphia in 1978 to work as a research librarian at Temple University, Tsang changed the name of MWGAJ to *Gay Insurgent: A Gay Left Journal.* This research journal had two goals—to increase knowledge and to preserve the material of the radical struggles of the era. Tsang's collection, organization, and preservation of the material of 1960s movements is some of the most significant work he has done for the LGBT and Asian American movements.

The independent alternative media was the network by which the many different facets of 1960s and 1970s movements communicated. Alternative media also contradicted prevailing stereotypes about racial and sexual "minorities" and was critical for exchanging information, connecting people, and disseminating ideas. Since the middle 1970s, Tsang's work has involved not only the production of that media but also its preservation. In 1991, Tsang compiled the microform masters of the U.S. Underground Alternative Press of the 1960s and 1970s, the first time they had been compiled in one place.

Tsang's work did not stop at preservation. He cofounded such organizations as Philadelphia's Asian Americans United in the early 1980s and the Alternative Research Center and Alliance Working for Asian Rights and Empowerment in the 1990s. Perhaps more significant for the Asian American LGBT movement, in 1979 with Don Kao, Tsang organized the first National Third World Lesbian and Gay Conference gathering of Asian American lesbians and gay men in Washington, D.C. Attendants included Mini Liu, later founder of the Committee Against Anti-Asian Violence, Siong-huat Chua, later founder of Boston Asian Gay Men and Lesbians, Richard Fung, later founder of Gay Asians Toronto, Tana Loy, and Michiyo Cornell.

In 1980, *Gay Insurgent* focused an issue on Asian American lesbians and gays, documenting the call to action, describing the events of the conference, and encouraging the recognition of Asian American lesbians and gays, by both Asians and non-Asians. Most conference speakers and *Gay Insurgent* writers echoed the critiques of racism and homophobia, essentialized racial binaries, white privilege, and capitalist hegemony, and most proclaimed the exhilaration of Asian American LGBT pride. Throughout this period, Tsang also kept in touch with the Hong Kong gay liberation movement, writing for *Far Eastern Economic Review*, and eventually organizing the first Tongzhi Conference with activists including Russell Leong, editor of *Amerasia Journal*, in Hong Kong in 1998. Tsang has continued his documentary project on a number of fronts. After working as reference librarian for the Community College of Philadelphia, as librarian of the Free Library of Philadelphia, and as founder and curator of the Lavender Archives, Tsang moved to the University of California, Irvine, where he is currently the bibliographer for the Library's social sciences data archive. He also teaches at Irvine and is the host of a weekly radio program on KUCI, 88.9 FM called "Subversity." In testimony to the subversive weight of Tsang's work and to the surveillance of radical activists by the state, the Central Intelligence Agency (CIA) began keeping a covert file on Tsang in 1979. In the late 1980s, in a case handled by the American Civil Liberties Union, he sued the CIA. In 1995 they settled with Tsang, paying him $46,000 and agreeing to stop surveillance of his work. In 2000, Tsang was awarded the Media Award by Orange County Culture Pride. Also in 2000, he was awarded the Jackie Eubanks Memorial Award by the American Library Association's Alternatives in Print Task Force. He is on the editorial board of the *Journal of Homosexuality* and on the advisory board of the Alternative Press Center.

Bibliography

Kindy, Kimberly. "Prying Eyes Were Watching UCI's Library Activists." *The Orange County Register* (25 January 1998): AO1.

GAY $2.50
INSURGENT
No. 6   a gay left journal   1980

WE'RE ASIANS GAY&PROUD

Daniel Chuen-Tuen Tsang. The Asian American and LGBT activist and scholar appears (fifth from left, wearing a mustache) on the cover of a special issue of *Gay Insurgent: A Gay Left Journal* in 1980. [Daniel C. Tsang]

Tsang, Daniel. "Daniel Tsang Papers, 1970–1978." Bentley Historical Library, University of Michigan.

———. "Gay Awareness." *Bridge: An Asian American Perspective* 3, no. 4 (February 1975): 44–45.

———. "Slicing Silence: Asian Progressives Come Out." In *Asian Americans: The Movement and the Moment*. Edited by Steve Louie and Glenn K. Omatsu. Los Angeles: UCLA Asian American Studies Center Press, 2001.

Tsang, Daniel, ed. *Gay Insurgent* 1 (1978).

———. *Midwest Gay Academic Journal* 1, no. 3 (1978).

Susie J. Lee

See also ASIAN AMERICAN LGBTQ ORGANIZATIONS AND PERIODICALS; CHUA, SIONG-HUAT; FUKAYA, MICHIYO; GAY LIBERATION FRONT.

TSUI, Kitty (b. 4 September 1952), writer, activist, and athlete.

Kitty Tsui ranks as an important figure in Asian American and LGBT movements because of her writing and activism in both communities. Tsui's writings are widely known for their critical perspective on the intersections of race, gender, and sexuality; for articulating the experiences of homophobia and heterosexism within culturally specific contexts; and for bridging the various communities of which she is a member.

Born in Kowloon, Hong Kong, and raised in England, Tsui is the oldest of four children. In 1968, Tsui's family immigrated to San Francisco. Tsui studied creative writing at San Francisco State University, where she became active in the Third World student movement. During the late 1960s and early 1970s, Third World student activists began to define, document, and create their own cultural histories, experiences, and institutions. As a part of this effort, Tsui and others focused on cultural production, specifically through the written word, to empower and increase the visibility and representation of Third World people in general and of Asian Americans in particular. As the director of the Third World Poetry series, Tsui helped provide an early public space for Third World writers and poets, including Ntozake Shange, Lawson Inada, and Paula Gunn Allen, who later became well known for their work. Tsui also participated in some of the earliest publications by and about Third World writers, including *Third World Women* (1972) which she coedited.

In addition to her growing consciousness and activism on race issues, in her early twenties Tsui became aware of her strong feelings for women. She had become friends with a coworker who came out to her as bisexual, and Tsui responded with many questions because she hungered for knowledge about lesbians. In the late 1970s, she came out publicly to the Asian American community in an article, "Coming Out: We Are Here in the Asian Community: A Dialogue with Three Asian Women," published in *Bridge*, a journal by and about Asian Americans. In this article, Tsui and others talked about the overlapping oppression that LGBT people experience along with other minorities, suffering not only because of their sexual orientation but also because of their membership in a minority group. They also expressed how much there was to learn and share about each other's experiences so that there could be better understanding between Third World people, Third World LGBT people, and the more-typically white majority of LGBT people.

The themes of shared oppression; the need for self-empowerment for Asian American women; and an understanding of how her multiple identities, as a Chinese American and as a woman, inform and transform her lesbianism run throughout Tsui's writing. Tsui expressed these themes early in her career through her participation in a collective of Asian American women writers called *Unbound Feet*, which included Nancy Hom, Genny Lim, Canyon Sam, Nellie Wong, and Merle Woo. Performances by *Unbound Feet* became venues for Asian American lesbians because they knew that Sam, Tsui, and Woo were lesbians and that their material reflected the experience of being Asian American and lesbian.

Tsui's multiple identities as a woman, a Chinese American, and a lesbian constitute the main themes of her landmark book, *The Words of a Woman Who Breathes Fire*. Many of Tsui's other writings—articles, short stories, and poetry—also address these themes, as well as issues of sex, erotica, sadomasochism, and power. As Karin Aguilar-San Juan noted in "Landmarks in Literature by Asian American Lesbians," published in *Signs*, Tsui emerged as one of the earliest foremothers of this body of literature and "offered us an image of a proud, defiant, 'no bullshit' woman, the dyke we all wanted to be."

In addition to her writing, Tsui has competed in Gay Games II, where she won a bronze medal for physique, and Gay Games III, where she won a gold medal for the first ever same-sex couples physique event.

Tsui has been writing and publishing for several decades, and her work has been included in more than seventy anthologies worldwide. She continues to help build the ever-growing body of literature by and about Asian American LGBT people that she helped start. Tsui responded to a question about stereotypes and how people do not know what it is like to be an Asian American lesbian in the "Coming Out" article: "Talk about it, write about it, spread the word, let it be known" (p. 24). Tsui has taken her own advice to heart and has helped countless people to read and learn about the complexity of the lives and loves of Asian American lesbians.

Bibliography

Aguilar-San Juan, Karin. "Landmarks in Asian American Lesbian Literature." *Signs* 18, no. 4 (summer 1993): 936–944.

Hom, Alice Y. Personal correspondence with author, April 2003.

Noda, Barbara, Kitty Tsui, and Z. Wong. "Coming Out: We Are Here in the Asian Community: A Dialogue with Three Asian Women." *Bridge Magazine* 7, no. 1 (spring 1979): 22–24.

Tsang, Daniel C. "Slicing Silence: Asian Progressives Come Out." In *Asian Americans: The Movement and the Moment.* Steve Louie and Glenn K. Omatsu, eds. Los Angeles: UCLA Asian American Studies Press, 2001: 220–239.

Alice Y. Hom

See also ALLEN, PAULA GUNN; ASIAN AMERICAN LGBTQ ORGANIZATIONS AND PERIODICALS; LITERATURE; WOO, MERLE.

TWO-SPIRIT FEMALES

Among Native American groups, at least forty had multiple-gender systems in which females identified as two-spirit. This identity has been given many labels by European and American travelers, officials, and scholars, but the French word *berdache* was the most common term associated with it. *Berdache* was derived from the Persian term *bardaj,* which referred to a boy slave kept for sexual purposes. A number of Native writers objected to the use of the term because it lumped together many different identities under one colonially imposed and stigmatized term. Paula Gunn Allen, in particular, argued that it was not relevant to females, and chose to use the terms "dyke" and "lesbian" in her groundbreaking essay "Beloved Women: Lesbians in American Indian Culture." Following the growth of a Native lesbian and gay movement in the 1980s, the term "two-spirit" was chosen in 1990 by Native American individuals attending the third Native American/First Nations Gay and Lesbian Conference. It was rapidly embraced by activists and Native scholars to encompass lesbians, gay men, bisexuals, and transgendered individuals both historically and at the turn of the twenty-first century. "Two-spirit" signifies the presence of both masculine and feminine in one person. Although on the one hand, this term is meant to be inclusive of both males and females, on the other, activists such as Beverly Little Thunder stress the need to continue to talk specifically about female two-spirits because they have been so invisible in the scholarly literature.

The literature on two-spirit people has blossomed since the early 1980s. From that time, in-depth scholarship and debates over terms and theories have meant the continued revision and reformulation of ideas about Native genders. This process signifies the importance of "getting it right," as so many Native activists and scholars have demanded of anthropologists and historians. One of the key debates tackles the question of whether two-spirit is a third gender, alternative gender, or something much more. Native and non-Native scholars have argued that many Native tribes have multiple-gender systems; others point to the flexibility of gender identities that may shift several times over a person's lifetime. Because being two-spirit is also a spiritual identity, some argue that it is not a gender at all. Carrie House points out in her 1997 essay "Navajo Warrior Women" that gender is a restrictive Western notion. Within certain Native cosmological views of the world, a two-spirit identity represents alternatives and possibilities, not genders. In addition, because two-spirit people see two ways, many are thought to have more spiritual power than ordinary humans. Thus, the concept of gender does not adequately correspond to many aspects of the two-spirit identity.

The persistence of two-spirits has also been hotly debated. Non-Native scholars declared that the last "true" two-spirit person disappeared in the early twentieth century. Many tribal groups and individuals, however, retained knowledge of such identities. Even in the face of sometimes extreme U.S. government repression and rejection by tribal leaders, individuals lived lives that reflected Native ideas about two-spirit identities.

Anthropological and Historical Evidence

Accounts from the late 1800s and early 1900s provide evidence of a long-standing and deeply respected institution of female two-spirits. Historically, as well as at the beginning of the twenty-first century, there was no one type of two-spirit female. Their identities varied according to the practices, beliefs, and histories of their tribal groups. The information that follows pertains to female two-spirits of Native American groups in the Southwest, specifically the Mojave, Maricopa, and Cocopa.

Among Southwest Indian groups, spiritual guidance from dreams was an important aspect of life. Dreams foretold the attainment of success or special skills and were faithfully followed by those who dreamt them. The female two-spirit, who was physically female, dreamed about becoming a different gender, sometimes while still in the womb or during childhood. In childhood, the female two-spirit displayed an interest in the activities of boys. Such a child avoided learning tasks that women did, playing instead with boys and making bows and arrows for hunting birds and rabbits. The Mojave *hwame* (female two-spirit) would not play with dolls and refused to shred bark or grind corn, tasks associated with women. Adults acknowledged this gender difference and taught such a child the skills that a boy learned.

Upon reaching puberty, the female two-spirit was initiated into the two-spirit identity. The Mojave publicly acknowledged the new status of the female two-spirit by performing an initiation ceremony. Following this ceremony the female two-spirit assumed a name befitting a man and had the right to marry a woman. At puberty the Cocopa *warrhameh*'s hair was dressed in the male style. Instead of receiving a chin tattoo as women did at puberty, the *warrhameh* had a nose piercing like a man's. These public rites validated the two-spirit's identity, signifying to the community that this person was a man.

As adults, female two-spirits engaged in men's tasks, such as hunting, trapping, cultivating crops, or in some cases fighting in battles. The Mojave *hwame* were said to be excellent providers; they hunted for meat or worked in the fields. *Hwame* were also known to be spiritually powerful, possessing the ability to cure certain diseases. Mojave *hwame* married women and cared for any children of their wives as if they were their own. The wife of a *hwame* was not stigmatized by such a marriage and—if the marriage ended—usually returned to a heterosexual relationship.

Negotiated Identities

Female two-spirits' identities, then and now, are constantly being negotiated and transformed. They have been shaped in part by the colonial presence of the U.S. government and its majority white citizens. The story of Masahai, a Mojave *hwame* who lived in the late 1800s under colonial rile, reflects the erosion of Native beliefs about the spiritual power of the *hwame* and the consequent loss of respect for those who lived as *hwame*. One hundred years later two-spirit people tell stories of identifying first as lesbian or gay like their white lesbian and gay counterparts in urban areas, and then learning about and identifying as two-spirit.

Native writers in the late twentieth and early twenty-first centuries argue against neat definitions and categories for two-spirit people. Like any identity, two-spirit is a continually changing and negotiated category. Beverly Little Thunder writes in 1997 in her essay "I Am a Lakota Womyn" that two-spirit people are all so different in so many ways. She identifies as a Lakota womyn and a mother who loves women and has no desire to be a man. Yet she can perform many tasks that are considered men's jobs. Other stories of female two-spirits tell of female cowboys or mannish females, or spiritual beliefs that have little or nothing to do with occupations or sexual orientation. Rather than confining two-spirit females to a particular pigeonhole, we are asked to remember that two-spirits are following the path they have been directed to follow, a path that takes many different forms.

Bibliography

Allen, Paula Gunn. "Beloved Women: Lesbians in American Indian Cultures." In *The Sacred Hoop: Recovering the Feminine in American Indian Traditions*. Boston: Beacon Press, 1986. An earlier version of the essay appeared in the journal *Conditions 7* in 1981.

Blackwood, Evelyn. "Sexuality and Gender in Certain Native American Tribes: The Case of Cross-Gender Females." *Signs: Journal of Women in Culture and Society* 10 (1984): 27–42.

Brant, Beth, ed. *A Gathering of Spirit: A Collection by North American Indian Women*. Ithaca, N.Y.: Firebrand Books, 1988.

Jacobs, Sue-Ellen, Wesley Thomas, and Sabine Lang, eds. *Two-Spirit People: Native American Gender Identity, Sexuality, and Spirituality*. Urbana: University of Illinois Press, 1997.

Lang, Sabine. *Men as Women, Women as Men: Changing Gender in Native American Cultures*. Translated from the German by John L. Vantine. Austin: University of Texas Press, 1998.

Roscoe, Will. *Changing Ones: Third and Fourth Genders in Native North America*. New York: St. Martin's Press, 1998.

Evelyn Blackwood

See also ALLEN, PAULA GUNN; BURNS, RANDY; CHURCHES, TEMPLES, AND RELIGIOUS GROUPS; MASAHAI AMATKWISAI; NATIVE AMERICANS; NATIVE AMERICAN LGBTQ ORGANIZATIONS AND PUBLICATIONS; NATIVE AMERICAN RELIGIONS AND SPIRITUALITIES; NATIVE AMERICAN STUDIES; NATIVE AMERICANS; PI'TAMAKAN; QANQON KAMEK KLAULA; RADICAL SPIRITUALITY AND NEW AGE RELIGION; TWO-SPIRIT MALES; WOMAN CHIEF.

TWO-SPIRIT MALES

Many Native American indigenous cultures have traditionally held feminine or androgynous males in high respect. Such males were sometimes referred to as *berdache* by early French explorers in North America. Because these androgynous males were commonly married to a masculine man or had sex with men, the term *berdache* had a clear homosexual connotation. Both the Spanish in Latin America and the English colonists in North America condemned them as sodomites.

The Religious Perspective

Rather than emphasizing the homosexual orientation of these feminine males, however, many Native American cultures focused on the spiritual gifts of such persons. American Indian traditionalists, even in the early twenty-first century, tend to see a person's basic character as a reflection of their spirit. Since everything that exists is thought to come from the spirit world, androgynous or transgender persons are seen as doubly blessed, having both the spirit of a man and the spirit of a woman. Thus, they are honored for having two spirits and are seen as more spiritually gifted than the typical masculine male or feminine female.

From this religious perspective, androgynous or transgender persons are commonly honored as sacred. Therefore, many Native American religions, rather than stigmatizing such persons, often looked to them as religious leaders and teachers. Because researchers are so dependent upon the written sources of early European explorers, it is difficult to say with certainty exactly how widespread were these traditions of respect. Quite similar religious traditions existed among the native peoples of Siberia and many other parts of Asia. Since the ancestors of Native Americans migrated from Siberia over fifteen thousand years ago, and since reports of highly respected two-spirit androgynous persons have been reported among indigenous Americans from Alaska in the north to Chile in the south, androgyny seems to be quite ancient among humans.

Though some anthropologists have linked two-spirit people with transsexuality, there was no tradition of Native Americans castrating two-spirit males. Rather than attempting to change the physical body, Native Americans emphasized a person's spirit, or character, as being most important. Instead of seeing two-spirit males as transsexual males who try to make themselves into women, it is more accurate to understand them as unique individuals who take on a gender status that is different from both men and women. This alternative gender status offers a range of possibilities, from only slightly effeminate men to androgynous or transgender persons and to those who completely cross-dress and act as women. The emphasis of Native Americans is not to force every person into one box, but to allow for the reality of diversity in gender and sexual identities.

Because so many eastern North American cultures were so quickly overwhelmed by the European invasion, there is not much evidence of two-spirit traditions in those societies. But the little evidence that does exist suggests that, especially before they converted to Christianity, these eastern Indians also respected two-spirit people. Most of the evidence for respectful two-spirit traditions is focused on the Native peoples of the Plains, the Great Lakes, the Southwest, and California. With over a thousand vastly different cultural and linguistic backgrounds, it is important not to overgeneralize for the indigenous peoples of North America. Some documentary sources suggest that a minority of societies treated two-spirit persons disrespectfully by kidding them or discouraging children from taking on a two-spirit role. However, many of the documents that report negative reactions are themselves suspect and should be evaluated critically in light of the preponderance of evidence that suggests a respectful attitude. In addition, some European commentators, from early frontier explorers to modern anthropologists, have been influenced by their homophobic prejudices to distort Native attitudes.

Economic Contributions

Two-spirit people were respected by Native societies not only due to religious attitudes, but also because of practical concerns. Since their gender roles involved a mixture of both masculine and feminine traits, two-spirit persons could do the work of both men and women. They were often considered hard workers and artistically gifted craftspersons, of great value to their extended families and communities. Among some groups, such as the Navajo, a family was believed to be economically advantaged by having a *nadleh* (literally translated as "one who is transformed") androgynous person as a relative. Two-spirit persons often assisted in raising their siblings' children, served as adoptive parents for homeless children, and took care of elderly relatives.

A feminine male who preferred to do women's work (gathering wild plants or farming domestic plants) was logically expected to marry a masculine male, who did men's work (hunting and warfare). Because a family needed both plant foods and meat, a masculine female hunter, in turn, usually married a feminine female to provide these complementary gender roles for economic survival. The gender-conforming spouse of two-spirit people did not identify as homosexual or as anything other than normal.

The Waning and Revival of Respect

In the twentieth century, as homophobic European Christian influences increased among many Native Americans, respect for same-sex love and for androgynous persons greatly declined. Two-spirit males were often forced, either by government officials, Christian missionaries, or their own communities, to conform to a masculine gender role. Some who could not conform went underground or committed suicide. With the imposition of European American marriage laws, the same-sex marriages of two-spirit people and their spouses were no longer legally recognized. But with the revitalization of Native American Red Power cultural pride in the 1960s and 1970s and the rise of gay and lesbian liberation movements at the same time, a new respect for androgyny started slowly reemerging among Indian people.

Because of this tradition of respect, in the 1990s many LGBT Native American activists in the United States and Canada rejected the French word *berdache* in favor of the term "two-spirit people" to describe themselves. Many non-Indians have incorporated knowledge of Native American two-spirit traditions into their increasing acceptance of same-sex love, androgyny, and transgender diversity. Native American same-sex marriages have been used as a model for legalizing same-sex marriages in the new millennium, and the spiritual gifts of androgynous persons have started to become more recognized.

Bibliography

Allen, Paula Gunn. *The Sacred Hoop: Recovering the Feminine in American Indian Traditions.* Boston: Beacon Press, 1986.

Jacobs, Sue-Ellen, Wesley Thomas, and Sabine Lang, eds. *Two-Spirit People: Native American Gender Identity, Sexuality, and Spirituality.* Urbana: University of Illinois Press, 1997.

Katz, Jonathan. *Gay American History: Lesbians and Gay Men in the U.S.A., a Documentary.* New York: Crowell, 1976.

Lang, Sabine. *Men as Women, Women as Men: Changing Gender in Native American Cultures.* Translated from the German by John L. Vantine. Austin: University of Texas Press, 1998.

Roscoe, Will. *The Zuni Man-Woman.* Albuquerque: University of New Mexico Press, 1991.

———. *Changed Ones: Third and Fourth Genders in Native North America.* New York: St. Martin's Press, 1998.

Roscoe, Will, ed. *Living the Spirit: A Gay American Indian Anthology.* New York: St. Martin's Press, 1988.

Williams, Walter L. *The Spirit and the Flesh: Sexual Diversity in American Indian Culture.* Boston: Beacon Press, 1986.

Walter L. Williams

See also ALLEN, PAULA GUNN; ANDROGYNY; BURNS, RANDY; CHURCHES, TEMPLES, AND RELIGIOUS GROUPS; KLAH, HASTÍÍN; NATIVE AMERICANS; NATIVE AMERICAN LGBTQ ORGANIZATIONS AND PUBLICATIONS; NATIVE AMERICAN RELIGION AND SPIRITUALITY; NATIVE AMERICAN STUDIES; OSH-TISCH; RADICAL SPIRITUALITY AND NEW AGE RELIGION; TWO-SPIRIT FEMALES; WE'WHA.

U

URBAN, SUBURBAN, AND RURAL GEOGRAPHIES

When and how dissident gender identities and sexual subcultures have emerged in U.S. society has largely depended upon where women and men who desired the social, emotional, and sexual companionship of members of their own sex have found themselves. Perhaps more accurately, it has depended upon where they believed they might find others with similar desires. Sometimes, LGBT Americans migrated to join already established communities. In other cases, however, they made room for themselves where none existed previously, either by creating new spaces and places over which they exercised some modicum of control or by developing tacit social protocols that allowed them to use existing venues in new and unintended ways.

Urban Geographies: Privacy in Public

Urban geographies have played an especially important role in the history of lesbian and gay identity formation in the United States. When the insular and atomized economy of household production gave way to the wage labor system during the nineteenth century, throngs of unmarried women and men flocked to cities in search of work. For some, urban life provided a new context in which they could begin to understand their same-sex desire as something they shared in common with others. Women and men who sought out same-sex sexual encounters were more likely to find partners in the crowded streets of New York or Chicago than in relatively sparsely populated small towns and rural districts. But

while living in a city may have improved one's chances of finding sexual partners, it did not necessarily make having sex easy. For members of the working class especially, living in a city meant living in extraordinarily close quarters. Most crowded into small and unsanitary tenements or lodged in inexpensive boarding houses and transient hotels. Privacy was a privilege enjoyed by relatively few. Instead, working men and women spent much of their lives in public or quasi-public space. They took meals in cafeterias and at inexpensive lunch counters. Before indoor plumbing was common, they often bathed at public baths. They also amused themselves on the streets, in public parks, and at public venues like dance halls and saloons. It was in these spaces that homosexuals sought out intimate contact with others. Paradoxically, it was often easier to steal a few moments of intimacy behind a hedge in a public park than in one's overcrowded room.

For those in the know, urban landscapes represented multiple geographies superimposed atop one another. On the surface was a workaday world consisting of all the familiar urban features—businesses, restaurants, apartment buildings. Not far beneath, however, was a dynamic network of well-known cruising spots, performance venues, gathering places, bars, red-light districts, and bathhouses that catered to the social needs and sexual desires of LGBT Americans. The fortunes of such spaces rose and fell along with the fortunes of the men and women who made use of them. But by the end of the twentieth century most major cities in the United States included specific areas or neighborhoods known colloquially as "gay ghettos." Greenwich Village and, more recently, Chelsea in

217

Urban Brownstones. Greenwich Village in New York City (along with, more recently, the Chelsea area just to the north) has long been one of the LGBT-friendly neighborhoods, in several American cities, that some people call "gay ghettos." [Bill Ross/corbis]

New York City; Dupont Circle in Washington, D.C.; West Hollywood in Los Angeles; "Boystown," or North Halstead, in Chicago; the Castro in San Francisco; and the Montrose neighborhood of Houston are just a few examples. At the end of the twentieth century, most of these neighborhoods included a healthy balance of conspicuously gay or gay-friendly businesses and gay households, a combination of urban amenities that has made them extremely convenient and extremely expensive places to live. Unsurprisingly, some of these revitalized neighborhoods have come under fire for their newfound socioeconomic exclusivity. Longtime residents of surrounding neighborhoods—especially longtime residents of color—have been outspoken critics of what they see as the fiscal opportunism of one social minority exacted against another. Gay and lesbian residents, in turn, have criticized affluent heterosexuals for being latecomers to urban renewal and for driving up housing costs in their now-trendy urban neighborhoods. The whole mess, commonly referred to as gentrification, has laid bare many of the antagonisms that continue to plague relations between members of communities that define themselves in terms of race, class, and sexuality, and it has done so in explicitly geographic terms.

Along with the growth of urban enclaves, the twentieth century also witnessed the emergence of a number of seasonal resort communities that cater primarily to an urban lesbian and gay clientele. Many of these communities have a long history of welcoming eccentric visitors into their midst. For example, Provincetown, Massachusetts, was well known as an artist's colony before it began catering to gay and lesbian vacationers from Boston, New England, and later the world. Fire Island, off Long Island, and Cherry Grove in particular, was also famous for attracting an unusually cosmopolitan set of women and men associated with the theater when gay New Yorkers elected to make it their "summer capital," to quote the anthropologist Esther Newton. But countless other resort communities have gained a reputation for attracting gay and lesbian visitors as well. Rehoboth Beach, Delaware, is extremely popular as a weekend retreat among the gay and lesbian elite of Philadelphia and Washington, D.C., and Saugatuck, Michigan, draws large crowds from Chicago and the surrounding Great Lakes region every year between Memorial Day and Labor Day.

Rural Geographies: Worlds Apart

If urban landscapes have provided LGBT persons with unique opportunities to build distinct subcultures organized around shared experiences and desires, nonmetropolitan landscapes have seen their fair share of homosexual behavior and gender nonconformity as well. While it is true that many lesbians and gay men have flocked to urban centers in the hope of escaping their sense of being different or alone, others have found considerable comfort in small towns and rural areas. This is especially true when their eccentric sex and gender ways have been regarded as familiar aspects of their natal community's local culture rather than overt challenges to it. Native North Americans, for example, have long honored the *berdache*, or "two-spirited" Man-Woman, as a sacred and integral member of their communities. And in *Sexual Behavior in the Human Male,* Alfred Kinsey and his colleagues insisted that "ranchmen, cattle men, prospectors, lumbermen, and farming groups in general" (p. 457) were widely known to engage in homosexual activity on a regular basis.

Indeed, throughout the nineteenth and twentieth centuries, nonmetropolitan America has accommodated a number of homosocial labor communities in which conventional gender norms and prohibitions against homosexual behavior were reorganized or set aside. Most

Suburban Housing Development. Post–World War II suburbia, designed to appeal to traditional nuclear families, has typically been a much less friendly environment for openly LGBT residents—especially same-sex couples—than urban enclaves. [Ed Wheeler/corbis]

famous, perhaps, are the "miner's balls" of the gold rush era, at which prospectors on the western frontier amused themselves by dancing in one another's arms. But there have also been other, considerably more widespread, rural labor communities in which homosociality and homosexuality were normal aspects of everyday life.

After the Civil War advances in agricultural mechanization dissolved countless jobs in rural areas and set tens of thousands of men adrift in search of temporary or seasonal work. In time, a vibrant homosocial culture emerged among them, especially among hoboes and tramps, reputedly the most shiftless of all casual laborers. Like sailors and prisoners, transient laborers organized the meaning of their same-sex sexual activities in highly gendered terms. Older men, known as "jockers" or "wolves," often asserted their social dominance over younger denizens of the road by taking the active or insertive role in anal intercourse. In turn, younger men, known as "punks," "lambs," "preshuns," and "gonsils," gained the benefit of mentorship and some modicum of protection from older men as long as they were willing to play the receptive role in such scenarios. Although transients regularly passed through urban working-class neighborhoods like Chicago's "hobohemia" or Minneapolis' "skid row," they spent the majority of their time riding the rails or on the road in search of work. And contrary to popular belief, it was outside of the city that homosexual relations flourished among hobos, tramps, and other migrants. As the sociologist Nels Anderson observed in *The Hobo,* his classic 1923 study of transients

in the United States, "out of town the pair can travel as companions aiding each other, [but] in the city they can get along better alone" (p. 147).

During the Great Depression many men who might previously have sought their fortunes on the road found opportunity in the Civilian Conservation Corps (CCC), one of the largest of President Franklin Roosevelt's New Deal recovery programs. Between 1933 and 1942, more than three million men between the ages of eighteen and twenty-three passed through the CCC for periods ranging in length from six months to two years. Mostly of rural extraction, "enrollees" quickly took it upon themselves to create a complex social world in which female impersonation and other kinds of campy display were important aspects of everyday life. Drag performances were popular forms of entertainment in many of the more than 1400 camps that were established throughout the country, mostly in extremely isolated and remote areas. Womanless weddings, a predominantly southern genre of folk performance, were also common affairs. CCC enrollees joined men throughout the country in their avid devotion to the physical culture movement. But the isolation of their all-male world allowed them to take this cult of male body worship to new extremes. Among other things, CCC enrollees founded hundreds of nudist clubs and regularly participated in all-male beauty contests.

In the post–World War II era, lesbian and gay subcultures thrived throughout the United States, and not just in coastal megalopolises. As the historian John

Howard has shown, "men like that" created a vibrant gay male culture that spanned the entire state of Mississippi by 1969, the year in which drag queens rose up in protest at New York's Stonewall Inn and launched the modern lesbian and gay movement. In the early 1970s feminists and lesbian separatists collaborated to spread word of a new women's geography that was emerging across the United States. Known collectively as "women's land," these territorial refuges from heterosociality and patriarchal culture included private homes, isolated communes, and annual women-only events like the Michigan Womyn's Music Festival. Vestiges of this once-extensive network still remain. But the movement has suffered considerably since internal debate broke out about a number of important issues, including whether or not male children should be allowed to accompany their mothers and sisters onto women's land. And even though the character of "rural" America changed dramatically during the twentieth century, organizations like the Radical Faeiries continue to nurture decidedly nonmetropolitan traditions of queer social unity.

Suburban Geographies: Cruising and the Cold War Consensus

In the United States, suburbanization has been under way in one form or another since at least the 1920s. But "suburbia" as it has generally come to be understood is primarily a post–World War II phenomenon. Following the war, returning veterans eagerly filled the sprawling communities of modest single-family homes that quickly grew up to meet them. In spatial terms, these communities reflected a new emphasis on privacy, consumerism, and conformity. Postwar prosperity brought with it increased social pressures to marry and have children—pressures that obviously weighed heavily on men and women who would have preferred to do neither. In many cases, "homophile" women and men sought refuge from these social mandates by settling in urban neighborhoods like those mentioned above. More often, however, men and women who had enjoyed intimate same-sex relationships during wartime set those experiences and desires aside, preferring instead to rejoin mainstream society in its pursuit of the "American dream."

In terms of their physical layout, postwar suburbs left little room for the kind of sexual subcultures that blossomed in U.S. urban centers. Detached single-family homes were designed to bring nuclear families closer together by insulating them from the troubles of the outside world. At the same time, however, they provided relatively little protection from the prying eyes of suspicious neighbors. During the McCarthy era, many Americans came to regard homosexuality as a criminal perversion

and a threat to national security. In their minds, adult women and men who chose not to involve themselves in marriages and nuclear families necessarily represented an affront to values that were supposedly shared in common by a vast majority of Americans. Needless to say, lesbian and gay households were few and far between in most postwar suburban neighborhoods.

Yet even amid unfriendly circumstances some women and many men managed to use the geographic specificities of postwar suburban landscapes to their advantage. On their way home from work in the city, men could find brief, anonymous sexual encounters with other men at the truck stops and public rest areas that grew up alongside new regional and interstate highways. They could cruise abandoned parking lots and underused suburban parks in search of sex. When shopping malls began to spring up in suburban areas, they too become anonymous spaces in which men could cruise for sexual partners without needing to explain their presence.

While many Americans welcomed the normalcy that suburban life supposedly represented, others eventually began to question the value of social isolation and compulsory familialism that suburban life occasioned. In different ways, and for very different reasons, prominent cultural figures such as *Playboy* publisher Hugh Hefner, feminist leader Betty Friedan, and Mattachine Society founder Harry Hay began to criticize mainstream Americans for their prudery, hypocrisy, and narrowly defined vision of the good life. They questioned the moral elision of sex, marriage, and reproduction, and in doing so they and others like them paved the way for many of the social and cultural upheavals of the 1960s and 1970s.

The task of reconstructing suburban America's lesbian and gay past is extremely difficult. Many people are still reluctant to talk about their sexual experiences publicly, and exceedingly few take the time to document such an intimate aspect of their lives. But regardless of how sexually diverse the suburban experience may or may not have actually been during the second half of the twentieth century, suburbs themselves continue to be associated with a class of Americans who are comparatively affluent, typically white, and overwhelmingly heterosexual.

The Continuing Debate to Define LGBT Space

Even as lesbians, gay men, and members of other sexual subcultures continued to increase their public visibility and expand their political influence by establishing themselves as significant and outspoken constituencies within certain urban voting districts, critics of the "gay lifestyle" continued to portray homosexuality as an isolated phenomenon indigenous to just a few scattered urban enclaves. On 22 August 2001, the *Washington Post* reported that the number of same-sex couples in the United States had exceeded half a million for the first time. In fact, during the 2000 Census, 594,391 couples identified themselves "same-sex domestic partners." Demographers agreed that this number certainly under-represented LGBT people in the United States, since it failed to capture members of same-sex couples who had elected not to report their relationship as a "domestic partnership" and it also did not include single lesbians and gay men. What it did represent, however, was a more than 300 percent increase over similar statistics gathered ten years earlier. In response, a spokesman for the Family Research Council noted that "what we've seen in the numbers thus far is that homosexuals are located by and large in urban areas. The fact that they are located mostly in cities does not indicate that homosexuality is wide-spread." However, given the fact that the same census revealed that more than 75 percent of Americans overall lived in statistically urban areas, one was left to wonder what it *did* indicate.

Perhaps one thing that statements such as this reveal is the extent to which subtly influencing public perception about the geography of sexual identity remains an important stratagem of both progay and antigay groups in the United States today. Conservatives insist that homosexuality is an urban, and therefore somehow atypical, experience. Queer activists, on the other hand, assert that "we are everywhere." That the geographic essence of sexual identity politics remains such an embattled issue may also begin to explain why the theme of out-of-place homosexuals seemed to capture the imagination of filmmakers and moviegoing audiences so completely as the twentieth century came to a close. Beginning in 1994 with the U.S. release of *The Adventures of Priscilla, Queen of the Desert*, Americans have been treated to a film about the special challenges of being queer in a rural or small-town environment at a rate of almost one per year. In 1995 heterosexual heartthrobs Patrick Swayze, Wesley Snipes, and John Leguizamo teamed up in *To Wong Foo, Thanks for Everything! Julie Newmar*, a film about three drag queens who find themselves stranded in a small Nebraska town when their lemon-yellow Cadillac breaks down during a cross-country trek from New York to Hollywood. In 1997, in *In & Out*, Kevin Kline portrayed a latently homosexual drama teacher from the small town of Greenleaf, Indiana, who reluctantly comes to accept his same-sex desire after a former student, played by Matt Dillon, outs him on national television. Other films that placed queer characters in small towns, rural areas, or on cross-country journeys included *Flirting with Disaster* (1996), *Waiting for Guffman* (1997), *Happy Texas* (1999), and *Big Eden*

(2001). All of them communicate a common sense of optimism about nonmetropolitan communities and their unique ability to overcome homophobia through a heightened sense of civic unity that is supposedly typical of small-town America.

Yet even as Hollywood was busy reversing the polarity of conventional wisdom regarding nonmetropolitan America's capacity to accept homosexuality, a few high profile incidents of antigay violence seemed to confirm popular wisdom about "rural" America's murderous hostility toward homosexuals and transgender individuals. The most famous of these occurred in October 1998 when Matthew Shepard, a young University of Wyoming student, was severely beaten and left for dead by Russell Henderson and Aaron McKinney, two Laramie miscreants who claimed, initially at least, that Shepard had propositioned them at a local tavern. Many journalists and some prominent gay rights organizations were quick to represent the incident as though it were illustrative of some inherent antagonism between people like Matt—gay people—and Main Street, U.S.A. In the end, of course, the Shepard case proved to be quite complicated. Not only did Matthew Shepard eventually emerge as a complicated individual with a broad range of relations to both town and country, Laramie, Wyoming, emerged as a new kind of American geography—both in the middle of nowhere and at the center of debate about the meaning of sex and sexual identity in the United States.

Bibliography

Anderson, Nels. *The Hobo: The Sociology of the Homeless Man.* Chicago: University of Chicago Press, 1923.

Chauncey, George. *Gay New York: Gender, Urban Culture, and the Making of the Gay Male World, 1890–1940.* New York: Basic Books, 1994.

Chauncey, George. "Privacy Could Only Be Had in Public: Gay Uses of the Streets." In *Stud: Architectures of Masculinity.* Edited by Joel Sanders. New York: Princeton Architectural Press, 1996, pp. 224–267.

D'Emilio, John. *Sexual Politics, Sexual Communities: The Making of a Homosexual Minority in the United States, 1940–1970.* Chicago: University of Chicago Press, 1983.

Howard, John. *Men Like That: A Southern Queer History.* Chicago: University of Chicago Press, 1999.

Humphreys, Laud. *Tearoom Trade: Impersonal Sex in Public Places.* Chicago: Aldine, 1970.

Johnson, Susan Lee. "Bulls, Bears, and Dancing Boys." In her *Roaring Camp: The Social World of the California Gold Rush.* New York: Norton, 2000, pp. 141–183.

Loffreda, Beth. *Losing Matt Shepard: Life and Politics in the Aftermath of Anti-Gay Murder.* New York: Columbia University Press, 2000.

Newton, Esther. *Cherry Grove, Fire Island: Sixty Years in American's First Gay and Lesbian Town.* Boston: Beacon Press, 1993.

Roscoe, Will. *The Zuni Man-Woman.* Albuquerque: University of New Mexico Press, 1991.

Weston, Kath. "Get Thee to a Big City: Sexual Imaginary and the Great Gay City." In her *Long Slow Burn: Sexuality and Social Science.* New York: Routledge, 1998, pp. 29–56.

Colin R. Johnson

See also CRUISING; GENTRIFICATION; GHETTOS AND NEIGHBORHOODS; RADICAL FAERIES; RESORTS.

V

VAN VECHTEN, Carl (b. 17 June 1880; d. 21 December 1964), writer, photographer, archivist.

Van Vechten was born in Cedar Rapids, Iowa, to Caucasian parents who believed in race and gender equality. While he was a student at the University of Chicago (1899–1903), Van Vechten built upon his knowledge of black art forms and introduced the student body to prominent local black talent. Upon graduation, Van Vechten became an arts critic for the *New York Times* and the *New York Press*. He used his position to introduce mainstream America to spirituals, the blues, jazz, and other black art forms.

Van Vechten met Walter White, an African American author who at the time was serving as secretary for the National Association for the Advancement of Colored People (NAACP), through their mutual publisher, Alfred A. Knopf, in 1924, and cemented a relationship with black American culture he would liken to an addiction. It took Van Vechten only days to succeed in his mission to acquaint himself with every important black figure in New York. Van Vechten had more to offer black Manhattan than his curiosity. He was the author of three popular novels: *Peter Whiffle* (1922), *The Blind Bow-Boy* (1923), and *The Tattooed Countess* (1924), all of them bearing the bold and unique style of their author. Van Vechten's success earned him a unique status with his publishers, Alfred and Blanche Knopf, whom Van Vechten counted among his closest friends. The Knopfs came to rely upon Van Vechten for suggestions about new authors worthy of publication, and he sent them, among others, James Weldon Johnson, Nella Larsen, and Langston Hughes.

In order to forge more connections between ambitious black artists and influential whites in New York, Van Vechten and his wife, the Russian actress Fania Marinoff, hosted numerous parties at their stylish midtown home. Van Vechten honed his party-giving skills when he helped organize the famous salons hosted downtown by his close friend Mabel Dodge Luhan in the 1910s. Prohibition was not an obstacle for Carl and Fania; they had a personal bootlegger who ran a speakeasy not far from their home. Significant relationships, personal and professional, were formed during these legendary evenings that were routinely written up in black newspapers. Walter White and other black notables referred to the Van Vechten–Marinoff home as the midtown office of the NAACP.

Van Vechten was a serious and dedicated patron of African American arts and culture. But he also enjoyed the black nightlife he discovered in Harlem cabarets, rent parties, and buffet flats. Uptown provided adventure and anonymity for the restless whites who journeyed there from downtown and beyond. During the 1920s and for the rest of his life, Van Vechten was famous for the Harlem tours he gave to curious out-of-town visitors. He was also often asked to serve as a judge at Harlem's famous drag balls.

Van Vechten made no secret of his sexual interests. His biographer, Bruce Kellner, maintains that the marriage between Carl and Fania had a sexual component for years, and then remained intensely romantic. Van Vechten was also romantically connected to many men throughout his life, including three men with whom he had successive long-term relationships—Donald Angus, a one-time stage manager; Mark Lutz, a journalist from Richmond, Virginia; and Saul Mauriber, who served as Van Vechten's lighting assistant in his career as a photographer. All of these men remained close to Carl and Fania after their romantic connections with Van Vechten had fizzled. Van Vechten and Lutz exchanged daily letters for thirty-three years. Van Vechten honored Lutz's wishes that Van Vechten's letters to Lutz be destroyed upon the journalist's death.

In the 1940s, Van Vechten became consumed with archiving. He established the James Weldon Johnson Memorial Collection of Negro Arts and Letters at Yale University; thereafter he spent his days urging prominent blacks to add their papers to the collection and sorting and arranging the material. Van Vechten created other collections at institutions around the United States, including the George Gershwin Memorial Collection of Music and Musical Literature at Fisk University. It was his explicit objective to build black collections at traditionally white institutions and vice versa. Today, Van Vechten's collections are among the most thorough accumulations of African American cultural history in the United States.

Concurrently, Van Vechten began compiling a personal collection to donate to Yale that was not to be opened until twenty-five years after his death. When library curators opened the sealed containers in 1989, they were surprised to find more than twenty scrapbooks full of sexually charged material. Homoerotic photographs, cartoons, and drawings abound in these scrapbooks, which are as explicit as they are delightfully humorous. The scrapbooks also contain serious material, such as news clippings about gay bashings, drag balls, and scandals about individuals caught in "perverse acts." Together, these scrapbooks provide an intimate and intriguing look at gay life during the pre-Stonewall period. Carl Van Vechten died in New York City.

Bibliography

Bernard, Emily, ed. *Remember Me To Harlem: The Letters of Langston Hughes and Carl Van Vechten, 1925–1964.* New York: Knopf, 2001.

Kellner, Bruce. *Carl Van Vechten and the Irreverent Decades.* Norman: University of Oklahoma Press, 1968.

Weinberg, Jonathan. " 'Boy Crazy': Carl Van Vechten's Queer Collection." *Yale Journal of Criticism* 7 (1994): 25–49.

Emily Bernard

See also BENTLEY, GLADYS; HARLEM RENAISSANCE; HUGHES, LANGSTON; LITERATURE; STEIN, GERTRUDE, AND ALICE B. TOKLAS; WALKER, A'LELIA.

VAN WATERS, Miriam (b. 4 October 1887; d. 17 January 1974), prison reformer.

Miriam Van Waters was the leading female penologist in twentieth-century America. She brought to juvenile courts and women's prisons a nonjudgmental approach to female sexuality that rested largely upon her strong Christian faith in personal redemption. Although she consciously rejected lesbian identity for herself, Van Waters deeply loved other women, tolerated prison homosexuality, and survived anti-lesbian attacks during her career.

The oldest of five children, Van Waters was raised in the rectory of her father's Portland, Oregon, Episcopal Church. She earned B.A. (1908) and M.A. (1910) degrees in psychology at the University of Oregon. While studying at Clark University, where she completed a doctorate in anthropology in 1913, Van Waters read the new scholarly literature on sexuality. She consciously rejected both Freudian interpretations and pathological notions of sexual deviance in favor of a culturally relativist approach. After recovering from tuberculosis, in 1917 she became superintendent of the Los Angeles County Juvenile Hall, and between 1920 and 1930 she served as an informal judge at the Los Angeles Juvenile Court, where she founded an experimental school for troubled girls. Van Waters lived with a network of female professional colleagues, who helped her raise the seven-year-old neglected child whom she met in 1929 when the child was a ward of the juvenile court; she renamed the girl Sarah Ann Van Waters and later adopted her. Her two popular books about delinquent youth, *Youth in Conflict* (1925) and *Parents on Probation* (1928), established her national reputation, and in 1929 she was elected president of the National Conference of Social Workers.

Van Waters came of age in an era when female intimacy remained normative, but over the course of her life romantic friendships lost their sexual innocence as doctors and psychologists labeled lesbianism as a pathology. Since adolescence, Van Waters had preferred the company of women. Her personal writing acknowledged a range of erotic desire, but she emphasized the power of sublimation to harness erotic energy into art, spirituality, or public service. Personally she attempted to restrain her passions toward both men and women. In the 1930s, she fell deeply, and mutually, in love with her older patron, the New Jersey philanthropist Geraldine Thompson.

As the charismatic superintendent of the Massachusetts Reformatory for Women from 1932 to 1957, Van Waters abolished uniforms and silence rules, established musical and theater clubs, and allowed cultural excursions and home visits. She drew upon women's maternal sentiments to bolster morale among inmates and staff. She also fostered personal ties with inmates, and she typically ignored evidence of overt lesbian relationships. This tolerance, as well as the open secret of her romantic friendship with Thompson, made Van Waters highly vulnerable to political critics of her liberal approach, who repeatedly tried to force her from office. One tactic to undermine the legitimacy of women reformers like Van Waters was to accuse them of lesbianism. In the late 1940s, for example, investigators grilled a former inmate to learn if any of the reformatory staff had "homosexual tendencies" or dressed mannishly. Anticipating a scandal, in 1948 Van Waters burned more than twenty years' worth of letters from Thompson.

In 1949, the state commissioner of corrections dismissed Van Waters from office, charging, among other things, that she failed to prevent the continuance of "unwholesome relationships." Van Waters denied all charges and demanded a hearing, which attracted national publicity. She defended her policies by minimizing the existence of homosexuality at the reformatory and refusing to label nonconforming women as lesbians. Media coverage both sensationalized prison lesbianism (the "doll racket") and reflected the shifting meaning of female intimacy. With the staunch support of Thompson, Eleanor Roosevelt, and dozens of women's, liberal, and church groups, and after weeks of public hearings and an appeal to the governor, Van Waters overturned the dismissal.

After her reinstatement, however, conservative state officials, spurred by cold war attacks on liberalism, curtailed her reforms. The Federal Bureau of Investigation monitored her mail for evidence of subversive activity. In 1956, amid renewed attacks on the reformatory, Van Waters suffered an aneurysm and she retired the following year. For the next sixteen years she lived in a Framingham household with two former inmates, where she died at age eighty-six.

Bibliography

Freedman, Estelle B. *Maternal Justice: Miriam Van Waters and the Female Reform Tradition.* Chicago: University of Chicago Press, 1996.

———. "The Prison Lesbian: Race, Class, and the Construction of the Aggressive Female Homosexual, 1915–1965." *Feminist Studies* 22 (summer 1996): 397–423.

———. "'The Burning of Letters Continues': Elusive Identities and the Historical Construction of Sexuality." *Journal of Women's History* 9 (winter 1998): 181–200.

Estelle B. Freedman

See also PRISONS, JAILS, AND REFORMATORIES: WOMEN'S; SAME-SEX INSTITUTIONS.

VIDAL, Gore (b. 3 October 1925), writer.

By his early twenties, Gore Vidal had published three novels, including *The City and the Pillar* (1948), a controversial book containing not only homosexual characters that were not pathological but also commentary about being openly gay and about homosexuality's existence throughout history. This early success put Vidal in the distinguished company of post–World War II American writers such as Tennessee Williams, Truman Capote, and Norman Mailer. Vidal has been publishing since 1946, and his body of work is vast and wide-ranging. He is known as a novelist, an essayist, a scriptwriter, and a memoirist. He has appeared in several films and ran unsuccessfully for the U.S. House of Representatives in New York State in 1960, the same year his cousin by marriage, John F. Kennedy, was elected president. Also in 1960, his play about Kennedy, *The Best Man,* opened on Broadway, where it had a tremendously successful run. It was revived to great acclaim forty years later.

Vidal was born Eugene Luther Vidal in West Point, New York, and grew up in Washington, D.C. His grandfather, Thomas P. Gore, was a blind U. S. senator from Oklahoma, and the young Vidal grew up by his grandfather's side, reading to him, assisting him in the Senate, and meeting many of his friends and colleagues, including, for example, Louisiana's notorious Huey P. Long. Vidal's investment in American political and social history and his outspoken views and controversial interpretations can be found in his seven-volume American Empire series of historical novels. The first in that group—*Washington, D.C.* (1967)—is set in the World War II era; the series concludes with *Burr* (1973), *Lincoln* (1984), and *The Golden Age* (2000), which are perhaps the most controversial in the series because of their historical revisionism.

The controversy around homosexual themes in *The City and the Pillar* was troublesome to Vidal's writing career. The *New York Times* refused to review his later novels for years to come (except in the Sunday *Book Review* section). During these financially troubled times, Vidal moved to Hollywood to write for television and film. His better-known work in the entertainment industry includes the screenplay for *Ben-Hur* (1959); *Visit to a Small Planet* (1955), a television movie; an adaptation of Tennessee Williams's *Suddenly Last Summer* (1959); and *Caligula* (1979). He discussed his work in Hollywood in the context of homosexuality and censorship in the film *Celluloid Closet* (1995) and performed in *Bob Roberts* (1994) and *Gattaca* (1997).

In addition to *The City and the Pillar*, Vidal has two other novels of great interest in terms of LGBT issues:

Gore Vidal. Usually genteel in manner but politically and sexually outspoken, the expatriate American novelist, essayist, and playwright relaxes at La Rondinaia, his longtime home in Ravello, Italy. [Jonathan Blair/corbis]

Myra Breckinridge (1968) and *Myron* (1974). *Myra* is a Hollywood novel whose protagonist is transsexual; it is a comic, pseudo-autobiographical novel, remarkable for its campiness and forward-looking on its complex of issues. *Myron* is a sort of prequel, depicting Myra's preoperative identity. Both books offer a much lighter tone than the 1948 novel.

In the 1960s, Vidal bought an Italian villa in Ravello with his companion of many years, Howard Austen. Vidal and Austen met, according to Vidal, "anonymously at the Everard Baths" in New York City in 1950. Accounting for the longevity of their relationship, Vidal has written: "'How,' we are often asked, 'have you stayed together for forty-four years?' The answer is, 'No sex.' This satisfies no one, of course, but there, as Henry James would say, it is" (1995, p. 132).

Living abroad for much of the last forty years has given Vidal an interesting observation point for his social and political writing, culminating perhaps with his National Book Award–winning essay collection *United States* in 1993. Two years later, Vidal published *Palimpsest,*

the first volume of his memoirs, which ends in the mid-1960s.

Never one to keep his controversial views to himself, in the 1990s Vidal wrote a "sympathetic" portrait of executed Oklahoma City bomber Timothy McVeigh based on letters the two men exchanged, and he wrote essays and gave speeches accusing the Bush family of having ties with Osama bin Laden. Vidal has cultivated what could be called a contentious relationship with his native country, but regardless of one's views of his outspokenness, it is clear that he speaks with an intelligence and a level of knowledge surpassed by few.

In 2003, a documentary called *The Education of Gore Vidal* was released. Writer and director Deborah Dickson provides an excellent introduction to the multifaceted Vidal, showing his political engagement, his literary achievements, and his celebrity. Some of the archival footage, for example, shows famous televised exchanges and arguments with the likes of Norman Mailer and William F. Buckley. The overwhelming portrait that emerges is one of a man of letters who has chronicled the twentieth century as a major participant and an incisive observer.

Bibliography

The Education of Gore Vidal. Directed and written by Deborah Dickson. 84 min. 2003. Videocassette.

"Gore Vidal." 2000. Available from www.kirjasto.sci.fi/vidal.htm

"The Gore Vidal Index." 2001. Available from www.pitt.edu/~kloman/vidalfintro.html

Kaplan, Fred. *Gore Vidal: A Biography.* New York: Doubleday, 1999.

Vidal, Gore. *Palimpsest: A Memoir.* New York: Random House, 1995.

Chris Freeman

See also BEATS; COMEDY AND HUMOR; LITERATURE; PULP FICTION: GAY.

VIOLENCE

Three types of violence are of major concern to LGBT people: domestic violence, anti-LGBT hate crimes, and murders committed by LGBT people that have influenced public perceptions of LGBT people as a group. Although these categories sometimes overlap, they provide a useful framework for examining the ways in which violence has affected not just the individuals involved, but also LGBT people in general.

The term "violence" as used here refers not only to physical assault with or without a weapon, but also to vandalism, harassment, and verbal/emotional/psychological battering, ranging from mild teasing to name-calling, taunts, and threats. Many experts on violence view these behaviors as points on a continuum, pointing out that the "milder" forms such as taunting help create a social climate in which the harsher forms are more likely to occur.

Domestic Violence

Domestic violence commonly refers to behaviors used by one person to gain and maintain control over another within the context of an intimate or family relationship. Behaviors may include physical acts like pushing, kicking, hitting, and sexual assault, as well as verbal, psychological, and emotional abuse. The abuse almost always occurs in private, and the victim typically keeps it hidden, in part out of shame and fear. The relationship may, in fact, look like an ideal one to friends and family, and the abuser may be a respected member of the community. According to the National Coalition of Anti-Violence Programs (NCAVP), domestic violence in the United States occurs with equal frequency across all lines—age, race, ethnicity, national origin, religion, socioeconomic status, and sexual orientation.

Before the second wave women's movement of the 1960s and 1970s, the issue of violence in heterosexual relationships—overwhelmingly perpetrated by men—was largely unacknowledged. The women's liberation movement changed this situation dramatically. Feminists pointed out the connections between domestic violence, other forms of violence against women, and male power and privilege. They organized to expose and address the problem of domestic abuse, and by the end of the 1980s a plethora of resources was available for battered women.

Ironically, the feminist analysis of domestic violence as a manifestation of institutionalized sexism made it easier to ignore the problem of domestic violence in same-sex relationships. If domestic violence is linked to men's greater size, power, and privilege relative to women, how could it occur between two women or two men, who would presumably be on equal footing? Yet over the past two decades, many researchers have come to believe that domestic violence is as likely to occur in LGBT as in non-LGBT relationships. To understand why this may be the case, transgender people and others point to the distinction between birth sex and gender identity. Because the two do not always correlate in an individual, gender differences may exist even in a same-sex relationship, and it may be the case that "masculine" LGBT people are more likely to commit violence against "feminine" partners.

To account for the dynamics of violence in same-sex and transgender relationships, some experts in the field also note that differences other than sex or gender identity, including race, health, size, ability, citizenship status, degree of "outness," socio-economic status, and age, may underlie an unequal balance of power in a relationship. For example a study in the December 2002 *American Journal of Public Health* looked at a sample of urban men who have sex with men. This study found that they are as likely to suffer partner abuse as are heterosexual women and identified two demographic factors—age under forty and HIV-positive status—that correlate with an increased risk of abuse.

Information about LGBT domestic abuse is still scarce compared with what is known about non-LGBT counterparts. Experts agree that the majority of instances of abuse in relationships go unreported. A number of factors related to the homophobia, heterosexism, and transphobia prevalent in American society accounts for the dearth of data, including

- the difficulty of finding representative samples from which to draw data since many LGBT people are closeted, and studies of violence in the general population do not ask about participants' sexual orientation or gender identity;

- LGBT people's fear of further stigmatizing their group by speaking out;

- individual LGBT people's fear of outing themselves to family, employers, or the community at large by seeking help (some perpetrators make this fear more immediate by threatening to out a partner if he/she tells anyone of the abuse);

- LGBT people's fears that police and service providers will be biased against them;

- lack of education about transgenderism as well as same-sex violence for police and service providers, who sometimes decide that violence is not present or is mutual when two women or two men are involved;

- lack of resources available to male and transgender victims of abuse, since most shelters and programs deal only with battered women-born women;

- lack of understanding of transgenderism among LGB people;

- the facts that domestic violence laws were written with heterosexual women-born-women in mind, and that same-sex relationships lack legal standing; and

- a practice adopted by some female perpetrators of identifying themselves to women's advocates as victims, making it all but impossible for providers to determine which partner is in fact the victim and which the perpetrator.

NCAVP's annual reports on LGBT domestic violence include personal narratives written by survivors of abusive relationships. In the 2001 report, one such narrative came from a transgendered Latina whose male partner abused her regularly over a twenty-year period. When she finally fought back and hit him with a lamp, he called the police and had her arrested. She spent four nights in a men's jail, where she was raped repeatedly. She reports that the police and the judge in her case referred to her as "he" and refused to believe she had not been the abuser. She was required by the court to attend a group for batterers for a year and was put into a group for male batterers. When she tried to leave her partner, she was refused admission to a shelter for battered women because she had been arrested and was not born a woman.

Beginning in the 1980s, scholars and activists began taking important steps to combat LGBT domestic violence. Groundbreaking books were published, articles in the LGBT press called attention to the problem, and in some locations programs were developed to support LGBT survivors and to encourage mainstream domestic violence agencies to deal more effectively with LGBT issues.

Anti-LGBT Hate Crimes

Hate crimes are crimes motivated by hatred of people of a certain race, ethnicity, gender, nationality, religion, sexual orientation, gender identity, or degree of physical or mental ability. Hate crimes differ from other crimes in that they are intended to threaten and intimidate an entire group. According to some definitions, anti-LGBT hate crimes include the sexual and physical assaults that have long occurred in institutions such as prisons and the violence that has often been committed against LGBT people by their families of origin. In the United States, forty-six states have hate crime laws under which a perpetrator may receive a harsher sentence if the crime is demonstrated to have been motivated by bias or hatred; however, fifteen states exclude crimes based on the victim's real or perceived sexual orientation, and only six include both sexual orientation and gender identity.

It is difficult to estimate the prevalence of hate crimes. The Federal Bureau of Investigation (FBI) gathers data from states and issues an annual report on hate crimes nationwide, but the FBI's numbers reflect only a percentage of the hate crimes that actually occur. Definitions and reporting requirements for hate crimes vary considerably from state to state, and, like domestic violence, hate crimes often go unreported. In a 1997 study of gay men and lesbians, Gregory Herek and two colleagues found that those who were victims of hate crimes were so severely traumatized and fearful that only one-third reported the crimes, as compared to two-thirds of the victims of non–bias-related crimes. For these reasons, added to the fact that not all states criminalize or track them, the prevalence of anti-LGBT hate crimes is difficult to assess.

There is, however, research on the percentage of lesbian and gay people who are targets of hate crimes. In a study conducted by Herek and his colleagues, one in four gay men and one in five lesbians had been victims of hate crimes since age sixteen, including vandalism, robbery, theft, physical or sexual assault, or assault with a weapon. According to Gender Education and Advocacy (GEA), a transgender person has been murdered at least once each month since 1989. As GEA notes, people who do not conform to gender norms are frequently targeted, regardless of whether they identify as transgendered or LGB. Nontransgendered heterosexuals may also be victims of anti-LGBT violence if they are perceived to be LGBT.

The NCAVP tracks anti-LGBT hate crimes reported to its member organizations, whether or not they were reported to authorities; however, its 2002 report on anti-LGBT violence includes data from only twelve LGBT antiviolence organizations, covering about 30 percent of the U.S. population. According to its figures, 1,968 anti-LGBT incidents were reported in 2002. In contrast, FBI figures for 2001, the most recent available, show that 1,393 anti-LGB crimes were reported to authorities nationwide, accounting for 14.3 percent of all hate crimes (anti-transgender hate crimes are not tracked).

Many people who commit hate crimes are ordinary young people not affiliated with any organized hate group and may not perceive what they did as wrong. For example, a study by Karen Franklin of the motivations for anti-LGBT violence found that among a group of young community college students, anti-LGBT harassment and violence were perceived as socially acceptable, especially by young men. Unfortunately, the prevalence of the "gay panic" defense—in which a defendant argues, often successfully, that he assaulted or murdered someone to defend himself against an unwanted sexual overture—lends credence to the views of these young people.

Historians have documented a long history of legal and extralegal hate-motivated violence against LGBT people, including violence committed by state authorities, police officers, military figures, religious leaders, scientific experts, institutional staff, families of origin, friends and peers, strangers and acquaintances, and sexual partners. In the late 1990s, several anti-LGBT crimes received significant public attention. The 1978 murder of one of the first openly gay elected officials, San Francisco Board of Supervisors member Harvey Milk, had a huge impact on the LGBT community in San Francisco and across the country. Milk and Mayor George Moscone were shot to death at City Hall by former city supervisor Dan White, who held strong anti-LGBT views. When White was sentenced to only seven years in prison for the two killings after his lawyers blamed his acts on the excess sugar in the Twinkies that he had consumed (he served six years and later committed suicide), LGBT people in San Francisco rioted in protest. Later, at the 1979 March on Washington for Gay and Lesbian Rights, tens of thousands of marchers reportedly chanted "Harvey Milk lives." Milk's stature as an icon of the early LGBT movement has continued to grow since his death. In 2000, *Time* magazine named Milk one of the one hundred most influential people of the twentieth century.

Other well-known LGBT victims of hate-inspired murders include Charlie Howard, a young gay man who was thrown from a bridge in Maine in 1984; Rebecca Wight, a lesbian who was killed and whose partner, Claudia Brenner, was shot while they were hiking the Appalachian Trail in 1988; Brandon Teena, a transgender person killed in Nebraska in 1993 and the subject of the film *Boys Don't Cry*; and gay college student Matthew Shepard, killed in 1998.

LGBT Murderers

LGBT people have been, like members of any group, both victims and perpetrators of violence. However, murders committed by LGBT people often become linked in the public mind with the perpetrator's sexual or gender identity. Sensationalized media accounts of homosexual murders have a history in the United States that dates back to the nineteenth century. Along with other fictional and nonfictional narratives, they have stigmatized LGBT people by linking them with violence, depravity, and insanity. Examining some well-known LGBT murder cases reveals how not only the crimes themselves, but also the discourse they generated, served to reinforce the link between "deviant" sexuality and violent behavior and to portray both as threats to society.

Lisa Duggan has done extensive research on the publicity surrounding a late-nineteenth-century violent crime: the 1892 murder of a young Memphis woman named Freda Ward by Alice Mitchell, who had planned to dress as a man so that the two could get married. After female relatives discovered and foiled the plan, not only

did Mitchell kill Ward, but also she was committed to an insane asylum and later killed herself. Duggan examines the narrative structure of the tellings and retellings of the Mitchell-Ward story and argues that in these various versions, the link between female sexuality and violence draws a clear boundary between the normalcy of the heterosexual family and the dangers that lurk outside its purview. It thus served as, among other things, a cautionary tale.

During the twentieth century, sensationalized murder cases have often centered on gay men, linking same-sex sexuality, moral depravity, and violence. One, the case of Leopold and Loeb, was dubbed at the time "the crime of the century." In 1924 two Chicago teenagers from well-to-do families, Nathan Leopold and Richard Loeb, kidnapped and killed a fourteen-year-old boy in order to demonstrate that they were so intelligent, they could commit a perfect crime. Leopold later said that he had joined Loeb in committing this and other crimes in exchange for Loeb's agreeing to have sex with him. The Leopold and Loeb case inspired many books, plays, and films, including Alfred Hitchcock's *Rope* (1948).

In the latter half of the twentieth century, two serial killers—John Wayne Gacy in the late 1970s and Jeffrey Dahmer in the early 1990s—victimized young men and were dubbed "homosexual killers" by the press. Ironically, Dahmer's arrest came not long after the release of the movie *The Silence of the Lambs*, whose villain, Hannibal Lecter, killed and cannibalized his victims. The media often referred to Dahmer as the real-life Hannibal Lecter, and the sensationalized coverage of the arrest and trial focused on Dahmer as a gay man who killed other gay men. During this period, members of the LGBT community in Milwaukee, where Dahmer committed his crimes, became targets of anti-LGBT rhetoric as well as physical attacks.

A 1997 notorious gay murder involved not only a gay male perpetrator, Andrew Cunanan, but also a gay male victim, Italian fashion designer Gianni Versace. The case was widely publicized because of Versace's fame, and although the two men were not lovers but acquaintances, the gay identity of both Cunanan and Versace was a central focus of media coverage.

Conclusion

The ongoing problems associated with violence—including domestic violence, hate crimes, and media portrayals of LGBT people as violent—make clear that civil and legal rights, while important, are not sufficient to protect LGBT people from the consequences of our society's heterosexism and homo- and transphobia. Yet significant progress has been made in recognizing and combatting many of these problems. High-profile hate crimes like the murder of Matthew Shepard have raised public awareness of anti-LGBT hate crimes in recent years. The LGBT community itself has begun to acknowledge the problem of LGBT domestic abuse; as a result, more resources are available than ever before for both victims and perpetrators. And organizations like the Gay and Lesbian Alliance against Defamation (GLAAD) regularly monitor media portrayals of LGBT people and communities and take action when necessary. While there is still much to be done, LGBT people and communities are slowly moving forward toward a society in which violence is no longer used as a weapon of hate and fear.

Bibliography

American Psychological Association Public Policy Office and Society for the Psychological Study of Social Issues. "Hate Crimes Today: An Age-Old Foe in Modern Dress." New York: APA, 1998. Available at http://www.apa.org/pubinfo/hate/

Brenner, Claudia, with Hannah Ashley. *Eight Bullets: One Woman's Story of Surviving Anti-Gay Violence.* Ithaca, New York: Firebrand Books, 1995.

Comstock, Gary David. *Violence against Lesbians and Gay Men.* New York: Columbia University Press, 1991.

Duggan, Lisa. "The Trials of Alice Mitchell: Sensationalism, Sexology, and the Lesbian Subject in Turn-of-the Century America." *Signs: A Journal of Women in Culture and Society* 18 (1993): 791–814.

Franklin, Karen. "Unassuming Motivations: Contextualizing the Narratives of Antigay Assailants." In *Stigma and Sexual Orientation: Understanding Prejudice against Lesbians, Gay Men, and Bisexuals.* Edited by Gregory M. Herek. Thousand Oaks, Calif.: Sage, 1998.

———. "Antigay Behaviors by Young Adults: Prevalence, Patterns, and Motivators in a Noncriminal Population." *Journal of Interpersonal Violence* 15, no. 4 (April 2000): 339–363.

Greenwood, Gregory L., et al. "Battering Victimization among a Probability-Based Sample of Men Who Have Sex with Men." *American Journal of Public Health* 92 (2002): 1964–1969.

Herek, Gregory, and Kevin T. Berrill. *Hate Crimes: Confronting Violence against Lesbians and Gay Men.* Newbury Park, Calif.: Sage Press, 1992.

Herek, Gregory M., J. Roy Gillis, Jeanine Cogan, and Eric K. Glunt. "Psychological Sequelae of Hate Crime Victimization among Lesbian, Gay, and Bisexual Adults." *Journal of Consulting and Clinical Psychology* 67 (1999): 945–951.

Jenness, Valerie, and Kendal Broad. Hate Crimes: New Social Movement's and the Politics of Violence. New York: Aldine, 1997.

Lobel, Kerry. *Naming the Violence: Speaking Out about Lesbian Battering.* Seattle: Seal Press, 1986.

National Coalition of Anti-Violence Programs. "Lesbian, Gay, Bisexual, and Transgender Domestic Violence in 2001." New York: NCAVP, 2002.

———. "2002 National Hate Crimes Report." New York: NCAVP, 2002. NCAVP reports available at www.avp.org/ncavp.htm

Public Broadcasting Corporation. "Assault on Gay America: The Life and Death of Billy Jack Gaither." Website based on the *Frontline* story that aired in February 2002. Available at http://www.pbs.org/wgbh/

Renzetti, Claire M., and Charles H. Miley, eds. *Violence in Gay and Lesbian Domestic Partnerships.* New York: Haworth Press, 1996.

Ristock, Janice L. *No More Secrets: Violence in Lesbian Relationships.* New York: Routledge, 2002.

Schmidt, Martha A. "Dahmer Discourse and Gay Identity: The Paradox of Queer Politics." *Critical Sociology* 20, no. 3 (1994): 81–106.

Saralyn Chesnut

See also ATLANTA; HATE CRIMES LAW AND POLICY; MILK, HARVEY; MITCHELL, ALICE; SEXUAL ABUSE, EXPLOITATION, HARASSMENT, AND RAPE; SUICIDE.

VISUAL ART: PAINTING, DRAWING, AND SCULPTURE

This is a composite entry; it is composed of the following three parts:

PAINTING, DRAWING, AND SCULPTURE: EIGHTEENTH AND NINETEENTH CENTURIES
James Smalls

PAINTING, DRAWING, AND SCULPTURE: 1890–1969
Christopher Reed

PAINTING, DRAWING, AND SCULPTURE: 1969–PRESENT
Tee A. Corinne

PAINTING, DRAWING, AND SCULPTURE: EIGHTEENTH AND NINETEENTH CENTURIES

More so in Europe than in the United States, the period from 1700 to 1890 gave rise to distinct homosexual and transgender identities, with particular links to the arts. The social and artistic visibility of men and women whose sexual preference was for members of the same sex and who transgressed normative sex and gender roles grew over these two centuries. The major factors that helped propel homosexuality and transgenderism to heightened exposure were urban expansion and the impact of intellectual, industrial, and political revolutions. In the urban centers of Europe, gays and lesbians gathered in bars, brothels, taverns, clubs, and other places. Admittedly, our understanding of attitudes towards homosexuality and transgenderism during this period in America is fragmentary due to a dearth of evidence. No evidence has emerged that suggests that colonial cities in America harbored a gay subculture such as that witnessed in London or Paris in the eighteenth and early nineteenth centuries. American men and women who wanted to have same-sex sex had to rely on "tenuous networks and chance encounters." Acts of homosexuality and transgenderism were condemned, and the notion of the homosexual or the invert as having a distinct sexual orientation or gender identity did not fully develop until the late nineteenth century.

Nevertheless, there are three principal ways to link LGBT history with the history of visual art in the United States in this period. First, there is evidence that suggests that some eighteenth-century and nineteenth-century American artists experienced same-sex desires, formed same-sex romantic attachments, and transgressed normative gender roles. Second, some eighteenth-century and nineteenth-century works of art represented same-sex desires, same-sex intimacies, and cross-gender phenomena. And third, some audiences, then and now, have perceived and experienced sexualities and genders that can be described as LGBT in eighteenth-century and nineteenth-century artists and art.

Male Artists

During the nineteenth century, American artists learned how to transfer the aestheticized aspects of homoerotic desire into their works, relying on the examples set by European artists such as Oscar Wilde, Robert de Montesquiou, Aubrey Beardsley, and Joséphin Peladan. In the United States, the inspiration for homosexual influence in the arts came from these and other dandified lovers of beautiful things. Influential literature such as Oscar Wilde's *The Portrait of Dorian Gray* (1895) and J.K. Huysman's *A Rebours* (Against the Grain) brought the hedonistic lifestyle of the aesthetic dandy across the Atlantic to North America. The introspective qualities of the aesthetes can be seen most profoundly in the works of Thomas Eakins and the photographer Fred Holland Day.

Beginning with Day's work of the 1880s and 1890s, the British aestheticism of Wilde and Beardsley found its way into the camera vision and work of several American photographers. Like them, Day was a highly educated and talented homosexual man whose works spoke to a homosexualized aestheticism based on exaltation of the male body beautiful coupled with religious and allegorical themes and conventions. Day, an exponent of photography as a fine art, pursued new and controversial imagery based on received ideas about the beauty of the classical male nude form. He often combined spiritual and sexual qualities in the same image, thus creating a state of introspection and veiled homoerotic desire. This was an approach that influenced later image-makers.

In Eakins's works—most notably *The Swimming Hole* (c. 1883–1885) and *The Wrestlers* (1899)—Walt Whitman's ideals of male bonding and comradeship as the foundation of American democracy can be found. Homoerotic friendships between men of different races occupied a central place in much nineteenth-century American literature and art. Many American artists voyeuristically profited from the erotic potential of the exotic other. In both the art and minds of nineteenth-century America, for example, Native American men were both feared and eroticized. Native American men were sexualized in part because numerous native cultures practiced and condoned what to westerners looked like cross-dressing and the breaching of gender norms. *Berdaches,* males who lived as women and females who lived as men, were considered integral, productive, and revered members of their communities. In some instances they were looked upon as shamans or deities. Many participated in same-sex sexual and emotional relationships. The Euro-American fascination with the *berdaches* was recorded in the 1830 watercolor sketch *Dance to the Berdache* by the American frontier artist George Catlin (National Museum of American Art, Washington, D.C.). In it, a standing figure "in Pocahontas garb" is shown accepting a ritual tribute of the tribe's men (Saslow, p. 5).

Male homosexuality is often most pronounced in male homosocial environments. This was particularly true on the western frontier, which spawned representations of masculine types that served as icons of manhood and erotic attraction for both men and women. Among these types were railroad workers, soldiers, miners, lumberjacks, and cowboys. Perhaps the most popular of these figures was Davy Crockett, who was visually displayed in dozens of almanacs. The subliminal eroticizing of such men became the stuff of some late nineteenth-century works of art and literature. Images by Eakins, Winslow Homer, Thomas Anshutz, and Frederic Remington speak to this fascination with the American manly type.

As an illustrator for *Harpers Weekly* from 1859 to 1867, Homer was sent to record the Civil War, during which he focused on scenes of camp life, showing soldiers in periods of boredom and loneliness. In descriptive ways, these works link war and homosexuality through the intimate comradeship that developed in the military.

His soldiers are thoughtful, quiet, and amazingly unheroic. They exhibit compassion and loving companionship between soldiers—the antithesis of the aggressive and all-male domain of war. The genre had previously been investigated in the military canvases of colonial era artists such as Benjamin West (*The Death of General Wolfe*, 1770, now at the National Gallery of Canada, Ottawa) and John Trumbull (*The Death of General Warren at the Battle of Bunker's Hill*, 1786, at the Yale University Art Gallery, New Haven, Connecticut)—both of whom produced paintings of bonding between men on the battlefield but whose works generally are not interpreted as homoerotic. Later in his career, Homer produced paintings of men relaxing or struggling with the sea. In the late nineteenth century, he took a trip to the Bahamas and painted scenes of sensuous and half-naked muscular black men at work and leisure.

Nineteenth-century masculine types constituted the subject of American painter Thomas Anshutz's 1880 painting *Steel Workers at Noon* (Fine Arts Museums of San Francisco, California). In it, Anshutz represented a group of men, some stripped to the waist, relaxing, exercising, and fooling around during a break at work. The men are carefully arranged in varied interlocking poses while displaying their masculine physiques. The artist has focused on the effects of labor on male bodies and minds while at the same time supplying the viewer with an eyeful of eroticized male flesh.

Female Artists

Female artists in eighteenth-century and nineteenth-century America confronted stereotypes of women's inferiority, passivity, and dependence. The unequal terms for acceptance into the art establishment that were imposed by men were challenged by female artists and activists such as Harriet Hosmer, Anna Klumpke, Anne Whitney, and (Mary) Edmonia Lewis. All of these women modeled their ambitions on the accomplishments of the highly successful French animal painter Rosa Bonheur, who became a source of inspiration for many lesbian and straight female artists of the nineteenth and early twentieth centuries. American painter Klumpke was a close friend of Bonheur. The two eventually lived together, and Klumpke became not only Bonheur's intimate companion, but also her official biographer. Although she was born in San Francisco, Klumpke spent most of her adolescent and adult years in Europe, where she received her artistic training as a painter. Her 1889 portrait *Elizabeth Cady Stanton at Seventy One* (National Portrait Gallery, Washington, D.C.) was highly praised and resulted in numerous portrait commissions. Her finest painting, however, is *Portrait of Rosa Bonheur* of 1898 (New York,

Metropolitan Museum of Art) in which she shows the then elderly and resolute artist seated at her easel before one of her paintings.

Harriet Hosmer, one of a very small number of women who became a member of the Rome Academy in 1858, led a group of American neoclassical expatriate female sculptors referred to as "the white marmorean flock." The phrase was coined by Henry James, the expatriate American writer who, in the 1870s, met Hosmer and her circle of female artists. The designation was derisive, intended to ridicule these women's white marble sculptures and their exclusion of men from their circle. Members of the white marmorean flock were feminists and abolitionists and believed in the struggles of liberation. Like male artists of the period, women of this elite circle accepted the contemporary vogue for neoclassicism but chose particular women from allegorical and classical history as subject matter. The women Hosmer chose to sculpt were often portrayed as "beautiful victims, powerless to overcome the many obstacles put in their struggle for independence" (Cooper, p. 56). Her most famous piece is *Xenobia in Chains* (1858; Wadsworth Atheneum, Hartford, Connecticut), a work that celebrates the stoic fortitude of the queen of Palmyra while in captivity. This and other works featuring female protagonists served as a visual metaphor and powerful symbol of women's struggle.

Hosmer called fellow sculptor Emma Stebbins her "wife" before Stebbins became the lifelong companion of the American actress Charlotte Cushman. Both Cushman and Hosmer were ambitious women determined to become famous. They were not only mavericks in excelling in the typically male domains of acting and sculpting, but were noteworthy for their social independence and their decisions to focus on professional careers over the obligations of marriage and family. Women in this world tended to band together and support one another emotionally as well as practically. Their intimate bonding often resulted in what has been called "romantic friendships," which, in turn, have sometimes been seen as lesbian liaisons. In the general society in which such relationships were formed, few were perceived as having sexual content. What was contested by society at large, however, was the seemingly "mannish" challenge to the male social preserve of independence that these women often exhibited. Again taking Bonheur's lead, some of these women walked around in men's clothing and smoked cigars or cigarettes in public. Women donning "mannish" dress and exhibiting male-associated behavior was often criticized even by other women. By the end of the nineteenth century, many men condemned such women who refused to respect the "natural" division between the sexes.

One woman of mixed African American and Native American heritage who was taken under Cushman's wing in 1865 in Rome was American sculptor (Mary) Edmonia Lewis, who "fascinated visitors with her 'brown hands working in the white marble'" (Tufts, p. 162). From the start, she held abolitionist and feminist convictions, both of which heavily influenced her work. She produced powerful sculptured portraits of known white and black abolitionists. Although her sexual preference remains unknown, Lewis never married or had children. She became part of the circle of women artists around Cushman and Hosmer. Her most famous work, *Forever Free* of 1867 (Howard University, Washington, D.C.), is triumphantly antislavery in perspective and was created to commemorate the Thirteenth Amendment to the Constitution. Her statue *Hagar* (1875; National Museum of American Art, Washington, D.C.) is decidedly feminist—a visual declaration of support to "all women who have struggled and suffered" (Peterson and Wilson, p. 82).

In late nineteenth-century Boston, close relationships between women of the middle and upper classes who lived together and celebrated their spinsterhood were referred to as "Boston marriages." Many painters and sculptors formed such relationships. These artists chose their artistic themes carefully, investing their beliefs in women's emancipation in indirect yet creative ways. Many artists chose scenes of women from classical history who expressed qualities of independence and individuality. Themes of emancipation and the equating of colonial slavery with women's condition as the "slaves" of men were also chosen. One such artist was Anne Whitney, who formed a long-enduring "Boston marriage" with the painter and poet Abby Adelaide Manning. Whitney thought sculpture a perfect medium for communicating her strong ideas of intellectual and physical freedom for women. She was also a staunch feminist and held abolitionist concerns. In 1864 she completed a work called *Africa*, a piece that "symbolized a race rising from slavery" (Cooper, p. 61). She also created several marble busts of Samuel Adams, Harriet Martineau, and Harriet Beecher Stowe.

There was an endearing bond between all of the women mentioned here. All attempted to assert their equality to men. Their works were informed by deeply held feminist and abolitionist ideas. As well, they all found support and strength from the "divine affection" of other women.

The Modern Homosexual and the Future of Art

The year 1869 is believed to be a watershed year in that it was the moment in which the German-Hungarian writer Karoly Maria Kertbeny coined the word "homosexuality."

Not long after he brought the word "heterosexuality" into existence as well. The actual naming of homosexuality was significant in that it provided to a repressed minority the name for a psychological and sociological identity and identification. At this critical point in history the conceptual contours and visual features of the modern homosexual were taking shape. After 1890 the links between homosexuality, transgenderism, and creativity grew ever stronger—forging extraordinary acts and works of LGBT visibility and pride.

Bibliography

Cooper, Emmanuel. *The Sexual Perspective: Homosexuality and Art in the Last 100 Years in the West.* London and New York: Routledge and Kegan Paul, 1986.

Katz, Jonathan. *Gay/Lesbian Almanac.* New York: Harper and Row, 1983.

Petersen, Karen, and J. J. Wilson, *Women Artists.* London: Women's Press, 1978.

Saslow, James M. *Pictures and Passions: A History of Homosexuality in the Visual Arts.* New York: Penguin Books, 1999.

Smalls, James. *Homosexuality in Art.* New York: Parkstone Press, 2003.

Tufts, Eleanor. *Our Hidden Heritage.* London: Paddington Press, 1974.

James Smalls

See also ART HISTORY; EAKINS, THOMAS; BROOKS, ROMAINE; KLUMPKE, ANNA; VISUAL ART: PHOTOGRAPHY.

PAINTING, DRAWING, AND SCULPTURE: 1890–1969

Far from being a tangential or minority concern, homosexuality is central to an understanding of the history of modern art. During this time, the alienated attitudes and coded expressions of the homosexual minority grew congruent with avant-garde art, while being "artistic" was increasingly perceived as both a medical symptom of and a social euphemism for homosexuality. A catalog of all twentieth-century artists who were or were thought to be homosexual, or who documented aspects of homosexuality in their work, or who reacted against associations of art and homosexuality by aggressive displays of homophobia or heterosexuality, would come close to a chronicle of twentieth-century U.S. art in its entirety. Exemplary case studies, however, can be used to trace the developing relationship between art and homosexuality during this period.

Various scholars have traced the processes through which homosexuality as an identity was invented by nineteenth-century scientists as part of a broader project to chart and describe human types. Scientists initially described homosexuality as a condition between male and female—some claimed it constituted its own interstitial "third sex"—and associated it with individuals' manifestation of behaviors or sensibilities believed to belong to the opposite sex. Androgyny, therefore, was closely associated with homosexuality, and art was associated with androgyny, since its practice connoted supposedly masculine attributes of ambition, skill, and learning while appreciation was associated with feminine sensitivity, beauty, and leisure.

Aesthetes as Homosexuals

The potential association of homosexuality and art as forms of androgyny was forcefully realized, especially for English-speaking audiences, in 1895, with the sensational trial and conviction of Oscar Wilde on sodomy charges. Wilde was not himself a visual artist, but as a famous British playwright, poet, novelist, journalist, and lecturer, he was the preeminent spokesman for the avant-garde contingent known as the Aesthetes. Aestheticism included the visual arts in its mission to subordinate ideas of truth or morality to aesthetics by assessing all experience as matters of aesthetic sensation. Wilde himself was a well-known critic and lecturer on both the fine and decorative arts. During his highly publicized trial, the prosecution linked testimony concerning his sexual activities with other men to the style and subjects of his own writings and the writings of other Aesthetes. The effect was to solidify for the public an association between aesthetics and homosexuality so that each was seen as evidence of the other. By 1897 the pioneering British sexologist Havelock Ellis had credited the publicity over Wilde's trials with granting widespread "definiteness and self-consciousness to the manifestation of homosexuality." A more colloquial indication of this in Britain may be found in E.M. Forster's early novel of homosexual identity, *Maurice* (written around 1910, but not published until 1971, after the author's death), in which, when the protagonist first looks for words to describe himself he says, "I'm an unspeakable of the Oscar Wilde sort."

Because the links between art and homosexuality were often forged by medical and legal authorities and promulgated by the press, their most immediate effect was on the educated urban bourgeoisie (working-class and rural conceptions of homosexual behavior in many areas remained unaffected by these new ideas into the second half of the twentieth century). In Boston, for instance, the photographer Fred Holland Day was at the center of a sophisticated circle of designers, artists, and writers who modeled themselves on the Aesthetes. Day's

publishing firm, Copeland and Day, between 1893 and 1899 issued American editions of the English Aesthetes' poems and images—including Wilde's *Salomé* (1894) with Aubrey Beardsley's illustrations—as well as work in the aesthetic style by American writers and artists. Day's own photographs, in which he posed semi-nude as the crucified Christ, received mixed reviews from a mystified American press, but were widely condemned in London by journalists more attuned to associations of aestheticism with homosexuality. The *British Journal of Photography* condemned Day as "the leader of the Oscar Wilde school." Provoked rather than chastened by such rebukes, Day's late work grew increasingly homoerotic. Especially after 1904, when a studio fire destroyed much of his early work, Day's images rehearsed the beauty of young men in aesthetic terms, using props to link his models to classical myths suggesting love between men and to other forms of aesthetic enjoyment, such as music.

Aestheticism and Lesbians: Barnes, Brooks, Stein

The link between aestheticism and homosexuality also affected American women artists, especially the group that gathered around the expatriate writer Natalie Barney in Paris. Modeling themselves on the Aesthetes, Barney and her friends published several lesbian love poems and novels during the first years of the twentieth century. The visual artists most closely associated with this circle were Djuna Barnes and Romaine Brooks. Though Barnes is today best known as a writer, she illustrated her early poems in Beardsley's style. Brooks's accomplished portraits of the women in this community record their appropriation of English gentlemen's clothing in paintings that assert aesthetic sensitivity through the subtle juxtaposition of shades of gray. Among the first self-representations of lesbian identity, these images shift the depiction of lesbianism away from erotic images designed to arouse men and toward a social category experienced by women themselves. The self-perception of the women in Barney's circle was very much a product of its time, reflecting medical models of homosexuality as a condition between conventional masculinity and femininity, and the association between homosexuality and art.

Barney's circle of Anglophone women was not the only expatriate group in Paris in the early twentieth century. Paris was the center of the art world and attracted artists ambitious to be "modern," including many English speakers, for whom modern art was closely associated with Wildean homosexuality. For many of the foreign artists in Paris, their status as expatriates—outsiders, freed from familial bonds and supervision—strengthened associations between avant-garde and homosexual identity. The most famous of these circles of English-speaking expatriates centered on another prominent American lesbian, Gertrude Stein. Stein's early medical training left her well versed in scientific theories that associated homosexuality with gender inversion and art. Claiming for herself the authority of both masculinity and artistry, Stein allied herself with the most famous modernists of her day. "Pablo [Picasso] and Matisse have a maleness that belongs to genius," Stein wrote, "*Moi aussi* [me too], perhaps" (Benstock, p. 189). Despite her public lifelong relationship with Alice B. Toklas, Stein's focus on modernist abstraction has led critics to assume that she was less affected by her homosexuality than Barney's artist colleagues. Such assumptions reflect the common reluctance to acknowledge the importance of homosexuality in the rise of abstract art, a history in which Stein's experimental prose style, her patronage of young artists, and the social circle she created all played a crucial role. All of these activities were influenced in important ways by her sexual identity.

Stein's lesbianism was equally important to her role as a patron who exerted great influence over other American women, especially the wealthy Cone sisters of Baltimore, Etta and Claribel. Etta's diaries suggest an early romance with Stein and her letters to Stein frankly discuss her attractions to women. Most contemporaries, however, saw Stein as closer to the more intellectual Claribel, a friend from medical school who became a prominent researcher and administrator. So close was their identification that Stein's 1912 essay "Two Women," nominally a word portrait of the Cone sisters, is also commonly read as describing Stein's relationship with Toklas. Under Stein's guidance, the Cones amassed one of the most important American collections of modernist French art, including works by Matisse, Gauguin, and Renoir. The Cones' collection focused on images of women in a range of genres—from nudes, through fashionable portraits, to a remarkable series of ten Matisse drawings of the strong-jawed Cone sisters looking remarkably like Picasso's famous portrait of Stein—as if to catalog the manifestations of modern womanhood from sensual "primitive" through fashionable lady to serious intellectual. Like Stein, the Cones saw their collection as an educational resource. They opened their home to scholars and other collectors, lectured on modern art, and lent pieces to museums, all with the goal of promoting modernism, a way of thinking they associated with women's voting rights and other feminist issues.

Stein was also a strong influence on aspiring male modernists. Some of her protégés—most notably the author Ernest Hemingway—were deeply troubled by their attraction to activities and individuals coded as homosexual; much of his fiction can be read as a reaction against such imputations. Others were fascinated by Stein's ability to make a success of both her unconventional domestic partnership and her experimental writing, which used the ambiguities of modernist abstraction to range freely through subjects that, described straightforwardly, would be scandalous or even illegal.

The painter Marsden Hartley was one of the ambitious, young American modernists Stein encouraged. On his first visit to Stein's home, Hartley admired her collection of cubist Picassos, which he sketched in letters documenting his fascination with their apparently random use of symbols: "names of people and words like *jolie* or *bien* and numbers like 75," as he put it (Weinberg, pp. 158–159). Hartley's memoirs recount how the first sight of this art made him feel "like a severed head living of itself by mystical excitation," going on to speculate that "maybe Gertrude lived by disembodiedness." Hartley's phrases connect coded art with a yearning to transcend a body that for both him and Stein was encumbered with stigmatized sexual desires. Seizing on his perception of abstraction as a code that escaped the regulations to which bodies were subjected, Hartley responded to the death of a German army lieutenant he loved by painting a series of abstract portraits, building his compositions around elements from the man's uniform and such symbols as the letters of his monogram and the numbers of his age. Exhibited in New York City in 1916, these paintings' quotations of German military insignia aroused political controversy, but were not seen as expressions of sexual identity. Only after Hartley's death did art historians decode personal references in his portraits, so that they are now commonly cited in studies of art and homosexuality. But to see these images as portraits is to miss what is most important about them: that the artist's passion for another man could find expression only in a language that was disembodied and indecipherable.

Romaine Brooks and Marsden Hartley might be described as opposite poles on the spectrum of possibility for modern artists' expression of homosexual identity in the first half of the twentieth century. Brooks's tasteful, carefully painted, emotionally reserved portraits of lesbians leave ambiguous her attitude toward what she clearly depicts. In contrast, Hartley's childlike colors, vigorous paint strokes, and frontal presentation convey a passionate personal commitment to his imagery, but his abstraction leaves what he depicts unclear. Between these poles of Brooks's aloofness and Hartley's obscurity, many other LGBT artists could be located, all intrigued by the associations of art with homosexuality yet prevented—by both social strictures and censorship laws—from expressing homosexual identity directly. Many artists during this period responded to these pressures by creating work they did not exhibit or publicize. Significant amounts of hidden homoerotic imagery have since emerged from painters like Charles Demuth and photographers like George Platt Lynes and Carl Van Vechten, among others. Many other artists are reputed to have created such work, only to have it destroyed by anxious families or friends after their deaths.

Postwar Repression and Coding

Anxiety over homosexuality increased with the social changes following World War II, as witnessed by the regular outbreak of sensationalized panics over sexual deviance, which in postwar political rhetoric was often linked to communist infiltration. Despite the fact that communist governments prohibited abstract art, politicians exploited modernism's international origins to condemn it as communist. Ironically, many mid-twentieth-century artists who rejected abstraction and retained realist styles—most prominently Paul Cadmus and Jared French—did so to sustain a tradition of homoerotic imagery they associated with Renaissance painting techniques. Their old-fashioned style gained them the mixed blessing of critical indifference as they sacrificed claims to be avant-garde for the freedom to explore homoerotic imagery.

More ambitious modernists often overcompensated for anxieties over imputations of social and sexual deviance by embracing stereotypical forms of American masculinity. The abstract expressionist painters banned homosexuals, as well as women and critics, from their "artists' club," and modernist critics policed even abstract art for signs of secrecy or effeminacy that might signal sexual deviation. Critical reviews by the influential Clement Greenberg, for instance, warned the heterosexual painter Robert Motherwell away from "archness like that of the interior decorator" and complained about "evasion" in the abstract art of the homosexual Mark Tobey, comparing him to female poets. Prescriptions of a masculine, often violent heterosexuality stunted the artistic careers of both women and gender-transgressive men. But homophobia also took its toll on successful artists, most notably Jackson Pollock, whose art of "violence, exasperation and stridency" was celebrated by Greenberg as "radically American." Such acclaim trapped both Pollock's art and life in highly scrutinized performances of masculinity, frustrating his development of new approaches to painting and contributing to his premature death in a drunken car crash, which also killed his female passenger.

Ironically, despite the art world's strenuous efforts to shake off associations with homosexuality in the 1950s, two of the artists who, in retrospect, emerged as exemplary of that era were not only gay, but—secretly—a couple. The art of Jasper Johns and Robert Rauschenberg refined many of the strategies of masking and coding pioneered by artists earlier in the century. Rauschenberg's 1953 exhibition of all-white paintings was widely seen as a challenge to the self-revelatory gestures of abstract expressionism. His *Erased de Kooning* (1953)—the marred sheet of paper from which he had erased a drawing by the abstract expressionist painter Willem de Kooning—challenged requirements that art express its creator. Rauschenberg's work after 1953 continued to refuse self-revelation, but his strategy shifted from presenting blankness to overwhelming the viewer with visual cues that frustrate claims of artistic self-expression. Rauschenberg's so-called Combines—large collages of paint strokes, texts, reproductions of other images, and stuck-on objects—present the viewer with an array of visual stimuli, much of it selected rather than produced by the artist. Although these works can be analyzed for subtle references to homosexuality, the onus of interpretation is on the viewer to attribute meaning to compositions where abstract expressionist splashes of paint seem to be just another kind of randomly discovered image.

Rauschenberg was joined in this phase of his career by a poet-turned-painter, Jasper Johns. Controversial recent scholarship has augmented long-standing analyses of works like Johns's *Target with Plaster Casts* (1955) and *Painting with Two Balls* (1960) as just critical response to abstract expressionism's claims for gestural self-expression, elucidating, as well, their allusions to the machismo of the art world and to the vulnerability of the closet. But like Demuth and Hartley, artists whom Johns admired, Johns's work was less an assertion of sexual identity than a display of codes that dares viewers to make sense of what they see.

Such coding may be, paradoxically, the clearest expression of homosexual identity in the art of the postwar decades, but that raises the question of why this secretive art became so central to the modernism of the 1950s. Sexual secrecy in general—and the secret of homosexuality in particular—animated much American high culture during the 1950s. The plays of Tennessee Williams—for instance, *Cat on a Hot Tin Roof* (1955) and *Suddenly Last Summer* (1958), both of which became major Hollywood films—trace the lethal ramifications of a homosexual secret, which is never actually named. The paradox of postwar culture's fascination with what it repressed may be the definitive characteristic of an era when a growing middle class defined itself by conformity to rigid standards of social and sexual propriety balanced by indulgence in social practices from psychoanalysis to detective novels structured around the revelation of secrets. Though it was not just homosexuality that was repressed during the 1950s, its perceived links to political subversiveness and mental illness—two other categories of repression—contributed to its status as the paradigmatic secret. This helps to explain Rauschenberg's and Johns's success with audiences (including dealers, collectors, critics, and museumgoers) who embraced these artists' subtle experiments with codes, masks, and ambiguous allusions. In what may be the ultimate paradox of a paradoxical era, the secretive, gay-coded art of Johns and Rauschenberg became, by the end of the 1950s, the most celebrated artistic expression of a culture intrigued by well-kept secrets.

End of Secrecy

The culture of secrets collapsed in the 1960s, when a militant youth culture and the sexual revolution challenged middle-class social norms. Pop Art, which defied injunctions to both heterosexuality and abstraction, was part of this challenge. Openly gay Pop artists like David Hockney and Andy Warhol made free use of homoerotic imagery, challenging the Wildean model of the avant-garde artist whose brilliance masks the secret of homosexuality. Making brilliant use, instead, of non-art visual sources like physique magazine illustrations and publicity photographs of handsome singers and movie stars, these Pop artists revealed the rich homoerotic conventions that, evading the scrutiny accorded avant-garde art, had developed in the popular culture. Both Warhol and Hockney, moreover, used their art to record their participation in celebrity social networks that accepted homosexuality. Pop Art's rejection of abstraction in favor of figuration and visual quotation is often cited as the origin of postmodernism on stylistic grounds. From the perspective of the history of sexuality, as well, Pop marked the end of an era in which the paradigm of the alienated avant-garde was crucially defined by association with the secretive homosexual.

Bibliography

Benstock, Shari. *Women of the Left Bank: Paris, 1900–1940.* Austin: University of Texas Press, 1986.

Chadwick, Whitney. *Amazons in the Drawing Room: The Art of Romaine Brooks.* Berkeley: University of California Press, 2000.

Cooper, Emmanuel. *The Sexual Perspective: Homosexuality and Art in the Last 100 Years in the West.* 2d ed. London: Routledge, 1994.

Craven, David. *Abstract Expressionism as Cultural Critique: Dissent during the McCarthy Era.* Cambridge, U.K.: Cambridge University Press, 1999.

Doyle, Jennifer, Jonathan Flatley, and José Esteban Muñoz, eds. *Pop Out: Queer Warhol.* Durham, N.C.: Duke University Press, 1996.

Gibson, Ann Eden. *Abstract Expressionism: Other Politics.* New Haven, Conn.: Yale University Press, 1997.

Jussim, Estelle. *Slave to Beauty: The Eccentric Life and Controversial Career of F. Holland Day, Photographer, Publisher, Aesthete.* Boston: Godine, 1981.

Katz, Jonathan. "The Art of Code: Jasper Johns and Robert Rauschenberg." In *Significant Others: Creativity and Intimate Partnership.* Edited by Whitney Chadwick and Isabelle de Courtivron. London: Thames and Hudson, 1993.

———. "Passive Resistance: On the Success of Queer Artists in Cold War American Art." *Image* (Winter 1996): 119–142.

Meyer, Richard. *Outlaw Representation: Censorship and Homosexuality in Twentieth-Century American Art.* New York: Oxford University Press, 2002.

Naifeh, Steven, and Gregory White Smith. *Jackson Pollock: An American Saga.* New York: Clarkson Potter, 1989.

Shand-Tucci, Douglass. *Boston Bohemia, 1881–1900.* Amherst, Mass.: University of Massachusetts Press, 1995.

Silver, Kenneth E. "Modes of Disclosure: The Construction of Gay Identity and the Rise of Pop Art." In *Hand-Painted Pop: American Art in Transition, 1955–62.* Edited by Russell Ferguson. Los Angeles: Museum of Contemporary Art, 1992.

Weinberg, Jonathan. *Speaking for Vice: Homosexuality in the Art of Charles Demuth, Marsden Hartley, and the First American Avant-Garde.* New Haven, Conn.: Yale University Press, 1993.

Christopher Reed

See also ART HISTORY; BARNES, DJUNA; BARNEY, NATALIE; BROOKS, ROMAINE; CADMUS, PAUL; HARTLEY, MARSDEN; HOCKNEY, DAVID; JOHNS, JASPER; RAUSCHENBERG, ROBERT; STEIN, GERTRUDE, AND ALICE B. TOKLAS; WARHOL, ANDY.

PAINTING, DRAWING, AND SCULPTURE: 1969–PRESENT

There are many histories of art produced by LGBT people in the United States since the Stonewall Riots of 1969. These histories often have distinct gender, economic, and political goals. Although post-Stonewall LGBT artists work in all styles and media, figurative and narrative art, rather than abstract imagery, have been the most visible and identifiable. The most notable effect of post-Stonewall LGBT movements on art can be seen in the shift into the public sphere of what had been private and hidden imagery. This relates to the establishment and promotion of venues for exhibiting LGBT artwork and the development of a series of theoretical discourses about the nature of LGBT art.

In the post-Stonewall era, public discourse about LGBT art was transformed. The LGBT and feminist press documented and publicized LGBT artists and shows. LGBT publications were interested in visual imagery and helped launch hundreds of careers, but they were also the vehicles for developing a knowledgeable public willing to support LGBT artistic work. LGBT community centers, women's bookstores, and gay and lesbian bookstores sold posters and note cards and often included space for the display of original art. Galleries were established to show work by LGBT artists and many feminist galleries exhibited work by lesbians. LGBT libraries and archives played key roles in preserving artwork and biographical information about artists. Nevertheless, geography, race, class, gender, and other factors all influenced the nature of support systems and the ability for artists to be recognized at regional and national levels.

The 1970s

The Stonewall Riots of 1969 contributed to an artistic explosion in which the pent-up creativity of several generations was expressed in a multitude of forms. During this period, the male nude body most directly conveyed male homosexual desire in art. Seductive stances, frontal nudity, and overt gay erotic activities increasingly appeared on canvas and in print.

Some well-known artists, such as David Hockney in Los Angeles and Andy Warhol in New York, both of whom had been openly gay before 1969, continued making gay-themed images after Stonewall. Hockney in particular used his gay friends, crushes, and lovers as the subjects of drawings and paintings. Others who have used gay friends and lovers for inspiration include George Dureau in New Orleans, who crafted idiosyncratic narratives in painting, photography, and sculpture, and Don Bachardy in Los Angeles, who made large-scale portrait drawings of his aging lover, author Christopher Isherwood.

Gay content was not central to other gay artists' work. Scott Burton in New York moved from installation art to geometric chair forms, which in the 1980s became monumental. Joe Brainard worked in collage, assemblage, painting, and drawing and associated with an older New York poetry and art scene that included bisexual artist Larry Rivers. Harlem Renaissance painter (Richard) Bruce Nugent saw renewed interest in his work after he appeared in the gay and lesbian interview film *Word Is Out* (1978), whereas sculptor Richmond Barthé, also active in the Harlem Renaissance, remained silent about his homosexuality and was obscure in his later years. Texas-based Forrest Bess, regarded by some as transgender, addressed androgyny in his life and in his mystical paintings, which included transsexual images and themes.

Prominent among lesbian artists producing lesbian-themed work in the 1970s was Lili Lakich, a founder of the Museum of Neon Art in Los Angeles. In portraits and self-portraits, Lakich pictured her relationships in honeycombed aluminum cutouts and neon tubing. Los Angeles sculptor Nancy Fried crafted sapphic domestic scenes in bread dough, which were then baked and painted. Working on the East Coast, Sudie Rakusin created amazon and goddess graphics that spoke to countercultural lesbian communities. In New York, sculptor Harmony Hammond, painter Louise Fishman, and sculptor Jody Pinto were featured in lesbian-themed shows while also exhibiting in mainstream art venues. Washington, D.C., painter Judy Castelli, diagnosed as schizophrenic, painted psychologically revealing self-portraits. Within the West Coast Latina/Latino muralist movement, there was at least one bisexual male, Carlos Almaraz, and three lesbians: Ester Medina Hernández, Irene Pérez, and Judith F. Baca. Of these, painter-printmaker Hernández crafted the most overtly lesbian-themed imagery, some of which has been reproduced as book cover art.

Some histories of the period claim that there was little sexual imagery made by women in the 1970s, yet sexually specific work by a number of artists, such as Noreen Scully in northern California, has been ignored. Female genitalia emerged during this period as liberationist iconography. In 1974, bisexual New York artist Betty Dodson published labia drawings in *Liberating Masturbation*. Bisexual artist Judy Chicago made vulval plates from 1974 to 1979. In the early 1970s in San Francisco, Jeri Robertson exhibited a giant labia painting in a lesbian bar. In Manhattan, Flavia Rando's painting of the same subject was displayed in and then removed from a women's restaurant. In 1975, Tee A. Corinne's *Cunt Coloring Book* was published in San Francisco, and *What Lesbians Do*, a book of sexually explicit drawings and poems by Marilyn Gayle and Barbary Katherine, was produced in Portland, Oregon.

Exhibitions in the 1970s

Exhibitions connect artists, audiences, and commentators. Open submission lesbian- and gay-related shows began in the early 1970s and curated shows began later in the decade. Open submission shows, often criticized for being aesthetically uneven, tend to have an exuberance and celebratory character. Curated shows usually aim, in some way, to define the field of LGBT art and aesthetics. Charles W. Leslie and J. Frederic Lohman, who initiated shows of gay art in their New York loft in 1969, ran the commercial Leslie-Lohman Gallery from 1975 to 1981. In the San Francisco Bay area in the 1970s, lesbian art shows took place in women's bars such as Scott's Pit (1973–1974) and the Bacchanal (1975–1980). By 1978 in Manhattan, Harmony Hammond curated a widely publicized and well-reviewed exhibit called "A Lesbian Show" in an informal, artist-run alternative space. A second show followed in 1980.

The 1980s

In the 1980s, the dialogue about LGBT art extended into books, university courses, and LGBT and queer studies venues. Some argued against using LGBT identity as a basis for producing or evaluating art, yet self-portraiture, portraiture, and lifestyle imagery—central to identity-based art—remained popular.

People of color became more visible across the range of queer cultural and political activities in the 1980s. In this period, art careers began for Hong Kong–born Horatio Hung-Yan Law, Chicago painter Juarez Hawkins, Korean-born Mi Ok Song Bruining, Yaqui (native Mexican) painter Mario Martinez, and Los Angeles painter Tony de Carlo. De Carlo's colorful paintings often showed aspects of his environment and daily life. Connecticut-based African American painter Lula Mae Blocton began exhibiting in lesbian-themed shows in 1980, the same year in which *Azalea: A Magazine by and for Third World Lesbians* produced a graphics issue featuring, among others, realist painter Diane Edison. California-based sculptor Fan Lee Warren and painter and mixed-media artist Glenn Ligon in New York have produced politically nuanced, racially referenced work. Lloyd Vega in New Jersey explored images of black male couples.

Published in 1981, painter Mary Meigs's autobiography, *Lily Briscoe: A Self-Portrait,* detailed her struggles as a lesbian who could believe in the importance of her art. Other artists who became known in the 1980s by producing LGBT-themed art include painters Max White in San Francisco and Lari Pittman in southern California. Pittman's large-format paintings gather imagery from a variety of sources. Painter Jonathan Weinberg distinguished himself as an art historian working on LGBT themes.

Conceptual frameworks shaped the sculpture of New Yorkers Robert Gober, Roni Horn, and Nayland Blake and southern California artist Millie Wilson. In contrast, there was a visceral physicality in the leather-masked heads of New York sculptor Nancy Grossman and the

Andy Warhol. The Pop Artist, who also created gay-themed artwork both before and after the Stonewall Riots of 1969, stands in front of his silk-screened images of Brillo soapboxes. **[AP/Wide World Photos]**

male torsos of Philip Hitchcock, who worked in Venice, California.

Exhibitions in the 1980s

The Women's Building in Los Angeles supported feminist and lesbian art education from 1973 until it closed in 1991. In 1980, it was the site of GALAS, the Great American Lesbian Art Show, which included over two hundred satellite shows held around the country. In 1981, the Hibbs Gallery in New York City sponsored a show and catalog of work by artists who had been featured in the *Advocate,* the LGBT magazine based in Los Angeles. In 1982, the New Museum of Contemporary Art in Manhattan mounted "Extended Sensibilities: Homosexual Presence in Contemporary Art," the first museum exhibit to examine gay and lesbian art issues. Although many saw the show as opening up new possibilities, no new major museum show of LGBT art occurred until 1995. "The Dynamics of Color: Lesbian Artists Respond to Racism,"

Keith Haring.
Drawings and installations
by the 1980s artist, whose
work often dealt with AIDS.
[Keith Haring]

held in a community center in a traditionally African American area of San Francisco in 1989, was the first show to exhibit work made primarily by lesbians of color.

Disability and HIV/AIDS Imagery

Disability, which had emerged as an art subject in lesbian communities during the 1970s, was featured in the 1980s in the wheelchair imagery of Connie Panzarino, a bisexual painter with severely limited mobility. Panzarino designed a graphic that incorporated the women's symbol, the clenched fist of power, and the universal wheelchair access logo.

Central to art making in the 1980s was the HIV/AIDS crisis, which outed many male artists who, in another era, might have remained private. Activist art took many forms. Some artists organized into groups such as Gran Fury, Art Positive, and GANG in New York City; Boy With Arms Akimbo in San Francisco; Helm's Angels in Chicago; and Stiff Sheets in Los Angeles.

Hundreds of artists have produced work associated with HIV/AIDS. David Wojnarowicz was one of the first artists to respond to the AIDS crisis. Other artists whose work is often identified with AIDS issues include Keith Haring, Juan González, and Donald Moffett, a cofounder of Gran Fury. Martin Wong, who often painted images of ethnic minorities other than his own, participated in AIDS-themed shows. Ohio-born painter Jerome Caja, exhibiting a camp persona, constructed glittering mixed-media paintings incorporating found objects, eye liner, and nail polish. Oregon painter Morgan Johnson imaged his partner the way the partner wished to be seen, avoid-

ing the visual manifestations of AIDS. Painter Frank Moore utilized an old master style to portray contemporary subjects, including HIV/AIDS. Some paintings by Ross Bleckner are understood to be memorials to those who have died of AIDS.

The Names Project AIDS Memorial Quilt began in San Francisco in 1985 as a way to remember those who have been lost to AIDS. In New York in 1991, the Estate Project for Artists with AIDS was formed in order to keep artwork, documentation, and biographical information from being lost.

The 1990s

Dominating queer art's critical discourse in the 1990s—egged on, perhaps, by controversies surrounding Robert Mapplethorpe's work and National Endowment for the Arts funding—an edgy, urban aesthetics sought to push the boundaries of what could be exhibited and published. A new generation of sexually explicit lesbian imagery emerged in paintings and drawings by Carrie Moyer and Nicola Tyson in New York and Judith Bamber and Monica Majoli in southern California. It appeared more subtly in the red-flocked, labia-like saddle sculptures of New Jersey artist Julia Kunin and the sensuality of paintings by Tucson-based Lorraine Inzalaco and New Yorker Patricia Cronin.

Sexually inflected art remained popular with gay male audiences. New Mexico artist Delmas Howe eroticized cowboy and leather imagery. Los Angeles nude-man-as-object figurative painter John Sonsini found an audience for his art. In New Orleans, after retiring from a

Divers. A work by Nicole Eisenman.

curatorial career, J. B. Harter pursued his passion for painting erotic images of men.

Throughout the 1990s, race and racism, in varying degrees, continued to influence those artists seen as significant. Equality, however, was still a goal rather than a reality. Within an expanding dialogue, some artists referenced specific cultural backgrounds; others did not. African Americans such as graphic artist Rupert Kinnard in Portland, Oregon, and Laura Irene Wayne in California imaged active black subjects. Paintings by Celia Herrera Rodriguez reflected Chicano, Native American, Pre-Columbian, and Mexican concerns. In Los Angeles, painter Miguel Angel Reyes often worked with VIVA, a

gay and lesbian Latino arts collective dedicated to increasing the visibility of queer Latino and Latina artists. Northern California–based Asian American painters Bernice Bing and Kim Anno preferred abstraction. Themes in the art of David Zamora Casas in San Antonio reflected his roots in Mexicano/Chicano culture and in queer and AIDS activism.

Narrative, identity, and culture shaped the work of other LGBT artists active in the 1990s. In New York, Deborah Kass reconstructed Andy Warhol's silk-screened images from lesbian and Jewish points of view and George Towne painted gay men, including those whose lovers had died of HIV/AIDS. During the 1990s, Chicago-based Hollis Sigler painted her visual journal of life with breast cancer. In Oakland, California, Jean Sirius responded to her lover's cancer with torn and cut paper imagery. In Philadelphia, Daniel Heyman and Mary Kerr independently pursued neo-naive figurative styles. In the Pacific Northwest, paintings by Sierra Lonepine Briano often referenced her Italian Catholic background. Lenore Chinn in San Francisco and David Alexander in New York City were known for portraits of domestic partners in personally referential settings. Working on the Maine coast, Robert Indiana, best known for his colorful geometric LOVE image, celebrated his love of men in gay-themed homages to the bisexual painter Marsden Hartley and totemic figures with erect penises.

In the 1990s, various LGBT artists who had been producing LGBT art in decades past continued to make and influence LGBT art. In the Northeast, Provincetown-based figurative painter Jane Kogan, known for her *Ladder* magazine covers in the late 1960s, pursued a regional career. In New York, Forrest Williams painted male figures that seem to echo, on a much larger scale, the earlier work of George Tooker. Paul Cadmus and his bisexual lover, Jared French, had explored queer sensibilities decades before Stonewall in paintings and photographs. Cadmus became popular with post-Stonewall generations because of his openness about his love of men, his use of the nude male body, and his exploration of gay themes. Tooker, too, continued to paint and has been willing to be written about as a gay artist, something not everyone of his generation is willing to do.

Of the older artists who reached a level of professional visibility prior to 1969, Oklahoma-born abstract painter Leon Polk Smith was most involved with gay liberation activities and left a legacy of scholarship funds for young gay artists. New York–based lesbian painter Nell Blaine was not involved with organized lesbian or gay activities, but the naming of her female partner in Blaine's *New York Times* obituary can be understood as a liberationist act.

Exhibitions in the 1990s

Some of the strongest LGBT shows in the 1990s that addressed race, ethnicity, and art have taken place in San Francisco. Since 1991, annual exhibitions of gay and lesbian Latina/Latino art have been held in the Mission Cultural Center during gay pride month (June). In "Situation: Perspectives on Work by Lesbian and Gay Artists," held in San Francisco in 1991, half of the lesbians were women of color. Adrienne Fuzee was the first openly lesbian African American curator working in the United States. Throughout the 1990s, she was active in the San

Francisco Bay area with LAVA (Lesbians in the Visual Arts) and the Queer Cultural Center, which she helped to found.

In New York City in 1990, Charles W. Leslie and J. Frederic Lohman established the Leslie-Lohman Gay Art Foundation, a major venue to show and archive gay (and some lesbian) art. The foundation's catalogs, newsletters, and Web presence (which includes a listing of who's who in queer art of the past and present) has, like books on the subject, aided the visibility of LGBT art.

"In A Different Light: Visual Culture, Sexual Identity, Queer Practice," the first major museum examination of LGBT art since the "Extended Sensibilities" show in 1982, was held at the University Art Museum, University of California at Berkeley, in 1995. It mixed together work by gay men, lesbians, bisexuals, and heterosexuals.

A high point of mainstream visibility for gay men was reached when seventeen gay and bisexual male artists—most showing gay-themed work—were among the seventy-five artists and artist's collaboratives represented in the 1991 Whitney Biennial. These included Keith Haring, who had died the previous year, Nayland Blake, Glenn Ligon, David Wojnarowicz, Robert Gober, Félix González-Torres, Ross Bleckner, Jasper Johns, Robert Rauschenberg, and Group Material, which was a collaborative effort of four gay artists, active since the early 1980s.

Into the New Millennium

In the past several years, the LGBT art world has become more interested in transgenderism. Gender issues, often important in LGB lives, become critical with artists whose self-identity and body are not congruent. Although these artists have been documented since the 1930s and earlier, accumulating information about contemporary gender variant artists is complicated by the desire of many to be known by their internal identity rather than as transsexuals. Information about transgender aspects of the work of Forrest Bess was not available before the mid-1990s. Groups such as the Transsexual Artists Guild (founded in 2000) seek to publicize the work of artists such as painter N. E. (Nathaniel Evan) Wolfe.

There are variations in gender dysphoric experience. Artist Cooper Lee Bombardier describes herself as a gender-bent renaissance cowboy. Gender activist Daphne Scholinski, a painter institutionalized as a teen, wrote *The Last Time I Wore a Dress* (1997). Writer, dancer, and visual artist Camille designed a stained glass skylight in San Francisco's LGBT Community Center as a memorial to children who have experienced psychiatric abuse.

New LGBT artists have also become more visible in the last several years. Many younger queer artists, such as Japanese-born Hiroshi Sunairi, use collaged imagery, often generated by computers. Young artists featured in the online Queer Arts Resource show "Generation Q: The First International Queer Youth Expo" include Missouri cyber abstract artist Victor Hsieh, Boston-based Mollie Biewald, Brooklyn sculptor Aaron Sciandra, and San Francisco-based Sara (Frog) Davidson.

Midcareer artists reach national audiences through innovative as well as traditional means. In 2001, Los Angeles artist Alma López generated controversy when her digital, photo-collaged Virgin of Guadalupe, who wears a bikini made of roses, was exhibited at the Museum of International Folk Art in Santa Fe, New Mexico.

Older LGBT artists continue to produce new work. In New Mexico, geometric abstract painter Agnes Martin paints elegant, minimalist stripes. In San Francisco, figurative expressionist painters Theophilus Brown and his long-term lover Paul Wonner maintained studios and painted regularly even after they entered retirement lodgings.

Many artists, although not closeted among friends, have not participated in the public dialogue about queer art. Often, information about the connections between their sexualities, their genders, and their art only becomes available after they die. These artists, active in the post-Stonewall years, include the Philippine-born Alfonso Ossorio, African American Beauford Delaney, Greek American Theodoros Stamos, bisexual figure painter Fairfield Porter, and bisexual abstract sculptor Richard Lippold.

Some artists fought public identification as bisexual or homosexual but have been outed by LGBT scholarship. These include Robert Rauschenberg, Jasper Johns, Louise Nevelson, and Ellsworth Kelly. Research has also uncovered closeted LGBT artists associated with Seattle: Mark Tobey, Guy Anderson, Morris Graves, and Leo Kenney.

Exhibitions, 2000 Forward

In 2002 at the State University of New York at Stony Brook, "Queer Visualities: Reframing Sexuality in a Post-Warhol World" was organized by photographer Carl Robert Pope Jr., one of the first African American men to curate a major show about gay, lesbian, or queer art in the United States.

Other venues supportive of LGBT art include the Queer Cultural Center in San Francisco and the Esperanza Center in San Antonio. Additionally, many LGBT community centers in the United States maintain

Target. One of a series by Jasper Johns, an older artist whose continuing work included representation in the 1991 Whitney Biennial, along with works by more than a dozen other gay or bisexual male artists (though Johns resists that identification of himself). [corbis]

exhibition space. Some of the most active include New York City, Philadelphia, New Orleans, San Francisco, Los Angeles (which shows artists from around the country), and Seattle (whose gallery focuses on regional artists).

Commonality and Divergence

The rise of the Internet in the late twentieth century has had a dramatic impact on how artists become known and how minorities within minorities become visible. Search engines are more democratic than curators and editors. Imagery by queer artists, once difficult to find and confined to a limited number of books and archives or obscured in storage in artist's studios, is now easily accessible. Technological developments have also made hardcopy publication, including self-publication, more affordable.

As the twenty-first century proceeds, LGBT artists continue to function, for the most part, in separate spheres defined by, for example, age, gender, geography, race, sexuality, orientation to LGBT communities and to the general public, and popular and critical reception. Those artists whose work has been featured in books, exhibition catalogs, and magazines are the best known. Others exhibit their work to local and regional audiences. Scholars and curators—not all of them queer—working within and outside of academic programs and museums continue to shape and reshape the ways in which LGBT art is understood, exhibited, and archived.

Bibliography

Blake, Nayland, Lawrence Rinder, and Amy Scholder, eds. *In a Different Light: Visual Culture, Sexual Identity, Queer Practice.* San Francisco: City Lights Books, 1995.

Cameron, Daniel. ed. *Extended Sensibilities: Homosexual Presence in Contemporary Art.* New York: New Museum of Contemporary Art, 1982.

Cooper, Emmanuel. *The Sexual Perspective: Homosexuality and Art in the Last 100 Years in the West.* 2d ed. London and New York: Routledge, 1990.

Corinne, Tee A. "How Lesbian Artists Support Their Art." *Journal of Lesbian Studies* 5, no. 3 (2001).

Cottingham, Laura. *Lesbians Are So Chic.* New York: Cassell, 1996.

Davalos, Karen Mary. *Exhibiting Mestizaje: Mexican (American) Museums in the Diaspora.* Albuquerque: University of New Mexico Press, 2001.

Davis, Whitney, ed. *Gay and Lesbian Studies in Art History.* New York: Harrington Park Press, 1994.

Fernandez, Dominique. *A Hidden Love: Art and Homosexuality.* New York: Prestel, 2002.

Gay and Lesbian Caucus of the College Art Association. *Bibliography of Gay and Lesbian Art.* New York: Gay and Lesbian Caucus of the College Art Association, 1994.

Hammond, Harmony. *Lesbian Art in America: A Contemporary History.* New York: Rizzoli, 2000.

Hammond, Harmony, and Lord, Catherine. *Gender, Fucked.* Seattle: CoCA (Center On Contemporary Art), 1996.

Kelley, Caffyn, ed. *Forbidden Subjects: Self-Portraits by Lesbian Artists.* North Vancouver, British Columbia: Gallerie, 1992.

Meyer, Richard. *Outlaw Representation: Censorship and Homosexuality in Twentieth-Century American Art.* New York: Oxford University Press, 2002.

Saslow, James M. *Pictures and Passions: A History of Homosexuality in the Visual Arts.* New York: Penguin Putnam, 1999.

Smalls, James. *Homosexuality in Art.* Paris: Parkstone Press, 2003.

Smyth, Cherry. *Damn Fine Art by New Lesbian Artists.* London: Cassell, 1996.

Tee A. Corinne

See also AIDS MEMORIAL QUILT—NAMES PROJECT; ART HISTORY; BACA, JUDITH; CADMUS, PAUL; HARING, KEITH; HARTLEY, MARSDEN; HOCKNEY, DAVID; ISHERWOOD, CHRISTOPHER; JOHNS, JASPER; MAPPLETHORPE, ROBERT; NUGENT, RICHARD BRUCE; RAUSCHENBERG, ROBERT; WARHOL, ANDY; WOJNAROWICZ, DAVID.

VISUAL ART: PHOTOGRAPHY

LGBT photography includes images made in many contexts. There is work by persons of any gender or sexuality, which was not necessarily intended for LGBT consumption, but has been appropriated by the LGBT community. There is work by persons of any identity or orientation that specifically addresses LGBT concerns. There is work by members of the LGBT community that does not address LGBT issues. Finally, there is work by photographers whose orientation is unknown and whose work does not reflect LGBT concerns, but whose relationship with a same-sex partner put them at the margins of society and may have altered their photographic viewpoint. In a discussion of LGBT photography, these categories are not mutually exclusive, and one photographer might participate in several categories at once or over the course of a career.

The Nineteenth Century

Beginning with photography's inception in 1839, the nude has been photographed for artistic, ethnographic, and erotic reasons. Because most photographers in the nineteenth century were heterosexual men, most photographs of the nude were of women and were designed for the male gaze. This does not mean that women did not view these images, and there were photographs of nude men. As with women, these were frequently artist's models, who posed in positions imitating ancient Greek statues. Over time, the classically posed male nude became a symbol for homosexual desire.

In 1873, Eadweard Muybridge (1830–1904) was commissioned by Leland Stanford, the president of the Central Pacific railroad and a racehorse breeder, to do studies of a horse in motion. Muybridge extended this project to include other animals (including humans), which were photographed at regular intervals as they performed various tasks. In 1887, his studies were published as *Animal Locomotion.* The 781 plates included images of men, women, and children (some nude, seminude, or draped in a gauzy fabric) performing a wide variety of activities such as running, skipping, and pouring water. While the purpose of these images was scientific, they offered a new vision of the human body. The artist Thomas Eakins (1844–1916) also experimented with the male nude. In the 1880s, Eakins took photographs of men wrestling, boxing out of doors, and jumping and lifting weights. He photographed himself and his male students swimming in 1883 as a study for a painting. This photograph, which became known for its naturalistic depiction of a group of nude men, demonstrated that male images of the nude did not need to be classically posed. The photograph, and others like it by Eakins, inspired the photographs of male nudes in natural settings and poses that emerged in the late nineteenth and early twentieth centuries.

1890 to 1920

This period saw the emergence of nudes and genre portraits created by both men and women, much of them made in the soft-focused painterly style called pictorialism. While the female nude was usually not seen as indicating or producing same-sex desire, when made by a woman, it could be construed as such. Anne Brigman (1868–1950) was a pictorial photographer whose soft-focus images often depicted her or her sister in natural settings in California. A declared pagan, Brigman often posed her female nudes in classical postures and used classical titles. In 1906, she became a member of the Photo-Secession, a small group of avant-garde photographers whose work was exhibited and published by Alfred Stieglitz.

Frances Benjamin Johnson (1864–1952) showed a similar independence in her work and life. She was a well-known portraitist who photographed many U.S. presidents, but her most artistically accomplished images were of the Hampton Institute, a historically black and Indian vocational school, which later became a black college. She made sympathetic portrayals of industrious students working and studying. An 1896 self-portrait, in which she sits with her skirt drawn up to reveal her legs crossed at the knee, holding a beer stein in one hand and a cigar in the other, is a symbolic portrait of an independent and assertive woman who felt confined by society. Alice Austen (1866–1952) evinced a similar independence of spirit. Born to a wealthy New York family, she documented her own social class extensively for over two decades, photographing a number of female couples and living with a woman. Austen later documented immigrant and working-class street life in lower Manhattan.

F(red) Holland Day (1864–1933) did the bulk of his photographic work between 1895 and 1917. A prominent pictorial photographer, Day's depiction of the crucifixion (taken on a hill outside Boston) shocked locals and critics alike. In the photograph, Day portrayed Christ, and he starved himself for a year to achieve sufficient emaciation. Seen retrospectively, in the age of AIDS, this image of a nearly nude emaciated man playing the part of Christ acquires new meanings related to involuntary sacrifice and social persecution. This was not Day's only male nude. In the 1890s, he posed nude youths in the woods outside Boston, and he is the first recorded photographer to work with a black male nude (his chauffeur).

Frank Eugene (1865–1936), also a member of the Photo-Secession, photographed the male nude as well as the female form. He sometimes used an etching needle on his negatives to obscure faces and body parts and to give his classically posed nudes painterly effects.

1920 to 1960

By the second decade of the twentieth century, the soft focus and painterly effects of pictorialism had largely given way to sharply focused images. Higher speed photographic emulsions also permitted shorter exposure times, allowing subjects to assume more informal and active poses. Nikolas Muray (1892–1965) was a photographer and champion fencer who represented the United States at the Olympic Games. He made his living as an advertising photographer and was the principal photographer for *Dance* magazine, for which he photographed many male ballet dancers whom he later photographed in the nude.

The 1920s and 1930s saw the emergence of a well-documented LGBT subculture in cities in Europe and the United States, and a number of noted American photographers recorded it. Margrethe Mather (1885–1952) was primarily lesbian and entered Hollywood culture with the help of a female patron. She made portraits of androgynous women, as well as photographs of hands, torsos, and other body parts in which the sex of the subject was not readily apparent. She also photographed overtly handsome men, who were often stripped to the waist to better record their neck and shoulder muscles. Mathers's interiors and still lifes may be said to reflect a camp aesthetic in their self-aware artificiality. Although her imagery is not overtly sexual, her treatment and selection of subject matter may be construed as reflecting and producing LGBT culture.

At the same time, Berenice Abbott (1898–1991) documented lesbian and gay artists and writers in Paris. She was a studio assistant to Man Ray from 1923 to 1929, during which time she opened her own portrait studio, where she photographed Jane Heap, Djuna Barnes, Thelma Wood, and Jean Cocteau. She returned to the United States in 1929 and began to document the changing face of New York in the 1930s, funded in part by a Works Progress Administration grant. In the 1940s, Abbott began to illustrate scientific principles and to write about large-format photography. Her partner, Elizabeth McCausland, was an early photography critic.

George Platt Lynes (1907–1955) worked in New York as a portrait photographer beginning in the mid-1920s and for three years in Hollywood in the 1940s. Lynes was also an advertising and fashion photographer, and his work appeared in *Town and Country, Harper's Bazaar,* and *Vogue.* However, it is his personal work, featuring dancers and male nudes, that has earned Lynes a place in photographic history. These large-format images evoke classical sculpture in their poses and props, as well as more contemporary surrealist imagery. A circa 1935 male nude, showing another man's hand reaching from behind to cover the genitals, is an early artistic photograph showing sexual contact. Using the pseudonym Roberto Rolf, Lynes published photographs in the German homoerotic magazine *Der Kreis* in 1954. Although Lynes destroyed many of his prints and negatives before his death from cancer in 1955, Dr. Alfred C. Kinsey was impressed by his work and arranged for the purchase of many of his photographs for the Kinsey Institute, which studies human sexual behavior.

Classical poses persisted in images of the male nude for art and physique magazines and books until the 1960s. These reproductions of male nudes attempted to avoid censorship because the shaven bodies and classical poses of the sitters transformed them into art—classical sculptures with flesh doubling as marble. Beginning in the 1950s, principally due to the efforts of Bob Mizer (1922–1992), individual studies began to appear in magazine format. Physique magazines had their origins in nineteenth-century and early twentieth-century photographs of male art models, some of whom, like Tony Sansone, were also bodybuilders. These images were sold as prints or as books or catalogs, from which prints of physically beautiful and fit men could be ordered.

The work of Minor White (1908–1976) subverted this trend by including vulnerable-looking men and male torsos in complex sequences of images in which each photograph was to be seen as an individual metaphor or equivalent. His emphasis on the photograph as metaphor was derived from Stieglitz's symbolic understanding of photography as "equivalent" to other aesthetic experiences such as music. The sequencing of these photographs increased the impact of each photograph as it interacted with others in the sequence. Although some of his nudes and sensitive emotional portraits of men were included in White's publications, many of his male nudes, like those of Lynes, were for his private consumption as a gay man. White was also a distinguished teacher. In 1946, he joined the faculty at the California School of Fine Arts (now the San Francisco Art Institute), where he participated in one of the country's first art photography departments. In 1953, he joined the staff at George Eastman House in Rochester, New York, and two years later became associated with the faculty of the Rochester Institute of Technology. From 1965 until his death in 1976, he

taught photography at the Massachusetts Institute of Technology. In 1952, White cofounded *Aperture* magazine, serving as editor in chief until 1964.

Ruth Bernhard (1905–) is best known for her landscape nudes and still lifes. In her work, one informs the other, and her nudes are anonymous, carefully posed images in which the female torso may resemble a natural landscape. Bernhard's work also contains strong design, as in *African* (1959), in which the pubic area of a kneeling black woman is clearly outlined as part of a torso, which is both dignified and strong. *Two Forms* (1963) shows a dark woman's torso pressed lightly and tenderly against that of a lighter woman. Bernhard's series of female nudes in boxes become metaphors for the female and lesbian body and the constraints placed on them by society.

1960 to 1980

In the decades after 1960, photographers began to photograph more marginalized members of society. The formal portrait and the staged photograph became major themes during this period. The photographer Diane Arbus (1923–1971) was the first to document LGBT people as part of a larger society. Her sitters, which ran the gamut from middle-aged, middle-class women to circus dwarfs, nudists, transvestite prostitutes, and children, were people she encountered on the streets and in other public places. Beginning in 1962, Arbus's use of flash coupled with a square-format, 2¼-inch camera was designed to reveal the details that made each subject a flawed, yet fascinating, individual. She often caught her subjects as they shifted from one emotion, position, or even gender to another. Her work links all humans through their vulnerability, their flaws, and their private psychological realities. One of the great photographers of the twentieth century, Arbus was awarded Guggenheim fellowships in 1963 and 1966. In 1972, a monograph on her work was published in conjunction with a major retrospective at the Museum of Modern Art in New York City. Her legacy was a vision of a world in which average humans are seen through the same lens as the marginalized.

The themes of private and personal transformation are also central to the work of Lucas Samaras (1936–). Trained originally as a sculptor, Samaras began making Polaroid self-portraits in 1969. In 1973, he began using the Polaroid process for the series *Photo-Transformations,* an examination of his body and his environment, using colored lights to transform both. In a second series, Samaras manipulated the surface of the print itself, using emulsion to obscure his body, change his sex, and even change from human to animal. In one transformation, his head became that of a werewolf. This autobiographical work references the self-discovery and transformation that Samaras underwent as a gay man. Like the freaks that are integrated into Arbus's larger culture, the werewolf portrait and other monstrous transformations are metaphors for how society views the outsider.

In the 1970s, photography was influenced by feminism, gay liberation, and a renewed interest in the constructed studio photograph. By 1978, these social and aesthetic changes gave rise to the first photography exhibition devoted to the male nude at the Marcuse Pfeifer Gallery in New York.

In 1971, George Dureau (1930–) began photographing a series of black and white men, some of whom were missing limbs. While their direct gazes and accessories identify these images as contemporary and homoerotic, the classicism of the poses uses the missing limbs to create references to Greek sculpture. Dureau's movement between black and white subjects, disabled and not, asks the viewer to rethink these categories in the larger context of gay and straight. Dureau was a major influence on Robert Mapplethorpe, who purchased his work.

In 1975, Judy Dater (1941–) and Jack Welpott (1923–) published a series of portraits, *Women and Other Visions.* Although the focus of these images was heterosexual women, lesbians, cross-dressed men and women, and adorned and unadorned male and female nudes were included as part of a continuum. The sitters gaze directly at the viewer, challenging a call to judgment, and the artfully arranged environments function as extensions of their personalities.

In 1976, Peter Hujar (1934–1987) published a monograph, *Portraits in Life and Death.* The portraits included Mexican mummies, young gay men who were nude and androgynous in a studio setting, and an image of the writer Susan Sontag, reclining on a bed after surviving cancer and mastectomies. A gay man, Hujar saw people on a journey from life into death, which erases all differences.

Arthur Tress (1940–) stages photographs that have the quality of a waking dream. His work is about power relationships—men to other men, the gay man to others, and a man to himself. His 1977 image "Superman Fantasy" showed a nude man with a Superman cutout superimposed over his body but revealing his genitals. Tress debunks Superman as a paper cutout, while at the same time highlighting the vulnerability of the nude man. The vulnerability of the male body, and specifically its genitalia, is a recurring theme in Tress's work and is part of a larger investigation into deep-rooted human fears.

Rather than concentrating on single images as a method for the exploration of the gay male psyche, Duane Michals (1932–) prefers to establish a dialogue using sequential images that tell a short story in photographs. Six to fifteen images recount an often life-changing chance encounter, which, because only the titles serve as text, may be read on several levels. In 1978, he created a series of ten photographs with handwritten titles that he called *Homage to Cavafy,* intending these images to stand as equivalents for Constantine P. Cavafy's poems. Like many of Michals's pieces, this series may be interpreted as involving the self and the other, eros, youth, aging, and death.

1980 to the Present

By the end of the 1970s, photographers started to exhibit the outer reaches of sexuality, concentrating on constructed and posed images in which sadomasochism, mythic depictions of humans, and the consequences of the AIDS epidemic were examined.

When the work of Joel-Peter Witkin (1939–) was exhibited at the San Francisco Museum of Modern Art in 1985, viewers encountered images that depicted private and staged theatrical events that made reference to classical mythology and well-known western European paintings. The sitters—dwarves, amputees, hermaphrodites, exhibitionists, transvestites, and others—took part in staged private theatrical events that moved from the realm of voyeurism into the realm of art with scratches on the emulsion, toning baths, and printing through tissue.

In 1983, Cynthia MacAdams (1939–) approached the mythic in a different way in her book *Rising Goddess.* As in her 1977 monograph *Emergence,* MacAdams concentrates on the female subject. In *Rising Goddess,* an Amazonian world of strong nude women and their female progeny is created through the use of infrared film, which gives an ethereal cast to her images.

Beginning in 1978 and continuing throughout the 1980s, Mariette Pathy Allen (1940–) created a body of work depicting transvestites old and young, with and without female costume, and at times posing with their wives and children. These straightforward images are devoid of campiness and concentrate on what it means to pass as female.

In the late 1980s, images of the AIDS epidemic began to receive attention. In 1988, Rosalind Solomon (1930–) created a portfolio called *Portraits in the Time of AIDS.* That same year, Nicholas Nixon (1947–) exhibited photographs of people with AIDS at the Museum of Modern Art. The AIDS Coalition to Unleash Power (ACT UP)

Robert Mapplethorpe. The photographer, the most important—and controversial—of the 1970s and 1980s, appears at an opening. [corbis]

protested against the exhibit for its unsympathetic portrayal of people with AIDS. ACT UP was also photographed at the Democratic National Convention in Atlanta, Georgia, by William Klein (1928–), the painter, filmmaker, and photographer.

The most important photographer to emerge in the 1970s and 1980s was Robert Mapplethorpe (1946–1989), whose carefully composed and printed images included portraits, male nudes, flowers, and sex acts centered around the culture of gay male sadomasochism. In 1988, the culmination of his life's work, the monograph and exhibit *The Perfect Moment* was organized by the Philadelphia Institute of Contemporary Art, where it was exhibited without incident. The exhibit was then canceled by the Corcoran Gallery in Washington, D.C, just before it was due to open. At the center of this controversy was the *X Portfolio,* which featured images of bondage and sadomasochistic sex. The exhibit later moved to the Contemporary Arts Center in Cincinnati, where it was shut down by the police. The center and its director, Dennis Barrie, were charged with obscenity and child pornography but were acquitted in a highly publicized trial.

The carefully seen and lighted studio image also informs the work of Bruce Weber (1946–) but has led to very different results. Weber is best known for his advertising work for Calvin Klein and Ralph Lauren. He specializes in fashion photography that features beautiful nude men in situations that suggest a story line and invite viewer participation in the fantasy before them.

In stark contrast to the carefully controlled work of Mapplethorpe and Weber stands the work of Nan Goldin (1953–). Her color photographs, although carefully composed, look like snapshots of the intimate moments of sex and love they depict. Goldin's work first achieved prominence with her 1986 book *The Ballad of Sexual Dependency,* in which gay and straight friends and lovers are revealed in intimate moments of pain and pleasure against the gritty claustrophobia of run-down apartments in lower Manhattan. A self-described bisexual, Goldin in 1988 did raw, natural-light self-portraits after undergoing drug rehabilitation, and later she continued to photograph her friends and lovers, some of whom were dying of AIDS. In 1993, she published *The Other Side,* the culmination of a decade-long investigation into the world of transsexuals and transvestites. Her subjects, from Berlin to Bangkok, were imaged in saturated color that increased both their glamour and a sense of the surreal.

In the late 1980s, Catherine Opie (1961–) gained international attention with her color portraits of members of the LGBT culture. Her portraits of people such as dyke daddies, performance transvestites, female-to-male transsexuals, and tattooed men and women reveal self-contained sitters who invite and return the viewer's gaze.

Toward the end of the twentieth century and into the twenty-first, women and people of color emerged as a force in American photography. In this context, the work of Laura Aguilar (1959–) and Gaye Chan (1957–) is of note. Aguilar, an overweight, dyslexic lesbian of mixed Mexican and Irish descent, responded to the challenge of being different by photographing differences, attempting to place herself within the different cultures she inhabited. She started exhibiting in 1985, and in 1990 she began her clothed and unclothed series, in which an individual or couple would pose once with clothing and once in the nude to form a diptych. In 1992, Aguilar showed the *Plush Pony* series, portraits of the clientele of a working-class lesbian Latina bar. Her richly printed large-format photographs include people of every body type, race, and sexuality. In 1993, her work was exhibited at the Venice Biennale.

Gaye Chan is a Hong Kong–born Asian American lesbian who teaches at the University of Hawaii. She trained as a graphic artist and also does installations that include photographs. Her photographic series *Angel in a Folding Chair* (1986–1988) is one of several showing lesbian relationships from the participant's point of view. Her carefully constructed photographs are intimate, use symbolic objects, and are full of graphic contrasts. Her postmodernist use of different media, and her postmodernist stance of making what is marginal to many the center of her explorations, are central to photography as it exists at the beginning of the twenty-first century.

Bibliography

"Against the Tide: The Homoerotic Image in the Age of Censorship and AIDS." *Amethyst* 7 (Spring–Summer 1991).

Barnes, Lawrence. *The Male Nude in Photography.* Waitsfield, Vt.: Crossroads Press, 1980.

"The Body in Question." *Aperture* 121 (Fall 1990). Boffin, Tessa, and Jean Fraser, eds. *Stolen Glances: Lesbians Take Photographs.* London: Pandora, 1991.

Censorship Art Journal 50, no. 3 (Fall 1991).

Crimp, Douglas. "The Boys in My Bedroom." *Art in America* 78, no. 2. (February 1990): 47–49.

Davis, Melody. *The Male Nude in Contemporary Photography.* Philadelphia: Temple University Press, 1991.

Ellenzweig, Allen. *The Homoerotic Photograph: Male Images from Durieu/Delacroix to Mapplethorpe.* New York: Columbia University Press, 1992.

Goldin, Nan. *The Other Side: 1972–1992.* New York: Scalo, 2000.

Goldin, Nan, et al. *The Ballad of Sexual Dependency.* New York: Aperture, 1986.

Grover, Jan Zita. "Dykes in Context, Some Problems in Minority Representation." In *The Contest of Meaning: Critical Histories of Photography.* Edited by Richard Bolton. Cambridge, Mass.: The MIT Press, 1989.

———. "Visible Lesions." *Afterimage* 17, no. 1 (Summer 1989): 10–16.

MacAdams, Cynthia. *Rising Goddess.* Dobbs Ferry, N.Y.: Morgan and Morgan, 1983.

Mapplethorpe, Robert. *Robert Mapplethorpe.* New York: The Whitney Museum of American Art, 1988.

Waugh, Thomas. *Hard to Imagine: Gay Male Eroticism in Photography and Film from Their Beginnings to Stonewall.* New York: Columbia University Press, 1996.

Diane Hulick

See also ART HISTORY; AUSTEN, ALICE; CENSORSHIP, OBSCENITY, AND PORNOGRAPHY LAW AND POLICY; EAKINS, THOMAS; HOCKNEY, DAVID; KLUMPKE, ANNA; LYNES, GEORGE PLATT; MAPPLETHORPE, ROBERT; MIZER, ROBERT; PHYSIQUE MAGAZINES AND PHOTOGRAPHS; RITTS, HERB; WEBER, BRUCE.

W

WADDELL, Thomas Joseph Michael (b. 1 November 1937; d. 11 July 1987), athlete, doctor.

After Elmer and Marion Flubacher divorced around 1950, their middle son Tom lived with Hazel and Gene Waddell, his ballet teacher and her gymnast husband, who later adopted him. Waddell told *Advocate* writer Randy Shilts, "I knew I was gay when I was very young. . . . I figured that if everyone really knew [I was gay], they would never like me . . ." (p. 9). So he concealed his sexual feelings for many years.

Waddell attended Massachusetts's Springfield College from 1955 to 1959 on a football scholarship, but changed his major from physical education when his best friend, a premed student, died in his arms after a gymnastics accident. Waddell enrolled in the New Jersey College of Medicine in 1961 and graduated in 1965. He especially enjoyed the freedom of being a doctor and practiced medicine for many years, part of that time serving as the personal physician to Saudi Arabia's royal family.

At age twenty-one Waddell fell in love for the first time. Sixty-three-year-old Enge Menaker told Tom, "You must never, ever, tell anybody that you're homosexual." Waddell could not reconcile Menaker's view with his own, later telling a reporter, "I've always wanted to come out because I hated living a lie. . . . I felt this was a restriction on my freedom and I would not be liberated until I could not think of [myself] being perverse" (Bluestein, p. 31).

Meanwhile, the U.S. Army drafted Waddell in 1966, and he served for two years. While working at the Walter Reed Army Medical Center in Washington, D.C., Tom trained for the 1968 U.S. Olympic decathlon team (after failing to qualify in 1960); astonishingly, the thirty-year-old Waddell not only qualified, but finished sixth at the Olympics in Mexico City, competing against the world's best decathletes. As he was training for the 1972 Olympics, Waddell suffered a knee injury while high jumping that abbreviated his Olympic career. Several years later, after coming out with little fanfare in two gay publications, Waddell revealed his homosexuality to a wider audience in *People* magazine in October 1976 (through an item about him and his then-partner Charles Deaton in the "Couples" section). Besides Menaker and Deaton, Waddell also paired with Lee Bryan and Zohn Artman, all notably older than Tom.

In June 1980, while watching a televised Gay Men's Bowling Tournament, Waddell conceived the idea of an athletic festival for gay men and lesbians as a way to alter perceptions about homosexuals and sports. Gay men in particular were perceived as "sissies" who could not play sports seriously or successfully. With Mark Brown and Paul Mart, Waddell founded San Francisco Arts and Athletics (SFAA) and further developed what became the Gay Games concept, initially described as the Gay Olympics. The first Gay Games began in San Francisco on 28 August 1982. Approximately thirteen hundred athletes from a dozen countries gathered to participate in sixteen sports. San Francisco again (1986), Vancouver (Canada) (1990), New York City (1994), Amsterdam (Netherlands) (1998), and Sydney (Australia) (2002) have hosted subsequent Gay Games. Sydney boasted over thirty events and more than ten thousand participants.

In 1982, the United States Olympic Committee (USOC) sued SFAA to retain rights to the word "Olympic," an action that many perceived as homophobic. Only nineteen days before Gay Games I began, a federal court declared that the USOC had exclusive possession of the word "Olympic" and could prohibit its use at will. The case reached the U.S. Supreme Court; while SFAA lost, the USOC ultimately removed its $96,000 lien from Waddell's home.

In the meantime, while preparing Gay Games I, Tom met fellow athlete Sara Lewinstein. They shared a then-uncommon vision for a lesbian and a gay man, as each wanted to parent a child. Sara proposed the radical concept that they parent together and Tom excitedly accepted. Jessica Waddell Lewinstein was born on 31 August 1983, and Tom and Sara married in 1985.

Just four weeks prior to Gay Games II, Waddell's doctor diagnosed him with pneumocystic carinii pneumonia, an AIDS-related opportunistic infection. Despite his serious illness, Waddell literally left his hospital bed to win a gold medal in the javelin competition. After a brave battle against AIDS, Waddell chose an overdose of morphine and died peacefully at his home with his friends beside him. Sports journalist Dick Schaap summarized Waddell as "sometimes stubborn, sometimes fickle, sometimes manipulative, and for a long time . . . dangerously promiscuous. But he managed to combine, in dazzling doses, strength and sensitivity, intelligence and courage, compassion and combativeness. He contradicted all the stereotypes of the athlete—and of the homosexual" (Waddell and Schaap, pp. 4–5). The Gay Games remain Waddell's enduring legacy.

Bibliography

Bluestein, Ron. "'Papa Games' in Profile." *Advocate,* 23 (December 1986): 28, 30–31, 112–113.

Shilts, Randy. "Dr. Tom Waddell." *Advocate* 28 (July 1976): 9–10.

Waddell, Tom, and Dick Schaap. *Gay Olympian: The Life and Death of Dr. Tom Waddell.* New York: Knopf, 1996.

Paul D. Cain

See also SPORTS.

WALKER, A'Lelia (b. 6 June 1885; d. 17 August 1931), entrepreneur, Harlem Renaissance hostess.

During the Harlem Renaissance, an era from the end of World War I to the beginning of the Great Depression and known for the cultural space it afforded black LGB people, A'Lelia Walker provided the most upscale social opportunities for those "in the life." Born in Vicksburg, Mississippi, she was named Leila by her parents, Sarah Breedlove and Moses McWilliams (she adopted the name "A'Lelia" as an adult). After Moses's death, the Walkers moved to St. Louis and then to Denver, where her mother married C. J. Walker and began to develop products to straighten and soften African American women's hair. Assisted by A'Lelia and motivated by a desire to give her only child a better life than the poverty and hardship she had known, Sarah ("Madam C. J.") Walker created a vast hair-care empire that made her the first self-made woman millionaire in the United States. Eventually settling in New York City, A'Lelia and her mother bought property on Harlem's Striver's Row and had a thirty-four room mansion built along the Hudson River that became known as Villa Lewaro (short for Leila Walker Robinson).

After her mother's death in 1919, Walker became the nominal president of the Walker Manufacturing Company, but she spent most of her time and money on entertaining, becoming what Langston Hughes described as "the joy-goddess of Harlem's 1920's." According to Hughes, the hundreds of lavish parties she threw during the decade "were as crowded as the New York subway at the rush hour," attracting everyone from European royalty and white New York socialites to black celebrities and notorious Harlem numbers runners and bootleggers. She especially sought the company of black LGB writers and artists, who gave her gatherings a distinctly gay character.

In 1927, Walker set out to do more for her LGB friends in the arts. Envisioning a place where writers and artists could meet, share ideas, and obtain cheap meals, she converted a floor of her Harlem townhouse into a club she called the "Dark Tower" after the title of Countee Cullen's column in *Opportunity.* She assembled a group of artists and writers to oversee the club's development, but not satisfied with their progress, she undertook the planning herself. The result was that rather than being an informal, inexpensive salon for the creative minds of the Renaissance, it became an upscale gathering place for white café society. The Dark Tower succeeded in drawing greater white attention to black art and literature, but it largely failed to serve the needs of the black LGB writers and artists it had originally been intended to support.

Little is known about Walker's sexual identity. She married three times, but the relationships were short-lived. By all accounts, she preferred instead to surround herself with attractive, light-skinned women like actress

Edna Thomas and Walker's constant companion and houseguest Mayme White. Among her friends were also a number of gay and bisexual men, including writers Countee Cullen and Richard Bruce Nugent, teacher Harold Jackman, white novelist Carl Van Vechten, and the organizers of her parties: voice teacher Caska Bonds and newspaper columnist Edward Perry. Members of Harlem society who did not approve of her choice of company either learned to keep quiet or found themselves left off future guest lists.

Because of her fondness for lesbians, gay men, and bisexuals, her family's working-class background, and her dark skin color, Walker was not accepted into the social circles of the black elite. She also met with disdain for her independence and nonconformity to the gender expectations for respectable African American women. Walker frequently wore jeweled turbans and carried a riding crop, which, along with being nearly six feet tall, gave her a striking presence.

Walker died suddenly of a heart attack in 1931 while on a trip to New Jersey with Mayme White to visit another close female friend. She was only forty-six, but had not listened to her doctors' warnings to lower her blood pressure and lose weight. Like her parties, her funeral was an extravagant, invitation-only affair, with many more people in attendance than could fit into the Harlem mortuary.

By the time of Walker's death, the Depression had had a devastating impact on the Renaissance, as white pleasure seekers no longer had money to spend in Harlem, and most African Americans, who did not have much to begin with, were affected even harder. Walker was not immune to great financial difficulties. With hair-care products an unnecessary and unaffordable expense for most African Americans, the company increasingly was unable to meet its bills and Walker had to mortgage Villa Lewaro to maintain her lavish lifestyle. Her parties became less opulent, if not less popular with black LGB people. Walker's passing marked the end of an era. Perhaps playing on words, Langston Hughes remarked that her death "was really the end of the gay times of the New Negro era in Harlem."

Bibliography

Bundles, A'Lelia. *On Her Own Ground: The Life and Times of Madam C. J. Walker*. New York: Scribner, 2001.

Garber, Eric. "A Spectacle in Color: The Lesbian and Gay Subculture of Jazz Age Harlem." In *Hidden from History: Reclaiming the Gay and Lesbian Past*. Edited by Martin Duberman, Martha Vicinus, and George Chauncey. New York: New American Library, 1989.

Hughes, Langston. *The Big Sea: An Autobiography*. New York: Knopf, 1940.

Lewis, David Levering. *When Harlem Was in Vogue*. New York: Oxford University Press, 1981.

Nugent, Richard Bruce. "On the Dark Tower." In *Gay Rebel of the Harlem Renaissance: Selections from the Work of Richard Bruce Nugent*. Edited by Thomas H. Wirth. Durham, N.C.: Duke University Press, 2002.

Wintz, Cary D. *Black Culture and the Harlem Renaissance*. Houston, Texas: Rice University Press, 1988.

Brett Beemyn

See also HARLEM RENAISSANCE.

WALKER, Mary Edwards (b. 26 November 1832; d. 21 February 1919), Civil War physician and social reformer.

Dr. Mary Edwards Walker is most probably the best-known cross-dressing woman from her era. Seeking an appointment as an army surgeon, she served as a medical officer during the Civil War, was captured by Confederate forces, and earned a Congressional Medal of Honor. After the Civil War, she was an outspoken proponent of various feminist causes such as dress reform and suffrage. Nevertheless, she is most often remembered for her audacity in wearing the full men's attire that she adopted later in life, including a frock coat, trousers, shirt, tie, and top hat. Though viewed in her time as a curiosity and an eccentric, Walker demonstrated the possibilities available for women who were willing to forgo accepted roles and norms of appearance during the second half of the nineteenth century.

The "burnt-over district" of upstate New York (named so because it was the site of intense revivalism and reform during the early nineteenth century) produced many notable reformers, including Mary Edwards Walker, who was born in Oswego in 1832. Her liberal parents permitted the youngest of their five daughters enough freedom in her childhood for her to see folly in traditional feminine dress. She was educated in local schools and attended Falley Seminary in Fulton, New York. In 1855, Walker graduated from Syracuse Medical College after completing a nonregular, or eclectic, program. In 1856 Walker married another doctor, Albert Miller, and practiced medicine with him for a few years. The marriage did not last, however, and Walker never adopted her husband's name.

In 1861, with the outbreak of the Civil War, Walker decided to seek a position as a surgeon in the Union Army. Over the next two years she alternated between

Dr. Mary Edwards Walker. The cross-dressing feminist activist poses in the usual men's attire of her later years, complete with top hat—and the Congressional Medal of Honor she received after her service as a medical officer in the Civil War. [corbis-Bettmann]

petitioning various offices in Washington, D.C., for a commission and volunteering her services in the field and in hospitals. To strengthen her case, she completed an additional degree at the New York Hageio-Therapeutic College, and her struggle for an appointment received public notice through press attention and her own writings. It is not clear if it was her sex, her nonregular medical training, or the combination that prevented her from achieving an official position. In 1863, she finally gained an appointment as an assistant surgeon assigned to the 52nd Ohio Infantry. She adopted the same uniform as the other officers. Walker was captured by Confederate forces in 1864 and was imprisoned in Richmond for several months before being released as part of a prisoner exchange. She then continued her medical service at an orphanage and a women's prison. In 1865 she was awarded the Congressional Medal of Honor. Walker proudly added the Medal of Honor to her attire and continued to wear it even after it was revoked (along with 910 others) in 1917, on the grounds that she had not been in actual combat with an enemy. (President Carter signed a bill reinstating Walker's medal posthumously in 1977.)

In the years after the Civil War, Dr. Walker gave her time to various reform causes. She was president of the National Dress Reform Association and was active in suffrage work. She was dedicated to these causes and traveled in the United States and England to speak on them, but, as she moved from appearing in a "bloomer" outfit to a regular men's suit, she became an embarrassment and distraction to the movements. In 1871, she wrote *Hit*, a mostly autobiographical work. In 1878, she followed this with *Unmasked; or, The Science of Immorality*. In this second book she wrote explicitly about women's sexuality, expressing her own conservative attitudes. Addressed to men but concerned with women's oppression, she condemned the double standard and all sexual activity except marital intercourse for the purpose of procreation.

Walker's later life was difficult. In 1887 she toured as part of a sideshow. She was denied a Civil War pension. She returned to her home town where she died in 1919 and was buried in her frock coat in the family plot.

Bibliography

Katz, Jonathan, ed. *Gay American History: Lesbians and Gay Men in the U.S.A.* New York: Crowell, 1976.

Leonard, Elizabeth D. *Yankee Women: Gender Battles in the Civil War.* New York: Norton, 1994.

Trisha Franzen

See also TRANSSEXUALS, TRANSVESTITES, TRANSGENDER PEOPLE, AND CROSS-DRESSERS; WAR.

WALSH, David (b. 11 November 1872; d. 11 June 1947), U.S. senator.

Born in Leominster, Massachusetts, in 1872 to Irish immigrants James and Bridget Walsh, David Walsh grew up in poverty, supported by his older sisters after the early death of his father. After graduating from the College of the Holy Cross in 1893 and from Boston University Law School in 1897, he threw himself immediately into Democratic politics, winning election as a state representative in 1899. He won the lieutenant governorship in 1912, and served two one-year terms as governor of Massachusetts from 1914 to 1916, the first child of an immigrant to do so. Walsh left the state house for the U.S. Senate in 1918. Although defeated for reelection in 1924, he was appointed to fill an unfinished term in 1926, was reelected in 1928, and ultimately served twenty-six years in the Senate. In the 1930s, Walsh emerged as a prominent Democratic critic of New Deal domestic policies, and, as chair of the Naval Affairs Committee, he was an outspoken isolationist in the years before World War II.

Walsh never married and maintained privacy about his personal life, but his sexuality emerged as the subject of a significant political scandal in the spring of 1942. On 14 March 1942, New York City detectives and naval intelligence officers raided the home of Gustave Beekman at 329 Pacific Street, near the Brooklyn Navy Yard. Men regularly met at Beekman's house for companionship and sexual encounters; although there is no evidence that prostitution took place there, it was frequently described in the media as a "male brothel." On 30 April a Brooklyn court convicted Beekman of sodomy; in exchange for leniency in sentencing, he agreed to name patrons of the house. Among them was Walsh. On 1 May 1942, the *New York Post* reported that a "Senator X" was among the visitors to the Pacific Street house. Five days later, the paper named Walsh and insinuated a connection to espionage by noting that the house was also frequented by Germans who sought to ply war-related secrets from drunken sailors. (In fact, there is no evidence that the German citizens who frequented the house were spies.)

When the scandal broke, leading Democrats—including President Franklin Roosevelt himself—closed ranks to defend Walsh against what many believed was baseless character assassination. Walsh maintained his speaking commitments with no public acknowledgment of the scandal. Behind the scenes, however, he urged Senate majority leader Alben W. Barkley to intervene on his behalf. On 20 May 1942, Barkley addressed the issue in a speech on the Senate floor. He announced that "disgusting and unprintable" charges had been lodged against Walsh, but that an investigation by the Federal Bureau of

Investigation completely exonerated the senator. The matter was a simple case of mistaken identity, said Barkley; after further questioning, Beekman had recanted his story and acknowledged that another man named "Doc" better matched the physical description of the patron Beekman had identified.

The FBI report, however, does not quite match Barkley's characterization of it. One witness's statement cast doubt only on whether Walsh and "Doc" were the same person without suggesting that Walsh had never visited the house. Beekman, moreover, recanted only after six hours of grueling interrogation by FBI agents and later told the *Post* that he changed his story under duress. Having cooperated in hopes of leniency, Beekman found himself the fall guy for the cover-up. He was sentenced to the maximum term for his sodomy conviction and remained in prison until 1963.

Walsh survived the scandal, but his career soon came to an end. In 1946 he was soundly defeated in an election influenced by general sentiment against Democrats, specific hostility to his prewar isolationism, and, perhaps, lingering aspects of the scandal. Walsh's health subsequently declined and he died in July 1947. He had always dismissed the charges as "a diabolical lie" that targeted him for his isolationist views. But he was probably not so much the object of a deliberate campaign as the victim of a situation that his political opponents seized on in order to discredit him. Moreover, the scandal shows the powerful impact that accusations of homosexuality could have and demonstrates the close association in many Americans' minds between homosexuality and espionage, concerns that continued into the Cold War period.

Bibliography

Murphy, Lawrence R. "The House on Pacific Street: Homosexuality, Intrigue, and Politics during World War II." *Journal of Homosexuality* 12 (Fall 1985): 27–49.

Wayman, Dorothy G. *David I. Walsh: Citizen Patriot.* Milwaukee, Wis.: Bruce Publishing, 1952.

Christopher Capozzola

See also POLITICAL SCANDALS.

WAR

At first glance, wars seem to promote gender and sexual dichotomies and hierarchies, bringing to mind images of muscled, battle-scarred men standing in defense of tearful women and helpless children. The trauma, violence, and chaos of war can reinforce prescriptive models of appearance and behavior, and war's aftermath is often characterized by efforts to reinscribe gender and sexual norms that were altered during the war. But armed conflict has also provided crucial opportunities for individuals and institutions to challenge and even subvert gender and sexual norms. Both women and men have found inspiration for changes in their appearances and behavior during wartime, altering their perceptions of gender norms and sexual possibilities. Whether it is women passing as men in order to take up arms, or young men finding new horizons of sexual opportunity through their military service, soldiers, sailors, airmen, and marines have always pushed the boundaries of gender and sexual convention.

Armed conflict has also had a complex impact on the discourse of rights and the reality of opportunity in the United States. Military service has been a stepping-stone to citizenship and political power for racial minorities, immigrants, and women. Though war is often conceived of as a collective sacrifice rather than an individual effort, servicemembers who bore arms on behalf of their nation have returned to civilian life with a sense of entitlement and authority, spawning U.S. social movements, political change, and social and cultural transformation. The LGBT people who have served in the military during times of war have—with varying degrees of success—asserted their rights to the privileges of veterans because they shouldered the burdens of wartime military duty.

Of course, the transformations wrought by war have varied depending on the timing, type, and scope of conflict. Fully understanding the impact of a specific war on society requires a particularized, in-depth study. But because wars tend to affect social and cultural norms related to gender and sexuality in identifiable ways, we can draw some useful generalizations about war's potential for initiating change in U.S. culture and society.

Cross-Dressing Women

War has often created an opportunity for women and men to break out of the roles and behaviors assigned to their sex by dominant social and cultural practice. Some of the new roles that women took on during wartime have included serving as soldiers by dressing as men. Deborah Samson, who enlisted as Robert Shurtleff (also Shirtliffe), served for three years as a volunteer from Massachusetts in the Revolutionary War. Enlisted in 1778, Sampson successfully concealed her identity for seventeen months. Later the U.S. Congress officially acknowledged her as a veteran of the war. The legend of Molly Pitcher, which celebrates heroic women fighting for independence, was based on women like Margaret Corbin,

who took the place of her husband when he fell in battle; she helped to fire artillery during the 1776 British attack on Fort Washington. Corbin's contribution to the war fit more easily than that of other women into existing paradigms of female behavior because she followed her husband's lead, and because her work in cooling the artillery with water could be feminized by recasting her role as providing drinking water to parched men on the firing line.

Many other women performed vital roles during U.S. wars, serving as nurses, surgeons, spies, soldiers, and in other capacities without achieving the legendary status of Molly Pitcher—or the postwar recognition and accolades accorded men. In the War of 1812, a few intrepid women fought while disguised as men, including Lucy Brewer, who served as a marine aboard the USS *Constitution*, nicknamed Old Ironsides. During the Civil War, dozens of women cross-dressed in order to serve in military uniform. They include Loreta Janeta Velazquez (Lieutenant Harry T. Buford in the Confederate Army) and Sarah Emma Edmonds (Private Franklin Thompson of the Union Army's Second Michigan Volunteer Infantry), who fought and spied for their respective sides. The motivations of these women and others who hid their sex in order to bear arms included elements of patriotism as well as wanderlust. They sought to experience the challenges and deprivations of war firsthand and to avenge lost lovers and family members. But each elected to take the risk of posing as a man in order to escape the limitations of female roles. The exigencies of war encouraged and validated a particular variety of gender deviance that has helped to shape the history of gender and sexual nonconformity in the United States.

GI Drag

Cross-dressing of a different sort became popular among soldiers during World War II. Irving Berlin's all-soldier revue *This Is the Army*, a show that raised money for the Army Emergency Relief Fund and opened to packed houses in New York City on 4 July 1942, provided a model for similar shows in many military units. Soldiers staged their own theatrical productions complete with female impersonators, singing, and dancing. Popular during World War II, such shows continued to be a feature of many units after the war as soldiers and sailors relied on comic relief to ease the tension of remote tours and lengthy deployments during the Cold War. GI drag was simply campy fun to many soldiers, who participated but did not see same-sex desire as a subtext of the shows. To some spectators, GI drag shows mocked soldiers who were inclined toward homosexual or transgender behavior, playing on stereotypes to ridicule and differentiate such appearances and actions from those of "normal" troops. But for many gay troops, the implicit homoeroticism of drag shows created public spaces for bending gender norms and exploring same-sex attraction.

Sexual Opportunity

Many young Americans entered wartime military service with relatively little sexual experience and with limited if any exposure to potential sexual partners from outside their immediate communities. Military service during war was a time of increased sexual opportunity for many of these still-maturing servicemembers. They forged close friendships with persons from different social backgrounds and geographic regions and learned about different regional cultures in the United States and foreign cultures overseas. Often isolated in single-sex environments—particularly onboard ships and at remote outposts—some servicemembers negotiated the alienation and rigors of military life by seeking intimacy from fellow troops. From Walt Whitman (who was a volunteer nurse and not a member of the military) during the Civil War to Perry Watkins during the Vietnam War, men and women who experienced same-sex attraction were likely to find fertile ground for emotional and sexual experimentation in the wartime military.

During and after World War II, servicemen encountered LGBT subcultures in many of the port cities near military bases, including New York City, Philadelphia, Miami, Chicago, San Diego, and San Francisco. On their way to remote tours of duty in Europe or Asia, servicemembers often spent a few days on liberty before they left the United States and again upon their return, adding even more military personnel to the population of servicemembers stationed near major cities. Mobilization for World War II, and to a lesser degree for the Korean and Vietnam Wars, brought thousands of young men and women to urban centers. Movie theaters, bars, parks, hotels, and private homes became centers of homosexual connection and activity, and troops joined civilians in building a vibrant gay subculture. Lesbian subcultures flourished in the military as well, especially during World War II. Throughout the war sexually active servicewomen were considered a threat by the image-conscious leaders of the women's services. As a result, female soldiers were often more restricted than their male counterparts in terms of access to public facilities and sexual opportunities. Military investigators worked to expose and oust women who were thought to have homosexual tendencies, particularly after the end of the war. But lesbian troops found each other regardless, aware of the risks but unwilling to sacrifice their newfound connections to other women.

Military efforts to suppress homosexuality backfired when LGB troops used lists of off-limits bars to locate friendly hangouts or when they read descriptions of likely homosexuals, published for the benefit of military police and investigators to guide in the identification of sexual deviants, in order to avoid suspicion by dressing in inconspicuous ways. The armed forces' various efforts to screen out homosexuals probably deterred some potential recruits, but not many. During the Cold War—a period of time that included extended and costly "hot" wars in Korea and Vietnam—sexual experimentation among servicemembers was also encouraged by the sexual commerce that thrived around military posts in Asia. Much as the horrors of impending combat during war encouraged servicemembers to indulge in sexual acts that they might otherwise have resisted, the atmosphere of escapist self-indulgence that servicemen found in brothels and bars made sexual experimentation seem to be an expected rather than threatening behavior.

Triggers for Policy Change

Wars did more than create opportunities for gender deviance and sexual experimentation. They also led the U.S. military to scrutinize, and often adjust, its policies concerning same-sex sexual desire and behavior. The growing bureaucracy of the U.S. armed forces in the twentieth century is a rich source of historical data on how and when governmental policies about homosexuality shifted. Military regulations often explicitly expressed concerns and anxieties about sexual behavior that were felt, but not always articulated, in U.S. communities. For example, the Newport, Rhode Island, sting of 1919 reflected a concerted effort to identify and eliminate homosexual servicemembers. The investigations and trials that resulted brought nationwide publicity to a sexual subculture that had been flourishing in various parts of the country for decades, sparking both curiosity and outrage in the U.S. public.

During World War I, the U.S. Congress attempted to regulate "indecent" activity, most often construed to mean the use of female prostitutes, near military bases. But the congressional statutes were most infamously used to police male homosexuality rather than heterosexual commerce. In 1919 a Young Men's Christian Association (YMCA) near the Newport Naval Training Station and its chaplain, the Reverend Samuel Kent, were the primary targets of a navy investigation into alleged degenerates that caught sailors as well as civilians in its wide net. Kent, along with many of his friends and acquaintances, was tried and acquitted in both state and federal courts, the prosecution foiled by the fact that the undercover operatives who testified against Kent and others had also participated in "lewd" acts and were therefore not credible witnesses. The navy did not consider these "straight" men to be homosexuals, so they did not attempt to eliminate them through discharges. But the military's fine distinctions did not convince the courts that heard these witnesses testify about consensual sex acts in which they took part.

The navy's witchhunt, intended to expose sexual degenerates, left a documentary record of a subculture of gender nonconformity and homoerotic behavior. The men who participated were variously called "perverts," "fairies," "pogues," "queers," or "inverts," the latter a term indicating the medical assumption that men who dressed or acted in stereotypically feminine ways were plagued by sexual inversion, a distortion of "normal" masculine behavior and desire that led them to take on female gender characteristics and sexual roles. These men attended parties in which men dressed as women and sought out "trade," or "straight"-appearing men, for sexual encounters. The role of the Newport YMCA in facilitating sexual solicitation and the interaction of "feminized" men with others of like desires was of great concern to the navy, which court-martialed several sailors. They were convicted and sentenced to prison terms as long as twenty years, though all were later reduced.

The military took steps after the war to clarify its hostile stance toward same-sex sexual activity, specifying sodomy as a military crime in the 1920 Articles of War and redefining the term to include oral as well as anal sex. Policies governing entry into military service after 1920 attempted to screen out "sexual psychopaths" and sodomists as well as inverts. World War II initiated a new pattern of screening and eliminating suspected homosexuals, but young women and men continued to find ample opportunity for sexual experimentation and building LGBT subcultures within the ranks of the armed forces.

Wartime Personnel Needs

After World War II the military's policies regarding homosexuality in the ranks continued to evolve, marked by regulations that, while unevenly enforced, nonetheless ended the careers of many dedicated servicemembers. During the anticommunist fervor of the Cold War, government leaders associated homosexuality with weakness and vulnerability to blackmail (despite military-sponsored studies finding this association unfounded), leading the military to pursue discharges of LGBT servicemembers as security risks. Attempts to purge suspected homosexuals from the ranks occurred alongside crackdowns in civilian law enforcement with raids on LGB bars and arrests for consensual sexual activity. Both

Allan Bérubé's and Randy Shilts's studies of gays and lesbians in the U.S. military point out that the armed forces enforced its various bans against homosexuality most aggressively when personnel needs were low. During times of force reductions and drawdowns after major military efforts, discharges for and investigations of homosexuality grew in intensity. But when the need for service personnel was great, prosecution and investigation of suspected lesbians and gay men were not a high priority for military leaders. As a result, discharges based on sexual orientation dropped when the military was growing to fulfill wartime requirements.

Catalysts for Political and Social Change

The U.S. military has been consistently willing to embrace LGBT servicemembers to fulfill "manpower" needs, much as it turned to African American troops to increase the size of the Union Army during the Civil War or began to permit women to serve in larger numbers when the draft ended in 1973, cutting off the armed forces' supply of conscript troops. For veterans who fought during wars only to be denied basic rights upon their return to civilian life, wartime military service could be a radicalizing experience. The political aftermath of war often leads to more aggressive assertions of rights by individuals and disfranchised groups. Like African American veterans of World War II, many of whom became leaders in the civil rights movement, LGBT veterans were a key part of the fight to end discrimination based on sexual orientation and gender identity. Veterans like Margarethe Cammermeyer, Harvey Milk, Leonard Matlovich, Miriam Ben Shalom, Perry Watkins, and others publicized the plight of LGBT troops and helped to pressure the U.S. government to revise its policies concerning homosexuality in the ranks.

Bibliography

Bérubé, Allan. *Coming Out under Fire: The History of Gay Men and Women in World War Two.* New York: Free Press, 1990.

Chauncey, George, Jr. "Christian Brotherhood or Sexual Perversion? Homosexual Identities and the Construction of Sexual Boundaries in the World War One Era." *Journal of Social History* 19 (1985): 189–211.

Fraser, Antonia. *The Warrior Queens.* New York: Knopf, 1989.

Hall, Richard. *Patriots in Disguise: Women Warriors of the Civil War.* New York: Paragon House, 1993.

Humphrey, Mary Ann. *My Country, My Right to Serve: Experiences of Gay Men and Women in the Military, World War II to the Present.* New York: HarperCollins, 1990.

Meyer, Leisa D. *Creating GI Jane: Sexuality and Power in the Women's Army Corps during World War II.* New York: Columbia University Press, 1996.

Murphy, Lawrence R. *Perverts by Official Order: The Campaign against Homosexuals by the United States Navy.* New York: Haworth, 1988.

Shilts, Randy. *Conduct Unbecoming: Gays and Lesbians in the United States Military, Vietnam to the Persian Gulf.* New York: St. Martin's Press, 1993.

Whitman, Walt. *The Sacrificial Years: A Chronicle of Walt Whitman's Experiences in the Civil War.* Edited by John Harmon McElroy. Boston: Godine, 1999.

Elizabeth Lutes Hillman

See also ANTIWAR, PACIFIST, AND PEACE MOVEMENTS; MILITARY; MILITARY LAW AND POLICY; MILK, HARVEY; O'HARA, FRANK; SAMSON, DEBORAH; SULLIVAN, HARRY STACK; THOMPSON, FRANCES; WALKER, MARY; WHITMAN, WALT.

WARHOL, Andy (b. 6 August 1928; d. 22 February 1987), artist, writer, filmmaker.

Andy Warhol was one of the most influential cultural figures of the twentieth century. While best known as the Pop artist who produced Campbell's Soup can paintings and silkscreen paintings of Marilyn Monroe in the 1960s, Warhol was also a filmmaker, writer, photographer, commercial artist, magazine publisher, music producer, art collector, and all-around popular icon. The son of Slovakian working-class immigrants, Andrew Warhola was born and raised in Pittsburgh, Pennsylvania. A sickly child, Warhola collected comic strips and fanzine photographs of movie stars from an early age. With the encouragement of his mother, herself an amateur painter and collagist, Andrew developed his visual skills by drawing, painting, and making paper cutouts throughout his school years.

After graduating from the Carnegie Institute of Technology (now Carnegie Mellon University) with a bachelor of fine arts degree in pictorial design, Warhol moved to New York City in 1949 to launch his career as a graphic artist. By this time he had dropped the final "a" from his surname to make it sound less foreign. In the 1950s Warhol enjoyed great success as a commercial illustrator and designer. His professional output included graphic designs for *Glamour, Harper's Bazaar, Interiors, McCall's,* the *New York Times Fashion Special,* and *Vogue* as well as window displays for Bonwit Teller and Lord and Taylor department stores. It was, however, Warhol's advertising campaign for I. Miller Shoes that brought him the greatest degree of recognition during this period. From 1955 to 1957, I. Miller advertisements showcasing Warhol drawings appeared on a weekly basis in the Sunday *New York Times,* almost always in the pages

devoted to wedding announcements and engagements. From advertisements for ladies' shoes to shop windows celebrating the pleasures of potpourri, Warhol's commercial work of the 1950s was tailored to and closely associated with the female consumer. Warhol's professional association with femininity may have occasionally shaded into camp identification. In 1952, for example, when he received his first Art Director's Club Medal, a handwritten inscription on the envelope read "Andrew Warhol, her medal." And in a 1955 flyer he created as a professional calling card, Warhol used the figure of a female circus performer to stand as his surrogate.

In the early 1960s Warhol gradually abandoned his professional life as a commercial illustrator so he could concentrate on launching his career as a fine artist. In developing what would become his signature style of Pop art (deadpan if endlessly various repetitions of celebrity images and consumer product designs), Warhol moved away from the hand-drawn and flamboyantly decorative pictorial style of his commercial work. In tandem with this shift in his artistic output, Warhol reinvented his personal style of dress and self-presentation. Dispensing with the tweed jackets and white Oxford shirts he wore in the 1950s, Warhol emerged as a sixties hipster in black jeans, t-shirt, sunglasses, and, often, a leather jacket.

Late in 1963 Warhol established a studio in a former hat factory on East 47th Street in New York City. This loft, which was known as The Factory, provided the space for the production of Warhol's art and films, the latter of which he started shooting in 1963. No less importantly, the silvered space of The Factory (its walls were covered in silver paint and foil) became the gathering space for an extended social and creative circle of artists, poets, musicians (including Lou Reed and the Velvet Underground), speed freaks, hustlers, hangers-on, and Warhol-styled "superstars." During the early Factory years, Warhol produced some of his best-known Pop paintings, including the *Jackie* (Kennedy), *Elvis* (Presley), and *Electric Chair* silkscreens, as well as such films as *Empire* (1964; an eight-hour silent film of the Empire State Building) and *Blow Job* (1964; a thirty-minute silent film of a young man, shown only from the neck up, receiving fellatio).

In 1968 a radical feminist named Valerie Solanas shot Warhol in an assassination attempt in The Factory. After a two-month hospitalization, Warhol recovered and later sat for a portrait by Richard Avedon in which he displayed his scars. In 1969 Warhol published the first issue of *inter/VIEW* magazine, a monthly film journal that later evolved into a large format celebrity magazine featuring interviews of the famous by the famous. Among the many works Warhol produced in the 1970s were *Ladies and*

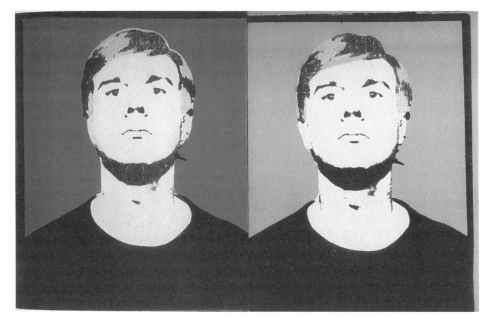

Self-Portrait. A 1964 silk screen by the hugely influential 1960s–1980s artist and celebrity Andy Warhol—who was famous far longer than the fifteen minutes he predicted for everyone else in the future. [Artists Rights Society]

Gentleman, a series of silkscreen portraits of drag queens, and *Torsos,* a series of homoerotic male nudes. During this period, Warhol went out virtually every night, often to the disco Studio 54, where he was frequently photographed with friends such as Halston, Bianca Jagger, and Liza Minelli.

During the 1980s Warhol made paintings on a monumental scale based on such disparate subjects as Leonardo da Vinci's *Last Supper* (1495–1497), Rorschach ink blots, and American dollar signs. For a series entitled *Oxidation Paintings,* the artist asked various men to urinate on chemically treated surfaces to produce abstract patterns that loosely mimicked the work of modernist painters such as Jackson Pollock. During this period, Warhol also mentored and occasionally collaborated with younger artists such as Jean-Michel Basquiat.

Warhol died in 1987 from complications following gall bladder surgery. His art, however, continues to be exhibited across the globe and the culture of celebrity he portrayed and helped to shape has become yet more powerful.

Bibliography

Doyle, Jennifer, Jonathan Flatley, and José Esteban Munoz. *Pop Out: Queer Warhol.* Durham, N.C., and London: Duke University Press, 1996.

Koestenbaum, Wayne. *Andy Warhol.* New York: Viking Press, 2001.

McShine, Kynaston. *Andy Warhol: A Retrospective.* New York: Museum of Modern Art, 1989.

Meyer, Richard. *Outlaw Representation: Censorship and Homosexuality in Twentieth-Century American Art.* Boston: Beacon Press, 2004.

Richard Meyer

See also ART HISTORY; FIERSTEIN, HARVEY; FILM AND VIDEO; SOLANAS, VALERIE; VISUAL ART.

WASHINGTON, D.C.

Evidence of an LGBT subculture in Washington, D.C., dates back to at least the 1890s. Medical professionals reported that African American men held an annual "drag dance" and that lesbians engaged in sexual activity in more private settings. Lafayette Park became such a center of gay male socializing and cruising that it caught the attention of local police and politicians. For much of the first half of the twentieth century, this one-block-square park directly across Pennsylvania Avenue from the White House was the epicenter of Washington's gay male world. By the 1920s a plainclothes police officer regularly patrolled the park. The great expansion in the city's population during the New Deal in the 1930s led to a dramatic increase in the size and visibility of the city's gay and lesbian subculture. Like New York City's Greenwich Village and Chicago's Towertown, the neighborhood around Lafayette Park featured rooming houses, restaurants, and cultural institutions that became centers of gay social life. Many gay men lived and socialized at the G Street Young Men's Christian Association (YMCA). Many of the cheap cafeterias in the neighborhood, such as

Childs and the Allies Inn, became frequent haunts of the gay men who lived in the YMCA or the nearby rooming houses.

With the repeal of Prohibition in 1933, bars catering to a gay and lesbian clientele opened in Washington. The Horseshoe, also known as Margaret's or Maggie's, was located in a basement on Seventeenth Street behind the Mayflower Hotel, whose gentlemen's bar also became known as a gathering spot for gay men. It featured a pianist named Howard who entertained patrons on the weekends. The Showboat at Thirteenth and H Streets had both a gay and lesbian following. Located in the dingy basement of an all-night cafeteria, the Showboat featured a pianist named Chloe and a butch lesbian singer named Lover Boy. A third bar, Carroll's, attracted both gay men and "rough trade" made up of men, many of whom were in the military, who would have sex with men but did not consider themselves gay. Carroll's was located on Ninth Street, a notorious strip of burlesque houses, bars, and tattoo parlors.

World War II brought thousands of men and women streaming through Washington, filling up its LGBT bars and cruising areas. The wartime atmosphere fostered a tolerant attitude. After the war, many gay men and women who had been stationed in and around Washington decided to stay. The G.I. Bill brought even more veterans to the area to attend the city's many colleges and universities. Georgetown developed a reputation as an enclave for gay men, lesbians, and other nonconformists, and new gay bars opened, including the Derby Room and the Chicken Hut for white patrons and the Nob Hill and Cozy Corner for blacks.

Lavender Scare

In the postwar years a sex crime panic swept the nation, and the *Washington Star* launched a campaign to highlight the threat posed by so-called sex criminals and the need to toughen existing sex laws. In 1947 the U.S. Park Service began its Pervert Elimination Campaign to arrest men cruising in Lafayette and Franklin Parks. Despite the efforts, three years later an exposé of Washington, D.C., by Jack Lait and Lee Mortimer called Lafayette Park "the chief meeting-place" for "fairies" (pp. 91–92). In June 1948, President Harry Truman signed the Miller Sexual Psychopath Law, which substantially increased the penalty for a variety of sexual crimes, codified the common law crime of sodomy, and sentenced recidivist offenders to indefinite confinement at St. Elizabeth's Hospital. Reacting to the police crackdown, some men challenged their arrests in court, winning important legal victories that helped to limit, but not end, police harassment.

At midcentury, such local matters as the gays in Lafayette Park would become caught up in the McCarthy-era campaign to rid the federal government of security risks, giving Washington's gay community a central role in national debates about homosexuality. In 1950, U.S. senator Joseph McCarthy made national headlines with his claim that the State Department was harboring security risks, including several homosexuals. One of his few documented cases of a security risk was a man who had been arrested in Lafayette Park. Corroborating McCarthy's claims, Lieutenant Roy Blick of the local vice squad testified before a Senate committee that the nation's capital was home to five thousand homosexuals and that three-quarters of them worked for the federal government. Another congressional committee launched an investigation into the presence of homosexuals in government and concluded that because homosexuals were vulnerable to blackmail, they posed a threat to national security. Under congressional pressure, federal government agencies began purging their rolls of suspected homosexuals in what has been called a "lavender scare." The security program of President Dwight D. Eisenhower codified this practice by specifically barring anyone guilty of "sexual perversion" from all federal civil service jobs.

Emergence of LGBT Rights Organizations

In 1956, Buell Dwight Huggins, a federal clerk-typist, formed a Washington chapter of the Mattachine Society (the national homophile organization) with the ambitious goal of changing "unjust laws." But the chapter retreated from its initial activist agenda when the national Mattachine leadership in California insisted it limit its activities to research and education. For several years it held monthly meetings, sponsored speakers, published a newsletter, and maintained a lending library. By the end of the decade the group had disbanded. Better known was H. Lynn Womack's Guild Press, publisher of physique magazines, whose mailing list included thousands of gay men. His victory in the U.S. Supreme Court case of *Manual Enterprises v. Day* (1962) affirmed the right to publish gay periodicals.

In November 1961 a small group of gay Washingtonians formed a new, independent organization, the Mattachine Society of Washington (MSW). Under the leadership of its president, Franklin Kameny, MSW promised to "act by any lawful means . . . to secure for homosexuals the right to life, liberty, and the pursuit of happiness." A civil liberties and social action organization, MSW radicalized the small homophile movement by adopting the methods of the black civil rights movement. With the primary goal of ending federal anti-LGB discrimination policies, MSW distributed press releases, lobbied government officials, supported court challenges, and organized public demonstrations. Its first picket of the White House on 17 April 1965 inspired a series of increasingly larger public demonstrations in front of the U.S. Civil Service Commission, the Pentagon, and the State Department. It published a small monthly magazine, the *Homosexual Citizen,* and in 1969 began publishing the *Gay Blade,* which later became an independent newspaper called the *Washington Blade.*

In June 1970, a year after the Stonewall Riots in New York City, a group of Washingtonians formed the local Gay Liberation Front, which adopted a more confrontational style than its predecessors and saw itself as part of a coalition of New Left organizations. With weekly meetings attracting over one hundred people, the GLF sponsored outdoor social events known as "gay-ins" and organized unannounced protests, or "zaps," that disrupted businesses and institutions considered to be homophobic. In May 1971, GLF members invaded an annual meeting of the American Psychiatric Association at the Shoreham Hotel. Though it lasted little more than a year, GLF's group house on S Street in Dupont Circle served as a de facto community center. In 1971, Rita Mae Brown, Charlotte Bunch, Joan Elizabeth Biren, and nine other women activists formed the Furies, a separatist lesbian-feminist collective that advocated lesbianism as a necessary political tactic to end male supremacy. They were best known for their widely distributed newspaper, *Furies,* which members continued to publish even after the group disbanded in 1972.

Political Victories under Home Rule

In the 1970s the U.S. Congress replaced the District of Columbia's appointed board of commissioners with a limited form of home rule. This allowed the LGBT community to enter local politics at the same time as other constituent groups. In the first election for a nonvoting delegate to the U.S. House of Representatives in 1971, volunteers blanketed the city, acquiring more than seven thousand signatures to secure a place for Franklin Kameny on the March ballot. With Paul Kuntzler serving as campaign manager, Kameny garnered nineteen hundred votes, coming in fourth in the six-way race. With an increased sense of the community's political potential, Kameny's campaign committee reorganized after the campaign into the Gay Activists Alliance (GAA/DC), a nonpartisan group dedicated to securing the full rights of citizenship for the gay and lesbian community of the District of Columbia through "peaceful participation in the political process." In addition to its political activism, GAA/DC sponsored weekly dances at a short-lived gay community center on Thirteenth and M Streets. Later

renamed the Gay and Lesbian Activists Alliance (GLAA), it remains one of the oldest, continuously active LGBT organizations in the United States.

During its first year, the GAA held a forum for candidates for the D.C. school board and rated candidates on their support of gay rights. After subsequent lobbying, the school board in 1972 enacted a resolution prohibiting sexual orientation discrimination within the school system, the first such resolution in the United States. The GAA later expanded its candidate forums and ratings process to include mayoral and council races. The GAA was instrumental in securing passage in 1973 by the D.C. Council of Title 34, a comprehensive human rights law, one of the first in the nation to ban discrimination against gays and lesbians in housing, employment, and public accommodations. In 1975 the GAA successfully lobbied the D.C. Council to eliminate funding for the police department's morals squad. That same year it also helped convince the council to allocate funds to establish the Gay Men's Veneral Disease Clinic.

In 1976 the Gertrude Stein Democratic Club was formed to provide financial and volunteer support to local pro-LGB candidates in the Democratic Party. In the 1978 Democratic mayoral primary, the club endorsed the candidacy of Marion Barry, who won an upset victory in the three-way race, thus ensuring his election as mayor. The *Washington Post* later gave credit to the gay community for providing Barry's margin of victory. In his first term as mayor, Barry appointed more than twenty openly gay leaders to his administration and headlines began asking whether Washington had become the "Gay Capital" of America. In another show of strength, three thousand protesters turned out in 1978 at the Washington Hilton to denounce Anita Bryant, the leader of the Save Our Children campaign.

The Proliferation of LGBT Institutions

The 1970s witnessed tremendous growth in LGBT social groups, religious organizations, and businesses, many of them located in the Dupont Circle neighborhood. In 1974, Deacon Maccubbin founded the Lambda Rising bookstore, which the following year sponsored the city's first gay pride block party in front of the store on Twentieth Street NW. On Capitol Hill, Mary Farmer opened the Lammas bookstore, which carried lesbian and feminist literature. The Whitman-Walker Clinic opened in 1978 on Seventeenth Street, bringing together a number of community health initiatives, including the Gay Men's Venereal Disease Clinic and the Lesbian Health and Counseling Center. Several large-scale dance clubs, such as the Lost and Found, opened in the warehouse district of southeast Washington. By 1980 the city boasted nearly one hundred gay organizations. That year the annual pride celebration outgrew the blocks around Twentieth Street, and the new pride organizers, P Street Festival Inc., moved the festivities to Rock Creek Park.

The city's black LGBT community was traditionally centered in private social clubs, since most LGBT establishments were segregated. Even the large gay bars that opened in the 1970s came under fire for discriminatory door policies. In 1978 the D.C. Coalition of Black Gays formed as a political advocacy group to rate political candidates and campaign against discrimination in gay clubs. In 1982 the coalition opened the Coffeehouse, which became an important performance center for minority artists. In May 1991, Welmore Cook and other activists organized the first black gay and lesbian pride event in Banneker Field, across from Howard University, to raise funds for African American AIDS groups.

When the Republican Party won control of the U.S. Senate in 1980, a rift developed between the D.C. Council and Congress, which had the power to veto local legislation. In 1981 the D.C. Council repealed the city's sodomy law, but Congress, exercising its oversight power, overturned the change under pressure from the Moral Majority. When the D.C. Court of Appeals ruled in 1987 that Georgetown University's refusal to recognize a gay and lesbian student group violated the city's Human Rights Act, Congress passed the Armstrong Amendment, exempting religiously affiliated educational institutions from the law's lesbian and gay antidiscrimination protections. Following a similar pattern, the D.C. Council passed a domestic partnership measure in 1992, but Congress held up its implementation until 2001.

During the 1980s, Acquired Immune Deficiency Syndrome (AIDS) devastated the gay male community. The Whitman-Walker Clinic expanded its treatment facilities, and in 1993 it opened both the Max Robinson Center to provide HIV and other services to southeast Washington and the Elizabeth Taylor Medical Center on Fourteenth Street NW. Steve Michaels and Wayne Turner founded a chapter of the AIDS Coalition to Unleash Power (ACT-UP/DC), which called attention to government inaction by holding public funerals for people who had succumbed to AIDS. Along with other groups, ACT UP protested actions of the U.S. Congress, which was holding up much local legislation designed to fight the AIDS epidemic, including authorization for a needle exchange program.

In the 1990s, LGBT cultural and political organizations continued to proliferate. Reel Affirmations, a gay and lesbian film festival, promoted LGBT cultural pro-

duction; the Lesbian Avengers' annual Dyke March sought to increase lesbian visibility; and the annual Walk Without Fear was organized to protest continuing anti-LGBT violence. Craig Dean and Patrick Gill, a gay Washington couple, received national media attention when they sued the District of Columbia for refusing to issue them a marriage license. A February 1992 raid on a private gay club, the Follies Theater, resulted in the arrest of eleven men on sodomy charges and reenergized efforts to repeal the city's antisodomy law. The next year the D.C. Council successfully repealed the sodomy law without any congressional intervention. Transgender rights came to the fore with the 1995 death of Tyra Hunter, a transgender citizen who was denied proper emergency treatment after a traffic accident. The incident sparked protests and pressure against the D.C. fire department. After intense lobbying by local LGBT organizations, the city reached an out-of-court settlement of the case in 1999. By the end of the decade, two openly gay candidates had won election to the D.C. Council: David Catania, a Republican, and Jim Graham, a Democrat.

D.C.: A Center of LGBT Life and Activism

According to the 1990 U.S. census, the first to ask about unmarried couples, Washington ranked as the city with the second largest number of gay and lesbian couples, behind only San Francisco. Census data indicated that 19 percent of D.C. households with unmarried "partners" (excluding "roommates") were same-sex households. The average percentage of same-sex households in the twenty largest U.S. cities was only 9 percent.

As the nation's capital, Washington has played host to many national marches and has been the headquarters of many national advocacy agencies. In 1977, Steve Endean became the first full-time federal gay lobbyist with the Gay Rights National Lobby. The first gay and lesbian March on Washington was held in October 1979 and drew thousands of LGBT persons to the nation's capital. The second March on Washington, in 1987, included a display of the Names Project's AIDS Memorial Quilt on the National Mall, a scene that was repeated in 1989, 1993, and 1996. Today a host of national gay organizations are located in Washington, including the National Gay and Lesbian Task Force and the Human Rights Campaign, which opened its own building near Dupont Circle in 2003.

Bibliography

Beemyn, Brett. "A Queer Capital: Lesbian, Gay, and Bisexual Life in Washington, D.C., 1890–1955." Ph.D. diss., University of Iowa, 1997.

D'Emilio, John. *Sexual Politics, Sexual Communities: The Making of the Homosexual Minority in the United States, 1940–1970.* Chicago: University of Chicago Press, 1983.

Dumas, Lorena. "The Sexual Orientation Clause of the District of Columbia Human Rights Act." *Law and Sexuality* 1 (Summer 1991).

Johnson, David K. *The Lavender Scare: The Cold War Persecution of Gays and Lesbians in the Federal Government.* Chicago: University of Chicago Press, 2003.

Lait, Jack, and Lee Mortimer. *Washington Confidential.* New York: Crown, 1951.

Russell, Ina, ed. *Jeb and Dash: A Diary of a Gay Life, 1918–1945.* Boston: Faber and Faber, 1993.

Valk, Anne M. "Living a Feminist Lifestyle: The Intersection of Theory and Action in a Lesbian Feminist Collective." *Feminist Studies* 28 (2002): 303–332.

Van Dyne, Larry. "Is DC Becoming the Gay Capital of America?" *Washingtonian*, September 1980.

White, Edmund. *States of Desire: Travels in Gay America.* New York: Dutton, 1980.

David K. Johnson

See also BARNEY, NATALIE; BROWN, RITA MAE; FURIES; GRAHN, JUDY; GRIMKÉ, ANGELINA WELD; HOMOPHILE MOVEMENT DEMONSTRATIONS; HOOVER, J. EDGAR; HUMAN RIGHTS CAMPAIGN; KAMENY, FRANKLIN; MARCHES ON WASHINGTON; MATTACHINE SOCIETY; NATIONAL GAY AND LESBIAN TASK FORCE (NGLTF); POLITICAL SCANDALS; STODDARD, CHARLES WARREN; WOMACK, H. LYNN.

WATERS, Ethel (b. 31 October 1896; d. 1 September 1977), singer, actress.

Ethel Waters, according to critic Ashton Stevens, was the greatest artist of her race and of her generation. She possessed a boundless talent that put her at the forefront of music, theater, and film from the 1920s to the 1950s. Born the illegitimate daughter of a teenage rape victim, Waters grew up in poverty in Chester, Pennsylvania. Starting as a shimmy dancer, Waters focused on singing after she won a talent contest at a Philadelphia saloon on her seventeenth birthday. She subsequently toured black theaters in the South as "Sweet Mama Stringbean," performing her showstopper, W. C. Handy's "St. Louis Blues," a song she had heard performed by a professional female impersonator. Waters's northern and pop-influenced approach to the blues, together with her impeccable diction, made her an immediate sensation. Dubbed "Long Goody" by rival Bessie Smith, Waters exerted an appeal that owed as much to her supple voice as to her lanky physique and sexual innuendo.

After winning a role in the all-black revue *Hello 1919!* at Harlem's Lafayette Theater, Waters moved to New York and began singing regularly at Edmond's Cellar. She commenced a long-term relationship with the dancer Ethel Williams, the twosome becoming known as "the two Ethels." In 1921, Waters made her first recording, "At the Jump Steady Ball" and "The New York Glide," for the Cardinal label. The next year, she joined the black-run Black Swan label and had an enormous hit with "Down Home Blues" and "Oh, Daddy." Waters broadened her repertoire, recording blues ("West End Blues," "Dying with the Blues") and songs now considered seminal vocal pop-jazz recordings ("Ethel Sings 'Em," "There'll Be Some Changes Made"). In 1922, while touring in New Orleans with a band led by Fletcher Henderson, the newly proclaimed "Queen of the Blues" purportedly became the first professional black artist to sing on radio. That same year, she also had her first star billing in the revue *Oh Joy*.

Moving to the Columbia label by the mid-1920s, Waters primarily recorded songs showcased in her musical revues. Such shows included the *Plantation Revue* in 1925 (in which she introduced "Dinah"), *Africana* in 1927 (marking her Broadway debut and garnering her acclaim as "Harlem's First Actress"). *Blackbirds of 1930* and *Rhapsody in Black* followed in 1930. She made her first film appearance in 1929 in *On with the Show*, in which she introduced "Am I Blue." In 1933, widespread fame came when she introduced "Stormy Weather" at the legendary Cotton Club, backed by Duke Ellington's orchestra. Impressed by her performance, songwriter Irving Berlin recruited her to appear in the show *As Thousands Cheer* later that year. In her numbers "Heat Wave," "Harlem on My Mind" (a parody of Josephine Baker), and "Supper Time" (about a woman whose husband has been lynched), Waters gained acclaim as a first-rate singer and actress, becoming the first black to play a leading role (while not in blackface) on Broadway alongside white co-stars. By 1934–1935, Waters had become the highest paid Broadway performer, thanks to her Broadway show *At Home Abroad* and radio broadcasts aired from her cabaret appearances. In 1939, she starred in the play *Mamba's Daughters*, becoming the first black female artist to hold a principal dramatic role on Broadway.

That same year she became the first black to have her own television show, *The Ethel Waters Show*. In the 1940s and 1950s, her successes were intermittent but noteworthy. She starred in the all-black Broadway show *Cabin in the Sky* (1940) and in the 1943 film version. In 1949, she received an Academy Award nomination for best supporting actress for her performance in *Pinky*. In 1950, she played the first black lead character on television in the series *Beulah*. That same year, she won a New York Drama Critics Award for best actress for her role in the Broadway drama *The Member of the Wedding* and in 1953 parlayed

Ethel Waters. An early photograph of the hugely popular blues, jazz, and pop singer, who also made significant contributions to Broadway, film, radio, and television from the early 1920s into the 1960s.

her role into her most acclaimed performance as an actress in the film version of the play.

In 1951, her autobiography *His Eye Is on the Sparrow* became a best-seller, startling readers with vivid descriptions of bigotry in the entertainment industry and her search for her mother's affection—and barely mentioning her two husbands, Ethel Williams, or other reputed female lovers. In 1953, she triumphed in her one-woman Broadway recital *At Home with Ethel Waters.* Starting in the late 1950s, she began performing regularly with Billy Graham's Crusades choir and made occasional television appearances, including an Emmy-nominated performance in "Goodnight, Sweet Blues" (1961), on the TV show *Route 66,* and an appearance with Diana Ross on the show *Hollywood Palace* (1969).

Although she died unjustifiably forgotten, in her pioneering career as a blues singer, jazz diva, and actress, Ethel Waters embodied the coming of age of the black entertainer in America.

Bibliography

Bogle, Donald. *Brown Sugar: Eighty Years of America's Black Female Superstars.* New York: Da Capo Press, 1980.

Bourne, Stephen. "Ethel Waters: Stormy Weather." *Capital Gay* (December 1993): 1–2.

———. "Sophisticated Ladies." *Diva* (August 1997): 26–28.

Cherry, Randall. "Ethel Waters: The Voice of an Era." In *Temples for Tomorrow: Looking Back at the Harlem Renaissance.* Edited by Geneviève Fabre and Michel Feith. Bloomington: Indiana University Press, 2001.

Giddins, Gary. "The Mother of Us All." In *Visions of Jazz: The First Century.* New York: Oxford University Press, 1998.

Harris, Sheldon. *Blue's Who's Who: A Dictionary of Blues Singers.* New York: Da Capo Press, 1981.

McCorkle, Susannah. "The Mother of Us All." *American Heritage* 45, no. 1 (February/March 1994): 60–73.

Pleasants, Henry. "Ethel Waters." In his *The Great American Popular Singers.* New York: Simon and Schuster, 1974.

Waters, Ethel, and Charles Samuels. *His Eye Is on the Sparrow: An Autobiography.* New York: Da Capo Press, 1992.

Woll, Allen. *Black Musical Theatre.* New York: Da Capo Press, 1991.

Randall Cherry

See also FEMMES AND BUTCHES; MUSIC: POPULAR.

WATERS, John (b. 22 April 1946), filmmaker, actor, writer.

For his fourth movie, *Mondo Trasho,* John Waters filmed a nude hitchhiker on the Johns Hopkins University campus in Baltimore during 1969 and found himself awaiting a judge's verdict on charges of conspiracy to commit indecent exposure. Judge Solomon Liss dismissed the charges, reading a poem instead of a sentence. "And so, go then and sin no more. Disrobe, if need be, but behind the door. And if again, you heed the call to art, rest assured, the judge will do his part." Waters had only begun to heed art's call.

The filmmaker made his first movie, *Hag in a Black Leather Jacket,* in 1964, an era when many young people in the United States were rebelling against the U.S. government's conduct of the Vietnam War and the country's attitudes toward racial equality and sexual behavior. His early career coincided as well with the development of alternative cinema in the United States. Like fellow gay filmmakers Andy Warhol and Kenneth Anger, Waters generally used nonprofessional actors in his movies, producing pictures on small budgets. All three made movies that featured characters from the LGBT communities, including drag queens and gay biker boys. More regularly than the others, Waters made movies that challenged the culture's gender and sexual boundaries. Many of his movies contained men playing women characters and women portraying men, and Waters has put on the screen lesbians having sex in a church, men masturbating in a movie theater, and bestiality.

The Maryland native, who set all of his movies in his beloved Baltimore, focused less on experimenting with the motion picture form than many other alternative filmmakers. Instead, he brought grossness and filth to the soap opera aspects of the movies. His *Pink Flamingos* (1972) contained copulation between a person and a chicken and the eating of dog feces. Despite its content being contrary to their Catholic beliefs, Waters's parents supported their son, going so far as to loan him the money to make the movie. *Premiere* magazine has named the film one of the one hundred movies that shook the movie world. Waters described "filth" as a code word for humor that was part hillbilly, part hippie, and part gay. He strove to make movies that "would make me and my friends laugh." His friends frequently worked as actors and crew for Waters's earlier movies; called "Dreamlanders," these friends represented a family to the filmmaker as well. His features often included has-beens and never-weres, but he did help create two stars, Divine, the three-hundred-pound cross-dresser, and Ricki Lake, the actress and talk-show host.

Waters fashioned a distinct image for himself. He presented a look that consisted of pencil-line mustache, pomade, and precariously held cigarette. His responses during interviews often included campy non sequiturs. These items represented "John Waters," the lewd outrager from Baltimore with the stuff that withers and weakens authority. During the late 1970s and early 1980s, his image provided audiences of specialized magazines, such as *Film Comment*, and the mid-Atlantic region's gay and lesbian and mainstream newspapers with a depiction of a successful gay man. Such images were much rarer in that era than they would become twenty years later.

In 1981 *Polyester* became Waters's first movie to receive a regular release, and moviegoers were given a "scratch-n-sniff" card with certain smells to experience along with the movie. As directors Tom Kalin and Gregg Araki began exploring issues of social alienation and the construction of sexual identities within queer cinema, Waters reached the mainstream with *Hairspray* (1988), a comedy that reappeared as a Broadway musical in 2002. His two films in the early 1990s, *Cry-Baby* (1990) and *Serial Mom* (1994), the latter a comedy about a sweet wife and mother who has a nasty homicide habit, starred major actors but did not achieve great commercial success. Meanwhile, Waters also participated in the expanded presence of gays and lesbians on television in the 1990s. His persona has made him a popular guest on David Letterman's *The Late Show*, where he has appeared several times; he also provided the voice of a gay kitsch collector on a 1997 *Simpsons* episode centered on homophobia and gay stereotypes. Once called "The Pope of Trash" by writer William S. Burroughs, Waters has shifted his method of pushing boundaries from creating extreme films to include appearing as himself within more mainstream media.

Bibliography

Daugherty, Timmerman, and Janet Stidman Eveleth. "Disparate Disobedients: John Waters and Philip Berrigan." *Maryland Bar Journal* 29, no. 1 (January 1996): 14–18.

Hightower, Scott. "Charles Laughton—John Waters." *Western Humanities Review* 52, no. 2 (1998): 169–171.

Pela, Robert L. *Filthy: The Weird World of John Waters*. Los Angeles: Alyson, 2002.

Rainer, Peter. "John Waters Gets DeMented, but He's All Wet." *New York*, 21 August 2000, p. 57.

Brett L. Abrams

See also FILM AND VIDEO.

WE'WHA (b. ca. 1849; d. December, 1896), potter, weaver, ethnographic consultant, tribal representative.

The most famous *lhamana*, or *berdache* ("two-spirit"), of the Zunis and arguably in all of Native American history, We'wha (WAY-wah) was born shortly after the United States took control of New Mexico in 1848 following the Mexican-American War, which set the stage for an influx of missionaries, anthropologists, Indian agents, traders, and settlers into the Zunis' homelands that threatened the tribe's cultural and economic survival. We'wha was a prominent player in the events of this period.

Having lost both parents in a smallpox epidemic, We'wha was raised by a paternal aunt. His interest in women's activities was apparent at an early age, and he learned weaving and pottery making from female relatives. Although he cross-dressed, *berdache* status within Zuni culture did not entail a social fiction of gender-crossing. An 1881 census lists We'wha's occupations as "Farmer; Weaver; Potter; Housekeeper." At that time, farming was considered a male pursuit, weaving was done by both men and women, and pottery and housework were women's activities. We'wha underwent the first of two initiations held for boys and became a member of the men's kachina society, which performed masked dances.

Male kinship terms were used in referring to him, and his male sex was freely acknowledged. (When speaking of We'wha in English, which requires gendered pronouns that the Zuni language lacks, Zunis past and present will say, "She is a man.") When We'wha died, he was dressed in both male and female clothing and was buried on the male side of a sex-segregated cemetery.

In 1879, an expedition of the newly-formed U.S. Bureau of Ethnology arrived at Zuni under the leadership of James Stevenson. Accompanying him was his wife, Matilda Coxe Stevenson, who took over his studies following his death in 1888. Matilda Stevenson soon discovered that the Zuni "girl" working at the Protestant mission was "especially versed in their ancient lore" and "possessed an indomitable will and an insatiable thirst for knowledge," making him an ideal anthropological informant (Stevenson, pp. 37, 310–11). We'wha facilitated Stevenson's research in various ways, even when Stevenson's brusque and officious bearing alienated other Zunis. (Present Zunis view Stevenson's impact on the tribe as largely detrimental.)

As a member of the kachina society and a curing or medicine society, We'wha was active in Zuni religion. According to Stevenson, he frequently offered prayers at feasts and "was the chief personage on many occasions" (Stevenson, p. 311). One ceremony required the participation of a *lhamana*—a dance held every four years to commemorate the merger of the Zunis with another people as told in mythology. A key figure in both the myth and the ceremony was Ko'lhamana (literally, supernatural *berdache*), whose costuming combined male and female symbols, along with those of hunting and farming, which were normally considered opposed pursuits. We'wha regularly performed this role.

In early 1886, We'wha traveled with the Stevensons to their home in Washington, D.C. Over the next six months, the Zuni "princess" (as he was identified in newspaper articles), attended society events, gave public demonstrations of weaving (and posed for a series of documentary photographs), assisted Matilda Stevenson and other researchers, befriended the Speaker of the U.S. House of Representatives and his wife, appeared in a major charity event at the National Theater, and called on President Grover Cleveland. Although We'wha's height and masculine demeanor were commented on in local newspapers, the Zuni *lhamana* was nonetheless taken to be a woman throughout his stay. (Although Stevenson herself described We'wha as the tallest and strongest member of the tribe, she was unaware of We'wha's true sex for some years; in her 1904 monograph she uses both male and female pronouns in referring to him.)

We'wha. In the ceremonial costume of Zuni women, the famous nineteenth-century Native American "two-spirit" holds a pottery bowl with sacred corn meal. [National Anthropological Archives, Smithsonian Institution, neg. no. 85-8666]

We'wha's conduct in Washington conformed to established patterns of Zuni diplomacy. Over the years, Zuni leaders had skillfully cultivated relations with the U.S. government hoping to protect their lands from encroachment. We'wha's demonstration of traditional arts also served to foster appreciation of his tribe's culture and Native Americans in general.

In 1892, We'wha adopted a different stance when the U.S. military intervened in tribal affairs. A young Zuni man was accused of witchcraft, a serious crime in many tribes, and tried by tribal authorities. White friends notified army officers at nearby Fort Wingate, and soldiers were sent to arrest the tribal leaders. When they arrived, however, they were confronted by the Zuni governor's brother—We'wha—and a scuffle ensued. Forced to retreat, the soldiers returned in a larger, heavily armed detachment and laid siege to the village. We'wha and other leaders were arrested and confined for a month.

Stevenson movingly described We'wha's death in her monograph. The loss of the renowned *lhamana* was viewed as a calamity by the tribe and became the occasion for another witchcraft trial and another military intervention resulting in a six month occupation by an army detachment and the detention of tribal leaders for a year and a half.

Bibliography

Roscoe, Will. *The Zuni Man-Woman.* Albuquerque: University of New Mexico Press, 1991.

———. "Was We'wha a Homosexual?: Native American Survivance and the Two-Spirit Tradition." *GLQ: A Journal of Lesbian/Gay Studies* 2(3) (1995): 193–235.

Stevenson, Matilda C. *The Zuñi Indians: Their Mythology, Esoteric Societies, and Ceremonies.* Bureau of American Ethnology Annual Report 23. Washington, D.C.: U.S. Government Printing Office, 1904.

Will Roscoe

See also NATIVE AMERICANS; NATIVE AMERICAN RELIGION AND SPIRITUALITY; TRANSSEXUALS, TRANSVESTITES, TRANSGENDER PEOPLE, AND CROSS-DRESSERS; TWO-SPIRIT MALES.

WEBER, Bruce (b. 29 March 1946), photographer, filmmaker.

By objectifying and eroticizing the athletic male body in his advertising photography of the 1980s, Bruce Weber revolutionized the depiction of men in U.S. visual culture. Weber's young muscular ideal remains a standard of masculine beauty in contemporary advertising.

Born in Greensburg, Pennsylvania, in 1946, Weber grew up in a family in which the making of home movies and photographs was an expression of belonging and love. Young Bruce's creativity was also fueled by the images of models and celebrities in his mother's fashion magazines. In this way the "fantasy life" Weber has described as essential to his art came into being.

After attending Denison University in Ohio, Weber moved to Manhattan in 1966 to study filmmaking at New York University. Photographers Diane Arbus and Lisette Model helped shape Weber's vision during his early years in New York City. Eschewing Arbus's "freaks" and Model's particularly nonidealized images, Weber nonetheless presents the viewer with equally compelling figures, typically remarkably beautiful men. Weber has recalled that Imogen Cunningham's nude photograph of her husband gave him "great inspiration and courage" to pursue his interest in the male nude when he was about twenty-one

years old. Herbert List's photographs of young men also informed Weber's work.

Weber was rocketed to fame by his 1982 photograph for Calvin Klein Underwear. Wearing nothing but Calvin Klein briefs, Tom Hinthaus, an Olympic pole-vaulter, leans with his eyes closed against a whitewashed wall on the Greek island of Santorini. A low vantage point forces the viewer to look up at the lean, muscular body of the athlete. His hands rest on spread thighs and frame the underwear and genitals evident beneath the fabric. By deploying fetishism and the idealized, objectified male body—conventions of overtly gay imagery—in the context of mass-market advertising, the photograph subtly queers the beholder's gaze.

Weber discusses the transitory nature of youthful beauty when describing his photographs. It seems significant then that Weber's coming of age as an artist coincided with the rise of AIDS in the 1980s and its devastating effect on the gay and arts communities of New York City. Weber's images had a great deal of currency with gay men in the 1980s. They appealed to—and helped construct—a body-conscious gay stereotype. At the same time, they offered a disavowal of the body ravaged by the disease as depicted later by Nicholas Nixon.

Weber's rise in the 1980s was meteoric. The prestigious Robert Miller Gallery in New York City began to show his work. His notoriety increased with the release of his photograph for Calvin Klein's Obsession fragrance products in 1985; it featured four nude men and two nude women. Art critic Paul Smith wrote in 1986, "Bruce Weber's work for fashion magazines and advertisers Calvin Klein and Ralph Lauren has established him as the preeminent fashion photographer in the '80s" (Smith, pp. 166–167). In 1987 Weber's *Studio Wall*, an installation of photographs, was included in the Whitney Museum's Biennial Exhibition. In the same year his first film, *Broken Noses*, debuted. Also in the 1980s, Weber published several books of his photographs.

In 1991 Weber photographed a 116-page magazine advertising supplement for Calvin Klein that appeared in *Vanity Fair.* Evident in this work is the cinematic style of much of Weber's still photography. Photograph after photograph of attractive young people beg the viewer's complicity in supplying a story line. The most celebrated image of the series features a beautiful male nude showering while clutching a pair of sopping wet Calvin Klein jeans to his crotch.

Previously evasive regarding his own sexuality, Weber began around 1989 to offer intimations of bisexu-

created work that is unwittingly political by implicating the viewer in an erotic and sexually ambiguous relationship with the idealized male body.

Bibliography

"Calvin Klein Jockeys for Space." *American Photographer* 10, no. 1 (January 1983): 15.

Kismaric, Carole, and Marvin Heiferman. *Talking Pictures: People Speak about the Photographs That Speak to Them.* San Francisco: Chronicle Books, 1994.

Smith, Paul. "Bruce Weber's Athletic Fashion." *Arts Magazine* 58, no. 10 (June 1984): 126–127.

———. Review of Bruce Weber's "O Rio de Janeiro" Exhibition at Robert Miller Gallery. *Art in America* 74, no. 11 (November 1986): 166–167.

Weber, Bruce. *Hotel Room with a View: Photographs by Bruce Weber.* Washington, D.C.: Smithsonian Institution Press, 1992.

———. *Branded Youth and Other Stories.* Boston: Bulfinch Press/Little, Brown, 1997.

Joseph J. Inguanti

See also ADVERTISING; FILM AND VIDEO; VISUAL ART: PHOTOGRAPHY.

Bruce Weber. The photographer is best known for eroticized, idealized males in advertisements and fashion shots since the early 1980s. [Reuters NewMedia, Inc./corbis]

ality in interviews and in his book essays. Perhaps not surprisingly, Weber's most engaging photographs of the 1990s are those that push the boundaries of what Eve Kosofsky Sedgwick has called "homosocial" interaction toward the homoerotic. This theme pervades Weber's photographic explorations of all-male milieus in his 1997 book *Branded Youth.* In *Scott and Jeremy, Wrestling Camp, University of Iowa,* a grinning college wrestler sits straddling his pinned opponent; the winner manipulates the loser's cheeks. The photo makes the viewer wonder whether these handsome young men are adversaries, lovers, or both.

Weber's most compelling work presents a world of idealized men where gay sex is suggested but never seen. This homoerotic desire is often displaced onto the products his photos advertise. While not an activist, Weber has

WEBSTER, Margaret (b. 15 March 1905; d. 13 November 1972), director, author, and actress.

Born in New York City, Webster descended from a British theatrical dynasty as the daughter of the actors Ben Webster and Dame May Whitty. As a child Webster appeared onstage with the legendary Ellen Terry and also acted with her parents. After more years of acting, including roles in *The Trojan Women* (1924) and John Barrymore's *Hamlet* (1925), she joined the Old Vic in 1929 and played Lady Macbeth during the 1932–1933 season.

In 1934, Webster began her work as a director, occasionally staging plays in London, but more often in the United States. She directed a wide variety of plays, but specialized in the works of William Shakespeare, staging notable productions of *Richard II* (1937) and *Hamlet* (1938), both starring Maurice Evans, followed by *Twelfth Night* (1941) with Helen Hayes in the cross-dressing role of Viola. Webster's work became so linked with the plays of Shakespeare that the press called her "the Bard's girl-friend."

Webster lived openly—if discreetly—as a lesbian. Among her relationships, she was involved for a time with Mady Christians, who acted in Webster's Shakespearean productions and is remembered in the title role of the gay playwright John Van Druten's *I*

Remember Mama (1944). A more celebrated actress (and director, theater manager, and writer), Eva Le Gallienne, was a more significant lover in Webster's life. Webster first met Le Gallienne as a child in the summer of 1913. They did not meet again until late 1937 when Le Gallienne, who had seen Maurice Evans in Webster's *Richard II* earlier that year, made a theatergoing trip to London. The two women found that they shared many of the same ideas and ambitions about the theater, especially the dream of establishing a nonprofit repertory theater company in the United States. Their intimate relationship began in 1941 and continued until 1954, after which Webster began a relationship with the novelist Pamela Frankau. The early 1950s proved a difficult time for Webster; she was summoned to appear before the House Un-American Activities Committee as a result of her penchant for joining many social and political organizations, but undoubtedly also because of her sexuality. Webster "named names," but later noted that the committee had not noticed that the names she named were mostly those of recently deceased individuals.

Following her direction of a successful 1941 production of *Macbeth*, starring Maurice Evans and Judith Anderson, Webster's most acclaimed production, *Othello*, with the celebrated African American actor Paul Robeson in the title role, was produced on Broadway in 1943. The cast of *Othello* also included José Ferrer as Iago, Uta Hagen as Desdemona, and Webster herself as Emilia. The extraordinary critical approval and popularity of *Othello* led producer Cheryl Crawford to back Webster's production of *The Tempest*, featuring the African American actor Canada Lee as Caliban. Opening in 1945 on a setting designed by an unbilled Le Gallienne, *The Tempest* was well-received by critics, although it was somewhat less commercially successful than *Othello*. More importantly, as a result of this production, Crawford, also a lesbian, maintained a working relationship with Webster and Le Gallienne throughout the 1940s.

The intense personal and professional relationship between Webster and Le Gallienne provided each the needed support to achieve some of the more outstanding theatrical efforts of their individual and joint careers during the 1940s. In 1944, Webster directed Le Gallienne in a critically applauded production of Chekov's *The Cherry Orchard*, followed in 1945 by *Terese*, a drama adapted from Emile Zola's *Térèse Raquin*, in a production that featured Webster's mother, who was then eighty years old.

Following the success of *Terese*, Le Gallienne, Crawford, and Webster joined to found the American Repertory Theatre (1946–1948), modeled on Le Gallienne's landmark Civic Repertory Theatre (1926–1933),

which had boldly demonstrated that a nonprofit, subsidized theater could succeed alongside the commercial theaters of Broadway. The American Repertory Theatre, which began operations in September 1946, was compromised by some unfortunate financial decisions and the difficulty of attracting name stage and screen actors to work in a theater in which the highest salary was five hundred dollars a week. Another problem, Webster and Le Gallienne believed, was that male actors resisted working with and for women. There is no evidence to suggest either Webster or Le Gallienne believed their sexual preferences caused some of the resistance, but in that era it is difficult to imagine that their lesbianism did not inspire prejudice. Some established actors, including Walter Hampden and Victor Jory, joined the American Repertory Theatre, and Webster and Le Gallienne selected a core of young actors to fill out the company, including Julie Harris, Anne Jackson, Eli Wallach, William Windom, and Efrem Zimbalist Jr. The theater began as a repertory with a four-play season: Shakespeare's *Henry VIII*, Henrik Ibsen's *John Gabriel Borkman*, J. M. Barrie's *What Every Woman Knows*, and George Bernard Shaw's *Androcles and the Lion*. Webster directed the Shakespeare and Shaw, while also acting in *John Gabriel Borkman*. Considerable money was lost during the first several months, and single-play runs of Sidney Howard's *Yellow Jack* and Le Gallienne's famous adaptation of *Alice in Wonderland* were added to bolster the theater's fortunes. By June 1947, the entire original capital investment of $300,000 had been lost, in part because the company was unable to convince both the stagehands' and musicians' unions to permit them to operate with a minimum number of union members employed. The American Repertory Theatre continued with individual productions of *Hedda Gabler*, directed by Le Gallienne, and *Ghosts*, directed by Webster, both of which were well-received, but not commercially successful enough to save the theater. The failure of the American Repertory Theatre signaled the beginning of the end of the Webster–Le Gallienne alliance.

After the American Repertory Theatre experience, Webster toured the United States with her own troupe, the Margaret Webster Shakespeare Company, from 1948 to 1951. In 1950, she made a transition to opera, earning the distinction of being the first woman to direct at the New York Metropolitan Opera. She occasionally returned to the theater to direct Shaw—*The Devil's Disciple* in 1950, *Saint Joan* in 1951, and *Back to Methuselah* in 1958—prior to her last significant production, *The Aspern Papers* in 1962. Webster authored several significant books on theater, including *Shakespeare without Tears* (1942), *The Same Only Different* (1969), and *Don't*

Put Your Daughter on the Stage (1972). She died on 13 November 1972 in Chilmark, Massachusetts.

Bibliography

Barranger, Milly S. *Margaret Webster: A Bio-Bibliography.* Westport, Conn.: Greenwood Press, 1994.

Le Gallienne, Eva. *With a Quiet Heart: An Autobiography.* Westport, Conn.: Greenwood Press, 1974.

Schanke, Robert A. *Eva Le Gallienne: A Bio-Bibliography.* New York: Greenwood Press, 1989.

———. *Shattered Applause: The Eva Le Gallienne Story.* New York: Barricade Books, 1995.

Sheehy, Helen. *Eva Le Gallienne: A Biography.* New York: Knopf, 1996.

Webster, Margaret. *Don't Put Your Daughter on the Stage.* New York: Knopf, 1972.

———. *The Same Only Different: Five Generations of a Great Theatre Family.* New York: Knopf, 1969.

———. *Shakespeare without Tears: A Modern Guide for Directors, Actors and Playgoers.* New York: McGraw-Hill, 1942; Mineola, N.Y.: Dover, 2000.

James Fisher

See also THEATER AND PERFORMANCE.

WEDDINGS. see MARRIAGE CEREMONIES AND WEDDINGS.

WELLES, Sumner (b. 14 October 1892; d. 24 September 1961), diplomat.

Raised in New York City by his wealthy parents, Benjamin and Frances Swan Welles, Benjamin Sumner Welles graduated from Harvard College in 1914 and entered the foreign service in 1915. His dignified manner, politeness, and independent wealth made him a natural diplomat. Welles rose to prominence at the State Department in the 1920s through various positions in Latin American affairs, but was forced out by President Calvin Coolidge in July 1925, in part because of Coolidge's disapproval of Welles's extramarital affairs. Welles had married Esther Slater of Boston in 1915, and the couple had two children. They divorced in 1923, perhaps because Welles had engaged in an affair with Mathilde Townsend Gerry, whom he later married in 1925 after her divorce from Peter Gerry, a prominent Rhode Island U.S. senator. Welles and Townsend remained married until her death in 1949; they had no children. Throughout his marriage to Townsend, rumors of Welles's homosexuality circulated in Washington, D.C., and his habits—which generally consisted of anonymous sexual encounters under the influence of alcohol—were an open secret within the State Department.

Welles's indiscretions, combined with political rivalry, eventually led to his downfall. President Franklin Roosevelt was much impressed with Welles's views on Latin American politics, and brought him into the new administration in 1933. Roosevelt had known Welles for years: Welles had roomed with Eleanor Roosevelt's brother at school and had even been a member of the couple's wedding party. Under FDR, Welles acted as the driving force behind the Good Neighbor policy, which sought to improve U.S. relations with Latin America through increased trade and an end to military occupations in some regions. Welles was named undersecretary of state in 1937, and FDR relied more and more on Welles's advice, as the world moved toward war and Secretary of State Cordell Hull, ill with tuberculosis, was increasingly unable to lead the State Department. Hull, however, viewed these developments with bitterness, as did another disgruntled State Department employee, William C. Bullitt. Bullitt had served as ambassador to the Soviet Union in 1933, and then as ambassador to France until its fall to the Nazis in 1940; during the war, he was frustrated at his exclusion from the inner circles of the Roosevelt administration, and he blamed Welles for his failures.

In September 1940 a number of leading politicians traveled to Alabama for the funeral of former U.S. House Speaker William Bankhead. On the train ride back to Washington, D.C., Welles drank heavily and allegedly propositioned several porters on the train. (Although the exact details will never be known, few scholars doubt that the incident actually took place.) News of Welles's indiscretion reached the president of the railroad company, and from there, to Bullitt, who seized on the incident as an opportunity to destroy his rival.

When rumors of Welles's alleged behavior reached the White House, Roosevelt was convinced that the charges were a smear tactic, but mounting evidence convinced him that something had to be done before word reached the press. Roosevelt initiated an investigation by the Federal Bureau of Investigation on 3 January 1941; FBI director J. Edgar Hoover reported back on 29 January that the allegations were likely true and also warned the president that Bullitt had been spreading the story around Washington. Roosevelt met with Bullitt on 23 April 1941, but fended off Bullitt's demand for Welles's immediate resignation, citing the demands of war mobilization. Meanwhile, Welles attempted, through Attorney General Francis Biddle, to squelch the story.

For a short time it appeared as if the incident had blown over. By 1942, Welles had effectively taken control of the State Department, due to his influence over Roosevelt and Hull's poor health. It was in the midst of this struggle for power at State that Bullitt and Hull teamed up to destroy Welles. On 24 October 1942, Hull met with Hoover and sought (unsuccessfully) to obtain a copy of the damning FBI report. Frustrated, Hull and Bullitt leaked the story to Maine's Republican U.S. Senator R. Owen Brewster, who met with Hoover on 27 April 1943 to inquire about Welles's actions. Hoover again refused to circulate the report; Brewster threatened to call for a Senate investigation in the middle of the next year's presidential campaign. On 4 May 1943, word reached the White House that Bullitt had leaked the story to publisher Cissy Patterson of the *Washington Times Herald*.

Roosevelt, who was deeply intolerant of homosexuality, nevertheless continued to protect his friend and trusted adviser. He even assigned a Secret Service agent to travel with Welles to prevent any repeat of indiscreet behavior. Finally, in the summer of 1943, Hull presented Roosevelt with an ultimatum, demanding that he fire either Hull or Welles. Roosevelt would have preferred to keep Welles, but knew that if he dismissed Hull and elevated Welles, it would only be a matter of time before Bullitt publicized the scandal—and Roosevelt's role in covering it up. Reluctantly, Roosevelt asked his trusted adviser to resign; Welles did so on 16 August 1943, after twenty-eight years of service in the State Department. Hull retired soon thereafter. Bullitt, who believed that the secretary's chair was now open to him, found that FDR had mobilized his political resources to exclude him completely from his administration.

Welles attempted to influence foreign policymaking through his public writings and speeches, but he never again held a government position. Increasingly isolated and in failing health, he turned to alcohol for solace. He died in September 1961 in New Jersey, at the home of his third wife, Harriette Post, whom he had married in 1952.

Bibliography

Bullitt, Orville H., ed. *For the President, Personal and Secret: Correspondence between Franklin D. Roosevelt and William C. Bullitt.* Boston: Houghton Mifflin, 1972.

Gellman, Irwin F. *Secret Affairs: Franklin Roosevelt, Cordell Hull, and Sumner Welles.* Baltimore: Johns Hopkins University Press, 1995.

Welles, Benjamin. *Sumner Welles: FDR's Global Strategist.* New York: St. Martin's Press, 1997.

Christopher Capozzola

See also POLITICAL SCANDALS.

WHITE, Edmund (b. January 13, 1940), writer.

Edmund White has made his private life unabashedly public, in his fiction, nonfiction, and interviews, revealing his most intimate details: his privileged but repressive Midwestern childhood, his sexual precocity, his life in New York City and presence at the Stonewall Riots, his years living in Paris, his friends and lovers—many dead from AIDS—and his own HIV-positive status.

Edmund Valentine White III was born in 1940 in Cincinnati, Ohio, and moved to the Chicago area at age seven when his parents divorced. He attended the all-male Cranbrook Academy and then the University of Michigan, where he majored in Chinese. In 1962, White moved to New York City, his home for the next twenty-one years. He worked as a staff writer and editor at Time-Life Books until 1970, when he quit to become a full-time writer and journalist.

White's first two published novels were lyrical in style and elliptical, even obscure, in narrative. *Forgetting Elena* (1973), praised by Vladimir Nabokov, concerns a highly stylized community, inspired by the gay society that White observed on Fire Island, even though the novel is not explicitly gay. *Nocturnes for the King of Naples* (1978), a series of dreamlike set pieces, is addressed by a young gay man to an absent older love. White also produced two nonfiction works, in a plainer style and with far more graphic gay sexual content: *The Joy of Gay Sex* (1977), coauthored with Charles Silverstein, and *States of Desire* (1980), a travelogue through gay sexual culture in several American cities.

White's next novel displayed both lyrical passages and a more direct style, along with an unapologetic frankness about gay sexuality. In *A Boy's Own Story* (1982), which draws on incidents in White's own adolescence, the narrator reminisces about growing up in the 1950s, his family dramas, and his sexual experiences and emotional confusion. The novel was an immediate success with readers both LGBT and straight. While working on the book, White read sections at the meetings of the Violet Quill Society, a group of gay writers that included Andrew Holleran and Felice Picano, among others.

In 1983, when White received a Guggenheim Fellowship to complete work on *Caracole,* he used the opportunity to move to Paris. *Caracole* (1985) is about a young man's initiation into a mysterious city that is both occupied Paris and 1980s New York. The book's heterosexual content puzzled much of White's newly found gay audience. White also finished *The Beautiful Room Is Empty* (1988), which again uses autobiographical elements to take the narrator of *A Boy's Own Story* into the 1960s, through college and a move to New York City, where he experiences the oppression of psychotherapy but also glimpses the possibility of freedom after the Stonewall Riots. While in Paris, White undertook a biography of Jean Genet, which would take him seven years to research and write. Published in 1993, *Genet* received the National Book Critics Circle Award. In the same year, the French government made White a *Chevalier de l'Ordre des Arts et Lettres*.

In 1989, White met Hubert Sorin, an architect who was married but gay. Soon after they began their relationship, Sorin was diagnosed with AIDS. In 1994, as Sorin's health deteriorated, they worked together on a project, eventually published as *Our Paris* (1995), with drawings by Sorin and text by White. Sorin died while he and White were traveling in Morocco.

White had written many essays and short stories over the years. A set of the essays were collected and published as *The Burning Library* (1994) and the short stories as *Skinned Alive* (1995). In further recognition of his growing eminence, White was accepted in 1996 into the American Academy of Arts and Letters, having been nominated by Ned Rorem. In his private life, he began a relationship in 1995 with Michael Carroll, an American writer twenty-five years his junior. He also wrote *The Farewell Symphony* (1997), which described the sexual culture of the 1970s and its devastation by AIDS in the 1980s. It is more strictly autobiographical than his two previous novels, in part because White was memorializing his gay world that was now disappearing.

White returned to the United States in 1998 to become a tenured full professor at Princeton University, directing the creative writing program there. He and Carroll moved to Manhattan in 1999. In 2000, the final novel in his autobiographical tetralogy was published: *The Married Man*, a fictionalized version of White's life with Sorin. Two works of nonfiction appeared at the same time: *Marcel Proust* (2000), a short biography, and the *Flaneur* (2001), a discursive stroll through Paris. White's novel *Fanny* is to be published in 2003. As of 2003, he is working on a memoir, to be called *My Lives*.

Bibliography

Barber, Stephen. *Edmund White: The Burning World*. New York: St. Martin's Press, 1999.

The Review of Contemporary Fiction 16, no. 3 (Fall 1996).

Woodhouse, Reed. "White Lies: Edmund White's Gay Fiction." In *Unlimited Embrace: A Canon of Gay Fiction, 1945–1995*. Amherst, Mass.: University of Massachusetts Press, 1998.

Michael Schwartz

See also LITERATURE; ROREM, NED.

WHITMAN, Walt (b. 31 May 1819; d. 26 March 1892), poet.

It would be difficult to overstate the significance of the life and writings of Walt Whitman to the histories and struggles of sexual minorities in the United States and abroad. At least since the 1860s, Whitman has served as a touchstone and a mentor for generations of gay men (and to a lesser extent, lesbians) who have been fortified by his depictions of same-sex affection and eroticism. Any account of his life must include not only his nearly forty-year revision of his magnum opus, *Leaves of Grass*, but also his dedicated Civil War service as a nurse in the hospitals in and around Washington, D.C., at a time when nursing was widely perceived as suitable only for women. As an American luminary later in his life he was visited by notables of all kinds, including Oscar Wilde, who arrived in 1882 at Whitman's home in Camden, New Jersey. This encounter remarkably places two of the most famous nineteenth-century advocates for the validity and value of same-sex affection between men in the same room at the same time—drinking, Whitman later said, elderberry wine. Whitman's writings have circulated in translation throughout the world and have often bolstered the forces of reform, and sometimes revolution, against censorship and repression. A partial list of the artists and writers whom Whitman strongly influenced—many of whom were LGBT—includes Willa Cather, Hart Crane, Thomas Eakins, Allen Ginsberg, Langston Hughes, Henry James, D.H. Lawrence, Federico García Lorca, Stéphane Mallarmé, José Martí, Pablo Neruda, Arthur Rimbaud, Charles Warren Stoddard, Bram Stoker, Algernon Charles Swinburne, John Addington Symonds, Henry David Thoreau, and William Carlos Williams.

Whitman began his working life in the rough-and-tumble world of urban journalism in and around New York City. In addition to reporting, editorializing, and reviewing, Whitman worked the mechanics of the printing trade as a compositor (typesetter), printer, and publisher. He never completely abandoned work with his hands, and throughout his writing life he repeatedly invoked a conception of poetic work that foregrounds the material and the corporeal. Against the epiphanic notion of transcendental literary creation popular at mid-century, Whitman insisted that he "made" poems, and his emphasis on the tangibility of the poet's work points us toward the central place he assigned the physical universe and the possibilities of erotic and sensual pleasures. For Whitman, the physical universe must always be permitted as central a position in the epistemology of "the soul" as the elements of the spiritual universe. As he writes in "Crossing Brooklyn Ferry" (1860): "I too had received identity by my body; / That I was, I

Walt Whitman. The nineteenth-century literary giant—whose primary life's work, the collection *Leaves of Grass,* celebrated the human spirit, the body, and America in verse that transformed modern poetry—said it best himself: "I am large, I contain multitudes." [National Archives and Records Administration (NARA)]

knew was of my body, and what I should be, I knew I should be of my body."

In Whitman's poetry, for probably the first time in American literature, the erotic possibilities of the body are not subordinated to the spiritual, the transcendent, and the metaphysical. This is the primary achievement of Whitman's work: he bequeathed to those who come after him the justification for taking seriously the physical and sexual demands of the body. Whitman published *Leaves of Grass,* his own declaration of bodily and poetic independence, on or around 4 July 1855, and his writings have been extraordinarily influential in enabling the similar declarations of erotic independence of many LGBT people ever since.

Whitman's liberation of the body from the constraints of religious and cultural subordination ("There will soon be no more priests," he confidently predicts in the 1855 "Preface" to *Leaves of Grass*), also made possible a cultural space for the depiction of active sexual desire by women. In what would become section eleven of the poem "Song of Myself," Whitman depicts a woman watching a group of men frolicking in water: "Twenty-eight young men bathe by the shore, / Twenty-eight young men, and all so friendly, / Twenty-eight years of womanly life, and all so lonesome." By episode's end, the woman has joined the men in the river, at least in her mind's eye: "Dancing and laughing along the beach came the twenty-ninth bather, / The rest did not see her, but she saw them and loved them."

In 1881, when the Boston District Attorney attempted to suppress overtly sexual passages in *Leaves of Grass,* he aimed especially at passages that demonstrated active female desire like this one. That is, while we often think of Whitman's homoerotic passages as the most controversial, the District Attorney's report suggests that, in the nineteenth century, even more dangerous was the possibility that women might take active possession of their erotic desires. And while Whitman did not always project such independent women—as even the title of his poem "A Woman Waits For Me" (1867) makes apparent—a range of nineteenth-century women, including Fanny Fern (Sara Willis Parton), Ann Gilchrist, and Kate Chopin, found much to admire and to build upon in his writings about women's sexual desires.

The same Boston District Attorney who censored the passage about the "twenty-ninth bather" barely noticed the 1860 "Calamus" cluster of poems that has represented for generations of gay men the very core of Whitman's homoeroticism. These poems present the affectionate and erotic bond between the speaker and his male lover within a framework that both treats openly, and takes seriously, the public and political consequences of such relationships. On the cusp of the American Civil War, Whitman links together a tender account of his lover's presence:

For the one I love most lay sleeping by me under the
  same cover in the cool night,
In the stillness, in the autumn moonbeams, his face was
  inclined toward me,
And his arm lay lightly around my breast—And that
  night I was happy.

               ("*Calamus 11*" [1860 Leaves of Grass]),

with the necessity of these ties between men for the survival of democracy:

States!
Were you looking to be held together by the lawyers?
By an agreement on a paper? Or by arms?
. . .
There shall from me be a new friendship—It shall be
  called after my name,

It shall circulate through The States, indifferent of place,
It shall twist and intertwist them through and around
each other.

("Calamus 5" [1860 Leaves of Grass])

The depiction of same-sex affection in the "Calamus" poems depends upon this inextricable connection between the personal and the political, the private and the public, which Whitman never repudiated; in his essay "Democratic Vistas" (1870–1871), he insists:

I confidently expect a time when there will be seen, running like a half-hid warp through all the myriad audible and visible worldly interests of America, threads of manly friendship, fond and loving, pure and sweet, strong and life-long, carried to degrees hitherto unknown . . . I say democracy infers such loving comradeship . . . , without which it will be incomplete, in vain, and incapable of perpetuating itself.

Thus twentieth-century activist groups like Queer Nation—which insisted on making visible in the public sphere the possibilities and the value of same-sex affections—may well claim allegiance with Whitman, whose nineteenth-century insistence on the inextricable alliance between homoeroticism and the democratic potential of America remains a connection many seek continually to declare.

Bibliography

Erkkila, Betsy. *Whitman the Political Poet.* New York: Oxford University Press, 1989.

Grossman, Jay, and Betsy Erkkila, eds. *Breaking Bounds: Whitman and American Cultural Studies.* New York: Oxford University Press, 1996.

Lynch, Michael. "'Here Is Adhesiveness': From Friendship to Homosexuality." *Victorian Studies* 29 (Autumn 1985): 67–96.

Martin, Robert K. *The Homosexual Tradition in American Poetry.* Austin: University of Texas Press, 1979.

Moon, Michael. *Disseminating Whitman: Revision and Corporeality in* Leaves of Grass. Cambridge, Mass.: Harvard University Press, 1991.

Shively, Charley, ed. *Calamus Lovers: Walt Whitman's Working-Class Camerados.* San Francisco: Gay Sunshine Press, 1987.

Jay Grossman

See also CATHER, WILLA; CRANE, HART; CROSS-CLASS SEX AND RELATIONSHIPS; EAKINS, THOMAS; FORD, CHARLES HENRI; GINSBERG, ALLEN; HARTLEY, MARSDEN; HUGHES, LANGSTON; LITERATURE; MATTHIESSEN, F. O; MUSIC: OPERA; STODDARD, CHARLES WARREN.

WICCA. see WITCHES AND WICCA.

WICKER, Randolfe (b. 1938), activist.

Randy Wicker, born Charles Hayden, grew up in Florida, New Jersey, and Virginia, claiming later that he felt no shame about his homosexuality. In the late 1950s, as an undergraduate at the University of Texas in Austin, he took to liberal student activism. After learning about the Mattachine Society of New York (an early homophile movement organization) from *ONE* magazine and the *Mattachine Review* (two of the most significant homophile publications of the period), he visited and then moved to Manhattan. Here his activism anticipated not only the future of gay politics but also the vision of an openly gay community with its own economy as a foundation for freedom and equality.

Wicker chafed at the Mattachine Society's faith that progress would come from research and education conducted by professional experts, and he responded with personal activism. In the early 1960s, he countered the view that homosexuality was a pathological psychological disorder by challenging experts in public forums. Presenting himself to reporters as a happy young homosexual who was raising important issues of civil rights, he won unprecedented coverage for this new perspective in newspapers and magazines with national reputations. Local radio and television appearances in which he personally spoke out about civil rights for homosexuals resulted in more media breakthroughs.

As the 1960s erupted with political activism, Wicker's new frontiers extended from tactics and issues to products, career lines, and even then-unfashionable patriotism. Usually he chose to identify himself as the head of the Homosexual League of New York. Its membership consisted of himself, his partner at the time, and whomever they could muster to participate in public demonstrations. Together with nongay contemporaries in the equally ad hoc Sexual Freedom League, Wicker and his Homosexual League picketed for everything from the right to birth control and abortion to legalizing prostitution and the use of marijuana.

On 19 September 1964, with a handful of peers recruited from the Mattachine Society of New York (MSNY) and the Sexual Freedom League, Wicker organized a small picket line to air issues pertaining to discrimination against homosexuals by the military, including violations of confidentiality involving draft records. In front of the Whitehall Induction Center in Manhattan, his picketers handed out a leaflet that proclaimed, precociously, "Army Invades Sexual Privacy."

In April 1965, on Easter Sunday, Wicker joined militants from MSNY on a picket line at the United Nations

that portrayed the homosexual's fight for equal rights as a global cause. This pioneering initiative was triggered by an article in a Cuban newspaper arguing that homosexuality was a "legacy of capitalism" that required "revolutionary social hygiene." Said the countering leaflet handed out by picketers: "We call upon the United Nations to invoke its Charter . . . which calls for 'promoting and encouraging respect for human rights and for fundamental freedoms without distinction as to race, sex, language, or religion.'" During the next several months, Wicker joined some of the historic homophile movement picket lines held at important federal buildings and national landmarks in Washington, D.C., and Philadelphia, to promote these same rights and freedoms in the United States.

Five years later, Wicker would write that the Castro government's intolerance for homosexuality had led him to shift his hope for social progress from "democratic socialism" to the American system of "free enterprise," despite all its lingering bigotry and discrimination. From an early age he had emulated his father, who was a businessman. In college, his business schemes had extended to a line of greeting cards with gay themes. Following his inroads with mainstream reporters, he had toyed with the idea of charging writers for guided tours of homosexual haunts in Greenwich Village.

In 1967, Wicker started one of the first businesses to produce pin-on buttons bearing liberal symbols and slogans. For Mattachine militants he had made a prototype the size of a dress shirt button, which was modeled after

one from the civil rights movement that featured a black equal sign on a white background. Its homophile movement counterpart bore a tiny lavender equal sign on white. With a later button Wicker promoted his ideal of male homosexual partnerships. On a rosy purple background, inside a graffiti-scrawl heart of luminous white, it coupled the names of his comic-book heroes: Batman and Robin.

In 1969, Wicker argued that self-employment and small business were the keys to homosexual freedom. One of the first leaflets circulated after the Stonewall Riots announced that "Randy Wicker, gay militant," would speak about "gay power" to "gay people" and "the general public" at the Electric Circus. This popular discotheque was located at St. Mark's Square near the psychedelic boutique that Wicker had opened with earnings from his button business. Wearing a shirt cut from cloth stamped with the stars and stripes of the American flag, he intended to deliver remarks praising business as a vehicle for integrating "gays" and "straights." As soon as he began to speak, however, a patron spewed antigay slurs that led to a fistfight.

Early in 1970 Wicker ended up in the Gay Activists Alliance. During the latter half of the 1960s he had developed his skills as a journalist by writing a column called "The Wicker Basket" for MSNY's newsletter. Now he became a regular contributor to an innovative commercial publication called *GAY*, a biweekly tabloid edited by Mattachine veterans Jack Nichols and his partner Lige Clarke. It featured articles by homosexual writers willing

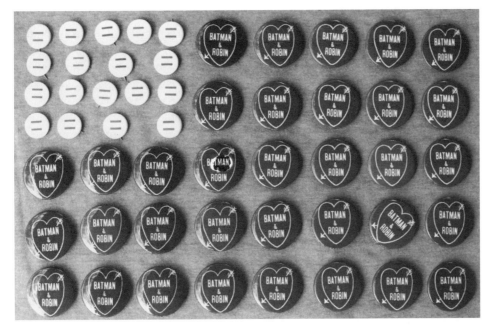

Equality and Love. This "flag" comprises Randy Wicker's lavender-on-white buttons for equal rights and rosy purple buttons celebrating Batman and Robin as partners of a different kind. [Toby Marotta GLBT Archive/Photo by Carrie Marotta]

to discuss their homosexuality personally and to reveal their views about sexual aspects of gay life previously considered too controversial for public discussion. It included explicit male erotica and advertising from any business willing to pitch for gay patronage. And it came to carry a regular column by Wicker (identified on its masthead as "Gay Businessman"), now working as a professional gay journalist, here and for the *Advocate,* to demonstrate, as the subtitle of one of his first articles declared, why "Money Offers A Key To Homosexual Freedom."

Bibliography

Cain, Paul D. *Leading the Parade: Conversations with America's Most Influential Lesbians and Gay Men.* Lanham, Md., and London: Scarecrow Press, 2002.

Clendinen, Dudley, and Adam Nagourney. *Out for Good: The Struggle To Build a Gay Rights Movement in America.* New York: Simon and Schuster, 1999.

D'Emilio, John. *Sexual Politics, Sexual Communities: The Making of a Homosexual Minority in the United States, 1940–1970.* Chicago: University of Chicago Press, 1983.

Duberman, Martin. *Stonewall.* New York: Dutton, 1993.

Marcus, Eric. *Making Gay History: The Half-Century Fight for Lesbian and Gay and Lesbian Equal Rights.* New York: Harper Perennial, 2002.

Marotta, Toby. *The Politics of Homosexuality: How Lesbians and Gay Men Have Made Themselves a Political and Social Force in Modern America.* Boston: Houghton Mifflin, 1981.

Miller, Neal. *Out of the Past: Gay and Lesbian History from 1869 to the Present.* New York: Vintage, 1995.

Teal, Donn. *The Gay Militants: How Gay Liberation Began in America, 1969–1971.* New York: St. Martin's Press, 1995.

Thompson, Mark, ed. *Long Road to Freedom: The Advocate History of the Gay and Lesbian Movement.* New York: St. Martin's Press, 1994.

Wicker, Randolphe. "A Businessman Sounds Off: Homosexual Freedom through Free Enterprise." *GAY* 2 (15 December 1969): 12–13.

Toby Marotta

See also HOMOPHILE MOVEMENT; MATTACHINE SOCIETY.

WIGGLESWORTH, Michael (b. 1631; d. 1705), minister.

Michael Wigglesworth arrived in New England at the age of seven with his parents. He attended Harvard College and taught there in the early 1650s before becoming a minister in Malden, Massachusetts, where he served as pastor until his death. Wigglesworth is perhaps most famous for his grim poem, *Day of Doom,* published in 1662. But his diary, written between 1653 and 1657, is invaluable to religious and cultural historians for its revelation of his interior life and anxieties. Wigglesworth agonized over his spiritual failings, including a "love" for his pupils that he considered sinful and that some scholars have identified as sexual in nature.

Wigglesworth worried constantly throughout the diary about his "sensuality" and "carnal spirit." He often felt overwhelmed by sexual cravings that led to "the ejection of seed" and wet dreams. "Last night," he wrote in February 1653, "a filthy dream and so pollution escaped me in my sleep, for which I desire to hang down my head with shame" (Morgan, p. 5). But this was by no means the only form of "carnality" that Wigglesworth feared. During his years as a Harvard tutor, Wigglesworth also lamented his "too much doting affection to some of my pupils" (Morgan, p. 9). "I find my spirit so exceedingly carried with love to my pupils," he wrote in one entry, "that I can't tell how to take up my rest in God. Lord for this cause I am afraid of my wicked heart. Fear takes hold of me" (Morgan, p. 11). In another he declared that the "filthy lust flowing from my fond affection to my pupils" made him "an object of God's loathing," just as his "sin" made him loathe himself; "pray God make it so more to me," he entreated (Morgan, p. 31).

Wigglesworth's references to "doting affection" and "filthy lust" have been interpreted as evidence of the young tutor's sexual attraction toward some of his students. Yet the language that Wigglesworth uses in these entries has to be placed carefully within its historical and cultural context. Godly New Englanders used words such as "lust," "carnality," and "concupiscence" to indicate not only sexual impulses but also sinfulness in general, including nonsexual failings such as sloth and greed. When Wigglesworth condemned himself for "sensuality," "fleshly lust," and "love of the creature," he referred to his distraction by worldly cravings ("creature comforts") and self-love ("vain thoughts and pride") at the expense of spiritual devotion (Morgan, pp. 5, 10). That words such as "lust" and "carnality" had sexual connotations and yet were often used to describe nonsexual sins reflects the Puritan belief that illicit sex was a quintessential expression of human depravity. But to assume that the language deployed by Wigglesworth in these passages must necessarily refer to sexual feelings is quite unwarranted.

It is clear that Wigglesworth cared deeply about the welfare of his pupils and that he was hurt when they displayed a lack of gratitude for his pedagogical attentions. As he wrote in one entry, "the unloving carriages of my pupils can go so to my heart" (Morgan, p. 3). Wigglesworth saw his affection for his students as distracting him from devotion to God, as did "ease and sloth and pleasure" (Morgan, p. 17). "There is much sensuality," he declared, "and doting upon the creature in my pursuit of the good of others; I cannot seek God's glory therein but am carried most with pity to man" (Morgan, p. 3). When Wigglesworth wrote of "the much distracted thoughts I find arising from too much doting affection to some of my pupils," he may well have been referring to his distraction from striving to deserve Christ's love by what he saw as a sinful preoccupation with human ties. When Wigglesworth lamented the "filthy lust flowing from my fond affection to my pupils," that sounds to a modern ear

like a clear admission of sexual attraction, yet he may have been thinking of his generally sinful fixation on this world at the expense of spiritual endeavor. The phrase "filthy lust" was often used to describe specifically sexual urges, but even if the feelings to which Wigglesworth referred were sexual, these were not necessarily directed toward his students: Puritans believed that diverse sins encouraged each other in a deadly symbiosis, and so he may have worried that excessive devotion to his pupils would prompt other forms of "carnality," including perhaps his masturbatory tendencies.

As we work to uncover long ignored or suppressed evidence relating to same-sex relations, we should beware of leaping to identify homoerotic impulses where they do not necessarily exist. Wigglesworth wrote that he had set up "a Sodom within the temple of the holy-ghost" (Morgan, p. 104). But Puritans often used Sodom as an example of general depravity and the divine judgment that such sinfulness called forth. The biblical city did not automatically invoke for them distinctly sexual, let alone specifically homoerotic, behavior. Puritans used a sexualized vocabulary to describe Christ's favors as well as the sins that alienated men and women from him. In common with other godly New Englanders, Wigglesworth envisioned spiritual faith as espousal to Jesus Christ, characterized any sinful tendency on his part as "whorish desertions" of his heavenly husband, and pined for the moment when his Lord would again "embrace me in the arms of his dearest love" (Morgan, pp. 13, 17). But to read such cravings as homoerotic, as have some scholars, is to ignore the gender fluidity within early modern culture that enabled men to envisage themselves as brides of Christ. Male Puritans were also expected to obey magistrates as a wife would her husband while embodying a masculine role as householders in their own homes.

It would be wrong to ignore the possibility that Wigglesworth was drawn sexually to some of his pupils. But his diary contains no unequivocal evidence that such was the case. If the young tutor's "feelings" for his students were sexual, he would most likely have understood them as one of many ways in which men and women could experience the effects of innate depravity. His theology taught him and he in turn would teach as a pastor that any individual could be tempted to commit any sin: all men and women were potential harlots; all could also hope to rest in the arms of their divine lover.

Bibliography

Crowder, Richard. *No Featherbed to Heaven: A Biography of Michael Wigglesworth 1631–1705.* East Lansing: Michigan State University Press, 1962.

Godbeer, Richard. *Sexual Revolution in Early America.* Baltimore: Johns Hopkins University Press, 2002.

Morgan, Edmund S., ed. *The Diary of Michael Wigglesworth, 1653–1657: The Conscience of a Puritan.* New York: Harper and Row, 1965.

Radel, Nicholas F. "A Sodom Within: Historicizing Puritan Homoerotics in the Diary of Michael Wigglesworth." In *The Puritan Origins of American Sex: Religion, Sexuality, and National Identity in American Literature.* Edited by Tracy Fessenden, Nicholas F. Radel, and Magdalena J. Zaborowska. New York: Routledge, 2001.

Richard Godbeer

WILHELM, Gale (b. 26 April 1908; d. 11 July 1991), writer.

Among Gale Wilhelm's six books of fiction published between 1935 and 1945 are two exquisitely crafted lesbian-themed novels, *We Too Are Drifting* (1935) and *Torchlight to Valhalla* (1938).

Born in Eugene, Oregon, the youngest of five children of Ethel Gale Brewer and Wilson Price Wilhelm, Gale Wilhelm was educated in Oregon, Idaho, and Washington. Around 1925, when Wilhelm was in her late teens, she moved to the San Francisco Bay area. During her ten years there, several of her sonnets were published in *Overland* magazine.

In 1934, while she was living in Berkeley, California, Wilhelm's first short story was published in *Literary America*, the New York-based monthly magazine edited by Kenneth Houston. More of her stories were published in 1934 and 1935. When Random House turned down her first novel, *We Too Are Drifting*, Houston recommended a New York literary agent, Frances Pindyck, who was instrumental in getting Random House to publish the book. Wilhelm dedicated it to Houston. Published in 1935, it received favorable reviews in the *New York Herald Tribune*, the *Nation*, the *New York World Telegram*, the *Daily Mirror*, the *Boston Transcript*, the *New Republic*, and elsewhere.

In 1935, Houston offered Wilhelm a job as an associate editor at *Literary America*. Wilhelm accepted and moved to New York City for a year (1935–1936). Her second novel, *No Letter for the Dead* (1936), was published by Random House before she returned to the West Coast. In 1938, she moved to Oakdale, California, to live with Helen Hope Rudolph Page who ran the Oakdale branch of the *Stockton Record*. The poet Carl Sandburg, who was a friend of Wilhelm and Page, wrote the flyleaf praise for Wilhelm's sixth novel. Wilhelm and Page remained together until Page's death in the late 1940s.

Wilhelm's second (and last) lesbian-themed novel, *Torchlight to Valhalla*, was published by Random House in 1938. The protagonists in both lesbian-themed novels are young, creative individuals who live in the San Francisco Bay area. After *Torchlight to Valhalla*, sapphic themes disappeared from Wilhelm's published writing. Three more novels—*Bring Home the Bride* (1940), *The Time Between* (1942), and *Never Let Me Go* (1945)—were published by William Morrow and Company.

In 1943, Wilhelm was awarded an honorary membership in the International Mark Twain Society and saw stories published in *Colliers* and the *Yale Review*. Publication of new writing ended in 1945, three years before Wilhelm reached age forty. Wilhelm returned to live in Berkeley, California, in 1948. In 1953, she moved into a house in the Berkeley hills where she lived with Kathleen Huebner for the remainder of her life.

Except for her last novel, Wilhelm's heterosexually themed books were not reprinted. Her lesbian-themed books, however, were extremely popular. *We Too Are Drifting*, with its girl-loses-girl ending, was reissued numerous times during the 1940s. During the 1950s, which witnessed the rise of the homophile movement and an increase in lesbian and gay male visibility, lesbianism was a popular theme in paperback novels. The emotionally positive *Torchlight to Valhalla* (under the title *The Strange Path*) was almost continuously in print from 1950 until the early 1960s.

In the 1970s, post-Stonewall lesbian and gay liberation brought a renewed interest in lesbian fiction. *Torchlight to Valhalla* (under its original title) was reprinted by Arno Press in 1975. In 1984, the lesbian publisher Naiad Press reissued *We Too Are Drifting* with editor Barbara Grier's summary of known biographical information on Wilhelm and a plea for help in locating the author. Help came in the form of an anonymous tip. Wilhelm was located and supplied information and photographs (old and new) of herself for the 1985 Naiad Press edition of *Torchlight to Valhalla*.

As an author of quality lesbian fiction, Wilhelm published her first sapphic novel seven years after Radclyffe Hall's international bestseller, *The Well of Loneliness* (1928), and it predates Djuna Barnes's *Nightwood* (1936) by a year. Mary Renault's *The Friendly Young Ladies* (1944; titled *The Middle Mist* in the United States) came out almost a decade later, followed, in 1952, by *The Price of Salt* by Claire Morgan (pseudonym of Patricia Highsmith). Barbara Grier believes that Wilhelm quit writing "because the world would not let her write the books she wanted" (personal interview, 14 November 2002).

Wilhelm died of cancer in Berkeley, California, at the age of eighty-three. Typescripts of her novels are held at the Bancroft Library, University of California, Berkeley. Some of her papers are in the Carl Sandburg Papers at the University of Illinois Library, Urbana-Champaign. Her correspondence with Barbara Grier is housed at the Hormel Gay and Lesbian Center of the San Francisco Public Library.

Bibliography

Grier, Barbara. Introduction to *Torchlight to Valhalla* by Gale Wilhelm. Tallahassee, Fla.: Naiad Press, 1985, xi–xiii.

———. Introduction to *We Too Are Drifting* by Gale Wilhelm. Tallahassee, Fla.: Naiad Press, 1986, 12–16.

Wilhelm, Gale. "Gale Wilhelm Writes." In her *Torchlight to Valhalla*. Tallahassee, Fla.: Naiad Press, 1985, viii–x.

Tee A. Corinne

See also LESBIAN PULP FICTION; LITERATURE.

WILLARD, Frances (b. 28 September 1839; d. 18 February 1898), educator, temperance and women's rights leader.

Frances Willard was one of the earliest "new women" of the nineteenth century. She sought education, rejected marriage, found life companions among women, traveled, built public careers, and fought for women's rights. At her prime in the 1880s, as president of the Women's Christian Temperance Union (WCTU), she was the most powerful woman in the United States, with a public following built on the contradictory foundations of personal charisma and ambition and the temperance movement's commitment to Victorian gender roles and women's traditional responsibilities in separate spheres. Willard's achievements, like those of many of her contemporaries, were not simply the accomplishments of an outstanding individual. To a significant degree Willard's ability to become a powerful leader depended upon her personal and professional relationships with other women, primarily her life partner, Anna Adams Gordon.

Her later prim public image is at odds with the rebellious young woman who preferred to be called "Frank." Frances Willard was born in Churchville in upstate New York, the daughter of Josiah Flint Willard and Mary Thompson Hill, and raised in the Midwest. She emerged from a secure childhood within the Protestant middle class where her mother encouraged this bright and creative daughter to relish the freedoms denied earlier generations of women. Willard disdained the feminine world's restrictions and enjoyed vigorous activities and

intellectual challenges. At college Willard continued her independent ways and rejoiced in breaking rules. She challenged the religious establishment by publicly announcing her religious doubts and was the object of many a "smash" (a nineteenth-century term for a passionate crush between young women) from other women students.

While she remained a radical in many ways, a series of personal and professional challenges appear to have caused her to redirect her life. A sickbed conversion and the death of her sister led Willard to focus her life on public religious service. After graduation from Northwestern Female College in Evanston, Illinois, Willard held a series of teaching posts and then traveled to Europe for an extended tour with Kate Jackson, the first of her companions, whose family financed the trip. A career then became a necessity following her father's death. In 1871 she became president of Evanston College for Ladies. After this institution merged with Northwestern University, she was appointed the first dean of women in 1873. However, Willard resigned from this post after a power struggle with Northwestern's male president. In 1874 Willard became the national corresponding secretary of the recently founded WCTU. The university position was the first of several attempts by Willard to work within male-dominated institutions, but she learned that men, from Northwestern president Charles Fowler to evangelist Dwight Moody, could not or would not work with a woman as a peer. Each time she was frustrated and returned to the WCTU.

In 1879 Willard became president of the WCTU, a position she held until her death. It is not clear if Willard's commitment was primarily to an evangelical mission against alcohol; what is clear is that the WCTU provided her with a paid position and a vehicle through which to fight for women's rights. She struggled within the temperance movement to broaden its goals to include a wide range of women's and political issues, including suffrage and socialism. Though the idea of women's suffrage as the "home protection ballot" did not originate with Willard, her genius was in seeing the power of this concept to allow women to embrace suffrage without abandoning their traditional responsibilities for family and home.

Willard's longest partnership was with Anna Adams Gordon. Willard's tremendous successes were possible to a great extent because Gordon brought order to the life of this charismatic but chaotic leader. Yet this was not a case of wifely devotion, but more a professional and personal partnership. Gordon was committed to the movement's goals as well as to Willard and she eventually became president of the WCTU in 1914.

One can only imagine what Frances Willard might have been able to accomplish in a less restrictive period, or what identities she might have claimed. While most women of her era had few choices but to marry, Willard chose to reject marriage. She found not only a means for financial independence, but also a means to use her gifts and express her ambition. She forged passionate relationships and political partnerships with other women during a time when dominant values denied women any autonomous sexuality. In a sense, the assumed asexuality of these women allowed them to create the relationships and families that sustained them in their numerous political involvements, especially the movement for women's rights.

Bibliography

Bordin, Ruth. *Frances Willard: A Biography.* Chapel Hill: University of North Carolina Press, 1986.

Leeman, Richard W. *"Do Everything" Reform: The Oratory of Frances E. Willard.* New York: Greenwood Press, 1992.

Willard, Frances Elizabeth. *Glimpses of Fifty Years: The Autobiography of an American Woman.* Chicago: Women's Christian Temperance Publication Association, 1889.

Trisha Franzen

See also FEMINISM; SMASHES AND CHUMMING.

WILLIAMS, Tennessee (b. 26 March 1911; d. 25 February 1983), author.

Thomas Lanier ("Tennessee") Williams was born in Columbus, Mississippi. His early years were troubled by differences with his parents; for example, although he won third place in a nationwide essay contest and always wanted to be a writer, his father forced him to quit the University of Missouri and work in a shoe factory. Williams finally received his B.A. degree in 1938 from the University of Iowa. In 1943 his mother authorized a frontal lobotomy on his sister Rose, and he cared for Rose for the rest of her life.

In 1939 Williams moved to New Orleans, where he took the name "Tennessee." There, in 1947, he met Frank Merlo, a former sailor in the U.S. Navy, who became Williams's companion until he died of lung cancer in 1961. Williams found solace in Merlo's Sicilian-American family. *The Rose Tattoo* (1951), the 1955 film version of which starred Anna Magnani and Burt Lancaster, is a sympathetic portrait of a big-hearted Italian woman who loves her philandering husband but who finds a better replacement after his death. Williams remained deeply depressed for most of the rest of his life, and became addicted to

Tennessee Williams. A 1960 photograph of one of the most important American playwrights, who poured his personal anguish and yearnings into his poetic—and sometimes outrageous—plays (and poems, short stories, and other works) during a prolific career that soared from the early 1940s into the 1960s. [corbis]

prescription drugs and alcohol. In 1969 his brother Dakin placed him in a St. Louis mental institution, where he suffered two massive heart attacks before being released. He died from choking on a bottle cap at his suite in the Hotel Elysée in New York City.

Williams's first major plays, *Candles to the Sun* and *The Fugitive Kind*, were produced in 1937 in St. Louis. Over the rest of his life, he wrote twenty-five full-length plays, numerous short plays, two novels, more than sixty short stories, an autobiography, and over one hundred poems.

Williams's most famous plays deal with domestic strife, insanity, and homosexuality, much of it inspired by his own domestic situation. Several are set in New Orleans and abound in local color; others reveal the tensions in upper-class family life in the South. *The Glass Menagerie* (1944), his first major success and for many his best play, was about a domineering mother who tries to marry off her disabled daughter, all the while stifling her poetic son, Tom. Williams won the Pulitzer Prize for *A*

Streetcar Named Desire (1947). *Streetcar*'s mentally unstable Blanche DuBois, who can be interpreted as either Williams's sister or himself, is driven mad by her brutal brother-in-law, Stanley Kowalski, whom Williams modeled on a coworker from his shoe factory days. His second Pulitzer Prize came for *Cat on a Hot Tin Roof* (1955), in which the attention of high school football hero Brick to his deceased buddy Skipper poisons his relationship with his wife, Maggie (the Cat), and his self-aggrandizing father, Big Daddy. Williams also treated homosexuality in *Suddenly, Last Summer* (1958), in which an aging mother tries to have her niece lobotomized because the latter might otherwise expose the homosexuality of the mother's deceased son, who was ripped to pieces by boys he propositioned.

Several of Williams's plays were adapted into excellent motion pictures. Roles in films based on Williams's plays were important in building a number of careers. Paul Newman starred in *Cat on a Hot Tin Roof* (1958) and *Sweet Bird of Youth* (1962) and directed *The Glass Menagerie* (1987). Marlon Brando played Stanley Kowalski in *Streetcar Named Desire* (1951), for which he received an Academy Award nomination for best actor, and appeared in *The Fugitive Kind* (1960). Elizabeth Taylor was in *Suddenly, Last Summer* (1959), *Cat on a Hot Tin Roof*; and, less fortunately, *Boom!* (1968), also starring Noël Coward. Vivien Leigh's portrayal of Blanche DuBois in *Streetcar Named Desire*, for which she won the Oscar for best actress in 1951, is one of the greatest performances in the history of cinema. She immortalized Williams's lines, "I don't want reality, I want magic" and "I have always depended on the kindness of strangers." Unfortunately, the classic films of Williams's plays were made in the 1950s and 1960s, when explicit references to homosexuality had to be excised, as in the 1964 film version of *Night of the Iguana*.

Not all of Williams's plays were successful. *Camino Real* (1953), which he thought his greatest achievement but which flopped on Broadway, features a variety of contemporary characters who cannot escape their stifling lives or the dictatorial society that is run for the benefit of idle rich people. The characters interact with Lord Byron, who is able to escape and forge a creative destiny, and Don Quixote, who fails despite heroic efforts. Few of Williams's post-1960 plays are regularly performed or remembered, but as with his poetry and his essays and short fiction, they are being reexamined and are gaining greater appreciation in the twenty-first century. His later works deal more with the depression and loneliness that afflicted him after Frank Merlo's death, rather than the sexual tensions characteristic of his early work. All of Williams's plays are now available from the Library of America.

Bibliography

Leverich, Lyle. *Tom: The Unknown Tennessee Williams.* New York: Crown, 1995.

Savron, David. *Communists, Cowboys, and Queers: The Politics of Masculinity in the Works of Arthur Miller and Tennessee Williams.* Minneapolis: University of Minnesota Press, 1992.

"The Tennessee Williams Annual Review." Available from http://www.tennesseewilliamsstudies.org.

Williams, Tennessee. *Memoirs.* New York: Bantam Books, 1976.

William Pencak

See also LITERATURE; THEATER AND PERFORMANCE.

WILSON, Lanford (b. 13 April 1937), playwright.

In New York's Greenwich Village in the early 1960s, Lanford Wilson emerged from the theatrical ferment at the Caffe Cino to become one of the most celebrated American playwrights of the last quarter of the twentieth century. Wilson arrived in New York City in 1962 by a circuitous route. Born in Lebanon, Missouri, and raised in rural Missouri, he attended Southwest Missouri State College and San Diego State College before moving to Chicago in 1957. While working as a graphic designer at an advertising agency and writing short stories on the side, Wilson discovered his talent for writing dialogue and enrolled in a playwriting course at the University of Chicago. There, Wilson found his life's calling.

The Madness of Lady Bright (1964), Wilson's third play to appear on Caffe Cino's tiny stage, has gone down in gay-play history as the first to feature a heretofore ignored type of gay man, a "preening screaming queen" (as the published play describes Leslie Bright). In the moments before a full-blown nervous breakdown, Bright recounts his loneliness and horror at growing old in a one-act play that is by turns self-dramatizing, hilarious, and immensely sad. Strikingly original for its time, *The Madness of Lady Bright* ran for 205 performances and attracted media attention as much for its large audience as for its subject matter; it has been variously credited for putting the Off-Off-Broadway theater movement on the map and preparing the way for other American dramatic works about gay men. In a study of Wilson's career, Gene Barnett has noted that the flamboyant and self-destructive Leslie Bright is a forerunner of the character Emory in Mart Crowley's *The Boys in the Band* (1968).

selected works of lanford wilson

The Madness of Lady Bright (1964). This one-act play about a desperate character with flair made history as a path-breaking original when first produced.

Lemon Sky (1970). Alan, the 29-year-old narrator, looks back at his naïve and hopeful seventeen-year-old self and reconsiders the hopes and dreams he had of reuniting with his long-estranged father. Paralleling Wilson's own experience, the play mines the theme of difficult family ties.

Fifth of July (1979). Set in rural Missouri, this perennially popular play features central characters who had all been to the city (and the world) before coming back to the country home for a dramatic reunion. The convergence of the events of the time (Vietnam, sex, drugs and rock 'n' roll) are central to the lives of Vietnam-veteran and double—amputee Ken Talley, his lover Jed, Ken's old college friends Gwen and Weston—but the main focus is on how to sustain a life and family while accommodating the past and preparing for the future.

Burn This (1987). Anna, a dancer, and Larry, a gay advertising executive, are grief-stricken following the sudden death of their beloved loft-mate Robbie. Into their walking-wounded safehouse storms Pale, Robbie's brother, whose guilt, rage, homophobia, and grief destabilize Anna and Larry's delicate equilibrium and alter the future landscape for all of Robbie's survivors.

A Poster of the Cosmos (1988). This emotionally charged one-act monologue presents a man being interrogated about his lover's death and his role in allowing his lover to die the way he wanted.

Wilson has said, "Not only do I hear the way people talk—and the specific rhythms of their speech—but I have a talent for reproducing that in an organized and exciting way" (Barnett, p. 150). And when he was given the opportunity to write full-length plays, he showed that his talent went far beyond the onetime tour-de-force of creating the Leslie Bright character. Whether in urban or rural settings, Wilson has consistently brought characters to vivid life in a daunting variety of work that spans everything from a small group of people at a rural Missouri archaeological dig (*The Mound Builders* [1976]) to a wildly diverse urban gang of night-crawlers (his first full-length play, *Balm in Gilead* [1965]).

Wilson's attraction to society's outsiders allowed him to explore from fresh, contemporary angles the complexities of family, community, loneliness, and the challenges to maintaining relationships (his favorite themes). In populating plays like *Balm in Gilead* and *Hot L Baltimore* (1973) with people he witnessed surviving by their wits in America's decaying cities, Wilson casually included gays, lesbians, sex workers, and other denizens of gritty settings. The popularity of these plays brought these new groups of characters, in their very ordinariness and individuality, into the mainstream of American theatre in the 1960s and 1970s.

Although Wilson has never shied away from focusing the spotlight on gay and lesbian issues and characters in his plays, he was for many years so discreet about his private life that reference books summed him up with lines such as "He is a bachelor and lives in Sag Harbor, New York." In a September 2002 *New York Times* interview, however, the usually reticent Wilson straightforwardly discussed the autobiographical origins of central gay characters in his most emotionally powerful plays.

In the dramatic forefront of American theater with seventeen full-length plays and over thirty one-act plays, he has pioneered the consideration of themes such as estrangement between fathers and gay sons (*Lemon Sky* [1970]), emergence of committed gay relationships among the Vietnam/Woodstock generation (*Fifth of July* [1978]) and grief over early deaths of gay friends (*Burn This* [1987] and *A Poster of the Cosmos* [1988]). Wilson's prominence and commercial clout meant that these works were widely produced and seriously reviewed even when his dramatic innovations were given short shrift in favor of discussions of the "controversial" main topic.

As if to form a stable artistic family like the ideal family he has searched for in his plays, Wilson founded the Circle Repertory Company in 1969 with his colleagues Marshall Mason, Rob Thirkield, and Tanya Berezin to nurture work they termed "lyric realism." From his base at that company, Wilson dramatized his times, his life as a gay man, and his fellow human beings in an intense and subtle body of work, including the Pulitzer Prize winning *Talley's Folly* (1979), that establishes his place in American theater alongside Tennessee Williams, Arthur Miller, and Eugene O'Neill.

Bibliography

Barnett, Gene A. *Lanford Wilson.* Boston: Twayne, 1987.

Bartow, Arthur. *The Director's Voice: Twenty-One Interviews.* New York: Theatre Communications Group, 1988.

Witches and Wicca. A woman in hood and cape takes part in a ceremony. [Brad and Sherry Steiger]

Daniels, Jeff. "Circle Repertory Company: 1969–1996." *American Theatre* 13, no. 10 (December 1996): 48.

Gusso, Mel. "A Playwright at Home with Life's Outsiders." *The New York Times* 15 September 2002: Section 2, AR 1, 22.

Jones, Chris. "The Glory Years: Lanford Wilson Returns to Form with a Compassionate New Play, Book of Days." *American Theatre* 15, no. 9 (November 1998): 20–22.

Ryzuk, Mary S. *The Circle Repertory Company: The First Fifteen Years.* Ames: Iowa State University Press, 1989.

John McFarland

See also THEATER AND PERFORMANCE.

WITCHES AND WICCA

Contemporary Witchcraft and Wicca are forms of earth-based spiritual and religious practices that come under the larger category of Paganism. There are many types of Witchcraft, and many Witches practice as solitaries, but there are some common threads shared by most. Witches recognize the divine as both Goddess and God, often using multiple pantheons from a variety of cultures. Witchcraft is a religion of divine immanence; God/dess is seen in all things, particularly in the realm of nature (which includes humans). As a result, Witches derive their rituals from the seasons and cycles of sun and moon. All initiates are priestesses and priests, personally responsible for their practice, their beliefs, and their behavior. Except in the minds of its detractors, Witchcraft is in no way related to Satanism, as Satan is a Christian concept; Witches do not believe in any embodied form of evil, though they do recognize that evil exists. Most Witches follow two ethical guidelines: (1) harm no one and do what you will, and (2) whatever you send out returns to you multiplied. These effectively inhibit the casting of damaging spells. Witches use magic within ritual circles to bring about needed change in themselves or their societies, to commune with the divine, to heal individuals and the earth, and to experience ecstatic states through drumming, chanting, and dancing. Witchcraft is a religion of the senses that affirms embodiment as a sacred gift and emphasizes the interconnectedness of all things.

Origins

While most practitioners use the terms "Witchcraft" and "Wicca" interchangeably, scholars tend to use "Wicca" only for Gardnerian Wicca, named for its founder Gerald Gardner. In creating (or rediscovering, as some Gardnerians maintain) the religion of Witchcraft in England in the 1930s and 1940s, Gardner reflected the attitudes of that time and place. His texts and rituals were hierarchical (with high priests and priestesses and three levels of initiation) and heterosexist at best, in keeping with his concept of Wicca as a fertility religion; some of his followers maintained that homosexuals could not be Witches. Nonetheless, the presence of Goddess in Gardnerian Wicca was of great interest to spiritual feminists of all genders in the United States, where initiates from England began to instruct new practitioners in the 1960s. Of even greater importance to queer people was "The Charge of the Star Goddess," reworked by Gardner's high priestess Doreen Valiente from Charles Leland's *Aradia* (1899). By affirming the sacredness of all forms of pleasure and love in the phrase "All acts of love and pleasure are My rituals," Gardner and Valiente inadvertently established a religious text that embraces all sexual and gender identities, and queer people became instrumental in establishing witchcraft in its many forms in the United States.

Dianic Wicca

Z (Zsuzsanna) Budapest, a lesbian hereditary Witch from Hungary, was the founder of the main branch of Dianic Witchcraft, which worships Goddess exclusively and restricts its circles to women (though there are Dianic groups that include men). She was the first woman to publish a manual for Witchcraft, *The Feminist Book of Lights and Shadows* (1976). Her students included Ruth Barrett, Kay Gardner, and Starhawk. In Dianic Witchcraft, Z created a spiritual basis for feminist activism against patriarchy, homophobia, racism, and all other forms of oppression. This was not well received by most Gardnerians and other formalists, for whom gender polarity and biological fertility were central to ritual and belief. Subsequent developments showed that such resistance was grounded in age-old social bias and not in the religion of Witchcraft itself. Indeed, Arthur Evans's study *Witchcraft and the Gay Counterculture* (1978) argued that the two groups had been linked throughout European history, particularly in the minds of the dominant cultures.

Radical Faeries and the Reclaiming Tradition

The year after his work was published, Evans put out a call for a spiritual conference for Radical Faeries. This was the beginning of another queer branch of Witchcraft in which gay and bisexual men claimed the spiritual aspects of their sexual identities and affirmed that their difference was and is a divine gift. Mitch Walker and J. Michael Clark were among those who contributed to this movement within a movement. Through play, openness, and such ritual creations as The Mud People and sacred tea dances, Radical Faeries broadened the spectrum of expression for Witchcraft, affirming men's place in the religion even as they challenged its more formalist aspects.

In the same year that the Radical Faeries first met in Arizona, Starhawk published *The Spiral Dance* (1979), one of the most widely read works on contemporary Witchcraft. From her teachers Victor and Cora Anderson and her work in San Francisco with Z Budapest and Diane Baker, Starhawk devised egalitarian classes that eventually evolved into the Reclaiming Collective. Teachers from Reclaiming offered weeklong intensive workshops known as Witch Camps, at first only in California, but soon throughout the United States, as well as Canada, Germany, and England. Starhawk's bisexuality, nonseparatist feminism, and commitment to nonviolent social change ensured that activism would rest at the heart of the Reclaiming Tradition, which is nonhierarchical, consensus-based, and committed to social transformation through shared empowerment and magical activism (witnessed in the antinuclear, queer rights, and antiglobalization movements). Creativity and ecstatic ritual are hallmarks of Reclaiming, inspired in part by the work of the Radical Faeries. Reclaiming is known to be welcoming of all orientations and gender identities; it

offers annual Queer Witch Camps and embraces transsexuals, gender benders, and queer folk of all descriptions. Other forms of Witchcraft, particularly those emphasizing trance, journeying, and ecstatic expression, also welcome transfolk, believing them to possess a multifaceted nature that gives greater facility in walking between worlds.

For millennia, traditions have named witches as those who sit at the edges of their societies, aware of multiple realities, carriers of difference. While many of today's Witches would claim (reminiscent of the early homophile movement) that theirs is a religion like any Western religion, only with many deities instead of one, other Witches affirm the marginal way and seek to change society for the better. They have embraced the queer people in their midst, and those queer people have found in many branches of Witchcraft a spiritual home.

Bibliography

Budapest, Zsuzsanna E. *The Feminist Book of Lights and Shadows.* Edited by Helen Beardwomon. Oakland, Calif.: Feminist Wicca, 1976. Reprinted as *The Holy Book of Women's Mysteries.* Berkeley, Calif.: Wingbow Press, 1989.

Conner, Randy P. *Blossom of Bone: Reclaiming the Connections Between Homoeroticism and the Sacred.* San Francisco: HarperSanFrancisco, 1993.

Conner, Randy P., David Hatfield Sparks, and Maria Sparks. *Cassell's Encyclopedia of Queer Myth, Symbol, and Spirit: Gay, Lesbian, Bisexual, and Transgender Lore.* New York: Cassell, 1998.

Evans, Arthur. *Witchcraft and the Gay Counterculture: A Radical View of Western Civilization and Some of the People It Has Tried to Destroy.* Boston: Fag Rag Books, 1978.

Starhawk. *The Spiral Dance: A Rebirth of the Ancient Religion of the Great Goddess.* 20th anniversary edition. San Francisco: HarperSanFrancisco, 1999.

Marilyn R. Pukkila

See also CHURCHES, TEMPLES, AND RELIGIOUS GROUPS; RADICAL FAERIES; RADICAL SPIRITUALITY AND NEW AGE RELIGION.

WITCHHUNTS. see GOVERNMENT AND MILITARY WITCHHUNTS.

WITTMAN, Carl (b. 24 February 1943; d. 22 January 1986), activist, writer, dancer.

Carl Wittman was a pioneering theorist and practitioner of community building and social justice for the modern LGBT movement in the United States. Born in Hackensack and raised in Paramus by his communist parents, the New Jersey native arrived at Swarthmore College near Philadelphia in 1960 just as the civil rights movement was expanding rapidly. In 1962, Wittman joined other white students on a summer civil rights project in Jackson, Tennessee, and in 1963 he became president of the Swarthmore Political Action Club. Under his leadership, the Swarthmore group worked with African American student activists demanding integration in Cambridge, Maryland, and engaged in civil disobedience in support of Chester, Pennsylvania, residents organizing for full and fair employment, equal access to quality education, universal medical care, and adequate housing.

Through this work, Wittman became a prominent figure in the early days of Students for a Democratic Society (SDS), the largest white student movement of the 1960s. Based on his experiences in Cambridge and Chester, Wittman authored "An Interracial Movement for the Poor?" with fellow SDS leader Tom Hayden. This document, which became the template for SDS's Economic Research and Action Projects (ERAP), synthesized the lessons learned by Old Left, civil rights, and labor organizers. Wittman outlined a strategy of social movement building through local community organizing around the intertwined issues of racism and poverty. Starting with the premises of racial and class equality and full participation by community members, neighborhood-based forums and discussions would generate a genuinely democratic society.

Wittman and Hayden led the ERAP organizing in Newark, but after Hayden reportedly declared that homosexuals were not welcome on the project, Wittman withdrew and launched a similar venture in Hoboken. In 1966, Wittman married his longtime Swarthmore friend and comrade Mimi Feingold, and the two left New Jersey for San Francisco in 1967, where they moved into a commune and joined the nascent draft resistance movement. In 1968, he invited those friends who had shared in the "community ceremony" of their wedding now to join him in publicly presenting a letter to his draft board declaring his refusal to cooperate with the Selective Service System. Soon after turning in his draft card, he wrote "Waves of Resistance," in which he addressed the gendered division of labor of antidraft work and heterosexual male fears of sexual assault while incarcerated for draft resistance.

Though heterosexually married, Wittman had begun having sex with men at age fourteen. Now, in contemplating noncooperation with the draft, writing "Waves of Resistance," participating in a gay protest against a local steamship line that shipped war materiel to Vietnam, and exploring San Francisco's homophile movement, Witt-

man began to synthesize his sexuality with his New Left politics of community. After separating from Feingold and coming out as gay, he penned "Refugees from Amerika: A Gay Manifesto," arguably the seminal theoretical essay of the new gay liberation movement. Begun before the 1969 Stonewall Riots (though published soon afterward), Wittman denounced gay male chauvinism, rejected marriage and mimicry of other heterosexual institutions, and condemned discrimination by legal, psychiatric, and government authorities. He called for forming coalitions with the women's, black, and Chicano movements, other white heterosexual radicals, homophiles, and members of the counterculture, and issued a call to "free ourselves: come out everywhere; initiate self defense and political activity; [and] initiate counter community institutions."

Early in 1971, Wittman and his boyfriend Stevens McClave moved to Wolf Creek, Oregon, where he and Feingold (along with several other friends) had purchased land just months before their 1969 separation. Once there, Wittman plunged into years of environmental organizing, joining efforts to block federal supervision of clear-cutting and aerial spraying of dioxin-based herbicides in the forests of southwestern Oregon. In 1973, he began a life partnership with Allan Troxler, a fellow antiwar activist and artist. The next year, the two collaborated with other men from Oregon and Iowa to launch *RFD*, a rural gay men's journal. Wittman also served as choreographer of the 1980 Oregon Shakespeare Festival. While he had danced since his college days, he discovered in Wolf Creek a passion for teaching folk dance that continued for the rest of his life. English and Scottish country dance encapsulated his life quest for cooperative community, bringing together lesbians, gay men, and heterosexuals in a nonsexist social arena, as he, Troxler, and their friends reformulated the steps to break down the gender roles inherent in the traditional dances.

When Troxler relocated to his native North Carolina, Wittman followed him to Durham in 1981. Once there, Wittman started teaching country dance classes and took a job as codirector of the North Carolina Public Interest Research Group. The couple spearheaded a campaign to block toxic dumping in their low-income neighborhood and shut down the local Armageddon Chemical Company recycling plant. Additionally, following the April 1981 fatal gay bashing of Ron Antonevich at the Little River, Wittman helped organize first a memorial rally and then in June, "Our Day Out," the first gay and lesbian pride march held in North Carolina.

In fall 1982, Wittman gathered a few friends to discuss reports of homophobic health care providers mistreating their lesbian and gay patients. These stories of neglect, ridicule, and harassment convinced them to organize to improve the quality of health care available to local lesbians and gay men. Wittman proposed the creation of a grassroots self-help organization modeled after 1970s feminist health clinics. They launched the North Carolina Lesbian and Gay Health Project (LGHP), which not only encouraged community members to take charge of their own health care but also proved to be the key community-building organization between gay men and lesbians in the Durham–Chapel Hill area for the next fourteen years.

Wittman gradually withdrew from the LGHP, however, as the rapidly escalating demands of the AIDS epidemic forced the organization to rely on the professional health care institutions that held little interest for him. His own health deteriorated over the next several years, and in December 1985, he was diagnosed with AIDS. Driven by his abiding skepticism toward authority and determined to maintain control over his last days, he eventually rejected hospitalization. On 22 January 1986, Wittman took a lethal dose of medication, but not before spending his last week working on his book about English country dance and gathering his family and friends for farewells in his final acts of community.

Bibliography

Frost, Jennifer. *"An Interracial Movement of the Poor": Community Organizing and the New Left in the 1960s.* New York: New York University Press, 2001.

Lekus, Ian. "Health Care, the AIDS Crisis, and the Politics of Community: The North Carolina Lesbian and Gay Health Project, 1982–1996." In *Modern American Queer History.* Edited by Allida Black. Philadelphia: Temple University Press, 2001.

Segrest, Mab. *Memoir of a Race Traitor.* Boston: South End Press, 1994.

Wittman, Carl. "Waves of Resistance." *Liberation* (November 1968): 29–33.

———. "A Gay Manifesto." In *Out of the Closets: Voices of Gay Liberation.* Edited by Karla Jay and Allen Young. New York: Douglas, 1972.

———. "Us and the New Left." *Fag Rag* (Fall 1978): 22–23.

Ian Lekus

See also ANARCHISM, SOCIALISM, AND COMMUNISM; ANTIWAR, PACIFIST, AND PEACE MOVEMENTS; BISEXUALITY, BISEXUALS, AND BISEXUAL MOVEMENTS; ENVIRONMENTAL AND ECOLOGY MOVEMENTS; GAY LIBERATION; NEW LEFT AND STUDENT MOVEMENTS.

WOJNAROWICZ, David (b. 14 September 1954; d. 22 July 1992), artist, writer, activist.

David Michael Wojnarowicz was one of the most intense and influential figures to emerge out of New York's East Village art scene in the 1980s. In both art and writing, Wojnarowicz drew on his difficult and sometimes harrowing life experience. Rather than using a straightforwardly autobiographical method, however, he opted for a complex layering of individual memory and collective history, of private fantasy and political reality.

To escape a physically abusive father, Wojnarowicz dropped out of high school at the age of sixteen and ran away from his family home in Red Bank, New Jersey. After hitchhiking his way across the country and back, Wojnarowicz settled in New York City, where he lived for a time on the streets and worked as a hustler.

In the mid-1970s, Wojnarowicz set out to produce what he called "an authentic version of history in the form of images/writings/objects that would contest state-supported forms of 'history.'" During these years, he worked on a film by and about heroin users; created a photographic series entitled "Arthur Rimbaud in New York," which pictured a male friend wearing a Rimbaud mask as he engaged in sundry activities (shooting up, masturbating, riding the subway); worked at the downtown music club Danceteria; stenciled graffiti images of burning houses and falling people throughout the city; and played in a rock band called 3 Teens Kill 4—No Motive, the name drawn from a tabloid headline.

In the early 1980s, Wojnarowicz devoted much of his art and writing to the quasi-public gay sex scene that took place in the abandoned warehouses lining the Hudson River on the West Side of New York City. Wojnarowicz sought to record what he called "the sounds, sights, smells, and movements as well as hallucinations inside these warehouses." During this period, Wojnarowicz began exhibiting his art—photographs, collages, paintings, and mixed-media work—in the East Village, which was developing into an increasingly visible venue for contemporary art and cultural production. In 1985, a work by Wojnarowicz was included in the Whitney Biennial, one of the most prestigious exhibitions of contemporary art in the United States.

In 1987, Wojnarowicz tested positive for HIV and his art increasingly addressed the psychological and political dimensions of the AIDS crisis. The artist also became involved in ACT UP, the AIDS Coalition to Unleash Power, a direct action political protest group. "When I was told that I'd contracted the virus," Wojnarowicz later wrote, "it didn't take me long to realize that I'd contracted a diseased society as well." In his art and writing of the late 1980s, Wojnarowicz framed AIDS as both an individual crisis and a social disaster.

In 1989, Wojnarowicz became embroiled in a national controversy over an exhibition about art, AIDS, and survival entitled *Witnesses: Against Our Vanishing.* The show, which was partially funded by the National Endowment for the Arts (NEA), was accompanied by a brief catalog that included an essay by Wojnarowicz entitled "Post Cards from America: X-Rays from Hell." In it, Wojnarowicz launched a wide-ranging indictment of American culture that focused with particular ferocity on issues of AIDS policy, the Catholic Church, and the federal government. As a result of Wojnarowicz's essay, the NEA attempted to retract its funding of the exhibition. Federal funding was ultimately restored to the show on the proviso that none of these monies be used for the catalog.

In1990, a conservative religious group called the American Family Association (AFA) targeted Wojnarowicz's art as exemplary of the "homosexual obscenity" that the NEA was allegedly funding. The group produced a flyer illustrated with images identified as the work of David Wojnarowicz, images which were, in fact, small details ripped from Wojnarowicz's larger photomontages, lithographs, and collages. Though Wojnarowicz's art was never comprised exclusively or even primarily of pornographic imagery, it was forcibly refashioned to appear as such within the context of the AFA's mailing. Wojnarowicz responded to the flyer by suing the AFA and its director, Reverend Donald Wildmon, for libel and copyright infringement. The suit, which Wojnarowicz won, marked the first time an artist pursued legal action against a Christian Right organization.

Wojnarowicz died as a result of AIDS in New York City in 1992. One week after his death, a memorial procession was held on the streets of Manhattan's East Village. Behind a banner reading "David Wojnarowicz/ 1954–1992 /Died of AIDS /Due to Government Neglect," participants carried placards with quotations from the artist's writing and reproductions of his visual art. At the conclusion of the march, the banner and placards were set on fire to create a symbolic funeral pyre, an image of private loss flaming into public protest.

Bibliography

Harris, Melissa, ed. *David Wojnarowicz: Brush Fires in the Social Landscape.* New York: Aperture, 1994.

Scholder, Amy, ed. *In the Shadow of the American Dream: The Diaries of David Wojnarowicz.* New York: Grove Press, 1999.

Wojnarowicz, David. *Close to the Knives: A Memoir of Disintegration.* New York: Vintage Books, 1991.

———. *Memories That Smell Like Gasoline.* San Francisco: Artspace Books, 1992.

Richard Meyer

See also COMICS AND COMIC BOOKS; VISUAL ART.

WOMACK, H. Lynn (b. 15 January 1923; d. September 1985), publisher, free speech advocate.

Herman Lynn Womack was born in Hazelhurst, Mississippi, the son of tenant farmers. As a Caucasian albino, Womack was taunted by his school classmates and found refuge in books. Holding down several part-time jobs, he worked his way through the University of Mississippi and then transferred to George Washington University in Washington, D.C., in 1941, where he worked part-time in various federal agencies. In the 1940s he was the headmaster at a boy's school and by 1955 had earned a B.A. degree and an M.A. degree in psychology from George Washington University and a Ph.D. in philosophy from Johns Hopkins University. He returned to George Washington to teach philosophy for several years, until his liberal ideology caused a falling out with his colleagues. Married for the first time at age twenty-one, Womack married twice and divorced twice before deciding that his primary erotic attraction was to other men. By that time a financial windfall from an investment he had made in a friend's business venture allowed him to leave academia and enter the business world. In 1952 he acquired the Guild Press with the goal of proving himself a successful gay entrepreneur.

Guild Press published physique magazines that featured beautiful, muscular young men in skimpy posing straps, along with a few bodybuilding tips. Ostensibly aimed at bodybuilders and artists and dedicated to the ancient Greek ideals of the perfection of the human body, Womack's publications were purchased mostly by gay men. Extremely lucrative, Guild Press had forty thousand subscribers by 1960, far more than any of the several explicitly gay periodicals and newsletters of the homophile movement. With new publications such as *Grecian Guild Pictorial, MANual, Fizeek,* and *Trim,* Womack expanded Guild Press into an extensive holding company that included the Potomac News Company, Manual Enterprises, and other subsidiaries.

In 1960 Womack was arrested and charged with sending obscene materials through the mail. Sentenced to one to three years in prison, Womack took advantage of the notion that homosexuals suffered from a psychological illness and arranged to be confined to St. Elizabeth's Hospital, from which he continued to run his business. When the postmaster general banned distribution of several of his periodicals as obscene, Womack took the case to the U.S. Supreme Court. Though the magazines were not explicitly gay, both sides argued that they appealed primarily to gay men. Womack's attorney argued that this was the basis of the postmaster general's claim that they were obscene, though they were no more explicit than magazines aimed at heterosexuals. In a 6 to 1 decision, the Supreme Court in *Manual Enterprises Inc. v. J. Edward Day, Postmaster General of the United States* (1962) found in Womack's favor and established the precedent that pornography had to be "patently offensive" to be banned as obscene. In the majority opinion, Justice John Marshall Harlan asserted that Womack's images were no more objectionable than portrayals of female nudes, suggesting that homosexuals and heterosexuals enjoyed equal protection under the First Amendment. The decision reinforced and clarified the right to publish gay material first established in *One, Incorporated v. Olsen* (1958), which the court had made with a one-sentence decision in favor of the homophile magazine.

Dismissed by critics as a pornographer, Womack was viewed by others as a champion of gay culture and the rights of gay men to express and affirm homosexual desire. His court victory paved the way for gay publications like *Drum*, founded in 1964, which combined gay news and features with physique photography. Sales soared as Guild Press publications became more provocative and more openly gay. In Washington, D.C., gay bars, the three-hundred pound Womack was hailed as a courageous defender of freedom of expression. In 1963 Womack began the Guild Book Service, a mail-order house for gay-themed literature. He launched the Grecian Guild, a gay pen-pal network, and published the International Guild Guide to the Gay Scene, one of the first directories of gay bars, baths, and clubs. He also opened a chain of adult bookshops, Village Books, in Washington, D.C., and the surrounding suburbs. In 1965, as obscenity laws further loosened, Womack began publishing nudist magazines featuring full frontal nudity. By then, total monthly sales of all physique magazines topped 750,000. Continually hounded by postal authorities, Womack's nudist magazines were also seized by the Federal Bureau of Investigation and temporarily banned from the mails. In 1970 Womack was arrested and convicted for publishing pornographic images of minors. To lessen his jail sentence, he agreed to sever all ties with the Guild Press and leave Washington. Though the Guild

Press soon folded, Womack later opened a mainstream bookstore in Norfolk, Virginia. He died in Boca Raton, Florida, in 1985.

Bibliography

D'Emilio, John. *Sexual Politics, Sexual Communities: The Making of a Homosexual Minority in the United States, 1940–1970.* Chicago: University of Chicago Press, 1983.

Hatton, Jackie. "The Pornography Empire of H. Lynn Womack: Gay Political Discourse and Popular Culture, 1955–1970." *Thresholds: Viewing Culture* 7 (1993): 9–32.

Murdoch, Joyce, and Deb Price. *Courting Justice: Gay Men and Lesbians v. The Supreme Court.* New York: Basic Books, 2001.

Streitmatter, Rodger, and John C. Watson. "Herman Lynn Womack: Pornographer as First Amendment Pioneer." *Journalism History* 28, no. 2 (Summer 2002): 56–65.

David K. Johnson

See also CENSORSHIP, OBSCENITY, AND PORNOGRAPHY LAW AND POLICY; PHYSIQUE MAGAZINES AND PHOTOGRAPHS; PUBLISHERS.

WOMAN CHIEF (c. 1814–1854), warrior, chief.

Woman Chief was born into the Gros Ventre tribe of what is now western Montana in about 1814. As a child she was captured and then adopted by the Crow people of what is now southeastern Montana and northern Wyoming. She began to express an interest in men's activities around the age of ten, and her Crow stepfather encouraged her by teaching her to hunt and ride.

Her career as a warrior began in her teens. During a Blackfoot attack on the Crows, her group took refuge in a nearby trading post. When the Blackfoot announced an interest in negotiating with the Crows, Woman Chief was the only person who would leave the post to talk to them. The Blackfoot shot at her instead of talking, but she escaped unharmed and shot at least three of the attackers in the process. A year later she led her first raid against the Blackfoot, during which she and her party stole approximately seventy horses. During the ensuing pursuit and battle she killed and scalped one Blackfoot warrior and counted coup on and seized the gun of a second. Counting coup was a battle tactic exclusive to Great Plains warriors, whereby power and prestige could be gained and bravery demonstrated by touching (but not killing) an enemy during combat and then escaping. As her daring accomplishments mounted, her people sang songs of her bravery and the tribe's elders believed she had a charmed life. She took the name Woman Chief and was invited into the men's councils. When she took over her family's lodge after her stepfather's death, she was ranked third out of 160 heads of families. According to one trader who knew her at Fort Union in the late 1840s and early 1850s, Woman Chief was the only known example of a woman attaining the status of chief among any of the Northern Great Plains tribes of the period.

Woman Chief was not the only woman in Northern Great Plains tribes like the Crows to participate in warfare. In these male-dominated horse cultures, masculine activities related to warfare, hunting, and horse-raiding conferred the greatest prestige. Not surprisingly some women sought such prestige for themselves. It was rare, however, for this behavior to involve more extensive adoption of the masculine role. In the case of Woman Chief, warfare was only one of the traditional masculine privileges she pursued. She also became wealthy by stealing horses and engaging in trade, and married four wives to process the numerous buffalo hides she obtained during hunting. A hunter could only trade as many hides and robes as his wives could process, and over the course of the nineteenth century, chiefs and warriors of the Northern Great Plains married more wives because of the growing focus on trading hides and robes as a secondary indicator of wealth and prestige. Woman Chief's wealth in horses and wives, therefore, reinforced her status as chief. There is no way of knowing whether these relationships involved sexual contact, but there is no indication that her tribe questioned her right as a chief to marry the women. She did not, however, wear men's clothing full-time: she only adopted a masculine style of dress when she was at war.

Woman Chief was killed by the Gros Ventre during the summer of 1854, when she was approximately forty years old. After the Treaty of Fort Laramie in 1851, during which the United States government negotiated with the Crows, Sioux, Northern Cheyennes, and four other tribes for the right to establish posts and roads across the Northern Great Plains, the Crows were interested in establishing more peaceful relations with the Blackfoot and Gros Ventres to the north and west. The Gros Ventres indicated a similar interest. Woman Chief decided to visit them to test their good faith, to potentially receive horses as gifts, and perhaps to visit the tribe of her birth. She was warned by her people not to go because of her reputation in battle against the Gros Ventres, but she went anyway. She encountered a large party of Gros Ventres and the contact was initially peaceful. When they discovered who she was, however, they killed her and her companions.

Bibliography

Denig, Edwin T. *Five Indian Tribes of the Upper Missouri: Sioux, Aricharas, Assiniboines, Crees, Crows.* Edited by John C. Ewers. Norman: University of Oklahoma Press, 1961

Ewers, John C. *Plains Indian History and Culture: Essays on Continuity and Change.* Norman and London: University of Oklahoma Press, 1997.

Lang, Sabine. *Men as Women, Women as Men: Changing Gender in Native American Cultures.* Translated from the German by John L. Vantine. Austin: University of Texas Press, 1988.

Lewis, Oscar. "Manly-Hearted Women among the Northern Piegan." *American Anthropologist* 43 (1941): 173–87.

Medicine, Beatrice. "'Warrior Women'—Sex Role Alternatives for Plains Indian Women." In *The Hidden Half: Studies of Plains Indian Women.* Edited by Patricia Albers and Beatrice Medicine. Lanham, Md., and London: University Press of America, 1983.

Schaeffer, Claude E. "The Kutenai Female Berdache." *Ethnohistory* 12, no. 3 (1965): 193–236.

Sheila McManus

See also MARRIAGE CEREMONIES AND WEDDINGS; TRANSSEXUALS, TRANSVESTITES, TRANSGENDER PEOPLE, AND CROSS-DRESSERS; TWO-SPIRIT FEMALES.

WOMEN'S STUDIES AND FEMINIST STUDIES

Women's studies and feminist studies first took shape as academic concentrations in the 1970s. Scholar-activists established the first women's studies program at San Diego State University in 1970 and founded the National Women's Studies Association (NWSA) in 1977. A constellation of factors fed into the environment generating women's studies and continued to influence the discipline as it grew. The majority of teachers and scholars coming to women's studies at its inception brought extensive experiences as political activists from civil rights, antiwar, antipoverty, and New Left campaigns. Developing hand in hand with the broader women's movement, women's studies and feminist studies began theorizing the experiences, roles, and statuses of women in various sectors of society, in multiple regions of the world, and in historical contexts. Feminist studies brought to this general focus on women a critique of all forms of domination, an emphasis on cooperation, and a belief in the integration of theory and practice. While somewhat different in purpose and focus, women's studies and feminist studies generally function as a single discipline within academia.

Much like the diverse women and multidimensional culture of feminism it seeks to analyze, women's studies coexists in complex relationship with LGBT cultures and LGBT studies. The two sets can be described as both distinct and overlapping, each defined by a range of concerns and conflicts particular to its population but intersecting where the concerns and conflicts are shared. Within academic institutions, for instance, LGBT studies, queer studies, and sexuality studies now often exist as separate concentrations from women's, feminist, and gender studies, but in many cases LGBT, queer, and sexuality studies concentrations are housed in women's, feminist, and gender studies units. And in some instances women's, feminist, and gender studies programs and departments have been renamed to reflect heightened attention to LGBT, queer, and sexuality issues.

Theoretical tensions and cultural conflicts characterize the history of these relationships. Beverly Guy-Sheftall notes in her 1995 report to the Ford Foundation on the status of women's studies that despite the important work of the women's studies movement since its inception, many advocates, especially women of color and lesbians, have found themselves frustrated by persistent assertions of universal sisterhood that fail to capture the diversity of women's experiences. Nevertheless, the activists, scholars, theorists, artists, and others populating LGBT and women's studies environments frequently exist in and influence both places. Lesbians in particular have both contributed to and critiqued women's studies since the early 1970s. The Lesbian Studies Caucus, in fact, emerged at the founding convention of the NWSA when, in a dramatic moment, student and faculty representatives took the podium, demonstrating to the assembly that lesbians were diverse, nonstereotypical, and deserving of organizational representation.

The 1970s

The heteronormative, white, and middle-class conceptual frameworks typifying first wave and early second wave feminist public discourse in the women's movement carried over into early women's studies scholarship. Marilyn Frye, in her speech for the Lesbian Perspectives on Women's Studies panel at the 1980 NWSA conference, described women's studies as basically and pervasively heterosexual, a fact that she, as a lesbian, found overwhelming and deeply disappointing. From the beginning, women's studies attracted a diverse population of women, but the predominant discourse during the first decade assumed a single reality that ignored difference. In particular, the dominant paradigm privileged the concept of gender over other categories of analysis such as sexual-

bell hooks. The Distinguished Professor of English at City College of New York (née Gloria Watkins, but she teaches and writes under this name, without capital letters) is a scholar and prolific author on feminism, race, cultural politics, and other subjects. [**Pinderhughes Photography, Inc.**]

ity and race. This conceptual framework subsumed the experiences of lesbians, women of color, and women who were members of both groups under a universalizing and inaccurate sign of white, heterosexual womanhood.

The organizational development process and trials of the NWSA offer a window on the relationship between women's studies and LGBT concerns. Several years after Catherine Stimpson called for a national women's studies organization in 1973, the NWSA founding convention took place at the University of San Francisco. Amid the excitement and enthusiasm for the project, tensions that would characterize the NWSA for years to come immediately flared around organizational structure and along sexuality, race, and class fault lines.

Attention to representation was, from the beginning, very important to the NWSA, but proved difficult to work out practically. Women in the Third World Women's Caucus (now Women of Color Caucus) and the Lesbian Caucus had difficulty with the association and also with working together. Theoretically, the overall intention at the founding convention was to resist any tactics that would divide participants. For example, the organization was called on from the beginning to defend women's studies against lesbian baiting, or blaming lesbians for social backlash against feminism. Despite these efforts to maintain solidarity against homophobic censure, members of the Lesbian Caucus found themselves silenced and denied participation in the process of countering such attacks on the NWSA. They also encountered blame and disapproval within the women's studies movement. Lesbian issues were repeatedly tabled as dangerous to the legitimacy of women's studies and of secondary concern to the primary objective of establishing women in academia and fighting for women's rights in the wider society. Feminist academic and public discourse revolved primarily around male violence against women, sex discrimination in education and the workplace, sexual exploitation through pornography, and women's reproductive health, including birth control and abortion rights. It also tended to use a gender-binary framework that categorized people as essentially female or essentially male, without recognizing fluidity, ambiguity, and change in sex, gender, and sexuality.

Homophobia and heterosexism within women's studies inhibited lesbian leadership, forcing deeper into the closet many people who were active in furthering the goals of women's studies. Even so, by the end of the 1970s a great deal had been accomplished. Although there were tensions between the two constituencies, women of color and lesbians were vocal in pushing the NWSA to take greater organizational responsibility and in challenging the organization's normative environment. Women of color (including lesbians) critiqued the elision of racial-ethnic, class, and cultural difference in definitions of womanhood, and lesbian feminists (including women of color) began critiquing institutionalized heterosexism and the invisibility of lesbians within the new scholarship on women. Both groups generated scholarly networks and publications. For example, Carroll Smith-Rosenberg's groundbreaking essay "The Female World of Love and Ritual: Relations between Women in Nineteenth-Century America" was published in 1975 in the first volume of the feminist journal *Signs*. Two other examples of early publications, both produced by the Feminist Press, are the collection *Lesbian Studies* (1982), edited by Margaret Cruikshank, and the foundational volume in black women's studies, *All the Women Are White, All the Blacks Are Men, but Some of Us Are Brave* (1982), edited by Gloria Hull, Patricia Bell-Scott, and Barbara Smith.

Scholarship and research by and about lesbians and women of color created critical oppositional discourses that challenged mainstream women's studies. The Combahee River Collective outlined the reasons for black

lesbian feminist solidarity with black men (1977), Adrienne Rich framed the concept of "compulsory heterosexuality" (1980), and Lillian Faderman rediscovered lesbians in history (1981). Esther Newton described the transgressive identities of female impersonators and the character of women-centered community (1972, 1973). Elizabeth Lapovsky Kennedy and Madeline Davis began ethnographic explorations of the intersections of race, class, and sexual identity (1993). Nevertheless, lesbian epistemology and concerns remained largely in the shadows of academic analysis and sociopolitical focus during the early second wave of the feminist movement. Academia certainly did not yet offer a safe space for LGBT people to be open about their sexual and gender identities.

The 1980s

Privileging gender over race and sexuality fractured women's studies and the feminist movement. Identity politics, later reincarnated as the politics of difference, became influential in women's studies during the 1980s. Lesbians of color theorized various approaches to women's studies that accounted for the multiple and intersecting dimensions of identity and oppression. During this same period self-defined sex-radical lesbians along with gay men began to forge a paradigm of sexual freedom articulated to some extent in opposition to what they framed as "big mother feminism" (mainstream feminist discourse), sparking the so-called gay-straight split and the sex wars.

In the 1980s, grassroots activism, theorizing, and scholarship by women of color concerned about civil, women's, and lesbian rights began to find a greater audience in academia. African American, Latina, Asian American, and Native critiques challenged the universalizing methods of white women's studies scholars for eliding race, racism, and questions of economy from analyses of patriarchy. They also criticized "additive" models, emphasizing, for example, that the experiences of African American women could not be captured simply by adding together the experiences of African American men and those of white women. While activists countered homogeneity in the women's movement, cultural and academic presses published a variety of influential works written by women of color and/or incorporating analyses of race-class-gender interaction.

This Bridge Called My Back: Writings by Radical Women of Color (1981), edited by Latina lesbians Cherríe Moraga and Gloria Anzaldúa, and *Home Girls* (1983), edited by Barbara Smith, represented a sea change within women's studies. In 1987 Juanita Ramos brought out the first Latina lesbian anthology, *Compañeras: Latina*

Lesbians. Other volumes addressing Latino-Latina and African American LGBT issues followed, including *Chicana Lesbians: The Girls Our Mothers Warned Us About* (1991), edited by Carla Trujillo, and Makeda Silvera's *Piece of My Heart: A Lesbian of Colour Anthology* (1991). The first Asian Pacific Islander lesbian anthology, *Between the Lines,* was published in 1987. Paula Gunn Allen's *Sacred Hoop: Recovering the Feminine in American Indian Traditions* (1986) includes a chapter on lesbians in Native American cultures. In 1988 Menominee poet Chrystos criticized homophobia, sexism, and white women's racism in a scathing and beautiful collection titled *Not Vanishing* (1988).

During this period many lesbians left mainstream women's movement organizations, including the NWSA. Simultaneously, sex-radical lesbians expressed growing tension around the privileging of gender over sexuality and began treating the two as autonomous or partially autonomous from one another. Gayle Rubin marked this shift most notably in her influential essay "Thinking Sex" (1994). Many lesbian sex-radicals felt that they had more in common with gay men than with heterosexual women and that the key axis of their oppression was sexual orientation rather than sex-gender. They were concerned that sexuality not be conflated with or subsumed by gender in theoretical, scholarly, and political work.

They were also concerned that women's studies had conceptualized sexuality as something dangerous and hurtful rather than liberating and pleasurable for women, and that much women's studies scholarship on rape, pornography, sex work, and sadomasochism conceptualized women as sexual victims rather than agents. Often aligning themselves with gay men and transsexuals, sex-radical lesbians struck out against "revolutionary feminist orthodoxy." Feminism, as a result of its censure of "unacceptable" sexual behavior, was labeled by many sex-radicals as erotophobic and antisex. Over time, a split emerged between revolutionary feminism, dedicated to women's liberation and gender theory, and sex-radical lesbians, dedicated to LGBT liberation. Among the better-known figures in the first group were Andrea Dworkin and Catharine MacKinnon; the latter group included, in addition to Rubin and Moraga, Pat Califia, Amber Hollibaugh, Joan Nestle, and Carol Vance. While in many respects these were distinct groups with different purposes and mutual animosity, there continued to be lesbians in the gender-theory camp and sex-radical lesbians who considered themselves feminist. And although problems continued, women's studies scholars and theorists increasingly addressed LGBT issues, and many LGBT studies scholars and theorists engaged in productive dialogue with women's studies.

The 1990s

While lesbians of color, lesbian feminists, and sex-radical lesbians were re-visioning feminism and women's studies, the NWSA reached a critical point. Having attempted a nonhierarchical governance structure during its first two decades, the organization transitioned to a hierarchical, democratic structure following its meltdown at the 1990 Akron, Ohio, conference. The Akron episode centered on the firing of an NWSA staff member and black woman, Ruby Sales, an action that brought to a head a longstanding sense among both women of color and lesbians that they were marginalized within the NWSA. It pushed everyone, especially lesbians of color, into an emotionally and ontologically painful position. Many women of color left the NWSA at this point, while others stayed with the organization. Over the ensuing years, intensive work and negotiation were required to salvage the organization. Since 1997 the NWSA structure has been reconfigured to include permanent seats on the governing board for both the Women of Color Caucus and the Lesbian Caucus. This move finally eased the competition between the two for representation, although not necessarily the loyalty dilemma for lesbians of color.

The decade also witnessed the rapid development and consolidation of LGBT studies in colleges and universities, as well as a trend for transforming women's studies programs into gender studies programs. While LGBT studies focused on analyzing sexuality, sexual orientation, and gender identity, gender studies expanded the domain of women's studies to incorporate analyses of the constructed gender of men, gender relations, and gender's role in shaping society, culture, and politics. Important contributions by Judith Butler, Teresa de Lauretis, Gayle Rubin, and Monique Wittig, among others, helped to develop new conceptions of sex, gender, sexuality, and their interrelationships. In so doing, they helped to redefine relationships between women's studies, gender studies, and LGBT studies.

These changes coincided with an increasing deployment of the term "queer," a concept unaligned with any specific identity category and meant to circumvent, subvert, and radically challenge the stability of the categories "heterosexual," "gay," and "lesbian." Shortly after Queer Nation started advocating in 1989 that "Fags and Dykes Bash Back," queer theorists Butler and de Lauretis, as well as Leslie Feinberg, David Halperin, and Eve Kosofsky Sedgwick, offered analyses of an increasingly complex configuration of genders and sexualities. Even as comedian and actor Ellen DeGeneres contributed to the mainstreaming of lesbian and gay identities as relatively stable categories by coming out on national television in 1996, Annamarie Jagose published *Queer Theory: An Introduction* (1996) to explain a line of thinking that aimed at radically transgressing any concrete forms of identity.

The lines of critique initiated by people of color, LGBT studies scholars, and queer theorists during the 1980s and early 1990s have since gone global in the form of postcolonial feminisms that frame the analysis of sexism, patriarchy, and identity within the context of colonial history and neocolonial power relations. Trinh T. Minh-ha in *Woman, Native, Other: Writing Postcoloniality and Feminism* (1989) was an early representative of this approach. *The New Lesbian Studies: Into the Twenty-First Century* (1996), edited by Bonnie Zimmerman and Toni A. H. McNaron, is a collection of essays that queries the intersections of queer theory, lesbian studies, and postcolonial feminist critique. In one of the essays, "Lesbian Studies and Postmodern Queer Theory," Harriet Malinowitz discusses the impact of queer on lesbian identity. Jo Whitehorse Cochran speaks in another essay, "From a Long Line of Contrary Folks," of an innate drive among Native American lesbians for family, tribe, and community for the sake of survival. Connie Chan in "Don't Ask, Don't Tell, Don't Know: Sexual Identity and Expression among East Asian–American Lesbians," theorizes cultural differences in expressions of sexuality and sexual orientation. The essays in this collection build on at least two decades of women's studies scholarship on sex, gender, and sexuality outside of the United States.

The Twenty-First Century

The founding mothers of the women's studies movement have recently taken steps to chronicle the development of their field. Nevertheless, the history remains relatively obscure and the dimensions complex. On approximately 615 college and university campuses in the United States, women's studies now enjoys program or departmental status. The movement has made its mark on nearly all subject areas, even as the bulk of academic funding continues to be funneled toward older, male-dominated disciplines. Moreover, the NWSA has survived ideological and fiscal trauma. Bonnie Zimmerman's 1999 presidential address in Albuquerque described the NWSA as an organization that created a space in which the intellectual work of the women's movement, the lesbian movement, the transgender movement, the queer movement, and the women of color movement could take place.

Third wave feminism and women's studies still wrestle with the category of gender. Frameworks for recognizing, analyzing, and addressing the ongoing second-class

status of women in the world are still needed, but the challenges of racial-ethnic, class, and sexual difference must also be addressed. Women's studies debates over dimensions of identity and power relations have become increasingly sophisticated and also frequently overlap with LGBT discourse. Indeed, since the 1960s, LGBT issues have shifted from having marginal status to being an area of focus within feminist academia. Feminist theorists addressing LGBT issues have the task of reconciling several currents in LGBT culture. Queer theory offers insights into the fluidity of sex, gender, and sexuality and a promise of freedom from externally imposed categories of identity. The long struggle for civil rights seems finally to be affording LGBT people an eddy in the mainstream, allowing some to have greater access, acceptance, and social power. Patterns of unjust economic and racial power relations referenced by postcolonial feminisms and by such social critics as Smith (1998) persist, however, maintaining the socially marginalized status quo for many LGBT people.

Despite the years of debate and the growth of a transnational feminist critique, the relatively marginal status of women of color, even within lesbian academic circles, still persists. Willa Taylor, former chair of the National Black Lesbian and Gay Leadership Forum, challenged participants in the NWSA First Lesbian Institute, held in 2000, to address the ongoing omission of women of color from the national agendas of lesbian, gay, and women's organizations. She pointed out, in particular, the invisibility and absence of lesbians of color and the fact that discussion at the national level fails to address the chief concerns of women of color. The prevailing focus of lesbian and gay rights groups on gays in the military and on marriage rights, for instance, obscures the issues of child care, jobs, equitable housing, and redistribution of wealth that weigh more heavily on women and men in communities of color than does the right to marry.

Women's studies in the new millennium continue adapting and evolving. While third wave women's studies incorporates transnational issues and concepts of hybrid identity in ways not fully articulated by second wave theorists, contemporary analyses reflect the radical critique of sex, gender, and sexuality that arose out of the second wave sex wars and queer theory and activism. The contemporary subject is a third wave queer identity born of the issues that have spurred women's studies through nearly half a century of growth. Poet Staceyann Chin, recently firing up the LGBT cultural scene, is one example of this complex identity and the constant negotiations to which women's studies has struggled to be accountable. A Chinese-Jamaican-American hybrid, wearing hair reminiscent of radical black-is-beautiful 1970s activists, Chin pounds out in spoken word a searing critique of American racism and xenophobia. Tensile and sometimes barefoot, body draped in androgynous clothing, she breaks down persistent homophobia and the necessity of passing as straight into clear, ugly truth. Detailing experiences of partner violence, Chin ends her performance with a flourish, unzipping her drab clothing to dazzle her audience with a high-femme scarlet bustier. Chin's identity is mutable, multiply positioned, and critically grounded in social dynamics of oppression and resistance. So, too, is women's studies.

Bibliography

Allen, Paula Gunn. *Sacred Hoop: Recovering the Feminine in American Indian Traditions*. Boston: Beacon, 1986.

Butler, Judith. *Gender Trouble: Feminism and the Subversion of Identity*. New York: Routledge, 1990.

Chin, Staceyann. *Stories Surrounding My Coming*. New York: loudPress, 2001.

Chrystos. *Not Vanishing*. Vancouver, Canada: Press Gang, 1988.

Chung, Cristy, Alison Kim, and Kaweah Lemeshewsky, eds. *Between the Lines: An Anthology by Pacific Asian Lesbians of Santa Cruz, California*. Santa Cruz, Calif.: Herbooks, 1987.

Combahee River Collective. "A Black Feminist Statement (1977)." In their *The Combahee River Collective Statement: Black Feminist Organizing in the Seventies and Eighties*. Albany, N.Y.: Kitchen Table/Women of Color, 1986.

Cruikshank, Margaret. *Lesbian Studies: Present and Future*. New York: Feminist Press, 1982.

Faderman, Lillian. *Surpassing the Love of Men: Romantic Friendship and Love between Women from the Renaissance to the Present*. New York: Morrow, 1981.

Feinberg, Leslie. *Transgender Warriors: Making History from Joan of Arc to Dennis Rodman*. Boston: Beacon, 1997.

Gonzalez, Maria C. "This Bridge Called NWSA." *NWSA Journal* 14, no. 1 (spring, 2002).

Guy-Sheftall, Beverly, with Susan Heath. *Women's Studies: A Retrospective: A Report to the Ford Foundation*. New York: Ford Foundation, 1995.

Halperin, David M. "Homosexuality: A Cultural Construct: An Exchange with Richard Schneider." In his *One Hundred Years of Homosexuality and Other Essays on Greek Love*. New York: Routledge, 1990.

Howe, Florence, ed. *The Politics of Women's Studies: Testimony from Thirty Founding Mothers*. New York: Feminist Press, 2000.

Hull, Gloria, Patricia Bell Scott, and Barbara Smith, eds. *All the Women Are White, All the Blacks Are Men, but Some of Us Are Brave: Black Women's Studies*. Old Westbury, N.Y.: Feminist Press, 1982.

Jagose, Annamarie. *Queer Theory: An Introduction*. New York: New York University Press, 1996.

Kennedy, Elizabeth Lapovsky, and Madeline D. Davis. *Boots of Leather, Slippers of Gold: The History of a Lesbian Community*. New York: Routledge, 1993.

Lesbian Herstory Project. Available from www-lib.usc.edu/~retter/chrono.html.

Lesbians of Color Archive. Available from www-lib.usc.edu/~retter/lochrono.html.

Moraga, Cherríe, and Gloria Anzaldúa, eds. *This Bridge Called My Back: Writings by Radical Women of Color*. New York: Kitchen Table, 1981.

Newton, Esther. *Mother Camp: Female Impersonators in America*. Englewood Cliffs, N.J.: Prentice-Hall, 1972.

"Queer Theory: Lesbian and Gay Sexualities." *differences* 3, no. 2 (1991).

Ramos, Juanita, ed. *Compañeras: Latina Lesbians: An Anthology*. New York: Latina Lesbian History Project, 1987.

Rich, Adrienne. "Compulsory Heterosexuality and Lesbian Existence." *Signs* 5 (1980): 631–660.

Rubin, Gayle. "Thinking Sex: Notes for a Radical Theory of the Politics of Sexuality." In *Pleasure and Danger: Exploring Female Sexuality*. Edited by Carole S. Vance. Boston: Routledge, 1984.

Rubin, Gayle, with Judith Butler. "Interview: Sexual Traffic." *differences* 6, nos. 2–3 (summer–fall 1994): 62–99.

Sedgwick, Eve Kosofsky. *Epistemology of the Closet*. Berkeley: University of California Press, 1990.

Silvera, Makeda, ed. *Piece of My Heart: A Lesbian of Colour Anthology*. Toronto: Sister Vision, 1991.

Smith, Barbara. *The Truth That Never Hurts: Writings on Race, Gender, and Freedom*. New Brunswick, N.J.: Rutgers University Press, 1998.

———, ed. *Home Girls: A Black Feminist Anthology*. New York: Kitchen Table, 1983.

Smith-Rosenberg, Carroll. "The Female World of Love and Ritual: Relations between Women in Nineteenth-Century America." *Signs* 1 (1975): 1–29.

Trinh, T. Minh-ha. *Woman, Native, Other: Writing Postcoloniality and Feminism*. Bloomington: Indiana University Press, 1989.

Trujillo, Carla, ed. *Chicana Lesbians: The Girls Our Mothers Warned Us About*. Berkeley: Third Woman, 1991.

Tucker, Farley. "Speaking, Silence, and Shifting Listening Space: The NWSA Lesbian Caucus in the Early Years." *NWSA Journal* 14, no. 1 (spring, 2002).

Wittig. Monique. *The Straight Mind and Other Essays*. Boston: Beacon, 1992.

Zimmerman, Bonnie, and Toni A. H. McNaron, eds. *The New Lesbian Studies: Into the Twenty-First Century*. New York: Feminist Press, 1996.

Aryana F. Bates

See also FEMINISM; GENDER AND SEX; LGBTQ STUDIES; QUEER THEORY AND QUEER STUDIES; WOO, MERLE.

WOO, Merle (b. 24 October 1941), activist, teacher, poet.

Merle Woo was born to a Korean mother and Chinese father in San Francisco, where she has spent most of her life. She came out as a lesbian in the late 1970s, and has fought for LGBT rights and other social causes ever since.

Woo grew up in San Francisco's Chinatown with her parents Helene, a clerical worker, and Richard, a butcher. Striving to give their daughter the best education possible, the Woos sent Merle to Catholic schools, which they considered superior to public schools. In 1965, Woo received a bachelor's degree in English from San Francisco State University (SFSU). Four years later, she completed a master's degree at SFSU, also in English. Woo entered the Ph.D. program in English at the University of California, Berkeley, but withdrew in 1971 because the program felt too elitist to her. While in college, she married and had two children, Emily and Paul. In this respect, her life resembles that of other lesbian feminist writers of her generation, such as Audre Lorde or Adrienne Rich, who also married and had children before coming out.

Woo's first exposure to radical activism came during the Third World Student Strike at SFSU in 1968–1969, which called for the establishment of an ethnic studies program and for affirmative action. Woo attributes both her radical consciousness and her first job as a lecturer in the newly founded Educational Opportunity Program at SFSU to the strike. Since 1969, she has been active in the Asian American, feminist, and LGBT liberation movements and has fought for immigrants' and workers' rights. Woo also joined two feminist social organizations, Radical Women and the Freedom Socialist Party. She has been particularly outspoken about the need to build coalitions between various groups in the fight against economic and social oppression.

Between 1969 and 1997, Woo taught educational, ethnic, and women's studies at various universities. Despite increasing opposition, she remained committed to her goal of creating an active exchange between the community and the classroom throughout this time. She tried to incorporate her activism into her teaching and strove to include material by feminist, queer, and international writers. In 1977, Woo left her position at SFSU to work as a part-time lecturer in Asian American studies at the University of California, Berkeley, where she taught until her contract was terminated under a new employment rule in 1982. Convinced that her termination was at least partially due to her activism and outspokenness against university policies, Woo sued the university for violation of free speech and employment rights. With much support from her students and colleagues, she gained reinstatement in 1984, but was transferred from Asian American studies to the Graduate School of Education. When her contract was not renewed in 1986, she filed a complaint with the American Federation of Teachers on the basis of racial and sexual discrimination. Still fighting for reinstatement in 1991, she was diagnosed with breast cancer and decided to drop her claims to focus on her health. Woo then returned to SFSU to teach in the Women's Studies department. During the 1990s, she found herself in increasing disagreement with the department's curriculum and consequently resigned from her position in 1997.

Besides being an activist and a teacher, Woo is a well-known poet and writer. Her collection of poetry, *Yellow Woman Speaks*, was published in 1986, and her poems have also appeared in numerous anthologies. Woo was one of the first Asian American authors to write explicitly lesbian poetry. More broadly speaking, she uses her poetry to think through the issues in her life and activism; many of her poems are autobiographical and political. Among her prose writings, "Letter to Ma," published in *This Bridge Called My Back* (1981), is probably most well-known. Here Woo addresses the position of Asian American women in their communities and in American society at large, especially in relation to the experience of sexism and racism, and Woo discusses her life as an activist and her complicated relationship with her mother.

As of 2003, Woo is a full-time activist and writer. As relentless as ever, she continues her fight against homophobia, racism, sexism, and economic exploitation.

Bibliography

Huang, Su-Ching. "Merle Woo." In *Asian American Poets: A Bio-Bibliographical Critical Sourcebook*. Edited by Guiyou Huang. Westport, Conn.: Greenwood Press, 2002.

Woo, Merle. "Letter to Ma." In *This Bridge Called My Back: Writings by Radical Women of Color*. Edited by Cherríe Moraga and Gloria Anzaldúa. Watertown, Mass.: Persephone Press, 1981.

———. "Our Common Enemy, Our Common Cause: Freedom Organizing in the Eighties." In *Apartheid U.S.A.* Edited by Audre Lorde. New York: Kitchen Table Press, 1986.

———. *Yellow Woman Speaks*. New York: Kitchen Table Press, 1986.

———. "Forging the Future, Remembering Our Roots: Building Multicultural, Feminist, Lesbian and Gay Studies." In *Tilting the Tower: Lesbians, Teaching, Queer Subjects*. Edited by Linda Garber. New York and London: Routledge, 1994.

Mary Woolley. The president of Mount Holyoke College, a former professor of history at Wellesley College, poses in an academic gown for this 1903 photograph, taken toward the beginning of her half-century relationship with Jeanette Marks. [corbis]

———. "Three Decades of Class Struggle on Campus: A Personal History." In *Legacy to Liberation: Politics and Culture of Revolutionary Asian Pacific America.* Edited by Fred Ho et al. Edinburgh: AK Press, 2000.

Melanie E. S. Kohnen

WOOLLEY, Mary (b. 13 July 1863; d. 5 September 1947), and Jeanette MARKS (b. 16August 1875; d. 15 March 1964), educators and women's rights activists.

In 1895, Mary ("May") Woolley, the first female student at Brown University, took up a position as an instructor of history at Wellesley College. Jeannette Marks arrived on the campus the same year as a first-year student. Despite (or perhaps because of) the differences in their ages and stations, the two rather quickly developed the kind of strong attachment that was not unusual between teachers and students in women's institutions. In 1900, Woolley, who had moved rapidly up the ranks at Wellesley, was offered and accepted the presidency of Mount Holyoke College. Confronting her emotional con-

nection to Marks and the prospect of imminent separation, the two women pledged their ardent, exclusive, and lifelong love for each other and exchanged a ring and a pin. Woolley then arranged for Marks to be offered an instructorship in the department of literature at Mount Holyoke so that they could be together. From her home on the first floor of the building that housed students and instructors, Woolley climbed the stairs every evening to give a kiss to her beloved.

Until 1937, when Woolley retired as president of Mount Holyoke, they worked and lived together at the college, after 1909 residing together in a new president's house. Marks, whose primary ambition was to write, became head of the English department after receiving a master's degree from Wellesley. Their relationship, although unnamed, caused some criticism, especially when faculty—many of whom were themselves involved in what was called "twosing"—perceived Woolley to be granting Marks special privileges. There were even attempts by the trustees to get rid of Woolley, whose feminist principles and progressive positions they found as intolerable as her relationship with Marks. When Woolley learned that her successor was to be a man, she objected publicly and then cut off all contact with Mount Holyoke in the 1930s when she retired.

In her book *Miss Marks and Miss Woolley* (1978), Mount Holyoke alumna Anna Mary Wells, who discovered the love letters of the two women, portrays Marks as an arrogant and unpopular teacher who was never happy at the college and who held the emotional upper hand in the relationship. Wells, who admits her shock at discovering the letters despite long-standing rumors about the relationship, also refuses to believe that there could have been any physical relationship between the two women. Instead, she takes refuge in the notion of romantic friendship, although she does admit that Marks probably had knowledge of lesbianism and at least unconsciously understood that her inclinations ran in that direction. "I despise conventionality.... I would not take a kingdom for the proof at the dinner table as well as in the quiet of our bedroom that you depend upon me; there is no gift equal to the dignity you can confer on me in that way," Marks wrote to Woolley in 1905 (Wells, p. 93). Later Marks expressed interest in the topic of homosexuality and even considered writing a book about it. Wells concludes that she consciously suppressed rather than repressed her desires, and that Woolley's behavior was entirely innocent.

Lillian Faderman, in *To Believe in Women*, devotes a chapter to Woolley and is much kinder to Marks. She points to the eroticism of Woolley's letters to Marks (few of Marks's have survived), and emphasizes the ways that the two women's relationships facilitated their contributions to women's education, women's rights, peace, and civil liberties. Woolley, named one of the twelve greatest living women in the country by *Good Housekeeping* in 1930, served as a delegate to the international Disarmament Conference in 1932, a fitting recognition of her stature and contributions to the cause of peace.

Woolley and Marks moved in a world of women couples, and, like others such as M. Carey Thomas, president of Bryn Mawr College, they straddled the worlds of acceptable female friendships and deviant lesbian relationships. Woolley seemed unconcerned about what people—including her trustees—might think of their relationship, while Marks was more anxious. After Woolley's death, Marks wrote her biography, never mentioning their relationship. Yet a friend, also in a relationship with a woman, commented that it read as if Marks "'had kissed each sentence as she wrote it down'" (Faderman, p. 236).

Bibliography

Faderman, Lillian. *To Believe in Women: What Lesbians Have Done for America—A History.* Boston: Houghton Mifflin, 1999.

Rupp, Leila J. "'Imagine My Surprise': Women's Relationships in Mid-Twentieth Century America." In *Hidden From History: Reclaiming the Gay and Lesbian Past.* Edited by Martin Bauml Duberman, Martha Vicinus, and George Chauncey, Jr. New York: New American Library, 1989.

Rupp, Leila J., and Verta Taylor. *Survival in the Doldrums: The American Women's Rights Movement, 1945 to the 1960s.* New York: Oxford University Press, 1987.

Wells, Anna Mary. *Miss Marks and Miss Woolley.* Boston: Houghton Mifflin, 1978.

Leila J. Rupp

See also BATES, KATHARINE LEE; COLLEGES AND UNIVERSITIES; ROMANTIC FRIENDSHIP AND BOSTON MARRIAGE; SAME-SEX INSTITUTIONS; SMASHES AND CHUMMING.

WORKPLACE MOVEMENTS. see EMPLOYMENT AND OCCUPATIONS.

Y

YOUNG MEN'S CHRISTIAN ASSOCIATION (YMCA).
see SAME-SEX INSTITUTIONS.

YOURCENAR, Marguerite (b. 8 June 1903; d. 17 December 1987), novelist.

Marguerite Yourcenar was born Marguerite de Crayencour in Brussels, Belgium. Her father, a French aristocrat, immediately requested that she be granted French citizenship. Her mother died shortly after giving birth, and Marguerite and her father moved to France. Marguerite was privately educated in the classics. Her career as a writer began in 1919 when her father published her long prose poem, *Le Jardin des Chimères*. Yourcenar published her first novel, *Alexis, ou le traité du vain combat,* in 1929. In it, the protagonist, Alexis, writes a letter to his wife explaining that he must leave her because of his attraction to other men. Declaring his intent to be true to himself, Alexis rejects common assumptions of the time that sexual attraction to other men was a disease, madness, or sin. In this, it is similar to most of Yourcenar's works, which address traditionally socially unacceptable forms of love, including homosexuality, bisexuality, and incest.

Alexis introduces other themes that would shape Yourcenar's writing: the difficulty of knowing oneself as well as the confusion of love. For Yourcenar, sexual orientation is not the only source of love's complexities: she also explores the relationship between love and power, the gap between physical pleasure and spiritual love, and the link between attraction and cruelty. This last theme appeared in a greater degree in two later novels. *La*

Nouvelle Eurydice (1931) and *Le Coup de Grace* (1939) examine love triangles in which one of the protagonists expresses hostility toward a woman who attracts him. In each case, a second male, to whom the first is also attracted, completes the triangle.

These novels were written during a productive period in Yourcenar's life. From 1929 to 1939 Yourcenar traveled throughout Europe and published nine books. At the end of this period, she moved to the United States with the American academic Grace Frick. After the move, Yourcenar wrote very little. Instead, she reread the classics and taught comparative literature at Sarah Lawrence College in New York. Then, in 1949, Yourcenar received a trunk of her belongings that contained a manuscript; it was the germ of what would become *Les mémoires d'Hadrien* (1951). The writing and publication of this novel ushered in a second period of intense productivity and led to growing critical acclaim. During the next thirty-five years, Yourcenar received numerous honors, including elections to the French Legion of Honor (1971), the French Academy (1980, as the first woman elected to this body), and the American Academy of Arts and Letters (1982). Many of her works were reissued by the French publisher Gallimard in its prestigious Pléiade series. Her works were also translated into English (several of them by Grace Frick).

Despite critical success, Yourcenar did not escape criticism of her work or her personal life. Believing that readers should search for meaning in the written work and not in the author's life, she employed a variety of means to distance her works from her personal life. These

299

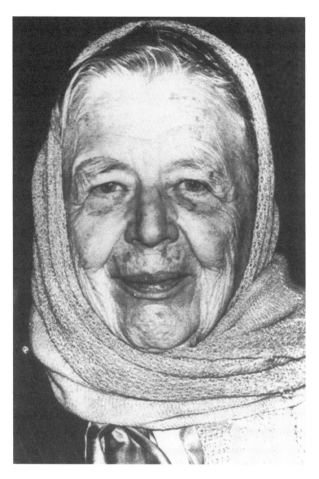

Marguerite Yourcenar. The French (and later American) novelist's critically successful works, which explore the complexities of love, earned her many honors; among them, she was the first woman elected to the prestigious French Academy. [Laffont Jean Pierre/corbis Sygma]

included the use of the pseudonym Yourcenar (which became her legal name upon her naturalization as a U.S. citizen), the focus on male protagonists, and reliance on history and myth. While most critics have respected her privacy, others have speculated on the nature of her relationship with Grace Frick. Some characterize it as an abusive relationship of convenience, in which Frick subordinated herself to Yourcenar's work, while others have intimated that Yourcenar's preference for spending time with Frick in their Maine cottage kept the author from making the sorts of connections that would have furthered her career.

Some critics have objected to Yourcenar's reliance on male protagonists, some of which express misogynist views. Others, wishing to claim her as a "woman writer," have been dismayed by her insistence that she did not believe in such a distinction. Finally, critics have been divided over her insistence on a classical style in a period when more experimental forms of writing were in fashion. However, while Yourcenar's style was rooted in tradition, her subject matter was radical and often scandalous. Some have suggested that her style served to make her subject matter more palatable to the general public, while others have argued that her style was inextricably linked to her belief in universal ideals and values. She was also an activist, supporting such causes as the environment, racial equality, and AIDS research.

Bibliography

Horn, Pierre L. *Marguerite Yourcenar.* Boston: Twayne, 1985.

Savigneau, Josyane. *Marguerite Yourcenar: Inventing a Life.* Translated by Joan E. Howard. Chicago: University of Chicago Press, 1993.

Shurr, Georgia Hooks. *Margeurite Yourcenar: A Reader's Guide.* Lanham, Md.: University Press of America, 1987.

Victoria E. Thompson

See also LITERATURE.

YOUTH AND YOUTH GROUPS

During the last decade of the twentieth century, there was a phenomenal increase in the number of LGBT and queer youth groups. This remarkable surge, from just a few hundred to several thousand, was fueled by a series of momentous events and circumstances. Higher visibility of LGBT adults, landmark court decisions, the tremendous growth of Internet access, and the outrage following the brutal murders of Nebraska transgender teen Brandon Teena in 1993 and University of Wyoming student Matthew Shephard in 1998 created an atmosphere ripe for youth activism.

Before the 1980s there were no high school youth groups for LGBT youth, and before the 1990s just a few hundred for college and university students. Support programs sponsored by community organizations existed for the most part only in major urban areas. Scholars of pre-Stonewall LGBT history have demonstrated that despite these lack of resources, LGBT youth found their way to many of the main institutions and spaces of LGBT social life, including bars, clubs, coffeehouses, restaurants, house parties, cruising areas, public parks, beaches, sports teams, YMCAs, bathhouses, and tearooms. In the late 1960s and early 1970s, LGBT youth played major radicalizing roles in the shift from homophile politics to gay liberationist and lesbian feminist politics. Not long after the 1969 Stonewall Riots, LGBT youth in major urban areas began founding groups such as Gay Youth. Nevertheless,

Youth Pride. Hundreds of college and high school students gather in Boston on 17 May 1997 for a Gay-Straight Youth Pride March, to celebrate the formation of Gay-Straight Alliances in more than one hundred high schools all over Massachusetts; by 2000, there were about six hundred, and about sixteen hundred three years after that. [AP Photo/Patricia McDonnell]

many LGBT youth led isolated and closeted lives without any means of affirming their sexualities and genders.

The Community at Large

Beginning in the 1980s community-based organizations took steps to reach out to youth in providing direct services and social outlets. By the end of the twentieth century every major urban locale, most mid-sized cities, and many small towns formed support groups to respond to the emotional and social needs of LGBT youth. As of 2003 there were more than four thousand such groups nationwide, according to the National Youth Advocacy Center (NYAC). These groups sponsor a wide range of activities, including LGBT and queer proms, lavender graduation ceremonies for high school and college seniors, conferences, field trips, mental health services, and HIV/AIDS counseling. Hundreds of organizations for LGBT and queer youth of color provide similar services in multilingual and ethnically supportive environments.

The College Scene

In 1967 Stephen Donaldson, then a student at Columbia University in New York City, founded the Student Homophile League, the first LGBT student activist group in the country. The next year at Cornell University, students formed the Cornell Student Homophile League. Similar organizations soon cropped up at New York University and the City University of New York. However, it took fifteen years before other colleges and universities began to establish LGBT student groups in large numbers.

College and university students have been at the forefront not only of organizing youth, but also of providing national organizations with energetic volunteers in their grassroots efforts. Although many institutions of higher learning have nondiscrimination policies that include sexual orientation, and some cover gender identity as well, such policies have not necessarily been a guarantee of protection for students. On-campus LGBT and queer organizations have been key in rallying students in times of crisis in the aftermath of homophobic and transphobic harassment. They also serve as crucial support systems and as educational resources for the general student population. Many hold annual "Pride Week" festivals that usually include noted guest speakers, performers, and film showings. In addition, student groups frequently host national organizing conferences.

Although many historically black colleges and universities (HBCU) have been slower to organize LGBT and queer groups, the oldest HBCU, Howard University in Washington, D.C., formed an LGBT group, the Lambda Student Alliance, in 1979. A sizable number of religious schools (with the exception of ultraconservative right-wing Christian schools), especially Jesuit institutions, also have LGBT and queer student groups. As of 2003 seventeen Jesuit colleges and universities had officially recognized LGBT students groups. At predominantly white schools, students of color have formed offshoots of the main LGBT groups in order to create even more supportive environments. In 1990, for example, students at Smith College in Northampton, Massachusetts, founded Prism, a group that provides support and resources for LBT and queer students of color.

In 1986 Washington, D.C., attorney Vernon L. Strickland established a gay fraternity, Delta Lambda Phi (DLP), for gay male students. By 2003 the DLP had eighteen chapters across the country. A lesbian sorority, Lambda Delta Lambda (LDL), came into existence at the University of California at Los Angeles in 1988 and grew to four chapters. However by the turn of the twenty-first century, LDL suffered from a decline in membership and a fluctuating number of chapters.

Secondary Schools

In 1984 HMI, in collaboration with the New York City Board of Education, founded the Harvey Milk High School, the first and largest accredited public school serving the educational needs of LGBT and queer youth. In Dallas, the Walt Whitman Community School, a private school for LGBT and queer youth, was established in 1997.

As the LGBT and queer population became more visible in the late 1980s and 1990s in popular culture, politics, and sports, LGBT and queer youth began coming out publicly at younger ages in high school and many even in middle school. This lowering of the "coming out" age, coupled with an increase in outreach programs for LGBT and queer youth, led to high school students organizing LGBT and queer youth groups in their schools. They are most frequently called the Gay-Straight Alliance (GSA). The first high school GSAs were formed in Massachusetts in 1989 in private schools. Within two years of Matthew Shephard's murder in 1998, which served as a wake-up call to LGBT and queer youth, their parents, and community advocates, six hundred GSAs were established. As of 2003 there were sixteen hundred, according to the Gay, Lesbian, and Straight Education Network (GLSEN). The creation of these organizations has gone smoothly for many students, but significant backlash from the Religious Right has often been a result. However, with the help of the Lambda Legal Defense Fund (LLDF), the American Civil Liberties Union (ACLU), and groups such as GLSEN, most resistance has been met with legal triumphs when students have sued school administrators and school districts for the right to create a GSA. These victories have come about when the ACLU and LLDF have argued successfully that GSAs are permitted under the First Amendment and the federal Equal Access Act.

Groups for At-risk Youth

In large cities, many at-risk LGBT and queer youth who are runaways and/or homeless are members of loose-knit groups that simulate traditional family units. The AIDS epidemic has led social service agencies to reach out to these at-risk youth and organize groups for them, but such services are scarce and only present in large metropolitan areas.

Many black and Latino male and transgender youngsters on the piers of New York City and other major urban centers join "houses," tight-knit groups usually led by an older person. The houses help youngsters navigate the often dangerous streets of hustlers, violence, and prostitution. These houses organize "balls," popular and extravagant fashion performances set to hip-hop and other forms of street music in which the kids perform and compete against each other. These balls and the lives of black and Latino youth on the piers were depicted in filmmaker Jennie Livingston's 1990 documentary *Paris Is Burning*. Vogueing, a type of dance performance showcased at balls, was made popular worldwide in 1993 by pop culture icon Madonna in her song and video "Vogue."

The Internet

As it has done for society at large, the Internet has given LGBT and queer youth innumerable ways of interacting with each other and the larger LGBT and queer community. Youth can now easily find supportive organizations, LGBT and queer youth-oriented publications, and various types of online communities. Politically, the Internet has been an important tool, providing youth with extensive information on grassroots organizing and the legal resources provided by national LGBT and queer organizations.

Bibliography

Buckel, David. Lambda Legal Defense and Education Fund. 1997. "The Equal Access Act: What Does It Mean?" Available from http://www.lambdalegal.org/cgi-bin/iowa/documents/record?record=78

———. Lambda Legal Defense and Education Fund. 1997. "Legal Perspectives on Ensuring a Safe and Nondiscriminatory School Environment for Lesbian, Gay, Bisexual, and Transgendered Students." Available from http://www.lambdalegal.org/cgi-bin/iowa/documents/record?record=706

Evans, Nancy J., and Vernon A. Wall, eds. *Beyond Tolerance: Gays, Lesbians and Bisexuals on Campus*. Alexandria, Va.: American College Personnel Association, 1991.

Faderman, Lillian. *Odd Girls and Twilight Lovers: A History of Lesbian Life in the Twentieth Century*. New York: Penguin, 1992.

Gay, Lesbian and Straight Education Network. 2001. "National School Climate Survey." Available from http://www.glsen.org/binary-data/GLSEN_ARTICLES/pdf_file/1029.pdf

———. 2002. "State of the States 2002: GLSEN's Policy Analysis of Lesbian, Gay, Bisexual and Transgender (LGBT) Safer Schools Issues." Available from http://glsen.org/binary-data/GLSEN_ARTICLES/pdf_file/1397.pdf

Gay, Lesbian and Straight Education Network, and Lambda Legal Defense and Education Fund. 2002. "A Guide to Effective Statewide Laws/Policies: Preventing Discrimination against LGBT Students in K-12 Schools." Available from http://www.lambdalegal.org/binary-data/LAMBDA_PDF/pdf/61.pdf

Herdt, G. "Gay and Lesbian Youth: Emergent Identities and Cultural Scenes at Home and Abroad." *Journal of Homosexuality* 17 (1989): 1–42.

Herdt, G., and A. Boxer. *Children of Horizons: How Gay and Lesbian Youth Are Forging a New Way out of the Closet.* Boston: Beacon Press, 1993.

Ireland, Doug. "Gay Teens Fight Back." *The Nation,* 21 January 2000, 21–23.

Lambda Legal Defense and Education Fund. 2002. "Youth in the Margins: A Report on the Unmet Needs of Lesbian, Gay, Bisexual, and Transgender Adolescents in Foster Care Including a Survey of Fourteen States and Proposals for Reform." Available from http://www.lambdalegal.org/binary-data/LAMBDA_PDF/pdf/27.pdf

McMurtrie, B. "Boston College Expects to Establish Group to Support Gay Students." *The Chronicle of Higher Education,* 21 February 2003, A30.

Savin-Williams, Ritch C. *Gay and Lesbian Youth: Expressions of Identity.* Washington, D.C.: Hemisphere, 1990.

Tuller, David. "A New Dimension in Snapshot of Gay Teenagers." *New York Times,* 24 December 2002, F7.

Woog, Dan. *School's Out: The Impact of Gay and Lesbian Issues on America's Schools.* Boston: Alyson Publications, 1995.

Cheryl L. Coward

See also AMERICAN CIVIL LIBERTIES UNION (ACLU); ASIAN AMERICAN LGBTQ ORGANIZATIONS AND PERIODICALS; COLLEGES AND UNIVERSITIES; GAY, LESBIAN, AND STRAIGHT EDUCATION NETWORK (GLSEN); LAMBDA LEGAL DEFENSE; NORTH AMERICAN MAN/BOY LOVE ASSOCIATION (NAMBLA); SUICIDE.

Z

ZAHARIAS, MILDRED ELLA. see DIDRIKSON, MILDRED ELLA.

ZANE, ARNIE. see JONES, BILL T., AND ARNIE ZANE

ZOOLOGY. see BIOLOGY AND ZOOLOGY.

ZULMA (b. 12 October 1953; d. 1972?), sex worker.

The "nonfiction novel" *Zulma*, written by Elaine Hollingsworth in 1974, is typical of a wave of sensationalist paperbacks about transexuality, which were popular in the United States from the 1950s through the 1970s. Hollingsworth based *Zulma*, however, on tape-recorded interviews with the eponymous narrator, and claims that the book followed the interview transcripts closely. A careful reading of the text makes it clear that Zulma shaped her story with her audience in mind—Hollingsworth was a beautiful, relatively wealthy, white woman and a U.S. citizen, who posed as a social worker in order to secure the interviews in a Tijuana jail—and that Hollingsworth herself, at least through the questions she asked and her editorial practices, then reshaped the story to conform with her professional interest in Hollywood cinema and her ideas about what makes a life interesting (perhaps, too, to make the book more marketable). Nonetheless, read with caution, *Zulma* offers a unique life history of a transgender Mexican migrant sex worker.

Zulma was the name preferred by Miguel (last name unknown), who was born in Acapulco, Mexico, and one of fourteen siblings. His factory-worker father migrated to San Francisco; at age seven, Miguel joined him in California while his siblings stayed behind, as his interest in his sisters' dolls targeted him for bullying. Moving to the United States did not discourage Miguel's femininity: by age nine he was wearing lipstick. He soon began a sexual relationship with a schoolteacher. Zulma described their first encounter as a seduction, but since he was ten at the time, it reads more as a rape. Miguel found sex painful and frightening, at least at first. However, the two-year relationship was useful: Miguel received affection, money, and help with his English. Miguel's feminine self-presentation through dress, makeup, and expressions of sexual desire for men caused conflict with his father, who threatened to kill him. When his mother arrived in California, Miguel worried about bringing shame to his family. So he left home at age twelve.

Miguel ran away to Los Angeles in 1965 and began selling sex in partnership with Phaedra, a white transvestite whose younger brother had befriended Miguel in San Francisco. Phaedra renamed Miguel "Zulma." They begin to work together, selling sex and stealing wallets. Zulma staved off the physical changes of puberty with electrolysis for her face and armpits and silicone for her hips and cheekbones. But she wanted a sex-change operation, which for legal reasons she could not have until she turned eighteen. Hollingsworth writes that the working partnership with Phaedra ended when Zulma was fifteen and Phaedra, having finally gotten her own sex change, moved to Europe.

By then Zulma had built a strong social network in Los Angeles by making friends, selling sex, and finding romantic partners across lines of class, ethnicity, and gender and sexual identities. For example, of the men she called "husband," one preferred to think of Zulma as a man and himself as homosexual, while the other two preferred to think of Zulma as a woman and themselves as straight. Use of this network as a source of information and material support enabled Zulma to avoid prostitution some of the time and, except for two incidents, to escape the physical violence that sex workers often face (although she was once beaten badly enough to require hospitalization). Her ability to survive and earn money easily made her proud, but her success required her to maintain a youthful, feminine look—a source of both anxiety and pleasure for Zulma. At age sixteen she started taking hormones in preparation for a sex-change operation, along with amphetamines to counteract the sleepiness and weight gain associated with estrogen.

By her eighteenth birthday, in 1971, Zulma had found a surgeon in Tijuana, saved enough money for a sex-change operation and breast implants, and completed the requisite psychological counseling and hormone shots. But after an evening spent celebrating her impending operation, Zulma was arrested in Tijuana for drunkenness. She fought back, her biological sex was discovered, and she was sentenced to six months in La Mesa Penitentiary. In La Mesa, Zulma suffered from beatings, rapes, and thefts. She made life tolerable by trading sex for food, shelter, and protection, while earning extra money by keeping house for an American imprisoned for drug possession (in Mexican prisons, wealthier prisoners are permitted to purchase more living space and hire servants).

Elaine Hollingsworth met Zulma while visiting this American. Fascinated by Zulma's stories and charm, Hollingsworth decided to record her life history, hoping to produce a book and a film script. (Prison authorities tolerated Hollingsworth's repeated visits because she convinced them that she was a social worker, although in fact she was an actor whose Hollywood career included ten films.) Hollingsworth finished the interviews a week before Zulma left prison. Zulma planned to return to prostitution until her operation; after that, she dreamed of a life as a Beverly Hills housewife or Acapulco businesswoman. But two weeks after her release in 1972, her body was found, stabbed, in a Tijuana dump. She was eighteen years old.

Hollingsworth published her book two years later, to little notice; her script never found a producer; and the interview tapes disappeared. The nonfiction novel *Zulma* remains the only record of Miguel/Zulma's existence.

Bibliography

Carrillo, Hector. *The Night Is Young: Sexuality in Mexico in the Time of AIDS.* Chicago: University of Chicago Press, 2002.

Hollingsworth, Elaine. *Zulma.* New York: Warner Paperback Library, 1974.

Prieur, Annick. *Mema's House, Mexico City: On Transvestites, Queens, and Machos.* Chicago: University of Chicago Press, 1998.

Stryker, Susan. *Queer Pulp.* San Francisco: Chronicle Books, 2001.

Anne Rubenstein

See also TRANSSEXUALS, TRANSVESTITES, TRANSGENDER PEOPLE, AND CROSS-DRESSERS.

appendix:
repositories with lgbt materials in the u.s. and canada

Established at the 1988 annual meeting of the Society of American Archivists, the Lesbian and Gay Archives Roundtable (LAGAR) helps researchers locate and access sources needed to write about LGBT history. LAGAR also advocates the responsible preservation of relevant documents by encouraging all archival repositories to document LGBT issues that relate to their existing collections and missions. It also encourages people who know about worthy documents to help place them in an appropriate archives.

Creating and maintaining a comprehensive guide to repositories of primary sources on LGBT topics is a crucial service that LAGAR provides. Working from Elizabeth Knowlton's "Documenting the Gay Rights Movement," (*Provenance: Journal of the Society of Georgia Archivists*, v. 5, no. 1, 1987), a 1987 list by the International Association of Lesbian and Gay Archives and Libraries (IALGAL), and a list maintained by LAGAR member Douglas Haller, in 1996 members of LAGAR's Directory Committee (Kim Brookes, Chair; Scott Andrew Bartley, Mimi Bowling, James Cartwright, John Paul Deley, Susan Edwards, Paula Jabloner, Brenda Marston, Mark Martin, Stephen Novack, Nancy Richard, Susan von Salis, and Rich Wandel) made telephone calls, conducted surveys, and followed up with approximately 140 institutions. Detailed data, including contact information, access policies and services for researchers, collection descriptions, and collecting policies, were gathered and in 1998 published online as "Lavender Legacies: Guide to Sources in North America" (http://www.archivists.org/saagroups/lagar/home.htm). An abbreviated and updated version of this appears here as a useful guide to both researchers and potential donors of historical papers, both in the United States and Canada.

The committed group of archivists who volunteered to ensure this 2003 version contained current, accurate information consisted of Cheryl Beredo, Aimee Brown, John Paul Deley, Laura Elizabeth Helton, Stephen Janick, Stephen E. Novak, Deborah A. Richards, and Amy Schindler.

The repositories listed here all maintain non-circulating collections. Most contain unique items such as personal letters, diaries, correspondence, and minutes from organizations. Collections of ephemera (flyers, posters, political buttons, and other objects generally not created with the intention of a long life) and non-circulating collections of printed items, rare books, and pamphlets are also included. The variety of institutions includes state archives, college and university libraries, manuscript repositories, public libraries, and community-run historical societies. Some focus exclusively on LGBT materials; others have a broader focus. In order to be included in this guide, repositories must provide some access to researchers, though the extent of these services varies greatly. Information was accurate as of 2003, and it is recommended to call or check the organization's website for updates and changes.

Brenda Marston

UNITED STATES

CALIFORNIA

AIDS History Project

Location: University of California at San Francisco Library and Center for Knowledge Management
Archives and Special Collections
530 Parnassus Ave.
San Francisco, CA 94143-0840

Telephone: 415-476-8112

Contact: Lisa Mix, Manager, Archives and Special Collections

Email: archives-info@library.ucsf.edu

Website: http://www.library.ucsf.edu/collres/archives/

Collecting areas: Additional phases of the AIDS History Project are currently being considered. A natural area in which the AIDS History Project could expand is documentation of the community research effort.

Bullough Collection on Human Sexuality
Special Collections and Archives

Location: University Library
California State University, Northridge
18111 Nordhoff St.
Northridge, CA 91330-8326

Telephone: 818-677-2597 or 818-677-2832

Contact: Tony Gardner, Curator of Special Collections and Archives

Email: Tony.Gardner@csun.edu

Website: http://library.csun.edu/spcoll/hbspcoll.html

Collecting areas: All areas of human sexuality.

Exodus Trust Archives of Erotology

Location: 1523 Franklin Street
San Francisco, CA 94109

Telephone: 415-928-1133

Contact: Ted McIlvenna

Email: drted@iashs.edu

Website: http://www.iashs.edu/

Collecting areas: Twenty-six specialty libraries which include books, art, film, erotic memorabilia, manuscripts, and dissertations.

Gay, Lesbian, Bisexual, Transgender Historical Society

Location: 657 Mission St., #300
San Francisco, CA 94105

Mailing address: P.O. Box 424280
San Francisco, CA 94142

Telephone: 415-777-5455

Contact: Kim Klausner, Library and Archives Director

Email: archives@glbthistory.org

Website: http://www.glbthistory.org

Collecting areas: Organizational records, personal papers, ephemera, and periodicals relating primarily to the LGBT history and culture of Northern California, but also including material from groups around the world and LGBT life before 1970.

James C. Hormel Gay & Lesbian Center

Location: San Francisco Public Library
100 Larkin Street
San Francisco, CA 94102

Telephone: 415-557-4566

Contact: Jim Van Buskirk, Program Manager

Email: jimv@sfpl.org

Website: http://sfpl4.sfpl.org/glcenter/home.htm
http://sfpl4.sfpl.org/librarylocations/main/glcarchival.htm

Collecting areas: The gay and lesbian collections contain unpublished materials focusing on northern California, while published works are national and international in scope. Particular attention is paid to materials dealing with people of color, people with disabilities, youth, the elderly, and other traditionally under-served groups. Formats include books, magazines, manuscripts, films, videos, photographs, posters, recordings, ephemera, and memorabilia.

June L. Mazer Lesbian Archives

Location: 626 No. Robertson Blvd.
West Hollywood, CA 90069

Telephone: 310-659-2478

Email: mazercoll@earthlink.net

Website: http://www.lesbian.org/mazer

Collecting areas: Throughout California, especially Southern California. Also includes material from other regions throughout the United States, Canada, Europe, Africa, and Asia. The majority of these materials are publications.

Lambda Archives of San Diego

Location: 1010 University Ave., Box 1885
San Diego, CA 92103-3395

Telephone: 619-260-1522

Contact: Sharon Parker, Board president

Email: lghssd@aol.com

Website: http://www-rohan.sdsu.edu/~clgoyne/lghssd/homepage.html

Collecting areas: Emphasis on the history and activities of LGBT people in the San Diego County (California) / Tijuana (Baja California Norte, Mexico) Region. Also includes information on LGBT culture worldwide.

Lavender Library, Archives and Cultural Exchange

Location: 1414 21st Street
Sacramento, CA 95815

Mailing address: P.O. Box 987
Sacramento, CA 95812

Telephone: 916-492-0558

Contact: Michael Colby

Email: sacmwb@pacbell.net

Website: http://www.lavenderlibrary.org

Collecting areas: The collection policy of LLACE is to collect, preserve, and celebrate the history and culture of the LGBT community, with special emphasis on the community in the Sacramento area.

Oakland Museum of California
History Department
Location: 1000 Oak Street
Oakland, CA 94607-4892

Telephone: 510-238-3842

Contact: Aimee Klask

Email: aklask@museumca.org

Website: http://www.museumca.org

Collecting areas: Keeping with the museum's California theme, it has a collection of costumes from the legendary drag performer José Sarria, and material from the annual San Francisco Lesbian, Gay, Bisexual, Transgender Pride Parade. The Museum also collects artifacts from the queer community in California.

ONE Institute and Archives
Location: 909 W Adams Blvd.
Los Angeles, CA 90007

Telephone: 213-741-0094

Contact: Stuart Timmons, Executive Director

Email: askone@oneinstitute.org

Website: http://www.oneinstitute.org/
http://www.oneinstitute.org

Collecting areas: ONE Institute and Archives is international with a special focus on the LGBT history of Los Angeles. ONE also includes the Lesbian Legacy Collection (Yolanda Retter, Curator); the Twice Blessed Jewish LGBT Collection; AIDS History Project; and Performing Arts Collections. (Some of these collections have websites linked to ONE's web address.) Other collection areas include grassroots organizing, particularly the homophile and Gay Liberation Front eras, art and imagery, and LGBT people of color.

San Francisco Performing Arts Library & Museum
Location: 401 Van Ness Ave., Fourth Floor
San Francisco, CA 94102

Telephone: 415-255-4800

Contact: David Humphrey, Director; or Kirsten Tanaka, Head Librarian

Email: Info@sfpalm.org

Website: http://www.sfpalm.org

Collecting areas: History of the performing arts in the San Francisco Bay Area: Dance, Music, Opera, Theater (including mime, puppetry and especially musical theater), and Theatrical Design.

Stanford University
Special Collections
Location: Green Library
557 Escondido Mall
Stanford, CA 94305-6004

Contact: Steven Mandeville-Gamble, Manuscripts, 650-725-3478, stevenmg@sulmail.stanford.edu; John Mustain, Rare Books, 650-725-6964, jmustain@sulmail.stanford.edu; Margaret (Maggie) Kimball, University Archivist, 650-725-1161, mkimball@sulmail.stanford.edu.

Website: http://garamond.stanford.edu/depts/spc/

Collecting areas: Strengths include Mexican American collections; American literary collections from the mid-twentieth century onward; the history of science and technology, and United States history. Collections with gay and lesbian content are acquired as they fit into the main curatorial collecting areas.

University of California
Bancroft Library
Location: Berkeley, CA 94720-6000

Telephone: 510-642-6481

Email: Bancref@library.berkeley.edu

Website: http://bancroft.berkeley.edu/ and http://sunsite.berkeley.edu/gaybears/

Collecting areas: Sexual Orientation and Social Conflict Collection covers the period from the late nineteenth century to the present. While the emphasis is on California and the West, much of the earlier material has a national focus. The Gay Bears! Collection includes oral history interviews with alumni/ae from the 1940s to the present.

University of California, Los Angeles
Department of Special Collections
Location: Charles E. Young Research Library
Room A1713
P.O. Box 951575
Los Angeles, CA 90095-1575

Telephone: 310-825-4988

Contact: Public Services Division

Email: spec-coll@library.ucla.edu

Website: http://www.library.ucla.edu/libraries/special/scweb/

Collecting areas: LGBT materials primarily in support of long-standing collecting areas: local imprints, literature, and culture.

COLORADO

Colorado Historical Society
Stephen H. Hart Library
Location: 1300 Broadway
Denver, CO 80203

Telephone: 303-866-2305

Email: research@chs.state.co.us

Website: http://coloradohistory.org

Collecting areas: Any material related to *Romer v. Evans* (the 1996 Supreme Court case that struck down Colorado's Amendment 2, which prohibited Colorado state government from banning discrimination based on sexual orientation), or to Colorado LGBT history.

Gay, Lesbian, Bisexual, and Transgender Center of Colorado
Terry Mangan Library
Location: 1050 Broadway
Denver, CO 80203

Mailing address: P.O. Box 9798
Denver, CO 80209

Telephone: 303-733-7743

Contact: Leonard Latham

Email: info@coloradoglbt.org

Website: http://coloradoglbt.org

Collecting areas: The Terry Mangan Library is a community library of approximately 5,000 volumes. Holdings include books, periodicals, and primary source material documenting local gay and lesbian history. Donations are accepted.

CONNECTICUT

Gender Equity Archives
Location: Elihu Burritt Library
Central Connecticut State University
1615 Stanley Street
New Britain, CT 06050

Telephone: 860-832-2098 or 860-832-2086

Contact: Francis J. Gagliardi or Ewa Wolynska

Email: gagliardi@ccsu.edu; wolynska@ccsu.edu

Website: http://wilson.ctstateu.edu/lib/archives/equity/

Collecting areas: This collection's mission is to acquire, preserve, and disseminate materials relating to the lesbian, gay, bisexual, and transgender communities in Connecticut. Materials include photographs, journals, diaries, flyers, records of organizations, playbills, postcards, T-shirts, buttons, and gay and lesbian pulp fiction. The archive also collects periodicals from Connecticut, New England, and New York (in this order of priority).

DISTRICT OF COLUMBIA

Rainbow History Project
Mailing address: P.O. Box 11018
Washington, D.C. 20008

Telephone: 202-907-9007

Contact: Mark Meinke, Bruce Pennington, or John Olinger

Email: info@rainbowhistory.org.

Website: http://www.rainbowhistory.org

Collecting areas: Not currently collecting because of a lack of space and archival expertise.

FLORIDA

Stonewall Library & Archives
Location: 1717 N. Andrews Ave.
Fort Lauderdale, FL 33311

Telephone: 954-763-8565

Contacts: Rob Nathans, President; Steve Kerr, Librarian; Paul Fasana, Archivist

Email: info@stonewall-library.org

Website: http://www.stonewall-library.org

Collecting areas: Published and archival materials in all formats relating to lesbian, gay, bisexual, and transgender culture and history, with emphasis on materials relating to the Southeast (east of Houston, Texas, and south of Washington, D.C.)

GEORGIA

Atlanta History Center
Location: 130 West Paces Ferry Road NW
Atlanta, GA 30305

Telephone: 404-814-4040

Email: information@atlantahistorycenter.com
Reference@AtlantaHistoryCenter.com

Website: http://www.atlantahistorycenter.com

Collecting areas: The collection documents the gay and lesbian community in Atlanta. The major holding is the "Atlanta Lesbian and Gay History Thing, 1957–1994," which includes 48.25 cubic feet of gay and lesbian publications from throughout the Southeast, business and organization papers pertaining to gay rights and AIDS, and various personal papers of gay and lesbian activists in Georgia.

IDAHO

Boise State University
Albertsons Library
Location: 1910 University Drive
Boise, ID 83725

Telephone: 208-426-3958

Contact: Alan Virta

Email: avirta@boisestate.edu

Website: http://library.boisestate.edu/special

Collecting areas: Materials documenting history of LGBT people in Idaho.

ILLINOIS

Gerber/Hart Library
Location: 1127 W. Granville Ave.
Chicago, IL 60660

Telephone: 773-381-8030

Email: info@gerberhart.org

Website: http://www.gerberhart.org/

Collecting areas: Personal papers and records of organizations related to the gay, lesbian, bisexual, and transgender community of Chicago, Illinois, and the Midwest region of the United States (Illinois, Indiana, Ohio, Missouri, Kansas, Nebraska, South Dakota, North Dakota, Minnesota, Iowa, Wisconsin, and Michigan).

Leather Archives and Museum
Location: 6418 N. Greenview Ave.
Chicago, IL 60626

Telephone: 773-761-9200

Contact: Rick Storer, Executive Director

Email: archives@leatherarchives.org

Website: http://www.leatherarchives.org

Collecting areas: The policy of the Leather Archives and Museum (LA&M) is to collect and expend its resources in the storage, preservation, restoration and exhibition of the artifacts and evidence of Leather/SM/Fetish lives, lifestyles and organizations, including but not limited to fraternal and commercial organizations, and without regard to sexuality, race, gender, orientation or age-group representation.

Lesbian, Gay, Bisexual and Transgender Religious Archives Network

Location: Chicago Theological Seminary
5757 S. University Avenue
Chicago, IL 60637-1507

Telephone: 773-322-0290

Contacts: Mark Bowman, Project Coordinator; James Carson, Archivist; Doris Malkmus, Archivist

Email: info@lgbtran.org

Website: http://www.lgbtran.org

Collecting areas: The LGBTRAN can best be viewed as a "virtual" archive. It serves a resource for LGBT religious leaders and groups in determining how to preserve their historical records, and provides an information clearinghouse for these archival collections in a central electronic directory for the use of historians, researchers and other interested persons. Extensive information on the history of LGBT religious movements is available on the Web site. This group's overarching purpose is to ensure the preservation and accessibility of the voices and experiences of LGBT religious leaders and organizations.

Northwestern University Library

Charles Deering McCormick Library of Special Collections

Location: 1970 Campus Drive
Evanston, IL 60208-2300

Telephone: 847-491-2895

Contact: Scott Krafft

Email: s-krafft@northwestern.edu

Website: http://www.library.northwestern.edu/spec

Collecting areas: There are some 4,000 women's periodicals including a great many lesbian titles, largely from 1965 to the present. The Women's Monographic Collection contains a wide range of materials on lesbians, including ephemera. The Gay Collection is adding historical periodicals (1930's, 1940's), monographs, and ephemera at an increasing rate.

INDIANA

Kinsey Institute for Research in Sex, Gender, and Reproduction

Location: Morrison Hall 313
Indiana University
Bloomington, IN 47405

Telephone: 812-855-7686

Contacts: Shawn C. Wilson, User Services Coordinator; Catherine Johnson, Curator; Liana Zhou, Head of Library

Email: libknsy@indiana.edu

Website: http://www.kinseyinstitute.org

Collecting areas: The Institute collects scientific and scholarly works relevant to the study of human sexuality, gender, and reproduction; it also seeks to document changing cultural mores regarding sexuality by collecting popular culture materials. Both contemporary and historical items are sought. The library also has a large holding of films and videos, sound recordings, comic books, newspapers and vertical files that are related to LGBT issues and history.

Up The Stairs Community Center Archives and Resource Library

Location: 514 E Washington Blvd.
Fort Wayne, IN 46802-3212

Telephone: 260-422-2450

Email: utslib@hotmail.com

Website: http://www.gayfortwayne.com/utscc/livrary.htm
http://www.gayfortwayne.com/utscc/

Collecting areas: The oldest LGBT collection in Indiana is a free-lending library of over 3,000 circulating items and an archive of local and regional history. The circulating collection is searchable on the website and includes books for children, teens, and adults both in fiction and non-fiction as well as videos, DVDs, and music CDs.

KANSAS

Sunflower Archives, Inc.

Location: P.O. Box 201
Olathe, KS 66051-0201

Telephone: 913-780-3430

Contact: Michael Foubert

Email: Mfarchive@aol.com

Collecting areas: Local gay and lesbian historical materials for the purposes of preservation and research.

KENTUCKY

Williams-Nichols Library and Archive for Gay and Lesbian Studies

Location: University of Louisville
Ekstrom Library, Special Collections
Belknap Campus
Louisville, KY 40292

Contact: 502-852-6762 (Delinda Buie, curator) or 502-636-0935 (David Williams)

Email: KyArchives@aol.com

Collecting areas: National in scope, with special emphasis on LGBT history in Kentucky, Indiana, Ohio, and Tennessee.

LOUISIANA

Tulane Manuscripts Department
Special Collections

Location: Tulane Libraries, Jones Hall
Tulane University
New Orleans, LA 70118

Telephone: 504-865-5685

Contact: Leon C. Miller, Manuscripts Librarian

Email: lmiller@tulane.edu

Website: http://specialcollections.tulane.edu

Collecting areas: The Tulane Manuscripts Department supports Tulane University's mission by acquiring, preserving, and making available records and papers pertaining primarily to the social and cultural development of New Orleans, and secondarily to the state of Louisiana as a whole. Women's studies and LGBT studies are among its primary collection interests.

MASSACHUSETTS

Archive Project

Location: 317 Pleasant St.
Northampton, MA 01060

Telephone: 413-585-0369

Contact: Phil Gauthier, archivist

Email: gokey3@hotmail.com

Collecting areas: The Archive Project's largest focus is the Radical Faerie community in New England. It also has materials relating to the growth of the gay communities of Western Massachusetts, and community and institutional responses to the AIDS crisis.

Bear History Project

Location: Nashoba Institute, Inc.
P.O. Box 926
Fitchburg, MA 01420

Telephone: 978-343-4631

Contact: Les Wright

Email: curator@bearhistory.com

Website: http://www.bearhistory.com

Collecting areas: Bears, gay masculinity, non-hegemonic masculinity, art. The Human Sexuality Collection at Cornell University is this project's archival repository.

Bloom Alternative Press Collection

Location: Amherst College Library
Archives and Special Collections
Amherst College
P.O. Box 5000
Amherst, MA 01002-5000

Telephone: 413-542-2299

Contact: Daria D'Arienzo, Head of Archives and Special Collections

Email: archives@amherst.edu

Website: http://www.amherst.edu/library/archives/

The History Project

Location: 46 Pleasant St.
Cambridge, MA 02139-3838

Contact: Libby Bouvier, Pat Gozemba, Neal Kane

Email: info@historyproject.org

Website: http://www.historyproject.org

Collecting areas: THP collects materials (in all media) which document the Lesbian, Gay, Bisexual and Transgender histories and communities of Boston. It also has a formal agreement with Northeastern University to collaborate in identifying LGBT collections which fit into the NU Archives collecting focus.

Northeastern University Library

Archives and Special Collections Department

Location: 92 Snell Library
360 Huntington Avenue
Boston, MA 02115

Telephone: 617-373-2351

Contact: Joan Krizack, University Archivist and Head, Special Collections Department

Email: archives@neu.edu

Website: http://www.lib.neu.edu/archives

Collecting areas: Northeastern is actively collecting LGBT organizational records.

Schlesinger Library on the History of Women in America

Location: Radcliffe Institute for Advanced Study
10 Garden Street
Cambridge, MA 02138

Telephone: 617-495-8647

Email: slref@radcliffe.edu

Website: http://www.radcliffe.edu/schles

Collecting areas: Anything that falls into the collecting scope will be considered: U.S. women (primarily 19th and 20th century), social activism, social welfare and reform, employment, the professions, suffrage, labor, women's rights, government, politics, education, medicine/health, and the family. LBT collections include Alix Dobkin, Charlotte Bunch, Holly Near, Adrienne Rich, and others.

Sexual Minorities Archives

Location: P.O. Box 60402
Florence, Massachusetts 01062-0402

Telephone: 413-584-7616

Contact: Bet Power, Curator and Director

Email: betpower@yahoo.com

Collecting areas: SMA collects lesbian, gay, bisexual, transgender, intersex, S/M, and fetish literature (books, periodicals, newsletters), history, art, music, personal papers, organizational papers, memorabilia, and ephemera.

Smith College Archives

Location: Alumnae Gymnasium, Smith College
Northampton, MA 01063
Telephone: 413-585-2970

Contact: Nanci Young

Email: nyoung@smith.edu

Website: http://www.smith.edu/libraries/libs/archives

Collecting areas: Contains the records of the Smith Spectrum (formerly known as the Lesbian, Bisexual, Transgender Alliance), 1983–present, and its predecessor organization, the Lesbian Alliance. Other records in the Archives, including letters, journals, diaries, buildings files, photographs, and scrapbooks can assist in illuminating lesbian, bisexual, and transgender life at Smith College.

Sophia Smith Collection
Location: Smith College
Northampton, MA 01063
Telephone: 413-585-2970

Contact: Sherrill Redmon, Director; Amy Hague, Curator; Susan Barker, Admin. Asst.

Email: ssc-wmhist@smith.edu

Website: http://libraries.smith.edu/ssc

Collecting areas: Reproductive rights and birth control, women's rights, the contemporary women's movement, lesbian life and culture, U.S. women working abroad, working women, and women in the labor movement.

MICHIGAN

Lesbian, Gay, Bisexual, and Transgender Materials in Special Collections
Location: Michigan State University Libraries
Special Collections Division
100 Library
East Lansing, MI 48824

Telephone: 517-353-8700

Contact: Peter Berg, Kristine Baclawski, Gerald Paulins, Randall Scott

Email: berg@pilot.msu.edu; baclaws1@msu.cdu, paulins@pilot.msu.edu; scottr@pilot.msu.edu

Website: http://www.lib.msu.edu/coll/main/spec_col/radicalism/glbt/index.htm

Collecting areas: In-depth resource of cross-disciplinary materials representing diverse viewpoints on the construction and development of gender and sexual identities, homosexuality, bisexuality, and related topics. Special attention has been given to the cultural and political experiences of diverse and marginalized groups of people, including particular contributions from people of various sexual identities, especially those from minority groups.

University of Michigan Special Collections Library Labadie Collection
Location: University of Michigan
711 Hatcher Library
Ann Arbor, MI 48109-1205

Telephone: 734-764-9377
Contact: Julie Herrada, Curator

Email: special.collections@umich.edu

Website: http://www.lib.umich.edu/spec-coll/labadie

Collecting areas: In addition to anarchism, the collection's strengths include civil liberties (with an emphasis on racial minorities), socialism, communism, sexual freedom, women's liberation, gay liberation, the underground press, and student protest, among others. Since 2000, the collection also includes the National Transgender Library & Archive. In total the Labadie Collection contains 120 manuscript collections, 1,000 photographs, 50,000 books and 8,000 periodicals (including nearly 800 currently received titles), over 6,000 subject vertical files, and several hundred posters and buttons.

MINNESOTA

Jean-Nickolaus Tretter Collection in GLBT Studies
Location: Special Collections and Rare Books
University of Minnesota Libraries
111 Elmer L. Andersen Library
222 21st Ave. S.
Minneapolis, MN 55455

Telephone: 612-624-7526

Contact: Jean-Nickolaus Tretter

Email: trett007@umn.edu

Website: http://www.trettercollection.org

Collecting areas: The University of Minnesota Libraries have assumed responsibility for the materials and are willing and able to assume curatorial responsibility for additional materials as collected or donated. Additionally, the Schochet Center for GLBT Studies at the University of Minnesota (http://www.glbt studies.umn.edu/) will help build the collection with donated materials, as well as offer some financial support for acquisitions.

Minnesota Historical Society
Location: 345 Kellogg Blvd. West
St. Paul, MN 55102-1906

Telephone: 651-296-2143, 651-296-2620

Contact: Kathryn Otto, Head of Reference

Email: reference@mnhs.org; craig.wright@mnhs.org

Website: http://www.mnhs.org/library/search/index.html

Collecting areas: Materials relating directly to Minnesota.

Quatrefoil Library
Location: 1619 Dayton Avenue
St. Paul, MN 55104

Telephone: 651-641-0969

Contact: Kathy Robbins

Email: quatrefoillibrary@yahoo.com

Website: http://www.qlibrary.org

Collecting areas: The Quatrefoil Library houses published LGBT materials, including books, newspapers, magazines, newsletters, videos, DVDs, audiocassettes, and CDs.

NEVADA

Las Vegas Gay Archives

Location: University of Nevada at Las Vegas
Special Collections
4505 Maryland Pkwy
Box 457010
Las Vegas, NV 89154-7010

Telephone: 702-895-2234

Contact: Su Kim Chung, Manuscripts Librarian

Email: skchung@unlv.edu

Website: http://www.library.unlv.edu/speccol/index.html

Collecting areas: The Las Vegas Gay Archives represent one of the collecting initiatives within the manuscripts section of UNLV Special Collections. They include personal papers and organizational records of notable figures, organizations, and businesses in the Las Vegas gay community. The collection is supported by a number of rare monographs and journals that chronicle gay history and the development of the gay community in the United States.

NEW JERSEY

Rutgers Special Collections and University Archives

Location: Rutgers University Libraries
169 College Avenue
New Brunswick, NJ 08901-1163

Telephone: 32-932-7006

Contact: David Kuzma, Reference Archivist

Email: kuzmadav@rci.rutgers.edu

Website: http://www.libraries.rutgers.edu/rul/libs/scua/scua.shtml

Collecting areas: History of New Jersey and Rutgers University. Includes materials from statewide and regional LGBT organizations, as well as those of Rutgers.

NEW YORK

Black Gay and Lesbian Archive Project

Location: 12 West 130th Street, #3
New York, NY 10037

Telephone: 212-491-2226

Contact: Steven G. Fullwood, Project Director

Email: bglanyc@yahoo.com

Collecting areas: Materials produced by and about lesbian, gay, bisexual, transgender, same-gender-loving, queer, questioning, and "in-the-life" people of African descent, nationally and internationally. Formats include audiotapes, books, broadsides, dramatic works, film, flyers, journals, magazines, monographs, newsletters, newspapers, organizational records, palm cards, pamphlets, photographs, poetry, posters, prints, slides, and video.

Human Sexuality Collection

Location: Cornell University
2B Carl A. Kroch Library
Ithaca, NY 14853

Telephone: 607-255-3530

Contact: Brenda J. Marston

Email: bjm4@cornell.edu

Website: http://rmc.library.cornell.edu/HSC/

Collecting areas: The Human Sexuality Collection seeks to preserve and make accessible primary sources that document historical shifts in the social construction of sexuality, with a focus on U.S. lesbian and gay history, bisexual and transgender issues and individuals, and the politics of pornography. The Collection is actively expanding and seeks especially gifts of personal papers, organizational records, rare books, and periodicals that document marginalized groups. Through this program, Cornell University is working to ensure that a more complete historical record of sexuality and gender will be available to researchers.

National Archive of Lesbian, Gay, Bisexual, and Transgender History

Location: Lesbian, Gay, Bisexual, and Transgender Community Center
208 West 13th Street
New York, NY 10011

Telephone: 212-620-7310

Contacts: Rich Wandel, Archivist/Historian

Email: archive@gaycenter.org

Website: http://www.gaycenter.org/archives/index.htm

Collecting areas: The Archive collects LGBT materials from all times and places, and in all forms except books. The center has a separately operating lending library that does accept books.

Lesbian Herstory Archives

Mailing address: LHEF, Inc.
P.O. Box 1258
New York, NY 10116

Contact: Deborah Edel, Co-Coordinator

Telephone: 718-768-DYKE (3953)

Website: http://www.lesbianherstoryarchives.org/

Collecting areas: All aspects of lesbian history and culture (international in scope). The Lesbian Herstory Archives collects and preserves any materials that are relevant to the lives and experiences of lesbians: books, magazines, journals, news clippings (from establishment, feminist or lesbian media), bibliographies, photos, historical information, tapes, films, diaries, oral histories, poetry and prose, biographies, autobiographies, notices of events, posters, graphics, and other memorabilia. Appointments must be made prior to visits.

The New York Public Library

Location: Manuscripts and Archives Division
Humanities and Social Sciences Library
Fifth Avenue and 42nd Street, Room 324
New York, NY 10018-2788

Telephone: Reference: 212-930-0801; Curator: 212-930-0804

Contact: William Stingone, Curator of Manuscripts

Email: Reference: mssref@nypl.org;
Curator: wstingone@nypl.org

Website: http://www.nypl.org (parent); http://www.nypl.org/research/chss/spe/rbk/igic.html (LGBT info); http://www.nypl.org/research/chss/spe/rbk/mss.html (divisional information, including some finding aids).

Collecting areas: Personal papers, organizational records, and ephemera, particularly from New York and the Northeast region of the United States.

Pat Parker/Vito Russo Center Library

Location: The Lesbian, Gay, Bisexual, and Transgender Community Center
208 West 13th Street
New York, NY 10011

Telephone: 212-620-7310

Contact: Librarian

Email: library@gaycenter.org

Website: http://www.gaycenter.org/library

Collecting areas: The Pat Parker/Vito Russo Center Library is New York's largest lending library of LGBT material, including over 12,000 circulating titles of fiction and non-fiction and over 600 circulating videos by, about, or of interest to the LGBT community.

Schomburg Center for Research in Black Culture

Location: The New York Public Library
515 Malcolm X Boulevard
New York, NY 10037-1801

Contact: Diana Lachatanere

Telephone: 212-491-2225

Email: scmarbref@nypl.org

Website: http://www.nypl.org/research/sc/sc.html

Collecting areas: Black gay and lesbian life, any time period, geographical area, all formats.

Tamiment Library & Robert F. Wagner Labor Archives

Location: New York University
70 Washington Square South
New York, NY 10012

Telephone: 212-998-2630

Contact: Gail Malmgreen, Associate Head for Archival Collections

Email: gail.malmgreen@nyu.edu

Website: http://www.nyu.edu/library/bobst/research/tam

Collection areas: This archive documents American radical, labor, and progressive social movements. Includes material related to LGBT trade unionists, activists, and organizations, including the Gay and Lesbian Labor Network, Leslie Cagan, Connie Kopelov, and the Out At Work Collection.

NORTH CAROLINA

Duke University
Rare Book, Manuscript, and Special Collections Library
Mailing address: P.O. Box 90185
Durham, NC 27708

Telephone: 919-660-5828

Contact: Laura Micham

Email: laura.m@duke.edu; cwhc@duke.edu; special-collections@duke.edu

Website: http://scriptorium.lib.duke.edu/specoll
http://scriptorium.lib.duke.edu/

Collecting areas: LGBT activism and literature, including a lesbian and gay pulp fiction collection

OHIO

Northeast Ohio Lesbian/Gay Archives
Location: Western Reserve Historical Society
10825 East Blvd.
Cleveland, OH 44106

Telephone: 216-721-5722

Contacts: Curator of Manuscripts for collection development; Reference for reference access

Email: reference@wrhs.org

Website: http://www.wrhs.org

Collecting areas: This archive collects personal papers, organizational records, and publications of the Ohio counties Loraine, Medina, Cuyahoga, Lake, Geauga, and Ashtabula.

Oberlin College Archives
Location: 420 Mudd Center
Oberlin, OH 44074
Telephone: 440-775-8014

Contact: Roland M. Baumann

Email: Archives.Office@oberlin.edu

Website: www.oberlin.edu/archive/

Collecting areas: The College Archives acquires documentary material that reports on the sexual orientation subcommittee of the student body and the Alumni Association. It also collects the personal papers of artists, faculty, staff, and graduates. Of principal importance are the records of the Lesbian, Gay, Bisexual, Transgendered Union (LGBTU), 1971–2000; Oberlin Lambda Alumni (OLA), 1987–2000, a self-defined group under the Oberlin Alumni Association; Papers of John Young '83, 1979–2001; Papers of Jan Cooper, 1987–1997; and Papers of Joseph Plaster, 1999–2000; plus various files regarding sexual orientation and intense relationships with the same sex in established institutional record groups.

Ohio Lesbian Archives
Location: P.O. Box 20075
Cincinnati, Ohio 45220

Telephone: 513-541-1917 (2)

Contact: Karen Phebe Beiser or Victoria Ramstetter

Email: ohiolesbianarchives@yahoo.com

Website: http://www.geocities.com/ohiolesbianarchives

Collection area: The Ohio Lesbian Archives collects lesbian materials relating to the Cincinnati tri-state area.

Popular Culture Library

Location: Bowling Green State University
Jerome Library, 4th Floor
Bowling Green, OH 43403

Telephone: 419-372-2450

Contact: Colleen Warner

Email: pcldesk@bgnet.bgsu.edu

Collecting areas: Major subject strengths of the Popular Culture Library include: popular fiction in the romance, mystery, science fiction, western, and adventure genres, the performing arts and entertainment industry, the graphic arts and mass communications, foodways and cookery, sports, recreation and travel, popular religion and the supernatural, teen culture and counterculture, folklore, and wit and humor.

OREGON

Oregon Historical Society

Location: 1200 SW Park Avenue
Portland, OR 97205-2483

Telephone: 503-306-5240

Contact: Library Reference

Email address: libreference@ohs.org

Website: http://www.ohs.org

Collecting area: Materials related to Oregon and the Pacific Northwest.

University of Oregon
Division of Special Collections and University Archives

Location: Knight Library
Eugene, Oregon 97403-1299

Telephone: 541-346-1906

Contact: Linda Long

Email: llong@oregon.uoregon.edu

Website: http://libweb.uoregon.edu/speccoll/index.html

Collecting areas: The Division of Special Collections and University Archives seeks to support graduate and faculty research, stimulate undergraduate instruction on the University of Oregon campus, and to respond to the needs of scholars by collecting, preserving, and providing access to primary source materials on lesbian, gay, bisexual, and transgender studies. A particular focus is the development of archival records and personal papers relating to the rich history of lesbian communities in Oregon.

PENNSYLVANIA

Gay, Lesbian, Bisexual, and Transgender Library/Archives of Philadelphia

Location: William Way LGBT Community Center
1315 Spruce St.
Philadelphia, PA 19107

Telephone: 215-732-2220

Email: williamwaylibrary@yahoo.com

Website: http://www.waygay.org

Collecting areas: The Library/Archives collects publications, organizational and personal papers, business records, audiovisual materials, and ephemera created by, dealing with, or of special interest to gay men, lesbians, bisexual men and women, and transgender individuals. As a secondary focus, it collects selected works about feminism and feminist organizations. The collections include materials from around the world.

Temple University Special Collections

Location: Paley Library
Philadelphia, PA 19122

Telephone: 215-204-8230

Contact: Thomas M. Whitehead

Email: whitetm@astro.ocis.temple.edu

Website: http://www.library.temple.edu/speccoll/

Collecting areas: Collecting gay and lesbian printed and manuscript materials in the Contemporary Culture Collection, a unit of Special Collections Department. The most extensive archival collection is the archives of PLGTF (Philadelphia Lesbian and Gay Task Force).

University of Pennsylvania Archives and Records Center

Location: North Arcade
Franklin Field
Philadelphia, PA 19104-6320

Telephone: 215-898-7025

Contact: Amey Hutchins, Public Services Archivist

Email: uarc@pobox.upenn.edu

Website: http://www.archives.upenn.edu

Collecting areas: Materials that relate to the university and to the university community.

RHODE ISLAND

Brown University The John Hay Library

Mailing address: Box A
Providence, RI 02912

Telephone: 401-863-1514

Contact: Rosemary L. Cullen

Email: Rosemary_Cullen@brown.edu

Website: http://www.brown.edu/Facilities/University_Library/libs/hay/index.html

Collecting areas: Literary works relating to gays and lesbians, with a small component of history and sociology; left- and right-wing pamphlet collections and manuscript collections of individuals and organizations such as ACT UP/RI. Particular interests include pre-Stonewall literature, and gay men's pulp fiction erotica.

TEXAS

Archives of the Episcopal Church

Mailing address: P.O. Box 2247
Austin, TX 78768

Telephone: 512-472-6816

Contact: Mark J. Duffy, Director

Email: research@episcopalarchives.org

Website: http://www.episcopalarchives.org

Collecting areas: Records of prominent Episcopal organizations and individuals involved in LGBT ministry, and issues of full recognition.

Archives for Research on Women and Gender Project

Location: University of Texas at San Antonio
Archives Department
801 South Bowie St.
San Antonio, TX 78205-3296

Telephone: 210-458-2381

Email: archives@utsa.edu

Website: http://www.lib.utsa.edu/Archives

Collecting areas: The archives actively collects materials related to women and gender in South Texas. Gay, lesbian, bisexual, and transgender persons and organizations are included in this collecting focus. The Archives does not accept textiles, paintings, or monotypes in oil or any other media, or large artifacts that require specialized housing. It is best equipped to preserve paper and photographic media, and small ephemera items.

Charles Botts Memorial Archives
Resurrection Metropolitan Community Church

Location: 2025 West 11th
Houston, TX 77008

Telephone: 713-861-9149

Contact: Ralph Lasher

Email: mccr@airmail.net

Website: http://www.resurrectionmcc.org

Collecting areas: Wealth of gay and lesbian literature dating back to the 19th century and a large collection of letters, brochures, clippings, books, periodicals, and newspapers from and about the LGBT community in Houston and throughout the world.

Gulf Coast Archive and Museum of Gay, Lesbian, Bisexual and Transgender History, Inc.

Mailing address: P.O. Box 130192
Houston, TX 77219

Telephone: 713-227-5973

Contact: Bruce Reeves or Judy Reeves

Email: info@gcam.org

Website: http://www.gcam.org

Collecting areas: Collects any LGBT materials, including erotica, but the focus is the Gulf Coast.

HAPPY Foundation

Location: 411 Bonham
San Antonio, TX 78205

Telephone: 210-227-6451

Contact: Gene Elder

Collecting areas: Texas LGBT history.

Resource Center of Dallas

Location: 2701 Reagan
Dallas, TX 75219

Telephone: 214-540-4451

Contact: Nicole Pool, Librarian

Email: library@resourcecenterdallas.org

Website: http://www.resourcecenterdallas.org

Collecting areas: The library has about 5,000 monographic titles which are predominantly gay- and lesbian-oriented. There are some archival materials which might be of historical interest to the gay and lesbian community for north Texas, but the material is not cataloged or organized in any systematic way.

University of Texas at Austin
Harry Ransom Humanities Research Center

Mailing address: Attn: Office of Research Librarian
P.O. Box 7219
Austin, TX 78713

Telephone: 512-471-9119

Contact: Tara Wenger

Email: reference@hrc.utexas.edu

Website: http://www.hrc.utexas.edu

Collecting areas: The Ransom Center collects British, French, and American literary manuscripts. A few collections of note are Radclyffe Hall and Oscar Wilde.

Woman's Collection
Texas Woman's University Libraries

Mailing address: P.O. Box 425528
Denton, TX 76204-5528

Telephone: 940-898-3754

Contact: Dawn Letson

Email: womansc@twu.edu

Website: http://venus.twu.edu/www/twu/library/wmcopy.html
http://www.twu.edu/library

Collecting areas: Texas women and Texas women's organizations only.

WASHINGTON

Northwest Lesbian and Gay History Museum Project

Location: 1122 East Pike Street
PMB #797
Seattle, WA 98122

Telephone: 206-903-9517

Contact: Ruth Pettis

Email: gayhistnw@aol.com

Website: http://home.earthlink.net/~ruthpett/lgbthistorynw/index.htm

Collecting areas: The Northwest Lesbian and Gay History Museum Project conducts oral histories with members of the local and regional LGBT population and their supporters. It collects images of venues, people, and events associated with local/regional LGBT history, and does limited collecting of flyers, posters, newsletters, and other documents.

University of Washington Libraries Manuscripts, Special Collections, and Archives
Mailing address: P.O. Box 352900
Seattle, WA 98195

Contact: Karyl Winn, Curator of Manuscripts (for papers and records of non-University individuals and organizations); Nicolette Bromberg, Curator of Photographs and Graphics; John Paul Deley, University Archivist (for University records, including those of student groups; faculty papers)

Telephone: 206-543-1929

Email: mssarch@u.washington.edu (for textual archives matters); photos@u.washington.edu (for photo archives matters)

Website: http://www.lib.washington.edu/SpecialColl/

Collecting areas: Late twentieth-century papers, records, and photographs of and about sexual minorities in the Greater Seattle area, Western Washington, and at the University of Washington; photographs also cover early twentieth-century subjects.

Western Washington University
Center for Pacific NW Studies
Goltz-Murray Archives
Location: Bellingham, WA 98225

Telephone: 360-650-7747

Contact: Elizabeth Joffrion

Email: elizabeth.joffrion@wwu.edu

Website: http://www.acadweb.wwu.edu/cpnws

Collecting areas: Collections focus on organizations and individuals in the Pacific Northwest, including the band Motherlode and Hands Off Washington. The archive also collects materials of Bellingham and WWU groups.

WISCONSIN

Marquette University
Department of Special Collections and
University Archives
Mailing address: 1415 W. Wisconsin Ave.
P.O. Box 3141
Milwaukee, WI 53201-3141

Contact: Phil Runkel, Archivist

Telephone: 414-288-7256

Email: Phil.Runkel@marquette.edu

Website: http://www.marquette.edu/library/collections/archives/index.html

Collecting areas: Marquette solicits national records and personal papers documenting the involvement of Catholic organizations, movements, and individuals in promoting social action and social change in gay and lesbian rights and women's rights, among many other areas.

Wisconsin State Historical Society
Location: 816 State St.
Madison, WI 53706

Telephone: 608-264-6460

Email: archref@whs.wisc.edu

Website: http://www.wisconsinhistory.org/archives/index.html

Collecting areas: The Society collects mass communication, film and theater research, social action collections, public records of state and local government, maps, labor, and broadcasting, particular to Wisconsin and the trans-Allegheny West.

CANADA

NOVA SCOTIA

Nova Scotia Archives and Records Management
Location: 6016 University Avenue
Halifax, NS B3H 1W4

Telephone: 902-424-6055

Contact: Reference and Retrieval Staff

Email: nsarm@gov.ns.ca

Website: http://www.gov.ns.ca/nsarm

Collecting areas: Nova Scotia Archives and Records Management acquires government and private-sector records of provincial significance.

ONTARIO

Hamilton-Wentworth Lesbian and Gay Archives
Location: 230 Caroline Street South
Hamilton, ON L8P 3L4

Telephone: 905-528-0156

Contact: Michael Johnstone

Email: michael.johnstone@sympatico.ca

Collecting areas: Contemporary and historic material relating to the lives of lesbians and gays in the Hamilton and Southern Ontario area, including newsletters, photographs, and audiovisual material.

SASKATCHEWAN

Saskatchewan Archives Board
Location: Room 91, Murray Building
University of Saskatchewan
3 Campus Drive
Saskatoon, SK S7N 5A4

Telephone: 306-933-5832

Contact: Reference Archivist

Email: info.saskatoon@archives.gov.sk.ca

Website: www.saskarchives.com

Collecting areas: History of the province of Saskatchewan. Includes two significant fonds related to LGBT history: the Neil Richards fonds and the Douglas Wilson fonds.

systematic outline of contents

This systemic outline provides a framework for the *Encyclopedia*, providing a general overview of the conceptual scheme and directing readers to those entries associated with particular subjects of interest. The outline is divided into thirteen categories and fourteen sub-categories.

1. People
   Artists (Film, Radio, Television, Music, Dance, Visual Arts)
   Athletes
   Colonial and Revolutionary War Figures
   Movement Activists
   Other Historical Figures
   Political, Educational, Reform, and Religious Figures
   Scientists, Sexologists, and Social Scientists
   Writers
2. Politics
   LGBTQ Movement Events
   LGBTQ Movement Organizations
   LGBTQ Movements
   LGBTQ Publishing, Publications, and Presses
   Social Movements, Political Parties, and Elections
   Scandals and Witchhunts
3. Culture and Arts
4. Academic Disciplines and Fields of Inquiry
5. Identities, Communities, and Cultures
6. Geographies

7. Law and Public Policy
8. Economics and Labor
9. Sex, Sexuality, Intimacy, and Relationships
10. Religion and Spirituality
11. Language, Symbols, Signs, and Concepts
12. Social Life, Issues, and Institutions
13. Social, Cultural, and Political Processes

Because the section headings are not mutually exclusive, certain entries are repeated in more than one section.

1. PEOPLE

Artists (Film, Radio, Television, Music, Dance, Visual Arts)
Ailey, Alvin
Anger, Kenneth
Arzner, Dorothy
Austen, Alice
Baca, Judy
Baker, Josephine
Barber, Samuel, and Gian Carlo Menotti
Bennett, Michael
Bentley, Gladys
Bernstein, Leonard
Bourbon, Ray (Rae)
Brooks, Romaine
Cadmus, Paul
Cage, John
Chambers, Jane
Copland, Aaron
Cukor, George

Cunningham, Merce
Cushman, Charlotte
Demuth, Charles
Eakins, Thomas
Eichelberger, Ethyl
Eltinge, Julian
Fierstein, Harvey
Haring, Keith
Hart, Lorenz
Hartley, Marsden
Hockney, David
Hunter, Alberta
Joffrey, Robert
Johns, Jasper
Jorgensen, Christine
Jones, Bill T., and Arnie Zane
Kirstein, Lincoln
Klah, Hastíín
Klumpke, Anna
Liberace
Lynes, George Platt
Mapplethorpe, Robert
Mizer, Robert
Oliveros, Pauline
Porter, Cole
Rainey, Ma
Rauschenberg, Robert
Reyes, Rodrigo
Riggs, Marlon
Ritts, Herb
Robbins, Jerome
Rorem, Ned
Sarria, José
Shawn, Ted
Smith, Bessie
Sondheim, Stephen
Strayhorn, Billy
Tavera, Hank

Fierstein, Harvey
Ford, Charles Henri
Fornes, Maria Irene
Foster, Jeannette
Fugate, James Barr
Gidlow, Elsa
Gilman, Charlotte Perkins
Ginsberg, Allen
Goodman, Paul
Grahn, Judy
Grimké, Angelina Weld
Gunn, Thom
H.D.
Hansberry, Lorraine
Hart, Alan
Hart, Lorenz
Hemphill, Essex
Highsmith, Patricia
Hughes, Langston
Isherwood, Christopher
Islas, Arturo
Jewett, Sarah Orne
Johnston, Jill
Kenny, Maurice
Kim, Willyce
Kirstein, Lincoln
Kramer, Larry
Le Guin, Ursula K.
Lobdell, Lucy Ann
Locke, Alain
Lorde, Audre
Ludlam, Charles
Matthiessen, F. O.
Maupin, Armistead
McCullers, Carson
McKay, Claude
McNally, Terrence
Millay, Edna St. Vincent
Millett, Kate
Monette, Paul
Moraga, Cherríe
Niles, Blair
Nin, Anaïs
Noda, Barbara
Nugent, Richard Bruce
O'Hara, Frank
Parker, Pat
Piñero, Miguel
Poma, Edgar
Preston, John
Prime-Stevenson, Edward I.
Ramos Otero, Manuel
Rechy, John
Reyes, Rodrigo
Rich, Adrienne
Rorem, Ned
Rule, Jane
Russo, Vito
Sánchez, Luis Rafael
Sarton, May
Shockley, Ann Allen
Smith, Barbara

Smith, Lillian
Stein, Gertrude, and Alice B. Toklas
Stoddard, Charles Warren
Taylor, Valerie
Thurman, Wallace
Tsui, Kitty
Van Vechten, Carl
Vidal, Gore
White, Edmund
Whitman, Walt
Wilhelm, Gale
Williams, Tennessee
Wilson, Lanford
Woo, Merle
Yourcenar, Marguerite

2. POLITICS

LGBTQ Movement Events
Homophile Movement
  Demonstrations
Marches on Washington
Pride Marches and Parades
Stonewall Riots

LGBTQ Movement Organizations
African American LGBTQ
  Organizations and Periodicals
AIDS Coalition to Unleash Power
  (ACT UP)
AIDS Memorial Quilt—NAMES
  Project
AIDS Service Organizations
American Civil Liberties Union
  (ACLU)
Asian American LGBTQ
  Organizations and Periodicals
Bisexuality, Bisexuals, and Bisexual
  Movements
Black and White Men Together
  (BWMT)
Center for Lesbian and Gay Studies
  (CLAGS)
Churches, Temples, and Religious
  Groups
Combahee River Collective
Community Centers
Daughters of Bilitis
Disability, Disabled People, and
  Disability Movements
Erickson Educational Foundation
Furies
Gay Activists Alliance
Gay and Lesbian Alliance Against
  Defamation (GLAAD)
Gay Liberation Front
Gay, Lesbian, and Straight Education
  Network (GLSEN)
History Projects, Libraries, and
  Archives
Human Rights Campaign
Janus Society
Lambda Legal Defense

Latina and Latino LGBTQ
  Organizations and Periodicals
Lesbian Avengers
Lesbian Herstory Archives
Mattachine Society
National Gay and Lesbian Task Force
  (NGLTF)
Native American LGBTQ
  Organizations and Periodicals
North American Man/Boy Love
  Association (NAMBLA)
ONE Institute
Parents, Families, and Friends of
  Lesbians and Gays (PFLAG)
Queer Nation
Radical Faeries
Radicalesbians
Samois
Society for Human Rights
Society for Individual Rights
Third World Gay Revolution
Transgender Organizations and
  Periodicals
Youth and Youth Groups

LGBTQ Movements
Gay Liberation
Homophile Movement
Lesbian Feminism

LGBTQ Publishing, Publications, and Presses
Advocate
Drum
Gay Community News
Homophile Press
Ladder
Lesbian Connection
Mattachine Review
Newspapers and Magazines
ONE
Physique Magazines and
  Photographs
Publishers
Pulp Fiction: Gay
Pulp Fiction: Lesbian

Social Movements, Political Parties, and Elections
Anarchism, Socialism, and
  Communism
Antiwar, Pacifist, and Peace
  Movements
Democratic Party
Electoral Politics
Environmental and Ecology
  Movements
Feminism
Labor Movements and Labor Unions
New Left and Student Movements
New Right
Poor People's Movements
Republican Party

directory of contributors

Julie Abraham
Emory University
   Literature: 1969–Present

Brett L. Abrams
American University, Washington,
D.C.
   Icons
   Liberace
   Waters, John

Barry D. Adam
University of Windsor
   Monogamy and Nonmonogamy

Katherine Adams
University of Tulsa
   Brown, Rita Mae

Mary Louise Adams
Queen's University, Kingston,
Ontario
   Shawn, Ted

Pam Edwards Allara
Brandeis University
   Demuth, Charles

Rebecca T. Alpert
Temple University
   Anti-Semitism
   Jews and Judaism

Edward Alwood
Quinnipiac University
   Mattachine Review
   Gay and Lesbian Alliance Against
   Defamation (GLAAD)

Paul Attinello
University of Newcastle upon Tyne
   Choruses and Bands
   Music Studies and Musicology

David S. Azzolina
University of Pennsylvania
   Drum
   Philadelphia

Lee Badgett
University of Massachusetts,
Amherst
   Boycotts
   Economics

Holly A. Baggett
Southwest Missouri State University
   Anderson, Margaret, and Jane
   Heap

Jane R. Ballinger
California State Polytechnic
University, Pomona
   Lesbian Connection
   Newspapers and Magazines

André Balog
Graduate Center of the City
University of New York
   Stein, Gertrude, and Alice B.
   Toklas

Aryana Bates
College of New Jersey
   African American Religion and
   Spirituality
   Race and Racism
   Women's Studies and Feminist
   Studies

Joseph Bean
Kahului, Hawaii
   Leathersex and Sexuality

Irenee R. Beattie
Ohio State University
   Marriage Ceremonies and
   Weddings

Rodger L. Beatty
University of Pittsburgh
   Health and Health Care Law and
   Policy

David P. Becker
Portland, Maine
   Hartley, Marsden

Brett Beemyn
Ohio State University
   Bisexuality, Bisexuals, and
   Bisexual Movements
   Grimké, Angelina Weld
   Walker, A'Lelia

Pablo Ben
University of Chicago
   Intersexuals and Intersexed People
   Le Guin, Ursula K.

James J. Berg
Minnesota State Colleges and
Universities
   Isherwood, Christopher

Michael H. Berglund
University of Tulsa
   Cather, Willa
   Dickinson, Emily

Emily Bernard
University of Vermont
  Hughes, Langston
  Van Vechten, Carl

Linda A. Bernhard
Ohio State University
  Health, Health Care, and Health
    Clinics

Amy Beth
Lesbian Herstory Archives
  Lesbian Herstory Archives

Evelyn Blackwood
Purdue University
  Two-Spirit Females

Warren J. Blumenfeld
Colgate University
  Stereotypes

Peter Boag
University of Colorado at Boulder
  Portland, Oregon
  Seattle

Michael Borgstrom
University of California, Davis
  Slavery and Emancipation

Danielle Bouchard
University of Minnesota
  Film and Video Studies

Libby Bouvier
*The History Project Documenting
LGBT Boston*
  Boston

Angela Bowen
*California State University, Long
Beach*
  Combahee River Collective
  Cornwell, Anita
  Lorde, Audre

Nan Alamilla Boyd
Sonoma State University
  San Francisco
  Society for Individual Rights

Jeanne Boydston
University of Wisconsin, Madison
  Smashes and Chumming

Stacy L. Braukman
*Radcliffe Institute for Advanced
Study, Harvard University*
  Cohn, Roy
  Government and Military
    Witchhunts
  Hay, Harry

Jennifer Brier
University of Illinois at Chicago
  AIDS and People with AIDS
  AIDS Service Organizations

Patricia M. Broderick
Boston College
  Colleges and Universities

Michael Bronski
*Independent Scholar and Journalist,
Cambridge, Massachusetts*
  Pornography
  Preston, John
  Pulp Fiction: Gay

Kathleen M. Brown
University of Pennsylvania
  Hall, Thomasine/Thomas

Robin Jarvis Brownlie
University of Manitoba
  Brant, Beth
  Masahai Amatkwisai
  Native American LGBTQ
    Organizations and Periodicals
  Qánqon-Kámek-Klaúla

Chris Bull
The Advocate
  Goodstein, David

Vern Bullough
*Independent Scholar, Westlake
Village, California*
  Prime-Stevenson, Edward I.
  Sexually Transmitted Diseases
  Situational Homosexuality

Richard Burns
*The Lesbian, Gay, Bisexual and
Transgender Community Center,
New York*
  Community Centers

Sean Cahill
*National Gay and Lesbian Task
Force*
  Antidiscrimination Law and
    Policy
  Education Law and Policy

Patricia A. Cain
University of Iowa College of Law
  Lambda Legal Defense
  Liquor Control Law and Policy
  Privacy and Privacy Rights

Paul D. Cain
Independent Scholar, Reno, Nevada
  Grier, Barbara
  Kopay, David
  Shelley, Martha
  Waddell, Tom

Patrick Califia
*Independent Scholar and Writer,
San Francisco*
  Androgyny

  Sadomasochism, Sadists, and
    Masochists
  Sex Acts
  Sex Clubs
  Suicide

Debra Campbell
Colby College
  Daly, Mary

Christopher Capozzola
*Massachusetts Institute of
Technology*
  AIDS Memorial Quilt–NAMES
    Project
  Walsh, David
  Welles, Sumner

Steven Capsuto
*Gay, Lesbian, Bisexual &
Transgender Archives of
Philadelphia, William Way
Community Center*
  Advocate
  Comedy and Humor
  Gittings, Barbara, and Kay Tobin
    Lahusen
  Homophile Press
  Television

Jane Caputi
Florida Atlantic University
  Radical Spirituality and New Age
    Religion

Peter Carpenter
University of California, Los Angeles
  Cunningham, Merce
  Dance

James P. Cassaro
University of Pittsburgh
  Sondheim, Stephen

Susan E. Cayleff
San Diego State University
  Didrikson, Mildred Ella
  King, Billie Jean

Anne Charles
University of New Orleans
  Barnes, Djuna

Elise Chenier
McGill University
  Bars, Clubs, and Restaurants
  Prisons, Jails, and Reformatories:
    Men's
  Sexual Psychopath Law and Policy

Randall Cherry
Paris, France
  Waters, Ethel

Saralyn Chesnut
Emory University
Atlanta
Bookstores
Publishers
Violence

Peter G. Christensen
Cardinal Stritch University
Capote, Truman

David S. Churchill
University of Manitoba
Goodman, Paul
Radical Faeries

Richard D. H. Clark
Tulane University
New Orleans

Suzanne Clark
University of Oregon
Millay, Edna St. Vincent

John M. Clum
Duke University
Albee, Edward
Fierstein, Harvey
Hart, Lorenz
Ludlam, Charles

Michael L. Cobb
University of Toronto
Literary Criticism and Theory

Cheryl Cole
University of Illinois at Urbana-Champaign
Richards, Renée

Diana Collecott
Durham University
H.D.

Anne Collinson
Ohio State University
Baker, Josephine
Baker, S. Josephine
Lesbian Feminism

Gregory Conerly
Cleveland State University
African American LGBTQ
Organizations and Periodicals
Black and White Men Together
(BWMT)
Boozer, Melvin
Third World Gay Revolution

Blanche Wiesen Cook
*Graduate Center of the City
University of New York*
Roosevelt, Eleanor, and Lorena
Hickock

Tom Cook
*Gay and Lesbian Archives of the
Pacific Northwest*
Hart, Alan

Robert Corber
Trinity College
Baldwin, James

Tee A. Corinne
Sunny Valley, Oregon
Austen, Alice
Brooks, Romaine
Gidlow, Elsa
Klumpke, Anna
Visual Art: Painting, Drawing, and
Sculpture: 1969–Present
Wilhelm, Gale

Roger Corless
Duke University
Buddhists and Buddhism

Cheryl Coward
Dartmouth College
Sports
Youth and Youth Groups

Corey K. Creekmur
University of Iowa
Actors and Actresses
Homoeroticism and
Homosociality
Music: Popular

Julie Davids
*New York City AIDS Housing
Network*
Kuromiya, Kyoshi

Thomas F. DeFrantz
*Massachusetts Institute of
Technology*
Ailey, Alvin
Bennett, Michael
Joffrey, Robert
Robbins, Jerome

John D'Emilio
Chicago, Illinois
National Gay and Lesbian Task
Force (NGLTF)
Rustin, Bayard

Jigna Desai
University of Minnesota
Film and Video Studies

Aaron H. Devor
University of Victoria
Erickson Educational Foundation
Tipton, Billy

Carlos Dews
*Carson McCullers Center for Writers
and Musicians*
McCullers, Carson

Ann Dils
*University of North Carolina,
Greensboro*
Jones, Bill T., and Arnie Zane

L. Mara Dodge
Westfield State College
Prisons, Jails, and Reformatories:
Women's

Zachary A. Dorsey
University of Texas, Austin
Music: Broadway and Musical
Theater

Alexander Doty
Lehigh University
Anger, Kenneth
Arzner, Dorothy
Cukor, George

Lisa Duggan
New York University
Hall, Murray
LGBTQ Studies
Mitchell, Alice
Sex Panics
Sex Wars
Sexual Orientation and Preference

Vicki L. Eaklor
Alfred University
Human Rights Campaign

Gerald Early
Washington University in Saint Louis
Cullen, Countee

Alice Echols
University of California, Los Angeles
Furies
Morgan, Robin
Radicalesbians

Mary Elliott
University of California, Berkeley
Bannon, Ann
Pulp Fiction: Lesbian

W. Mason Emnett
Georgetown University Law Center
Discrimination

Jeff Escoffier
Independent Scholar, New York City
Businesses
Sexual Revolutions

William N. Eskridge Jr.
Yale University
Crime and Criminalization
Federal Law and Policy
Immigration, Asylum, and
Deportation Law and Policy

Kristin G. Esterberg
University of Massachusetts, Lowell
New Right

Shelly Eversley
Baruch College, City University of New York
Beats
Locke, Alain

Lillian Faderman
California State University, Fresno
Ben, Lisa
Foster, Jeannette
Lobdell, Lucy Ann
Romantic Friendship and Boston
Marriage

Marilyn R. Farwell
University of Oregon
Rich, Adrienne

Fred Fejes
Florida Atlantic University
Florida
Media Studies and Journalism

Roderick A. Ferguson
University of Minnesota
African American Studies

James Fisher
Wabash College
Kramer, Larry
Ritts, Herb
Webster, Margaret

Dayo Folayan Gore
Brooklyn, New York
Murray, Pauli

Karen A. Foss
University of New Mexico
Milk, Harvey

Gillian Frank
Brown University
Gilman, Charlotte Perkins

Trisha Franzen
Albion College
Anthony, Susan B.
Shaw, Anna Howard
Walker, Mary
Willard, Frances

Estelle B. Freedman
Stanford University
Davis, Katharine
Van Waters, Miriam

Bruce Freeman
University of Calgary
Gender and Sex

Chris Freeman
St. John's University
Maupin, Armistead
Monette, Paul
Tilden, William
Vidal, Gore

Elizabeth Freeman
University of California, Davis
Queer Nation

Andrea Friedman
Washington University in St. Louis
Censorship, Obscenity, and
Pornography Law and Policy

Marcia M. Gallo
City University of New York
Ladder
American Civil Liberties Union
(ACLU)
Daughters of Bilitis
Eckstein, Ernestine
Glenn, Cleo
Lyon, Phyllis, and Del Martin

Linda Garber
Santa Clara University
Grahn, Judy

Jane Gerhard
Harvard University
Atkinson, Ti-Grace
Millett, Kate
Solanas, Valerie

Lorine Getz
University of North Carolina, Charlotte
Fuller, Margaret

Stephanie Gilmore
Ohio State University
Feminism
Lesbian Feminism
Memphis
Public Festivals, Parties, and
Holidays

R.J. Gilmour
York University
Piercings, Tattoos, and Scars

Richard Godbeer
University of California, Riverside
Colonial America
Sension, Nicholas
Wigglesworth, Michael

Lynn Gorchov
Oberlin College
Buffalo
Psychology, Psychiatry,
Psychoanalysis, and Sexology

Deborah B. Gould
University of Chicago
AIDS Coalition to Unleash Power
(ACT UP)

Ron Gregg
Film and Video

Jay Grossman
Northwestern University
Matthiessen, F. O.
Whitman, Walt

Laila S. Haidarali
York University
Primus, Rebecca, and Addie
Brown
Rainey, Ma
Smith, Bessie
Thompson, Frances

Donald P. Haider-Markel
University of Kansas
Colorado
Political Science

Judith Hallett
University of Maryland
Classical Studies

Michael W. Handis
City University of New York
Bates, Katharine Lee
Burns, Randy
Piñero, Miguel

Laura A. Harris
Pitzer College
Hansberry, Lorraine
Harlem Renaissance

Peter Hegarty
University of Surrey
Sullivan, Harry Stack

Linda Heidenreich
Washington State University
Anzaldúa, Gloria

Laura Hershey
Cripcommentary.com, Denver, Colorado
Disability, Disabled People, and
Disability Movements

Elizabeth Lutes Hillman
Rutgers School of Law
Military Law and Policy
War

James H. Hodnett
Ohio State University
Psychotherapy, Counseling, and
Recovery Programs

Patrick Holland
University of Guelph
Tourism

Will C. Holmes
University of Georgia
Hammond, James Henry
Smith, Lillian

Alice Y. Hom
Occidental College
Fukaya, Michiyo
Kim, Willyce
Tsui, Kitty

Evalie Horner
University of Washington
Femmes and Butches

Helen Lefkowitz Horowitz
Smith College
Thomas, M. Carey

John Howard
University of London
Mississippi

Nadine Hubbs
University of Michigan
Thomson, Virgil

Diana Hulick
Mesa, Arizona
Visual Art: Photography

Gerald Hunt
Ryerson University
Employment and Occupations

Joseph J. Inguanti
*Southern Connecticut State
University*
Weber, Bruce

Janice M. Irvine
*University of Massachusetts,
Amherst*
Kinsey, Alfred C.

Huda Jadallah
*University of California, Santa
Barbara*
Arab Americans

Karla Jay
New York City
Literature: 1890–1969

Joe E. Jeffreys
New York University
Eichelberger, Ethyl
Theater and Performance

Valerie Jenness
University of California, Irvine
Hate Crimes Law and Policy

Colin R. Johnson
University of Michigan
Urban, Suburban, and Rural
Geographies

David K. Johnson
Writer, Chicago, Illinois
Cory, Donald Webster
Kameny, Franklin
Washington, D.C.
Womack, H. Lynn

Jay Emerson Johnson
*The Center for Lesbian and Gay
Studies in Religion and Ministry*
Protestants and Protestantism

Phylis Johnson
*Southern Illinois University,
Carbondale*
Radio

Jordy Jones
University of California, Irvine
Alcohol and Drugs
Transgender Organizations and
Periodicals

Elizabeth Kaminski
Ohio State University
Public Festivals, Parties, and
Holidays

AnaLouise Keating
Texas Woman's University
Allen, Paula Gunn

Nancy J. Kennedy
*Center for Substance Abuse
Prevention, Rockville, Maryland*
Health and Health Care Law and
Policy

Julie J. Kilmer
Elmhurst College
Heterosexism and Homophobia

Samantha J. King
University of Arizona
Physical Education

Gary Kinsman
Sudbury, Ontario
Capitalism and Industrialization

Terence Kissack
City University of New York
Anarchism, Socialism, and
Communism
Gay Liberation
Gay Liberation Front
Goldman, Emma
Stoddard, Charles Warren

George Klawitter
St. Edward's University
Gunn, Thom

Melanie E. S. Kohnen
Brown University
Woo, Merle

Karen Christel Krahulik
Duke University
Resorts

Vikki Krane
Bowling Green State University
Navratilova, Martina

Marie J. Kuda
Oak Park, Illinois
Taylor, Valerie

Kevin K. Kumashiro
*Center for Anti-Oppressive
Education, El Cerrito, California*
Asian American LGBTQ
Organizations and Periodicals
Education
Gay, Lesbian, and Straight
Education Network (GLSEN)

Lawrence La Fountain-Stokes
University of Michigan
Puerto Rico
Ramos Otero, Manuel

Susie J. Lee
Cornell University
Tsang, Daniel

Ian Lekus
Duke University
Antiwar, Pacifist, and Peace
Movements
New Left and Student Movements
Wittman, Carl

Patrick J. Leonard
*Independent Scholar, Braintree,
Massachusetts*
Samson, Deborah

Karen Leong
Arizona State University
Noda, Barbara

Ellen Lewin
University of Iowa
Family Issues

Craig M. Loftin
University of Southern California
Kepner, James
Legg, Dorr
Murphy, Frank
ONE Institute
Political Scandals

Agnes Lugo-Ortiz
Dartmouth College
Sánchez, Luis Rafael

330

Kathryn A. Lyndes
Chicago, Illinois
  Rape, Sexual Assault, and Sexual
    Harassment Law and Policy

Mary Jo Mahoney
Elmira College
  Sarton, May

Martin F. Manalansan IV
*University of Illinois at Urbana-
Champaign*
  Anthropology

Toby Marotta
*Independent Scholar, Tucson,
Arizona*
  Gay Activists Alliance
  Rodwell, Craig
  Wicker, Randolfe

Brenda Marston
*Rare and Manuscript Collections,
Cornell University Library*
  History Projects, Libraries, and
    Archives

Jeff Maskovsky
Philadelphia, Pennsylvania
  Kuromiya, Kyoshi

Daniel E. Mathers
University of Cincinnati
  Copland, Aaron
  Rorem, Ned

Steven Maynard
*Queen's University, Kingston,
Ontario*
  Cross-Class Sex and Relationships
  Intergenerational Sex and
    Relationships
  Tearooms (Bathrooms)

John McFarland
*Writer and Critic, Seattle,
Washington*
  Ford, Charles Henri
  McNally, Terrence
  Wilson, Lanford

Sheila McManus
University of Lethbridge
  Pi'tamakan
  Woman Chief

Martin Meeker
University of California, Berkeley
  ONE
  Call, Hal
  Homophile Movement
  Mattachine Society

Lisa Merrill
Hofstra University
  Cushman, Charlotte

Richard Meyer
University of Southern California
  Cadmus, Paul
  Mapplethorpe, Robert
  Warhol, Andy
  Wojnarowicz, David

Joanne Meyerowitz
Indiana University
  Benjamin, Harry
  Lawrence, Louise

Heather Lee Miller
Ohio State University Press
  Prostitution, Hustling, and Sex
    Work

Laura M. Miller
Vanderbilt University
  Auden, W. H.
  Cheever, John
  Ginsberg, Allen

Liz Millward
York University
  Gentrification
  Ghettos and Neighborhoods

Henry L. Minton
University of Windsor
  Henry, George
  Hooker, Evelyn

Martha Mockus
*State University of New York, Stony
Brook*
  Music: Women's

Ken Mondschein
*Independent scholar and writer,
New York City*
  Sex Toys

Bonnie J. Morris
George Washington University
  Music: Women's Festivals

Donald Morton
Syracuse University
  Cultural Studies and Cultural
    Theory

Greg Mullins
The Evergreen State College
  Bowles, Paul, and Jane Bowles
  Burroughs, William S.
  Mizer, Robert

Kevin Mumford
Towson University
  Beam, Joseph

Kevin Murphy
Wesleyan University
  New York City

Michael J. Murphy
Washington University in Saint Louis
  Eakins, Thomas
  Eltinge, Julian
  Fashion, Style, and Clothing
  Haring, Keith
  Kirstein, Lincoln

David A. B. Murray
York University
  Mead, Margaret
  Nationalism

Stephen O. Murray
*El Instituto Obregón, San Francisco,
California*
  Benedict, Ruth
  Language
  Sociology

Christopher Nealon
University of California, Berkeley
  Crane, Hart
  Physique Magazines and
    Photographs

Joan Nestle
*Lesbian Herstory Archives/Lesbian
Herstory Education Foundation,
Inc.; University of Melbourne*
  Hampton, Mabel

Caryn E. Neumann
Ohio State University
  Addams, Jane
  Bean, Babe
  Bonnet, Jeanne
  Dunbar-Nelson, Alice
  Fornes, Maria Irene
  Johnston, Jill
  Oliveros, Pauline
  Shockley, Ann Allen

Jorge Olivares
Colby College
  Arenas, Reinaldo

Christa M. Orth
University of Oregon
  Labor Movements and Labor
    Unions

Ricardo L. Ortiz
Georgetown University
  Los Angeles and West Hollywood
  Rechy, John

Jon Panish
Palomar College
  Strayhorn, Billy

William Pencak
Pennsylvania State University
  Alger, Horatio
  Cage, John
  Crisp, Quentin

Music: Classical
Music: Opera
Williams, Tennessee

Judith A. Peraino
Cornell University
Olivia Records

Lea Pierce
The Gay Outlook
Niles, Blair

John D. Poling
Independent Scholar, Clinton, Illinois
Chicago

Howard Pollack
University of Houston
Porter, Cole

Claire Bond Potter
Wesleyan University
Hoover, J. Edgar

Nichole Suzanne Prescott
State University of New York, Stony Brook
Barney, Natalie
Essentialism and Constructionism

Jaclyn Iris Pryor
University of Texas, Austin
Chambers, Jane
Performance, Theater, and Dance Studies

Marilyn R. Pukkila
Colby College
Witches and Wicca

Meredith Raimondo
Oberlin, Ohio
Closet
Safer Sex

David Rayside
University of Toronto
Electoral Politics
Family Law and Policy
Frank, Barney
Military
Noble, Elaine

Scott Rayter
Camp
Russo, Vito

Chandan Reddy
University of Washington
Migration, Immigration, and Diaspora

Christopher Reed
Lake Forest College
Art History
Hockney, David

Johns, Jasper
Lynes, George Platt
Rauschenberg, Robert
Visual Art: Painting, Drawing, and Sculpture: 1890–1969

Robert Reid-Pharr
City University of New York
Hemphill, Essex
Riggs, Marlon

Yolanda Retter Vargas
University of Southern California; ONE Institute and Archives
Baca, Judy
Cameron, Barbara
Chrystos
Córdova, Jeanne
Díaz-Cotto, Juanita
Latina and Latino LGBTQ Organizations and Periodicals
Latinas and Latinos

Tim Retzloff
University of Michigan
Jones, Prophet
Michigan

Robert B. Marks Ridinger
Northern Illinois University
Fugate, James Barr
Parker, Pat

Craig A. Rimmerman
Hobart and William Smith Colleges
Democratic Party
Republican Party

Ruthann Robson
City University of New York School of Law
Employment Law and Policy
Rights of Association and Assembly

Don Romesburg
University of California, Berkeley
Bourbon, Ray (Rae)
Boy Scouts and Girl Scouts

Horacio N. Roque Ramirez
University of California, Santa Barbara
Latina and Latino Studies
Poma, Edgar
Reyes, Rodrigo
Tavera, Hank

Vernon A. Rosario
University of California, Los Angeles
Medicine, Medicalization, and the Medical Model

Will Roscoe
Independent Scholar, San Francisco
Kenny, Maurice
Klah, Hastíin

Lozen
Osh-Tisch
We'wha

Darren Rosenblum
New York City
Sodomy, Buggery, Crimes Against Nature, Disorderly Conduct, and Lewd and Lascivious Law and Policy

Terry Rowden
The College of Wooster
Thurman, Wallace

Lori Rowlett
University of Wisconsin–Eau Claire
Muslims and Islam
Symbols

Anne Rubenstein
York University
Zulma

Gayle Rubin
University of Michigan
Samois

Leila J. Rupp
University of California, Santa Barbara
Drag Queens and Kings
Same-Sex Institutions
Woolley, Mary and Jeanette Marks

Dereka Rushbrook
University of Arizona
Geography

Rosaura Sánchez
University of California, San Diego
Islas, Arturo

Catriona Sandilands
York University
Carson, Rachel
Environmental and Ecology Movements
Jewett, Sarah Orne

Jeffrey Santa Ana
Mount Holyoke College
Bishop, Elizabeth

Steven P. Schacht
State University of New York, Plattsburgh
Sarria, José

Marilyn R. Schuster
Smith College
Rule, Jane

Michael Schwartz
The Gay & Lesbian Review, Boston
White, Edmund

Karen C. Sendziak
Gerber/Hart Library, Chicago
Gerber, Henry
Hart, Pearl
Society for Human Rights

David Serlin
Bard College
Bathhouses
Bentley, Gladys
Jorgensen, Christine
Money, John, and Anke Ehrhardt

Edward H. Sewell Jr.
Virginia Tech
Advertising

Hasan Shafiqullah
Brooklyn, New York
Transgender and Gender
Impersonation Law and Policy

Michael D. Shanklee
University of Pittsburgh
Health and Health Care Law and
Policy

Michael Sherry
Northwestern University
Barber, Samuel, and Gian Carlo
Menotti
Bernstein, Leonard

Charles Shively
University of Massachusetts
Chua, Siong-huat
North American Man/Boy Love
Association (NAMBLA)

Audrey M. Skeete
*African American Religion and
Spirituality*

James Smalls
University of Maryland
Visual Art: Painting, Drawing, and
Sculpture: 18th and 19th
Centuries

Hazel Smith
University of Canberra
O'Hara, Frank

Nadine Smith
Equality Florida
Lesbian Avengers
Marches on Washington

Adam Sonstegard
University of California, Davis
Literature: 18th and 19th
Centuries

Tamara Shircliff Spike
Florida State University
Native American Religion and
Spirituality

Kimberly Springer
Portland State University
Smith, Barbara

Michele Spring-Moore
Columbus, Ohio
Howe, Marie Jenney
Poor People's Movements

Jeanne Stanley
University of Pennsylvania
Friendship

Marc Stein
York University
Class and Class Oppression
Coming Out and Outing
Gay Community News
Interracial and Interethnic Sex
and Relationships
Janus Society
Polak, Clark
Policing and Police

Linnea Stenson
University of Minnesota
Highsmith, Patricia

Michael R. Stevenson
Ball State University
Sex Education

Timothy Stewart-Winter
University of Chicago
Center for Lesbian and Gay
Studies (CLAGS)
Cruising
Gyms, Fitness Clubs, and Health
Clubs
Pride Marches and Parades
Public Sex

Susan Stryker
*GLBT Historical Society, San
Francisco*
Brewster, Lee
Erickson, Reed
Prince, Virginia
Rivera, Sylvia
Sullivan, Lou

Ira Tattelman
*Independent Scholar, Washington,
D.C.*
Architecture

Karen Taylor
Ohio State University
Psychotherapy, Counseling, and
Recovery Programs

Peter Taylor
Santa Clara University
McKay, Claude

Verta Taylor
*University of California, Santa
Barbara*
Drag Queens and Kings

Griff Tester
Ohio State University
Tricking

Anne N. Thalheimer
Simon's Rock College of Bard
Comics and Comic Books
Northampton

Polly J. Thistlethwaite
*Graduate Center of the City
University of New York*
Prostitution, Hustling, and Sex
Work Law and Policy

Kara Thompson
University of California, Davis
Transsexuals, Transvestites,
Transgender People, and Cross-
Dressers

Victoria E. Thompson
Arizona State University
Nin, Anaïs
Yourcenar, Marguerite

Daniel Tsang
Santa Ana, California
Asian American and Pacific
Islander Studies
Asian Americans and Pacific
Islanders

Jeffrey A. Tucker
University of Rochester
Delany, Samuel

William B. Turner
University of Wisconsin–Milwaukee
History
Parents, Families, and Friends of
Lesbians and Gays (PFLAG)
Queer Theory and Queer Studies

Nella Van Dyke
Washington State University
Marriage Ceremonies and
Weddings

Ruth Vanita
University of Montana
Hindus and Hinduism

Fred Wasserman
The Jewish Museum, New York
Stonewall Riots

Jacqueline S. Weinstock
Burlington, Vermont
Friendship

Yvonne Welbon
Our Film Works, Chicago
  Ellis, Ruth

Kevin White
University of Portsmouth
  Homosexuality and
    Heterosexuality

Patricia White
Swarthmore College
  Film and Video Festivals

Melissa M. Wilcox
Whitman College
  Catholics and Catholicism
  Churches, Temples, and Religious
    Groups
  Perry, Troy

Walter L. Williams
*University of Southern California
and the International Gay and
Lesbian Review*
  Native American Studies
  Native Americans
  Two-Spirit Males

Kari J. Winter
*State University of New York,
Buffalo*
  Hunter, Alberta

Thomas H. Wirth
Elizabeth, New Jersey
  Nugent, Richard Bruce

Les Wright
Mount Ida College
  Bears

Judy Tzu-Chun Wu
Ohio State University
  Chung, Margaret

Yvonne Yarbro-Bejarano
Stanford University
  Moraga, Cherríe

Jacqueline N. Zita
University of Minnesota
  Biology and Zoology
  Philosophy

index

Association of Latin Men for Action (ALMA), 2:147

Association of Lesbian and Gay Asians (ALGA), 1:97

Association of Suburban People, 2:252

Astarte (ballet), 2:99

Astraea Lesbian Action Foundation, 1:234

Asylum, based on sexuality, 2:81, 141

"At Baia" (H. D.), 2:1

At Saint Judas's (Fuller), 1:210; 3:181

At Seventy (Sarton), 3:82

Atalanta (newsletter), 1:102

ATEAC. *See* Aid to End AIDS Committee

ATHE. *See* Association for Theatre in Higher Education

Atheneum Review (newsletter), 2:59

Athey, Ron, 1:289

Athletes. *See* Sports

Athletic Model Guild (AMG), 2:206, 272, 409

Atkins, Gary, 2:241, 417, 418

Atkinson, John Augustus, *Men in Hot Baths*, 1:124

Atkinson, Nicole, 3:37

Atkinson, Ti-Grace, 1:100–101
    Amazon Odyssey, 1:101
    on feminism *vs.* lesbianism, 3:10
    in The Feminists, 1:100–101
    on marriage, 1:100–101
    in National Organization for Women, 1:100; 2:163
    Solanas (Valerie) and, 1:100; 3:143

Atlanta (Georgia), 1:101–103
    African Americans in, 1:102; 2:458
    Black Gay Pride in, 2:458
    bookstores in, 1:102
    gay liberation in, 1:102
    Hotlanta in, 2:457–458
    lesbian feminism in, 1:102
    Little Five Points neighborhood of, 1:102
    Olympics in (1996), 1:102–103
    Pride celebrations in, 1:101, 102
    Queer Nation chapter in, 2:480
    scholarship on, 1:101–102
    World War II in, 1:101–102

Atlanta Lesbian Feminist Alliance (ALFA), 1:102; 2:47; 3:145

Atlantic City (New Jersey), as resort, 2:375; 3:32

Atlantic Monthly, The (magazine), 2:95

Atlantis: Model 1924 (Delany), 1:296

At-risk youth, groups for, 3:302

AT&T, 1:343, 344; 2:227
    advertisements by, 1:8

Attinello, Paul, 2:305

Attom, Patches, 2:356

Aucoin, Kevyn, 1:373, 374

Auden, George, 1:103

Auden, W. H., 1:103–104
    Age of Anxiety (ballet) based on, 3:44
    Bernstein (Leonard) inspired by, 1:289
    and Isherwood (Christopher), 1:103, 104; 2:90, 91
    and McCullers (Carson), 2:218
    Rich's (Adrienne) book introduced by, 3:34
    and Stravinsky (Igor), 2:293
    works of, 1:104

Audre Lorde Project, 2:257; 3:1

Austen, Alice, 1:104–105; 2:336; 3:245

Austen, Alice Cornell, 1:104

Austen, Howard, 3:226

Austen, Roger, 2:408

Austin, John, 2:137

Austin (Texas), bars in, 1:121

Austin History Center, 2:46

Austin Latina/o Lesbian Gay, Bisexual and Transgender Organization (ALLGO), 2:140, 146

Austin Lesbian Activism, 2:46

Australia, lesbian organizations in, 1:293

Authority, The (comic book series), 1:251

Autobiographies, 2:199

Autobiography in Search of a Father (Johnston), 2:101

Autobiography of Alice B. Toklas, The (Stein), 2:189; 3:149–150

Autobiography of Roy Cohn, The (Zion), 1:232

Avalon, Frankie, 2:296

Avant-garde movement, 2:289

Avatar, 3:59

Avedon, Richard, 3:259

Aversion conditioning therapy, 2:448

Avicolli-Mecca, Tommi, 1:437

Aw Shucks! (Shigata Ga Nai) (Noda), 2:348

Award Books, 2:469

Awards, literary, 1:470; 2:463–464

Aware Talk Radio (radio program), 3:14

Ayala, George, 2:150

"Aye, and Gomorrah …" (Delany), 1:295

Azalea: A Magazine by and for Third World Lesbians, 1:19; 3:239

B

BAAITS. *See* Bay Area American Indian Two-Spirits

Babbitt, Milton, 3:143

Babe. *See* Didrikson, Mildred Ella

Babel-17 (Delany), 1:295

Babes in Arms (musical), 2:283

Babies Welfare Association, 1:110

Babuscio, Jack, 1:189, 191

Babycakes (Maupin), 2:238

Baca, Judy, 1:107–108
    in muralist movement, 1:107–108; 3:238

BACCAR. *See* Boston Area Coalition for Cuban Aid and Resettlement

Bacchanal, 2:208; 3:239

Bachardy, Don, 2:91; 3:238

Bachelor societies, Asian American, 1:88, 94; 3:64

Bachelors' Journal, 1:152

"Back to Africa" movement, 2:10

"Backrooms," 2:338

Bad Attitude (magazine), 1:205; 2:343, 410; 3:102

Baden-Powell, Robert, 1:160

Badgeley, Christian, 3:37

Badgett, M. V. Lee, 1:327

Baehr v. Lewin, 1:368; 2:130, 131

Baehr v. Miike, 1:364

Baez, Joan, 1:143; 2:356

Bagemihl, Bruce, 1:138, 140–141
    on spirituality, 3:10

BAGL. *See* Bay Area Gay Liberation

BAGMAL. *See* Boston Asian Gay Men and Lesbians

Bailey, Ann, 1:152

Bailey, Derrick Sherwin, 2:442

Bailey, J. Michael, 2:248; 3:104

Bailey, Robert, 1:447; 2:399, 400

Bailey-Boushay House, 3:84

Bajour, 1:134

Baker, Blanche, 2:358

Baker, David G., 2:399

Baker, Diane, 3:284

Baker, Gilbert, 3:167

Baker, Jack, 1:297

Baker, Josephine, 1:108–109, *109*
    in France, 1:108–109
    in Harlem Renaissance, 1:13

Baker, Orlando Daniel Mosher, 1:110

Baker, S. Josephine, 1:109–110

Baker, William Howard, 1:108

Baker Memorial Library, 1:351

Baker v. State (Vermont), 1:364, 368

Baker v. Wade, 2:130

Boston College, 1:285, 286

Boston Globe (newspaper), Frank's (Barney) interview with, 1:412

Boston marriages, 1:413; **3:46–49**
  between Addams and Starr, 1:6
  among artists, 3:233
  between Bates and Coman, 1:122
  definitions of, 1:6, 153; 3:47
  description of, 1:276; 2:229
  Gilman (Charlotte Perkins) and, 1:455
  between Jewett and Fields, 1:153; 2:96; 3:47
  in literature, 2:185–186
  between Lowell and Russell, 1:153
  between Manning and Whitney, 1:153; 3:233
  origin of term, 3:47
  outsiders misunderstanding, 2:52
  at Wellesley College, 1:122
  between Woolley and Marks, 1:122

Boston Medical and Surgical Journal, 1:154

Boston Sex Scandal, The (Mitzel), 2:349–350

Boston/Boise Committee, 1:216; 2:349

Bostonians, The (James), 2:185, 188

Boswell, John, 1:362
  on gays in Catholic Church, 1:200
  on history of violence against LGBT people, 2:19
  on LGBT history, 2:40
  on same-sex unions in ancient Greece, 2:228

Boté. See Two-spirit females and males

Bottoms, Sharon, 1:362

Boucher, Sheila Williams, Ginsberg (Allen) and, 1:130

Bouguereau, William-Adolphe, 2:118

Bouillon, Joseph Jean Étienne, 1:109

Boulanger, Nadia, 2:287–288; 3:190

Bouley, Charles "Karel," II, 3:14

Boulez, Pierre, 1:185

Bourbon, Ray (Rae), **1:157–158,** 247

Bourbon Street Awards, 2:331

Bourdet, Edouard, 2:336
  The Captive, 2:369; 3:181, 182

'Bout Time, 1:121

Boutilier, Clive Michael, 2:80

Boutilier v. INS, 2:80, 94, 389

Bow, Clara, in Arzner (Dorothy) films, 1:86, 87

Bowen, Bertha, 1:304

Bowers v. Hardwick
  and AIDS activism, 1:34
  criticism of, 3:140

demonstration in opposition to, 1:*265;* 2:418

homosexual *vs.* heterosexual sodomy in, 1:314

impact on state laws, 1:265, 367

and institutional closet, 1:228

Lambda Legal Defense in, 2:130

and March on Washington (1987), 2:223, 418

origination of case in Atlanta, 1:102

privacy rights in, 2:130, 431; 3:140

reversed by Supreme Court in *Lawrence v. Texas,* 1:265, 314, 365, 367; 2:131, 432; 3:39, 140–141

Romers v. Evans influence on, 1:54

Bowery (New York City neighborhood), 2:335

Bowie, David, 1:143; 2:77, 297

Bowles, Jane Auer, **1:158–160**
  and tourism in Tangiers, 3:194–195

Bowles, Paul, **1:158–160,** *159;* 2:292
  and Ford (Charles Henri), 1:408
  Rorem (Ned) and, 3:51
  and tourism in Tangiers, 3:194–195

Bowman, Karl M., 2:151, 451; 3:107

Bowman, Parke, 2:462

Boxing, paintings on, 1:323

Boy George, 2:77, 297, 298

Boy Scouts of America (BSA), **1:160–163,** *314,* 315
  discrimination in, 1:161–162; 2:131
    Supreme Court on, 1:162; 2:131; 3:39–40
  establishment of, 1:160
  membership criteria for, 1:160–163
  mission of, 1:160
  religion in, 1:161

Boyce, William, 1:160

Boycotts, **1:163–165**
  against Colorado, 1:164
  against Coors, 1:163–164; 2:125
  against Cracker Barrel, 1:164
  definition of, 1:163
  against Disney, 1:164
  effectiveness of, 1:164–165
  against United Airlines, 1:164

Boyd, Linda, 1:188

Boyd, Nan Alamilla, 1:390
  on class dynamics, 1:222
  on San Francisco, 1:222; 2:43, 46, 391
  Wide-Open Town, 1:119; 2:43

Boyfrank, Manual, 1:451

Boys Don't Cry (film), 1:400; 3:198, 229

Boys in the Band, The (Crowley), 1:189; 2:200, 369–370; 3:182, 282

Boys in the Band, The (film), 1:189, 397; 2:242

Boys in the Sand (film), 1:397

Boys of Boise, The (Gerassi), 2:82

Boy's Own Story, A (White), 3:272

Boys With Arms Akimbo, 3:240

Boy-Wives and Female Husbands: Studies in African Homosexualities (Murray and Roscoe), 2:43

Brace, Charles Loring, 1:49

Bracho, Ricardo A., 2:149

Bradford, Jim, 1:211

Bradford, William, 3:69

Bradley, Marion Zimmer, 1:292; 2:471
  in *Ladder,* 2:127

Bradley's, 2:206

Braille, feminist literature in, 1:307

Brainard, Joe, 3:238

Brancusi, Constantin, 1:301
  in *Little Review,* 1:58

Branded Youth (Weber), 3:269

Brandeis, Louis, 2:430

Branding, 2:387

Brando, Marlon, 3:282

Brandon, Teena. *See* Teena, Brandon

Brandon House, 2:409, 469

Brandt, Paul, 1:224

Brant, Beth E., **1:165–166;** 2:320

Braschi, Miguel, 1:368

Braschi v. Stahl Associates, 1:69, 368

Bratt, Benjamin, 2:388

Bravman, Scott, 2:486

Brazil
  Bishop (Elizabeth) in, 1:145–146
  race relations in, 1:145–146

Bread and Roses (women's organization), 1:387

Bread and Wine (Delany), 1:296

Breakfast at Tiffany's (Capote), 1:195, 196

"Breaking the Silence" (Tsang), 1:93

Breast cancer, in lesbians, 2:27

Breathing Show, The (Jones), 2:103

Breathless Orgasm, The (Money), 2:275

Brecht, Bertolt, 3:78

Breeder, 2:134

Brehony, Kathleen, 3:47–48

Brennan, Frank, 2:112

Brenner, Claudia, 3:229

Brenner, Johanna, 1:452

Bressan, Arthur, 2:410
  Buddies, 1:398
  Gay USA, 1:397

Brett, Philip, 2:304–305

Brewer, Ethel Gale, 3:279

Brewer, Lucy, **3:**256

Brewster, Anne Hampton, **1:**282

Brewster, Lee, **1:166–167; 2:**338

  in Queens Liberation Front, **1:**166; **3:**197

Brewster, R. Owen, **3:**272

Briano, Sierra Lonepine, **3:**242

Brick Oven Tea Room, **1:**154

Bricknell, Charles H., **3:**70

Bridge: An Asian American Perspective (Lim and Yung), **2:**348

Bridge, The (Crane), **1:**263

Bridge (magazine), **1:**89; **3:**210, 212

Bridgers, Aaron, **3:**160

Bridges, Alicia, **2:**357

Bridgewater State College, **1:**234

"Brief History of Chinese Lesbianism, A" (Sasha), **1:**216

Brigadoon (musical), **2:**286

Briggs, John, **3:**153, 177

Briggs Initiative (California), **1:**337, 463; **2:**417

  Córdova (Jeanne) fighting, **1:**259

  Milk (Harvey) fighting, **2:**266

  rejection of, **1:**334; **2:**332

Bright, Susie, on lesbian feminism, **1:**389

Brigman, Anne, **3:**245

Brill, Abraham, **2:**245, 446

Bring Home the Bride (Wilhelm), **3:**279

Bringing Up Baby (film), **1:**270

Britain. *See* Great Britain

British Journal of Photography, **3:**234

Britten, Benjamin, **2:**292, 304

  Auden (W. H.) and, **1:**104

Broadway, **2:282–286,** *284, 285;* **3:**181–182

  actors in, **1:**2; **2:**283

  creators of, **2:**283–284

  drag and, **2:**285–286

  Fierstein (Harvey) on, **1:**393

  form and structure of, **2:**283

  Hart's lyrics and, **2:**14–15

  icons in, **2:**78, 286

  LGBT characters in, **2:**284–285

  Porter (Cole) on, **2:**412

  queering, **2:**286

Brock, Lilyan, *Queer Patterns*, **2:**471

Brody, Jennifer, **2:**182

Broken Column, The (Kahlo), **1:**308

Broken Noses (film), **3:**268

"Broken Tower" (Crane), **1:**263

Bromfield Street Educational Foundation, **1:**433

Bronski, Michael, **1:**149; **2:**36

  Gay Community News and, **1:**433

on GLAAD, **1:**432

Bronski Beat, **2:**297

Bronx Hospital, **2:**246

Brook Farm, Fuller (Margaret) and, **1:**423

Brooklyn Daily Eagle, **1:**116

Brooklyn Heights (New York City neighborhood), **2:**337

Brooks, John Ellingham, **1:**167

Brooks, Romaine, **1:167–168**

  Barney (Natalie) and, **1:**117, 167, 168; **3:**234

  paintings of, **1:**167–168

  self-portrait of, *1:168*

Brooten, Bernadette, **1:**200

Brothels

  same-sex relationships in, **3:**64

  See also Prostitution

"Brother Sun" (camp), **2:**303

Brother to Brother: New Writings by Black Gay Men (Beam and Hemphill), **1:**25, 126; **2:**30

"Brothers, The" (Cheever), **1:**208

Brothers (TV show), **3:**180

Brown, Addie, **1:**11; **2:421–422; 3:**47, 63–64

Brown, Charles Brockden, *Ormond: or The Secret Witness*, **3:**47

Brown, Claude, **1:**50

Brown, Darrel, **1:**51

Brown, Howard, **2:**311

Brown, James, **2:**296

Brown, Jenny, **1:**110

Brown, Joe E., **1:**395

Brown, John, **2:**68

Brown, Judith C., **1:**200; **3:**10

Brown, Julia, **1:**168

Brown, Kathleen, **2:**391

Brown, Mark, **3:**251

Brown, Michael, **1:**230, 449, 450

Brown, Ralph, **1:**168

Brown, Rita Mae, **1:168–170,** *169;* **2:**342

  activism of, **1:**168–169

  in Furies, **1:**169, 424; **2:**166; **3:**262

  and *Furies* (newspaper), **2:**462

  in Gay Liberation Front, **3:**11

  The Hand That Cradles the Rock, **1:**169

  on Kopay (David), **2:**119

  in *Ladder*, **1:**292; **2:**127

  mystery series of, **1:**169

  Navratilova (Martina) and, **3:**145

  in NOW, **1:**169, 385; **2:**163; **3:**10–11

  A Plain Brown Rapper, **1:**169; **2:**166

  and *Quest* (journal), **1:**426

  in Radicalesbians, **1:**169; **3:**11

Rubyfruit Jungle, **1:**169, 249; **2:**180, 462, 473

  scripts by, **1:**169

  Shelley (Martha) and, **3:**11, 120

Brown, Rupert, "Contact Is Not Enough," **3:**151

Brown, Stephen, **1:**289

Brown, Theophilus, **3:**243

Brown, Willie, **3:**76

Brown Berets, **2:**145

Brown Health Center, **1:**212; **2:**29

Browne, Bothwell, **1:**2; **3:**72

Browning, Elizabeth Barrett, **1:**282

Brownmiller, Susan, **3:**10

  Against Our Will, **3:**100

Brownworth, Victoria A., **1:**309, 312

Bruce, Earle, **3:**134

Bruchac, Joseph, **2:**110

Bruining, Mi Ok Song, **3:**239

Brutalism, in architecture, **1:**80

Bryan, Lee, **3:**251

Bryant, Anita

  anti-LGBT sentiment represented by, **1:**398

  backlash led by, **1:**69; **3:**84

  gay pride marches in response to, documentary about, **1:**397

  on homosexuality as curable disease, **2:**63

  and Miami campaign against gay rights, **1:**406

  protests against, **1:**102; **3:**262

  Save Our Children campaign of, **1:**334, 337; **2:**81, 332, 442

  sex panics and, **3:**95

  Southern Baptist Convention address by, **1:**102

  stereotypes and, **3:**153

  television coverage of, **3:**177

Brydon, Charles, **2:**312

Bryher, **2:**1

Bryn Mawr College, **3:**187, 188

BSA. *See* Boy Scouts of America

Buchanan, James, **2:**395

Buchanan, Pat

  on gay rights, **3:**26

  on *Tongues Untied*, **1:**32; **3:**37

Buchanan, Robert J., **2:**400

Buchsbaum, Alan J., **1:**80

Buck, Claire, **2:**2

Buckley, William F., **1:**431; **3:**226

Budapest, Zsuzsanna, **3:**284

Buddhists and Buddhism, **1:170–171**

  and Cage's (John) music, **1:**185; **2:**289

  homosexuality in, **1:**170

Grecian Guild, 3:288

Grecian Quarterly (magazine), 2:409

Greece

  ancient

    hermaphrodites in, 2:87–88

    homoeroticism in, 1:224–227

    same-sex unions in, 2:228

    tourism in, 3:194

Greek Homosexuality (Dover), 1:225

"Greek Love at Rome" (Williams), 1:227

Greeley, Horace, 1:423

Green, Diana, 1:251

Green, James, 2:43

Green, Jesse, *The Velveteen Father,* 1:362

Green, Richard, 1:352, 354

Green Lantern (comic book series), 1:251

Green Table, The (ballet), 2:99

Greenberg, Clement, 3:236

Greenberg, David, 3:136

Greenberg, Steve, 2:98

Greenburg, Richard, *Take Me Out,* 3:182

Greenery Press, 3:59

Greenleaf Press, 2:409, 469

Greenwich Village (New York City), 1:447, 452; 2:336–337; 3:*219*

  Ford (Charles Henri) in, 1:408

  Oscar Wilde Memorial Bookshop in, 1:458

  and Socialist Party, 1:55

Greer, Michael, 1:247

Gregg, Frances, 2:1

Gregory, Roberta, 1:250

Gregory-Lewis, Sasha, 1:464

Grey, Antony, 1:351

GRID. *See* Gay-Related Immune Deficiency

Grier, Barbara, 1:406, **469–470**

  collecting LGBT records, 2:44

  in Daughters of Bilitis, 1:292, 293; 2:54, 59

  Ladder edited by, 2:128, 163

  and LGBT publishing, 2:463

  preparation for retirement, 2:464

  Taylor (Valerie) and, 3:171

  Wilhelm (Gale) and, 3:279, 280

Griffes, Charles Tomlinson, 2:287

Griffin, Pat, 2:381

Griffin, Susan

  and Shameless Hussy Press, 2:462

  in WomanSpirit movement, 3:9

  and Women's Press Collective, 1:468

Grimké, Angelina Weld, 1:**470–471**; 2:10, 12

bisexuality of, 1:142

  codes in works of, 2:190; 3:63

  in Harlem Renaissance, 1:13

  romantic friend of, 1:414

Griski, Vincent, 2:376

Griswold v. Connecticut, 2:80, 431; 3:39, 140

GRNL. *See* Gay Rights National Lobby

Gross, Alfred A., 2:31–32

Gross, Emily, same-sex relationships of, 1:382

Gross, Terry, Bannon (Ann) interviewed by, 1:113

Gross Clinic, The (Eakins), 1:324

Grosser, Maurice, 2:287; 3:190

Grossman, Nancy, 3:239

Grosz, Elizabeth, 2:379

Grotesque, Gay, 2:189

Group Material, 3:242

Grove, Bill, 3:160

Grove Press, 2:469

Growing Up Absurd (Goodman), 1:462

Gruen, John, on Ailey (Alvin), 1:44

GSA. *See* Girl Scouts of America

GSAs. *See* Gay-straight alliances

Guardian Angels, 2:479

Guba, Emil F., *Deborah Samson,* 3:70

Gubbay, Jacob, 1:218

Gucci Group, 1:372

Guggenheim, Peggy, 1:116

Guggenheim Museum, 1:84, 85

Guide (biweekly), 2:349

Guide to Gay and Lesbian Resources (University of Chicago), 1:234

Guidebooks, 1:178; 3:195, 288

Guild Book Service, 3:288

Guild Press, 2:409, 462; 3:288–289

  closure of, 3:289

  growth of, 3:288

  mail-order business of, 1:179; 3:288

  photographs published by, 1:179

  physique magazines of, 1:179; 3:288–289

  Supreme Court on, 3:261

  Womack (H. Lynn) at, 1:178; 3:261, 288–289

Guiler, Hugh, 2:345

Gulf Coast Womyn's Festival, 2:303

Gulf War. *See* Persian Gulf War

Gumby, Alexander, 1:13; 2:11

Gunderson, Steve, 1:412

Gunn, Thom, 1:**471–472**, *472*; 2:50

Gunthrie, Will, 3:14

Gurdjieff, George, 1:58

Gustav-Wrathall, John Donald, 1:473; 2:82

Guthrie, Woody, 2:356

Gutierrez, Eric-Steven, 3:5

Gutiérrez, Juan Pablo, *Ya Vas Carnal,* 3:33

Gutiérrez, Ramón, 1:221; 2:42, 85, 150

Guy-Sheftall, Beverly, 3:290

Guzman, Mary, 2:149

Gwinn, Mamie, 1:414

  in Friday Evening Club, 3:187

  Thomas (M. Carey) and, 3:63, 187

Gyms, 1:**472–474**

  and gay male body image, 1:374

  and lesbians, 1:473, 474

  and photography, 2:408

  and pornography, 1:473; 2:409

Gyn/Ecology: The Metaethics of Radical Feminism, 1:285–286

Gypsy (musical), 3:43, 143

H

H. D. (Hilda Doolittle), 2:1–2

  in *Little Review,* 1:57

HA! (TV show), 1:248

Hacker, Marilyn, 1:295

Hackman, Gene, 1:398

Hadden, Samuel, 1:233

Hadith, 2:307

Haeberle, Steven H., 2:400

Haeckel, Ernst, 2:88

Hag in a Black Leather Jacket (film), 3:265

Hagar (Lewis), 3:233

Hagen, Uta, 3:270

Hagerty, Tom, 2:416

Haggadah (Shelley), 3:121

Haider-Markel, Donald P., 2:400, 401

Haifetz v. Rizzo, 3:38

Haight-Ashbury, drug use in, 1:48

Haile, Berard, 2:117

Haines, William, 1:2, 395

Hair (musical), 2:284

Hairspray (film), 3:266

Hairspray (musical), 2:78

  Fierstein (Harvey) in, 1:394

Haitians, with AIDS, 1:27, 28

HAL. *See* Homophile Action League

Halberstam, Judith, 1:190

  Female Masculinity, 2:172, 182–183; 3:205

"Halcyon" (H. D.), 2:1

Hale, Jacob, 2:377, 379; 3:207

Half-man/half-woman. *See* Two-spirit females and males

Halfway Home (Monette), 2:274

Hall, Adrian, 1:336

Health care workers
   and AIDS stigma, 2:29
   associations for, 1:344
   disclosure by LGBT people to, 2:28
   homophobia of, 1:311, 312; 2:28, 34
Health clubs. *See* Gyms
Healthy People 2010 Companion Document on LGBT Health (Gay and Lesbian Medical Association), 2:26, 27
Healthy People 2010 initiative, 2:25
Healthy People initiative, 2:25
Healy v. James, 3:38
Heap, Jane, **1:57–58**
   Anderson's (Margaret) relationship with, 1:57–58
   Little Review edited by, 1:57–58
   photographs of, 3:245
Heaphy, Brian, 1:416, 418
Hearst, William Randolph, 1:79
Hearst Castle, 1:79
Heart Is a Lonely Hunter, The (McCullers), 2:191, 217
HeartBeat (TV show), 3:178
Heather Has Two Mommies (Newman), 1:360; 3:91–92
Heavenly Breakfast: An Essay on the Winter of Love (Delany), 1:296
Heavy metal, 2:297
Hebrew Bible, 2:96
Hebrew Union College (HUC), 2:98
Hedwig and the Angry Inch (film), 1:398, 400
Hedwig and the Angry Inch (musical), 2:286; 3:182
Hefner, Hugh, 3:220
Heggie, Jake, 2:293, 294
Heldke, Lisa, 2:379
Helen Ford (Alger), 1:50
Helen in Egypt (H. D.), 2:1
Hellfire Club, 3:91
   See also Chicago Hellfire Club
Hellman, Lillian, 1:203; 2:293
   The Children's Hour, 2:369; 3:182
Helms, Jesse
   and funding for AIDS education, 1:298
   and funding for art, 1:84
   and funding for education, 3:25
   and Harkin (Tom), 2:479
   and Maupin (Armistead), 2:238
   and NEA "decency clause," 1:205; 2:333
   and radio regulation, 3:13
   and safer sex education, 3:61
   on *Tongues Untied*, 3:36–37

Helms Amendment (1987), 1:205; 2:80; 3:25
Helm's Angels, 3:240
Hemingway, Ernest, 3:31, 149, 235
   The Sun Also Rises, 1:415
Hemmings, Clare, 1:390
Hemophiliacs, AIDS among, 1:27, 42
Hemphill, Essex, **2:30–31**
   Brother to Brother, 1:25, 126
Henderson, Clay, 3:14
Henderson, Fletcher, 3:264
Henderson, Jeffrey, 1:225, 226
Henderson, Russell, 3:221
Hendrix, Jimi, 2:297
Hennings, Thomas, Jr., 2:*359*
Henry, Aaron, 2:270
Henry, George, **2:31–32**, 447
   Sex Variants, 3:134
   sexual survey by, 2:170
Henry, Sweet Henry (musical), 1:134
Henry Ford Hospital, 2:253
Henry Foundation, 2:32
Henry Regnery and Sons, 3:171
Henry Street Settlement, 2:336
Henry VIII, 1:263
Henry-Anderson, Violet Winifred Leslie, 1:453
Hepatitis, 3:114
Hepburn, Audrey, 1:396
Hepburn, Katharine, 1:4, 273, 274, 395
   in Arzner (Dorothy) films, 1:86, 87
Her (H. D.), 2:2
Herbert, John, *Fortune and Men's Eyes*, 2:424
Herdt, Gilbert
   Gay Culture in America, 1:65–66
   Ritualized Homosexuality in Melanesia, 1:65
HERE. *See* Hotel and Restaurants Employees; Human Equal Rights for Everyone
Hereditary factor in homosexuality. *See* Genetic research
Herek, Gregory M.
   on hate crimes, 3:228
   "Psychological Heterosexism in the United States," 3:152
Here's Love, Bennett (Michael) in, 1:134
"Heritage" (Cullen), 1:275
Heritage Foundation, 1:164
Herman, Jerry, 1:393
Hermaphrodeities (Kaldera), 3:9
Hermaphrodites with Attitude (newsletter), 2:89
Hermaphroditism, **2:87–88**
   definition of, 2:132

psychosexual, 2:244, 246
   See also Intersexuals and intersexed people
Hermaphroditism and the Medical Invention of Sex (Dreger), 2:88
Hermaphroditus, 2:87
Hermes (journal), 1:224
Hermit Songs (Ailey), 1:44; 2:288
Hernández, Ester Medina, 3:238
Hernandez brothers, 1:250
Hernández Valadéz, Manuel, in Gay Latino Alliance, 3:33
Heroes and Saints (Moraga), 2:278
Herpes simplex virus (HSV), 3:115
Herrick, Rebekah, 2:401
Herring, Phillip, 1:116
Herter, Hans, 1:224
Hertzog, Mark, 2:400
Hess, Elizabeth, 3:111
Heterodoxy Club, 1:110; 2:67–68, 336; 3:111
Heteronormativity, 1:330, 331; 2:12
Heterosexism, **2:32–35**
   capitalism and, 2:34
   in colonial America, 2:34
   definition of, 2:32
   explanations for, 2:33–34
   expressions of, 2:33
   vs. homophobia, 2:33
   nationalism and, 2:313
   origin and use of term, 2:32
   responses to, 2:35
Heterosexuality, **2:60–64**
   in 19th century, 2:60–61
   in 20th century, early, 2:61–62
   AIDS and, 2:63
   challenging space determined by, 1:448–449
   during Cold War, 2:62
   creation of, 1:356; 2:41–42
   Freud (Sigmund) on, 2:61, 245
   gay liberation and, 2:62–63
   Kinsey (Alfred) on, 2:62
   lesbian feminist criticism of, 2:166
   medical model of, 2:60–61
   queer theory and, 2:64
   on sexual continuum, 2:62, 247
Hewetson, Dick, 2:45
Hewstone, Miles, "Contact Is Not Enough," 3:151
Heyman, Daniel, 3:242
Heyward, Carter, 2:443
Hi Time (radio show), 1:207
Hibbs Gallery, 3:239
Hicklin rule, 1:203, 204

Model, Lisette, 3:268

Model Penal Code (1962), 1:211

Modern Language Association (MLA), 2:182

LGBT caucuses in, 1:233, 344

"Modern Romance, A" (Gregory), 1:250

Modernism, in visual art, 3:235–236

Modernization, in anthropology, 1:64

"Modes of Disclosure" (Silver), 1:84

Modine, Matthew, in *And the Band Played On*, 1:30

Moffett, Donald, 3:240

Moffitt, Betty Jerman, 2:112

Moffitt, Randy, 2:112

Moffitt, Willis B., 2:112

Mohave tribe, 2:232–233

Mohawk Trail (Brant), 1:165

MOHR. *See* Michigan Organization for Human Rights

Moja = Gay and Black (periodical), 1:19

Mojave tribe, two-spirit females in, 3:213–214

Moldenhauer, Jearld, 2:45

Mollie and the King of Tears, La (Islas), 2:92

Molloscum contagiosum, 3:116

Mom Chung, 1:217

Mommy Queerest (Thompson), 1:362

Mona's, 1:47, 118, 119, 135, 317, 318; 3:72

Mondale, Walter, 2:70

Mondo Trasho (film), 3:265

Monette, Paul, 2:273–274

Borrowed Time, 2:209

Money, John, 2:274–275, 450

Benjamin (Harry) and, 3:204

on biological sex, 2:88–89

EEF supporting work of, 1:352, 354

and nature *vs.* nurture debate, 1:140

research by, 1:233; 2:274–275

and Richards (Renée), 3:35

in Task Force on Homosexuality, 2:24

Monk, Meredith, 1:288

Monkees, 3:175

Monkey Run Road (Jones and Zane), 2:102

Monogamy, 2:275–277

AIDS and, 2:277

Christianity and, 2:275

history of, 2:276

among lesbians *vs.* among gay men, 2:276

vs. polygamy, 2:275

vs. promiscuity, 2:275–276

same-sex marriage and, 2:276

sexual exclusivity as, 2:276–277

vs. tricking, 3:208–209

Monograph of the Pheasants, A (Niles), 2:344

Monroe, Eason, 1:53

Monroe, Marilyn, 2:77; 3:259

Monson, Jennifer, 1:287, 289

Montagnier, Luc, 1:30

Montaigne, "On Friendship," 3:48

Montana

antidiscrimination laws in, 1:68

privacy rights in, 2:432

Monteagudo, Jessie, 2:142

Montealegre, Felicia, 1:136

Montesquiou, Robert de, and visual art, 3:231

Montgomery, Jeffrey, 2:253

Montgomery, Sarah, 3:163

Moody, Dwight, 3:280

Moon, Michael, 2:82, 188

Moonshadow and Mirage (periodical), 3:197

Moore, Alan, 1:250

Moore, Charles Willard, 1:80

Moore, Frank, 3:167, 240

Moore, Marianne, 1:145; 2:1

Moore, Sara Jane, 2:431

Moore, Steve, 1:191

Moore, Terry, 1:251

Moorehead, Agnes, 1:3

Moraga, Cherríe, 1:389; 2:278–279

and Fornes (Maria Irene), 1:410

Giving Up the Ghost, 2:278

Heroes and Saints, 2:278

The Hungry Woman, 2:278, 279

on identity, 2:138

on interracial sex, 2:86

The Last Generation, 2:279

on lesbian feminism, 2:166

Loving in the War Years, 1:75; 2:278

plays of, 2:149

in sex wars, 3:102, 292

Shadow of a Man, 2:278

This Bridge Called My Back, 1:75; 2:84, 149, 170, *198*, 278, 320, 348, 462; 3:292

Waiting in the Wings, 2:279

Moral Majority, 2:70, 332, 439; 3:24

Moral Majority Report, 3:95

Moral reform, feminists and, 1:383–384

Morales, Edward, 2:138

Morality of Gay Rights, The (Ball), 1:364

Moran, Jeffrey, *Teaching Sex*, 3:92

Moran, Red, 3:141

"Morbidification of Love between Women, The" (Faderman), 2:39

"More Gender Trouble: Feminism Meets Queer Theory" (Butler), 2:482, 484, 485

Morena, Naomi Littlebear, 2:140

Mores Tales of the City (Maupin), 2:238

Morford, Sam, 2:338

Morgan, Claire. *See* Highsmith, Patricia

Morgan, Julia, 1:79

Morgan, Marion, 1:86

Morgan, Robin, 2:279–280

Sisterhood Is Powerful, 2:279; 3:142

Morgan, Tracy, 2:383

Morgenthau, Robert, 1:231

Mormon Church, ordination policies of, 2:443

Morocco

Bowles (Jane and Paul) in, 1:159–160

Burroughs (William S.) in, 1:176

tourism in, 3:194–195

Morocco (film), 1:394

Morphological research, 1:139–140

Morris, Jim, 1:247

Morris, Mark, 1:289

Morris, Mitchell, 2:305

Morris, Rosalind, 1:67

Morrison, Marc, 1:347

Morrison v. State Board of Education, 1:347

Morrissey, Paul, 1:396

Mortgaged Heart, The (McCullers), 2:217

Mortimer, Lee, 3:261

Moscone, George, 2:70, 265, 266; 3:77, 229

Moses, Daniel David, 2:320

Mosse, George, 2:313

Mostel, Zero, 3:143

"Mother and Daughter" (Noda), 2:348

Mother Bound (Johnston), 2:101

Mother Camp (Newton), 1:65, 189; 2:171

Mother Earth (journal), 1:460

Mother Millett (Millett), 2:269

"Mother of the World." *See* Mead, Margaret

Mother of Us All, The (opera), 2:287, 292; 3:190

Motherhood, 1:359–360

anthropological studies of, 1:66

child custody issues, 1:359, 369–370

surrogate, 1:370

voluntary, 1:384

"Mother's Story, A" (Allen), 1:51

Smith, Lillian (chorus girl), 3:129

Smith, Lillian Eugenia (writer), **3:130–131**

Smith, Lucy, 3:188

Smith, Lula Carson. *See* McCullers, Carson

Smith, Margarita, 2:217

Smith, Martha Nell, 1:304

Smith, Mary Rozet, 1:6, 414

Smith, Michael, Black and White Men Together founded by, 1:146, 147

Smith, Neil, 1:446

Smith, Oliver, 1:287

Smith, Patti, 2:222, 298
    Burroughs (William S.) and, 1:177

Smith, Paul, 3:268

Smith, Raymond A., 2:401

Smith, Scott, 2:265

Smith, Willi, 1:372, 374

Smith College, 1:233, 234; 2:47, 350, 351; 3:301–302

Smith-Rosenberg, Carroll, 1:413; 2:185
    Disorderly Conduct, 2:171
    on female homosocial world, 2:51
    and LGBT history, 2:40
    on separate spheres of women and men, 1:222, 303
    "The Female World of Love and Ritual," 2:39; 3:47, 291

Smiths, 2:297

"Smoke, Lilies and Jade" (Nugent), 2:11, 190, 203, 352

SNCC. *See* Student Nonviolent Coordinating Committee

Snelling, Paula, 3:130

Snipes, Wesley, 3:221

Snitow, Ann, *Powers of Desire*, 2:171

"Snow queens," 1:90; 2:86

Snyder, Gary, 1:130; 2:193

Soap (TV show), 3:177

Soares, Lota de Macedo, Bishop (Elizabeth) and, 1:145–146

Soble, Alan, 2:378, 379

Sobule, Jill, 1:144

Socarides, Charles, 2:248, 449, 451, 452

Soccer, women's, 3:146

Social and Public Art Resource Center (SPARC), 1:107, 108

Social Construction of Reality, The (Berger and Luckmann), 3:135

Social constructionism. *See* Constructionism

Social control, and sexuality, 1:355

"Social Evil of Chicago, The" (Busse), 1:209–210

Social history, 2:41–42

Social justice, 2:378

Social movements, new, sociology on, 3:136–137

Social Problems (journal), 3:135

Social purity movement, 1:383

Social space, 1:192–193, 194

Social workers, homophobia of, 1:311, 312

Socialism, **1:54–57**
    attitude toward homosexuality in, 1:54
    in black feminism, 1:24
    diversity of membership, 1:55
    electoral success of, 1:55
    and feminism, 1:386–387
    in New York City, 2:336
    sexual politics of, 1:55, 56
    in Third World Gay Revolution, 3:186
    See also Communism

Socialization, and sexuality, 1:355

Society and the Healthy Homosexual (Weinberg), 2:33

Society for Comparative Philosophy, 1:454

Society for Ethnomusicology, 2:305

Society for Human Rights, 1:210; 2:53, 393; **3:131–132**
    bisexuals excluded from, 1:142
    demise of, 3:131–132
    establishment of, 3:131
    First Amendment protection of, 3:38
    Gerber (Henry) and, 1:451
    purpose of, 3:131

Society for Individual Rights (SIR), 2:55; **3:132–134**
    committee structure of, 3:133
    cooperation in, 3:133–134
    establishment of, 2:178; 3:74, 80, 132
    funding for, 3:80
    goals of, 3:132
    legal guidance by, 3:133
    political agenda of, 3:132–133
    in San Francisco, 1:379
    Sarria (José) in, 3:80
    social activities of, 3:133
    Tavern Guild and, 2:178

Society for Lesbian and Gay Philosophy, 2:377

Society for Music Theory, 2:305

Society for the Scientific Study of Sex, 1:133

Society for the Study of Social Problems (SSSP), 3:135

Society for the Suppression of Vice, 2:336

Society for Women in Philosophy (SWIP), 2:377

Society of American Archivists, 2:46

Society of Dance History Scholars Conference, 1:288

Society of Janus, 2:156; 3:59, 67

Society of Lesbian and Gay Anthropologists (SOLGA), 1:66

Society of Medical Psychoanalysts, 2:247

Society of Women Geographers (SWG), 2:344

Society Page (bar), 2:330

Sociology, **3:134–138**
    on bisexuality, 3:137
    early research in, 3:134–135
    funding for, 3:137
    interactionist wing of, 3:135
    labeling theory in, 3:135
    on new social movements, 3:136–137
    origin of term, 3:134
    on sexual preference *vs.* orientation, 3:104–105
    of sport, 2:381–382
    on transgenderism, 3:137

Sodomite, 1:193, 240

Sodomy
    by African Americans, 1:11, 12
    arrests for, 2:391, 392
    biblical texts on, 2:438
    Catholic Church on, 1:200
    in colonial era
        capital punishment for, 2:373–374, 439–440
        laws on, 1:151–152, 153, 238–240, 263; 2:390, 392; 3:138–139
        literature on, 2:184–185
        tolerance of, 3:85–86
        use of term, 2:132, 184
    consensual, 1:265
    definitions of, 3:138, 139
    First Amendment and, 3:39
    law and policy on, 1:314; **3:138–141**
        (*See also under specific states*)
        in 19th century, 1:264
        in 20th century, 1:264–265
        after Civil War, 1:264
        in colonial era, 1:151–152, 153, 238–240, 263; 2:390, 392; 3:138–139
        expansion of definition, 3:139
        in Great Britain, 1:263; 3:138
        in India, 2:37

Sodomy *(continued)*
    Lambda Legal Defense on, **2:**130, 131; **3:**140
    March on Washington (1987) on, **2:**224
    March on Washington (1993) on, **2:**225
    in military, **1:**346, 376; **2:**259, 262
    opposition to, **3:**139–141, *140*
    oral sex in, **3:**139, 140
    privacy arguments attacking, **2:**431
    in Puerto Rico, **2:**465
    punishment for, **3:**139
    and rape in legal system, **3:**19
    repeal of, **2:**442
    Supreme Court on (*See under* Supreme Court)
    in literature
      condemnations of, **2:**184–185
      definitions of, **2:**184
    among Native Americans, **1:**237; **2:**317
    origin of term, **2:**132
    use of term, **2:**132, 184
    violence as government sanction for, **2:**19
Soft Machine, The (Burroughs), **1:**177
Softball, **3:**145
Soilers, The (film), **1:**394
Sojourner (newspaper), **1:**155
Sojourner Truth Press, **2:**462
Soka Gakkai International (SGI), **1:**171
Sokolowski, Thomas, **1:**85
Sol 13, Interior (13 Sun Street) (Sánchez), **3:**78
Solanas, Dorothy Bondo, **3:**141
Solanas, Louis, **3:**141
Solanas, Valerie, **3:**141–143, *142*
    and Atkinson (Ti-Grace), **1:**100; **3:**143
    on marriage, **1:**100
    S.C.U.M. Manifesto, **3:**142
    Up Your Ass, **3:**141
    Warhol (Andy) and, **3:**141–143, 259
Soldier drag queens, **1:**317
SOLGA. *See* Society of Lesbian and Gay Anthropologists
Solie, R. A., **2:**305
Solomon, Alisa, **1:**206
Solomon, Carl, **1:**457; **2:**193
Solomon, Maynard, **2:**305
Solomon, Rosalind, *Portraits in the Time of AIDS,* **3:**247
Solomon-Godeau, Abigail, **1:**84
Solti, Sir George, **2:**290

SOME. *See* Save Our Moral Ethics
Some Like It Hot (film), **1:***319;* **2:**286
Somerville, Jimmy, **2:**305
Somerville, Siobhan, **1:**12; **2:**85, 446
    and African American studies, **1:**26
    Queering the Color Line, **1:**26; **2:**41; **3:**1–2
    on race and homosexuality, **3:**125
Something Moving (record), **2:**300
"Somewhere" (song), **2:**284
Sonbert, Warren, **3:**44
Sondheim, Herbert, **3:**143
Sondheim, Janet Fox, **3:**143
Sondheim, Stephen, **2:**283; **3:**143–144
    Company, **1:**134; **3:**143
    Follies, **1:**134
    West Side Story lyrics by, **3:**43, 143
"Song of Myself" (Whitman), **2:**186; **3:**274
Song of the Lark, The (Cather), **1:**198; **2:**292
Song of the Loon, The (Amory), **2:**470
Songs of Bilitis (Louys), **1:**290
Songs of Jamaica (McKay), **2:**219
Sonic Meditations (Oliveros), **2:**355
Sonnabend, Joseph, on AIDS, **1:**28
Sonsini, John, **3:**240
Sontag, Susan, **1:**188, 189, 276, 409; **3:**247
Sonthoff, Helen, **3:**52
Sophie's Parlor (radio program), **3:**13
Sorère, Gabrielle, **1:**288
Sorin, Hubert, **3:**273
Sororities, **1:**235
    lesbian, **3:**302
Soul on Ice (Cleaver), **2:**328
Souter, David, **3:**39
South Africa, protections for LGBT people in, **1:**365
South Asian Lesbian and Gay Association (SALGA), **2:**257
South Asian Lesbian and Gay Association of New York (SALGA-NYC), **1:**98
South Bay Queer and Asian (SBQA), **1:**99
South Beach (Miami, Florida)
    gentrification of, **1:**407, 446
    as resort, **3:**31
South Carolina, sodomy laws in, **3:**139
South Dakota, sex toys in, **3:**99
South End Steam Baths, **3:**82
South Pacific (musical), **2:**285
South Today (magazine), **3:**130
Southeast Asian Transgender AIDS Prevention Program, **1:**99

Southern Baptist Church, anti-gay stances of, **1:**363
Southern Baptist Convention, Disney boycotted by, **1:**164
Southern California Gay Liberation Front, **2:**23
Southern Christian Leadership Conference (SCLC), **3:**55
Southern Decadence, **2:**331
Southern Lady, The (Coleman), **2:**468
Southern literature, **2:**190–191
Southern Seating, **1:**354
Southern Women's Music and Comedy, **2:**303
South-Sea Idylls (Stoddard), **2:**186; **3:**126, 154, 155
Southwest Asian and North African Bay Area Queers (SWANABAQ), **1:**77
Sowerby, Leo, **3:**51
Spain, same-sex marriage in, **1:**365
Spanish language, discrimination against, **3:**4
SPARC. *See* Social and Public Art Resource Center
Sparks, David, *Cassell's Encyclopedia of Queer Myth, Symbol, and Spirit,* **3:**9
Sparks, Mariya, *Cassell's Encyclopedia of Queer Myth, Symbol, and Spirit,* **3:**9
Spatial closet, **1:**229
Speak Its Name (theater company), **1:**212
Speak Out, **2:**70
Speakeasies, **1:**118, 154, 246, 317; **2:**336–337
Spear, Allan, **1:**337; **2:**346
Spears, Britney, **3:**41
Spears, Jay, **2:**91
Specialty publications, **2:**343
Speckart, Harriet, **2:**413
"Spectacle of Color, A" (Garber), **1:**25
Spectre: Paper of Revolutionary Lesbians (periodical), **2:**164
Speech, patterns of, **2:**135
Speed. *See* Methamphetamine
Spencer-Devlin, Muffin, **3:**146
Spender, Stephen, **1:**104
Sperry, Almeda, **1:**461
Spickard, Paul, **2:**84, 85
Spider's House, The (Bowles), **1:**159
Spielberg, Steven, in Boy Scouts, **1:**162
Spike (club), **2:**338
Spinsters Ink, **2:**463
Spiral Dance, The (Starhawk), **3:**284
Spirit and the Flesh, The: Sexual Diversity in American Indian Culture (Williams), **1:**65; **2:**320, 323
Spiritsong (record), **2:**300